REAL-WORLD APPLICATIONS OF GENETIC ALGORITHMS

Edited by **Olympia Roeva**

Real-World Applications of Genetic Algorithms
Edited by Olympia Roeva

Published by InTech

Janeza Trdine 9, 51000 Rijeka, Croatia

Publishing Process Manager Marina Jozipovic

Technical Editor Teodora Smiljanic

Cover Designer InTech Design Team

Additional hard copies can be obtained from orders@intechopen.com

Real-World Applications of Genetic Algorithms, Edited by Olympia Roeva
p. cm.
ISBN 978-953-51-0146-8

For EU product safety concerns:
IN TECH d.o.o., Prolaz Marije Krucifikse Kozulić 3, 51000 Rijeka, Croatia,
info@intechopen.com or visit our website at intechopen.com.

Meet the editor

Dr. Olympia Roeva received the M.Sc. degree (1998) and Ph.D. degree (2007) from the Technical University – Sofia, Bulgaria. At present she is an associate professor in Department of Bioinformatics and Mathematical Modeling, Institute of Biophysics and Biomedical Engineering, Bulgarian Academy of Sciences. Dr. Roeva is one of the scientists playing a significant role in the renovation of International Journal Bioautomation. She has received various scientific awards, including a Diploma from Union of Scientists in Bulgaria for High Scientific Achievements 2008. Her research interests are in the fields of modeling, optimization and control of cultivation processes, functional state modeling approach, metaheuristic algorithms and generalized nets.

Contents

Preface

Genetic Algorithms are a part of *Evolutionary Computing*, which is a rapidly growing area of *Artificial Intelligence*. The popularity of *Genetic Algorithms* is reflected in the increasing amount of literature devoted to theoretical works and real-world applications in both scientific and engineering areas. The useful application and the proper combination of the different *Genetic Algorithms* with the various optimization algorithms is still an open research topic.

This book addresses some of the most recent issues, with the theoretical and methodological aspects, of evolutionary multi-objective optimization problems and the various design challenges using different hybrid intelligent approaches. Multi-objective optimization has been available for about two decades, and its application in real-world problems is continuously increasing. Furthermore, many applications function more effectively using a hybrid systems approach. Hybridization of *Genetic Algorithms* is getting popular due to their capabilities in handling different problems involving complexity, noisy environment, uncertainty, etc. The book presents hybrid techniques based on *Artificial Neural Network, Fuzzy Sets, Automata Theory, other metaheuristic* or *classical algorithms*, etc. The volume examines various examples of algorithms in different real-world application domains as *graph growing problem, speech synthesis, traveling salesman problem, scheduling problems, antenna design, genes design, modeling of chemical and biochemical processes* etc.

The book, organized in 17 chapters, begins with several applications of *Hybrid Genetic Algorithms* in wide range of problems. Further, some applications of *Genetic Algorithms* and other heuristic search methods are presented.

The objective of *Chapter 1* is to model and to optimize the process performances simultaneously in the plasma-catalytic conversion of methane such that the optimal process performances are obtained at the given process parameters. A *Hybrid Artificial Neural Network-Genetic Algorithm* (*ANN-GA*) is successfully developed to model, to simulate and to optimize simultaneously a catalytic-dielectric-barrier discharge plasma reactor. The integrated *ANN-GA* method facilitates powerful modeling and multi-objectives optimization for co-generation of synthesis gas, C_2 and higher hydrocarbons from methane and carbon dioxide in a dielectric barrier discharge plasma reactor.

Chapter 2 presents a new fast and accurate electromagnetic optimization technique combining full-wave method of moments, bio-inspired algorithms, continuous *Genetic Algorithm* and *Particle Swarm Optimization*, and multilayer perceptrons *Artificial Neural Networks*. The proposed optimization technique is applied for optimal design of frequency selective surfaces with fractal patch elements. A fixed frequency selective surface screen geometry is chosen a priori and then a smaller subset of frequency selective surface design variables is optimized to achieve a desired bandstop filter specification.

The main contribution of the *Chapter 3* is the test of the *Hybrid MOEA-HCEDA Algorithm* and the quality index based on the Pareto front used in the graph drawing problem. The Pareto front quality index printed on each generation of the algorithm showed a convergent curve. The results of the experiments show that the algorithm converges. A graphical user interface is constructed providing users with a tool for a friendly and easy to use graphs display. The automatic drawing of optimized graphs makes it easier for the user to compare results appearing in separate windows, giving the user the opportunity to choose the graph design which best suits their needs.

Chapter 4 studies metaheuristics based on the *Automata Theory* for the multi-objective optimization of combinatorial problems. The *SAMODS* (*Simulated Annealing inspired Algorithm*), *SAGAMODS* (*Evolutionary inspired Algorithm*) and *EMODS* (using *Tabu Search*) algorithms are presented. Presented experimental results of each proposed algorithm using multi-objective metrics from the specialized literature show that the *EMODS* has the best performance. In some cases the behavior of *SAMODS* and *SAGAMODS* tend to be the same – similar error rate.

Chapter 5 presents a *Hybrid Genetic Algorithm* (*Genetic Algorithm* linked to a *Simulated Annealing*) intended to solve the Flexible Job-Shop Scheduling Problem procedure able to schedule the production in a Job-Shop manufacturing system. The authors show that this *Hybrid Genetic Algorithm* yields more solutions in the Approximate Pareto Frontier than other algorithms. A platform and programming language independent interface for search algorithms has been used as a guide for the implementation of the proposed hybrid algorithm.

Chapter 6 suggests mathematical programming models and a *Hybrid Parallel Genetic Algorithm* (*HPGA*) for reliability optimization with resource constraints. The considered algorithm includes different heuristics such as swap, 2-opt, and interchange for an improvement solution. The experimental results of *HPGA* are compared with the results of existing meta-heuristics. The suggested algorithm presents superior solutions to all problems and found that the performance is superior to existing meta-heuristics.

Chapter 7 discusses the effectiveness of *Genetic Algorithms* in determining the optimal values of hyper-parameters of Least Squares-Support Vector Machines to solve power tracing problem. The developed hybrid *Genetic Algorithm-Support Vector Machines* (*GA-*

SVM) adopts real and reactive power tracing output determined by Superposition method as an estimator to train the model. The results show that *GA-SVM* gives good accuracy in predicting the generators' output and compared well with Superposition method and load flow study.

Chapter 8 provides an insight into the general reasoning behind selection of the *Genetic Algorithms* control parameters, discuss the ways of boosting the algorithm efficiency, and finally introduce a simple *Global-local Hybrid Genetic Algorithms* capable of fast and reliable optimization of multi-parameter and multi-extremum functions. The effectiveness of the proposed algorithm is demonstrated by numerical examples, namely: synthesis of linear antenna arrays with pencil-beam and flat-top patterns.

Chapter 9 introduces a hybrid methodology, the *Heuristics Backtracking*, an approach that combines a search algorithm, the backtracking, integer linear programming and *Genetic Algorithms* to solve the three dimensional knapsack loading problem considering weight distribution. The authors show that the *Heuristics Backtracking* achieved good results without the commonly great trade-off between the utilization of container and a good weight distribution. Some benchmark tests taken from literature are used to validate the performance and efficiency of the *Heuristics Backtracking* methodology as well as its applicability to cutting-stock problems.

Chapter 10 introduces two *Hybrid Genetic Algorithms* to solve the sequence-dependent setup times single machine problem. The proposed approaches are essentially based on adapting highly specialized genetic operators to the specificities of the studied problem. The numerical experiments demonstrate the efficiency of the hybrid algorithms for this problem. A natural conclusion from these experimental results is that *Genetic Algorithms* may be robust and efficient alternative to solve this problem.

Chapter 11 presents the Group Method of Data Handling-type Neural Network with Genetic Algorithm used to develop the early egg production in *broiler breeder*. By means of the Group Method of Data Handling Algorithm, a model can be represented as a set of quadratic polynomials. Genetic Algorithms are deployed to assign the number of neurons (polynomial equations) in the network and to find the optimal set of appropriate coefficients of the quadratic expressions.

Chapter 12 discusses some of the computational issues for evolutionary searches to find gene-regulatory sequences. Here the *retroGenetic Algorithm* technique is introduced. Proposed *Genetic Algorithm* crossover operator is inspired by retroviral recombination and in vitro DNA shuffling mechanisms to copy blocks of genetic information. The authors present particular results on the efficiency of *retroGenetic Algorithm* in comparison with the standard *Genetic Algorithm*.

Chapter 13 examines the use of *Genetic Algorithms* and *Ant Colony Optimization* for parameter identification of a system of nonlinear differential equations modeling the fed-batch cultivation process of the bacteria *E. coli*. The results from both metaheuristics *Genetic Algorithms* and *Ant Colony Optimization* are compared using the modified Hausdorff distance metric, in place of most common used – least squares regression. Analyzing of average results authors conclude that the *Ant Colony Optimization* algorithm performs better for the considered problem.

Chapter 14 presents a brief description about the estimation problem of a formant synthesizer, such as the Klatt. The combination of its input parameters to the imitation of human voice is not a simple task, because a reasonable number of parameters have to be combined and each of them has an interval of acceptable values that must be carefully adjusted to produce a specific voice. The authors conclude that it is necessary to develop a more efficient mechanism for evaluating the quality of the generated voice as a whole, and include it in the *Genetic Algorithm speech framework*.

Chapter 15 discusses about how *Genetic Algorithm* and heuristic search can solve the scheduling problem. As a case study the *"Universitas Pelita Harapan"* timetable is considered. The authors propose the architecture design of the system and show some experiments implementing the system.

The objective of *Chapter 16* is to show a set of single-objective and *multi-objective Genetic Algorithms*, designed by the Optical Communications Group at the University of Valladolid, to optimize the performance of semi-static *Wavelength-Routed Optical Networks* (*WRONs*). The fundamentals of those algorithms, i.e., the chromosome structures, their translation, the optimization goals and the genetic operators employed are described. Moreover, a number of simulation results are also included to show the efficiency of *Genetic Algorithms* when designing *WRONs*.

Finally, *Chapter 17* gives an overview of existing *surrogate* modeling techniques and issues about how to use them for optimization. *Surrogate* modeling techniques are of particular interest for engineering design when high-fidelity, thus expensive analysis codes (e.g. computation fluid dynamics and computational structural dynamics) are used.

The book is designed to be of interest to a wide spectrum of readers. The authors hope that the readers will find this book useful and inspiring.

Olympia Roeva
Institute of Biophysics and Biomedical Engineering
Bulgarian Academy of Sciences
Sofia,
Bulgaria

1

Different Tools on Multi-Objective Optimization of a Hybrid Artificial Neural Network – Genetic Algorithm for Plasma Chemical Reactor Modelling

Nor Aishah Saidina Amin[1,*] and I. Istadi[2]
[1]*Chemical Reaction Engineering Group, Faculty of Chemical Engineering, Universiti Teknologi Malaysia, Johor Bahru,*
[2]*Laboratory of Energy and Process Engineering, Department of Chemical Engineering, Diponegoro University, Jl. Prof. H. Soedarto, SH., Semarang,*
[1]*Malaysia*
[2]*Indonesia*

1. Introduction

Simultaneous modeling and optimization allows a cost-effective alternative to cover large number of experiments. The model should be able to improve overall process performance particularly for the complex process. A hybrid Artificial Neural Network - Genetic Algorithm (ANN-GA) was developed to model, to simulate, and to optimize simultaneously a catalytic–plasma reactor. The present contribution is intended to develop an ANN-GA method to facilitate simultaneous modeling and multi-objective optimization for co-generation of synthesis gas, C_2 and higher hydrocarbons from methane and carbon dioxide in a dielectric-barrier discharge (DBD) plasma reactor. The hybrid approach simplifies the complexity in process modeling the DBD plasma reactor.

A hybrid of ANN-GA method has been used for integrated process modelling and multi-objectives optimization. The detail hybrid algorithm for simultaneous modelling and multi-objective optimization has been developed in previous publication which focused on plasma reactor application (Istadi & Amin, 2005, 2006, 2007). They reported that the hybrid ANN-GA technique is a powerful method for process modelling and multi-objectives optimization (Nandi *et al.*, 2002, 2004; Ahmad *et al.*, 2004; Stephanopoulos & Han, 1996; Huang *et al.*, 2003; Radhakrishnan & Suppiah, 2004; Fissore *et al.*, 2004; Nandi *et al.*, 2002, 2004; Ahmad *et al.*, 2004; Kundu *et al.*, 20009; Marzbanrad & Ebrahimi, 2011; Bhatti *et al.*, 2011). The method is better than other technique such as response surface methodology (RSM) (Istadi & Amin, 2006, 2007), particularly for complex process model. The RSM proposes a quadratic model as empirical model for representing the effect of independent variables toward the targeting response. Therefore, all models which may not follow the quadratic trend are forced to the

* Corresponding Author

quadratic model. Disadvantage of the RSM method is then improved by the hybrid ANN-GA. In the later method, an empirical mathematical modelling of catalytic cracking was conducted by ANN strategy, while the multi-objectives optimization of operating conditions to reach optimal responses was performed using GA method.

In terms of single-response optimization applications, the selection of optimization method is very important to design an optimal catalyst as well as the relations between process parameters and catalytic performances (Wu *et al.*, 2002). Pertaining to the catalyst design, some previous researchers introduced ANN to design the catalysts (Hattori & Kito, 1991, 1995; Hou *et al.*, 1997). The ANN is feasible for modeling and optimization, and consequently, large number experiments can be avoidable (Wu *et al.*, 2002). According to the complex interaction among the catalyst compositions, the process parameters and the metal-support interaction with no clear reaction mechanism as in CO_2 OCM process, the empirical models are more useful in the catalyst design especially in the optimization studies. The reason is that the phenomenological modeling of interactions in the catalyst design is very complex. Unfortunately, a single-response optimization is usually insufficient for the real CO_2 OCM process due to the fact that most responses, i.e. methane conversion, product selectivity and product yield, are dependent during the process. Therefore, simultaneous modeling and multi-objective optimization techniques in complex plasma reactor is worthy. A simultaneous multi-objective optimization is more realistic than a single-response from reliability point of view. Empirical and pseudo-phenomenological modeling approaches were employed by previous researchers (Wu *et al.*, 2002; Larentis *et al.*, 2001; Huang *et al.*, 2003) for optimizing the catalytic process. The empirical modeling is efficient for the complex process optimization, but the drawback is that the model has no fundamental theory or actual phenomena meaning.

Pertaining to multi-objective optimization, a graphical multi-responses optimization technique was implemented by previous researchers for xylitol crystallization from synthetic solution (de Faveri *et al.*, 2004), but it was not useful for more than two independent variables or highly nonlinear models. In another study, a generalized distance approach technique was developed to optimize process variables in the production of protoplast from mycelium (Muralidhar *et al.*, 2003). The optimization procedure was carried out by searching independent variables that minimize the distance function over the experimental region in the simultaneous optimal critical parameters. Recently, robust and efficient technique of elitist Non-dominated Sorting Genetic Algorithm (NSGA) was used to obtain solution of the complex multi-objective optimization problem (Huang *et al.*, 2003; Nandasana *et al.*, 2003; Zhao *et al.*, 2000; Nandi *et al.*, 2004). A hybrid GA with ANN was also developed (Huang *et al.*, 2003) to design optimal catalyst and operating conditions for O_2 OCM process. In addition, a comprehensive optimization study of simulated moving bed process was also reported using a robust GA optimization technique (Zhang *et al.*, 2002b).

Several methods are available for solving multi-objective optimization problem, for example, weighted sum strategy (The MathWorks, 2005; Youness, 2004; Istadi, 2006), ε-constraint method (Yu *et al.*, 2003; The MathWorks, 2005; Youness, 2004), goal attainment method (Yu *et al.*, 2003; The MathWorks, 2005), NSGA (Nandasana *et al.*, 2003; Zhang *et al.*, 2002b; Yu *et al.*, 2003), and weighted sum of squared objective function (WSSOF) (Istadi & Amin, 2006b, 2007; Istadi, 2006) to obtain the Pareto set. The NSGA method has several advantages (Zhang *et al.*, 2002b): (a) its efficiency is relatively insensitive to the shape of the

Pareto-optimal front; (b) problems with uncertainties, stochasticities, and discrete search space can be handled efficiently; (c) spread of the Pareto set obtained is excellent, and (d) involves a single application to obtain the entire Pareto set. Among the methods, the NSGA is the most powerful method for solving a complex multi-responses optimization problem. In the multi-objective optimization of the CO_2 OCM process, the goal attainment combined with hybrid ANN-GA method was used to solve the optimization of catalytic-plasma process parameters. The multi-objective optimization strategy was combined simultaneously with ANN modelling and GA optimization algorithm. The multi-objective optimization deals with generation and selection of non-inferior solution points or Pareto-optimal solutions of the responses / objectives corresponding to the optimal operating parameters. The DBD plasma-catalytic coupling of methane and carbon dioxide is an intricate process within the plasma-catalytic reactor application. A hybrid ANN-GA modelling and multi-objective optimization was developed to produce a process model that simulated the complex DBD plasma - catalytic process. There were no previous researchers focused on the simultaneous modelling and multi-objective optimization of DBD plasma - catalytic reactor using the hybrid ANN-GA.

The objective of this chapter is to model and to optimize the process performances simultaneously in the DBD plasma-catalytic conversion of methane to higher hydrocarbons such that the optimal process performances (CH_4 conversion and C_2 hydrocarbons yield) are obtained at the given process parameters. In this Chapter, multi-objective optimization of two cases, i.e. C_2 hydrocarbon yield and C_2 hydrocarbons selectivity, and C_2 hydrocarbons yield and CH_4 conversion, to produce a Pareto Optimal solution is considered. In the process modeling, a number of experimental data was needed to validate the model. The ANN-based model required more example data which were noise-free and statistically well-distributed. Therefore, design of experiment was performed using central composite design with full factorial design for designing the training and test data sets. The method was chosen in order to provide a wider covering region of parameter space and good consideration of variable interactions in the model. This chapter is organized according to sections 1, 2, 3 and 4. After Introduction in section 1, section 2 covers design of experiment and strategy for simultaneous modeling and optimization including hybrid ANN-GA algorithm. In section 3, multi-objective optimization of methane conversion to higher hydrocarbons process over plasma - catalytic reactor is applied. In this section, ANN simulation of the DBD plasma - catalytic reactor performance is also presented with respect to the two cases. The final section, section 4 offers conclusions about the chapter.

2. Design of experiment, modeling, and optimization strategies

2.1 Central composite design for design of experiment

Central Composite Design for four factors was employed for designing the experimental works in which variance of the predicted response Y at some point X is only a function of distance from the point to the design centre (Montgomery, 2001). Hence, the variance of Y remained unchanged when the design is rotated about the centre. In the design, standard error, which depends on the coordinates of the point on the response surface at which Y is evaluated and on the coefficients β, is the same for all points that are same distance from the central point. The value of a for star point with respect to design depends on the number of points in the factorial portion of the design which is given in Equation (1) (Montgomery, 2001; Clarke & Kempson, 1997).

$$a = (n_c)^{1/4} \quad (1)$$

where n_c is number of points in the cube portion of the design (n_c = 2^k, k is number of factors). Since there are four parameters/factors in this experiment, the n_c number is equal to 2^4 (= 16) points, and a=2 according to Equation (1).

An experimental design matrix revealed in Table 1 consists of sets of coded conditions expressed in natural values (Istadi & Amin, 2006a) with a two-level full factorial design (n_c), star points (n_s) and centre points (n_0). Based on this table, the experiments for obtaining the responses of CH_4 conversion ($X(CH_4)$), C_2 hydrocarbons selectivity ($S(C_2)$) and C_2 hydrocarbons yield ($Y(C_2)$) were carried out at the corresponding independent variables. Number experimental data were used for validating the hybrid ANN-GA model of the catalytic-plasma CO_2 OCM process. Sequence of the experimental work was randomized in order to minimize the effects of uncontrolled factors. The experimental data from catalytic-plasma reactor operation with respect to combination of four factors including their respected responses (plasma-catalytic reactor performances: CH_4 conversion, C_2 hydrocarbons selectivity, C_2 hydrocarbons yield, and H_2 selectivity) are presented in Table 2.

Factors	Range and levels				
	$-a$	-1	0	+1	$+a$
CH_4/CO_2 Ratio (X_1), [-]	0.8	1.5	2.5	3.5	4.2
Discharge voltage (X_2), kV	12.5	13.5	15.0	16.5	17.5
Total feed flow rate (X_3), cm^3/min	18	25	35	45	52
Reactor temperature (X_4), ^oC	81	150	250	350	418

Note: -1 (low level value); +1 (high level value); 0 (centre point); $+\alpha$ and $-\alpha$ (star points)

Table 1. Central Composite Design with fractional factorial design for the catalytic DBD plasma reactor (Istadi, 2006)

2.2 Simultaneous modelling and multi-objective optimization

The integrated ANN-GA strategy meets the objective based on two steps: (a) development of an ANN-based process model which has inputs of process operating parameters of plasma – catalytic reactor, and output(s) of process output/response variable(s), i.e. yield of C_2hydrocarbons or hydrogen, or methane conversion; and (b) development of GA technique for multi-objective optimization of the ANN model. Input space of the ANN model is optimized using the GA technique such that the optimal response(s) or objective(s) are obtained corresponding to the optimal process parameters. The developed simultaneous algorithm is presented in a hybrid Algorithm of ANN-GA schematically for simultaneous modeling and optimization.

In the GA, a population of strings (called chromosomes), which encode individual solutions towards an optimization problem, adjusts toward better solutions. The solutions are represented in binary strings. The evolution begins from a population of randomly generated individuals and grows to produce next generations. In each generation, the fitness of each individual in the new population is evaluated and scored (recombination and mutation) to form a new population. During the fitness evaluation, the resulted ANN model is used. The new population is then used in the next iteration. The algorithm terminates when either a maximum generations number has been reached, or a best fitness level has been approached for the population. The multi-objective optimization can be formulated by converting the problem into a scalar single-objective optimization problem which is solvable by unconstrained single-response optimization technique. Many methods can be used for converting the problems into scalar optimization problem, such as weighted sum of squared objective functions (WSSOF), goal attainment, weighted sum strategy, and ε-constraint method.

Schematic diagram of the feed-forward ANN used in this model development is depicted in Figure 1. Detail stepwise procedure used for the hybrid ANN-GA modelling and multi-objectives optimization is modified from the previous publications (Istadi, 2006; Istadi & Amin, 2007). The modified algorithm is described in this section and is depicted schematically in Figure 2. The fit quality of the ANN model was checked by a correlation coefficient (R) or a determination coefficient (R^2) and Mean Square Error (MSE). The ANN model generated was repeated until the R^2 reached higher than 0.90. The commonly employed error function to check the fit quality of the model is the MSE as defined in Equation (2).

$$MSE = \frac{1}{N_p\,K}\sum_{i=1}^{i=N_p}\sum_{k=1}^{k=K}\left(t_{i,k}-y_{i,k}\right)^2 \quad (2)$$

where N_p and K denote the number of patterns and output nodes used in the training, i denotes the index of the input pattern (vector), and k denotes the index of the output node. Meanwhile, $t_i{,}k$ and $y_i{,}k$ express the desired (targeted or experimental) and predicted values of the kth output node at i^{th} input pattern, respectively.

With respect to the ANN modelling, a feed-forward ANN model was used in this model development which was trained using back-propagation training function. In general, four steps are developed in the training process: assemble the training data, create the network object, train the network, and simulate the network response to new inputs. The schematic of the feed-forward neural network used in the model development is depicted in Figure 1. As shown, the network consists of three layers nodes, i.e. input, hidden, and output layers comprising four numbers of each processing nodes. Each node in the input layer is linked to all nodes in the hidden layer and simultaneously the node in the hidden layer is linked to all nodes in the output layer using weighting connections (W). The weights are adjusted in the learning process in which all the patterns of input-output are presented in the learning phase repeatedly. In addition, the feed-forward neural network architecture also addresses the bias nodes which are connected to all nodes in subsequent layer, and they provide additional adjustable parameters (weights) for the fitting.

From Figure 1, $\boldsymbol{W}^H$ and $\boldsymbol{W}^O$ denote the weights between input and hidden nodes and between hidden and output nodes, respectively. Meanwhile, $\boldsymbol{y}^H$ and $\boldsymbol{y}^O$ denote the outputs vector from hidden and output layers, respectively. In this system, $\boldsymbol{b}^H$ and $\boldsymbol{b}^O$ signify the scalar bias corresponding to hidden and output layers, respectively. The weighted input (**W**) is the argument of the activation/transfer function *f*, which produces the scalar output *y*. The activation function net input is a summing function (n^H or n^O) which is the sum of the weighted input (W^H or W^O) and the bias *b*. In order that the ANN network accurately approximates the nonlinear relationship existing between the process inputs and outputs, it needs to be trained in a manner such that a pre-specified error function is minimized. There are many learning algorithms available and the most popular and successful learning algorithm used to train multilayer network is back-propagation scheme. Any output point can be obtained after this learning phase, and good results can be achieved.

Process variables				Responses/ Dependent variables (%)			
CH_4/CO_2 ratio (X_1)	Discharge voltage (X_2)	Total feed flow rate (X_3)	Reactor Temperature (X_4)	X(CH_4) (Y_1)	S(C_{2+}) (Y_2)	S(H_2) (Y_3)	Y(C_{2+}) (Y_4)
3.5	16.5	45	150	21.45	26.13	13.24	5.61
3.5	16.5	25	150	23.48	33.41	12.13	7.85
* 3.5	13.5	45	350	18.76	28.43	13.16	5.33
1.5	16.5	25	350	27.55	27.47	8.11	7.57
3.5	13.5	25	350	20.22	35.21	12.87	7.12
1.5	13.5	45	150	23.11	26.98	8.01	6.24
1.5	16.5	45	350	28.03	24.45	7.48	6.85
* 1.5	13.5	25	150	30.02	24.15	8.54	7.25
0.8	15.0	35	250	32.14	12.54	5.17	4.03
4.2	15.0	35	250	21.12	34.77	13.99	7.34
2.5	12.5	35	250	18.55	29.76	10.22	5.52
2.5	17.5	35	250	41.32	28.01	10.12	11.57
2.5	15.0	18	250	38.65	31.77	11.32	12.28
* 2.5	15.0	52	250	20.88	30.00	11.56	6.26
2.5	15.0	35	81	25.49	28.04	9.87	7.15
2.5	15.0	35	418	26.74	32.55	10.41	8.70
2.5	15.0	35	250	25.77	31.33	11.55	8.07
2.5	15.0	35	250	23.41	30.74	9.87	7.20
2.5	15.0	35	250	25.14	29.65	10.44	7.45
* 2.5	15.0	35	250	26.11	28.14	9.54	7.35

Note: *X*, *S*, and *Y* denote conversion, selectivity and yield, respectively, and C_{2+} comprises C_2H_4, C_2H_6, C_2H_2, C_3H_8.

* These data were used as test set.

X_1 (CH_4/CO_2 feed ratio); X_2 (Discharge voltage, kV); X_3 (Total feed flow rate, cm^3/min); X_4 (Reactor wall temperature, ^oC); Pressure: 1 atm; Catalyst loading: 5 gram; Frequency: 2 kHz (pulse)

Table 2. Experimental data of hybrid catalytic DBD plasma reactor at low temperature (Istadi, 2006)

Therefore, an input vector from the training set is applied to the network input nodes, and subsequently outputs of the hidden and output nodes are computed. The outputs are computed as follows: (a) the weighted sum of all the node-specific input is evaluated, which is then transformed using a nonlinear activation function (*f*), such as tangent-sigmoid (tansig) and linear (purelin) transfer functions for hidden and output layers, respectively; (b) the outputs from the output nodes $\{y_{i,k}\}$ are then compared with their target values $\{t_{i,k}\}$, and the difference is used to compute the MSE (Equation 2); (c) upon the *MSE* computation, the weight matrices W^H and W^O are updated using the corresponding method (Levenberg-Marquardt) (Hagan & Menhaj, 1994; Yao *et al.*, 2005).

In the back-propagation training method, the input *x* and target *t* values were normalized linearly to be within the range [-1 1]. The normalization of inputs and outputs leads to avoidance of numerical overflows due to very large or very small weights (Razavi *et al.*, 2003; Bowen *et al.*, 1998; Yao *et al.*, 2005). This normalization was performed to prevent mismatch between the influence of some input values to the network weights and biases. Network training was performed using Levenberg-Marquardt algorithm due to its fast convergence and reliability in locating the global minimum of the mean-squared error (*MSE*) (Levenberg-Marquardt) (Hagan & Menhaj, 1994; Yao *et al.*, 2005). The transfer function at the hidden layer nodes is tangent sigmoid, which is nonlinear but differentiable. The output node utilizes the linear transfer function so that the input values *n* equal to the output values *y*. The normalized output values y_n are retransformed to its original range (Razavi *et al.*, 2003; Bowen *et al.*, 1998; Yao *et al.*, 2005).

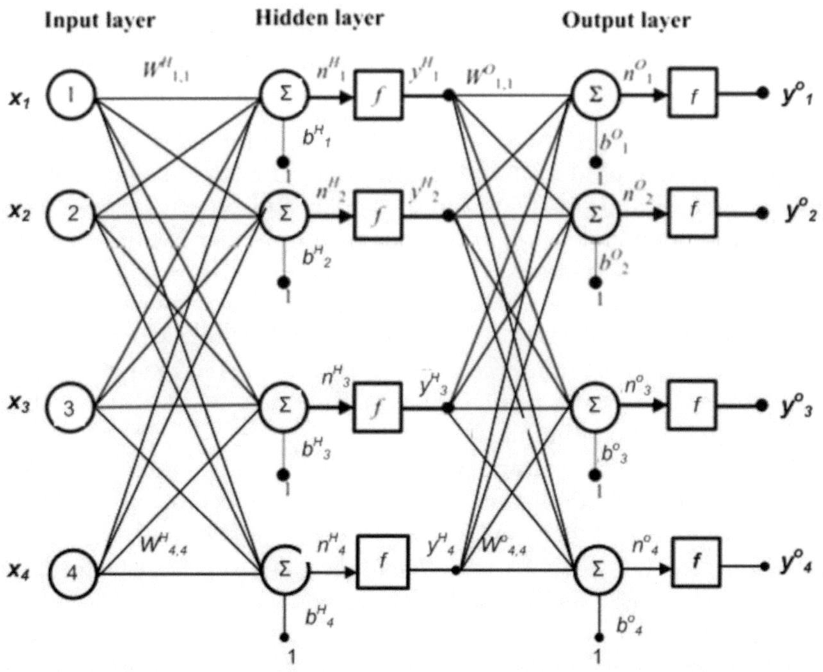

Fig. 1. A schematic diagram of the multi-layered perceptron (MLP) in feed-forward neural network with back-propagation training (X_1: CH_4/CO_2 ratio; X_2: discharge voltage; X_3: total feed flow rate; X_4: reactor temperature; $y^o{}_1$: CH_4 conversion; $y^o{}_2$: C_2 hydrocarbons selectivity; $y^o{}_3$: Hydrogen selectivity; and $y^o{}_4$: C_2 hydrocarbons yield)

In terms of multi-objective optimization, GA was used for solving the scalar optimization problem based on the principle of survival of the fittest during the evolution. The GA implements the "survival of the fittest" and "genetic propagation of characteristics" principles of biological evolution for searching the solution space of an optimization problem. In nature, individuals must adapt to the frequent changing environment in order to survive. The GA is one of the strategic randomized search techniques, which are well known for its robustness in finding the optimal or near-optimal solution since it does not depend on gradient information in its walk of life to find the best solution. Various kinds of algorithm were reported by previous researchers (Tarca *et al.*, 2002; Nandi *et al.*, 2002, 2004; Kundu *et al.*, 2009; Bhatti *et al.*, 2011).

The GA uses and manipulates a population of potential solutions to find optimal solutions. The generation is complete after each individual in the population has performed the genetic operators. The individuals in the population will be better adapted to the objective/fitness function, as they have to survive in the subsequent generations. At each step, the GA selects individuals at random from the current population to be parents and uses them to produce the children for the next generation. Over successive generation, the population evolves toward an optimal solution. The GA uses three main types of rules at each step to create the next generation from the current population: (a) *Selection rules* select the individuals, called parents, that contribute to the population at the next generation; (b) *Crossover rules* combine two parents to form children for the next generation; (c) *Mutation rules* apply random changes to individual parents to form children.

The detail stepwise procedures for the hybrid ANN-GA algorithm for simultaneous modelling and optimization are described below and are depicted schematically in Figure 2:

Step 1. **(Development of an ANN-based model):** Specify input and output experimental data of the system used for training and testing the ANN-based model. Create the network architecture involving input, hidden and output layers. Investigate the optimal network architecture (optimal number of hidden layer) and make sure that the network is not overfitted.

Step 2. **(Training of the ANN-based model):** Normalize the experimental input and output data to be within the range [-1 1]. The normalization is performed to prevent mismatch between the influence of some input values to the network weights and biases. Train the network using the normalized data by utilizing a robust training algorithm (Levenberg-Marquardt).

Step 3. **(Initialization of solution population):** Set the initial generation index (*Gen*) to zero and the number of population (N_{pop}). Set the number of independent variables (*nvars*). Generate a random initial population of N_{pop} individuals. Each individual possesses vector entries with certain length or called as *genes* which are divided into many segments based on the number of decision variables (*nvars*).

Step 4. **(Fitness computation):** In this step the performance (fitness) of the solution vector in the current population is computed by using a fitness function. Normalize the solution vector $\boldsymbol{x}_j$ to be within the range [-1 1]. Next, the vector $\boldsymbol{x}_j$ is entered as inputs vector to the trained ANN-based model to obtain the corresponding outputs $\boldsymbol{y}_j$, $\boldsymbol{y}_j=f(\boldsymbol{x}_j,\boldsymbol{W}, \boldsymbol{b})$. Re-transform the output vector $\boldsymbol{y}_j$ to the original values that are subsequently utilized to compute the fitness value/scores of the solution.

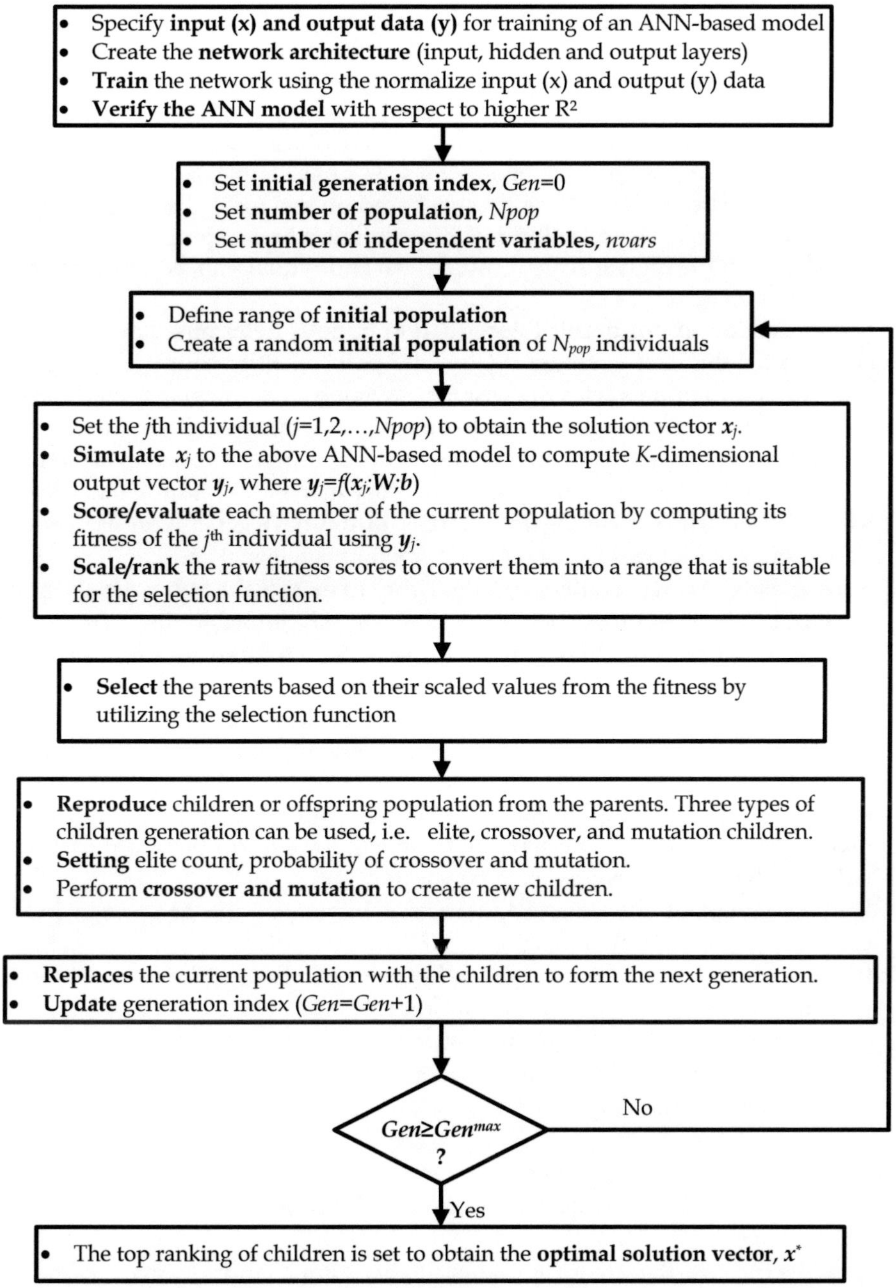

Fig. 2. Flowchart of the hybrid ANN-GA algorithms for modelling and optimization

Step 5. (Scaling the fitness scores): Scale/rank the raw fitness scores to values in a range that is suitable for the selection function. In the GA, the selection function uses the scaled fitness values to choose the parents for the next generation. The range of the scaled values influences performance of the GA. If the scaled values vary too widely, the individuals with the highest scaled values reproduce too rapidly, taking over the population gene pool too quickly, and preventing the GA from searching other areas of the solution space. On the other hand, if the scaled values vary only a little, all individuals have approximately the same chance of reproduction and the search will progress slowly. The scaling function used in this algorithm scales the raw scores based on the rank of each individual instead of its score. Because the algorithm minimizes the fitness function, lower raw scores have higher scaled values.

Step 6. (Parents selection): Choose the parents based on their scaled values by utilizing the selection function. The selection function assigns a higher probability of selection to individuals with higher scaled values. An individual can be selected more than once as a parent.

Step 7. (Reproduction of children): Reproduction options determine how the GA creates children for the next generation from the parents. **Elite count** (E_{child}) specifies the number of individuals with the best fitness values that are guaranteed to survive to the next generation. Set elite count to be a positive integer within the range: $1 \leq E_{child} \leq N_{pop}$. These individuals are called elite children. **Crossover fraction** (P_{cross}) specifies the fraction of each population, other than elite children, that are produced by crossover. The remaining individuals in the next generation are produced by mutation. Set crossover fraction to be a fraction between 0 and 1.

- **Crossover**: Crossover enables the algorithm to extract the best genes from different individuals by selecting genes from a pair of individuals in the current generation and recombines them into potentially superior children for the next generation with the probability equal to *crossover fraction* (P_{cross}) from Step 7.
- **Mutation:** Mutation function makes small random changes in the individuals, which provide genetic diversity and thereby increases the likelihood that the algorithm will generate individuals with better fitness values.

Step 8. (Replaces the current population with the children): After the reproduction is performed and the new children are obtained, the current populations are replaced with the children to form the next generation.

Step 9. Update/increment the generation index): Increment the generation index by 1: *Gen*=*Gen*+1.

Step 10. (Repeat Steps 4-9 until convergence is achieved): Repeat the steps 4-9 on the new generation until the convergences are met. The GA uses the following five criteria to determine when the algorithm stops:

- *Generations*: the algorithm stops when the number of generation reaches the maximum value (Gen_{max}).
- *Fitness limit*: the algorithm stops when the value of the fitness function for the best point in the current population is less than or equal to *Fitness limit*.
- *Time limit*: the algorithm stops after running for an amount of time in seconds equal to *Time limit*.
- *Stall generations*: the algorithm stops if there is no improvement in the objective function for a sequence of consecutive generations of length *Stall generations*.
- *Stall time limit*: the algorithm stops if there is no improvement in the objective function during an interval of time in seconds equal to *Stall time limit*.The algorithm stops if any one of these five conditions is met.

Step 11. (Assign the top ranking of children to the optimal solution vector): After the GA convergence criteria is achieved, the children possessing top ranking of fitness value is assigned to the optimized population or decision variable vector, x^*.

There is a vector of objectives, $\boldsymbol{F}(\boldsymbol{X}) = \{F_1(\boldsymbol{X}), F_2(\boldsymbol{X}),..., F_M(\boldsymbol{X})\}$ where M denotes the number of objectives, that must be considered in chemical engineering process. The optimization techniques are developed to find a set of decision parameters, $\boldsymbol{X}=\{X_1, X_2, ..., X_N\}$ where N is the number of independent variables. As the number of responses increases, the optimal solutions are likely to become complex and less easily quantified. Therefore, the development of multi-objectives optimization strategy enables a numerically solvable and realistic design problem (Wu *et al.*, 2002; Yu *et al.*, 2003). In this method, a set of design goals, $F^* = \{F_1^*, F_2^*, ..., F_M^*\}$ is associated with a set of objectives, $\boldsymbol{F}(\boldsymbol{X}) = \{F_1(\boldsymbol{X}), F_2(\boldsymbol{X}),..., F_M(\boldsymbol{X})\}$. The multi-objectives optimization formulation allows the objectives to be under- or over-achieved which is controlled by a vector of weighting coefficient, $w=\{w_1, w_2, ..., w_M\}$. The optimization problem is formulated as follow:

$$\underset{\gamma,\, x \in \Omega}{\text{minimize}}\ \gamma \quad \text{subject to} \quad \begin{aligned} F_1(x) - w_1\gamma &\le F_1{}^* \\ F_2(x) - w_2\gamma &\le F_2{}^* \end{aligned} \tag{3}$$

Specification of the goals, (F_1^*, F_2^*), defines the goal point. The weighting vector defines the direction of search from the goal point to the feasible function space. During the optimization, γ is varied which changes the size of the feasible region. The constraint boundaries converge to the unique solution point (F_{1s}, F_{2s}).

3. Results and discussion

3.1 Development and testing of artificial neural network – Genetic algorithm model

In developing a phenomenological model, it is mandatory to consider detailed kinetics of stated multiple reactions in the conservation equations. However, due to the tedious procedures involved in obtaining the requisite kinetic information within phenomenological model, the empirical data-based ANN-GA modelwas chosen for maximizing the process performances. In this study, simultaneous modeling and multi-objectives optimization of catalytic-plasma reactor for methane and carbon dioxide conversions to higher hydrocarbons (C_2) and hydrogen was done. The purpose of multi-objectives optimization is to maximize the process performances simultaneously, i.e. CH_4 conversion (Y_1) and C_2 hydrocarbons yield (Y_4). Accordingly, four parameters namely CH_4/CO_2 ratio (X_1), discharge voltage (X_2), total feed flow rate (X_3), and reactor temperature (X_4), generate input space of the ANN model. In the ANN model, the four parameters and four targeted responses (CH_4 conversion ($y^o{}_1$), C_2 hydrocarbons selectivity ($y^o{}_2$), Hydrogen selectivity ($y^o{}_3$), and C_2 hydrocarbons yield ($y^o{}_4$) were developed and simulated.

Regarding the simultaneous modeling and optimization using the ANN-GA method (Figure 2), accuracy of the hybrid method was validated by a set of simple discrete data extracted from a simple quadratic equation (i.e. $y= -2x^2 + 15x + 5$). From the testing, the determination coefficient (R^2) of the method closes to 1 means the empirical method (ANN-GA) has a good fitting, while the relative error of the optimized results (comparison between GA results and analytical solution) are below 10%.

In this chapter, Multi Input and Multi Output (MIMO) system with 4 inputs and 4 outputs of the ANN model was developed. Prior to the network training, numbers of experimental data (Table 2) were supplied into the training. The data were obtained based on the experimental design (central composite design) as revealed in Tables 1 and 2. In each network training, the training data set was utilized for adjusting the weight matrix set, *W*. The performance of the ANN model is considered as fitness tests of the model, i.e. MSE, R, and epoch number (epochs). Comparison of the ANN model performance for various topologies was performed. The MSE decreases and R increases with increasing number of nodes in the hidden layer. However, increasing number of hidden layer takes more time in computation due to more complexity of the model. Therefore, optimization of layer number structure is important step in ANN modeling.

The ANN model fitness in terms of comparison between targeted (t) and predicted (y) performances is shown in Figures 3 and 4. In the figures, the ANN models are fit well to the experimental data which is demonstrated by high determination coefficients (R^2) of 0.9975 and 0.9968 with respect to CH_4 conversion (y_1) and C_2 hydrocarbons yield (y_2) models, respectively. The high R^2 and low MSE value implies a good fitting between the targeted (experimental) and the predicted (calculated) values. Therefore, the ANN-based models are suitable for representing the plasma-catalytic conversion of methane and carbon dioxide to higher hydrocarbons. From the simulation, the hybrid ANN-GA algorithm is supposed to be powerful for simultaneous modeling and optimizing process conditions of the complex process as inline with the previous literatures (Istadi & Amin, 2006, 2007) with similar algorithm. The R^2 by this method is high enough (higher than 0.95). The ANN-GA model has advantageous on the fitted model which is a complex non linear model. This is to improve the weaknesses of the response surface methodology that is forced to quadratic model.

3.2. Multi-objective oOptimization of DBD plasma - Catalytic reactor performances

In this study, simultaneous modeling and multi-objective optimization of catalytic-plasma reactor for methane and carbon dioxide conversions to higher hydrocarbons (C_2) and hydrogen was performed. The multi-objective optimization is aimed to maximize the CH_4 conversion (Y_1) and C_2 hydrocarbons yield (Y_4) simultaneously. Accordingly, four respected parameters, namely CH_4/CO_2 ratio (X_1), discharge voltage (X_2), total feed flow rate (X_3), and reactor temperature (X_4) are optimized stated as input space of the ANN model. In the ANN model, the four parameters and four targeted responses (CH_4 conversion ($y^o{}_1$), C_2 hydrocarbons selectivity ($y^o{}_2$), hydrogen selectivity ($y^o{}_3$), and C_2 hydrocarbons yield ($y^o{}_4$)) were developed and simulated. In this case, two responses or objectives can be optimized simultaneously to obtain optimum four respected process parameters, i.e. CH_4 conversion and C_2 hydrocarbons yield ($y^o{}_1$ and $y^o{}_4$), CH_4 conversion and C_2hydrocarbon selectivity ($y^o{}_1$ and $y^o{}_2$), or CH_4 conversion and hydrogen selectivity ($y^o{}_1$and $y^o{}_3$). For maximizing F_1 and F_4 (CH_4 conversion and C_2hydrocarbons yield, respectively), the actual objective functions are presented in Equation 4 which is one of the popular approaches for inversion (Deb, 2001; Tarafder *et al.*, 2005). The equation was used due to the default of the optimization function is minimization.

$$F_i = \frac{1}{1+F_{i,o}} \tag{4}$$

where $F_{i,o}$ denotes the real objective functions, while F_i is the inverted objective functions for minimization problem.

For the multi-objectives optimization, the decision variables/operating parameters bound were chosen from the corresponding bounds in the training data as listed in Table 3. Meanwhile, Table 4 lists the numerical parameter values used in the GA for all optimization runs. In this optimization, rank method was used for fitness scaling, while stochastic tournament was used for selection method to specify how the GA chooses parents for the next generation. Meanwhile, scattered method was chosen for crossover function and uniform strategy was selected for mutation function. From the 40 numbers of population size, two of them are elite used in the next generation, while 80% of the rest population was used for crossover reproduction and 20% of them was used for mutation reproduction with 5% rate.

Operating Parameters	Bounds
CH_4/CO_2 feed ratio	$1.5 \leq X_1 \leq 4.0$
Discharge voltage (kV)	$12 \leq X_2 \leq 17$
Total feed flow rate (cm^3/min)	$20 \leq X_3 \leq 40$
Reactor temperature (°C)	$100 \leq X_4 \leq 350$

Table 3. Operating parameters bound used in multi-objectives optimization of DBD plasma reactor without catalyst

Computational Parameters	Values
Population size	40
Elite count	2
Crossover fraction	0.80
Number of generation	20
Fitness scaling function	fitscalingrank
Selection function	selectiontournament
Crossover function	crossoverscattered
Mutation function	mutationuniform
Mutation probability	0.05

Table 4. Computational parameters of GA used in the multi-objectives optimization

The Pareto optimal solutions owing to the simultaneous CH_4 conversion and C_2 hydrocarbons yield and the corresponding four process parameters are presented in Figure 5. The Pareto optimal solutions points are obtained by varying the weighting coefficient (w_k) in Equation (3) (goal attainment method) and performing the GA optimization corresponding to each w_k so that the γ reaches its minimum value ($F_k(x)$-$w_k.\gamma \leq F_k$) (goal). From Figure 5, it was found in the Pareto optimal solution that if CH_4 conversion improves, C_2hydrocarbons yield deteriorates or vice versa. Theoretically, all sets of non-inferior/Pareto optimal solutions are acceptable. The maximum CH_4 conversion and C_2 hydrocarbons yield of 48 % and 15 %, respectively are recommended at corresponding optimum process parameters of CH_4/CO_2 feed ratio 3.6, discharge voltage 15 kV, total feed flow rate 20 cm^3/min, and reactor temperature of 147 °C. Larger CH_4 amount in the feed and higher feed flow rate enhance the C_{2+} hydrocarbons yield which is corroborated with the results of Eliasson *et al.* (2000). From the Pareto optimal solutions and the corresponding optimal operating parameters, the suitable operating conditions ranges for DBD plasma reactor owing to simultaneous maximization of CH_4 conversion and C_2hydrocarbons yield can be recommended easily.

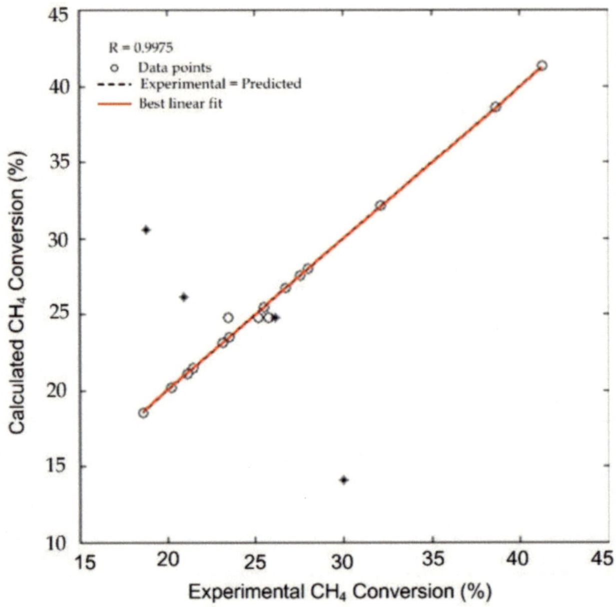

Fig. 3. Comparison of targeted (experimental) and predicted (calculated) CH_4 conversion of the ANN model (R^2=0.9975) (* : test set data)

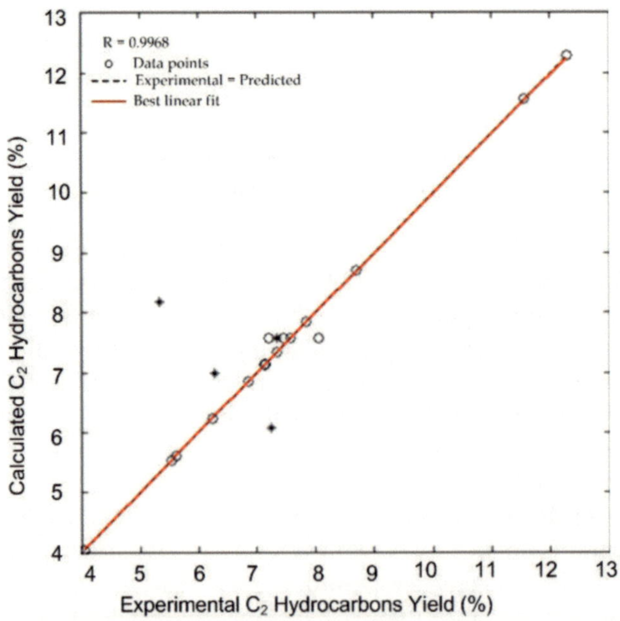

Fig. 4. Comparison of targeted (experimental) and predicted (calculated) C_2 hydrocarbons yield of the ANN model (R^2=0.9968) (* : test set data)

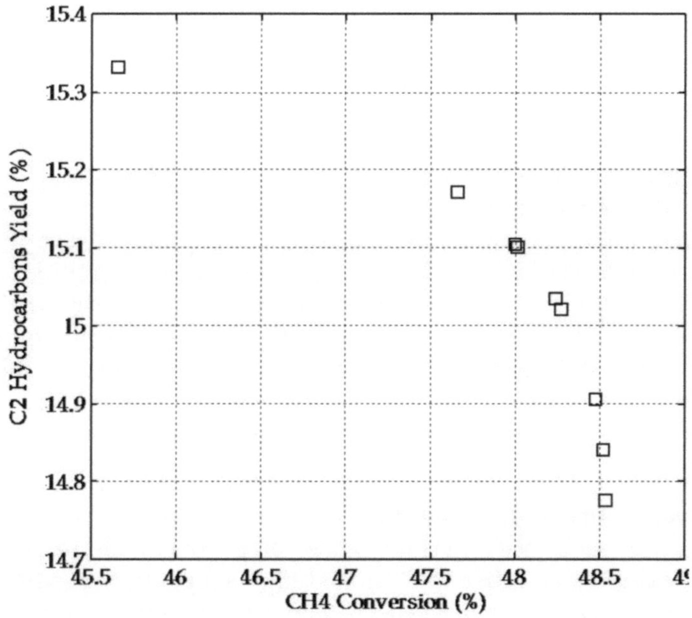

Fig. 5. Pareto optimal solutions with respect to multi-objectives optimization of CH_4 conversion (Y_1) and C_2hydrocarbons yield (Y_2).

3.3 Effect of hybrid catalytic-plasma DBD reactor for CH_4 and CO_2 conversions

When a gas phase consisting electrically neutral species, electrons, ions and other excited species flow through the catalyst bed, the catalyst particles become electrically charged. The charge on the catalyst surface, together with other effects of excited species in the gas discharge leads to the variations of electrostatic potential of the catalyst surface. The chemisorption and desorption performances of the catalyst therefore may be modified in the catalyst surface (Jung *et al.*, 2004; Kraus *et al.*, 2001). Effects of these modifications on methane conversion are dependent on the amount and concentration of surface charge and the species present at the catalyst surface (Kim *et al.*, 2004). The combining DBD plasma and a heterogeneous catalyst are possible to activate the reactants in the discharge prior to the catalytic reaction, which should have positive influences on the reaction conditions.

Comparison of the application of DBD plasma technology in CH_4 and CO_2 conversion with catalyst is studied in this research. Since most of the energetic electrons are required to activate the CH_4 and CO_2 gases in a discharge gap, special consideration must be taken in the designing a reactor that maximizes the contact time between the energetic electrons and the neutral feed gas species. The catalyst located in the discharge gap is an alternative way to increase the time and area of contact between gas molecules and energetic electrons in addition to other modification of electronic properties. The energetic electrons determine the chemistry of the conversions of both gases (Eliasson *et al.*, 2000; Yao *et al.*, 2000; Zhou *et al.*, 1998). The nature of dielectric and electrode surfaces is also an important factor for products distribution of CH_4 and CO_2 conversions using the DBD.

In the catalytic DBD plasma reactor system, the catalyst acts as a dielectric material. Most of the discharge energy is used to produce and to accelerate the electrons generating highly active species (metastable, radicals and ions). The combined action of catalysts and a non-equilibrium gas discharge leads to an alternative method for production of syngas and hydrocarbons from CH_4 and CO_2. When an electric field is applied across the packed dielectric layer, the catalyst is polarized and the charge is accumulated on the dielectric surface. An intense electric field is generated around each catalyst pellet contact point resulting in microdischarges between the pellets. The microdischarges in the packed-bed of catalyst produced energetic electrons rather than ions. The microdischarges induced a significant enrichment of electrons that were essential for the sustainability of plasmas. Methane and carbon dioxide were chemically activated by electron collisions. Liu *et al.* (1997) concluded that the electronic properties of catalysts have an important role in oxidative coupling of methane using DBD plasma reactor. The electronic properties and catalytic properties can be expected to be changed if the catalyst is electrically charged.

From the non-catalytic DBD plasma reactor, it is shown that the plasma process seems to be less selective than conventional catalytic processes, but it has high conversion. The conventional catalytic reactions on the other hand can give high selectivity, but they require a certain gas composition, an active catalyst, and high temperature condition (endothermic reaction). In the hybrid catalysis-plasma, the catalyst has important roles such as increasing the reaction surface area, maintaining and probably increasing the non-equilibrium properties of gas discharge, acting as a dielectric-barrier material, and improving the selectivity and efficiency of plasma processes by surface reactions. The catalyst placed in the plasma zone can influence the plasma properties due to the presence of conductive surfaces in the case of metallic catalysts (Heintze & Pietruszka, 2004; Kizling & Järås, 1996). The catalyst can also change the reaction products due to surface reactions. The heating and electronic properties of the catalyst by the plasma induce chemisorption of surface species. A synergy between the catalyst and the plasma is important so that the interactions lead to improved reactant conversions and higher selectivity to the desired products. However until now, the exact role of the catalyst in the DBD plasma reactor is still not clear from the chemistry point of view. Even the kind of plasma reactor determines the product selectivity (Gordon *et al.*, 2001). The most significant influence of the plasma was observed at low temperatures (Liu *et al.*, 2001b) at which the catalysts were not active. At higher temperatures the catalysts became active; nonetheless, the plasma catalytic effect was still observed (Huang *et al.*, 2000).

3.4. Simulation of DBD plasma - Catalytic reactor performances

This section demonstrates ANN simulation for the effect of operating parameters (X_1, X_2, X_3, X_4) in catalytic DBD plasma reactor on CH_4 conversion (y_1) and C_2 hydrocarbons yield (y_4). The simulation results were presented in three dimensional surface graphics (Figures 6 to 13). From the results, the CH_4 conversion and C_2 hydrocarbons yield are affected by CH_4/CO_2 feed ratio, discharge voltage, total feed flow rate, and reactor wall temperature from the ANN-based model simulation.

Figures 6, 7, 8, and 9 simulates the effect of discharge voltage, CH_4/CO_2 feed ratio, total feed flow rate, and reactor temperature on the methane conversion. Increasing the discharge voltage improves methane conversion significantly. That is true because energy of energetic

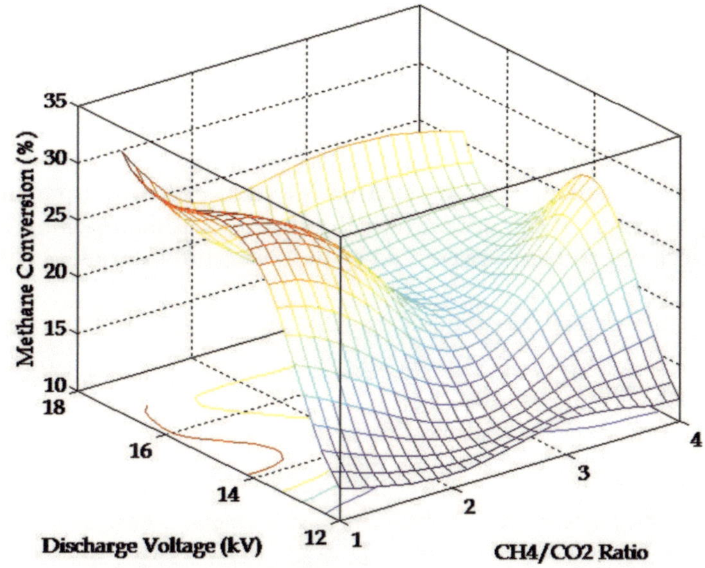

Fig. 6. Effect of discharge voltage (X_2) and CH_4/CO_2 ratio (X_1) toward methane conversion (y_1)

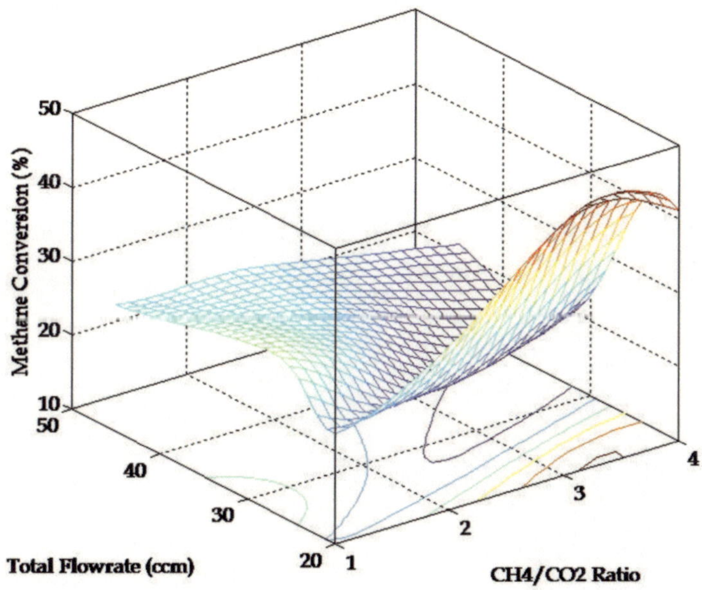

Fig. 7. Effect of total flow rate (X_3) and CH_4/CO_2 ratio (X_1) toward methane conversion (y_1)

electrons is dependent on the discharge voltage. Higher the discharge voltage, higher the energy of electrons flows from high voltage electrode to ground electrode. Increasing the CH_4 concentration in the feed favors the selectivity of C_2 hydrocarbons and hydrogen significantly, but the C_2 hydrocarbons yield is slightly affected due to the decrease of CH_4 conversion. It is suggested that the CH_4 concentration in the feed is an important factor for the total amount of hydrocarbons produced. However, increasing CH_4/CO_2 ratio to 4 reduces the methane conversion considerably and leads to enhanced C_2 hydrocarbons selectivity and H_2/CO ratio. It is confirmed that CO_2 as co-feed has an important role in improving CH_4 conversion by contributing some oxygen active species from the CO_2. This phenomenon is corroborated with the results of Zhang *et al.* (2001).

Effect of total feed flow rate on methane conversion is displayed in Figures 7 and 8. From the figures, total feed flow rate has significant effect on methane conversion. Higher the total feed flow rate, lower methane conversion. This is due to primarily from short collision of energetic electrons with feed gas during flow through the plasma reactor. Therefore, only a few reactant molecules that has been cracked by the energetic electrons.

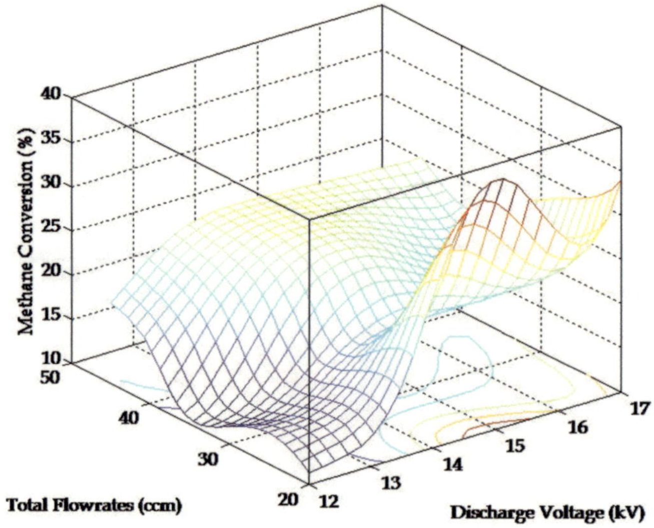

Fig. 8. Effect of total flow rate (X_3) and discharge voltage (X_2) toward methane conversion (y_1)

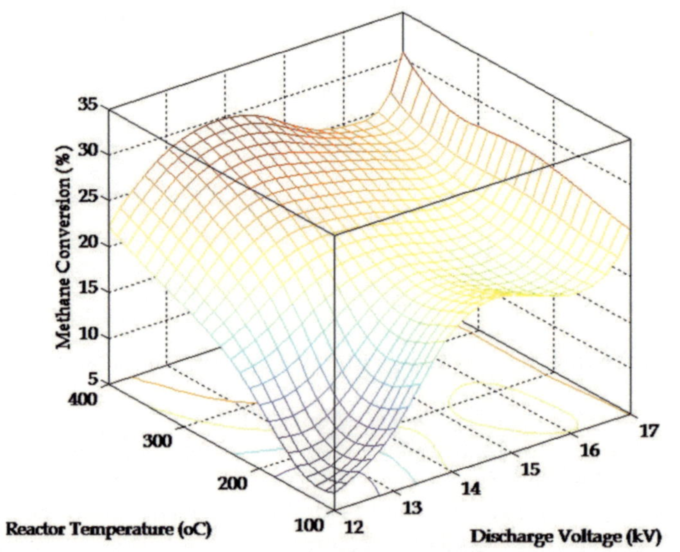

Fig. 9. Effect of reactor temperature (X_4) and discharge voltage (X_2) toward methane conversion (y_1)

Figures 10, 11, 12, and 13presents the effect of discharge voltage, CH_4/CO_2 feed ratio, total feed flow rate, and reactor temperature on the C_2 hydrocarbons yield. The yield of gaseous hydrocarbons (C_2) increases with the CH_4/CO_2 feed ratio as exhibited in Figure. It is possible to control the composition of C_2 hydrocarbons and hydrogen products by adjusting the CH_4/CO_2 feed ratio. Increasing CH_4/CO_2 ratio above 2.5 exhibits dramatic enhancement of C_2hydrocarbons yield and lowers CH_4 conversion slightly. In this work, the composition of the feed gas is an essential factor to influence the product distribution. Obviously, more methane in the feed will produce more light hydrocarbons.

In comparison with non-catalytic DBD plasma reactor, the enhancement of reactor performance is obtained when using the hybrid catalytic-DBD plasma reactor (Istadi, 2006). The CH_4 conversion, C_2 hydrocarbons selectivity, C_2 hydrocarbons yield and H_2 selectivity of catalytic DBD plasma reactor is higher than that without catalyst (Istadi, 2006). The catalyst located in the discharge gap can increase the time and area of contact in addition to other modification of electronic properties. Therefore, collision among the energetic electrons and the gas molecules is intensive. Through the hybrid system, the chemisorption and desorption performances of the catalyst may be modified in the catalyst surface (Jung *et al.*, 2004; Kraus *et al.*, 2001) which is dependent on the amount and concentration of surface charge and the species on the catalyst surface (Kim *et al.*, 2004). The results enhancement was also reported by Eliasson *et al.* (2000) over DBD plasma reactor with high input power 500 W (20 kV and 30 kHz) that the zeolite catalyst introduction significantly increased the selectivity of light hydrocarbons compared to that in the absence of zeolite.

Varying the discharge power/voltage affects predominantly on methane conversion and higher hydrocarbons (C_2) yield and selectivity. At high discharge voltage the CH_4 conversion becomes higher than that of CO_2 as presented in Table 2, since the dissociation energy of CO_2 (5.5 eV) is higher than that of CH_4 (4.5 eV) as reported by Liu *et al.* (1999a). More plasma species may be generated at higher discharge voltage. Previous researchers suggested that the conversions of CH_4 and CO_2 were enhanced with discharge power in a catalytic DBD plasma reactor (Caldwell *et al.*, 2001; Eliasson *et al.*, 2000; Zhang *et al.*, 2001) and non-catalytic DBD plasma reactor (Liu *et al.*, 2001b). From Figures10 and 12, the yield of C_2 hydrocarbons decreases slightly with the discharge voltage which is corroborated with the results of Liu *et al.* (2001b). This means that increasing discharge power may destroy the light hydrocarbons (C_2-C_3). In this research, the lower range of discharge power (discharge voltage 12 - 17 kV and frequency 2 kHz) does not improve the H_2 selectivity over DBD plasma reactor although the catalyst and the heating was introduced in the discharge space as exhibited in Figures 9 and 13. Eliasson *et al.* (2000) reported that higher discharge power is necessary for generating higher selectivity to higher hydrocarbons (C_{5+}) over DBD plasma reactor with the presence of zeolite catalysts. Higher discharge power is suggested to be efficient for methane conversion. As the discharge power increases, the bulk gas temperature in the reaction zone may also increase.

The total feed flow rate also affects predominantly on residence time of gases within the discharge zone in the catalytic DBD plasma reactor. Therefore, the residence time influences collisions among the gas molecules and the energetic electrons. Increasing the total feed flow rate reduces the residence time of gases and therefore decreases the C_2 hydrocarbons yield dramatically as demonstrated in Figures 11 and 12. A lower feed flow rate is beneficial for producing high yields light hydrocarbons (C_{2+}) and synthesis gases with higher H_2/CO

ratio as reported by Li *et al.* (2004c). The hydrogen selectivity is also affected slightly by the total feed flow rate within the range of operating conditions. Indeed, the total feed flow rate affects significantly on the methane conversion rather than yield of C_2 hydrocarbons. Actually, the low total feed flow rate (high residence time) leads to high intimate collision among the gas molecules, the catalyst and high energetic electrons. The high intensive collisions favor the methane and carbon dioxide conversions to C_{2+} hydrocarbons.

From Figures 9 and 13, it is evident that the current range of reactor temperature only affects the catalytic - DBD plasma reactor slightly. The methane conversion and C_2 hydrocarbons yield is only affected slightly by reactor wall temperature over the CaO-MnO/CeO_2 catalyst. This may be due to the altering of the catalyst surface phenomena and the temperature of energetic electrons is quite higher than that of reactor temperature. The adsorption-desorption, heterogeneous catalytic and electronic properties of the catalysts may change the surface reaction activity when electrically charged. However, the chemistry and physical phenomena at the catalyst surface cannot be determined in the sense of traditional catalyst. Some previous researchers implied that the synergistic effect of catalysis-plasma only occurred at high temperature where the catalyst was active. Huang *et al.* (2000) and Heintze & Pietruszka (2004) pointed out that the product selectivity significantly improved only if the temperature was high enough for the catalytic material to become itself active. Zhang *et al.* (2001) also claimed that the reactor wall temperature did not significantly affect the reaction activity (selectivity) over zeolite NaY catalyst under DBD plasma conditions at the temperature range tested (323-423 K). Particularly, increasing the wall temperature at the low temperature range tested did not affect the reaction activity under plasma conditions. In contrast, some other researchers suggested that the synergistic effect of catalysis - plasma may occur at low temperature. Based on the ANN-based model simulation, it can be suggested that low total feed flow rate, high CH_4/CO_2 feed ratio, high discharge voltage and proper reactor temperature are suitable for producing C_{2+} hydrocarbons and synthesis gas over catalytic DBD plasma reactor.

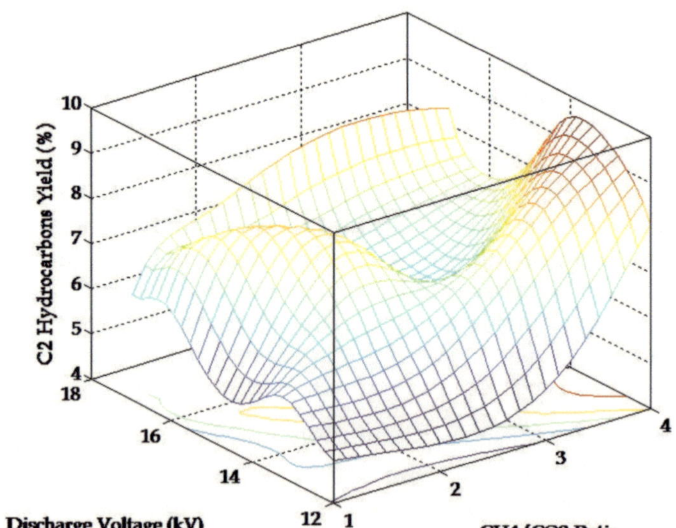

Fig. 10. Effect of discharge voltage (X_2) and CH_4/CO_2 ratio (X_1) toward C_2 hydrocarbons yield (y_4)

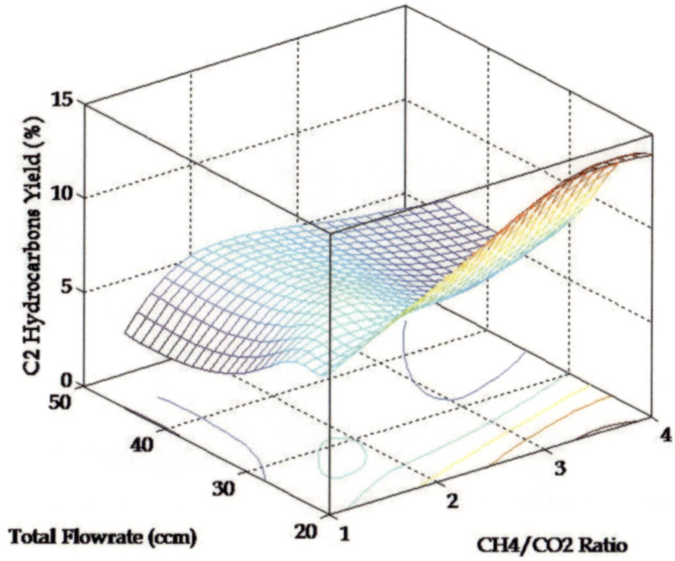

Fig. 11. Effect of total feed flowrate (X_3) and CH_4/CO_2 ratio (X_1) toward C_2 hydrocarbons yield (y_4)

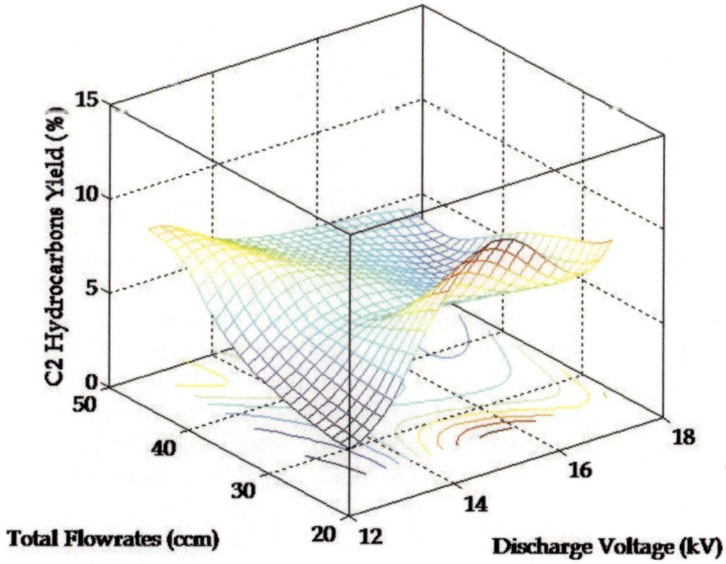

Fig. 12. Effect of total feed flowrate (X_3) and discharge voltage (X_2) toward C_2 hydrocarbons yield (y_4)

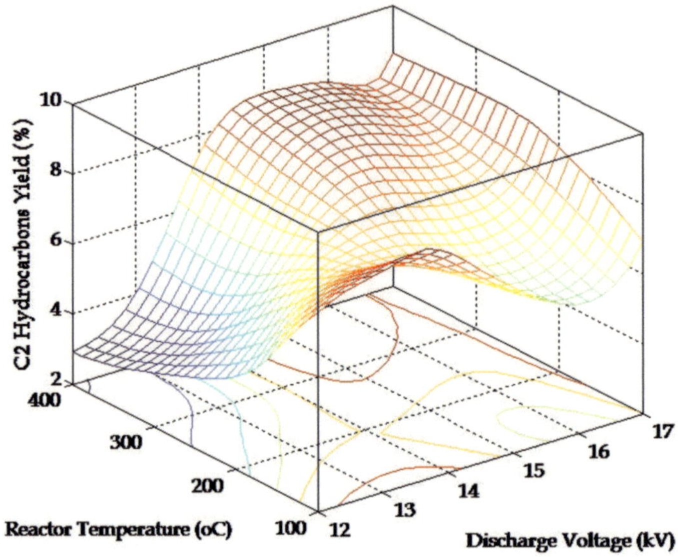

Fig. 13. Effect of reactor temperature (X_4) and discharge voltage (X_2) toward C_2 hydrocarbons yield (y_4)

4. Conclusions

A hybrid ANN-GA was successfully developed to model, to simulate and to optimize simultaneously a catalytic–DBD plasma reactor. The integrated ANN-GA method facilitates powerful modeling and multi-objective optimization for co-generation of synthesis gas, C_2 and higher hydrocarbons from methane and carbon dioxide in a DBD plasma reactor. The hybrid approach simplified the complexity in process modeling of the DBD plasma reactor. In the ANN model, the four parameters and four targeted responses (CH_4 conversion ($y^o{}_1$), C_2 hydrocarbons selectivity ($y^o{}_2$), hydrogen selectivity ($y^o{}_3$), and C_2 hydrocarbons yield ($y^o{}_4$) were developed and simulated. In the multi-objectives optimization, two responses or objectives were optimized simultaneously for optimum process parameters, i.e. CH_4 conversion ($y^o{}_1$) and C_2 hydrocarbons yield ($y^o{}_4$). Pareto optimal solutions pertaining to simultaneous CH_4 conversion and C_2 hydrocarbons yield and the corresponding process parameters were attained. It was found that if CH_4 conversion improved, C_2 hydrocarbons yield deteriorated, or vice versa. Theoretically, all sets of non-inferior/Pareto optimal solutions were acceptable. From the Pareto optimal solutions and the corresponding optimal operating parameters, the suitable operating condition range for DBD plasma reactor for simultaneous maximization of CH_4 conversion and C_2 hydrocarbons yield could be recommended easily. The maximum CH_4 conversion and C_2 hydrocarbons yield of 48 % and 15 %, respectively were recommended at corresponding optimum process parameters of CH_4/CO_2 feed ratio 3.6, discharge voltage 15 kV, total feed flow rate 20 cm^3/min, and reactor temperature of 147 ^oC.

5. Abbreviations

ANN	: artificial neural network
GA	: genetic algorithm

ANN-GA	: artificial neural network - genetic algorithm
DBD	: dielectric-barrier discharge
NSGA	: non-dominated sorting genetic algorithm
CO_2 OCM	: carbon dioxide oxidative coupling of methane
O_2 OCM	: oxygen oxidative coupling of methane
CCD	: central composite design
MSE	: mean square error
MLP	: multi-layered perceptron
WSSOF	: weighted sum of square objective function
MIMO	: multi input multi output

6. References

Ahmad, A.L., Azid, I.A., Yusof, A.R., & Seetharamu, K.N. (2004). Emission control in palm oil mills using artificial neural network and genetic algorithm. *Comp. Chem. Eng.* 28: 2709-2715

Bhatti, M.S., Kapoor, D., Kalia, R.K., Reddy, A.S., Thukral, A.K. (2011). RSM and ANN modeling for electrocoagulation of copper from simulated wastewater: Multi objective optimization using genetic algorithm approach. *Desalination*. 274:74-80

Bowen, W.R., Jones, M.J., & Yousef, H.N.S. (1998). Dynamic Ultrafiltration of Proteins - A Neural Network Approach. *J. Membrane Sci.* 146: 225-235

Caldwell, T.A., Le, H., Lobban, L.L., & Mallinson, R.G. (2001).Partial Oxidation of Methane to Form Synthesis Gas in a Tubular AC Plasma Reactor. in Spivey, J.J., Iglesia, E. and Fleisch, T.H. Eds. *Studies in Surface Science and Catalysis 136*, Amsterdam: Elsevier Science B.V. 265-270

Clarke, G.M., & Kempson, R.E. (1997). *Introduction to the Design and Analysis of Experiments.* London: Arnold

Deb, K. (2001). *Multi-objective Optimization Using Evolutionary Algorithms.*Chichester, UK: John Wiley & Sons

Eliasson, B., Liu, C.J., & Kogelschatz, U. (2000). Direct Conversion of Methane and Carbon Dioxide to Higher Hydrocarbons using Catalytic Dielectric-Barrier Discharges with Zeolites. *Ind. Eng. Chem. Res.* 39: 1221-1227

Fissore, D., Barresi, A.A., & Manca, D. (2004). Modelling of methanol synthesis in a network of forced unsteady-state ring reactors by artificial neural networks for control purposes. *Chem. Eng. Sci.* 59: 4033-4041

Gordon, C.L., Lobban, L.L., & Mallinson, R.G. (2001).Selective Hydrogenation of Acetylene to Ethylene during the Conversion of Methane in a Catalytic DC Plasma Reactor. In: *Studies in Surface Science and Catalysis 136*, Pivey, J.J., Iglesia, E. and Fleisch, T.H. Eds. Amsterdam: Elsevier Science B.V. 271-276

Hagan, M.T., & Menhaj, M. (1994). Training Feedforward Networks with the Marquardt Algorithm. *IEEE Trans. Neural Network.* 5: 989-993

Hattori, T., & Kito, S. (1991). Artificial Intelligence Approach to Catalyst Design. *Catal. Today.* 10: 213-222

Hattori, T., & Kito, S. (1995). Neural Network as a Tool for Catalyst Development. *Catal. Today.* 23: 347-355

Heintze, M., & Pietruszka, B. (2004). Plasma Catalytic Conversion of Methane into Syngas: The Combined Effect of Discharge Activation and Catalysis. *Catal. Today.* 89: 21-25

Hou, Z.Y., Dai, Q.L., Wu, X.Q., &Chen, G.T. (1997). Artificial Neural Network Aided Design of Catalyst for Propane Ammoxidation. *Appl. Catal. A: Gen.* 161: 183-190

Huang, A., Xia, G., Wang, J., Suib, S.L., Hayashi, Y., & Matsumoto, H. (2000). CO_2 Reforming of CH4 by Atmospheric Pressure AC Discharge Plasmas. *J. Catal.* 189: 349-359

Huang, K., Zhan, X.L., Chen, F.Q., Lü, & D.W. (2003). Catalyst Design for Methane Oxidative Coupling by Using Artificial Neural Network and Hybrid Genetic Algorithm. *Chem. Eng. Sci.* 58: 81-87

Istadi, I. (2006). Catalytic Conversion of Methane and Carbon Dioxide in Conventional Fixed Bed and Dielectric Barrier Discharge Plasma Reactors. *PhD Thesis.* UniversitiTeknologi Malaysia, Malaysia

Istadi, I. & Amin, N.A.S. (2005). A Hybrid Numerical Approach for Multi-Responses Optimization of Process Parameters and Catalyst Compositions in CO_2 OCM Process over CaO-MnO/CeO_2 Catalyst. *Chem. Eng. J.*, 106: 213-227

Istadi, I., & Amin, N.A.S. (2006a). Optimization of Process Parameters and Catalyst Compositions in CO_2 Oxidative Coupling of Methane over CaO-MnO/CeO_2 Catalyst using Response Surface Methodology. *Fuel Process. Technol.* 87: 449-459

Istadi, I., & Amin, N.A.S. (2006b). Hybrid Artificial Neural Network−Genetic Algorithm Technique for Modeling and Optimization of Plasma Reactor. *Ind. Eng. Chem. Res.* 45: 6655-6664

Istadi, I., & Amin, N.A.S. (2007). Modelling and optimization of catalytic–dielectric barrier discharge plasma reactor for methane and carbon dioxide conversion using hybrid artificial neural network—genetic algorithm technique. *Chem. Eng. Sci.* 62: 6568-6581

Jung, S.H., Park, S.M., Park, S.H., & Kim, S.D. (2004). Surface Modification of Fine Powders by Atmospheric Pressure Plasma in A Circulating Fluidized Bed Reactor. *Ind. Eng. Chem. Res.* 43: 5483-5488.

Kim, S.S., Lee, H., Na, B.K., & Song, H.K. (2004). Plasma-assisted Reduction of Supported Metal Catalyst using Atmospheric Dielectric-barrier Discharge. *Catal. Today.* 89:193-200

Kizling, M.B., & Järås, S.G. (1996). A Review of the Use of Plasma Techniques in Catalyst Preparation and Catalytic Reactions. *Appl. Catal. A: Gen.* 147:1-21

Kraus, M., Eliasson, B., Kogelschatz, U., & Wokaun, A. (2001). CO_2 Reforming of Methane by the Combination of Dielectric-Barrier Discharges and Catalysis. *Phys. Chem. Chem. Phys.* 3:294-300

Kundu, P.K., Zhang, Y., Ray, A.K. (2009). Multi-objective optimization of simulated counter current moving bed chromatographycs reactor for oxidative coupling of methane. *Chem. Eng. Sci.* 64: 4137-4149

Larentis, A.L., de Resende, N.S., Salim, V.M.M., & Pinto J.C. (2001). Modeling and Optimization of the Combined Carbon Dioxide Reforming and Partial Oxidation of Natural Gas. *Appl. Catal. A: Gen.* 215: 211-224

Li, M.W., Xu, G.H., Tian, Y.L., Chen, L., & Fu, H.F. (2004c). Carbon Dioxide Reforming of Methane Using DC Corona Discharge Plasma Reaction. *J. Phys. Chem. A.* 108: 1687-1693

Liu, C.J., Mallinson, R., & Lobban, L. (1999a). Comparative Investigations on Plasma Catalytic Methane Conversion to Higher Hydrocarbons over Zeolites. *Appl. Catal. A: Gen.* 178: 17-27

Liu, C.J., Xue, B., Eliasson, B., He, F., Li, Y., &Xu, G.H. (2001b). Methane Conversion to Higher Hydrocarbons in the Presence of Carbon Dioxide using Dielectric Barrier-Discharge Plasmas. *Plasma Chem. Plasma Process.* 21: 301-309

Marzbanrad, J., Ibrahimi, M.R. (2011). Multi-Objective optimization of alumunium hollow tubes for vehicle crash energy absorption using a genetic algorithm and neural networks. *Thin Structure,* 49: 1605 - 1615

Montgomery, D.C. (2001). *Design and Analysis of Experiments.* New York: John Wiley & Sons

Nandasana, A.D., Ray, A.K., & Gupta, S.K. (2003). Dynamic Model of an Industrial Steam Reformer and Its Use for Multiobjective Optimization. *Ind. Eng. Chem. Res.* 42: 4028-4042

Nandi, S., Badhe, Y., Lonari, J., Sridevi, U., Rao, B.S., Tambe, S.S., & Kulkarni, B.D. (2004). Hybrid Process Modeling and Optimization Strategies Integrating Neural Networks/Support Vector Regression and Genetic Algorithms: Study of Benzene Isopropylation on Hbeta Catalyst. *Chem. Eng. J.* 97: 115-129

Nandi, S., Mukherjee, Tambe, S.S., Kumar, R., & Kulkarni, B.D. (2002). Reaction Modeling and Optimization Using Neural Networks and Genetic Algorithms: Case Study Involving TS-1 Catalyzed Hydroxylation of Benzene. *Ind. Eng. Chem. Res.* 41: 2159-2169

Radhakrishnan, V.R., & Suppiah, S. (2004). *Proceeding of the 18th Symposium of Malaysian Chemical Engineers.* UniversitiTeknologiPetronas, Perak, Malaysia

Razavi, S.M.A., Mousavi, S.M., & Mortazavi, S.A. (2003). Dynamic Prediction of Milk Ultrafiltration Performance: A Neural Network Approach. *Chem. Eng. Sci.* 58: 4185-4195

Stephanopoulos, G., & Han, C. (1996). Intelligent systems in process engineering: a review. *Comp. Chem. Eng.* 20: 743-791

Tarafder, A., Rangaiah, G.P., & Ray, A.K. (2005). Multiobjective Optimization of An Industrial Styrene Monomer Manufacturing Process. *Chem. Eng. Sci.* 60: 347-363

Tarca, L.A., Grandjean, B.P.A., & Larachi, F. (2002).Integrated Genetic Algorithm - Artificial Neural Network Strategy for Modelling Important Multiphase-Flow Characteristics. *Ind. Eng. Chem. Res.* 41: 2543-2551

The Mathworks. (2005). *Genetic Algorithm and Direct Search Toolbox for Use with MATLAB.* Natick, MA: The Mathworks, Inc

Wu, D., Li, Y., Shi, Y., Fang, Z., Wu, D., & Chang, L. (2002). Effects of the Calcination Conditions on the Mechanical Properties of a PCoMo/Al_2O_3Hydrotreating Catalyst. *Chem. Eng. Sci.* 57: 3495-3504

Yao, H.M., Vuthaluru, H.B., Tadé, M.O., & Djukanovic, D. (2005). Artificial Neural Network-Based Prediction of Hydrogen Content of Coal in Power Station Boilers. *Fuel.* 84: 1535-1542

Yao, S.L., Ouyang, F., Nakayama, A., Suzuki, E., Okumoto, M., & Mizuno, A. (2000). Oxidative Coupling and Reforming of Methane with Carbon Dioxide Using a High-Frequency Pulsed Plasma. *Energy Fuels.* 14: 910-914

Youness, E.A. (2004). Characterization of Efficient Solutions of Multi-Objective E-Convex Programming Problems. *Appl. Math. Comp.* 151: 755-761

Yu, W., Hidajat, K., & Ray, A.K. (2003). Application of Multiobjective Optimization in The Design and Operation of Reactive SMB and Its Experimental Verification. *Ind. Eng. Chem. Res.* 42: 6823-6831

Zhang, K., Kogelschatz, U., & Eliasson, B. (2001). Conversion of Greenhouse Gases to Synthesis Gas and Higher Hydrocarbons. *Energy Fuels*. 15: 395-402

Zhang, Z., Hidajat, K., & Ray, A.K. (2002b). Multiobjective Optimization of SMB and Varicol Process for Chiral Separation. *AIChE J*. 48: 2800-2816.

Zhao, W., Chen, D., & Hu, S. (2000). Optimizing Operating Conditions Based on ANN and Modified Gas. *Comp. Chem. Eng*. 24: 61-65

Zhou, L.M., Xue, B., Kogelshatz, U., & Eliasson, B. (1998). Non-Equilibrium Plasma Reforming of Greenhouse Gases to Synthesis Gas. *Energy Fuels*. 12:1191-1199

2

Application of Bio-Inspired Algorithms and Neural Networks for Optimal Design of Fractal Frequency Selective Surfaces

Paulo Henrique da Fonseca Silva[1], Marcelo Ribeiro da Silva[2], Clarissa de Lucena Nóbrega[2] and Adaildo Gomes D'Assunção[2]
[1]*Federal Institute of Education, Science and Technology of Paraiba, IFPB,*
[2]*Federal University of Rio Grande do Norte, UFRN,*
Brazil

1. Introduction

Technological advances in the field of microwave and communication systems and the increase of their commercial applications in recent years have resulted in more stringent requirements for innovative design of microwave passive devices, such as: antennas, filters, power splitters and couplers, frequency selective surfaces, etc. To be competitive in the commercial marketplace, microwave engineers may be using computer-aided design (CAD) tools to minimize cost and design cycle times. Modern CAD tools have become an integral part of the microwave product cycle and demand powerful optimization techniques combined with fast and accurate models so that the optimal solutions can be achieved, eventually guaranteeing first-pass design success. The target of microwave device design is to determine a set of physical parameters to satisfy certain design specifications (Mohamed, 2005).

Early methods of designing and optimizing microwave devices by hand are time and labor intensive, limit complexity, and require significant expertise and experience. Many of the important developments in microwave engineering were made possible when complex electromagnetic characteristics of microwave devices were represented in terms of circuit equivalents, lumped elements and transmission lines. Circuit simulators using empirical/analytical models are simple and efficient, reduce optimization time, but have limited accuracy or validity region. Although circuit simulator is still used today it suffers from some severe limitations (the most serious of them is that it considers only fundamental mode interactions) and requires corrections in the form of post manufacturing tuning (Fahmi, 2007).

While developments in circuit simulators were taking place, numerical electromagnetic (EM) techniques were also emerging. With the computational power provided by modern computers, the use of accurate full-wave electromagnetic models by EM simulators for design and optimization of microwave devices became possible. By using full-wave electromagnetic methods higher order modes are taken into consideration and microwave devices can be rigorously characterized in the designs so that simulation and experimental results are in close agreement. This is particularly of interest for the rapid large scale production of low-cost high performance microwave devices reducing or eliminating the need of post manufacturing tuning (Bandler et al., 1994; Fahmi, 2007).

The EM simulators can simulate microwave device structures of arbitrary geometrical shapes and ensure a satisfactory degree of accuracy up to millimeter wave frequencies (Mohamed, 2005). These simulators are based on EM field solvers whose function is to solve the EM problem of the structure under analysis, which is described by the Maxwell´s equations. Thus, the design of electromagnetic structures is usually a very challenging task due to the complexity of the models involved. In the majority of cases, there are no simple analytical formulas to describe the performance of new microwave devices. However, the use of EM field solver for device optimization is still a time consuming procedure and need heavy computations. For complex problems, resulting in very long design cycles, this computational cost may be prohibitive (Haupt & Werner, 2007).

Actually, many approaches are available to implement optimization using full-wave methods. For instance, the exploitation of commercial EM software packages inside the optimization loop of a general purpose optimization program. New techniques, such as geometry capture (Bandler et al., 1996) (suitable for automated EM design of arbitrary three-dimensional structures), space mapping (Bandler et al., 1994) (alternative design schemes combining the speed of circuit simulators with the accuracy of EM solvers), adjoint network concept (Nikolova et al., 2004), global optimization techniques based on bio-inspired algorithms, knowledge based methods, and artificial neural networks (ANNs), establish a solid foundation for efficient optimization of microwave device structures (Haupt & Werner, 2007; Zhang & Gupta, 2000; Silva et al., 2010a).

This chapter presents a new fast and accurate EM optimization technique combining full-wave method of moments (MoM), bio-inspired algorithms, continuous genetic algorithm (GA) and particle swarm optimization (PSO), and multilayer perceptrons (MLP) artificial neural networks. The proposed optimization technique is applied for optimal design of frequency selective surfaces with fractal patch elements. A fixed FSS screen geometry is choose a priori and then optimizing a smaller subset of FSS design variables to achieve a desired bandstop filter specification.

A frequency selective surface (FSS) is a two-dimensional array of periodic metallic elements on a dielectric layer or two-dimensional arrays of apertures within a metallic screen. This surface exhibits total reflection or transmission for patch and aperture elements, respectively. The most important parameters that will determine the overall frequency response of a FSS are: element shape, cell size, orientation, and dielectric layer properties. FSSs have been widely used as spatial filters for plane waves in a variety of applications, such as: microwave, optical, and infrared filters, bandpass radomes, microwave absorbers, polarizers, dichroic subreflectors, antenna systems, etc. (Munk, 2000).

Several authors proposed the design of FSS using fractals. In this chapter, different fractal geometries are considered, such as: Koch, Dürer's pentagon, and Sierpinski. While the use of space-filling fractal properties (e.g., Koch, Minkowski, Hilbert) reduce the overall size of the FSS elements (Oliveira et al., 2009; Campos et al., 2010), the attractive features of certain self-similar fractals (e.g., Sierpinski, Gosper, fractal tree, etc.) have received attention of microwave engineers to design multiband FSS. Many others self-similar geometries have been explored in the design of dual-band and dual polarized FSS (Gianvittorio et al., 2001).

The self-similarity property of these fractals enables the design of multiband fractal elements or fractal screens (Gianvittorio et al., 2003). Furthermore, as the number of fractal iterations increases, the resonant frequencies of these periodic structures decrease, allowing the construction of compact FSSs (Cruz et al., 2009). In addition, an FSS with fractal elements present resonant frequency that is almost independent of the plane-wave incidence angle.

There is no closed form solution directly from a given desired frequency response to the corresponding FSS with fractal elements. The analysis of scattering characteristics from FSS devices requires the application of rigorous full-wave techniques. Besides that, due to the computational complexity of using a full-wave simulator to evaluate the FSS scattering variables, many electromagnetic engineers still use trial-and-error process until to achieve a given design criteria. Obviously this procedure is very laborious and human dependent. On the other hand, calculating the gradient of the scattering coefficients in terms of the FSS design variables is quite difficult. Therefore, optimization techniques are required to design practical FSSs with desired filter specifications. Some authors have been employed neural networks, PSO, and GA for FSS design and optimization (Manara et al., 1999; Hussein & El-Ghazaly, 2004; Silva et al., 2010b).

The main computational drawback for EM optimization of FSSs based on bio-inspired algorithms relies on the repetitive evaluation of numerically expensive fitness functions. Due the expensive computation to calculate the scattering variables for every population member at multiple frequencies over many generations, several schemes are available to improve the GA performance for optimal design of FSSs, such as: the use of fast full-wave methods, micro-genetic algorithm, which aims to reduce the population size, and parallel GA using parallel computation. However, despite of these improvements done on the EM optimization using genetic algorithms, all the same several hours are required for expensive computational simulations of GA optimization (Haupt & Werner, 2007; Silva et al., 2010b).

The application of ANNs as approximate fitness evaluation tools for genetic algorithms, though suggest often, had seldom been put to practice. The combination of ANNs and GAs has been applied mainly for the construction of optimized neural networks through GA-based optimization techniques. Few applications of ANNs to GA processing have been reported for EM optimization of microwave devices.

The advantages of the MoM-ANN-GA/PSO optimization technique are discussed in terms of convergence and computational cost. This technique is applied for optimal design of bandstop FSS spatial filters with fractal elements considering the resonant frequency (*fr*) and bandwidth (*BW*) bandstop specifications. Some FSS prototypes with fractal elements are built and measured. The accuracy of the proposed optimization technique is verified by means of comparisons between theoretical and experimental results.

2. An overview of bio-inspired optimization technique

The idea of blending full-wave methods, artificial neural networks, and bio-inspired optimization algorithms for electromagnetic optimization of FSS spatial filters was first proposed in 2007 (Silva et al., 2007). This optimization technique named MoM-ANN-GA replaces the computational intensive full-wave method of moments simulations by a fast and accurate MLP neural network model of FSS spatial filter, which is used to compute the cost (or fitness) function in the genetic algorithm iterations.

The proposed bio-inspired EM optimization technique starts with the definition of a FSS screen geometry that is choose a priori. A full-wave parametric analysis is carried out for accurate EM characterization of FSS spatial filter scattering properties. From obtained EM dataset, a MLP network is trained to establish the complicated relationships between FSS design variables and frequency response. Then, in order to overcome the computational requirements associated with full-wave numerical simulations, the developed MLP model is used for fast and accurate evaluation of fitness function into bio-inspired algorithm simulations. From the optimal design of FSS parameters, FSS prototypes are fabricated and measured for verification of optimization methodology. Fig. 1 gives a "big picture" overview of proposed bio-inspired EM optimization technique.

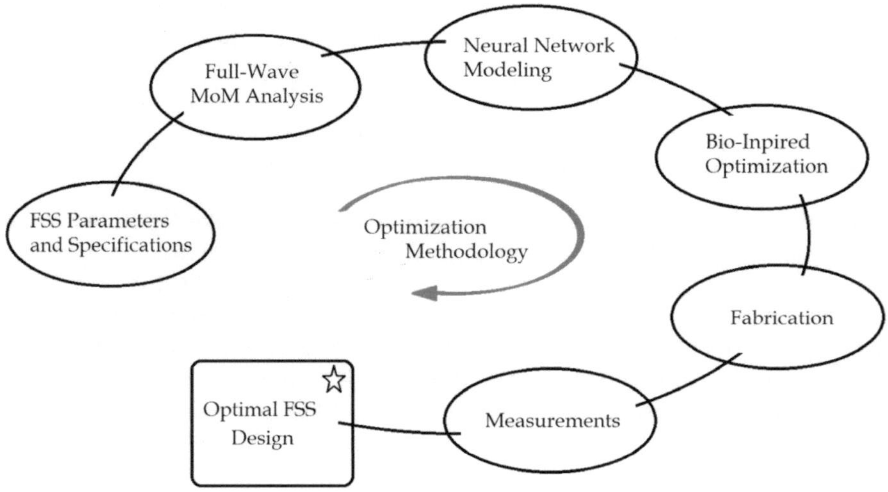

Fig. 1. An overview of proposed bio-inspired optimization technique

This section is a brief introduction that provides an overview of the proposed optimization technique to be presented. The overview includes fundamentals of multilayer perceptrons, continuous genetic algorithm, and particle swarm optimization.

2.1 Artificial neural networks

Since the beginning of the 1990s, the artificial neural networks have been used as a flexible numerical tool, which are efficient for modeling of microwave devices. In the CAD applications related to microwave engineering, the use of ANNs as nonlinear models becomes very common. Neural network models trained by accurate EM data (obtained through measurements or by EM simulations) are used for fast and accurate design/optimization of microwave devices. In addition, the use of previously established knowledge in the microwave area (as empirical models) combined with the neural networks, results in a major reliability of the resulting hybrid model - with a major ability to learn nonlinear input-output mappings, as well as to generalize responses, when new values of the input design variables are presented. Another important advantage is the data amount reduction necessary for the neural networks training. Some hybrid modeling techniques have been proposed for the use with empirical models and neural networks, such as: Source Difference Method, PKI (Prior Knowledge Input), KBNN (Knowledge Based

Neural Network), and SMANN (Space Mapping Artificial Neural Network) (Zhang & Gupta, 2000).

Versatility, efficient computation, reduced memory occupation, stability of learning algorithms, and generalization from representative data, are some characteristics that have motivated the use of neural networks in many areas of microwave engineering as models for complex ill-defined input-output mappings in new, not well-known microwave devices (Santos et al., 1997; Patnaik & Mishra, 2000; Zhang & Gupta, 2000). As mentioned previously, the electromagnetic behavior of a microwave device is extremely complex and simple empirical model cannot accurately describe its behavior under all conditions. Only with a detailed full-wave device model, more accurate results can be found. In general, the quality of simulation is decided by the accuracy of device models. On the other hand, a very detailed model would naturally slow down the program. A compromise between accuracy and speed of computation has to be struck. Using neural networks enables to overcome this problem (Silva et al., 2010a).

The multilayer perceptrons is the most used artificial neural network for neuromodeling applications. Multilayer perceptrons artificial neurons are based on the nonlinear model proposed by (McCulloch & Pitts, 1943; Rosenblatt, 1958, as cited in Haykin, 1999). In this model, neurons are signal processing units composed by a linear combiner and an activation function, that can be linear or nonlinear, as shown in Fig. 2.

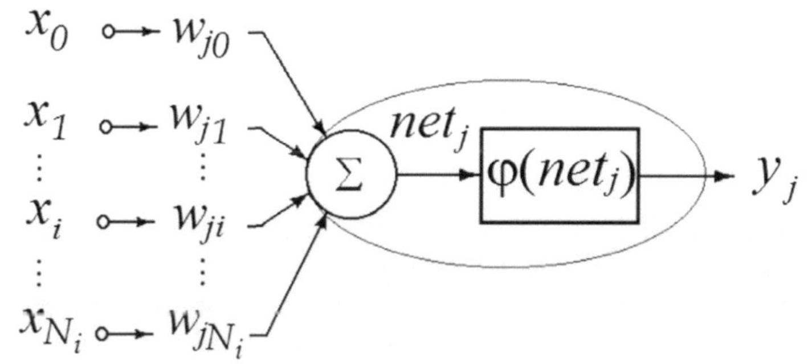

Fig. 2. Nonlinear model of an artificial neuron

The input signals are defined as x_i, $i = 0,1,\cdots,N_i$, where N_i is the number of input units. The output of linear combiner corresponds to the neuron level of internal activity net_j, as defined in (1). The information processed by neuron is storage in weights w_{ji}, $j = 1,\cdots,N_j$, where N_j is the number of neurons in a given neural network layer; $x_0 = \pm 1$ is the polarization potential (or threshold) applied to the neurons. The neuron output signal y_j is the value of the activation function $\varphi(\cdot)$ in response to the neuron activation potential net_j, as defined in (2).

$$net_j = \sum_{i=0}^{Ni} w_{ji} \cdot x_i \tag{1}$$

$$y_j = \varphi(net_j) \tag{2}$$

Multilayer perceptrons presents a feed forward neural network (FNN) configuration with neurons set into layers. Each neuron of a layer is connected to those of the previous layer, as illustrated in Fig. 3. Signal propagation occurs from input to output layers, passing through the hidden layers of the FNN. Hidden neurons represent the input characteristics, while output neurons generate the neural network responses (Haykin, 1999).

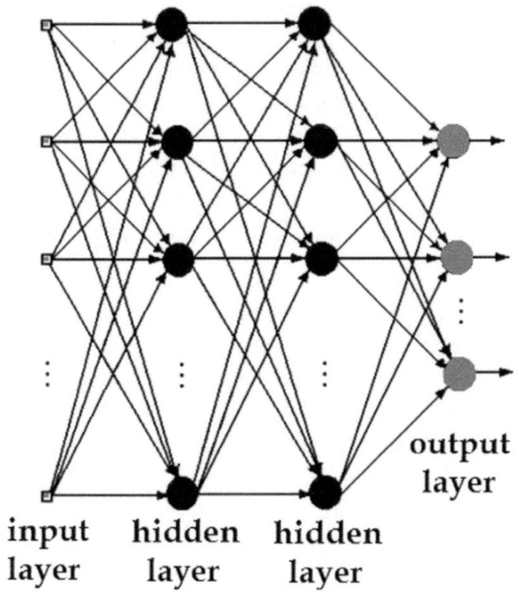

Fig. 3. Feed forward neural network configuration with two hidden layers

The design of a MLP model consists by three main steps: i) configuration - how layers are organized and connected; ii) supervised learning - how information is stored in neural network; iii) generalization test - how neural network produces reasonable outputs for inputs not found in the training set (Haykin, 1999). In this work, we use feed forward neural networks and supervised learning to develop MLP neural network models.

In the computational simulation of supervised error-correcting learning, a training algorithm is used for the adaptation of neural network synaptic weights. The instantaneous error $\mathbf{e}(\mathrm{n})$, as defined in (3), represents the difference between the desired response $\mathbf{d}(\mathrm{n})$, and the neural network output $\mathbf{y}(n)$, at the n-th iteration, corresponding to the presentation of the n-th training example, $(\mathbf{x}(\mathrm{n});\mathbf{d}(\mathrm{n}))$. Training examples variables are normalized to present unitary maximum absolute value. So, when using a given MLP model, prior scaling and de-scaling operations may be performed into input and output signals of MLP neural network, according to (4) and (5), respectively.

$$\mathbf{e}(n) = \mathbf{y}(n) - \mathbf{d}(n) \tag{3}$$

$$\overline{\mathbf{x}} = \mathbf{x} / \mathbf{x}_{\max} \tag{4}$$

$$\mathbf{y} = \overline{\mathbf{y}} \cdot \mathbf{y}_{\max} \tag{5}$$

Supervised learning has as objective the minimization of the sum squared error SSE(t), given in (6), where the index t, represents the number of training epochs (one complete presentation of all training examples, $n = 1, 2, \ldots, N$, where N is the total number of examples, is called an epoch).

$$SSE(t) = \frac{1}{N \cdot N_j} \sum_{n=1}^{N} \sum_{j=1}^{Nj} \frac{1}{2} e_j(n)^2 \quad (6)$$

Currently, there are several algorithms for the training of MLP neural networks. The most popular training algorithms are those derived from back-propagation algorithm (Rumelhart, Hinton, & Williams, 1986, as cited in Haykin, 1999). Among the family of back-propagation algorithms, the RPROP algorithm shows to be very efficient in solving complex modeling learning tasks.

After neural network training, we hope that MLP weights will storage the representative information contained on training dataset. The trained neural network is tested in order to verify its capability of generalizing to new values that do not belong to the training dataset. Therefore, the MLP neural network operates like a "black box" model inside a given region of interest, which was previously defined when the training dataset was generated.

2.2 Bio-inspired optimization algorithms

Bio-inspired algorithms, which are stochastic population-based global search methods inspired by nature, such as simulated annealing (SA), genetic algorithm and particle swarm optimization are effective for optimization problems with a large number of design variables and inexpensive fitness function evaluation (Haupt, 1995; Haupt & Werner, 2007; Kennedy & Eberhart, 1995). However, the main computational drawback for optimization of microwave devices relies on the repetitive evaluation of numerically expensive fitness functions. Finding a way to shorten the optimization cycle is highly desirable (Silva et al., 2010b). For instance, several GA schemes are available in order to improve its performance, such as: the use of fast full-wave methods, micro-genetic algorithm, which aims to reduce the population size, and parallel GA using parallel computation (R. L. Haupt & Sue, 2004).

Bio-inspired algorithms start with an initial population of candidate individuals for the optimal solution. Assuming an optimization problem with N_{var} input variables and N_{pop} individuals, the population at the i-th iteration is represented as a matrix $\boldsymbol{P}(i)_{Npop \times Nvar}$ of floating-point elements, denoted by $p^i_{m,n}$, with each row corresponding to an individual. Under GA and PSO jargons, the individuals are named *chromosomes* and *particles* (or agents), respectively.

2.2.1 Continuous genetic algorithm

Continuous genetic algorithm is very similar to the binary-GA but works with floating-point variables. Continuous-GA chromosomes are defined in (7) as a vector with N_{var} floating-point optimization variables. Each chromosome is evaluated by means of its associated cost, which is computed through the cost function E given in (8).

$$chromosome(\mathrm{i},m) = \left[p_{m,1}^{i},\ p_{m,2}^{i},\ \ldots,\ p_{m,N\mathrm{var}}^{i} \right],\quad m = 1,2,\ldots,Npop \tag{7}$$

$$\cos t(\mathrm{i},m) = \mathbf{E}\left(chromosome(\mathrm{i},m)\right) \tag{8}$$

Based on the cost associated to each chromosome, the population evolves through generations with the application of genetic operators, such as: selection, crossover and mutation. Flow chart shown in Fig. 4(a) gives an overview of continuous-GA.

Mating step includes roulette wheel selection presented in (Haupt & Werner, 2007; R. L. Haupt & Sue, 2004). Population selection is performed after the N_{pop} chromosomes are ranked from lowest to highest costs. Then, the N_{keep} most-fit chromosomes are selected to form the mating pool and the rest are discarded to make room for the new offspring. Mothers and fathers pair in a random fashion through the blending crossover method (R. L. Haupt & Sue, 2004). Each pair produces two offspring that contain traits from each parent. In addition, the parents survive to be part of the next generation. After mating, a fraction of chromosomes in the population will suffer mutation. Then, the chromosome variable selected for real-value mutation is added to a normally distributed random number.

Most users of continuous-GA add a normally distributed random number to the variable selected for mutation with a constant standard deviation (R. L. Haupt & Sue, 2004). In particular, we propose a new real-value mutation operator for continuous-GA as given in (9), where p_{max} and p_{min} are constant values defined according to the limits of the region of interest composed by input parameters. Function *randn*() returns a normal distribution with mean equal to zero and standard deviation equal to one.

This mutation operator was inspired by simulating annealing cooling schedules (R. L. Haupt & Sue, 2004). It is used to improve continuous-GA convergence at the neighbourhood of global minimum. The quotient function Q given in (10) is crescent when the number of iterations increases and the global cost decreases. Thus, similar to the decrease of temperature in a simulating annealing algorithm, the standard deviation is decreased when the number of continuous-GA iterations is increased. The parameter A is a constant value and B is a value of cost function neighbour to the global minimum. The continuous-GA using the real-value mutation definition given in (9) and (10) is denominated improved genetic algorithm.

$$p_{m,n}^{i+1} = p_{m,n}^{i} + randn()\cdot\frac{\left(p_{\max} - p_{\min}\right)}{Q\left(i, global\cos t(i)\right)} \tag{9}$$

$$Q\left(i, global\cos t(i)\right) = \begin{cases} A, & global\cos t(i) \geq B \\ A + i\cdot\left[\log\left(global\cos t(i)\right)\right]^{2}, & global\cos t(i) < B \end{cases} \tag{10}$$

2.2.2 Particle swarm optimization

Particle swarm optimization was first formulated in 1995 (Kennedy & Eberhart, 1995). The thought process behind the algorithm was inspired by social behavior of animals, such as bird flocking or fish schooling. PSO is similar to continuous-GA since it begins with a random initial population. Unlike GA, PSO has no evolution operators such as crossover and mutation. Each particle moves around the cost surface with an individual velocity. The implemented PSO algorithm updates the velocities and positions of the particles based on the local and global best solutions, according to (11) and (12), respectively.

$$v_{m,n}^{i+1} = C\left[r_0 v_{m,n}^{i} + \Gamma_1 \cdot r_1 \cdot \left(p_{m,n}^{local\,bes(i)} - p_{m,n}^{i} \right) + \Gamma_2 \cdot r_2 \cdot \left(p_{m,n}^{global\,best(i)} - p_{m,n}^{i} \right) \right] \quad (11)$$

$$p_{m,n}^{i+1} = p_{m,n}^{i} + v_{m,n}^{i+1} \quad (12)$$

Here, $v_{m,n}$ is the particle velocity; $p_{m,n}$ is the particle variables; r_0, r_1 and r_2 are independent uniform random numbers; Γ_1 is the cognitive parameter and Γ_2 is the social parameter; $p_{m,n}^{local\,best(i)}$ is the best local solution and $p_{m,n}^{global\,best(i)}$ is the best global solution; C is the constriction parameter (Kennedy & Eberhart, 1995). If the best local solution has a cost less than the cost of the current global solution, then the best local solution replaces the best global solution. PSO is a very simple bio-inspired algorithm, easy to implement and with few parameters to adjust. Flow chart shown in Fig. 4(b) gives an overview of PSO algorithm.

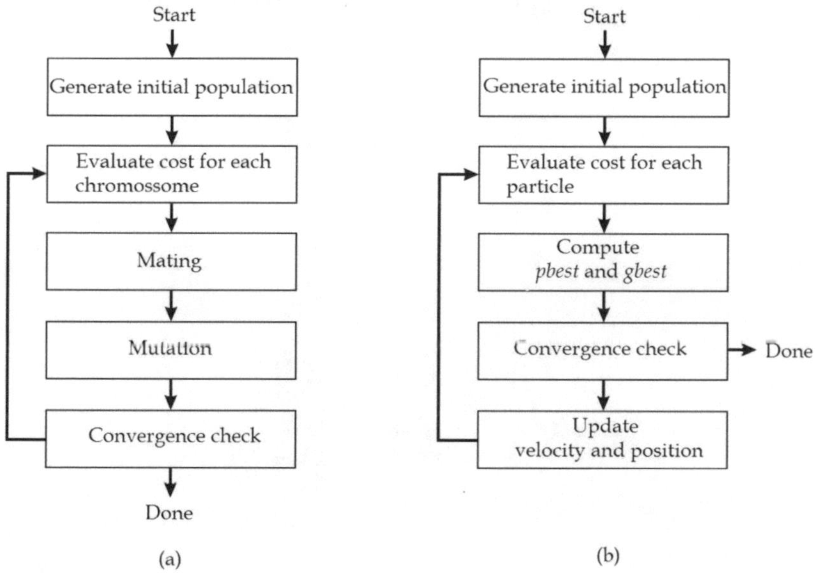

Fig. 4. Flow charts of (a) continuous-GA and (b) PSO algorithm.

3. FSS design considerations

Frequency selective surfaces (FSSs) are used in many commercial and military applications. Usually, conducting patches and isotropic dielectric layers are used to build these FSS structures. FSS frequency response is entirely determined by the geometry of the structure in one period called a unit cell. In this section is presented some considerations about the design of FSS with fractal elements for operation at the X-band (8–12 GHz) and Ku-band (12–18 GHz). FSS fabrication and measurement procedures are summarized.

3.1 Design of FSS using fractal geometries

FSS with fractal elements has attracted the attention of microwave engineering researchers because of its particular/special features. The design of a FSS with pre-fractal elements is a very competitive solution that enables the fabrication of compact spatial filters, with better performances when compared to conventional structures (Oliveira, et al., 2009; Campos et al., 2010). Several fractal iterations can be used to design a FSS with multiband frequency response associated to the self-similarity contained in the structure. Various self-similar fractals elements (e.g., Koch, Sierpinski, Minkowski, Dürer's pentagon) were previously used to design multiband FSSs (Gianvittorio et al., 2003; Cruz et al., 2009; Trindade et al., 2011).

Fig. 5 illustrates the considered periodic array in this chapter. The periodicity of the elements is given by t_x=W_c, in the x axis, and t_y=L_c, in the y axis, where W_c is the width and L_c is the length of the unit cell element; in addition, W is the width and L is the length of the patch. The design of fractal patch elements depend of desired FSS filter specifications, such as: bandstop attenuation, resonant frequency, quality factor, fabrication restrictions, etc.

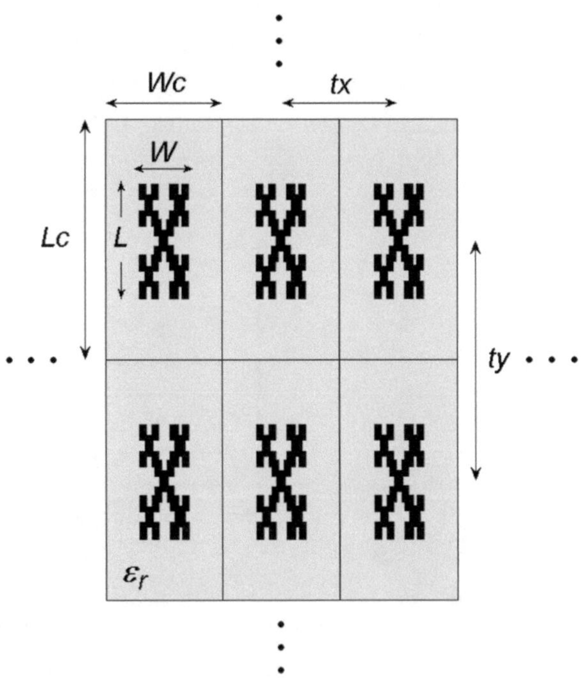

Fig. 5. Periodic array of fractal patch elements

3.1.1 Koch island fractal

The Koch island fractal patch elements were obtained assuming a rectangular construction, fractal iteration-number (or level), k=0,1,2, and a variable fractal iteration-factor $r = 1/a$, where a belongs to interval $3.05 \le a \le 10.0$. The geometry of the Koch island fractal patch elements is shown in Fig. 6, considering for k=0,1,2, and a=4. The rectangular patch element (fractal initiator) dimensions are (mm): W=4.93, L= 8.22, t_x=8.22, and t_y=12.32.

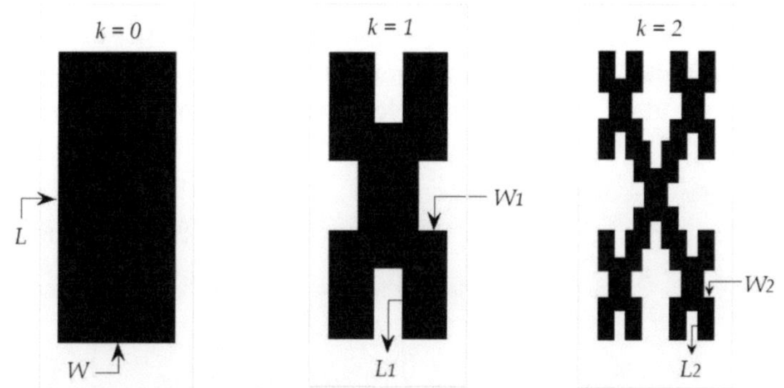

Fig. 6. Koch Island fractal patch elements (a=4)

The Koch curve begins as a straight line corresponding to each side of the conventional rectangle. Next, the Koch element in the first fractal iteration is obtained by removing four scaled rectangles (with the width and length of the initiator rectangle scaled by the fractal iteration-factor) that lies at the center of each side of the initiator rectangle. The same construction is applied for others Koch iterations (see Fig. 6). After the k-th fractal iteration, the dimensions of scaled rectangles are given in (13) through the substitution of the dummy variable ℓ_k by the width W_k or length L_k of the k-th scaled rectangle.

$$\ell_k = \begin{cases} \dfrac{\ell_{k-1}}{a}, & k=1 \\ \dfrac{(\ell_{k-2}-\ell_{k-1})}{2a} & k=2,3,\ldots \end{cases} \tag{13}$$

3.1.2 Dürer's pentagon fractal

The Dürer's pentagon fractal geometry was generated with the application of iterated function system (Trindade et al., 2011). From a regular pentagon patch element (L=10 mm and t_x=t_y=16.5 mm), that corresponds to the fractal initiator element, we use a fractal iteration-factor $r = 0.382$ for the generation of Dürer's pentagon elements at levels k=1,2, and 3, where $L_k = L \cdot r^k$. Therefore, six small-scale copies of the initiator element are generated in a given fractal iteration, N = 6, resulting in a fractal dimension $D = \log(N) / \log(1/r)$, where D=1.8619. The geometry of the Dürer's pentagon fractal is shown in Fig. 7.

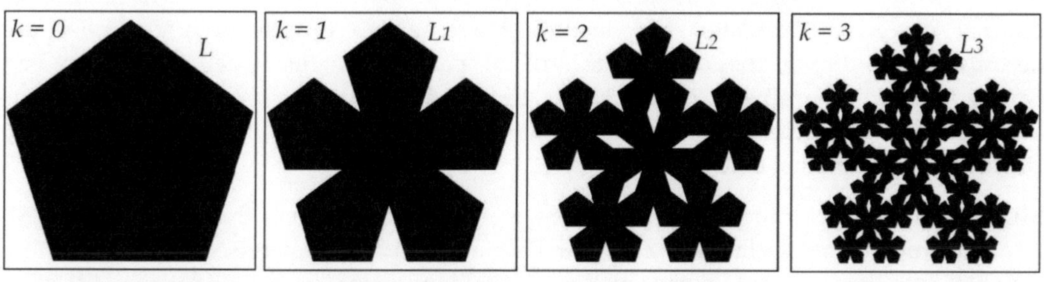

Fig. 7. Dürer's pentagon fractal patch elements

3.1.3 Sierpinski island fractal

The Sierpinski island fractal patch elements were designed based on Sierpinski curve fractal geometry. From an regular octagon patch element (L=3.6 mm and t_x=t_y=16.0 mm), that corresponds to the fractal initiator element, we used a fractal iteration-factor $r = 1/2$, and a number of five small-scale copies $N = 5$, resulting in a fractal dimension $D = \log(N)/\log(1/r)$, where D=2.3219. The geometry of the Sierpinski island fractal patch elements is shown in Fig. 8.

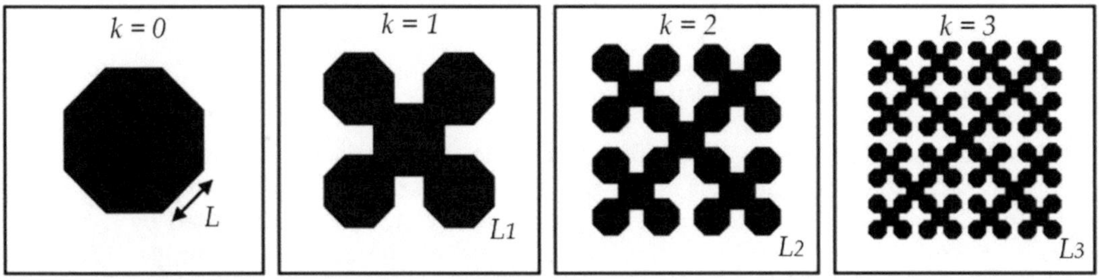

Fig. 8. Sierpinski Island fractal patch elements

3.2 Fabrication and measurement of frequency selective surfaces

The frequency selective surfaces using fractal geometries were built as periodic arrays of patch fractal elements. FSS is mounted on a dielectric isotropic layer. FSS spatial filter prototypes were fabricated using conventional planar circuit technology, with low-cost fiberglass (FR-4) substrate with 1.5 mm of height and a relative permittivity of 4.4.

The setup to measure the FSS transmission coefficients included: two horn antennas, two waveguides (cut-off frequency, 6.8 GHz), a network analyzer (model N5230A, Agilent Technologies), which operates from 300 KHz up to 13.5 GHz, beyond coaxial/waveguide transitions, handles and connectors. A fixed distance was adopted between the horn antennas in order to guarantee the operation in the far field region. The FSS filter prototypes were placed between the horn antennas for the measurement procedure (see Fig. 9).

4. Optimal design of fractal frequency selective surfaces

In this section are presented some applications of proposed optimization technique for optimal design of bandstop FSS spatial filters. Three optimization examples are described considering the use of FSS fractal patch elements: Koch island, Dürer's pentagon, and Sierpinski island. The EM characterization of these FSSs was accomplished by means of a full-wave parametric analysis through the use Ansoft Designer™ commercial software.

MLP neural network models for these FSSs were developed using the conventional EM-ANN neuromodeling technique (Zhang & Gupta, 2000). The supervised training of MLP weights was done through the well-established resilient back-propagation (RPROP) algorithm with standard training parameters (Ridmiller & Braun, 1993).

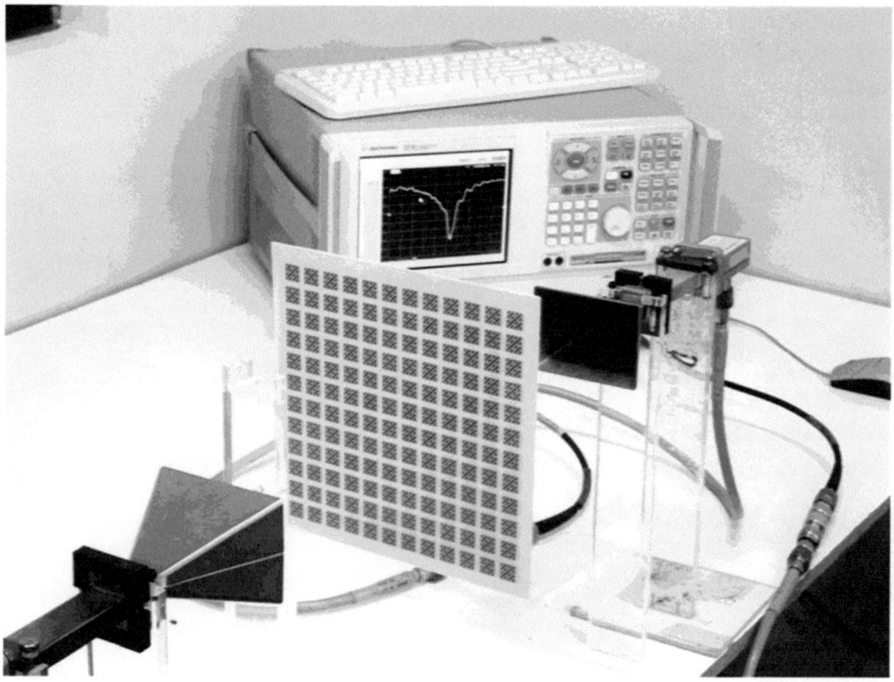

Fig. 9. Photograph of the Sierpinski FSS prototype and the measurement setup

4.1 FSS with Koch island fractal patch elements

In order to control the FSS resonant frequency and bandwidth, the shape of Koch island fractal patch elements is adjusted by fractal parameters: iteration-factor and iteration-number. The input design variables (k, a, ε_r) are limited to design region of interest defined by the following discrete values selected for MoM full-wave parametric analysis:

- Fractal iteration-number (or level): k=[1, 2]
- Fractal iteration-factor: $r = 1/a$, a=[3, 4, 5, 6, 7, 9]
- Relative permittivity: ε_r=[2.2, 3.0, 4.0, 4.8, 6.15, 7.0]
- Dielectric layer thickness: h=1.5 mm
- Scaling factors for training dataset: $\mathbf{x}_{\max} = [1, 9, 7]$ and $\mathbf{y}_{\max} = [19.05, 4.58]$

Considering for design input variables (k, a, ε_r), a MLP model was trained to approach the resonant frequency $fr(k, a, \varepsilon_r)$ and bandwidth $BW(k, a, \varepsilon_r)$ of the FSS spatial filters. The minimal MLP configuration able to solve the FSS modeling problem was defined with four input units, five hidden units, and two output units. The MLP configuration is illustrated in Fig. 10. The minimum number of five hidden neurons was found by means of a trial and error procedure and training restarts (Cruz et al., 2009).

Using sigmoid activation function, the outputs of MLP model are computed by (14).

$$\mathbf{y} = \mathbf{V} \cdot \left[-1, \ \frac{1}{1 + \exp(-\mathbf{W} \cdot \mathbf{x})} \right] \tag{14}$$

Where **W** and **V** are the MLP weight matrix, **x**=[-1, *k-1*, *a*, ε_r]^T and **y**=[*fr*, *BW*]^T are the MLP input and output vectors, respectively. The resultant MLP trained weight values are given by (15) and (16).

$$\mathbf{W} = \begin{bmatrix} 3.4476 & 0.4761 & 9.3218 & -0.1876 \\ 1.0630 & -0.3178 & 0.4056 & -2.0478 \\ 5.6533 & 5.2681 & 2.0179 & 1.9425 \\ 0.9611 & -4.0685 & 3.1393 & -0.1349 \\ 5.0429 & -12.4751 & 13.4767 & 1.5855 \end{bmatrix} \quad (15)$$

$$\mathbf{V} = \begin{bmatrix} -0.0572 & 0.1656 & 2.1679 & 0.1640 & 0.0936 & 0.2227 \\ 0.1059 & 0.2534 & 0.7188 & 0.2979 & 0.4961 & 0.2441 \end{bmatrix} \quad (16)$$

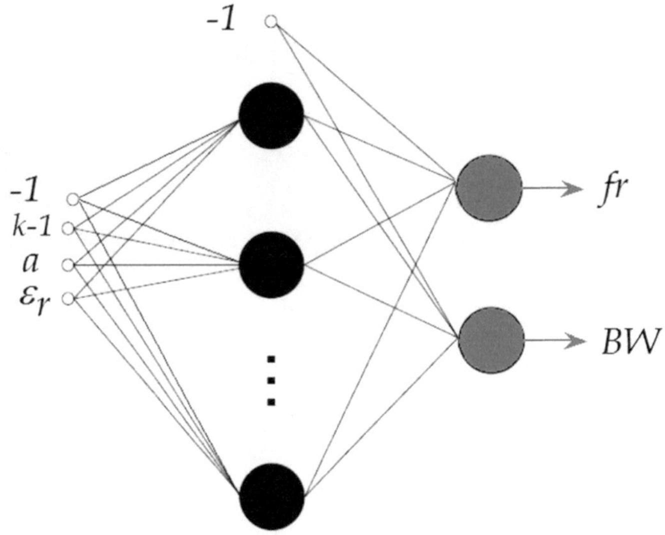

Fig. 10. Multilayer perceptron configuration

The MLP model for FSS filter design is CPU inexpensive, easy to implement and accurate. In addition, it requires small size EM dataset to learning the model of input/output mapping. The MLP model is used for evaluation of cost function in the bio-inspired optimization algorithm for FSSs with Koch island fractal patch elements.

The FSS set of design variables [*k*, *f*, *BW*] composed the input data for bio-Inspired optimization algorithms and are chosen by the user, within the region of interest of MLP model: (*k*=1,2), (2,7<*fr*<19) GHz, and (1.5<*BW*<4.5) GHz. Given a FSS filter desired specification (*f*, *BW*), the goal of bio-inspired optimization is to find an optimal solution (ε_r, *a*) for a given fractal level *k* that minimizes the quadratic cost function as defined in (17).

$$\mathbf{E}(i,m) = \frac{\left[f - fr\left(\mathbf{p}_m^i\right)\right]^2}{f^2} + \frac{\left[BW - BW\left(\mathbf{p}_m^i\right)\right]^2}{BW^2} \quad (17)$$

The individuals $\mathbf{p}_m^i = [\varepsilon_{rm}^i, a_m^i]^T$ evolve from the initial population given according to (18). The center of initial population $(\varepsilon_{rm}^0, a_m^0)$ in the searching space was chosen equal to (3.0, 8.5). When the population evolves, each individual is constrained to the region of interest using (19). The dummy variable ξ can be replaced by variables ε_r or a.

$$\mathbf{p}_m^0 = [randn()/5 + \varepsilon_{rm}^0 \quad randn()/5 + a_m^0] \tag{18}$$

$$\xi_m^k = \min\left(\max\left(\xi_m^k, \xi_{\min}\right), \xi_{\max}\right) \tag{19}$$

In this first FSS optimization example, we intended to verify the execution of continuous-GA and improved-GA algorithms. The algorithms start with the same initial population with 25 individuals distributed according to (18) and subject to restriction given in (19). We use the following FSS design specification: k=2, f=10.0 GHz, and BW=2.10 GHz.

Assuming the GA parameters: crossover probability=0.6, mutation rate=0.2, A=30, B=10^{-9}, $Nvar$=2, and $Npop$=25, we simulated up to 600 iterations. In Fig. 11(a) is presented the initial, intermediate, and final populations, as well as, the continuous-GA path plotted over the cost surface contours. Fig. 11(b) shows the same results for the improved-GA.

The observed zigzag paths at flat regions of the cost surface contribute to slow down the convergence of genetic algorithms. The final population of the continuous-GA algorithm oscillates around the global minimum of cost function (see Fig. 11(a)), while the improved-GA final population is closely to the global minimum (see Fig. 11(b)).

Fig. 12(a) shows the global cost evolution for the best individual of continuous-GA and improved-GA populations. It is observed that improved-GA converges closely to global minimum. The final global cost values for improved-GA and continuous-GA were 2.91×10^{-10}, and 1.26×10^{-13}, respectively. The optimized values of design parameters, $a = 5$ and $\varepsilon_r = 4.4$, were obtained (see final population in Fig. 11(b)).

To verify the optimization results, a FSS prototype with Koch island fractal patch elements was built and bandstop properties of this spatial filter were measured. In Fig. 12(b) is presented the simulated and measured FSS transmission. The obtained numeric results are presented in Table 1, and are in excellent agreement with desired FSS design specifications.

		Ansoft Designer™		Measured	
a	ε_r	f_r (GHz)	BW (GHz)	f_r (GHz)	BW (GHz)
5	4.4	9.97	2.10	10.00	1.73

Table 1. Simulated and measured results of optimized FSS

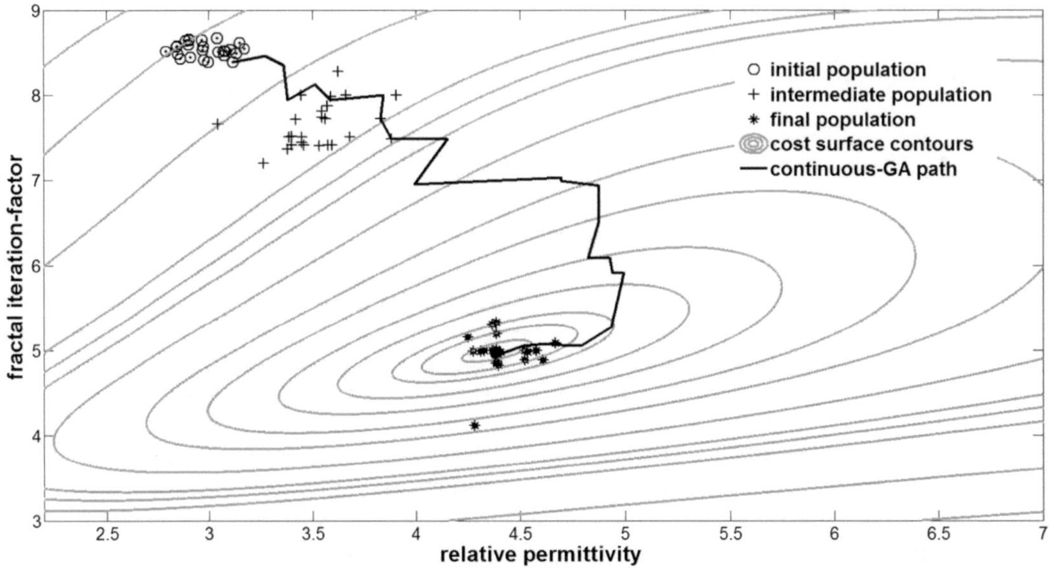

(a)

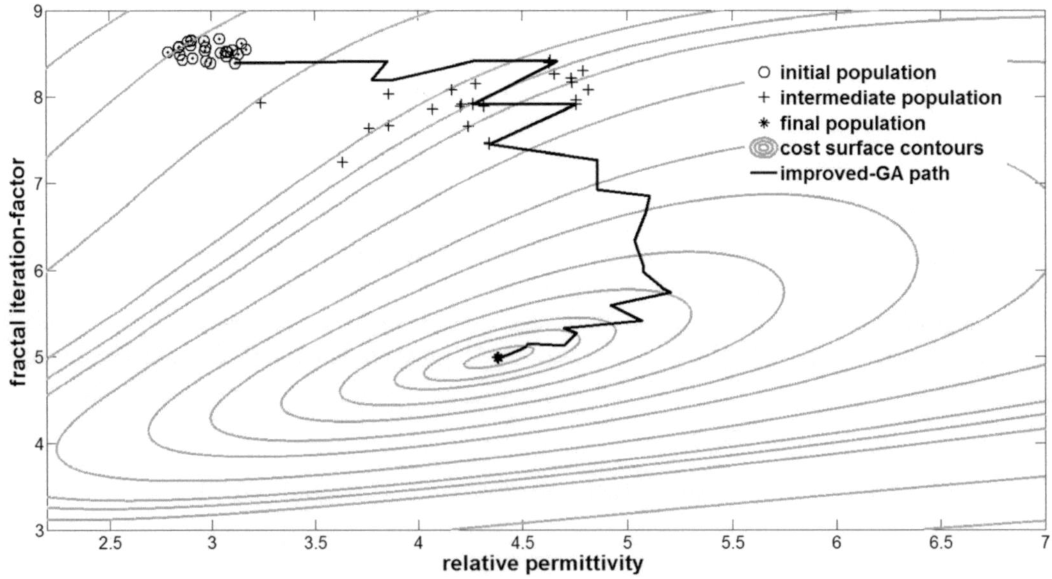

(b)

Fig. 11. Initial, intermediate, and final populations and GA paths plotted over the cost surface contours: (a) continuous-GA and (b) improved-GA.

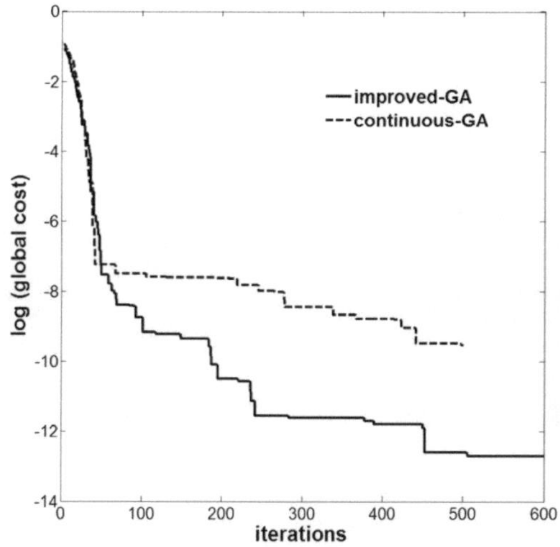

(a)

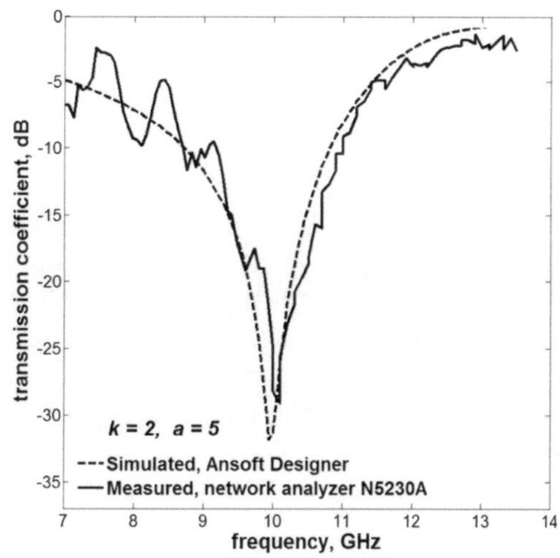

(b)

Fig. 12. (a) Evolution of global cost for continuous-GA and improved-GA. (b) Comparison between the simulated and measured FSS transmission (k=2, ε_r=4.4, and a =5)

4.2 FSS with Dürer's pentagon patch elements

The Dürer's pentagon geometry was used to design a FSS consisting of a periodic array of fractal patch elements. The input design variables (k, $\tan\delta$, t_x, ε_r) are limited to design region of interest defined by the following discrete values selected for parametric analysis:

- Fractal iteration-number (or level): k=[0, 1, 2, 3]
- Patch element periodicity: t_x=t_y= [16.5, 17, 18, 19, 20, 21, 22, 23, 24, 25] mm
- Relative permittivity: ε_r=[2.33, 3.5, 4.4, 6.15, 10.2]
- Loss tangent: $\tan\delta$ = [0.0014, 0.012, 0.02, 0.0025, 0.0035]
- Dielectric layer thickness: h=1.5 mm

Considering for design input variables (k, $\tan\delta$, t_x, ε_r), a MLP model was trained to approach the resonant frequency and bandwidth of the bandstop FSS spatial filters. The minimal MLP configuration able to solve the FSS modeling problem was defined with five input units, ten hidden units, and two output units.

The MLP model outputs are shown in Fig. 13(a) and 13(b), considering the limits of the desired region of interest of the design input variables. The MLP model is able to interpolate the training examples corresponding to ε_r=[2.33, 3.5, 6.15, 10.2] and presents generalization ability for new inputs within the region of interest, ε_r=4.4. Thus, the MLP model learns the EM behavior of FSS filters becoming available this EM knowledge for future utilization.

In this second FSS optimization example, we verify the performance of continuous-GA and PSO. The algorithms start with the same initial population with $Npop$=25 individuals $\mathbf{p}_m^i = [\varepsilon_{rm}^i, t_{xm}^i]^T$ distributed according to (18) with $(\varepsilon_{rm}^0, t_{xm}^0)$ = (9.0, 24).

The FSS set of design variables [k, f, BW] composed the input data for bio-Inspired optimization algorithms and are chosen by the user, within the region of interest of MLP model: (k=0,1,2,3), (4.9<fr<13.9) GHz, and (0.6<BW<4.6) GHz. In this example, we use the following FSS design specification: k=1, f=8.2 GHz and BW=2.78 GHz.

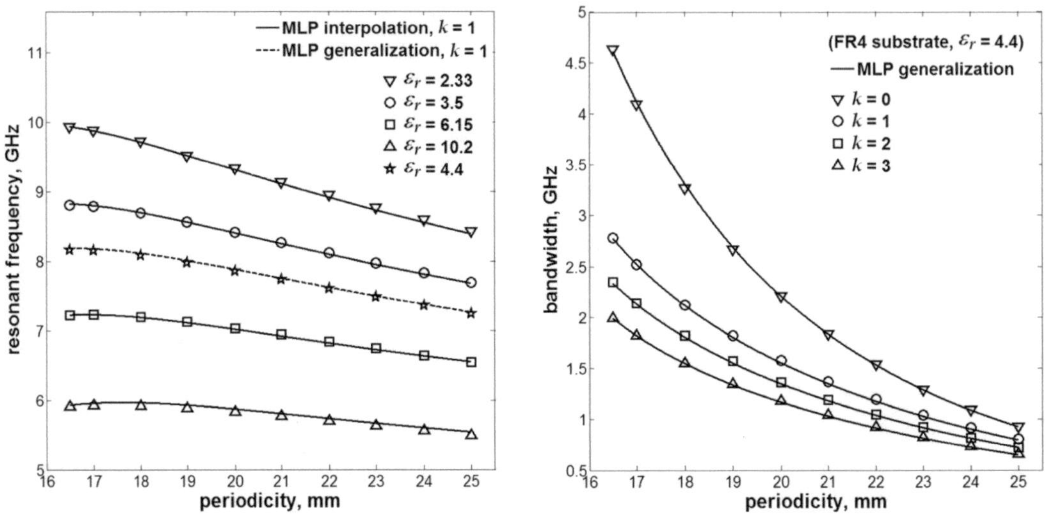

(a) (b)

Fig. 13. (a) FSS resonant frequency as a function of periodicity and relative permittivity. (b) FSS bandwidth as a function of periodicity and fractal iteration-number

Assuming the genetic algorithm parameters: crossover probability=0.6, mutation rate=0.2, A=30, B=10^{-9}, $Nvar$=2 and $Npop$=25, we simulated up to 250 GA-iterations. Fig. 14(a) shows the initial, intermediate and final populations, and the continuous-GA path plotted over the cost surface contours. The optimal solution was: ε_r=4.4 and t_x=t_y=16.5 mm.

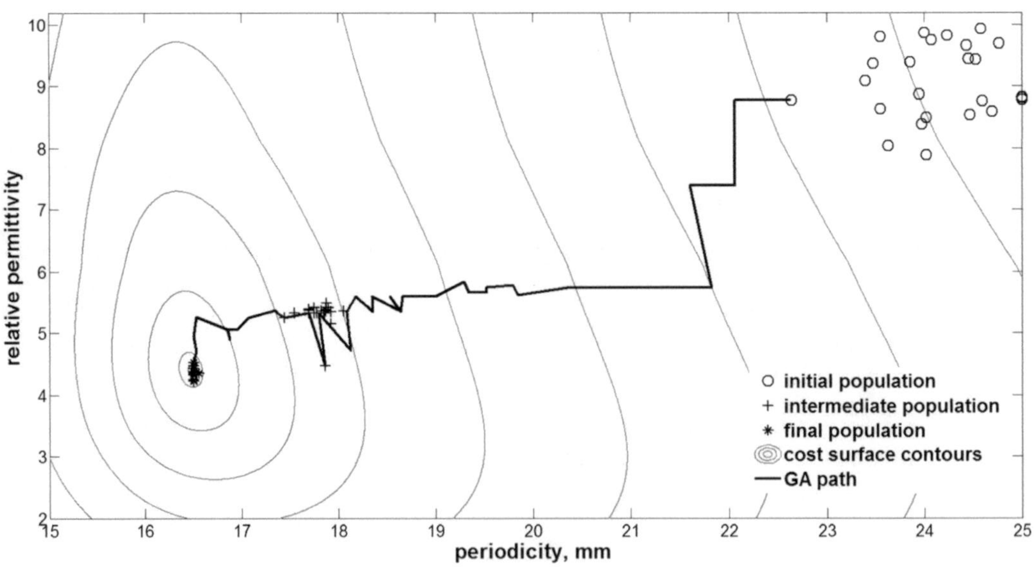

(a)

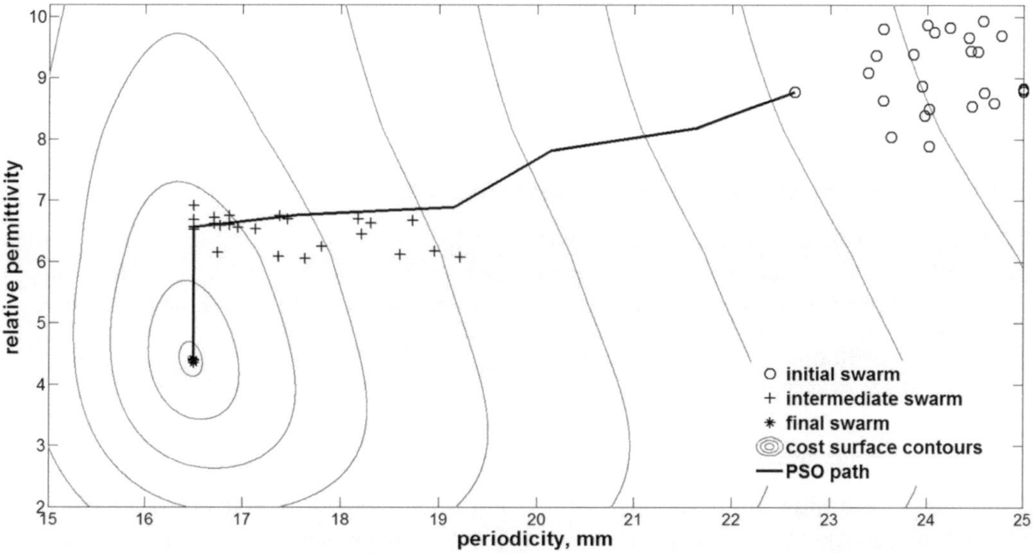

(b)

Fig. 14. Initial, intermediate, and final populations and bio-inspired algorithm paths plotted over the cost surface contours: (a) continuous-GA and (b) PSO.

The PSO algorithm with parameters $\Gamma_1 = \Gamma_2 = 2, C = 1.3$ and the same initial population was used for FSS optimization. Fig. 14(b) shows the PSO path plotted over the cost surface contours. In this simulation, the PSO algorithm converges to the global minimum of cost function after 96 iterations. In this case, the optimal solution was: ε_r=4.4 and t_x=t_y=16.5 mm.

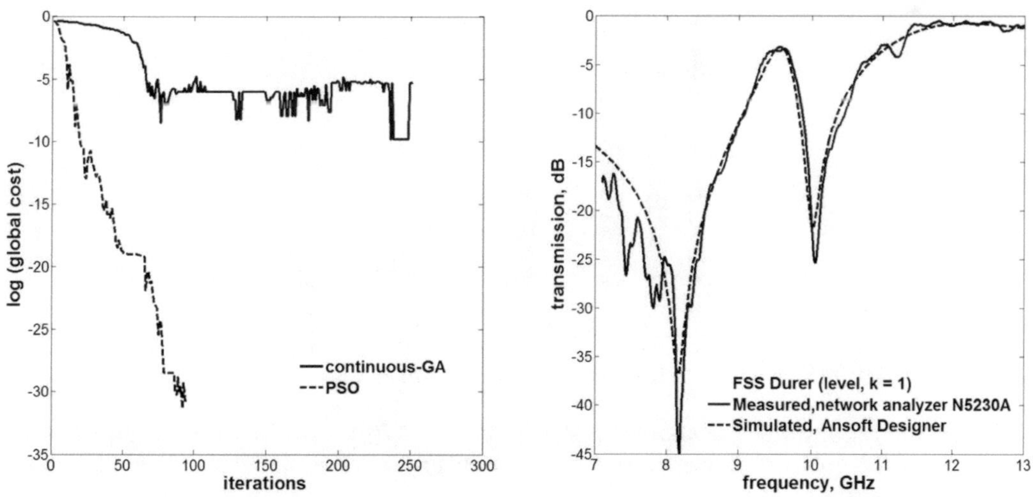

Fig. 15. (a) Evolution of global cost for continuous-GA and PSO. (b) Comparison between the simulated and measured FSS transmission (k=1, ε_r=4.4, and t_x=t_y=16.5 mm).

Fig. 15(a) shows the evolution of the average global cost for continuous-GA and PSO populations. We observe that the PSO algorithm is limited in precision to the round off error of the computer (≈10^{-31}). In Fig. 15(b) is presented a comparison between the simulated and measured results for the transmission coefficient (dB) of the optimized FSS with Koch fractal patch elements. The simulated and measured results are in excellent agreement with desired FSS design specifications.

4.3 FSS with Sierpinski ilsland fractal patch elements

The Sierpinski island fractal geometry was used to design a FSS consisting of a periodic array of fractal patch elements. The input design variables (k, t_x, ε_r) are limited to design region of interest defined by the following discrete values selected for parametric analysis:

- Fractal iteration-number (or level): k=[1, 2, 3]
- Patch element periodicity: t_x=t_y=[15, 16, 17, 18, 19, 20, 21, 22, 23, 24, 25] mm
- Relative permittivity: ε_r=[2.2, 2.94, 4.4, 6.15, 10.2]
- Dielectric layer thickness: h=1.5 mm

Considering for design input variables (k, ε_r, t_x), a MLP model was trained to approach the resonant frequency and bandwidth of the FSS filters with Sierpinski island fractal patch elements. Fig. 16 shows the variation of sum squared error given in (6) as a function of the number of MLP hidden units. The minimal MLP configuration able to solve the FSS modeling problem was defined with four input units, fifteen hidden units, and two output units.

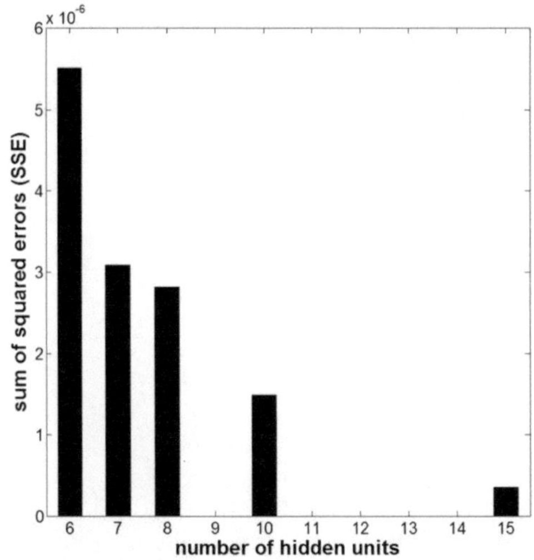

Fig. 16. Variation of SSE as a function of MLP hidden units

The MLP model outputs are shown in Fig. 17(a) and 17(b). Considering the limits of the desired region of interest of the input design variables, the MLP model is able to interpolate the training dataset.

In this third FSS optimization example, we intended to verify the execution of continuous-GA, improved-GA, and PSO. The algorithms start with the same initial population with $Npop$=100 individuals $\mathbf{p}_m^i = [\varepsilon_{rm}^i, t_{xm}^i]^T$ distributed according to (18), with $(\varepsilon_{rm}^0, t_{xm}^0)$ = (8.5, 22) and subject to restriction given in (19).

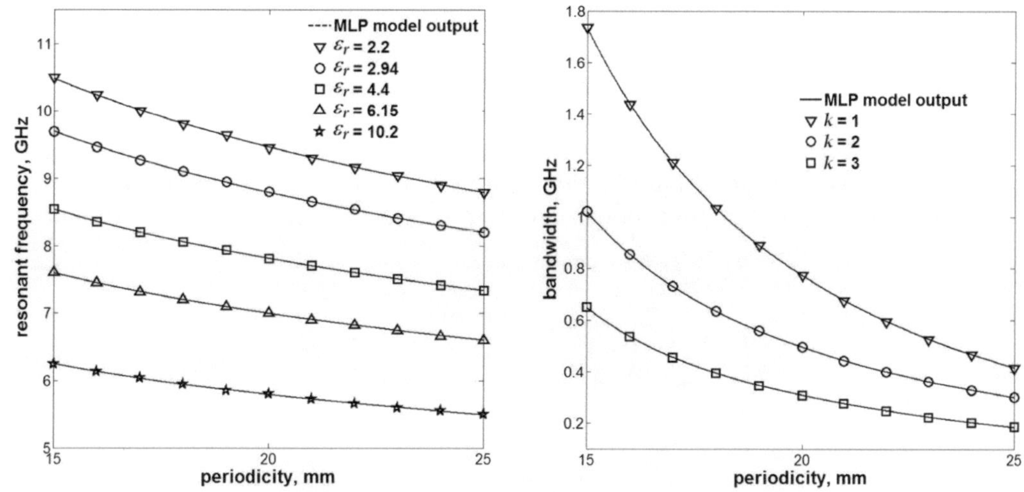

Fig. 17. (a) FSS resonant frequency as a function of periodicity and relative permittivity. (b) FSS bandwidth as a function of periodicity and fractal levels

The FSS design variables [*k*, *f*, *BW*] composed the input data for bio-Inspired optimization algorithms and are chosen by the user within the region of interest of MLP model: (k=1,2,3), ($3.1<fr<10.5$) GHz, and ($0.15<BW<1.7$) GHz. We used the following input data for simulation of bio-inspired optimization: k=1, f=8.37 GHz and BW=1.44 GHz.

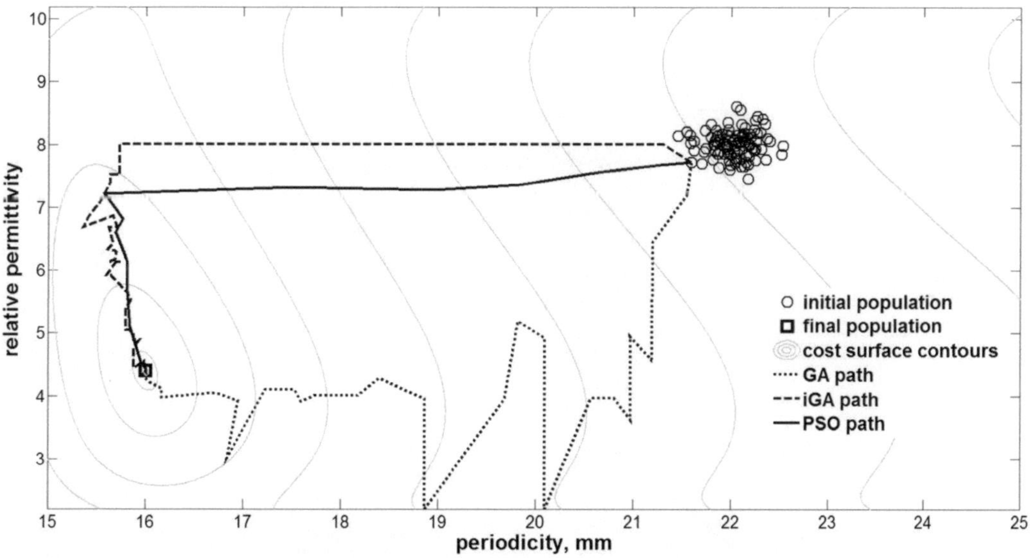

Fig. 18. Bio-inspired algorithm paths plotted over the cost surface contours, initial, intermediate, and final populations

In Fig. 18 is presented the initial, intermediate, and final populations, as well as, the bio-inspired algorithm paths plotted over the cost surface contours. In this case, the optimal solution founded was: ε_r=4.4 and t_x=t_y=16.0 mm.

Fig. 19(a) shows the evolution of the global cost for bio-inspired algorithms. PSO algorithm converges to the global minimum of cost function after 93 iterations. Improved-GA and continuous-GA converge after 185 and 211 iterations, respectively. In this example, implemented bio-inspired algorithms are limited in precision to the round off error of the computer ($\approx 10^{-31}$). In Fig. 19(b) is presented a comparison between the CPU requirement as a function of bio-inspired algorithm iterations. From this result, was observed that the CPU spent-time of bio-inspired optimization is determined by MLP model CPU requirement.

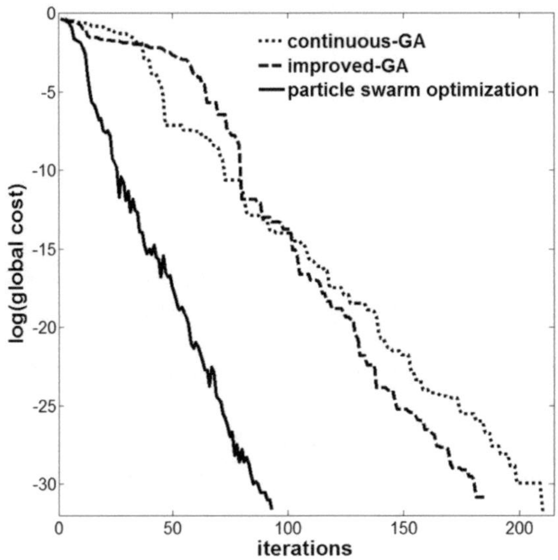

(a)

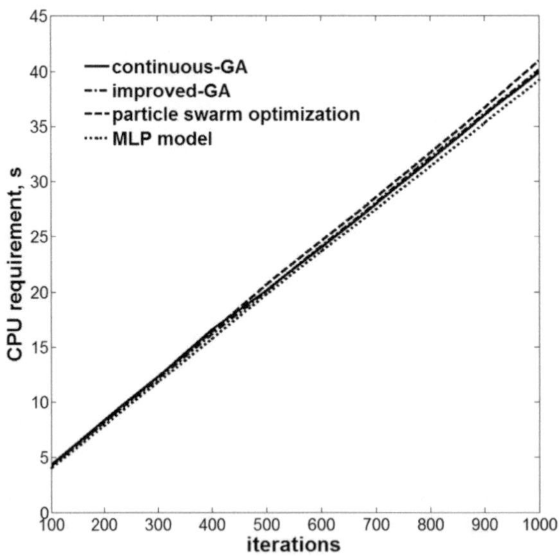

(b)

Fig. 19. (a) Evolution of global cost for implemented bio-inspired algorithms. (b) CPU requirement as a function of bio-inspired algorithm iterations ($Npop$=100)

Fig. 20(a) shows a photograph of the fabricated FSS prototype with Sierpinski island fractal patch elements considering the optimal design parameters: k=1, ε_r=4.4, and t_x=t_y=16.0 mm. In Fig. 20(b) is presented a comparison between the simulated and measured results for the transmission coefficient (dB) of the optimized FSS. The simulated and measured results are in good agreement with desired FSS design specifications (f=8.37 GHz and BW=1.44 GHz).

(a)

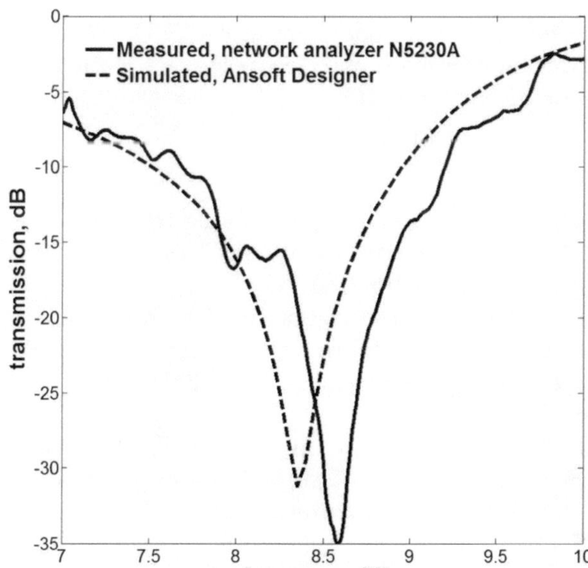

(b)

Fig. 20. (a) Built FSS prototype with Sierpinski island fractal patch elements (k=1, ε_r=4.4, and t_x=t_y=16.0 mm). (b) Comparison between the simulated and measured FSS transmission

5. Conclusion

This chapter described a new EM optimization technique blending full-wave method of moments, MLP artificial neural networks and bio-inspired algorithms for optimal design of frequency selective surfaces with fractal patch elements. Three fractal geometries were considered: Koch island, Dürer's pentagon and Sierpinski island. The use of fractal geometries to design FSS on isotropic dielectric substrates becomes possible the control of its frequency responses without increase its overall size. The MLP models were trained with accurate EM data provided by FSS simulations based on the method of moments. The computation of cost function of bio-inspired algorithms was done throught the use of developed MLP models. This procedure results in fast and accurate bio-inspired optimization algorithms. According to the obtained results, genetic algorithms present zigzag paths at flat regions of the cost surface that contribute to slow down the algorithm convergence. The introdution of a new mutation operation avoid the oscilation of continuous-GA final population around the global minimum of cost function. The improved-GA final population closely to the global minimum improves the GA convergence. PSO algorithm showed to be faster and easier to implement. This makes the optimization through PSO a powerful tool in synthesizing FSS structures. The idea of blending bio-inspired algorithms and artificial neural networks to optimize frequency selective surfaces shows to be very interesting, due to its great flexibility and easy application to structures that do not have a direct fitness function. The MoM-ANN-GA/PSO proposed technique is accurate and CPU inexpensive, which are most desired characteristics in the development of computer-aided design tools for EM optimization.

6. Acknowledgment

This work was supported by CNPq, under contracts 479253/2009-9 and 307256/2009-0, by Federal Institute of Education, Science and Technology of Paraíba (IFPB) and by Federal University of Rio Grande do Norte (UFRN).

7. References

Bandler, J. W. et al. (1994). Space Mapping Technique for Electromagnetic Optimization. *IEEE Transactions on Microwave Theory and Techniques*, Vol.42, No.12, (December 1994), pp. 2536-2544, ISSN 0018-9480

Bandler, J. W. et al. (1996). Parameterization of Arbitrary Geometrical Structures for Automated Electromagnetic Optimization, *Proceedings of IEEE MTT-S International Microwave Symposium Digest*, pp. 1059-1062, ISBN 0-7803-3246-6, San Francisco, CA, USA, August 17-21, 1996

Campos, A. L. P. S., Oliveira, E. E. C. & Silva, P. H. F. (2010). Design of Miniaturized Frequency Selective Surfaces Using Minkowski Island Fractal, *Journal of Microwaves, Optoelectronics and Electromagnetic Applications*, Vol.9, No.1, (June 2010), pp. 43-49, ISSN 1516-7399

Cruz, R. M. S.; Silva, P. H. F. & D'Assunção, A. G. (2009). Neuromodeling Stop Band Properties of Koch Island Patch Elements for FSS Filter Design, *Microwave and Optical Technology Letters*, Vol.51, No.12, (December 2009), pp. 3014-3019, ISSN 1098-2760

Fahmi, M. (November 2007). Computer Aided Design of Wide-Band Microwave Components, In: *Digital Repository at the University of Maryland,* 18.10.2011, Available from http://drum.lib.umd.edu/handle/1903/7693

Gianvittorio, J. P. et al., (2001). Fractal FSS: Various Self-Similar Geometries Used for Dual-Band and Dual-Polarized FSS. *Proceedings of the IEEE Antennas and Propagation Society International Symposium*, pp. 640-643, ISBN 0-7803-7070-8, Boston, MA , USA, July 8-13, 2001

Gianvittorio, J. P. et al., (2003). Self-Similar Prefractal Frequency Selective Surfaces for Multiband and Dual-Polarized Applications, *IEEE Transactions on Antennas and Propagation,* Vol.51, No. 11, (November 2003), pp. 3088-3096, ISSN 0018-926X

Haupt, R. L. (1995). An introduction to Genetic Algorithms for Electromagnetics. *IEEE Antennas Propagation Magazine*, Vol.37, No.2, (April 1995), pp. 7-15, ISSN: 1045-9243

Haupt, R. L. & Haupt, S. E. (2004). *Practical Genetic Algorithms,* 2nd ed., Wiley, ISBN 978-0-471-45565-3, New Jersey, NJ, USA

Haupt, R. L. & Werner, D. H. (2007). *Genetic algorithms in electromagnetics.* Willey, ISBN 978-0-471-48889-7, Hoboken, NJ, USA

Haykin, S. (1999). *Neural Networks: A Comprehensive Foundation,* (2nd ed.), Prentice-Hall, ISBN 0-13-273350-1, Upper Saddle River, NJ, USA

Hussein, Y. A. & El-Ghazaly, S. M. (2004). Modeling and Optimization of Microwave Devices and Circuits Using Genetic Algorithms, *IEEE Transactions on Microwave Theory and Techniques*, Vol.52, No.1, (January 2004), pp. 420-435, ISSN 0018-9480

Kennedy, L. & Eberhart, R. C. (1995). Particle swarm optimization. *Proceedings of the IEEE International Conference on Neural Networks*, pp. 1942-1948, ISBN 0-7803-2768-3, Perth, WA , Australia, November 27-01, 1995

Manara, G. et al., (1999). Frequency Selective Surface Design Based on Genetic Algorithm, *Electronics Letters*, Vol.35, No.17, (August 1999), pp. 400-401, ISSN 0013-5194

Mohamed, A. S. (August 2005). Recent Trends in CAD Tools for Microwave Circuit Design Exploiting Space Mapping Technology, In: *CiteSeer,* 18.10.2011, Available from http://sos.mcmaster.ca/theses/ahmed%20mohamed/

Munk, B. A. (2000). *Frequency-Selective Surfaces: Theory and Design*. Wiley, ISBN 0-471-37047-9 New York, NY, USA

Nikolova, N. K. et al. (2004). Adjoint Techniques for Sensitivity Analysis in High-Frequency Structure CAD, *IEEE Transactions on Microwave Theory and Techniques,* Vol.52, No.1, (January 2004), pp. 403-419, ISSN 0018-9480

Patnaik, A. & Mishra, R. K. (2000). ANN Techniques in Microwave Engineering. *IEEE Microwave Magazine,* Vol.1, No.1, (March 2000), pp. 55-60, ISSN 1527-3342

Ridmiller M. & Braun, H. (1993). A Direct Adaptative Method for Faster Backpropagation Learning: the RPROP Algorithm. *Proceedings of the IEEE International Conference on Neural Networks,* pp. 586-591, ISBN 0-7803-0999-5, San Francisco, CA , USA, March 28-01, 1993

Santos, A. L., Romariz, A. R. S. & Carvalho, P. H. P. (1997). Neural model of electrical devices for circuit simulation. *Proceedings of the SBMO/IEEE MTT-S International Microwave and Optoelectronics Conference,* Vol. 1, No.1, pp. 253-258, ISBN 0-7803-4165-1, Natal, Brazil, August 11-14, 1997

Silva, P. H. F., Lacouth, P., Fontgalland, G., Campos, A.L.P.S. & D'Assuncao, A.G. (2007). Design of Frequency Selective Surfaces Using a Novel MoM-ANN-GA Technique.

Proceedings of the SBMO/IEEE MTT-S International Microwave and Optoelectronics Conference, Vol.1, No.1, pp. 275-279, ISBN 978-1-4244-0661-6, Salvador, Brazil, October 29-1, 2007

Silva, P. H. F. et al. (2010a). Neuromodeling and Natural Optimization of Nonlinear Devices and Circuits, In: *System and Circuit Design for Biologically Inspired Intelligent Learning,* Turgay Temel, pp. 326-348, IGI Global, ISBN 978-1-60960-020-4, New York, NY, USA

Silva, P. H. F. et al. (2010b). Blending PSO and ANN for Optimal Design of FSS Filters With Koch Island Patch Elements. *IEEE Transactions on Magnetics,* Vol.46, No.8, (August 2010), pp. 3010-3013, ISSN 0018-9464

Trindade, J. I. A. et al. (2011). Analysis of Stop-Band Frequency Selective Surfaces With Dürer's Pentagon Pre-Fractals Patch Elements. *IEEE Transactions on Magnetics,* Vol.47, No. 5, (May 2011), pp. 1518-1521, ISSN 0018-9464

Oliveira, E. E. C.; Campos, A. L. P. S. & Silva, P. H. F. (2009). Miniaturization of Frequency Selective Surfaces Using Fractal Koch Curves. *Microwave and Optical Technology Letters,* Vol.51, No.8, (August 2009), pp. 1983-1986, ISSN 1098-2760

Zhang, Q. J. & Gupta, C. (2000). *Neural Networks for RF and Microwaves Design,* Artech House, ISBN 1-781-769-9750, Norwood, MA, USA

3

Evolutionary Multi-Objective Algorithms

Aurora Torres, Dolores Torres, Sergio Enriquez,
Eunice Ponce de León and Elva Díaz
University of Aguascalientes,
México

1. Introduction

The versatility that genetic algorithm (GA) has proved to have for solving different problems, has make it the first choice of researchers to deal with new challenges. Currently, GAs are the most well known evolutionary algorithms, because their intuitive principle of operation and their relatively simple implementation; besides they have the ability to reflect the philosophy of evolutionary computation in an easy and quick way.

As time goes by, human beings are more sophisticated. Every time we demand better performance of the equipment and techniques in the solution of more complex problems; forcing problem-solvers to use non-exhaustive solution techniques, although this could means the loss of accuracy. Non conventional techniques provide a solution in a suitable time when other techniques can be extraordinarily slow. Evolutionary algorithms are metaheuristics inspired on Darwin's theory of the survival of the fittest. A feature shared by these algorithms is that they are population-based, so each population represents a group of possible solutions to the problem posed; and only will transcend to the next generation those individuals with the best performance. At the end of the evolutionary process, the population is formed by the better individuals only. In general, all metaheuristics have shown their efficiency in solving complex optimization problems with one goal, so having to work simultaneously with more than one target, and therefore having to determine not only one answer but a set of them; population-based metaheuristics like evolutionary algorithms seem to be the most natural technique to address this type of optimization.

This chapter presents the theoretical description of the multi-objective optimization problem and establishes some important concepts. Later the most well known algorithms that initially were used for solving this problem are presented. Among these algorithms excels the GA and some modifications to it. The chapter also briefly discusses the estimation of the distribution algorithm (EDA), which was also inspired on the GA. Subsequently, the drawing graphs problem is established and solved. This problem, like many other of real life is inherently multi-objective. The proposed solution to this problem uses a hybrid EDA combined with a hill-climbing algorithm, which handled three simultaneous objectives: minimizing the number of crossing edges in the graph (total number of crossing edges of the graph have to be minimized), minimizing the graph area (total space used by the graph have to be as small as possible) and minimizing the graph aspect ratio (the graph have to be in a perfect square Visualized area). This section includes the description of the used approach and a group of experimental results, as well as some conclusions and future work. Finally, the last section of this chapter is a brief reflection on the future of multi-objective optimization research. On it, we capture some concerns and issues that are relevant to the development of this area.

2. Multi-objective optimization

Optimization in both mathematics and computing, refers to the determination of one or more feasible solutions that corresponds to an extreme value (maximum or minimum), according to one or more objective functions. To find the extreme solutions of one or more objective functions can be applied in a wide range of practical situations, such as to minimize the manufacturing cost of a product, to maximize profit, to reduce uncertainty, and so on. The principles and methods of optimization are used in solving quantitative problems in disciplines such as physics, biology, engineering, economics, and others. The simplest optimization problems involve functions of a single variable and can be solved by differential calculus. When researchers work with optimization, we could find two main types: mono-objective optimization and multi-objective optimization (MOO), depending on the number of optimization functions. The optimization can be subject to one or several constraints. The constraints are conditions that limit the selection of the values variables can take. This area has been approached for different techniques and methods.

Probably, the main difficulty of modelling mono-objective problems consists on obtaining just one equation for the complete problem. This stage could be too complicated to reach (Collette & Siarry, 2002). Due to the difficulty of finding an equation for a problem where many factors can influence, multi-objective optimization gives a very important advantage. Nevertheless, multi-objective optimization let us use some equations for reaching more than one objective; this property adds complexity to the model. As complexity of problems is increased, it is necessary to use new tools; for example: lineal programming that was created to solve optimization problems that involve two or more entrance variables.

2.1 Global optimization

Global optimization is the process of finding the global maximum or minimum (it will depend on the problem to be solved), inside a space S. Formally, it could be defined as (Bäck, 1996):

Definition 1. Given a function $f(\vec{x}) : \Omega \subseteq S = \mathbb{R}^n \rightarrow \mathbb{R}$, $\Omega \neq \emptyset$, for $\vec{x} \in \Omega$ the value $f^* \triangleq f(\vec{x}^*) > -\infty$ is named the global minimum if and only if

$$\forall \vec{x} \in \Omega : f(\vec{x}^*) \leq f(\vec{x}) \tag{1}$$

This way, $\vec{x}$ is the global minimum, $f(\vec{x}^*)$ is the objective function and the set Ω is the feasible region inside the set S. The problem of determining the global minimum is called "*problem of global optimization*". When the problem to optimize is mono-objective, the solution is unique. But this is not the case of multi-objective optimization problems (MOOP), they usually give a group of solutions that satisfy all objectives presented in vectors. Then, the decision maker (the human with this work) selects one or more of that vectors which represent acceptable solutions of the problem according to their own point of view (Coello et al., 2002).

2.2 General multi-objective optimization problem

MOOP also called multi-criteria optimization, multi-performance or vector optimization problem, can be defined (in words) as the problem of finding a vector of decision variables which satisfies constraints and optimizes a vector function whose elements represent the objective functions (Osyczka, 1985). These functions form a mathematical description of performance criteria which are usually in conflict with each other. Hence, the term "*optimize*" means finding such a solution which would give the values of all the objective functions acceptable to the decision maker (Coello, 2001).

2.2.1 Decision variables

Decision variables are numeric values, which should be selected in a problem of optimization. These variables are represented for x_i where $i = 1,2, \dots, n$.

The vector of n decision variables $\vec{x}$ is represented by:

$$\vec{x} = \begin{bmatrix} x_1 \\ x_2 \\ \vdots \\ x_n \end{bmatrix} \tag{2}$$

2.2.2 Constraints

Constraints imposed by the nature and environment of certain studied case, will be found in most of optimization problems. These conditions can be physical limitations, space or resistance obstacles, or restrictions in the time for the realization of a task, among others. So, certain solution is considered acceptable, if at least it satisfies these constraints. The constraints represent dependences between the parameters and the decision variables in the optimization problem. We can identify two different types of constraints; constraints of inequality:

$$g_i(\vec{x}) \leq 0 \qquad i = 1,2, \dots, m \tag{3}$$

and the equality constraints:

$$h_i(\vec{x}) = 0 \qquad i = 1,2, \dots, p \tag{4}$$

It is necessary to highlight that p should be smaller than n, because the number of equality constraints should be smaller than the number of decision variables, since if $p \geq n$ the problem is known as over constrained (Ramírez, 2007), and this means that will have more unknown variables than equations. Those constraints can be explicit (described by one algebraic expression), or implicit (in which case, an algorithm or method have to exist to calculate this constraints for any vector $\vec{v}$).

2.2.3 Objective functions

To know how good a solution is, it is necessary to have a criterion to evaluate it. This measure should be expressed as an algebraic function of the decision variables and it is known as objective function. It is possible that researches do not have this mathematical model, so, at least it is needed to have some mechanisms to determine the quality of the solutions, which can vary depending on the problem.

In many problems of the real world, objective functions are in conflict one to each other and even in the same problem some of them can be functions to minimize while the remaining ones have to be maximized. The vector of objective functions $\vec{f}(\vec{x})$ is defined as follow:

$$\vec{f}(\vec{x}) = \begin{bmatrix} \vec{f}_1(\vec{x}) \\ \vec{f}_2(\vec{x}) \\ \vdots \\ \vec{f}_k(\vec{x}) \end{bmatrix} \quad (5)$$

The set where R denotes the real numbers by $\mathbb{R}^n$ is called Euclidian space of n dimensions. For the multi-objective optimization problem are considered two Euclidian spaces: the one of the decisions variables and the one of the objective functions. Each point in the first space represents a solution and it can be mapped in the space of the objective functions and then the quality of each solution can be determined. The general MOOP can be formally defined as:

Definition 2. Find the vector $\vec{x}^* = [x_1^*, x_2^*, \dots, x_n^*]^T$ which will satisfy the m inequality constraints:

$$g_i(\vec{x}) \leq 0 \quad i = 1,2,\dots,m \quad (6)$$

the p equality constraints

$$h_i(\vec{x}) = 0 \quad i = 1,2,\dots,p \quad (7)$$

and will optimize the vector function

$$\vec{f}(\vec{x}) = [f_1(\vec{x}), f_2(\vec{x}), \dots, f_k(\vec{x})]^T \quad (8)$$

In other words, MOOP consists on determining the set of values for the decision variables $x_1^*, x_2^*, \dots, x_n^*$ which satisfy equations (6) and (7) and simultaneously optimize (8). Constraints given in (6) and (7) the feasible region of Ω and any point $\vec{x} \in \Omega$ is a feasible solution. The vector of functions $\vec{f}(\vec{x})$ map the group of feasible solutions Ω to the group of feasible objective functions. The k objective functions in the vector $\vec{f}(\vec{x})$ represent the criterion that can be expressed in different units. The restrictions $g_i(\vec{x})$ and $h_i(\vec{x})$ represent constraints applied to the decision variables. The vector $\vec{x}^*$ represents the group of optimal solutions.

2.3 Multi-objective optimization type of problems

In the area of multi-objective problems, three variants could be found; the first of them consists on minimizing the whole set of objective functions, the second consists on maximizing them and the third one is a mixture of minimization and maximization of the objective functions.

When we are in the third case, is very common that all the functions be transformed to their minimization version or maximization one, as it is preferred. So, the next equation can be used:

$$\max(f_i(\vec{x})) = -\min(-f_i(\vec{x})) \quad (9)$$

In the same way, inequality constraints (6) can be transformed multiplying by -1 and changing the sign of the inequality as follows:

$$-g_i(\vec{x}) \geq 0 \quad i = 1,2,\dots,m \quad (10)$$

2.4 The ideal vector

The ideal vector $\vec{f}_i^\star$ is formed as $\vec{f}_i^\star = [\vec{f}_1^\star, \vec{f}_2^\star, \cdots, \vec{f}_k^\star]^T$, where $f_i^\star$ denotes the optimal for the i-th objective function. If the objectives were not in conflict, then would exist a unique point $\vec{x}^\star$ (in the space of the decision variables), but this situation is very exceptional in the real world.

The most accepted notion of optimum in the multi-objective environment was formulated by Francis Ysidro Edgeworth in 1881 and generalized after by Vilfredo Pareto in 1896.

2.5 Pareto – optimality

The concept of Pareto Optimum (also called Efficiency of Pareto, in honour of his discoverer, Vilfredo Pareto), is a concept of the economy with application in that discipline and in social sciences and engineering.

According to Pareto, a specific situation X is superior or preferable to other situation Y when the pass from Y to X supposes an improvement for all the members of the society, or an improvement for some, without the other ones be harmed. In other words, in economy and political economy, the concept of "*Optimum of Pareto*" simply indicates a situation in which cannot improve the situation of somebody without making worse the others' situation.

As already was said, the concept was born in economics, but its scope covers any situation with more than one objective to optimize.

Pareto optimality

We say that a vector of decision variables $\vec{x}^* \in S$ is Pareto optimal if there is not another $\vec{x} \in S$ such that $f_i(\vec{x}) \leq f_i(\vec{x}^*)$ for all i = 1, ... k and $f_j(\vec{x}) < f_j(\vec{x}^*)$ for at least one j. In other words, this definition establishes $\vec{x}^*$ is Pareto optimal if there no exists a feasible vector of decision variables $\vec{x} \in S$ which would decrease some criterion without causing a simultaneous increase in at least one other criterion. Unfortunately, this concept almost always gives not a single solution, but rather a set of solutions called the Pareto optimal set. The vectors $\vec{x}^*$ corresponding to the solutions included in the Pareto optimal set are called non-dominated ones. The plot of the objective functions whose non-dominated vectors are in the Pareto optimal set that is called the Pareto front (Coello, 2011).

2.6 Pareto dominance

Formally, it is said that a vector $\overline{u} = [u_1, u_2, \dots, u_k]^T$ dominates a vector $\overline{v} = [v_1, v_2, \dots, v_k]^T$ if and only if $\overline{u}$ is partially less than v. In other words:

$$\forall i \in \{1,2,\dots,k\}, u_i \leq v_i \wedge \exists i \in \{1,2,\dots,k\} : u_i < v_i \tag{11}$$

And it is denoted by: $\vec{u} \preceq \vec{v}$.

Considering a MOOP $\vec{f}(\vec{x})$, then the Pareto optimal set P* is defined as:

$$\mathcal{P}^* = \{\vec{x} \in \Omega \mid \neg \exists\ \vec{y} \in \Omega\ \vec{f}(\vec{y}) \preceq \vec{f}(\vec{x})\} \tag{12}$$

2.7 Pareto front

The Pareto Front concept is defined formally as follow:

Considering a MOOP $\vec{f}(\vec{x})$ and a Pareto optimal set P^*; the Pareto Front $\mathcal{PF}^*$ is defined as

$$\mathcal{PF}^* = \{\vec{f} = [f_1(\vec{x}),\ f_2(\vec{x}), \dots, f_k(\vec{x})]^T \mid \vec{x} \in \mathcal{P}^*\} \tag{13}$$

Figures 1, 2, 3 and 4 show some Pareto fronts for two objective functions (f1 and f2). In all mentioned figures, the front is the set of points marked with a line. Figure 1 for example, presents the case in which both objective functions are minimized.

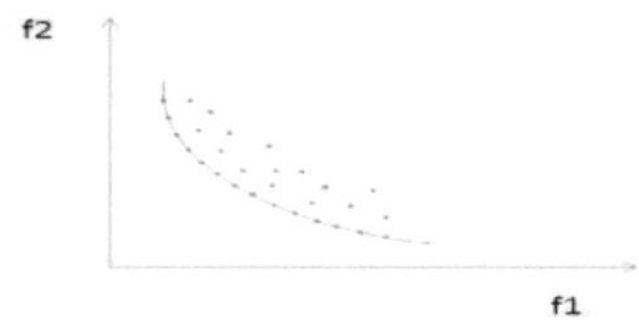

Fig. 1. Pareto front for the minimization of two objective functions (f1 and f2)

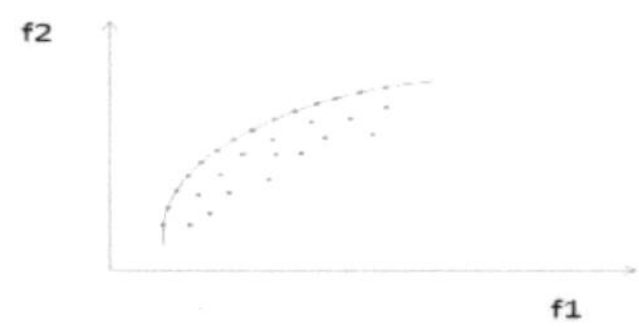

Fig. 2. Pareto front for the minimization of f1 and the maximization of f2

Figure 2 shows the Pareto front for the minimization of function f1 and the maximization of function f2. As the reader can see, the front is formed by the solutions that are bigger on f2 but smaller on f1.

In figure 3, it is presented the Pareto front for the maximization of the two objective functions. Here the solutions on the front are those with the biggest value on function f1 and the biggest value on f2 too.

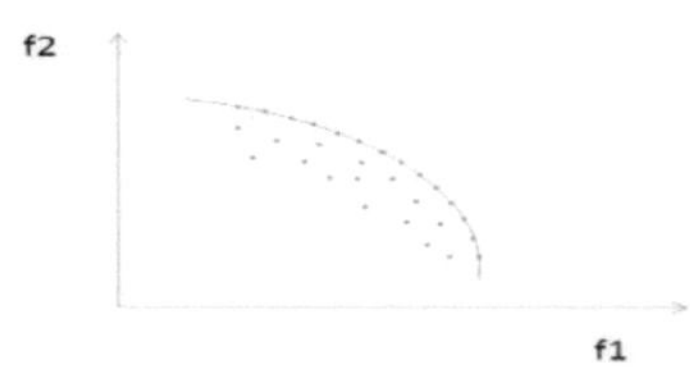

Fig. 3. Pareto front for the maximization of f1 and the maximization of f2

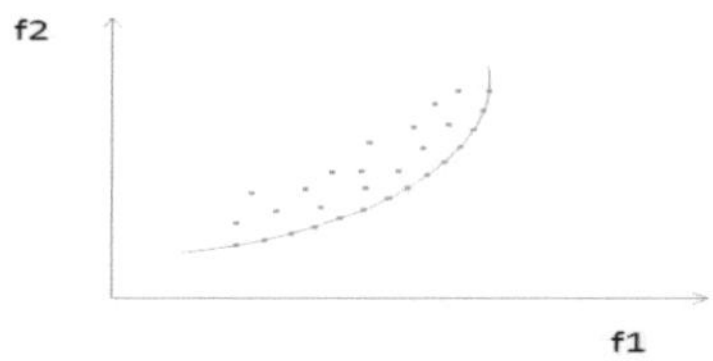

Fig. 4. Pareto front for the maximization of f1 and the minimization of f2

Finally, figure 4 shows the shape of the Pareto front when f1 is maximized while f2 is minimized. In this figure it can be seen that the Pareto front is formed by solutions that exhibit a high fitness on f1 but low fitness on f2.

Normally, it is impossible to find a mathematical expression that allows us to determine the whole set of points conforming the $\mathcal{PF}^*$. To determine this group, usually are calculated the $\vec{f}$ of an enough number of points in Ω (feasible region). If the number of points calculated is appropriate, then can be determined which solutions are not dominated ones and this way the Pareto front can be obtained. Not dominated solutions don't have any relationship to each other, on the fact they are members of the Pareto optimal. This set corresponds to the non dominated solutions that conform the Pareto front.

According with the definition of Pareto optimal, to get the solutions, it is necessary to make a commitment among the functions, in other words, improving an objective will be reflected as the deterioration of another. This is one of the main concepts in multi-objective optimization. The commitment is subjected to questions in some cases, maybe not in the totality of cases. But we could generate better results in terms of quality and smaller cost, only changing the formulation of the problem (Zeleny, 1997).

2.8 Strong and weak Pareto dominance

Besides the Pareto optimality concept, there are some other concepts very important in MOOP, two of them are called: weak Pareto dominance and strong Pareto dominance. A vector is a weak Pareto optimal if does not exist another vector in which all components in the objective functions space are better. Formally it can be defined as: A solution $\vec{x}^* \in \Omega$ is a weakly not dominated solution if does not exist another solution $\vec{x} \in \Omega \mid f_i(\vec{x}) < f_i(\vec{x}^*)$, for $i = 1,2,\dots,k$.

The concept of strong Pareto dominance could be summarized as follows: A solution $\vec{x}^* \in \Omega$ is a strongly not dominated solution if does not exist another solution $\vec{x} \in \Omega \mid f_i(\vec{x}) \leq f_i(\vec{x}^*)$, for $i = 1,2,\dots,k$ and also exists at least a value $j \mid f_j(\vec{x}) < f_j(\vec{x}^*)$

3. Multi-objective evolutionary algorithms

Although apparently the only source of motivation for using evolutionary algorithms to solve multi-objective problems arises from a single source (Goldberg 1989), this field has become very wide in recent years. As discussed in the introduction to this chapter, the parallel nature of evolutionary algorithms make them a tool with great potential when trying to find a group of solutions on an optimization problem.

This section will discuss the first multi-objective optimization algorithms (MOAs) used, passing from those that handle the problem as if it were a single objective problem, to those that make use of EDAs. EDAs are particularly important in this chapter, because towards the end of it, the problem of graph drawing is addresses by this type of metaheuristics.

The field of both mono-objective and multi-objective optimization has been benefited from a significant number of classical techniques, but quantity of new techniques have been recently included. A particularly successful approach is the application of evolutionary computation. Because this chapter deals with the solution of multi-objective problems with heuristic tools, we will start describing the general operation of an evolutionary algorithm.

An evolutionary algorithm begins with the creation (initialization) of a population of individuals (possible solutions to the problem) "*Pt*", usually created by a random procedure or knowledge-driven problem-information. Thereafter, the algorithm performs an iterative process that evaluates the quality of each individual in the population and starts a process of transformation of the current population by certain operators. The most common operators are selection, crossover, mutation and elitism. The iterative process stops when one or more predetermined criteria are met. Figure 5 shows the general procedure of an evolutionary algorithm. In this figure each apostrophe represents a new transformation of the current population, while "*t*" indicates the generation number.

An Evolutionary Optimization Procedure

```
t=0;
Initialization (P_t);
do
    Evaluation(P_t);
    P_t' = Selection (P_t);
    P_t'' = Variation (P_t');
    P_t+1 = Elitism (P_t, P_t'');
while (Termination(P_t,P_t+1));
```

Fig. 5. General Evolutionary Optimization Procedure (Deb, 2008)

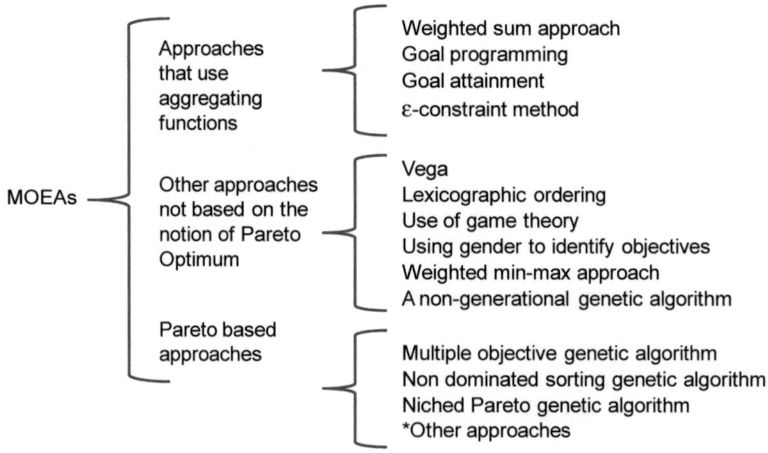

Fig. 6. Classification of Multi-Objective Evolutionary Algorithms

Even though the evolutionary multi-objective optimization field is very young (less than twenty years), it is already considered as a well-established research and application area; according to Deb (Deb, 2008) there are hundreds of doctoral theses on this topic, and are dozens of books devoted to it too.

Some of the reasons why evolutionary algorithms (EAs) have become so popular are:

1. EAs do not require any derivative information
2. EAs are relatively simple to implement
3. EAs are flexible and have a wide-spread of applicability (Deb, 2008)

Marler and Arora (Marler and Arora, 2004) propose a general classification of all multi-objective optimization methods according to the decision maker (DM) intervention. These researchers distinguished the next categories:

- Methods with a priori articulation of preferences
- Methods with a posteriori articulation
- Methods with no articulation of preferences.

The first category focuses on those methods where the user (DM) can specify certain preferences since the beginning of the process; which may be articulated in terms of goals, levels of importance of the objective functions, etc. The second category refers to the group of methods that begin the search for the Pareto set without additional information, but as the search process progresses, the method has to be assisted by the introduction of some preferences provided by the DM. Finally, when the DM is not able to define specifically what he prefers, it is necessary to employ methods that do not require any articulation of preferences. These methods are those that make up the third category of Marler and Arora. For more details see (Marler and Arora, 2004).

Speaking more specifically about multi-objective evolutionary algorithms (MOEAs), we can find another widely accepted classification. This classification groups them as follows:

- Those algorithms that do not incorporate the concept of Pareto optimality in their selection mechanism.
- Those algorithms that rely in the population according to whether an individual is dominated or not.

Considering this last classification and the one used by Coello (Coello, 1999), main multi-objective evolutionary algorithms can be grouped in the way shown in Figure 6.

In this chapter we will use mainly the latter classification, because our interest is in those techniques that come from the evolutionary computation. Since explaining all the algorithms of the previous classification would be very extensive, we will focus on discussing only the most used of them.

3.1 Approaches that use aggregative functions

The most commonly used methods for solving multi-objective problems, also called "*basic methods*" (Miettinen, 2008) are those who handle problems as if they were single-objective problems. These methods consist on the transformation of the problem so that they can be solved by optimizing a single objective function. The tendency to transform a multi-objective problem to the form of a single-objective one, responds to the fact that single-objective optimization techniques are better known than those that include optimization based on several functions. The intuitive nature of these techniques, besides the fact that GAs use scalar fitness, makes aggregative functions the first option for solving multi-objective problems. Aggregative functions are combinations either linear or nonlinear of all objectives into a single one. Although there are some drawbacks in using arithmetic combinations of objectives, these techniques have been used extensively since the late sixties, when Rosenberg published his work (Rosenberg, 1967). Even though Rosenberg did not use a multi-objective technique, his work showed that it was feasible to use evolutionary search techniques to handle multi-objective problems. The two techniques that best represent this kind of approaches are: Weighted Sum Method and ε-Constraint Method.

Readers interested on techniques in this group, can consult "*A comprehensive Survey of Evolutionary-Based Multi-objective Techniques*" (Coello, 1999).

3.1.1 Weighted sum method

The goal of this method is constituted by the sum of all objectives of the problem, using different coefficients for each one. The coefficients used represent the level of importance assigned to each of the objectives. So the optimization problem becomes a problem of scale optimization as follows:

$$\text{minimize } \sum_{i=1}^{k} w_i f_i(\vec{x}) \tag{14}$$

Where $w_i \geq 0$ is the weighting coefficient that represents the relative importance of the i-th objective. It is usually assumed that

$$\sum_{i=1}^{k} w_i = 1 \tag{15}$$

The normalization above takes place because the results obtained by this technique may have significant variations to small changes in the coefficients and avoids that different magnitudes confuse the method. Very often it is need to perform a set of experiments before determining the best combination of weights. When the decision maker has some a priori knowledge about the problem, it is feasible and beneficial to introduce this information in modelling. At the end of the process is the decision maker the one who should make the most appropriate solution according to his experience and intuition. There are several variations of this method, for example, adding constant multipliers to scale objectives in a better way. This was the first method used for the generation of non inferior solutions for multi-objective optimization (Coello 1998), perhaps because it was implied by Kuhn and Tucker in their seminar work on numerical optimization (Kuhn and Tucker, 1951). Computationally speaking, this method is efficient and it has proven to have the ability of generating non-dominated solutions which are often used as a starting point for other techniques; nevertheless, its main drawback is the enormous complexity to determine the appropriate weights when there is no information about the problem. In the case that there is no information about the problem, the literature suggests using simple linear combinations of the objectives to adjust the weights iteratively. In general this technique is not suitable in the presence of search spaces non-convex (Ritzel et al., 1994), because the alteration of the weights can produce jumps between several vertex, leaving undetected intermediate solutions.

3.1.2 ε-constraint method

The operating principle of this method is to optimize only one objective at a time, leaving the rest of them as constraints that must be limited by certain permitted levels ε_j. The objective that is optimized, is the one considered as the principal or most important f1. ε_j levels are then altered to generate the Pareto optimal entire set. This method can be formulated as follows:

$$\text{minimize } f_l(\vec{x}) \tag{16}$$

$$subject\ to\ f_j(\vec{x}) \leq \varepsilon_j\ for\ all\ j = 1, \ldots, k, j \neq l \tag{17}$$

where $l \in \{1,\ldots,k\}$ and ε_j are upper bounds for the objectives $(j \neq l)$. The search stops when the decision maker finds a satisfactory solution. This method was introduced by Haimes et al in (Haimes et al., 1971). It is possible that this procedure should be repeated for different values of the index l. In order to obtain a set of appropriate values of ε_j is very common to use independent GAs or other techniques for optimizing each objective function. The main weakness of this method is related to its huge consumption of time, however, its relative ease, has made it very popular especially in the community of GAs.

3.2 Other approaches not based on the notion of Pareto optimum

Although techniques mentioned in the previous sub-section have proven to be useful for solving multi-objective optimization problems, we must not forget that they do it as if it were a problem with a single objective. The search for other alternatives resulted in the development of the techniques in the second category according to Figure 6. Techniques in this category introduced two very important elements: the use the populations and the use of special handling of objectives. To illustrate this group of techniques, the Vector Evaluated Genetic Algorithm (VEGA) and the lexicographic ordering are going to be discussed. VEGA is so important because it was the first GA used as a tool for solving MOOP. On the other hand, during the decade of the 80's and early 90's, the MOEAs were characterized by the use of aggregative techniques (already discussed), target vector optimization and lexicographic ordering; so, it would be illustrative to review this last one.

3.2.1 Vector Evaluated Genetic Algorithm (VEGA)

The first multi-objective genetic algorithm was implemented by Schaffer (Schaffer, 1984), and it was inspired on the "*simple GA*" (SGA). After making some modifications to the first implementation, Schaffer named it "*Vector Evaluated Genet Algorithm*" (Schaffer, 1985). Schaffer proposed the creation of one sub-population per each objective function of the problem on each generation of the algorithm. So, assuming a population size of N for a problem with k objective functions, k subsets (sub-populations) of size N/k should be generated; then the k sub-populations must be shuffled together to obtain the new population of size N. Finally, the GA will apply classical operators. Figure 7 shows the selection scheme of VEGA.

The main weakness of this algorithm comes from the fact that it promotes the conservation of solutions with very good performance in only one of the k objectives of the problem, by eliminating the solutions that have what Schaffer called "*middling*" performance (acceptable performance in all objective functions). The problem mentioned is known in genetics like "*speciation*", and it is obviously undesirable in solving multi-objective problems because it goes against the goal of finding compromise solutions.

In more general terms, the performance of this method is compared with the linear combination of objectives, where the weights depend on the distribution of the population in each generation as demonstrated by Richardson et al (Richardson et al., 1989). Therefore this technique has not the ability to produce Pareto optimal solutions in the presence of non-convex search spaces.

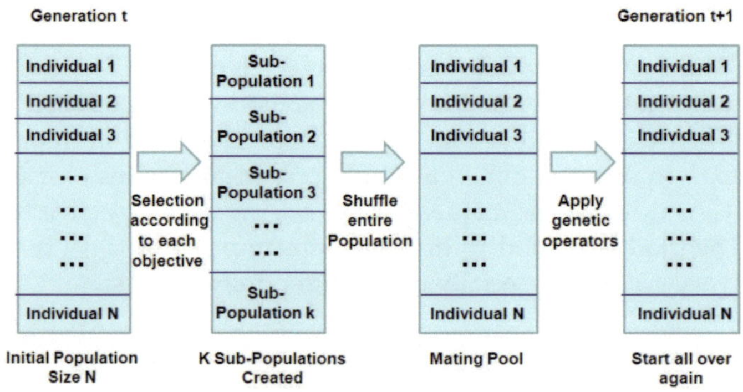

Fig. 7. Scheme of VEGA selection

3.2.2 Lexicographic ordering

This method, which is commonly grouped with the methods that articulate some preferences a priori according with the Marler and Arora's classification (Marler and Arora, 2004), or the named as a priori methods (Miettinen, 2008), begins with the arrangement of all objective functions according to their relative importance. Subsequently, the most important objective function is minimized subject to the original constraints. Then, we formulate a similar problem with the second most important objective function and an extra restriction. This procedure is repeated until the k objectives have been considered. The first problem to be solved, assuming that f_1 is the most important objective, has the following form:

$$\text{minimize } f_1(\vec{x}) \tag{18}$$

$$subject\ to\colon\ g_j(\vec{x}) \leq 0 \quad j = 1,2\ldots,m \tag{19}$$

By solving (5) and (6), we obtain $\overrightarrow{x_1}^*$ and $f_1^*=f(\overrightarrow{x_1}^*)$, and then, the next problem is formulated:

$$\text{minimize } f_2(\vec{x}) \tag{20}$$

$$subject\ to\colon\ g_j(\vec{x}) \leq 0 \quad j = 1,2\ldots,m \tag{21}$$

$$f_1(\vec{x}) = f_1^* \tag{22}$$

Once the problem in (7), (8) and (9) is solved, $\overrightarrow{x_2}^*$ and $f_2^*=f(\overrightarrow{x_2}^*)$ are obtained. This procedure is then repeated over and over, until all objective functions have been taken into account. The final solution obtained $\overrightarrow{x_k}^*$ is considered the best solution of the problem.

The greatest strength of this method lies in its simplicity, and its greatest weakness comes from the high level of dependence of their performance with the order of importance chosen for each objective function. Because this method takes into account one objective at a time, it tends to promote only certain goals, when there are others in the problem, making the process to converge to a particular area of the Pareto front.

3.3 Pareto based approaches

As the reader may have observed, all techniques discussed so far produce Pareto front members implicitly, because they do not use the Pareto-optimality concept as a search mechanism, nevertheless there are also a set of methods that employ the definition of Pareto-optimality to conduct the search for solutions. In 1989 Goldberg suggested the use of a fitness function based on the concept of Pareto-optimality to deal with the problem of speciation identified by Schaffler. Goldberg's proposal was to find the set of individuals that are Pareto non-dominated by the rest of the population and assign them the rank 1, then removing them from contention, and then find a new set of non-dominated individuals and rank them as 2, and so forth. This technique is named Pareto ranking.

The main weakness of this method is that there is not yet an efficient algorithm to check non-dominance in a set of feasible solutions (Coello, 1996). As the size of population and the number of objective functions grow up, efficiency of algorithms is worse; however, Pareto ranking is the most appropriate method to generate an entire Pareto front in a single run of the GA (Coello, 1999). Several algorithms that use Pareto based approaches have been developed; next subsections will discuss some of them.

3.3.1 Multiple Objective Genetic Algorithm (MOGA)

A scheme in which the rank of an individual depends on the number of individuals from a certain population, by which it is dominated, was proposed by Fonseca and Fleming (Fonseca and Fleming, 1993). For example, lets suppose generation *t*, all non-dominated individuals are assigned rank 1, while dominated ones are assigned a rank of ($1+p_i^{(t)}$) where $p_i^{(t)}$ is the number of solutions that dominates the solution x_i. The individual x_i in the generation t, can be assigned the next rank.

$$rank(x_i, t) = 1 + p_i^{(t)} \tag{23}$$

Fitness assignment is performed in the following way (Fonseca and Fleming, 1993).

1. Population is sort by the assigned rank
2. Fitness is assigned to individuals by interpolating from the best (rank 1) to the worst (rank n). Interpolation is usually linear but it can be non linear.
3. The fitness of individuals with the same rank is averaged, so all of them will be sampled at the same rate.

A potential weakness of this algorithm is the premature convergence produced by a large selection pressure because of blocked selected fitness (Goldberg and Deb, 1991). To avoid this, Fonseca and Fleming used niche-formation method to distribute the population over the Pareto-optimal region; however instead of performing sharing on the parameters values, they used sharing on the objective function values.

This algorithm has been widely accepted and used because of its efficiency and relatively easy implementation. As other Pareto ranking techniques, this algorithm is highly dependent of an appropriate selection of the sharing factor, but Fonseca and Fleming developed a methodology to compute this factor for their approach (Fonseca and Fleming, 1993).

3.3.2 Non-dominated Sorting Genetic Algorithm (NSGA)

The NSGA was proposed by Srinivas and Deb (Srinivas and Deb, 1993). This method is characterized in that the fitness assignment is performed by a rank of dominance. It does not work with a functional value, but with a dummy fitness.

In the first step of this method, the population is ranked based on non-domination. All non-dominated individuals are put into a category with a dummy fitness proportional to population size. Then, this group of classified individuals is ignored and another layer of non-dominated individuals is considered. This process continues until all individuals in the population have been classified. Because individuals of the first front have the highest value of fitness, they will be copied more times than the rest of the population. This method allows the search of non-dominated regions with quick convergence results. The efficiency of this method lies in the way a group of objectives is replaced by a dummy function using a non-dominated sorting procedure. According with Srinivas and Deb, with this approach maximization and minimization with any number of objectives can be handled (Srinivas and Deb, 1994). Among other researchers, Coello has reported that this approach is less efficient than the MOGA, and more sensitive to the value of the sharing factor.

3.3.3 Niched Pareto Genetic Algorithm (NPGA)

A tournament selection scheme based on Pareto dominance was proposed by Horn and Nafpliotis (Horn and Nafpliotis, 1993). The main idea of this approach is to use tournament selection based on Pareto dominance with respect to a subset of the population (typically around 10 individuals). In case of ties (when both competitors were either dominated or non-dominated), the decision is made by fitness sharing in both, fitness function space and in the decision variables space.

3.4 Other approaches

Evolutionary algorithms have proved to be very efficient in solving several multi-objective optimization problems, because they have good ability of global exploration and fast convergence speed, all due to the use of nature-inspired operators (crossover, mutation, selection). However, they also have been criticized for the little use made of the information about the problem, the high random component they possess and the large number of evaluations of the problem they use. Some of these problems are being addressed through proposals such as EDAs and Scatter Search, in which operators are deterministic or employ techniques that reduce the number of evaluations.

Another recent trend to address the weaknesses of evolutionary algorithms is combining them with classical optimization methods or other metaheuristics. This type of technique has been used successfully in single-objective optimization, leading to what is called "*memetic algorithms*" (Moscato, 1999).

In this section, the general idea behind the EDA is discuss, because it is the technique used in solving the problem of drawing graphs. Section 4.2 of this chapter describes the used algorithm called "*Hybrid multi-objective optimization estimation of distribution algorithm*". This algorithm is a hybridized EDA with Hill Climbing.

The main idea behind EDAs is to use the probability distribution of the population in the reproduction of the new offspring. EDAs are a natural outgrowth of GA in which statistical information of the population is used to build a probability distribution. Then, this distribution is used to generate new individuals by sampling. Because probability distribution replaces Darwinian operators, this kind of algorithm is classified as non-Darwinian evolutionary algorithm.

The general procedure of the EDA can be sketched as shown in figure 8.

```
Template of the EDA algorithm
t=1
Generate randomly a population of n individuals
Initialize a probability model Q(x)
While Termination criteria are not met Do
  Create a population of n individuals by sampling from Q(x)
  Evaluate the objective function for each individual
  Select m individuals according to a selection method
  Update the probabilistic model Q(x) using selected population and f() values
  t=t+1
End While
Output: Best found solution or set of solutions
```

Fig. 8. Estimation of the Distribution Algorithm (Talbi, 2009)

EDAs are classified according to the level of variable-interaction they use in their probabilistic model:

- Univariate: This class of EDAs suppose that there is not interaction among problem-variables.
- Bivariate: This class of EDAs suppose that there is interaction between two variables.
- Multivariate: In this class of EDAs, the probabilistic distribution models the interaction among more than two variables.

Although initially EDAs were intended for combinatorial optimization, now they have been extended to the continuous domain. Nowadays the application field of EDAs not only addresses mono-objective optimization issues, but it has been created a discipline related to their application on multi-objective problems. The group of EDAs applied to multi-objective optimization is called "*multi-objective optimization EDAs*" (MOEDAs) (Marti, 2008). Most of the actual MOEAs are modified single-objective EDAs whose fitness assignments are replaced by multi-objective assignments.

According to some researchers, there are several aspects that are crucial in the implementation of multi-objective solutions when MOEDAs are used; some of them are:

- Fitness assignment: Since several objectives have to be taken into account; this aspect is very important and more complex than in single-objective optimization.
- Diversity preservation: In order to reach a good coverage of the Pareto front, population diversity is critical.

- Elitism: Elitism is the mechanism used to preserve non dominated solution through successive generations of the algorithm.

With these aspects in mind, next section will discuss the implementation of the proposed solution to the graph drawing problem.

4. An application of a multi-objective optimization hybrid estimation of distribution algorithm for graph drawing problem

Graph drawing problems are a particular class of combinatorial optimization problems whose goal is to find plane layout of an input graph in such a way that certain objective functions are optimized. A large number of relevant problems in different domains can be formulated as graph layout problems. Among these problems are optimization of networks for parallel computer architectures, VLSI circuit design, information retrieval, numerical analysis, computational biology, graph theory, graphical model visualization, scheduling and archaeology. Most interesting graph drawing problems are NP-hard and their decisional versions are NP-complete (Garey and Johnson, 1983), but, for most of their applications, feasible solutions with an almost optimal cost are sufficient. As a consequence, approximation algorithms and effective heuristics are welcome in practice (Díaz et al., 2002).

Visualization of complex conceptual structures is a support tool used on several engineering and scientific applications. A graph is an abstract structure used to model information. Graphs are used to represent information that can be modeled as connections between variables, and so, to draw graphs to put information in an understandable way. The usefulness of graphs visualization systems depends on how easy is to catch its meaning, and how fast and clear is to interpret it. This characteristic can be expressed through of aesthetic criteria (Sugiyama, 2002) as the edges' crossing minimization, the reduction of drawing area and the minimization of aspect ratio, the minimization of the maximum length of an edge, among others.

In our approach the three first objectives are used and we can make a multi-objective optimization formulation for the graph drawing problem. On the one hand, to enhance the legibility of the graph drawing is very important to keep as low as possible the number of crosses, as well as to keep a good aspect ratio in the draw. Another point is to maintain symmetric the drawing region (same drawing height and width). It is very desirable too, to keep the drawing area small. This last requirement avoids the waste of screen space. These objectives are in conflict with each other. To reach the minimum crossing edges in the graph drawing is frequently needed a bigger area. At the same time, for minimizing the aspect ratio of the graph is needed to draw the nodes in a symmetrically delimited region. The reduction of the used area increases the number of crosses because as closer the edges are, there is less space to do the crossing edges minimization. Besides, area reduction of the sketching also affects the symmetrical delimitation of the region used by the graph. The aspect ratio minimization is affected by the crossing edges minimization due that just to get a node outside the defined area contributes to the imbalance of the symmetry reached until that moment. So, the reduction of the drawing area affects directly the aspect ratio of the graph because generally this kind of reduction is not symmetric. A first approach of the multi-objective optimization problem for these three objectives for graph drawing could be found in (Enriquez et al., 2011).

4.1 Formulation of the multi-objective optimization for graph drawing problem

At the beginning, we have a graph given by its edges, that is, a pair of vertices. To each vertex is assigned a pair of coordinates. All coordinates of the vertices of the graph are randomly generated in the cartesian plane. If any two vertices have the same coordinates then new coordinates are randomly generated for one of them. The candidate solution is represented as a vector of pairs of coordinates. The input information, i.e., the list of edges of the graph is used by the algorithm to draw the edges in the best manner in order to fulfill a tradeoff between all considered objective functions.

In this chapter the following in conflict objectives have been considered:

- Minimization of the number of crossing edges in the graph: The total number of crossing edges of the graph has to be minimized (f1).
- Minimization of the graph area: to minimize the total space used by the graph (f2).
- Minimization of the graph aspect ratio: the graph has to be visualized in an approximate square area (f3).

The vector of the objective functions is denoted by F=(f1,f2,f3). The first function f1 is calculated as follows:

To draw a line between two vertices, $v_1(x_1, y_1)$ and $v_2(x_2, y_2)$ we use the following equation:

$$y - y_1 = \frac{y_2 - y_1}{x_2 - x_1}(x - x_1) \tag{24}$$

and solve the equation system for knowing if the two lines corresponding to edges have an intersection point. The function f1 sums the number of intersection points between edges of this drawing.

$$a_1 x + b_1 y = c_1 \tag{25}$$

$$a_2 x + b_2 y = c_2 \tag{26}$$

The second function f2 is defined as the area of the rectangle containing the graph drawing. The following formula is used:

$$S = (x_{max} - x_{min}) \cdot (y_{max} - y_{min}) \tag{27}$$

where $x_{min}$and x_{max} are the least and greatest values on the abscise axis, and y_{min} and y_{max} are the least and greatest values on the vertical axis. S is the value of the function f2.

Finally, the f3 function is obtained as a ratio of $(x_{max} - x_{min})$ on $(y_{max} - y_{min})$ or vice versa, depending on which was the least. f3 is the value of this ratio, and it is knowing as aspect ratio.

We use the Pareto front approach for the multi-objective optimization problem (Coello and López, 2009), (Deb, 2001) and we give the final Pareto front and also give as more promissory solution, that solution closest to the origin, because it resumes all objective tradeoffs. The distance to origin is calculated evaluating the Euclidean distance using the standardized values of the objectives of the problem.

4.2 Hybrid multi-objective optimization estimation of distribution algorithm

This section presents a description of the components of the proposed algorithm, which is built of three main components. One of them the Univariate Marginal Distribution Algorithm (UMDA) (Mühlenbein et al., 1998) adapted for multi-objective optimization problems is used for exploration of the search space, and the second component the Random Mutation Hill Climbing (RMHC) algorithm is used for the exploitation. Finally, a component for calculating the Pareto front is used.

The pseudocode of the multi-objective optimization evolutionary hill climbing estimation of distribution algorithm (MOEA-HCEDA) is as shows in figure 9.

```
MOEA-HCEDA

Pseudocode MOEA-HCEDA
ParetoInitialPopulation( );
 Repeat for ι = 1, 2, . . . until stop criterion is verified.
    Obtain estimate of joint probability distribution
    p_l(x) = ∏_{i=1}^{n} p_l(x_i)
    D_l ←Sample M individuals (new population) from p_l(x)
    RandomMutationHillClimbing_RMHC( );
    CalculateParetoPopulation();
End repeat
End MOEA-HCEDA
```

Fig. 9. Pseudocode of MOEA-HCEDA

```
RMHC

Pseudocode RandomMutationHillClimbing_RMHC
  Choose a binary string at random. Call this string best-evaluated solution.
  Mutate a bit chosen a random in best-evaluated.
  Compute the fitness of the mutated string. If the fitness is greater than the
        fitness of the best-evaluated, then set the best-evaluated to the mutated
        string.
  If the maximum number of function evaluations has been performed return the
        best evaluated, otherwise, go to step 2.
End RandomMutationHillClimbing_RMHC
```

Fig. 10. Pseudocode of RMHC

ParetoInitialPopulation( ): In the first step a random population with size 2*size of population is generated. After that, the first Pareto front is obtained using the dominance solution. The first approximated Pareto front is saved in D_0.

RandomMutationHillClimbing( ): In Random Mutation Hill Climbing (Mitchell et al., 1994), a string is chosen randomly and its fitness is evaluated. The string solution is mutated randomly choosing a single locus, and the new solution is evaluated. If mutation leads to an equal or higher fitness, the new string solution replaces the old. This procedure is iterated until the optimum has been found or a maximum number of function evaluations have been performed. The algorithm RMHC works as figure 10 shows.

CalculateParetoPopulation( ): In the first step, the last approximated Pareto front saved in D_{l-1} is joined with the recently generated population and saved in D_l. In the second step the new approximated Pareto front is calculated from $D_{l-1} \cup D_l$. The new approximated Pareto front is saved in D_{l-1}.

UMDA is a particular case of EDAs, introduced by Mühlenbein (Mühlenbein et al., 1998), where the variables are totally independent. The n-dimensional joint probability is a product of n univariate probability distributions (Larrañaga & Lozano, 2002).

Example:

$$p_l(x) = \prod_{i=1}^{n} p_l(x_i) \tag{28}$$

The joint probability distribution of each generation is estimated using the individuals $p_l(x)$ selected. The joint probability distribution factorizes as the product of independent univariate distributions.

4.3 Dominance index to evaluate solutions in Pareto front

This section describes how to define a measure of quality (dominance index) for each solution stored in the Pareto front. The objective of this dominance index is to order the elements of the Pareto front.

Definition. Dominance index of a solution $\vec{x}$: Let $\mathcal{P}_r, \mathcal{P}_s$ be two approximate Pareto fronts and let $r(\mathcal{P}_r)$ be the number of elements of $\mathcal{P}_r$ and $s(\mathcal{P}_s)$ the number of elements of $\mathcal{P}_s$. The dominance index of a solution $\vec{x}$ is defined as the number of times $n(\vec{x})$ that a solution $\vec{x}_r \in \mathcal{P}_r$ dominates solutions $\vec{x}_s \in \mathcal{P}_s$, divided by $s(\mathcal{P}_s)$.

4.4 Quality index to evaluate Pareto front performance

Based on the definition of dominance index of a solution $\vec{x}$, the quality index of Pareto front is constructed. Given two Pareto fronts, a relative evaluation of the first front $\mathcal{P}_r$ with respect to the second $\mathcal{P}_s$ can be given as follows:

Let $\vec{x}_i^{(r)}$ be one solution of the first Pareto front and let $n_i = n(\vec{x}_i^{(r)})$ be the number of times $\vec{x}_i^{(r)}$ dominates elements of the second Pareto front $\mathcal{P}_s$. To normalize this quantity in the dominance index definition, it is divided by the number of solutions of the second front $s(\mathcal{P}_s)$. The quantity obtained is the quality index to evaluate the solution $\vec{x}_i^{(r)}$.

Definition. Quality Index of the first Pareto front with respect to the second: Let now $\sum n_i$ be the sum of the number of times all the solutions of the first Pareto front dominate the solutions of the second front. To normalize this quantity, it is divided by the number of solutions in $\mathcal{P}_r$ front. This last quantity can be considered a relative quality index of the first Pareto front with respect to the second.

4.5 Experimental design

In a previous paper a factorial experiment was performed (Enriquez et al., 2011) where the best combination of factors found was: number of generations equal to 500 and population size equal to 150. These parameters were the ones that reached the best results of the algorithm. Seven graphs were selected from the papers (Rossete, 2000),(Branke, et al., 1997),(Eleoranta and Mäkinen, 2001), (Hobbs and Rodgers, 1998), (Rossete and Ochoa, 1998) to use them as benchmarks, but only the results of the composite graph (Enriquez et al., 2010) is commented in this chapter because this graph is the biggest one. It is a no planar graph with a total of 40 vertices and 69 edges. A total of ten runs for the combination of factors (500,150) were executed, each run has an output that is an approximation to the Pareto Front. The evaluation of the convergence to the Pareto front was performed with the quality index.

4.6 Results and discussion

The results of this experiment appear on table 1, figures 11, 12, 13, 14, 15, 16, and 17. Table 1 shows the best graphs obtained for ten repetitions of MOEA-HCEDA algorithm. For each of the best solution, the table shows run, graph number, total number of edges intersected, area size and aspect ratio. A distance to origin is used to evaluate the best solution obtained on each repetition. This distance is calculated evaluating the Euclidean distance using the standardized values of the three objectives of the problem. The optimal Pareto value is obtained in the graph 267 of the 5th repetition. The results show the average number crossing is 16.1, average area is 106318.6, and average aspect ratio is 1.0632.

		Objective Functions			
RUN	**GRAPH NUMBER**	**NCROSS**	**AREA**	**ASPECT RATIO**	**DISTANCE TO ORIGIN**
1	55	17	106446	1.079617834	0.679992707
2	115	18	89951	1.04778157	0.489841704
3	130	22	111132	1.058641975	0.702735094
4	230	10	128520	1.111764706	0.465940815
5	267	9	91506	1.003311258	0.343328661
6	303	12	155298	1.185082873	0.815347591
7	317	18	79520	1.014285714	0.368875792
8	420	16	93852	1.063973064	0.458813972
9	500	22	101661	1.064724919	0.559167084
10	520	17	105300	1.00308642	0.44348268
Total Average:		**16.1**	**106318.6**	**1.063227033**	

		The best solution obtained			
RUN	**GRAPH NUMBER**	**NCROSS**	**AREA**	**ASPECT RATIO**	**DISTANCE TO ORIGIN**
5	267	9	91506	1.0033113	0.343328661

Table 1. Best solution on each run

Figure 11 shows the average for ten runs of the Pareto front quality index printed on each generation of the algorithm, a convergent curve is showed. The results of the experiments showed that the algorithm converges to an optimal Pareto front.

Figures 12, 13, 14, 15, 16, and 17 show the evolution of graphs corresponding to run 5. Figure 12 shows the graph 16 of the generation 1. This graph has 412 edges crossing, 285270 total area and 1.01698 aspect ratio. Figure 13 shows the graph 2555 in the generation 100. This graph is better than the graph 16 because the edges crossing decrease to 29, total area decreases to 116620 and aspect ratio decreases to 1.0088. Figure 14 shows the graph 5822 of the generation 200. This graph is better in two objectives compared to 16th and 2555th graphs because the edges crossing decrease to 24, total area decreases to 110500 but the aspect ratio increases to 1.0461. Figure 15 shows the graph 10028 of the generation 300. This graph is better in two objectives than the other three graphs because the edges crossing decrease to 14, total area decreases to 109525 and the aspect ratio newly decreases to 1.0369. Figure 16 shows the graph 13924 of the generation 400. This graph is better in two objectives than the other four graphs because the total area decreases to 102700 and the aspect ratio decreases to 1.0284, the edges crossing is manteined in 14 crosses. Figure 17 shows the graph 17470 of the generation 500. This graph is the best in all objectives because the edges crossing decreases to 9, total area decrease to 91506 and aspect ratio decreases to 1.0033.

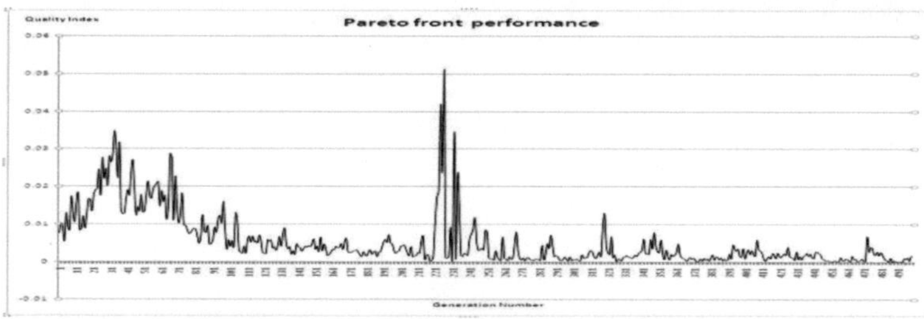

Fig. 11. Quality index for Pareto front comparison.

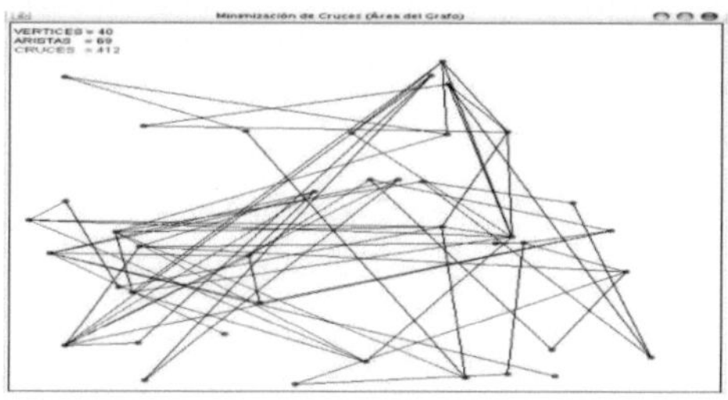

Fig. 12. Generation 1, graph 16.

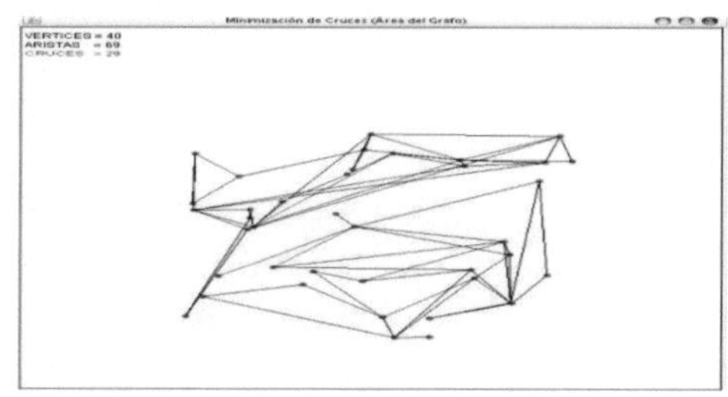

Fig. 13. Generation 100, graph 2555

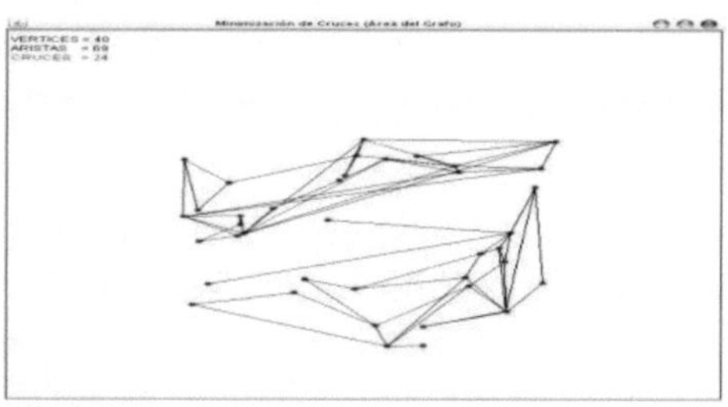

Fig. 14. Generation 200, graph 5822.

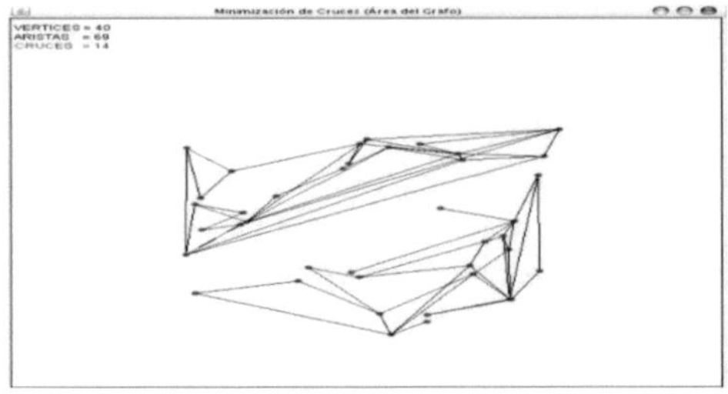

Fig. 15. Generation 300, graph 10028.

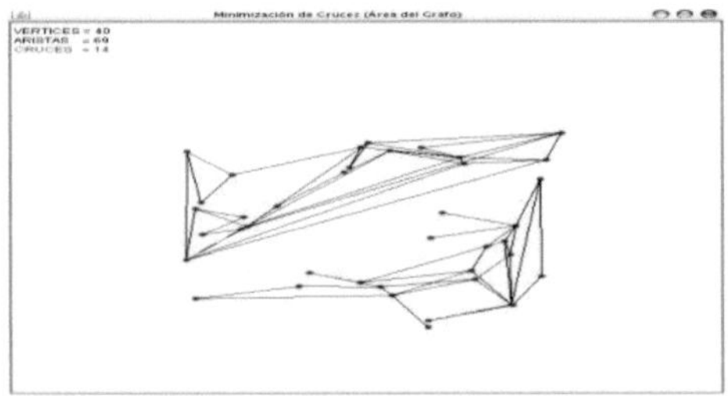

Fig. 16. Generation 400, graph 13924.

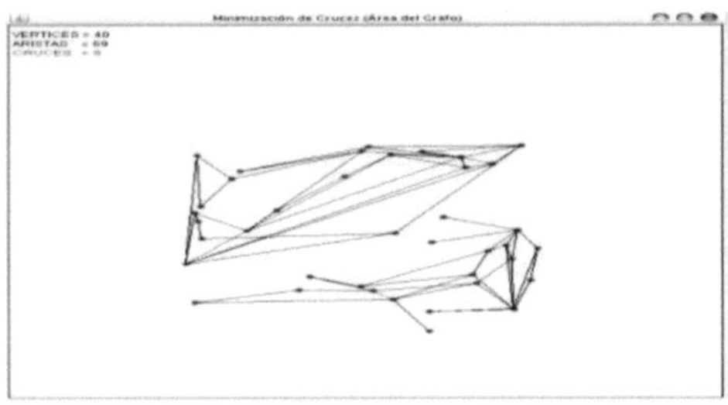

Fig. 17. Generation 500, graph 17470

4.7 Conclusions and future work

The main contributions of this application is the test of the hybrid MOEA-HCEDA algorithm and the quality index based on the Pareto front used in the graph drawing problem. The Pareto front quality index obtained on each generation of the algorithm showed a convergent curve. The results of the experiments showed that the algorithm converges. A graphical user interface was constructed providing users with a tool for a friendly and easy to use graphs display. The automatic drawing of optimized graphs makes it easier for the user to compare results appearing in separate windows, giving the user the opportunity to choose the graph design which best fits their needs.

To continue this research, the hybridization MOEA-HCEDA with others algorithms, for example using other types of EDAs is a next objective. The testing of the algorithms using others more complex benchmarks and, the comparison of the results between different variants is a very challenging and interesting task for future work. The graphical presentation can be friendlier and dispose other facilities as, for example, the printing of the results.

5. Future directions for research

Although there are many versions of evolutionary algorithms that are tailored to multi-objective optimization, theoretical results are apparently not yet available. Rudolph (1999) has shown that results known from the theory of evolutionary algorithms in case of single objective optimization do not carry over to the multi-objective case.

Assuming that the evolutionary algorithms are Markov processes, and that the fitness functions are partially ordered, Rudolph presented some theoretical results about the convergence of multi objective algorithms. In particular some properties of the operators have to be checked to establish the algorithm convergence. This theoretical analysis shows that a special version of an evolutionary algorithm converges with probability 1 to the Pareto set for the test problem under consideration, but this tools are not used frequently.

Although, there exist a number of multi-objective GA implementations and there exist a number of GA applications to multi-objective optimization problems, there not exists systematic study to speculate what problem features may cause a multi-objective GA to face difficulties. The systematic testing in a controlled manner on various aspects of problem difficulties is not so deeply addressed. Specifically, multi-modal multi-objective problems, deceptive multi-objective problems, multi-objective problems having convex, non-convex, and discrete Pareto-optima fronts, and non-uniformly represented Pareto-optimal fronts are not presented and systematically analyzed.

Although some studies have compared different GA implementations (Zitzler and Thiele, 1998), they all have presented a specific problem without an analysis about the complexity of the test problems. The test functions suggested until now in the literature provide various degrees of complexity but are not enough. The construction of test problems has been done without enough knowledge of how multi-objective GAs work. Thus, it will be worthwhile to investigate how existing multi-objective GA implementations work in the context of different test problems. It is intuitive that as the number of objectives increase, the Pareto-optimal region is represented by multi-dimensional surfaces. With more objectives, multi-objective GAs must have to maintain more diverse solutions in the non-dominated front in each iteration. Whether GAs are able to find and maintain diverse solutions, as demanded by the search space of the problem with many objectives would be a matter of interesting study. Whether population size alone can solve this scalability issue or a major structural change (implementing a better niching method) is imminent would be the outcome of such a study. Constraints can introduce additional complexity in the search space by inducing infeasible regions in the search space, thereby obstructing the progress of an algorithm towards the global Pareto-optimal front. Thus, creation of constrained test problems is an interesting area which should get emphasis in the near future. With the development of such complex test problems, there is also a need to develop efficient constraint handling techniques that would be able to help GAs to overcome hurdles caused by constraints. Some such methods are in progress in the context of single-objective GAs and with proper implementations they should also work in multi-objective GAs. Most multi-objective GAs that exist to date, work with the non-domination principle. It is a question if all solutions in a non-dominated set need not be members of the true Pareto optimal front, although some of them could be. This means that all non-dominated solutions found by a multi-objective optimization algorithm may not necessarily be Pareto-optimal solutions. Thus, while working with such algorithms, it is wise to check the Pareto-optimality of each of such solutions (by perturbing the solution locally or by using weighted-sum single-objective methods originating from these solutions). In this regard, it would be interesting to introduce special features (such as elitism, mutation, or other diversity-preserving operators), the presence of which may help us to prove convergence of a GA population to the global Pareto-optimal front. Some such proofs exist for single-objective GAs (Davis and Principe, 1991; Rudolph, 1994) and a similar proof may also be attempted for multi-objective GAs. Elitism is a useful and popular mechanism used in single-objective GAs. Elitism ensures that the best solutions in each generation will not be lost. They are directly carried over from one generation to the next and what is important is that these good solutions get a chance to participate in recombination with other solutions in the hope of creating better solutions. In the context of single-objective optimization, there is only one best solution in a population. But in multi-objective optimization, all non-dominated solutions of the first level are the best solutions in the population. There is no way to distinguish one solution from the other in the non-dominated set. Then if we like to introduce elitism in multi-objective GAs, should we carry over all solutions in the first non-dominated set to the next generation! This may mean copying many good solutions from one generation to the next, a process which may lead to premature convergence to non-Pareto-optimal solutions. How elitism should be defined in this context is an interesting research topic. In this context, an issue related to comparison of two populations also raises some interesting questions.

There are two goals in a multi-objective optimization—convergence to the true Pareto-optimal front and maintenance of diversity among Pareto-optimal solutions. A multi-objective GA may have found a population which has many Pareto-optimal solutions, but with less diversity among them. How would such a population be compared with respect to another which has a fewer number of Pareto-optimal solutions but with wide diversity? The practitioners of multi-objective GAs must have to settle for an answer for these questions before they would be able to compare different GA implementations or before they would be able to mimic operators in other single-objective GAs, such as CHC (Eshelman, 1990) or steady-state GAs (Syswerda, 1989). As it is often suggested and used in single-objective GAs, a hybrid strategy of either implementing problem-specific knowledge in GA operators or using a two-stage optimization process of first finding good solutions with GAs and then improving these good solutions with a domain-specific algorithm would make multi-objective optimization much faster than GAs alone.

Test functions test an algorithm's capability to overcome a specific aspect that a real-world problem may have. In this respect, an algorithm which can overcome more aspects of problem difficulty is naturally a better algorithm. This is precisely the reason why so much effort is spent on doing research in test function development. As it is important to develop better algorithms by applying them on test problems with known complexity, it is also equally important that the algorithms are tested in real-world problems with unknown complexity. Fortunately, most interesting engineering design problems are naturally posed as finding trade-offs among a number of objectives. Among them, cost and reliability are two objectives which are often the priorities of designers. This is because, often in a design, a solution which is less costly is likely to be less reliable and vice versa. In handling such real-world applications using single-objective GAs, often, an artificial scenario is created. Only one objective is retained and all other objectives are used as constraints. For example, if cost is retained as an objective, then an extra constraint restricting the reliability to be greater than 0.9 (or some other value) is used. With the availability of efficient multi-objective GAs, there is no need to have such artificial constraints (which are, in some sense, user-dependent). Moreover, a single run of a multi-objective GA may provide a number of Pareto-optimal solutions, each of which is optimal in one objective with a constrained upper limit on other objectives (such as optimal in cost for a particular upper bound on reliability). Thus, the advantages of using a multi-objective GA in real-world problems are many and there is the need for some interesting application case studies which would clearly show the advantages and flexibilities in using a multi-objective GA, as opposed to a single-objective GA.

We believe that more such mentioned studies are needed to understand better the working principles of a multi-objective GA. An obvious outcome of such studies would be the development of new and improved multi-objective GAs.

6. References

Bäck, T. (1996). Evolutionary Algorithms in Theory and Practice. Oxford University Press, ISBN 0-19-509971-0 New York, New York.

Branke, J., Bucher, F., and Schmeck, H. (1997). Using Genetic Algorithms for Drawing Undirected Graphs. In Allen, J. (Ed.), *Proceedings of 3rd Nordic Workshop on Genetics Algorithms and their Applications,* pp. 193-205 (1997).

Coello, C. (1996).*An Empirical Study of Evolutionary Techniques for Multiobjective Optimization. Engineering Design*. Doctoral thesis. Department of Computer Science, Tulane University, New Orleans, Louisiana, USA, April 1996.

Coello, C. (1999). A Comprehensive Survey of Evolutionary-Based Multiobjective Optimization Techniques. In Knowledge and Information Systems. Vol. 1, No.3 pp. 269-308., Aug.1999. Eberhart.

Coello, C., Van Veldhuizen, D., and Lamont, G. (2002). Evolutionary Algorithms for Solving Multi-Objective Problems. Kluwer Academic Publishers, ISBN 0-3064-6762-3 New York, New York.

Coello, C. (2011). Evolutionary Multiobjective Optimization, In: *Data Mining and Knowledge Discovery,* W. Pedrycz, (Ed.), pp. 444-447, John Wiley & Sons, ISSN 1942-4795, N.J, USA.

Coello, C. and López, A. (2009). Multi-Objective Evolutionary Algorithms: A Review of the State-of-the-Art and some of their Applications in Chemical Engineering. In *Multi-Objective Optimization Techniques and Applications in Chemical Engineering*. Rangaiah G. (ed), pp. 61-90, World Scientific, ISBN: 9812836519. Singapore.

Collette, Y. and Siarry, P. (2002). Multiobjective optimization: principles and case studies. Groupe Eyrolles , ISBN 978-3-540-40182-7, France.

Davis, T. and Principe, J. (1991). A simulated annealing like convergence theory for the simple genetic algorithm. Proceeding of the Fourth International Conference on Genetic Algorithms. ISBN 1-55860-208-9. pp. 174-181. San Diego, CA, USA, July 1991.

Deb, K. (2001). *Multi-Objective Optimization Using Evolutionay Algorithms,* John Wiley & Sons, Ltd, ISBN 0-471-87339-X. New York, N.Y, 2001.

Deb, K. (2008). Introduction to Evolutionary Multiobjective Optimization. In *Multiobjective Optimization. Interactive and Evolutionary Approaches*. Branke, J., Deb, K., Miettinen, K. and Slowinski, R.(Ed). Springer-Verlag Berlin Heidelberg, Germany.

Díaz, J., Petit, J., and Serna, M.(2002) A Survey of Graph Layout Problems. *ACM Computing Surveys*. Vol. 34, No. 3, (September 2002), pp. 313–356. New York, N.Y, USA.

Eloranta, T. and Mäkinen E. (2001). *TimGA* - A Genetic Algorithm for Drawing Undirected Graphs. *Divulgaciones Matemáticas,* Vol. 9 No.2, (October, 2001), pp. 155-171, ISSN 1315-2068.

Enríquez, S., Ponce de León, E., Díaz, E., Padilla, A. (2010).A Hybrid Evolutionary Algorithm for the Edge Crossing Minimization Problem in Graph Drawing. In *Advances in computer Science and Engineering,* Vol. 45, pp. 27-40. ISSN 1870-4069

Enríquez, S., Ponce de León, E., Díaz, E., Padilla, A, Torres, D., Torres, A., Ochoa A. (2011). An Evolutionary Algorithm for Graph Drawing with a Multiobjective Approach. In *Logistics Management and Optimization through Hybrid Artificial Intelligent Systems,* Carlos A. Ochoa, Carmen Chira, Arturo Hernández y Miguel Basurto, IGI Global, ISBN 13 :9781466602977

Eshelman, L. (1991). The CHC Adaptive Search Algorithm: How to Have Safe Search When Engaging. In *Nontraditional Genetic Recombination*. Rawlins G. (ed.), pp. 265-283. Proceedings of the First Workshop on Foundations of Genetic Algorithms. ISBN 1-55860-170-8, San Mateo, CA. USA.

Fonseca, C. and Fleming P. (1993). Genetic Algorithms for Multiobjective Optimization: Formulation, Discussion and Generalization. In *Proceeding of the Fifth International Conference on Genetic Algorithms.* Forrest, S. (Ed). Morgan Kauffman Publishers. pp. 416-423, San Mateo, California, 1993. Urbana-Champaign.

Garey, M. and Johnson, D. (1983). Crossing number is NP-complete. In SIAM Journal on Algebraic and Discrete Methods, Vol. 4 (March, 1982), pp. 312–316, ISSN 0895-4798.

Goldberg, D. (1989). Genetic Algorithms in Search Optimization & Machine Learning. Addison-Wesley.

Goldberg, D. and Den, K. (1991). A comparison of selection schemes used in genetic algorithms. In *Foundations of Genetic Algorithms* Rawlins, G. (Ed). Morgan Kaufmann. pp. 69-93., San Mateo, California, 1991.

Haimes, Y., Lasdon, L., Wismer, D. (1971). On a Bicriterion Formulation of the Problems of Integrated System Identification and System Optimization . IEEE. *Transaction on systems*, Man and Cibernetics Vol. 1. pp. 296-297.

Horn, J. and Nafpliotis, N. (1993). *Multiobjective Optimization using the Niched Pareto Genetic Algorithm.* Technical Report IlliGAl Report 93005, University of Illinois at Urbana-Champaign, Urbana, Illinois, USA, 1993.

Hobbs, M. and Rodgers, P. (1998). Representing Space: A Hybrid Genetic Algorithm for Aesthetic Graph Layout. In *FEA'98, Proceedings of 4th Joint Conference on Information Sciences, JCIS'98,* The Fourth Joint Conference on Information Sciences, Vol. 2, pp. 415-418.

Kuhn, H. and Tucker, A. (1951). Nonlinear programming. In *Proceedings of the Second Berkely Symposium on Mathematical Statistics and Probability.* Neyman, J. (ed). pp. 481-492. University of California Press. Berkely, California.

Larrañaga, P. and Lozano, J.(2002). *Estimation of Distribution Algorithms: A New Tool for Evolutionary Computation*. Kluwer Academic Publishers, ISBN 0-7923-7466-5. Norwell, Massachusetts, USA.

Marler, R. and Arora, J. (2004). Survey of Multi-Objective Optimization Methods for Engineering. In *Structural and Multidisciplinary Optimization*, Vol. 26, No. 6, pp. 369-395.

Marti, L., Garcia, J., Berlanga, A. and Molina, J. (2008). Model-building algorithms for multiobjective EDAs: Directions for improvement, *Evolutionary Computation, 2008. CEC 2008. (IEEE World Congress on Computational Intelligence).*ISBN 978-1-4244-1823-7, June, 2008.

Miettinen, K. (2008). Introduction to Noninteractive Approaches. In *Multiobjective Optimization. Interactive and Evolutionary Approaches*. Branke, J., Deb, K., Miettinen, K. and Slowinski R. (Eds). Springer-Verlag Berlin Heidelberg. Germany.

Mitchell, M., Holland, J. and Forrest, S. (1994). "When Will a Genetic Algorithm Outperform Hill Climbing?", *Advances in Neural Information Processing Systems*, Vol. 6, pp. 51-58.

Moscato, P. (1999). Memetic algorithms: a short introduction, In *New Ideas in Optimization,* Corne, D., Dorigo, M. and Glover, F., pp. 219-234, McGraw-Hill, ISBN 0-07-709506-5, UK Maidenhead, UK, England.

Mühlenbein, H., Mahnig, T. and Ochoa, A.(1998). Schemata Distributions and Graphical Models. *In Evolutionary Optimization, Journal of Heuristic*, Vol. 5, No. 2, pp. 215-247.

Ramírez, M. (2007). *Técnicas Evolutivas Multiobjetivo Aplicadas en el Diseño de Rutas en Vehículos Espaciales*. Doctoral thesis, México, DF.

Richardson, J., Palmer, M., Liepins, G. and Hilliard, M. (1989). Some guidelines for genetic algorithms with penalti functions. In *Proceedings of the Third International Conference on Genetic Algorithms*. Schaffer J. (ed), Morgan Kaufmann Publishers. pp. 191-197, George Mason University.

Ritzel, B., Eheart, W. and Ranjithan S. (1994). Using genetic algorithms to solve a multiobjective groundwater pollution containment problem. *Water Resources Research*, doi:10.1029/93WR03511. Vol. 30 No. 5. pp. 1589-1606. May 1994.

Rosenberg, R. (1967). *Simulation of genetic populations with biochemical properties*. PhD thesis, University of Michigan, Ann Harbor, Michigan, 1967.

Rossete, A. and Ochoa, A. (1998). Genetic Graph Drawing. *In Proceedings of 13th International Conference of Applications of Artificial Intelligence in Engineering, AIENG'98*, Adey, R. A., Rzevski, G., Nolan, P. (Ed.) Galway, Computational Mechanics Publications, pp. 37-40.

Rossete, A. (2000). Un Enfoque General y Flexible para el Trazado de Grafos, Doctoral Thesis, Faculty of Industrial Enginering, CEIS, La Habana, Cuba.

Rudolph, G. (1994). Convergence Analysis of Canonical Genetic Algorithms. *In Transactions on Neural Networks IEEE*, Vol. 5, No. 1, (January, 1994). pp. 96-101, ISSN: 1045-9227.

Rudolph, G. (1999). *On a multi-objective evolutionary algorithm and its convergence to the Pareto set*. Technical Report No. CI-17/98. Dortmund, Germany: Department of Computer Science/XI, University of Dortmund.

Schaffer, J. (1984). *Some Experiments in Machine Learning Using Vector Evaluated Genetic Algorithms.* Doctoral Thesis, Nashville, TN; Vanderbilt University.

Schaffer, J. (1985). Multiple Objective Optimization with Vector Evaluated Genetic Algorithms. In *Proceedings of the First International Conference on Genetic Algorithms and their Applications*, pp. 93-100. July, 1985, Pittsburgh, Pa.

Srinivas, N. and Deb, K. (1993). *Multiobjective Optimization using nondominated sorting.* Technical report. Genetic algorithms, Department of Mechanical Engineering, Indian Istitute of Technology, Kanput, India, 1993.

Srinivas, N. and Deb, K. (1994). Multiobjective Optimization using Nondominated Sorting. In *Genetic Algorithms. Evolutionary Computation*, Vol. 2, No. 3, pp 221-248.

Sugiyama, K. (2002). *Graph Drawing and Applications for Software and Knowledge Engineers*, Japan Advanced Institute of Science and Technology, Vol. 11, p. 218.

Syswerda, G. (1989). Uniform Crossover in Genetic Algorithms. In Proceeding of the 3rd International Conference on Genetic Algorithms, pp. 2-9, ISBN:1-55860-066-3. San Francisco, CA, USA. 1989.

Talbi, E. (2009). *Methaheuristics. From Design to Implementation.* John Wiley & Sons, Inc, Publication, ISBN 978-0-470-27858-1, New Jersey.

Zeleny, M. (1997). Towards the Tradeoffs-Free Optimality in MCDM, In *Multicriteria Analysis*, J. Climaco, (Ed). , pp. 596-601, Springer-Verlag, ISBN 9783540620747, Berlin, Heidleberg.

Zitzler, E. and Thiele, L. (1998). Multiobjective optimization using evolutionary algorithms—A comparative case study. In *Proceedings of the 5th International Conference on Parallel Problem Solving from Nature.* pp. 292-301, ISBN:3-540-65078-4, Springer-Verlag, London, UK. 1998.

Evolutionary Algorithms Based on the Automata Theory for the Multi-Objective Optimization of Combinatorial Problems

Elias D. Niño
Universidad del Norte
Colombia

1. Introduction

In this chapter we are going to study metaheuristics based on the Automata Theory for the Multi-objective Optimization of Combinatorial Problems. As well known, Combinatorial Optimization is a branch of optimization. Its domain is optimization problems where the set of feasible solutions is discrete or can be reduced to a discrete one, and the goal is to find the best possible solution(Yong-Fa & Ming-Yang, 2004). In this field it is possible to find a lot of problems denominated NP-Hard, that is mean that the problem does not have a solution in Polynomial Time. For instance, problems such as Multi-depot vehicle routing problem(Lim & Wang, 2005), delivery and pickup vehicle routing problem with time windows(Wang & Lang, 2008), multi-depot vehicle routing problem with weight-related costs(Fung et al., 2009), Railway Traveling Salesman Problem(Hu & Raidl, 2008), Heterogeneous, Multiple Depot, Multiple Traveling Salesman Problem(Oberlin et al., 2009) and Traveling Salesman with Multi-agent(Wang & Xu, 2009) are categorized as NP-Hard problems.

One of the most classical problems in the Combinatorial Optimization Field is the Traveling Salesman Problem (TSP), it has been analyzed for years(Sauer & Coelho, 2008) either in a Mono or Multi-objective way. It is defined as follows: "Given a set of cities and a departure city, visit each city only once and go back to the departure city with the minimum cost". Basically, that is mean, visiting each city once, to find an optimal tour in a set of cities, an instance of TSP problem can be seen in figure 1. Formally, TSP is defined as follows:

$$min \sum_{i=1}^{n} \sum_{j=1}^{n} C_{ij} \cdot X_{ij} \quad (1)$$

Subject to:

$$\sum_{j=1}^{n} X_{ij} = 1, \forall i = 1, \ldots, n \quad (2)$$

$$\sum_{j=1}^{n} X_{ij} = 1, \forall j = 1, \ldots, n \quad (3)$$

$$\sum_{i \in \kappa} \sum_{j \in \kappa} X_{ij} \leq |\kappa| - 1, \forall \kappa \subset \{1, \ldots, n\} \quad (4)$$

$$X_{ij} = 0, 1 \forall i, j \quad (5)$$

Where C_{ij} is the cost of the path X_{ij} and κ is any nonempty proper subset of the cities $1, \ldots, m$. (1) is the objective function. The goal is the optimization of the overall cost of the tour. (2), (3) and (5) fulfills the constrain of visiting each city only once. Lastly, Equation (4) set the subsets of solutions, avoiding cycles in the tour.

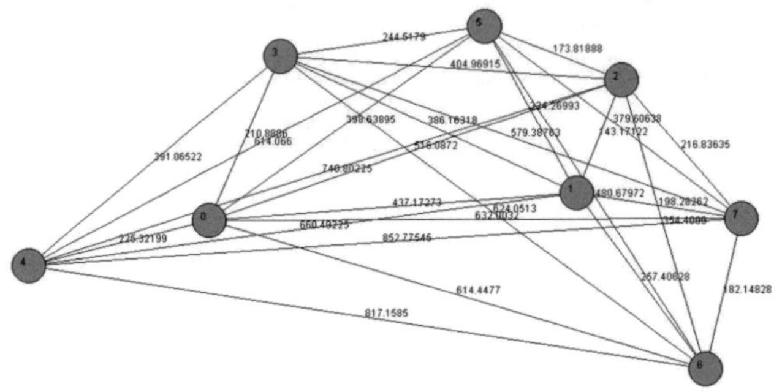

Fig. 1. TSP instance of ten cities

TSP has an important impact on different sciences and fields, for instance in Operations Research and Theoretical Computer Science. Most problems related to those fields, are based in the TSP definition. For instance, problems such as Heterogeneous Machine Scheduling(Kim & Lee, 1998), Hybrid Scheduling and Dual Queue Scheduling(Shah et al., 2009), Project Management(de Pablo, 2009), Scheduling for Multichannel EPONs(McGarry et al., 2008), Single Machine Scheduling(Chunyue et al., 2009), Distributed Scheduling Systems(Yu et al., 1999), Relaxing Scheduling Loop Constraints(Kim & Lipasti, 2003), Distributed Parallel Scheduling(Liu et al., 2003), Scheduling for Grids(Huang et al., 2010), Parallel Scheduling for Dependent Task Graphs(Mingsheng et al., 2003), Dynamic Scheduling on Multiprocessor Architectures(Hamidzadeh & Atif, 1996), Advanced Planning and Scheduling System(Chua et al., 2006), Tasks and Messages in Distributed Real-Time Systems(Manimaran et al., 1997), Production Scheduling(You-xin et al., 2009), Cellular Network for Quality of Service Assurance(Wu & Negi, 2003), Net Based Scheduling(Wei et al., 2007), Spring Scheduling Co-processor(Niehaus et al., 1993), Multiple-resource Periodic Scheduling(Zhu et al., 2003), Real-Time Query Scheduling for Wireless Sensor Networks(Chipara et al., 2007), Multimedia Computing and Real-time Constraints(Chen et al., 2003), Pattern Driven Dynamic Scheduling(Yingzi et al., 2009), Security-assured Grid Job Scheduling(Song et al., 2006), Cost Reduction and Customer Satisfaction(Grobler & Engelbrecht, 2007), MPEG-2 TS Multiplexers in CATV Networks(Jianghong et al., 2000), Contention Awareness(Shanmugapriya et al., 2009) and The Hard Scheduling Optimization(Niño, Ardila, Perez & Donoso, 2010) had been derived from TSP. Although several algorithms have been implemented to solve TSP, there is no one that optimal solves it. For this reason, this chapter discuss novel metaheuristics based on the Automata Theory to solve the Multi-objective Traveling Salesman Problem.

This chapter is structured as follows: Section 2 shows important definitions to understand the Multi-objective Combinatorial Optimization and the Metaheuristic Approximation. Section 3, 4 and 5 discuss Evolutionary Metaheuritics based on the Automata Theory for the Multi-objective Optimization of Combinatorial Problems. Finally, Section 6 and 7 discuss the Experimental Results of each proposed Algorithm using Multi-objective Metrics from the specialized literature.

2. Preliminaries

2.1 Multi-objective optimization

The Multi-objective optimization consists in two or more objectives functions to optimize and a set of constraints. Mathematically, the Multi-objective Optimization model is defined as follows:

$$optimize \quad F(X) = \{f_1(X), f_2(X), \ldots, f_n(X)\} \tag{6}$$

Subject to:

$$H(X) = 0 \tag{7}$$

$$G(X) \leq 0 \tag{8}$$

$$X_l \leq X \leq X_u \tag{9}$$

Where $F(X)$ is the set of objective functions, $H(X)$ and $G(X)$ are the constraints of the problem. Lastly, X_l and X_u are the bounds for the set of variables X.

Unlike to Mono-objective Optimization, Multi-objective Optimization deal with searching a set of Optimal Solutions instead of a Optimal Solution. For instance, table 1 shows three solutions for a particualr Mono-objective Problem. If we suppose that those are related to a maximization problem then the Optimal Solution (found) is the solution 1 otherwise (minimization) will be the solution 2. On the other hand, in table 2 can be seen three solutions for a particular Tri-objective Problem. Thus, if we suppose that all the components of the solutions are related with a minimization problem, solution 2 is a *dominated solution* due to all the components (0.8, 0.9 and 1.0) are the biggest values. On the other hand, solution 0 and 1 are *no-dominated solutions* due to in the first and second component (0.6 and 0.4) solution 0 is bigger than the relative components of the solution 1 but in the third component (0.5) solution 0 is lower than the same component in solution 1. Both examples show the

k	$F(X_k)$
0	10
1	20
2	5

Table 1. Solutions for a particular Mono-objective Problem

difference between Mono-objective and Multi-objective Optimization. While the first deal with finding the Optimal Solution, the last does with finding a set of Optimal Solutions. In Combinatorial Optimization, the set of Optimal Solution is called *Pareto Front*. It contains all the no-dominated solutions for a Multi-objective Problem. Figure 2 shows a Pareto Front for a particular Tri-objective Problem. Lastly, it is probably that some Multi-objective Problems

k	$F(X_k) = \{f_0(X_k), f_1(X_k), f_2(X_k)\}$
0	$\{0.6, 0.4, 0.5\}$
1	$\{0.2, 0.3, 0.8\}$
2	$\{0.8, 0.9, 1.0\}$

Table 2. Solutions for a particular Tri-objective Problem

have an infinite Pareto Front, in those cases is necessary to determinate how many solutions are required, for instance, using a maximum number of solution permitted in the Pareto Front.

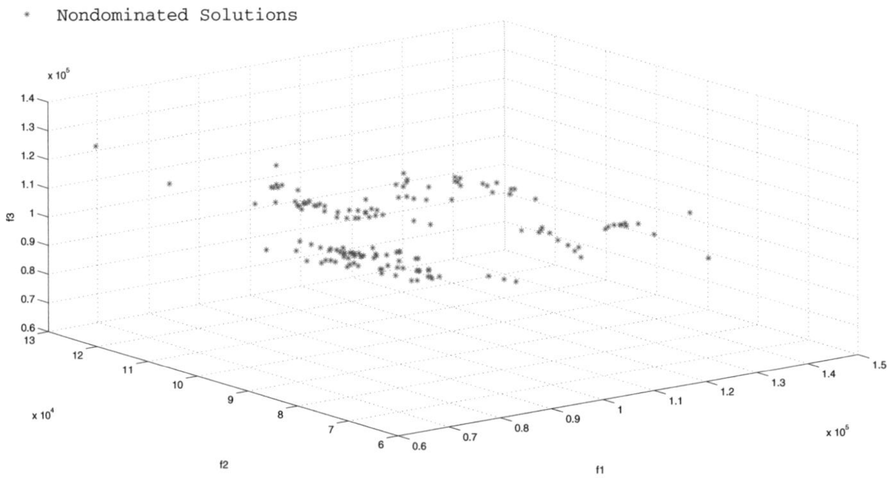

Fig. 2. Pareto Front for a particular Tri-objective Problem

2.2 Tabu search

Tabu Search(Glover & Laguna, 1997) is a basic local search strategy for the Optimization of Combinatorial Problems. It is defined as follows: Given S as the Initial Solutions Set.

Step 1. Selection. Select $x \in S$

Step 2. Perturbation. Perturbs the solution x for the purpose of knowing its Neighborhood $(N(x))$. Perturbing a solution means to modify the solution x in order to obtain a new solution $(x_i^{'})$. The solutions found are called Neighbors, and those represent the Neighborhood. For instance, figure 3 shows three perturbations for a x solutions and the new solutions $x_1^{'}$,$x_2^{'}$ and $x_3^{'}$ found. The perturbation can be done according to the representation of the solutions. Regularly, the representations of the solutions in Combinatorial Problems are based on Discrete Structures such as Vectors, Matrices, Queues and Lists. Lastly, good solutions are added to S.

Setp 3. Check Stop Condition. The stop condition can be delimited using rules such as number of execution without improvement or maximum number of iteration exceeded.

Recently, novels Tabu Search inspired Algorithms have been developed in order to solve Combinatorial Problems such as Permutation Flow Shop Scheduling(Ren et al., 2011), Displacement based on Support Vector(Fei et al., 2011), Examination Timetabling Problem(Malik et al., 2011), Partial Transmit Sequences for PAPR Reduction(Taspinar et al., 2011), Inverse Problems(An et al., 2011), Fuzzy PD Controllers(Talbi & Belarbi, 2011b), Instrusion Detection(Jian-guang et al., 2011), Tel-Home Care Problems(Lee et al., 2011), Ant Colony inspired Problems(Zhang-liang & Yue-guang, 2011), Steelmaking-Continuous Casting Production Scheduling(Zhao et al., 2011), Fuzzy Inference System(Talbi & Belarbi, 2011a) and Coordination of Dispatchable Distributed Generation and Voltage Control Devices(Ausavanop & Chaitusaney, 2011).

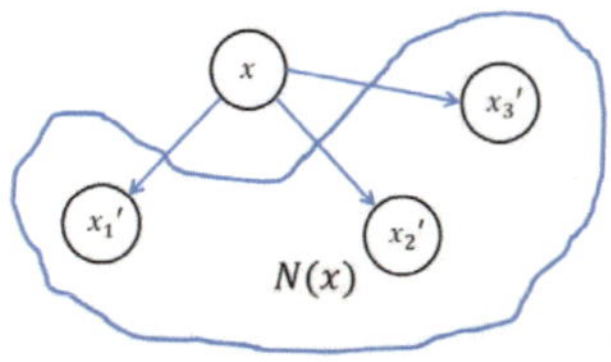

Fig. 3. The Neighborhood of a solution x is known after being perturbed

2.3 Genetic algorithms

Genetic Algorithms are Algorithms based on the Theory of Natural Selection(Wijkman, 1996). Thus, Genetic Algorithms mimics the realBehavior Genetic Algorithms(Fisher, 1930) through three basic steps: Given a set of Initial Solutions S

Step 1. Selection. Select solutions from a population. In pairs, select two solutions $x, y \in S$

Step 2. Crossover. Cross the selected solutions avoiding local optimums.

Step 3. Mutation. Perturbs the new solutions found for increasing the population. The perturbation can be done according to the representation of the solution. In this step, good solutions are added to S

Figure 4 shows the basics steps of a Genetic Algorithm. The most known Genetic

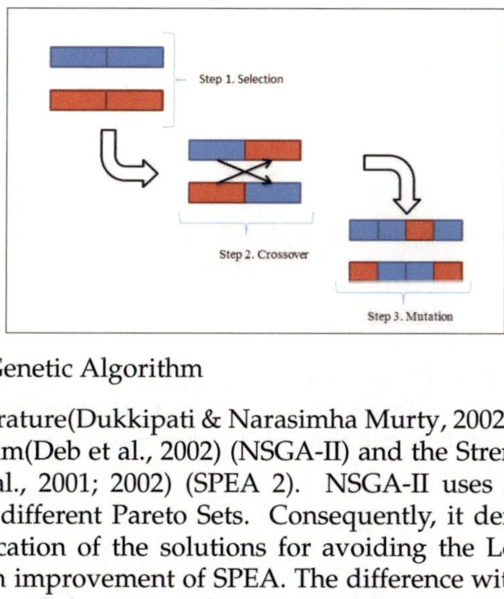

Fig. 4. Basics steps of a Genetic Algorithm

Algorithms from the literature(Dukkipati & Narasimha Murty, 2002) are the Non-Dominated Sorting Genetic Algorithm(Deb et al., 2002) (NSGA-II) and the Strength Pareto Evolutionary Algorithm 2(Zitzler et al., 2001; 2002) (SPEA 2). NSGA-II uses a no-dominated sort for sorting the solutions in different Pareto Sets. Consequently, it demands a lot of time, but it allows a global verification of the solutions for avoiding the Local Optimums. On the other hand, SPEA 2 is an improvement of SPEA. The difference with the first version is that SPEA 2 works using strength for every solution according to the number of solutions that it dominates. Consequently, at the end of the iterations, SPEA 2 has the non dominated solutions stronger avoiding Local Optimums. SPEA 2 and NSGA-II have been implemented to solve a lot of problems in the Multiobjective and Combinatorial Optimization fiel. For instance, problems such as Pattern-recognition based Machine Translation System(Sofianopoulos & Tambouratzis, 2011), Tuning of Fuzzy Logic controllers for a heating(Gacto et al., 2011), Real-coded Quantum Clones(Xiawen & Yu, 2011), Optimization Problems with Correlated Objectives(Ishibuchi et al., 2011), Production Planning(Yu et al., 2011), Optical and Dynamic Networks Designs(Araujo et al., 2011; Wismans et al., 2011), Benchmark multi-objective optimization(McClymont & Keedwell, 2011) and Vendor-managed Inventory(Azuma et al., 2011) have been solved using SPEA and NSGA-II.

2.4 Simulated Annealing algorithms

Simulated Annealing(Kirkpatrick et al., 1983) is a generic probabilistic metaheuristic based in the Annealing in Metallurgy. Similar to Tabu Search, Simulated Annealing explores the neighborhood of solutions being flexible with no-good solutions. That is mean, accepting bad solutions as well as good solution, but only in the first iterations. The acceptation of a bad solution is based on the Boltzmann Probabilistic Distribution:

$$P(x) = e^{\left(-\left(\frac{E}{T_i}\right)\right)} \tag{10}$$

Where E is the change of the Energy and T_i is the temperature in the moment i. In the first level of the temperature, bad solutions are accepted as well, anyways, when the temperature go down, Simulated Annealing behaves similar to Tabu Search (only accept good solutions).

Recentrly, similar to Genetic Algoritms and Tabu Search, many problems have been solved using Simulated Annealing metaheuristic. For instance, Neuro Fuzzy - SystemsCzabaski (2006), Contrast Functions for BSSGarriz et al. (2005), Cryptanalysis of Transposition CipherSong et al. (2008), Transmitter-Receiver Collaborative-Relay BeamformingZheng et al. (2011) and Two-Dimensional Strip Packing ProblemDereli & Sena Da (2007) have been solved through Simulated Annealing inspired algorithms.

2.5 Deterministic Finite Automata

Formally, a Deterministic Finite Automata is a Quint-tuple defined as follows:

$$A = (Q, \Sigma, \delta, q_0, F) \tag{11}$$

Set of transitions δ. The set of transitions (δ) describes the behavior of the automata. Let $a \in S$ and $q, r \in Q$, then the function is defined as follows:

$$\delta(q, a) = r \tag{12}$$

Example 1. Let $A = (Q, \Sigma, \delta, q_0, F)$, where $Q = \{q_0, q_1, q_2\}$, $S = \{0, 1\}$, $F = \{q_1\}$ and the set of transitions δ defined in table 3, the representation of A using a state diagram can be derived as shown in figure 5. Notice that each state of DFA has transitions with all the elements of Σ.

	0	*1*
q_0	q_2	q_0
q_1	q_1	q_1
q_2	q_2	q_1

Table 3. Set of transitions for the DFA of example 1

2.6 Metaheuristic Of Deterministic Swapping (MODS)

Metaheuristic Of Deterministic Swapping (MODS) (Niño et al., 2011) is a local search strategy that explores the Feasible Solution Space of a Combinatorial Problem supported in a data structure named Multi Objective Deterministic Finite Automata (MDFA) (Niño, Ardila, Donoso & Jabba, 2010). A MDFA is a Deterministic Finite Automata that allows the

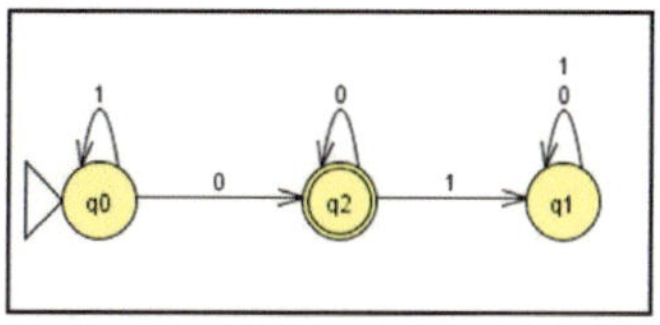

Fig. 5. Automata state diagram for the example 1.

representation of the feasible solution space of a Combinatorial Problem. Formally, a MDFA is defined as follows:

$$M = (Q, \Sigma, \delta, Q_0, F(X)) \tag{13}$$

Where Q represents all the set of states of the automata (feasible solution space), Σ is the input alphabet that is used for δ (transition function) to explore the feasible solution space of a combinatorial problem, Q_0 contains the initial set of states (initial solutions) and $F(X)$ are the objectives to optimize.

Example 1. MDFA for a Scheduling Parallel Machine Problem:

A Company has three machines. It is necessary to schedule three processes in parallel P_1,P_2 and P_3. Each process has a duration of 5, 10 y 50 minutes respectively. If the processes can be executed in any of the machines, how many manners the machines can be assigned to the processes? Given the Bi-objective function in (10), what is the optimal Pareto Front?

$$F(X) = \left\{ f_1(X) = \sum_{i=1}^{3} i \cdot X_i, f_2(X) = \sum_{i=1}^{3} \left(\frac{1}{i}\right) \cdot X_i \right\} \tag{14}$$

First of all, we need to build the MDFA. For doing this, we must define the states of the MDFA setting the structure of the solution for each state. Therefore, if we state that $X_q = (P_k, P_i, P_j)$ represents the solution for the state q: machine 1 executes the process P_k, machine 2 executes the process P_i and machine 3 executes the process P_j then the arrays solution for each state will be $X_q0 = (P_1, P_2, P_3)$, $X_q1 = (P_1, P_3, P_2)$, $X_q2 = (P_2, P_1, P_3)$, $X_q3 = (P_2, P_3, P_1)$, $X_q4 = (P_3, P_1, P_2)$ y $X_q5 = (P_3, P_2, P_1)$. Now, we have six states q_0,q_1,q_2,q_3,q_4 and q_5, those represent the feasible solution space of the Scheduling problem proposed. The set of states for the MDFA of this problem can be seen in figure 6. Once the set of states is defined, the Input Alphabet

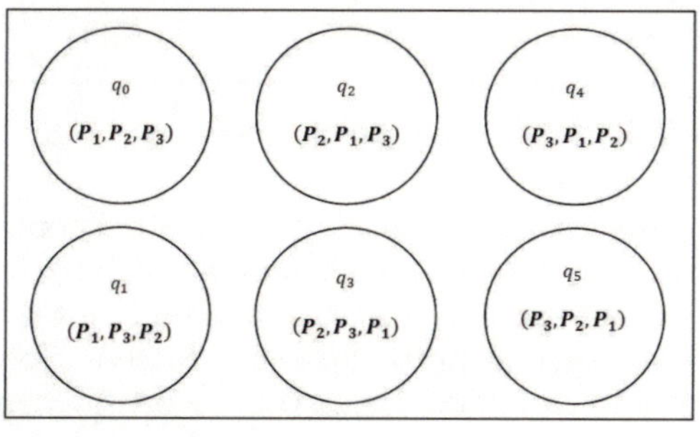

Fig. 6. Set of states for the MDFA of example 2

(Σ) and the Transition Function (δ) be done. It is very important to take into account, first, the bond of both allows to perturb the solutions in all the possible manners, in other words, we can change of state using the combination of Σ and δ. Obviously, doing this, we avoid unfeasible solutions. Regarding the proposed problem, we propose the set Σ as follows:

$$\Sigma = \{(P_1, P_2), (P_1, P_3), (P_2, P_3)\} \tag{15}$$

Hence, it is elemental that $\delta(q_0, (P_1, P_2)) = q_2$, $\delta(q_0, (P_1, P_3)) = q_5$, ... , $\delta(q_5, (P_2, P_3)) = q_3$. At this part, the transitions has been defined therefore the MDFA can be seen in figure 7.

Finally, the solution of each state is replaced in (10). The results can be seen in table 4 and the Optimal Pareto Front is shown in figure 8.

State	Assignments			Times			$F(X)$	
q_i	M_1	M_2	M_3	M_1	M_2	M_3	$f_1(X)$	$f_2(X)$
q_0	P_1	P_2	P_3	10	50	5	125	36.66
q_1	P_1	P_3	P_2	10	5	50	170	29.16
q_2	P_2	P_1	P_3	50	10	5	85	56.66
q_3	P_2	P_3	P_1	50	5	10	90	55.83
q_4	P_3	P_1	P_2	5	10	50	175	26.66
q_5	P_3	P_2	P_1	5	50	10	135	33.33

Table 4. Values of $F(X)$ for the states of example 2

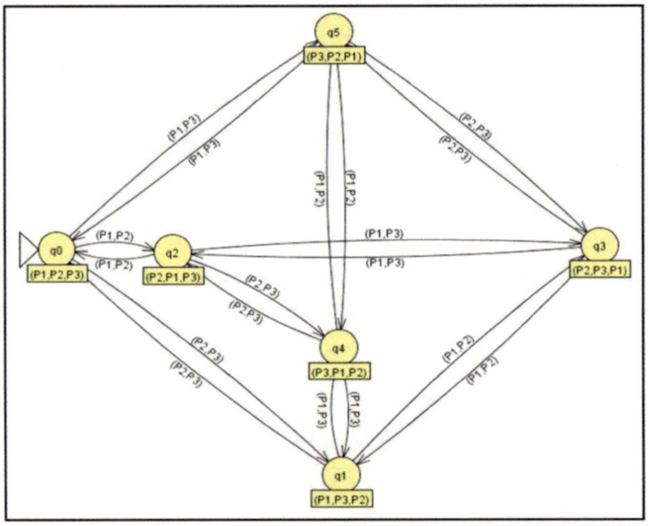

Fig. 7. MDFA for example 2, Parallel execution of processes

As can be seen in figure 7, the feasible solution space for this problem was described using a MDFA. Also, unfeasible solutions are not allowed because of the definition of Σ. Nevertheless, the general problem was not solved, only a particular case of three variables (machines) was done. For this reason, it was easy to draw the entire MDFA. However, problems like this are intractable for a large number of variables, in other words, when the number of variables grow the feasible solution space grows exponentially. In this manner, it is not a good idea to draw the entire feasible solution space and pick the best solutions. Thus, what should we do in order to solve any combinatorial problem, without taking into account its size, using a MDFA? Looking an answer to this question, MODS was proposed.

MODS explores the feasible solution space represented through a MDFA using a search direction given by an elitist set of solutions (Q_*). The elitist solution are states that, when

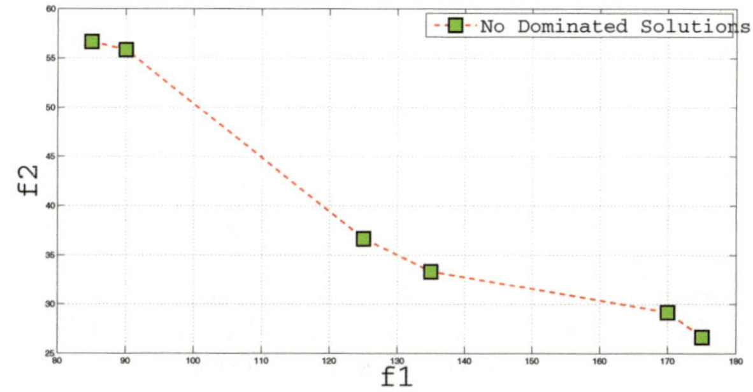

Fig. 8. Pareto Front for the MDFA of example 2, Parallel execution of processes

were visited, their solution dominated at least one solution of an element in Q_ϕ. Q_ϕ contains all the states with non-dominated solutions. Due to this, it can be inferred that the elements of Q_* are contained in Q_ϕ, for this reason is true that:

$$Q_\phi = Q_\phi \cup Q_* \tag{16}$$

Lastly, the template algorithm of MODS is defined as follows:

Step 1. Create the initial set of solutions Q_0 using a heuristic relative to the problem to solve.

Step 2. Set Q_ϕ as Q_0 and Q_* as ϕ.

Step 3. Select a random state $q \in Q_\phi$ or $q \in Q_*$

Step 4. Explore the neighborhood of q using δ and Σ. Add to Q_ϕ the solutions found that are not dominated by elements of Q_f. In addition, add to Q_* those solutions found that dominated at least one element from Q_ϕ.

Step 5. Check stop condition, go to 3.

3. Simulated Annealing Metaheuristic Of Deterministic Swapping (SAMODS)

Simulated Annealing & Metaheuristic Of Deterministic Swapping(Niño, 2012) (SAMODS) is a hybrid local search strategy based on the MODS theory and Simulated Annealing Algorithm for the Multiobjective Optimization of combinatorial problems. Its main propose consists in optimizing a combinatorial problem using a Search Direction and an Angle Improvement. SAMODS is based in the next Automata:

$$M = (Q, Q_0, P(q), F(X), A(n)) \tag{17}$$

Alike MODS, Q_0 is the set of initial solutions, Q is the feasible solution space and $F(X)$ are the functions of the combinatorial problem. $P(q)$ and $A(n)$ are defined as follows:

$P(q)$ is the *Permutation Function*, formally it is defined as follows:

$$P(q) : Q \to Q \tag{18}$$

P receives a solution $q \in Q$ and perturbs it returning a new solution $r_i \in Q$. The perturbation can be done based on the representation of the solutions. An example of some perturbations based on the representation of the solution can be seen in figure 15.

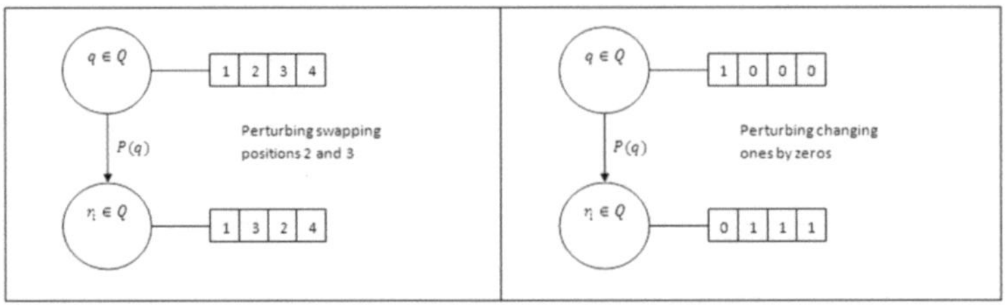

Fig. 9. Different representation and perturbation of solutions.

$A(n)$ is the *Weight Function*. Formally, it is defined as follow:

$$A(n) : \mathbb{N} \rightarrow \Re^n \tag{19}$$

Where n is the number of objectives of the problem.

Function A receives a natural number as parameter and it returns a vector with the weights. The weight values are randomly generated with an uniform distribution. Those represent the weight to assign to each function of the combinatorial problem. The weight values returned by the function fulfill the next constrain:

$$\sum_{i=1}^{n} \alpha_i = 1, 0 \leq \alpha_i \leq 1 \tag{20}$$

Where α_i is the weight assigned to function i. Table 5 shows some vectors randomly generated by $A(n)$.

Input Parameter	*Function*	*Vector of Weights*
2	$A(2)$	$\{0.6, 0.4\}$
3	$A(3)$	$\{0.2, 0.4, 0.4\}$
4	$A(4)$	$\{0.3, 0.8, 0.1, 0.0\}$

Table 5. Some weight vectors generated by A(n)

But, what is the importance of those weights? The weights, in an implicit manner, allow setting the angle direction to the solutions. The angle direction is the course being followed by the solutions for optimizing F(X). Hence, when the weights values are changed, the angle of optimization is changed and a new search direction is obtained. For instance, different search directions for different weight values are shown in figure 16 in a Bi-objective combinatorial problem. Due to this, (6) is rewritten as follows:

$$F(X) = \sum_{i=1}^{n} \alpha_i \cdot f_i(X) \tag{21}$$

Where n is the number of objectives of the problem and α_i is the weight assigned to the function i. The weights fulfills the constrain established in (20).

SAMODS main idea is simple: it takes advantage of the search directions given by MODS and it proposed an angle direction given by the function $A(n)$. Thus, there are two directions; the first helps in the convergence of the Pareto Front and the second helps the solutions to find neighborhoods where $F(X)$ is optimized. Due to this, SAMODS template is defined as follows:

Step 1. Setting sets. Set Q_0 as the set of Initial Solutions. Set Q_ϕ and Q_* as Q_0.

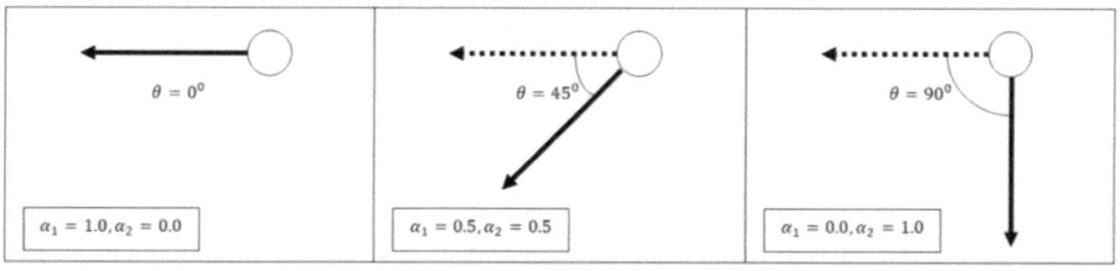

Fig. 10. Different angles given by different weights for a Bi-objective Problem.

Step 2. Settings parameters. Set T as the initial temperature, n as the number of objectives of the problem and ρ as the cooler factor.

Step 3. Setting Angle. If T is equal to 0 then got to 8, else set $T_{i+1} = \rho \times T_i$, randomly select $s \in Q_\phi$, set $W = A(n) = \{w_1, w_2, \cdots, w_n\}$ and go to step 4.

Step 4. Perturbing Solutions. Set $s' = P(s)$, add to Q_ϕ and Q_* according to the next rules:

$$Q_\phi = Q_\phi \cup \left\{s'\right\} \Leftrightarrow (\nexists r \in Q_\phi)(r \quad dominated \quad to \quad s') \tag{22}$$

$$Q_* = Q_* \cup \left\{s'\right\} \Leftrightarrow (\exists r \in Q_*)(s' \quad dominated \quad to \quad r) \tag{23}$$

If Q_ϕ has at least one element that dominated to s' go to step 5, otherwise go to step 7.

Step 5. Guess with dominated solutions. Randomly generated a number $n \in [0, 1]$. Set z as follows:

$$z = e^{(-(\gamma / T_i))} \tag{24}$$

Where T_i is the temperature value in moment i and γ is defined as follows:

$$\gamma = \sum_{i=1}^{n} w_i \cdot f_i(s_X) - \sum_{i=1}^{n} w_i \cdot f_i(s'_X) \tag{25}$$

Where s_X is the vector X of solution s, s'_X is the vector X of solution s', w_i is the weight assigned to the function i and n is the number of objectives of the problem. If $n < z$ then set s as s' and go to step 4 else go to step 6.

Step 6. Change the search direction. Randomly select a solution $s \in Q_*$ and go to step 4.

Step 7. Removing dominated solutions. Remove the dominated solution for each set (Q_* and Q_ϕ). Go to step 3.

Step 8. Finishing. Q_ϕ has the non-dominated solutions.

As can be seen in figure 11, alike MODS, SAMODS removes the dominated solutions when the new solution found is not dominated. Besides, if the new solution found dominated at least one element from the solution set (Q_ϕ) then it will be added to the elitisms set (Q_*) that works as a search direction for the Pareto Front. As far as here, SAMODS could sounds as a simple local search strategy but not, when a new solution found is dominated, SAMODS tries to improve it using guessing. Guessing is done accepting dominated solution as good solutions. Alike Simulated Annealing inspired algorithms, the dominated solutions are accepted under the Boltzmann Distribution Probability assigning weights to the objectives of the problem. It is probably that perturbing a dominated solution, a non-dominated solution can be found as can be seen in figure 12. Due to this, local optimums are avoided. When the temperature is low, the bad solutions are avoided because z value is low therefore SAMODS accepts only non-dominated solutions. However, by that time, Q_ϕ will be leaded on by Q_*.

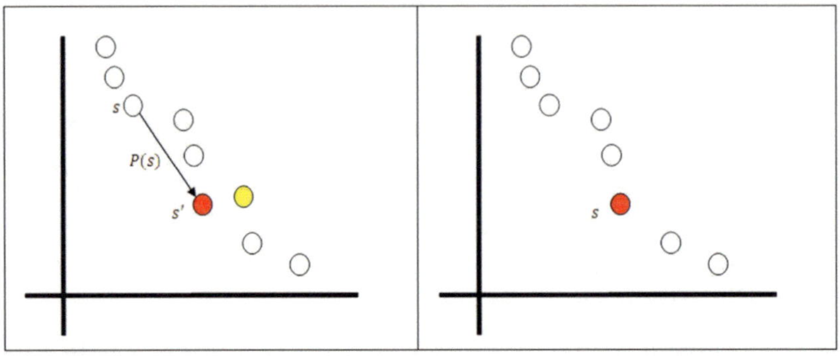

Fig. 11. Behavior of SAMODS when the new solution found is not dominated. Once a new solution found is non-dominated, it is added to the elitism set Q_* and the dominated solutions from Q_ϕ are removed.

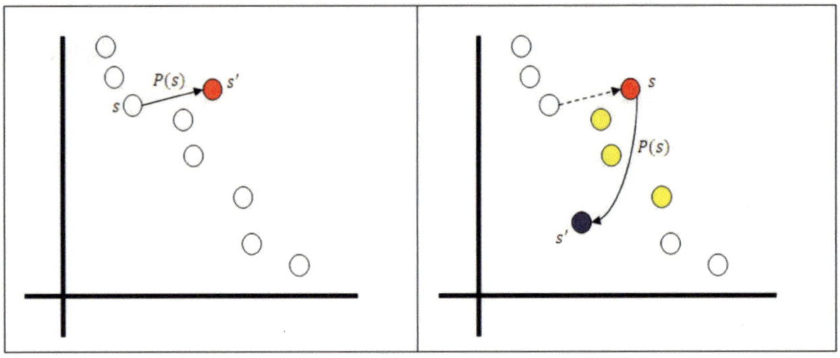

Fig. 12. Behavior of SAMODS when the new solution found is dominated. In this case, guessing gives a new solution non-dominated.

4. Genetic Simulated Annealing Metaheuristic Of Deterministic Swapping (SAGAMODS)

Simulated Annealing, Genetic Algorithm & Metaheuristic Of Deterministic Swapping(Niño, 2012) (SAGAMODS) is a hybrid search strategy based on the Automata Theory, Simulated Annealing and Genetics Algorithms. SAGAMODS is an extension of the SAMODS theory. It comes up as result of the next question: could SAMODS avoid quickly local optimums? Although, SAMODS avoids local optimums guessing, it can take a lot of time accepting dominated solutions for finding non-dominated. Thus, the answer to this question is based on the Evolutionary Theory. SAGAMODS proposes crossover step before SAMODS template is executed. Due to this, SAGAMODS supports to SAMODS for exploring distant regions of the solution space.

Formally, SAGAMODS is based on the next automata:

$$M = (Q, Q_S, C(q, r, k), F(X)) \tag{26}$$

Where Q is the feasible solutions space, Q_S is the initial solutions and $F(X)$ are the objectives of the problem. $C(q,r,k)$ is defined as follows:

Formally, *Cross Function K* is defined as follows:

$$C(q,r,k) : Q \to Q \tag{27}$$

Where $q,r \in Q$ and $k \in N$. q and r are named parents solutions and k is the cross point. The main idea of this function is cross two solutions in the same point and returns a new solution. For instance, two solutions of 4 variables are cross in figure 13. Obviously, the crossover is made regarding the representation of the solutions. Lastly, SAGAMODS template is defined

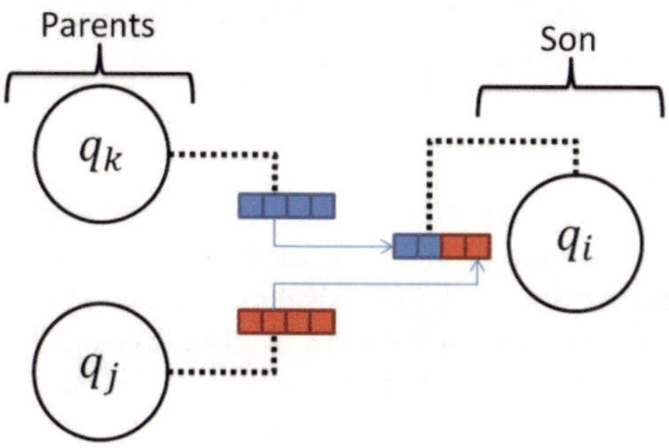

Fig. 13. Crossover between two solutions. Solutions of the states q_k and q_j are crossed in order to get state q_i

as follows:

Step 1. Setting parameters. Set Q_S as the solution set, x as the number of solutions to cross for each iteration.

Step 2. Selection. Set Q_C (crossover set) as selection of x solutions in Q_S, Q_M (mutation set) as ϕ and k as a random value.

Step 3. Crossover. For each $s_i, s_{i+1} \in Q_C / 1 \leq i < |Q_C|$:

$$Q_M = Q_M \cup \{C(s_i, s_{i+1}, k)\} \tag{28}$$

Step 4. Mutation. Set Q_0 as Q_M. Execute SAMODS as a local search strategy.

Step 5. Check stop conditions. Go to 2.

5. Evolutionary Metaheuristic Of Deterministic Swapping (EMODS)

Evolutionary Metaheuristic of Deterministic Swapping (EMODS), is a novel framework that allows the Multiobjective Optimization of Combinatorial Problems. Its framework is based on MODS template therefore its steps are the same: create Initial Solutions, Improve the Solutions (Optional) and Execute the Core Algorithm. Unlike SAMODS and SAGAMODS, EMODS avoids the slowly convergence of Simulated Annealing's method. EMODS explores different regions from the feasible solution space and search for non-dominated solution using Tabu Search.

The Core Algorithm is defined as follows:

Step 1. Set θ as the maximum number of iterations, β as the maximum number of state selected in each iteration, ρ as the maximum number of perturbations by state and Q_ϕ as Q_0

Step 2. Selection. Randomly select a state $q \in Q_\phi$ or $q \in Q_*$

Step 3. Mutation - Tabu Search. Set N as the new solutions found as result of perturbing q. Add to Q_ϕ and Q_* according to the next equations:

$$(Q_\phi = Q_\phi \cup \{q\}) \iff (\nexists r \in Q_\phi / q \quad is \quad dominated \quad by \quad r) \tag{29}$$

$$(Q_* = Q_* \cup \{q\}) \iff (\exists r \in Q_\phi / r \quad is \quad dominated \quad by \quad q) \tag{30}$$

Remove the states with dominated solutions for each set.

Step 4. Crossover. Randomly select states from Q_ϕ and Q_*. Generate a random point of cross.

Step 5. Check stop condition, go to 3.

Step 2 and 3 support the algorithm in removing dominated solutions from the set of solutions Q_ϕ as can be seen in figure 3. However, one of the most important steps in the EMODS algorithm is step 4. There, similar to SAGAMODS, the algorithm applies an Evolutionary Strategy based in the crossover step of Genetic Algorithms for avoiding Local Optimums. Due to the crossover is not always made in the same point (the k-value is randomly generated in each state analyzed) the variety of solutions found are diverse avoiding local optimums. An overview of EMODS behavior for a Tri-objective Combinatorial Optimization problem can be seen in figure 14

6. Experimental analysis

6.1 Experimental settings

The algorithms were tested using well-known instances from the Multi-objective Traveling Salesman Problem taken from TSPLIB(Heidelberg, n.d.). The instances worked are shown in table 6 and the input parameters for the algorithms are shown in table 7. The test of the algorithms was made using a Dual Core Computer with 2 Gb RAM. The optimal solutions were constructed based in the best non-dominated solutions of all algorithms in comparison for each instance worked.

6.2 Performance metrics

There are metrics that allow measuring the quality of a set of optimal solutions and the performance of an Algorithm (Corne & Knowles, 2003). Most of them use two Pareto Fronts. The first one is PF_{true} and it refers to the real optimal solutions of a combinatorial problem. The second is PF_{know} and it represents the optimal solutions found by an algorithm.

Generation of Non-dominated Vectors (GNDV) It measures the number of No Dominates Solutions generated by an algorithm.

$$GNDV = |PF_{know}| \tag{31}$$

A higher value for this metric is desired. *Rate of Generation of No-dominated Vectors (RGNDV)* This metric measures the proportion of the No Dominates Solutions (31) generated by an

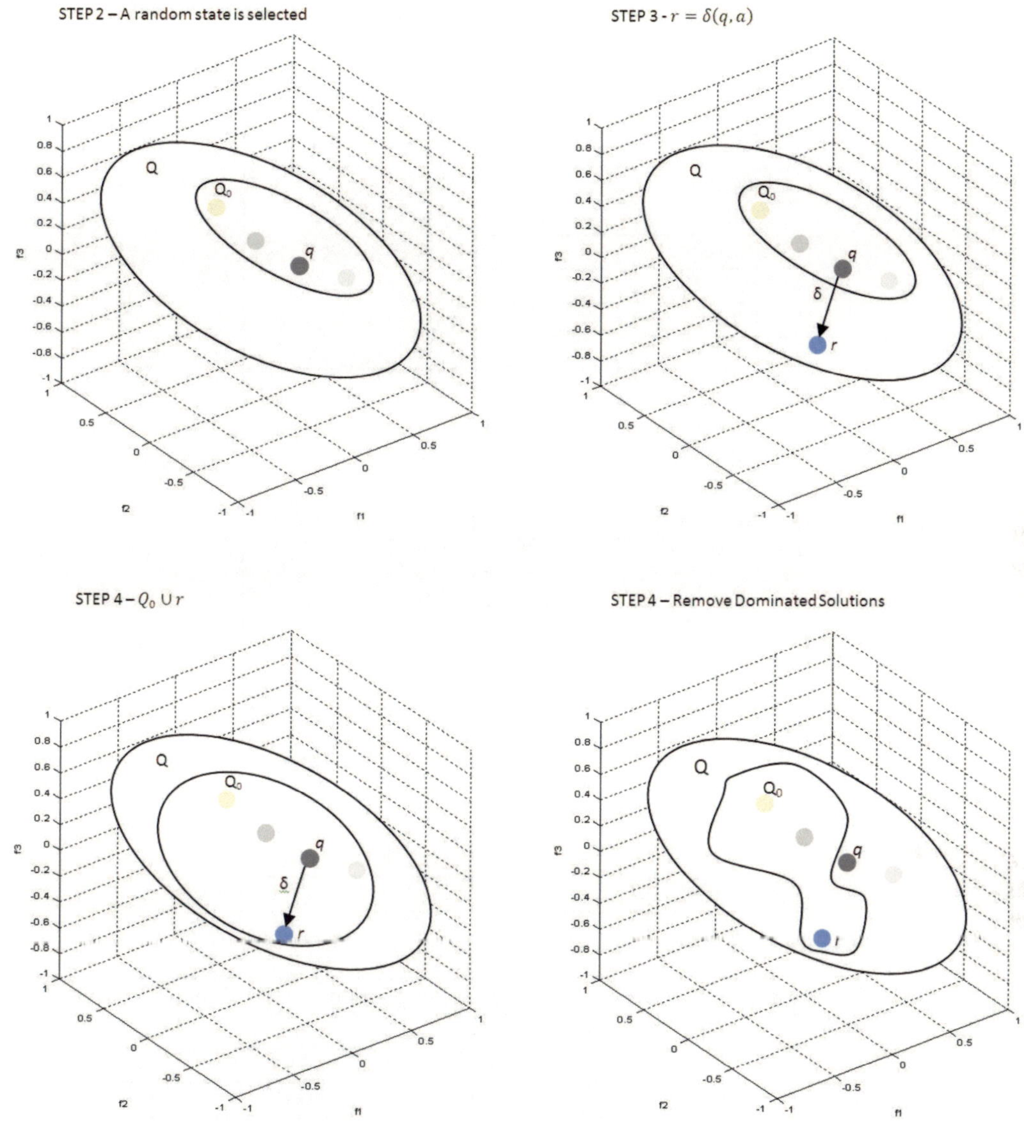

Fig. 14. An overview of EMODS behavior for a Tri-objective Problem.

algorithm and the Real Solutions.

$$RGNDV = \left(\frac{GNDV}{|PF_{true}|}\right) \cdot 100\% \tag{32}$$

A value closer to 100% for this metric is desired. *Real Generation of Non-dominated Vectors (ReGNDV)* This metric measures the number of Real Solutions found by an algorithm.

$$ReGNDV = |\{y | y \in PF_{know} \wedge y \in PF_{true}\}| \tag{33}$$

Combinatorial Problem Instance	Number of Objectives
KROAB100	2
KROAC100	
KROAD100	
KROAE100	
KROBC100	
KROBD100	
KROBE100	
KROCD100	
KROCE100	
KRODE100	
KROABC100	3
KROABD100	
KROABE100	
KROACD100	
KROACE100	
KROADE100	
KROBCD100	
KROBCE100	
KROBDE100	
KROCDE100	
KROABCD100	4
KROABCE100	
KROABDE100	
KROACDE100	
KROBCDE100	
KROABCDE100	5

Table 6. Instances worked for testing the proposed algorithms.

Algorithm	Max. Iterations	Max. Perturbations	Initial Temperature	Cooler Value	Crossover Rate
MODS	100	80	NA	NA	NA
SAMODS	100	80	1000	0.95	NA
SAGAMODS	100	80	1000	0.95	0.6
EMODS	100	80	NA	NA	0.6

Table 7. Parameters setting for each compared algorithm.

A value closer to $|PF_{true}|$ for this metric is desired.

Generational Distance (GD) This metric measures the distance between PF_{know} and PF_{true}. It allows to determinate the error rate in terms of the distance of a set of solutions relative to the real solutions.

$$GD = \left(\frac{1}{|PF_{know}|} \right) \cdot \left(\sum_{i=1}^{|PF_{know}|} d_i \right)^{(1/p)} \tag{34}$$

Where d_i is the smallest Euclidean distance between the solution i of FP_{know} and the solutions of FP_{true}. p is the dimension of the combinatorial problem, it means the number of objective functions. *Inverse Generational Distance (IGD)* This is another distance measurement between FP_{know} and FP_{true}:

$$IGD = \left(\frac{1}{|PF_{true}|}\right) \cdot \left(\sum_{i=1}^{|PF_{know}|} d_i\right) \tag{35}$$

Where d_i is the smallest Euclidean distance between the solution i of PF_{know} and the solutions of PF_{true}. *Spacing (S)* It measures the range variance of neighboring solutions in PF_{know}

$$S = \left(\frac{1}{|PF_{know}| - 1}\right)^2 \cdot \left(\sum_{i=1}^{|PF_{know}|} \left(\overline{d} - d_i\right)^2\right)^{(1/p)} \tag{36}$$

Where d_i is the smallest Euclidean distance between the solution i of PF_{know} and the rest of solutions of PF_{know}. $\overline{d}$ is the mean of all d_i. p is the dimension of the combinatorial problem.

A value closer to 0 for this metric is desired. A value of 0 means that all the solutions are equidistant.

Error Rate (ε) It estimates the error rate respect to the precision of the Real Algorithms Solutions (33) as follows:

$$\varepsilon = \left(\left|\frac{PF_{true}}{ReGNDV}\right|\right) \cdot 100\% \tag{37}$$

A value of 0% in this metric means that the values of the Real Pareto Front are constructed from the values of the Algorithm Pareto Front.

Lastly, notice that every metric by itself does not have sense. It is necessary to support in the other metrics for a real judge about the quality of the solutions. For instance, if a Pareto Front has a higher value in $GNDV$ but a lower value in $ReGNDV$ then the solutions has a poor-quality.

6.3 Experimental results

The tests made with Bi-objectives, Tri-objectives, Quad-objectives and Quin-objectives TSP instances are shown in tables 8, 9, 10 and 11 respectively. The average of the measurement is shown in table 12. Furthermore, a graphical comparison for bi-objectives and tri objectives instances worked is shown in figures 15 and 16 respectively.

6.4 Analysis

It can be concluded, that, in the case of two and three objectives, metrics such as S, IGD, GD and ε determine the best algorithm. In this case, the measurement of the metrics is similar for SAMODS and SAGAMODS. On the other hand, MODS has the most poor-quality measurement for the metrics used and EMODS has the best quality measurement for the same metrics.

Lastly, why are the results of the metrics similar for quint-instances? In this case, all the solutions for each solution set are in the optimal set. The answer to this question is based in the angle improvement. MODS as a local search strategy explore a part of the feasible solution using its search direction (Q_*). However, SAMODS and SAGAMODS, in addition, use a search direction given by the change of the search angle. While SAMODS was looking in a

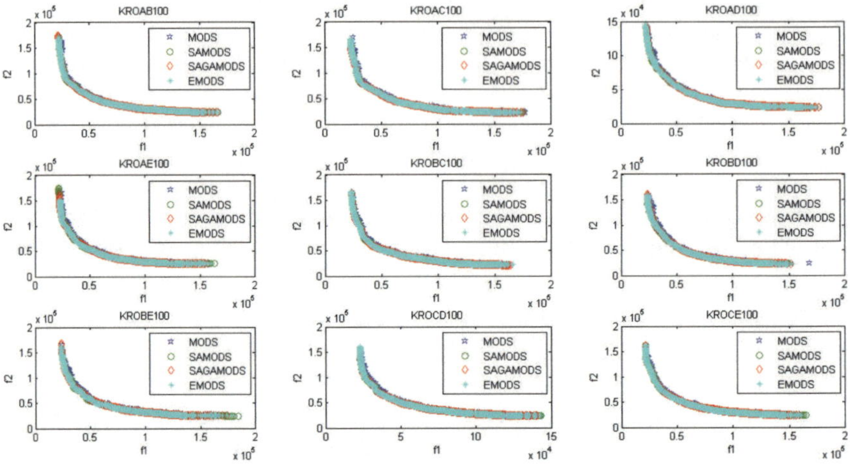

Fig. 15. Graphical comparison between MODS, SAMODS, SAGAMODS and EMODS for Bi-objective TSP instances.

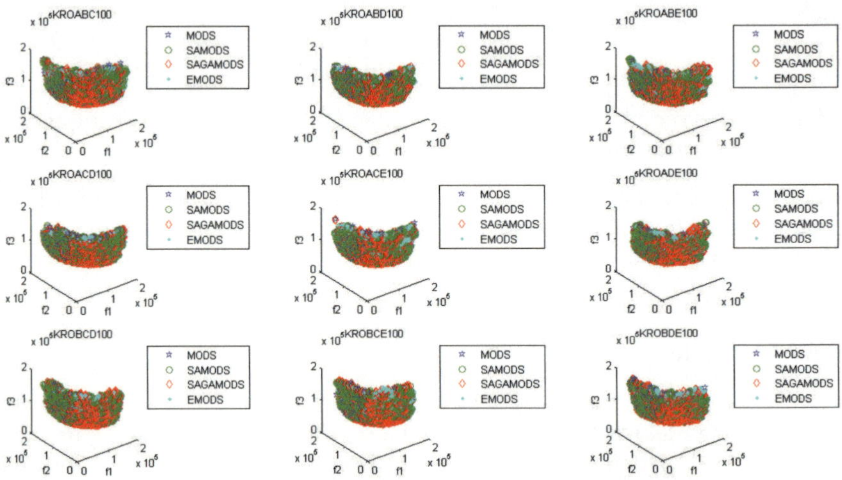

Fig. 16. Graphical comparison between MODS, SAMODS, SAGAMODS and EMODS for Tri-objective TSP instances.

part of the feasible solution space, SAGAMODS was doing the same in other. The same reason applies to EMODS. It can be possible because of the large size of the feasible solution space ($\Re^5$). The possibility of exploring the same part of the solution space for different algorithms is low.

Instance	*Algorithm*	*GNDV*	*RGNDV*	*ReGNDV*	$\left(\frac{ReGNDV}{GNDV}\right)\%$	*S*	*GD*	*IGD*	ε
AB	MODS	289	0.0189	0	0%	0.0193	21.2731	2473.4576	100%
	SAMODS	7787	0.5096	1247	16.01%	0.001	0.2404	229.2593	91.84%
	SAGAMODS	8479	0.5549	2974	35.07%	0.0007	0.1837	158.8229	80.54%
	EMODS	26125	1.7096	11060	42.33%	0.0002	0.0412	75.8814	27.62%
AC	MODS	217	0.0155	0	0%	0.034	28.575	2751.3232	100%
	SAMODS	6885	0.4927	2303	33.45%	0.0008	0.2297	179.0354	83.52%
	SAGAMODS	7023	0.5025	2431	34.61%	0.0008	0.2628	243.7536	82.6%
	EMODS	20990	1.502	9241	44.03%	0.0002	0.0617	119.8825	33.87%
AD	MODS	281	0.0187	0	0%	0.0139	20.4429	2198.883	100%
	SAMODS	6383	0.4253	1464	22.94%	0.0029	0.3188	275.9153	90.24%
	SAGAMODS	6289	0.4191	764	12.15%	0.0016	0.2835	211.7935	94.91%
	EMODS	17195	1.1458	12779	74.32%	0.0005	0.0521	53.5314	14.85%
AE	MODS	283	0.0189	0	0%	0.0533	21.3238	2433.63	100%
	SAMODS	5693	0.3804	1433	25.17%	0.0016	0.4308	402.0483	90.42%
	SAGAMODS	6440	0.4304	1515	23.52%	0.0013	0.3906	422.7859	89.88%
	EMODS	20695	1.383	12016	58.06%	0.0002	0.066	124.7197	19.7%
BC	MODS	298	0.0212	0	0%	0.0158	19.537	2411.8365	100%
	SAMODS	6858	0.488	789	11.5%	0.0024	0.3597	433.0882	94.39%
	SAGAMODS	6919	0.4923	2201	31.81%	0.0015	0.2378	192.5601	84.34%
	EMODS	21902	1.5584	11064	50.52%	0.0003	0.0582	115.5673	21.28%
BD	MODS	241	0.0198	0	0%	0.0239	21.7441	2251.0972	100%
	SAMODS	6844	0.561	2054	30.01%	0.0021	0.2542	248.0971	83.16%
	SAGAMODS	5934	0.4864	1971	33.22%	0.0018	0.2818	229.2093	83.84%
	EMODS	19420	1.5919	8174	42.09%	0.0003	0.0432	57.6434	32.99%
BE	MODS	280	0.0259	0	0%	0.0309	19.0193	2622.5243	100%
	SAMODS	6260	0.5789	952	15.21%	0.001	0.2601	245.1433	91.2%
	SAGAMODS	5802	0.5365	1622	27.96%	0.0025	0.3912	476.4848	85%
	EMODS	17362	1.6055	8240	47.46%	0.0004	0.0631	111.0209	23.8%
CD	MODS	286	0.022	0	0%	0.0184	18.0035	2040.9722	100%
	SAMODS	6171	0.4751	1912	30.98%	0.0007	0.2588	196.3394	85.28%
	SAGAMODS	6301	0.4851	994	15.78%	0.0014	0.2852	248.5855	92.35%
	EMODS	18628	1.434	10084	54.13%	0.0002	0.0426	48.3785	22.37%
CE	MODS	224	0.0187	0	0%	0.0285	23.1312	2245.6542	100%
	SAMODS	5881	0.4919	946	16.09%	0.0017	0.2894	242.2535	92.09%
	SAGAMODS	4613	0.3859	939	20.36%	0.0028	0.481	411.854	92.15%
	EMODS	15211	1.2724	10070	66.2%	0.0003	0.0339	22.2645	15.77%
DE	MODS	228	0.0147	0	0%	0.0477	23.6222	1864.9602	100%
	SAMODS	6110	0.3928	1157	18.94%	0.0022	0.2942	207.7947	92.56%
	SAGAMODS	7745	0.4979	407	5.26%	0.0012	0.2644	269.6204	97.38%
	EMODS	20058	1.2896	13990	69.75%	0.0005	0.0304	23.8829	10.06%

Table 8. Measuring algorithms performance for Bi-objectives instances of Traveling Salesman Problem with Multi-objective optimization metrics.

Instance	*Algorithm*	*GNDV*	*RGNDV*	*ReGNDV*	$\left(\frac{ReGNDV}{GNDV}\right)\%$	*S*	*GD*	*IGD*	*ε*
ABC	MODS	2115	0.0307	83	3.92%	0.1567	0.2819	3075.4309	99.88%
	SAMODS	12768	0.1853	227	1.78%	0.0722	0.0421	2256.4593	99.67%
	SAGAMODS	12523	0.1818	328	2.62%	0.073	0.0427	2220.5614	99.52%
	EMODS	70474	1.023	68254	96.85%	0.0477	0.001	5.6388	0.93%
ABD	MODS	1951	0.0292	74	3.79%	0.1524	0.305	3153.9212	99.89%
	SAMODS	12094	0.1811	317	2.62%	0.0746	0.0441	2270.3475	99.53%
	SAGAMODS	12132	0.1817	250	2.06%	0.0726	0.0441	2286.7374	99.63%
	EMODS	68001	1.0184	66133	97.25%	0.0471	0.0011	6.3212	0.96%
ABE	MODS	1931	0.0281	63	3.26%	0.1496	0.315	3278.1554	99.91%
	SAMODS	12461	0.1815	373	2.99%	0.0743	0.0438	2371.7641	99.46%
	SAGAMODS	12391	0.1805	370	2.99%	0.0745	0.0436	2304.3277	99.46%
	EMODS	70411	1.0257	67839	96.35%	0.0474	0.0012	8.0639	1.17%
ACD	MODS	2031	0.0305	66	3.25%	0.1425	0.2945	3213.7378	99.9%
	SAMODS	12004	0.1802	241	2.01%	0.0734	0.0444	2277.0343	99.64%
	SAGAMODS	12123	0.182	206	1.7%	0.0735	0.0442	2310.3683	99.69%
	EMODS	67451	1.0127	66090	97.98%	0.0468	0.001	4.5012	0.77%
ACE	MODS	1950	0.0306	57	2.92%	0.1628	0.3024	3215.8357	99.91%
	SAMODS	11382	0.1785	263	2.31%	0.074	0.0461	2271.6542	99.59%
	SAGAMODS	11476	0.18	303	2.64%	0.0734	0.0456	2241.9933	99.52%
	EMODS	64804	1.0162	63145	97.44%	0.048	0.0012	7.3103	0.98%
ADE	MODS	1824	0.0274	67	3.67%	0.1487	0.3289	3248.597	99.9%
	SAMODS	12149	0.1827	179	1.47%	0.0733	0.0442	2336.2798	99.73%
	SAGAMODS	11773	0.1771	258	2.19%	0.0771	0.0457	2346.6414	99.61%
	EMODS	67767	1.0193	65981	97.36%	0.0468	0.0011	5.7824	0.76%
BCD	MODS	2065	0.03	43	2.08%	0.1451	0.2927	3206.9305	99.94%
	SAMODS	13129	0.1908	260	1.98%	0.0712	0.0417	2387.8219	99.62%
	SAGAMODS	12889	0.1873	253	1.96%	0.0786	0.042	2308.1811	99.63%
	EMODS	70035	1.0176	68270	97.48%	0.0452	0.001	5.6235	0.81%
BCE	MODS	2009	0.0286	58	2.89%	0.1505	0.3065	3327.787	99.92%
	SAMODS	12992	0.1852	229	1.76%	0.0701	0.0428	2448.3577	99.67%
	SAGAMODS	12582	0.1794	201	1.6%	0.0736	0.0445	2503.0421	99.71%
	EMODS	71176	1.0147	69654	97.86%	0.0464	0.0011	7.8122	0.7%
BDE	MODS	2039	0.0316	45	2.21%	0.1532	0.2914	3252.7813	99.93%
	SAMODS	12379	0.192	205	1.66%	0.0728	0.0434	2401.8804	99.68%
	SAGAMODS	12427	0.1928	195	1.57%	0.0742	0.0431	2377.0621	99.7%
	EMODS	65509	1.0163	64015	97.72%	0.0476	0.0011	5.6322	0.69%
CDE	MODS	2010	0.0278	83	4.13%	0.1463	0.3022	3094.2824	99.89%
	SAMODS	13084	0.1807	399	3.05%	0.0712	0.0414	2193.6586	99.45%
	SAGAMODS	13009	0.1796	347	2.67%	0.0719	0.0418	2224.4738	99.52%
	EMODS	74063	1.0227	71589	96.66%	0.0453	0.0011	7.2279	1.14%

Table 9. Measuring algorithms performance for Tri-objective instances of TSP with Multi-objective optimization metrics.

Instance	*Algorithm*	*GNDV*	*RGNDV*	*ReGNDV*	$\left(\frac{ReGNDV}{GNDV}\right)$ %	*S*	*GD*	*IGD*	ε
ABCD	MODS	5333	0.0925	3303	61.94%	0.3497	0.0256	6030.5288	94.27%
	SAMODS	28523	0.4947	12178	42.7%	0.231	0.0042	3454.1238	78.88%
	SAGAMODS	36802	0.6382	14967	40.67%	0.2203	0.0031	3092.5232	74.04%
	EMODS	201934	3.502	27214	13.48%	0.1754	0.0005	1991.148	52.8%
ABCE	MODS	5533	0.0973	3439	62.15%	0.3452	0.0244	5861.8605	93.95%
	SAMODS	27684	0.4868	11471	41.44%	0.2331	0.0043	3444.6454	79.83%
	SAGAMODS	35766	0.6289	14552	40.69%	0.2232	0.0032	3118.6397	74.41%
	EMODS	204596	3.5976	27408	13.4%	0.1754	0.0005	1885.4464	51.81%
ABDE	MODS	5259	0.0942	3142	59.75%	0.3487	0.0256	5864.5036	94.37%
	SAMODS	27180	0.4869	11247	41.38%	0.232	0.0043	3398.9429	79.85%
	SAGAMODS	34930	0.6257	14472	41.43%	0.2236	0.0033	2986.5319	74.08%
	EMODS	195756	3.5067	26963	13.77%	0.1775	0.0005	1916.7141	51.7%
ACDE	MODS	5466	0.094	3400	62.2%	0.3405	0.0246	5617.5202	94.15%
	SAMODS	26757	0.4602	11336	42.37%	0.235	0.0044	3394.8396	80.5%
	SAGAMODS	34492	0.5932	14638	42.44%	0.2265	0.0033	2965.4482	74.83%
	EMODS	196800	3.3845	28774	14.62%	0.1764	0.0005	1793.4489	50.52%
BCDE	MODS	5233	0.0879	3082	58.9%	0.3499	0.0259	5677.9988	94.83%
	SAMODS	28054	0.471	11739	41.84%	0.2315	0.0042	3296.196	80.29%
	SAGAMODS	36258	0.6087	15145	41.77%	0.2218	0.0032	2902.8041	74.57%
	EMODS	203017	3.4083	29599	14.58%	0.1752	0.0005	1873.1748	50.31%

Table 10. Measuring algorithms performance for Quad-objectives instances of TSP with Multi-objective optimization metrics.

Instance	*Algorithm*	*GNDV*	*RGNDV*	*ReGNDV*	$\left(\frac{ReGNDV}{GNDV}\right)$ %	*S*	*GD*	*IGD*	ε
ABCDE	MODS	7517	0.0159	7517	100%	0.5728	0.0125	15705.6864	98.41%
	SAMODS	26140	0.0554	26140	100%	0.4101	0.0033	10801.6382	94.46%
	SAGAMODS	26611	0.0564	26611	100%	0.4097	0.0033	10544.8901	94.36%
	EMODS	411822	0.8723	411822	100%	0.3136	0.0001	950.4252	12.77%

Table 11. Measuring algorithms performance for Quint-objectives instances of TSP with Multi-objective optimization metrics.

Objectives	*Algorithm*	*GNDV*	*RGNDV*	*ReGNDV*	$\left(\frac{ReGNDV}{GNDV}\right)$ %	*S*	*GD*	*IGD*	ε
2	MODS	262.7	0.0194	0	0%	0.0286	21.6672	2329.4338	100%
	SAMODS	6487.2	0.4796	1425.7	22.03%	0.0016	0.2936	265.8974	89.47%
	SAGAMODS	6554.5	0.4791	1581.8	23.97%	0.0015	0.3062	286.547	88.3%
	EMODS	19758.6	1.4492	10671.8	54.89%	0.0003	0.0492	75.2773	22.23%
3	MODS	1992.5	0.0295	63.9	3.21%	0.1508	0.302	3206.7459	99.91%
	SAMODS	12444.2	0.1838	269.3	2.16%	0.0727	0.0434	2321.5258	99.6%
	SAGAMODS	12332.5	0.1822	271.1	2.2%	0.0743	0.0437	2312.3389	99.6%
	EMODS	68969.1	1.0187	67097	97.3%	0.0468	0.0011	6.3914	0.89%
4	MODS	5364.8	0.0932	3273.2	60.99%	0.3468	0.0252	5810.4824	94.31%
	SAMODS	27639.6	0.4799	11594.2	41.94%	0.2325	0.0043	3397.7495	79.87%
	SAGAMODS	35649.6	0.619	14754.8	41.4%	0.2231	0.0032	3013.1894	74.39%
	EMODS	200420.6	3.4798	27991.6	13.97%	0.176	0.0005	1891.9864	51.43%
5	MODS	7517	0.0159	7517	100%	0.5728	0.0125	15705.6864	98.41%
	SAMODS	26140	0.0554	26140	100%	0.4101	0.0033	10801.6382	94.46%
	SAGAMODS	26611	0.0564	26611	100%	0.4097	0.0033	10544.8901	94.36%
	EMODS	411822	0.8723	411822	100%	0.3136	0.0001	950.4252	12.77%

Table 12. Measuring algorithms performance for Multi-objectives instances of TSP with Multi-objective optimization metrics.

7. Conclusion

SAMODS, SAGAMODS and EMODS are algorithms based on the Automata Theory for the Multi-objective Optimization of Combinatorial Problems. All of them are derived from the MODS metaheuristic, which is inspired in the Theory of Deterministic Finite Swapping. SAMODS is a Simulated Annealing inspired Algorithm. It uses a search direction in order to optimize a set of solution (Pareto Front) through a linear combination of the objective functions. On the other hand, SAGAMODS, in addition to the advantages of SAMODS, is an Evolutionary inspired Algorithm. It implements a crossover step for exploring far regions of a solution space. Due to this, SAGAMODS tries to avoid local optimums owing to it takes a general look of the solution space. Lastly, in order to avoid slow convergence, EMODS is proposed. Unlike SAMODS and SAGAMODS, EMODS does not explore the neighborhood of a solution using Simulated Annealing, this step is done using Tabu Search. Thus, EMODS gets optimal solution faster than SAGAMODS and SAMODS. Lastly, the algorithms were tested using well known instances from TSPLIB and metrics from the specialized literature. The results shows that for instances of two, three and four objectives, the proposed algorithm has the best performance as the metrics values corroborate. For the last instance worked, quint-objective, the behavior of MODS, SAMODS and SAGAMODS tend to be the same, them have similar error rate but, EMODS has a the best performance. In all the cases, EMODS shows the best performance. However, for the last test, all the algorithms have different solutions sets of non-dominated solutions, and those form the optimal solution set.

8. Acknowledgment

First of all, I want to thank to God for being with me in my entire life, He made this possible. Secondly, I want to thank to my parents Elias Niño and Arely Ruiz and my sister Carmen Niño for their enormous love and support. Finally, and not less important, to thank to my beautiful wife Maria Padron and our baby for being my inspiration.

9. References

An, S., Yang, S., Ho, S., Li, T. & Fu, W. (2011). A modified tabu search method applied to inverse problems, *Magnetics, IEEE Transactions on* 47(5): 1234 –1237.

Araujo, D., Bastos-Filho, C., Barboza, E., Chaves, D. & Martins-Filho, J. (2011). A performance comparison of multi-objective optimization evolutionary algorithms for all-optical networks design, *Computational Intelligence in Multicriteria Decision-Making (MDCM), 2011 IEEE Symposium on*, pp. 89 –96.

Ausavanop, O. & Chaitusaney, S. (2011). Coordination of dispatchable distributed generation and voltage control devices for improving voltage profile by tabu search, *Electrical Engineering/Electronics, Computer, Telecommunications and Information Technology (ECTI-CON), 2011 8th International Conference on*, pp. 869 –872.

Azuma, R. M., Coelho, G. P. & Von Zuben, F. J. (2011). Evolutionary multi-objective optimization for the vendor-managed inventory routing problem, *Evolutionary Computation (CEC), 2011 IEEE Congress on*, pp. 1457 –1464.

Chen, K.-Y., Liu, A. & Lee, C.-H. (2003). A multiprocessor real-time process scheduling method, *Multimedia Software Engineering, 2003. Proceedings. Fifth International Symposium on*, pp. 29 – 36.

Chipara, O., Lu, C. & Roman, G.-C. (2007). Real-time query scheduling for wireless sensor networks, *Real-Time Systems Symposium, 2007. RTSS 2007. 28th IEEE International*, pp. 389 –399.

Chua, T., Wang, F., Cai, T. & Yin, X. (2006). A heuristics-based advanced planning and scheduling system with bottleneck scheduling algorithm, *Emerging Technologies and Factory Automation, 2006. ETFA '06. IEEE Conference on*, pp. 240 –247.

Chunyue, Y., Meirong, X. & Ruiguo, Z. (2009). Single-machine scheduling problem in plate hot rolling production, *Control and Decision Conference, 2009. CCDC '09. Chinese*, pp. 2500 –2503.

Corne, D. & Knowles, J. (2003). Some multiobjective optimizers are better than others, *Evolutionary Computation, 2003. CEC '03. The 2003 Congress on*, Vol. 4, pp. 2506 – 2512 Vol.4.

Czabaski, R. (2006). Deterministic annealing integrated with insensitive learning in neuro-fuzzy systems, *in* L. Rutkowski, R. Tadeusiewicz, L. Zadeh & J. Zurada (eds), *Artificial Intelligence and Soft Computing ICAISC 2006*, Vol. 4029 of *Lecture Notes in Computer Science*, Springer Berlin Heidelberg, pp. 220–229.

de Pablo, D. (2009). On scheduling models: An overview, *Computers Industrial Engineering, 2009. CIE 2009. International Conference on*, pp. 153 –158.

Deb, K., Pratap, A., Agarwal, S. & Meyarivan, T. (2002). A fast and elitist multiobjective genetic algorithm: Nsga-ii, *Evolutionary Computation, IEEE Transactions on* 6(2): 182 –197.

Dereli, T. & Sena Da, G. (2007). A hybrid simulated-annealing algorithm for two-dimensional strip packing problem, *in* B. Beliczynski, A. Dzielinski, M. Iwanowski & B. Ribeiro (eds), *Adaptive and Natural Computing Algorithms*, Vol. 4431 of *Lecture Notes in Computer Science*, Springer Berlin Heidelberg, pp. 508–516.

Dukkipati, A. & Narasimha Murty, M. (2002). Selection by parts: 'selection in two episodes' in evolutionary algorithms, *Evolutionary Computation, 2002. CEC '02. Proceedings of the 2002 Congress on*, Vol. 1, pp. 657 –662.

Fei, X., Ke, W., Jidong, S., Zheng, X. & Guilan, L. (2011). Back analysis of displacement based on support vector machine and continuous tabu search, *Electric Technology and Civil Engineering (ICETCE), 2011 International Conference on*, pp. 2016 –2019.

Fisher, R. (1930). *The genetical theory of natural selection*, Clarendon Press, Oxford.

Fung, R., Tang, J. & Zhang, J. (2009). A multi-depot vehicle routing problem with weight-related costs, *Computers Industrial Engineering, 2009. CIE 2009. International Conference on*, pp. 1028 –1033.

Gacto, M., Alcala, R. & Herrera, F. (2011). Evolutionary multi-objective algorithm to effectively improve the performance of the classic tuning of fuzzy logic controllers for a heating, ventilating and air conditioning system, *Genetic and Evolutionary Fuzzy Systems (GEFS), 2011 IEEE 5th International Workshop on*, pp. 73 –80.

Garriz, J., Puntonet, C., Morales, J. & delaRosa, J. (2005). Simulated annealing based-ga using injective contrast functions for bss, *in* V. Sunderam, G. van Albada, P. Sloot & J. Dongarra (eds), *Computational Science ICCS 2005*, Vol. 3514 of *Lecture Notes in Computer Science*, Springer Berlin Heidelberg, pp. 505–600.

Glover, F. & Laguna, M. (1997). *Tabu Search*, Kluwer Academic Publishers, Norwell, MA, USA.

Grobler, J. & Engelbrecht, A. (2007). A scheduling-specific modeling approach for real world scheduling, *Industrial Engineering and Engineering Management, 2007 IEEE International Conference on*, pp. 85 –89.

Hamidzadeh, B. & Atif, Y. (1996). Dynamic scheduling of real-time aperiodic tasks on multiprocessor architectures, *System Sciences, 1996., Proceedings of the Twenty-Ninth Hawaii International Conference on ,*, Vol. 1, pp. 469 –478 vol.1.

Heidelberg, U. O. (n.d.). Tsplib - office research group discrete optimization - university of heidelberg, URL: *http://comopt.ifi.uni-heidelberg.de/software/TSPLIB95/*.

Hu, B. & Raidl, G. (2008). Solving the railway traveling salesman problem via a transformation into the classical traveling salesman problem, *Hybrid Intelligent Systems, 2008. HIS '08. Eighth International Conference on*, pp. 73 –77.

Huang, Y., Brocco, A., Bessis, N., Kuonen, P. & Hirsbrunner, B. (2010). Community-aware scheduling protocol for grids, *Advanced Information Networking and Applications (AINA), 2010 24th IEEE International Conference on*, pp. 334 –341.

Ishibuchi, H., Akedo, N., Ohyanagi, H. & Nojima, Y. (2011). Behavior of emo algorithms on many-objective optimization problems with correlated objectives, *Evolutionary Computation (CEC), 2011 IEEE Congress on*, pp. 1465 –1472.

Jian-guang, W., Ran, T. & Zhi-Yong, L. (2011). An improving tabu search algorithm for intrusion detection, *Measuring Technology and Mechatronics Automation (ICMTMA), 2011 Third International Conference on*, Vol. 1, pp. 435 –439.

Jianghong, D., Zhongyang, X., Hao, C. & Hui, D. (2000). Scheduling algorithm for mpeg-2 ts multiplexers in catv networks, *Broadcasting, IEEE Transactions on* 46(4): 249 –255.

Kim, G. H. & Lee, C. (1998). Genetic reinforcement learning approach to the heterogeneous machine scheduling problem, *Robotics and Automation, IEEE Transactions on* 14(6): 879 –893.

Kim, I. & Lipasti, M. (2003). Macro-op scheduling: relaxing scheduling loop constraints, *Microarchitecture, 2003. MICRO-36. Proceedings. 36th Annual IEEE/ACM International Symposium on*, pp. 277 – 288.

Kirkpatrick, S., Gelatt, C. D. & Vecchi, M. P. (1983). Optimization by Simulated Annealing, *Science, Number 4598, 13 May 1983* 220, 4598: 671–680.
URL: *http://citeseerx.ist.psu.edu/viewdoc/summary?doi=10.1.1.18.4175*

Lee, H.-C., Keh, H.-C., Huang, N.-C. & Chang, W.-H. (2011). An application of google map and tabu-search algorithm for traveling salesman problem on tel-home care, *Electric Information and Control Engineering (ICEICE), 2011 International Conference on*, pp. 4764 –4767.

Lim, A. & Wang, F. (2005). Multi-depot vehicle routing problem: a one-stage approach, *Automation Science and Engineering, IEEE Transactions on* 2(4): 397–402.

Liu, J., Hamdi, M. & Hu, Q. (2003). Distributed parallel scheduling algorithms for high speed virtual output queuing switches, *Computer Systems and Applications, 2003. Book of Abstracts. ACS/IEEE International Conference on*, p. 27.

Malik, A. M. A., Othman, A. K., Ayob, M. & Hamdan, A. R. (2011). Hybrid integrated two-stage multi-neighbourhood tabu search-emcq technique for examination timetabling problem, *Data Mining and Optimization (DMO), 2011 3rd Conference on*, pp. 232 –236.

Manimaran, G., Shashidhar, M., Manikutty, A. & Murthy, C. (1997). Integrated scheduling of tasks and messages in distributed real-time systems, *Parallel and Distributed Real-Time Systems, 1997. Proceedings of the Joint Workshop on*, pp. 64 –71.

McClymont, K. & Keedwell, E. (2011). Benchmark multi-objective optimisation test problems with mixed encodings, *Evolutionary Computation (CEC), 2011 IEEE Congress on*, pp. 2131 –2138.

McGarry, M., Reisslein, M., Colbourn, C., Maier, M., Aurzada, F. & Scheutzow, M. (2008). Just-in-time scheduling for multichannel epons, *Lightwave Technology, Journal of* 26(10): 1204 –1216.

Mingsheng, S., Shixin, S. & Qingxian, W. (2003). An efficient parallel scheduling algorithm of dependent task graphs, *Parallel and Distributed Computing, Applications and Technologies, 2003. PDCAT'2003. Proceedings of the Fourth International Conference on*, pp. 595 – 598.

Niño, E. D. (2012). Samods and sagamods: Novel algorithms based on the automata theory for the multi-objective optimization of combinatorial problems, *International Journal of Artificial Intelligence - Special issue of IJAI on Metaheuristics in Artificial Intelligence* Pending: Pending.

Niño, E. D., Ardila, C., Donoso, Y. & Jabba, D. (2010). A novel algorithm based on deterministic finite automaton for solving the mono-objective symmetric traveling salesman problem, *International Journal of Artificial Intelligence* 5(A10): 101 – 108.

Niño, E. D., Ardila, C., Donoso, Y., Jabba, D. & Barrios, A. (2011). Mods: A novel metaheuristic of deterministic swapping for the multi Ű objective optimization of combinatorials problems, *Computer Technology and Application* 2(4): 280 – 292.

Niño, E. D., Ardila, C., Perez, A. & Donoso, Y. (2010). A genetic algorithm for multiobjective hard scheduling optimization, *International Journal of Computers Communications & Control* 5(5): 825–836.

Niehaus, D., Ramamritham, K., Stankovic, J., Wallace, G., Weems, C., Burleson, W. & Ko, J. (1993). The spring scheduling co-processor: Design, use, and performance, *Real-Time Systems Symposium, 1993., Proceedings.*, pp. 106 –111.

Oberlin, P., Rathinam, S. & Darbha, S. (2009). A transformation for a heterogeneous, multiple depot, multiple traveling salesman problem, *American Control Conference, 2009. ACC '09.*, pp. 1292 –1297.

Ren, W.-J., Duan, J.-H., rong Zhang, F., yan Han, H. & Zhang, M. (2011). Hybrid tabu search algorithm for bi-criteria no-idle permutation flow shop scheduling problem, *Control and Decision Conference (CCDC), 2011 Chinese*, pp. 1699 –1702.

Sauer, J. & Coelho, L. (2008). Discrete differential evolution with local search to solve the traveling salesman problem: Fundamentals and case studies, *Cybernetic Intelligent Systems, 2008. CIS 2008. 7th IEEE International Conference on*, pp. 1 –6.

Shah, S., Mahmood, A. & Oxley, A. (2009). Hybrid scheduling and dual queue scheduling, *Computer Science and Information Technology, 2009. ICCSIT 2009. 2nd IEEE International Conference on*, pp. 539 –543.

Shanmugapriya, R., Padmavathi, S. & Shalinie, S. (2009). Contention awareness in task scheduling using tabu search, *Advance Computing Conference, 2009. IACC 2009. IEEE International*, pp. 272 –277.

Sofianopoulos, S. & Tambouratzis, G. (2011). Studying the spea2 algorithm for optimising a pattern-recognition based machine translation system, *Computational Intelligence in Multicriteria Decision-Making (MDCM), 2011 IEEE Symposium on*, pp. 97 –104.

Song, J., Yang, F., Wang, M. & Zhang, H. (2008). Cryptanalysis of transposition cipher using simulated annealing genetic algorithm, *in* L. Kang, Z. Cai, X. Yan & Y. Liu (eds), *Advances in Computation and Intelligence*, Vol. 5370 of *Lecture Notes in Computer Science*, Springer Berlin Heidelberg, pp. 795–802.

Song, S., Hwang, K. & Kwok, Y.-K. (2006). Risk-resilient heuristics and genetic algorithms for security-assured grid job scheduling, *Computers, IEEE Transactions on* 55(6): 703 –719.

Talbi, N. & Belarbi, K. (2011a). Evolving fuzzy inference system by tabu search algorithm and its application to control, *Multimedia Computing and Systems (ICMCS), 2011 International Conference on*, pp. 1 –6.

Talbi, N. & Belarbi, K. (2011b). A self organized fuzzy pd controller using tabu search, *Innovations in Intelligent Systems and Applications (INISTA), 2011 International Symposium on*, pp. 460 –464.

Taspinar, N., Kalinli, A. & Yildirim, M. (2011). Partial transmit sequences for papr reduction using parallel tabu search algorithm in ofdm systems, *Communications Letters, IEEE* PP(99): 1 –3.

Wang, S.-Q. & Xu, Z.-Y. (2009). Ant colony algorithm approach for solving traveling salesman with multi-agent, *Information Engineering, 2009. ICIE '09. WASE International Conference on*, Vol. 1, pp. 381 –384.

Wang, Y. & Lang, M. (2008). Study on the model and tabu search algorithm for delivery and pickup vehicle routing problem with time windows, *Service Operations and Logistics, and Informatics, 2008. IEEE/SOLI 2008. IEEE International Conference on*, Vol. 1, pp. 1464 –1469.

Wei, Y., Gu, K., Liu, H. & Li, D. (2007). Contract net based scheduling approach using interactive bidding for dynamic job shop scheduling, *Integration Technology, 2007. ICIT '07. IEEE International Conference on*, pp. 281 –286.

Wijkman, P. (1996). Evolutionary computation and the principle of natural selection, *Intelligent Information Systems, 1996., Australian and New Zealand Conference on*, pp. 292 –297.

Wismans, L., Van Berkum, E. & Bliemer, M. (2011). Comparison of evolutionary multi objective algorithms for the dynamic network design problem, *Networking, Sensing and Control (ICNSC), 2011 IEEE International Conference on*, pp. 275 –280.

Wu, D. & Negi, R. (2003). Downlink scheduling in a cellular network for quality of service assurance, *Vehicular Technology Conference, 2003. VTC 2003-Fall. 2003 IEEE 58th*, Vol. 3, pp. 1391 – 1395 Vol.3.

Xiawen, Y. & Yu, S. (2011). A real-coded quantum clone multi-objective evolutionary algorithm, *Consumer Electronics, Communications and Networks (CECNet), 2011 International Conference on*, pp. 4683 –4687.

Yingzi, W., Xinli, J., Pingbo, H. & Kanfeng, G. (2009). Pattern driven dynamic scheduling approach using reinforcement learning, *Automation and Logistics, 2009. ICAL '09. IEEE International Conference on*, pp. 514 –519.

Yong-Fa, Q. & Ming-Yang, Z. (2004). Research on a new multiobjective combinatorial optimization algorithm, *Robotics and Biomimetics, 2004. ROBIO 2004. IEEE International Conference on*, pp. 187 –191.

You-xin, M., Jie, Z. & Zhuo, C. (2009). An overview of ant colony optimization algorithm and its application on production scheduling, *Innovation Management, 2009. ICIM '09. International Conference on*, pp. 135 –138.

Yu, G., Chai, T. & Luo, X. (2011). Multiobjective production planning optimization using hybrid evolutionary algorithms for mineral processing, *Evolutionary Computation, IEEE Transactions on* 15(4): 487 –514.

Yu, L., Ohsato, A., Kawakami, T. & Sekiguchi, T. (1999). Corba-based design and development of distributed scheduling systems: an application to flexible flow shop scheduling systems, *Systems, Man, and Cybernetics, 1999. IEEE SMC '99 Conference Proceedings. 1999 IEEE International Conference on*, Vol. 4, pp. 522 –527 vol.4.

Zhang-liang, W. & Yue-guang, L. (2011). An ant colony algorithm with tabu search and its application, *Intelligent Computation Technology and Automation (ICICTA), 2011 International Conference on*, Vol. 2, pp. 412 –416.

Zhao, Y., Jia, F., Wang, G. & Wang, L. (2011). A hybrid tabu search for steelmaking-continuous casting production scheduling problem, *Advanced Control of Industrial Processes (ADCONIP), 2011 International Symposium on*, pp. 535 –540.

Zheng, D., Liu, J., Chen, L., Liu, Y. & Guo, W. (2011). Transmitter-receiver collaborative-relay beamforming by simulated annealing, *in* Y. Tan, Y. Shi, Y. Chai & G. Wang (eds), *Advances in Swarm Intelligence*, Vol. 6729 of *Lecture Notes in Computer Science*, Springer Berlin Heidelberg, pp. 411–418.

Zhu, D., Mosse, D. & Melhem, R. (2003). Multiple-resource periodic scheduling problem: how much fairness is necessary?, *Real-Time Systems Symposium, 2003. RTSS 2003. 24th IEEE*, pp. 142 – 151.

Zitzler, E., Laumanns, M. & Thiele, L. (2001). Spea2: Improving the strength pareto evolutionary algorithm, *Technical Report 103*, Computer Engineering and Networks

Laboratory (TIK), Swiss Federal Institute of Technology (ETH) Zurich, Gloriastrasse 35, CH-8092 Zurich, Switzerland.

Zitzler, E., Laumanns, M. & Thiele, L. (2002). Spea2: Improving the strength pareto evolutionary algorithm for multiobjective optimization, *in* K. Giannakoglou, D. Tsahalis, J. Periaux, K. Papaliliou & T. Fogarty (eds), *Evolutionary Methods for Design, Optimisation and Control with Application to Industrial Problems. Proceedings of the EUROGEN2001 Conference,Athens, Greece, September 19-21, 2001,* International Center for Numerical Methos in Engineering (CIMNE), Barcelona, Spain, pp. 95–100.

5

Evolutionary Techniques in Multi-Objective Optimization Problems in Non-Standardized Production Processes

Mariano Frutos[1], Ana C. Olivera[2] and Fernando Tohmé[3]
[1]*Department of Engineering,*
[2]*Department of Computer Science & Engineering,*
[3]*Department of Economics,*
Universidad Nacional del Sur and CONICET,
Argentina

1. Introduction

To schedule production in a Job-Shop environment means to allocate adequately the available resources. It requires to rely on efficient optimization procedures. In fact, the Job-Shop Scheduling Problem (JSSP) is a NP-Hard problem (Ullman, 1975), so ad-hoc algorithms have to be applied to its solution (Frutos et al., 2010). This is similar to other combinatorial programming problems (Olivera et al., 2006), (Cortés et al., 2004). Most instances of the Job-Shop Scheduling Problem involve the simultaneous optimization of two usually conflicting goals. This one, like most multi-objective problems, tends to have many solutions. The Pareto frontier reached by an optimization procedure has to contain a uniformly distributed number of solutions close to the ones in the true Pareto frontier. This feature facilitates the task of the expert who interprets the solutions (Kacem et al., 2002). In this paper we present a Genetic Algorithm linked to a Simulated Annealing procedure able to schedule the production in a Job-Shop manufacturing system (Cortés et al., 2004), (Tsai & Lin, 2003), (Wu et al., 2004), (Chao-Hsien & Han-Chiang, 2009).

1.1 JSSP treatments: State of the art

The huge literature on the topic presents a variety of solution strategies that go from simple priority rules to sophisticated parallel branch-and-bound algorithms. A particular variety of scheduling problem is the JSSP. Muth and Thompson's 1964 (Muth & Thompson, 1964) book Industrial Scheduling presented the JSSP, basically in its currently known form. Even before, Jackson in 1956 (Jackson, 1956) generalized the flow-shop algorithm of Johnson (1954) (Johnson, 1954) to yield a job-shop algorithm. In 1955, Akers and Friedman (Akers & Friedman, 1955) gave a Boolean representation of the procedure, which later Roy and Sussman (1964) (Roy & Sussman, 1964) described by means of a disjunctive graph, while Egon Balas, already in 1969 (Balas, 1969), applied an enumerative approach that could be better understood in terms of this graph. Giffler and Thompson (1960) (Giffler & Thomson, 1960) presented an algorithm based on rule priorities to guide the search. For these reasons, the problem was already part of the folklore in Operations Research years before its official inception. The JSSP generated a huge literature. Its resiliency made it an ideal problem for further study. Besides, its usefulness made it a problem worth to scrutinize. Due to its complexity, several alternative presentations of the problem have been tried (Cheng & Smith, 1997), (Sadeh & Fox, 1995), (Crawford & Baker, 1994), (De Giovanni & Pezzella, 2010), in order to apply particular algorithms like Clonal Selection (Cortés Rivera et al., 2003), Taboo Search (Armentano & Scrich, 2000), Ant Colony Optimization (Merkle & Middendorf, 2001), Genetic Algorithms (Zalzala & Flemming, 1997), Priority Rules (Panwalker & Iskander, 1977), Shifting Bottlenecks (Adams et al., 1998), etc. The performance of these meta-heuristic procedures varies, and some seem fitter than others (Chinyao & Yuling, 2009).

1.2 Multi-objective optimization: Basic concepts

Our goal in this section is to characterize the general framework in which we will state the Job-Shop problem. We assume, without loss of generality, that there are several goals (objectives) to be minimized. Then, we seek to find a vector $\vec{x}^* = [x_1^*,...,x_n^*]^T$ of decision variables, satisfying q inequalities $g_i(\vec{x}) \geq 0,\ i = 1,...,q$ as well as p equations $h_i(\vec{x}) = 0,\ i = 1,...,p$, such that $\vec{f}(\vec{x}) = [f_1(\vec{x}),...,f_k(\vec{x})]^T$, a vector of k functions, each one corresponding to an objective, defined over the decision variables, attains its minimum. The class of the decision vectors satisfying the q inequalities and the p equations is denoted by Ω and each $\vec{x} \in \Omega$ is a feasible alternative. A $\vec{x}^* \in \Omega$ is Pareto optimal if for any $\vec{x} \in \Omega$ and every $i = 1,...,k$, $f_i(\vec{x}^*) \leq f_i(\vec{x})$. That is, if there is no $\vec{x}$ that improves some objectives without worsening the others. To simplify the notation, we say that a vector $\vec{u} = [u_1,...,u_n]^T$ dominates another, $\vec{v} = [v_1,...,v_n]^T$ (denoted $\vec{u} \prec \vec{v}$) if and only if $\forall i \in \{1,...,k\}$, $u_i \leq v_i \wedge \exists i \in \{1,...,k\} : u_i < v_i$. Then, the set of Pareto optima is $P^* = \{\vec{x} \in \Omega \mid \neg \exists \vec{x}' \in \Omega, \vec{f}(\vec{x}') \prec \vec{f}(\vec{x})\}$ while the corresponding Pareto frontier is $FP^* = \{\vec{f}(\vec{x}), \vec{x} \in P^*\}$. The search of the Pareto frontier is the main goal of Multi-Objective Optimization.

2. Flexible job-shop scheduling problem

The JSSP can be described as that of organizing the execution of n jobs on m machines. We assume a finite number of tasks, $\{J_j\}_{j=1}^n$. These tasks must be processed by a finite number of machines $\{M_k\}_{k=1}^m$. To process a task J_j in a machine M_k is denoted by O_{jk}^i, where i indicates the order in which a class of operations $\{S_j\}_{j=1}^n$ is applied on a task J_j. O_{jk}^i requires the uninterrupted use of a machine M_k for a period τ_{jk}^i (the processing time) at a cost υ_{jk}^i (see Table 1). A particular case is Flexible JSSP, in which the allocation of O_{jk}^i on M_k is undifferentiated, which means that each O_{jk}^i can be processed by any of the machines in $\{M_k\}_{k=1}^m$.

After allocating the operations, we obtain a finite class E of groupings of the $O_{jk}^i s$ on the same machine. We denote each of these groupings as E_k, for $k = 1,...,m$. A key issue here is the scheduling of activities, i.e. the determination of the starting time t_{jk}^i of each O_{jk}^i. The Flexible JSSP demands a procedure to handle its two sub-problems: the allocation of the $O_{jk}^i s$ on the different $M_k s$ and their sequencing, guided by the goals to reach. That is, to find optimal levels of Makespan (Processing Time) (see Eq. 1) and Total Operation Costs (see Eq. 2).

MF01 / Problem 3 × 4 with 8 operations (flexible)									
J_j	O_{jk}^i	M_1		M_2		M_3		M_4	
		τ_{j1}^i	υ_{j1}^i	τ_{j2}^i	υ_{j2}^i	τ_{j3}^i	υ_{j3}^i	τ_{j4}^i	υ_{j4}^i
J_1	O_{1k}^1	1	10	3	8	4	6	1	9
	O_{1k}^2	3	4	8	2	2	10	1	12
	O_{1k}^3	3	8	5	4	4	6	7	3
J_2	O_{2k}^1	4	7	1	16	1	14	4	6
	O_{2k}^2	2	10	3	8	9	3	3	8
	O_{2k}^3	9	3	1	15	2	10	2	13
J_3	O_{3k}^1	8	6	6	8	3	12	5	10
	O_{3k}^2	4	11	5	8	8	6	1	18

Table 1. Flexible Job-Shop Scheduling Problem

$$f1: C_{\max}^j = \sum_{i \in O(j)} \max_{k \in M}(t_{ij}^k + \tau_{ij}^k) \tag{1}$$

$$f2: \sum_j \sum_i \sum_k x_{jk}^i \upsilon_{jk}^i \tag{2}$$

Where $x_{jk}^i = 1$ if $O_{jk}^i \in E_k$ and 0 otherwise. On the other hand $\sum_k x_{jk}^i = 1$. Besides, $t_{jk}^i = max\ (t_{jh}^{(i-1)} + \tau_{jh}^{(i-1)},\ t_{pk}^s + \tau_{pk}^s,\ 0)$ for each pair O_{jh}^{i-1}, $O_{pk}^s \in E_k$ and all machines M_k, M_h and operations S_i, S_s.

3. Hybrid genetic algorithm

Due to its many advantages, evolutionary algorithms have become very popular for solving multi-objective optimization problems (Ztzler et al., 2001), (Coello Coello et al., 2002). Among the evolutionary algorithms used, some of the most interesting are Genetic Algorithms (GA) (Goldberg, 1989). To represent the individuals, we use a variant of (Wu et al., 2004). Since the Flexible JSSP has two subproblems, the Hybrid Genetic Algorithm (HGA) presented here operates over two chromosomes. The first one represents the allocation A_{jk}^i of each O_{jk}^i to every M_k. We denote with values between 0 and (m - 1) the allocation of each M_k, that is, for m = 4, we might have something like 0→M_1, 1→M_2, 2→M_3 and 3→M_4. The second chromosome represents the sequencing of the O_{jk}^i already assigned to each of the $M_k(\forall O_{jk}^i \in E_k)$. We denote with values between 0 and (n! - 1) the sequence of J_j in each M_k. That is, for n = 3, we may have 0→$J_1J_2J_3$, 1→$J_1J_3J_2$, 2→$J_2J_1J_3$, 3→$J_2J_3J_1$, 4→$J_3J_1J_2$ and 5→$J_3J_2J_1$ (see Table 2).

The algorithm NSGAII (Non-Dominated Sorting Genetic Algorithm II) (Deb et al., 2002), creates an initial population, be it random or otherwise. NSGAII uses an elitist strategy joint with an explicit diversity mechanism. Each individual candidate solution i is assumed to have an associated rank of non-dominance r_i and a distance d_i which indicates the radius of the area in the search space around i not occupied by another solution (see Eq. 3). A solution i is preferred over j if $r_i < r_j$. When i and j have the same rank, i is preferred if $d_i > d_j$. Let Y_i be an ordered class of individuals with same rank as i and f_j^{i+1} the value for objective j for the individual after i, while f_j^{i-1} is the value for the individual before i. $f_j^{\max}$ is the maximal value for j among Y_i while $f_j^{\min}$ is the minimal value among Y_i. The distances consider all the objective functions and attach an infinite value to the extreme solutions in Y_i. Since these yield the best values for one of the objective functions on the frontier, the resulting distance is the sum of the distances for the N objective functions.

MF01 / Problem 3 × 4 with 8 operations (flexible)						
J_j	O_{jk}^i	M_k / Chr.	M_1	M_2	M_3	M_4
			3	3	0	5
J_1	O_{1k}^1	2				
	O_{1k}^2	1				
	O_{1k}^3	0				
J_2	O_{2k}^1	1				
	O_{2k}^2	2				
	O_{2k}^3	3				
J_3	O_{3k}^1	0				
	O_{3k}^2	3				

0→$J_1J_2J_3$, 1→$J_1J_3J_2$, 2→$J_2J_1J_3$, 3→$J_2J_3J_1$, 4→$J_3J_1J_2$ and 5→$J_3J_2J_1$ / 0→MB_{1B}, 1→MB_{2B}, 2→MB_{3B}, 3→MB_4

Table 2. Chromosome encoding process

$$d_i = \sum_{j=1}^{N} (f_j^{i+1} - f_j^{i-1}) / (f_j^{max} - a_j^{min}) \tag{3}$$

Starting with a population P_t a new population of descendants Q_t obtains. These two populations mix to yield a new one, R_t of size $2N$ (N is the original size of P_t). The individuals in R_t are ranked with respect the frontier and a new population P_{t+1} obtains applying a tournament selection to R_t. After experimenting with several genetic operators we have chosen the uniform crossover for the crossover and two-swap for mutation (Fonseca & Fleming, 1995). After the individuals have been affected by these operators and before allowing them to become part of a new population we apply an improvement operator (Frutos & Tohmé, 2009). This operator has been designed following the guidelines of Simulated Annealing (Dowsland, 1993). This complements the genetic procedure. For the change of structure of both chromosomes we select a gene at random and change its value. This is repeated $M = (1/T) + \omega$, where T corresponds to the actual temperature determined up from a cooling coefficient (α) while ω is a control parameter ensuring sufficient permutations, particularly when the temperature is high. Summarizing all this, the relevant parameters for this phase of the procedure are the initial temperature (T_i), the final one (T_f), the cooling parameter (α) and the control parameter (ω). The general layout of the whole procedure is depicted in Fig. 1.

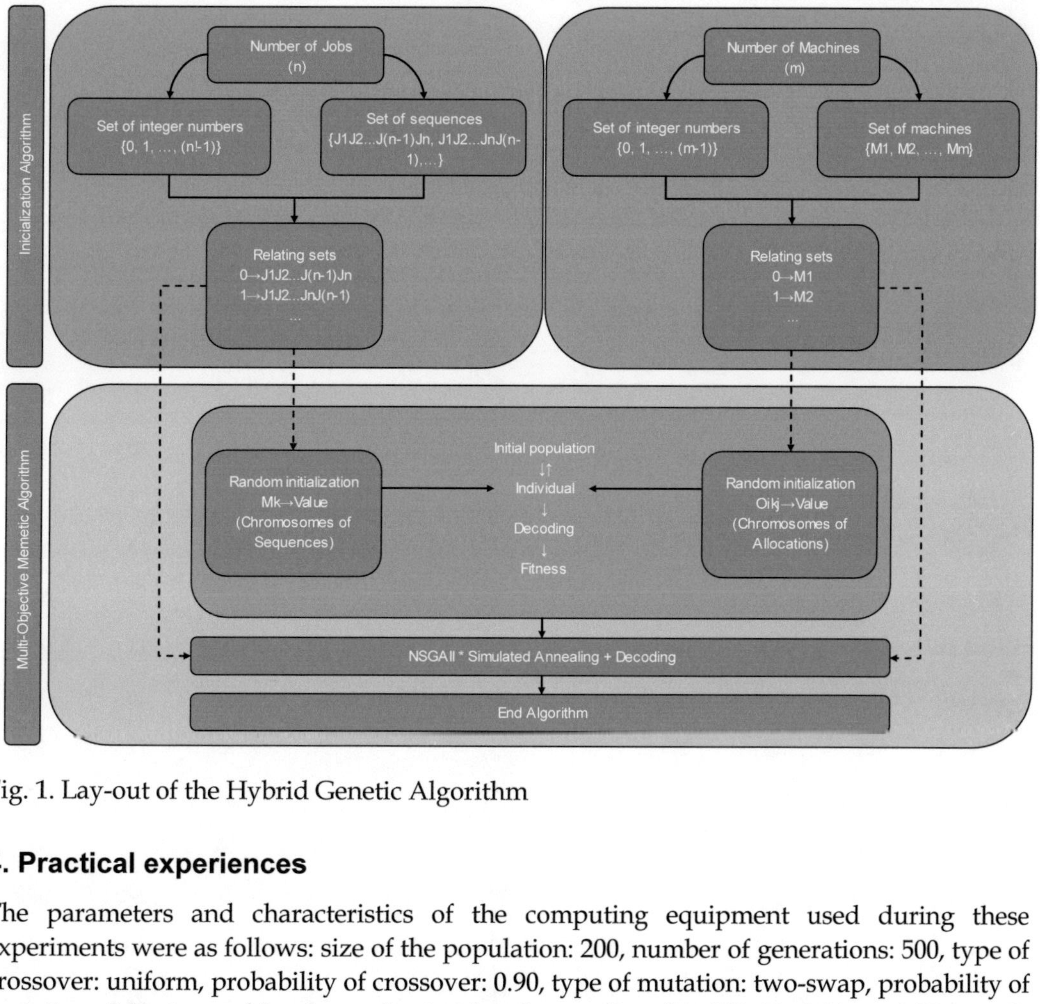

Fig. 1. Lay-out of the Hybrid Genetic Algorithm

4. Practical experiences

The parameters and characteristics of the computing equipment used during these experiments were as follows: size of the population: 200, number of generations: 500, type of crossover: uniform, probability of crossover: 0.90, type of mutation: two-swap, probability of mutation: 0.01, type of local search: simulated annealing (T_i: 850, T_f: 0.01, α: 0.95, ω: 10), probability of local search: 0.01, CPU: 3.00 GHZ and RAM: 1.00 GB. We worked with the PISA tool (A Platform and Programming Language Independent Interface for Search Algorithms) (Bleuler et al., 2003). The results obtained by means of HGA were compared to those yield by Greedy Randomized Adaptive Search Procedures (GRASP) (Binato et al., 2001), Taboo Search (TS) (Armentano & Scrich, 2000) and Ant Colony Optimization (ACO) (Heinonen & Pettersson, 2007). For the problems MF01, MF02, MF03, MF04 and MF05 (Frutos et al., 2010), we show the results for the multi-objective analysis based on Makespan (f_1, (1)) and Total Operation Costs (f_2, (2)). They were obtained by running each algorithm 10 times.

For each algorithm the sets of undominated solutions $P_1, P_2, ..., P_{10}$ were obtained as well as the superpopulation $P_T = P_1 \cup P_2 \cup ... \cup P_{10}$. From each superpopulation a class of undominated solutions was extracted, constituting the Pareto frontier for each algorithm. To obtain an approximation to the true Pareto front (Approximate Pareto Frontier), we take the fronts of each algorithm, from which all the dominated solutions are eliminated. These are detailed in Table 3 (MF01), Table 4 (MF02), Table 5 (MF03), Table 6 (MF04) and Table 7 (MF05), and are shown in Fig. 2 (MF01), Fig. 3 (MF02), Fig. 4 (MF03), Fig. 5 (MF04) and Fig. 6 (MF05).

MF01 / Problem 3 × 4 with 8 operations (flexible)										
	HGA [1]		GRASP [2]		TS [3]		ACO [4]		Approach	
Solutions	f_1	f_2	f_1	f_2	f_1	f_2	f_1	f_2	f_1	f_2
3x4_1	6	66	6	70	6	66	6	66	6	66
3x4_2	7	62	7	65	7	62	7	62	7	62
3x4_3	8	55	8	61	8	55	8	57	8	55
3x4_4	9	51	9	57	9	51	9	51	9	51
3x4_5	10	47	10	50	10	48	10	47	10	47
3x4_6	11	43	11	47	11	44	11	43	11	43
3x4_7	13	42	13	43	13	43	13	42	13	42
3x4_8	-	-	-	-	15	41	-	-	15	41
3x4_9	17	40	17	40	-	-	17	40	17	40
3x4_10	-	-	-	-	20	39	-	-	20	39
3x4_11	22	38	22	38	-	-	22	38	22	38
3x4_12	-	-	-	-	25	37	-	-	25	37
3x4_13	27	36	27	37	-	-	27	36	27	36
3x4_14	28	35	28	35	28	35	28	35	28	35
3x4_15	30	34	30	34	30	34	30	34	30	34
3x4_16	31	33	-	-	31	33	31	33	31	33
3x4_17	32	31	32	32	32	32	32	32	32	31
3x4_18	35	29	35	29	35	29	35	29	35	29
Mean Time	5,325 sec.		2,147 sec.		4,673 sec.		3,218 sec.		-	

[1](Frutos et al., 2010), [2](Binato et al., 2001), [3](Armentano & Scrich, 2000) and [4](Heinonen & Pettersson, 2007)

Table 3. Solutions for MF01

MF02 / Problem 4 × 5 with 12 operations (flexible)										
	HGA (1)		GRASP (2)		TS (3)		ACO (4)		Approach	
Solutions	f_1	f_2	f_1	f_2	f_1	f_2	f_1	f_2	f_1	f_2
4x5_1	16	148	16	152	16	148	16	148	16	148
4x5_2	17	142	17	146	17	142	17	142	17	142
4x5_3	19	139	19	140	19	139	19	140	19	139
4x5_4	20	135	20	136	20	136	20	135	20	135
4x5_5	22	130	22	132	22	130	22	130	22	130
4x5_6	25	124	25	128	25	124	25	124	25	124
4x5_7	26	122	26	122	26	122	26	122	26	122
4x5_8	28	118	28	118	28	118	28	118	28	118
4x5_9	-	-	-	-	30	117	30	117	30	117
4x5_10	31	115	31	116	31	115	-	-	31	115
4x5_11	34	108	34	110	34	110	34	108	34	108
4x5_12	38	102	38	102	-	-	38	102	38	102
4x5_13	39	99	39	100	39	99	39	99	39	99
4x5_14	42	95	42	97	42	95	42	95	42	95
4x5_15	45	90	45	94	45	90	45	94	45	90
4x5_16	50	81	50	83	50	83	50	81	50	81
4x5_17	52	79	52	79	52	79	53	79	52	79
4x5_18	56	68	56	72	-	-	56	72	56	68
4x5_19	-	-	-	-	57	67	-	-	57	67
4x5_20	58	65	-	-	58	65	58	65	58	65
4x5_21	61	60	61	60	61	60	61	60	61	60
4x5_22	63	57	63	58	63	58	63	58	63	57
4x5_23	-	-	-	-	-	-	65	55	65	55
4x5_24	66	53	66	53	66	53	66	53	66	53
4x5_25	67	50	67	52	67	50	-	-	67	50
4x5_26	-	-	-	-	68	48	-	-	68	48
4x5_27	69	42	69	46	69	42	69	42	69	42
4x5_28	71	36	71	36	71	36	71	36	71	36
Mean Time	15,885 sec.		6,405 sec.		13,940 sec.		9,602 sec.		-	

(1)(Frutos et al., 2010), (2)(Binato et al., 2001), (3)(Armentano & Scrich, 2000) and (4)(Heinonen & Pettersson, 2007)

Table 4. Solutions for MF02

MF03 / Problem 10 × 7 with 29 operations (flexible)										
	HGA (1)		GRASP (2)		TS (3)		ACO (4)		Approach	
Solutions	f_1	f_2	f_1	f_2	f_1	f_2	f_1	f_2	f_1	f_2
10x7_1	15	393	15	393	15	393	15	393	15	393
10x7_2	16	387	16	391	16	387	16	387	16	387
10x7_3	17	383	17	385	17	383	17	383	17	383
10x7_4	18	379	18	379	18	379	18	379	18	379
10x7_5	19	375	19	375	19	375	19	375	19	375
10x7_6	21	368	21	372	21	368	21	368	21	368
10x7_7	23	360	23	360	23	360	23	360	23	360
10x7_8	24	351	24	355	24	351	24	351	24	351
10x7_9	25	347	-	-	25	347	-	-	25	347
10x7_10	27	342	27	342	27	342	27	342	27	342
10x7_11	33	319	33	325	33	319	33	319	33	319
10x7_12	37	291	37	297	37	295	37	295	37	291
10x7_13	45	260	45	260	45	260	45	260	45	260
10x7_14	50	238	50	241	50	238	50	238	50	238
10x7_15	61	194	61	211	61	202	61	202	61	194
10x7_16	-	-	-	-	72	150	72	158	72	150
10x7_17	78	137	78	142	78	137	78	137	78	137
10x7_18	89	98	89	107	89	104	89	98	89	98
10x7_19	96	82	-	-	-	-	-	-	96	82
10x7_20	109	48	-	-	109	57	109	48	109	48
10x7_21	116	34	116	41	116	34	116	34	116	34
10x7_22	122	29	122	29	122	29	122	29	122	29
Mean Time	21,502 sec.		7,669 sec.		18,869 sec.		15,994 sec.		-	

(1)(Frutos et al., 2010), (2)(Binato et al., 2001), (3)(Armentano & Scrich, 2000) and (4)(Heinonen & Pettersson, 2007)

Table 5. Solutions for MF03

MF04 / Problem 10 × 10 with 30 operations (flexible)										
	HGA (1)		GRASP (2)		TS (3)		ACO (4)		Approach	
Solutions	f_1	f_2	f_1	f_2	f_1	f_2	f_1	f_2	f_1	f_2
10x10_1	7	282	7	282	7	282	7	282	7	282
10x10_2	8	267	8	274	8	267	8	267	8	267
10x10_3	10	254	10	254	10	254	10	254	10	254
10x10_4	11	241	11	246	11	241	11	241	11	241
10x10_5	13	224	13	224	13	224	13	224	13	224
10x10_6	15	205	15	205	15	205	15	205	15	205
10x10_7	16	198	16	198	16	198	16	198	16	198
10x10_8	-	-	-	-	18	186	-	-	18	186
10x10_9	19	176	19	185	19	176	19	180	19	176
10x10_10	23	148	23	148	23	148	23	148	23	148
10x10_11	25	137	25	137	25	137	25	137	25	137
10x10_12	28	113	-	-	-	-	-	-	28	113
10x10_13	29	107	29	115	29	107	29	111	29	107
10x10_14	31	87	31	96	31	90	31	90	31	87
10x10_15	33	78	33	83	33	78	33	78	33	78
10x10_16	34	73	34	73	34	73	34	73	34	73
10x10_17	36	62	36	67	36	62	36	62	36	62
10x10_18	37	58	37	58	37	58	37	58	37	58
10x10_19	38	57	38	57	38	57	38	57	38	57
10x10_20	41	51	41	54	41	55	41	55	41	51
10x10_21	44	49	44	51	44	49	44	49	44	49
10x10_22	47	43	47	48	-	-	-	-	47	43
10x10_23	50	42	50	42	50	42	50	42	50	42
10x10_24	53	40	53	40	53	40	53	40	53	40
10x10_25	-	-	-	-	-	-	56	37	56	37
10x10_26	57	34	57	34	57	34	57	34	57	34
10x10_27	60	30	60	30	60	30	60	30	60	30
Mean Time	31,439 sec.		11,214 sec.		27,590 sec.		22,999 sec.		-	

(1)(Frutos et al., 2010), (2)(Binato et al., 2001), (3)(Armentano & Scrich, 2000) and (4)(Heinonen & Pettersson, 2007)

Table 6. Solutions for MF04

MF05 / Problem 15 × 10 with 56 operations (flexible)										
	HGA (1)		GRASP (2)		TS (3)		ACO (4)		Approach	
Solutions	f_1	f_2	f_1	f_2	f_1	f_2	f_1	f_2	f_1	f_2
15x10_1	23	799	23	799	23	799	23	799	23	799
15x10_2	25	749	25	749	25	749	25	749	25	749
15x10_3	26	731	26	731	26	731	26	731	26	731
15x10_4	27	719	27	719	27	719	27	719	27	719
15x10_5	30	678	30	693	30	678	30	687	30	678
15x10_6	32	646	-	-	-	-	32	646	32	646
15x10_7	33	631	33	631	33	631	33	631	33	631
15x10_8	35	609	35	615	35	609	35	609	35	609
15x10_9	38	575	38	587	38	578	38	575	38	575
15x10_10	-	-	-	-	41	561	41	561	41	561
15x10_11	41	519	43	519	43	519	43	519	43	519
15x10_12	44	484	44	484	44	484	44	484	44	484
15x10_13	46	437	46	452	46	448	46	437	46	437
15x10_14	49	411	49	411	49	411	49	411	49	411
15x10_15	52	379	52	379	52	379	52	379	52	379
15x10_16	53	346	53	346	53	346	53	346	53	346
15x10_17	55	314	55	322	55	318	55	318	55	314
15x10_18	57	276	-	-	-	-	-	-	56	276
15x10_19	-	-	-	-	58	266	-	-	58	266
15x10_20	62	220	62	242	62	232	62	242	62	220
15x10_21	67	209	67	212	67	209	67	209	67	209
15x10_22	71	195	71	204	71	195	71	195	71	195
15x10_23	75	178	75	181	75	178	75	178	75	178
15x10_24	88	153	88	157	88	153	88	153	88	153
15x10_25	92	135	92	147	92	140	92	140	92	135
15x10_26	101	122	101	134	101	129	101	122	101	122
15x10_27	112	114	112	125	112	114	112	114	112	114
15x10_28	-	-	-	-	-	-	119	97	119	97
15x10_29	127	86	127	86	127	86	127	86	127	86
15x10_30	135	73	135	73	135	73	135	73	135	73
15x10_31	138	56	138	56	138	56	138	56	138	56
Mean Time	42,288 sec.		15,084 sec.		37,110 sec.		35,552 sec.		-	

(1)(Frutos et al., 2010), (2)(Binato et al., 2001), (3)(Armentano & Scrich, 2000) and (4)(Heinonen & Pettersson, 2007)

Table 7. Solutions for MF05

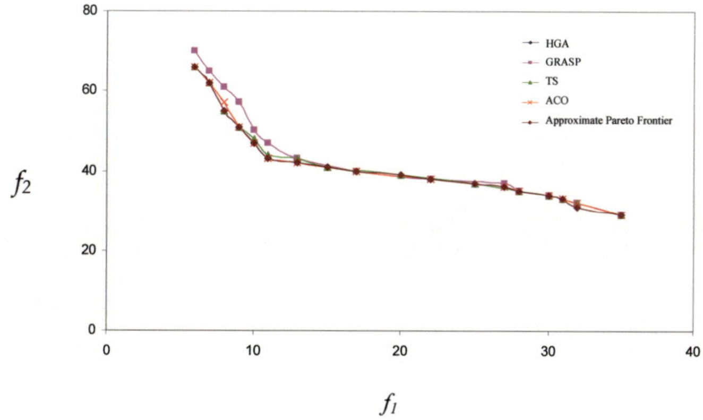

Fig. 2. Makespan *vs.* Total Operation Costs (MF01)

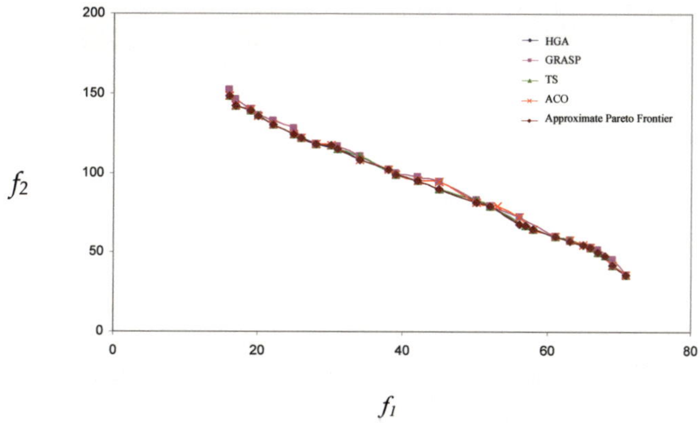

Fig. 3. Makespan *vs.* Total Operation Costs (MF02)

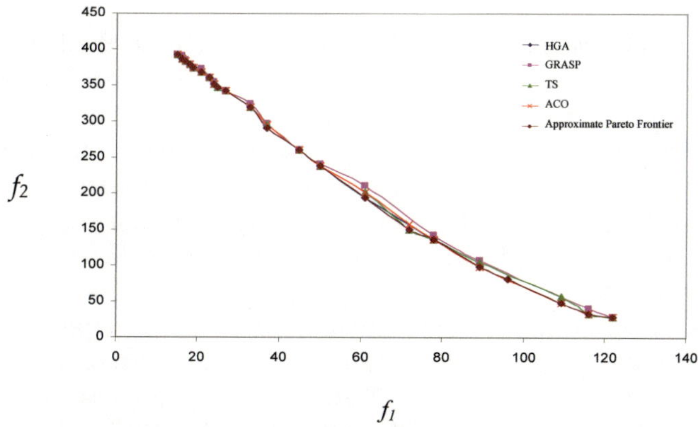

Fig. 4. Makespan *vs.* Total Operation Costs (MF03)

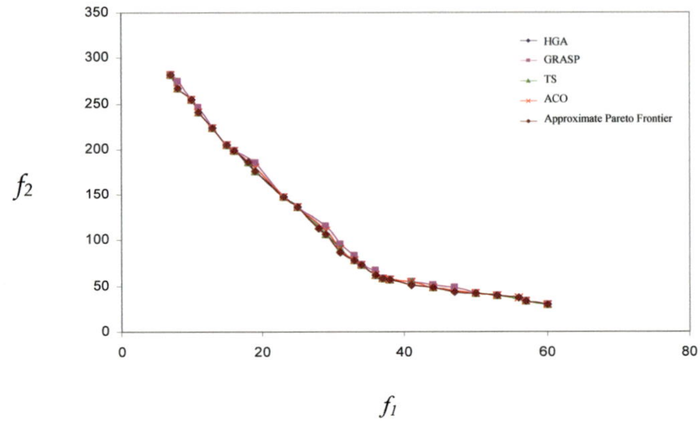

Fig. 5. Makespan *vs.* Total Operation Costs (MF04)

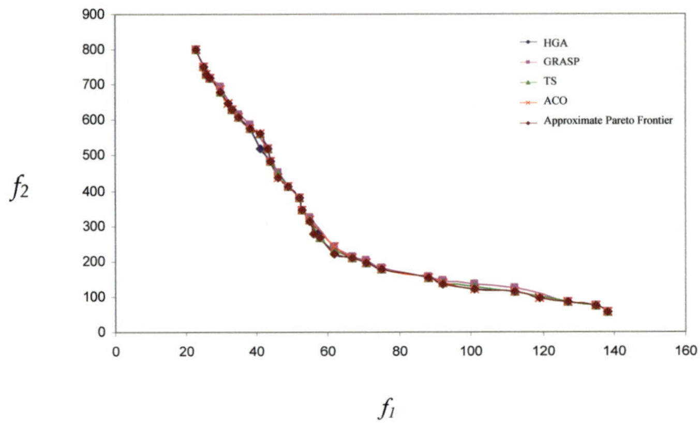

Fig. 6. Makespan *vs.* Total Operation Costs (MF05)

In order to compare the results of the algorithms and establish the better option for the Flexible JSSP, several tests were applied over the solutions. First, we consider a dominance ranking among the different algorithms. One-tailed Mann-Whitney rank sum (Conover, 1999) was run over the results (Ranktest, Table 8 (MF01), Table 9 (MF02), Table 10 (MF03), Table 11 (MF04) and Table 12 (MF05)). The outcomes are summarized in Table 1. None of the results for MF01, MF02, MF03, MF04 and MF05 is statistically significant at an overall significance level α=0.05. This indicates that no algorithm generate approximation sets that are significantly better. Next, we considered unary quality indicators using normalized approximation sets. Then, we applied the unary indicators (unary hypervolume indicator I_H, unary epsilon indicatior I_e^1 and R indicator I_{R2}^1) on the normalized approximation sets as well as on the reference set generated by PISA (I_H, I_e^1 and I_{R2}^1, Table 8 (MF01), Table 9 (MF02), Table 10 (MF03), Table 11 (MF04) and Table 12 (MF05)). Again, no significant differences were found at the 0.05 level.

Test for Problem MF01				
Ranktest				
	HGA	GRASP	TS	ACO
HGA	-	0,4668807	0,5248382	0,5000000
GRASP	0,5331193	-	0,5578024	0,5331193
TS	0,4751618	0,4421976	-	0,4751618
ACO	0,5000000	0,4668807	0,5248382	-
I_H				
	HGA	GRASP	TS	ACO
HGA	-	0,4849375	0,5193377	0,5451365
GRASP	0,5150625	-	0,5537379	0,5782757
TS	0,4806623	0,4462621	-	0,5793756
ACO	0,4548635	0,4217243	0,4206244	-
I_e^1				
	HGA	GRASP	TS	ACO
HGA	-	0,4668807	0,5000000	0,5248382
GRASP	0,5331193	-	0,5331193	0,5567435
TS	0,5000000	0,4668807	-	0,5578024
ACO	0,4751618	0,4421976	0,4751618	-
I_{R2}^1				
	HGA	GRASP	TS	ACO
HGA	-	0,4560385	0,4883887	0,5126501
GRASP	0,5439615	-	0,5207389	0,5438144
TS	0,5116113	0,4792611	-	0,5448488
ACO	0,4873499	0,4561856	0,4551512	-

Table 8. Comparing HGA, GRASP, TS and ACO (MF01)

Test for Problem MF02				
Ranktest				
	HGA	GRASP	TS	ACO
HGA	-	0,4507347	0,4364051	0,5123441
GRASP	0,5492653	-	0,4920168	0,5614884
TS	0,5635949	0,5079832	-	0,5792996
ACO	0,4876559	0,4385116	0,4207004	-
I_H				
	HGA	GRASP	TS	ACO
HGA	-	0,4554712	0,5065161	0,4369711
GRASP	0,5445288	-	0,5705083	0,5110457
TS	0,4934839	0,4294917	-	0,4532833
ACO	0,5630289	0,4889543	0,5467167	-
I_e^1				
	HGA	GRASP	TS	ACO
HGA	-	0,4385116	0,4876559	0,4207004
GRASP	0,5614884	-	0,5492653	0,4920168
TS	0,5123441	0,4507347	-	0,4364051

ACO	0,5792996	0,5079832	0,5635949	-
		I_{R2}^{1}		
	HGA	GRASP	TS	ACO
HGA	-	0,4283282	0,4763312	0,4109306
GRASP	0,5716718	-	0,5365099	0,4805909
TS	0,5236688	0,4634901	-	0,4262707
ACO	0,5890694	0,5194091	0,5737293	-

Table 9. Comparing HGA, GRASP, TS and ACO (MF02)

		Test for Problem MF03		
		Ranktest		
	HGA	GRASP	TS	ACO
HGA	-	0,6430292	0,5250930	0,5052068
GRASP	0,3569708	-	0,3782149	0,3627307
TS	0,4749070	0,6217851	-	0,4791809
ACO	0,4947932	0,6372693	0,5208191	-
		I_H		
	HGA	GRASP	TS	ACO
HGA	-	0,6619159	0,5139296	0,5409620
GRASP	0,3380841	-	0,3707768	0,3928425
TS	0,4860704	0,6292232	-	0,5454012
ACO	0,4590380	0,6071575	0,4545988	-
		I_e^{1}		
	HGA	GRASP	TS	ACO
HGA	-	0,6372693	0,4947932	0,5208191
GRASP	0,3627307	-	0,3569708	0,3782149
TS	0,5052068	0,6430292	-	0,5250930
ACO	0,4791809	0,6217851	0,4749070	-
		I_{R2}^{1}		
	HGA	GRASP	TS	ACO
HGA	-	0,6224702	0,4833028	0,5087244
GRASP	0,3775298	-	0,3486810	0,3694317
TS	0,5166972	0,6513190	-	0,5128990
ACO	0,4912756	0,6305683	0,4871010	-

Table 10. Comparing HGA, GRASP, TS and ACO (MF03)

		Test for Problem MF04		
		Ranktest		
	HGA	GRASP	TS	ACO
HGA	-	0,4840368	0,5910066	0,4641226
GRASP	0,5159632	-	0,6017605	0,4794311
TS	0,4089934	0,3982395	-	0,3824045
ACO	0,5358774	0,5205689	0,6175955	-
		I_H		
	HGA	GRASP	TS	ACO

HGA	-	0,5407021	0,5566027	0,6414813
GRASP	0,4592979	-	0,5359183	0,6250339
TS	0,4433973	0,4640817	-	0,6138640
ACO	0,3585187	0,3749661	0,3861360	-
		$I_e{}^1$		
	HGA	GRASP	TS	ACO
HGA	-	0,5205689	0,5358774	0,6175955
GRASP	0,4794311	-	0,5159632	0,6017605
TS	0,4641226	0,4840368	-	0,5910066
ACO	0,3824045	0,3982395	0,4089934	-
		$I_{R2}{}^1$		
	HGA	GRASP	TS	ACO
HGA	-	0,5084799	0,5234329	0,6032533
GRASP	0,4915201	-	0,5039812	0,5877861
TS	0,4765671	0,4960188	-	0,5772819
ACO	0,3967467	0,4122139	0,4227181	-

Table 11. Comparing HGA, GRASP, TS and ACO (MF04)

		Test for Problem MF05		
		Ranktest		
	HGA	GRASP	TS	ACO
HGA	-	0,4551815	0,4673350	0,4713557
GRASP	0,5448185	-	0,5207202	0,5201772
TS	0,5326650	0,4792798	-	0,5031851
ACO	0,5286443	0,4798228	0,4968146	-
		I_H		
	HGA	GRASP	TS	ACO
HGA	-	0,4983801	0,5501285	0,5160291
GRASP	0,5016199	-	0,5658896	0,5408593
TS	0,4498715	0,4341104	-	0,4854094
ACO	0,4839709	0,4591407	0,5145906	-
		$I_e{}^1$		
	HGA	GRASP	TS	ACO
HGA	-	0,4798228	0,5296443	0,4968146
GRASP	0,5201772	-	0,5448185	0,5207202
TS	0,4713557	0,4551815	-	0,4673350
ACO	0,5031557	0,4792798	0,5326650	-
		$I_{R2}{}^1$		
	HGA	GRASP	TS	ACO
HGA	-	0,4686801	0,5173445	0,4852773
GRASP	0,5313199	-	0,5321664	0,5086278
TS	0,4826555	0,4678336	-	0,4564823
ACO	0,5147227	0,4913722	0,5435177	-

Table 12. Comparing HGA, GRASP, TS and ACO (MF05)

Finally, we note that there are no major differences between the Pareto frontiers generated by the four algorithms. Therefore, we calculated the percentage of solutions provided by each algorithm that belong to the Approximate Pareto Frontier (see Table 13).

Percentage of solutions in the Approximate Pareto Frontier				
	HGA (1)	GRASP (2)	TS (3)	ACO (4)
MF01	83,33%	27,78%	61,11%	72,22%
MF02	85,71%	25,00%	75,00%	71,43%
MF03	95,45%	31,82%	77,27%	77,27%
MF04	92,59%	51,85%	81,48%	74,07%
MF05	90,32%	45,16%	70,97%	80,65%

(1) (Frutos et al., 2010), (2)(Binato et al., 2001), (3)(Armentano & Scrich, 2000) and (4)(Heinonen & Pettersson, 2007)

Table 13. Comparing HGA, GRASP, TS and ACO (MF01, MF02, MF03, MF04 and MF05)

5. Conclusions

We presented a Hybrid Genetic Algorithm (HGA) intended to solve the Flexible Job-Shop Scheduling Problem (Flexible JSSP). The application of HGA required the calibration of parameters, in order to yield valid values for the problem at hand, which constitute also a reference for similar problems. We have shown that this HGA yields more solutions in the Approximate Pareto Frontier than other algorithms. As said above, PISA has been used here as a guide for the implementation of our HGA. Nevertheless, PISA itself has features that we tried to overcome, making the understanding and extension of its outcomes a little bit hard. JMetal (Meta-heuristic Algorithms in Java) (Durillo et al., 2006) is already an alternative to PISA implemented on JAVA. We are currently experimenting with other techniques of local search in order to achieve a more aggressive exploration. We are also interested in evaluating the performance of the procedure over other kinds of problems to see whether it saves resources without sacrificing precision in convergence.

6. Acknowledgments

We would like to thank the economic support of the Consejo Nacional de Investigaciones Científicas y Técnicas (CONICET) and the Universidad Nacional del Sur (UNS) for Grant PGI 24/JO56.

7. References

Adams, J.; Balas, E. & Zawack, D. (1998). The Shifting Bottleneck Procedure for job shop scheduling, *Management Science*, Vol. 34 (3), pp 391-401.

Akers, S. B. & Friedman, J. (1955). A Non-Numerical Approach to Production Scheduling Problems, *Operations Research*, Vol. 3 (4), pp 429-442.

Armentano, V. & Scrich, C. (2000). Taboo search for minimizing total tardiness in a job-shop, *International Journal of Production Economics*, Vol. 63, pp 131-140.

Balas, E. (1969). Duality in Discrete Programming: The Quadratic Case, *Management Science*, Vol. 16 (1), pp 14-32.

Binato, S.; Hery, W. J.; Loewenstern, D. M. & Resende, M. G. C. (2001). A grasp for job shop scheduling, *Essays and Surveys in Meta-heuristics*, pp. 59-80.

Bleuler, S.; Laumanns, M.; Thiele, L. & Zitzler, E. (2003). PISA, A Platform and Programming Language Independent Interface for Search Algorithms, *Proceedings of Evolutionary Multi-Criterion Optimization*, pp. 494-508.

Chao-Hsien, J. & Han-Chiang, H. (2009). A hybrid genetic algorithm for no-wait job shop cheduling problems, *Expert Systems with Applications*, Vol. 36 (3), pp 5800-5806.

Cheng, C. C. & Smith, S. F. (1997). Applyng constraint satisfaction techniques to job shop scheduling, *Annals of Operations Research*, Vol. 70, pp 327-357.

Chinyao, L. & Yuling, Y. (2009). Genetic algorithm-based heuristics for an open shop scheduling problem with setup, processing, and removal times separated, *Robotics and Computer-Integrated Manufacturing*, Vol. 25 (2), pp 314-322.

Coello Coello, C. A.; Van Veldhuizen, D. A. & Lamont, G. B. (2002). Evolutionary Algorithms for Solving Multi-Objective Problems, *Kluwer Academic Publishers*, New York.

Conover, W. (1999). Practical Nonparametric Statistics. *John Wiley & Sons*, New York.

Cortés Rivera, D.; Coello Coello, C. A. & Cortés, N. C. (2004). Job shop scheduling using the clonal selection principle, *ACDM'2004*, UK.

Cortés Rivera, D.; Coello Coello, C. A. & Cortés, N. C. (2003). Use of an Artificial Immune System for Job Shop Scheduling, *Proceedings of Second International Conference on Artificial Immune Systems*, Edinburgh, Scotland. Springer-Verlag, Lecture Notes in Computer Science, Vol. 2787, pp 1-10.

Crawford, J. M. & Baker, A. B. (1994). Experimental Results on the Application of Satisfiability Algorithms to Scheduling Problems, *Computational Intelligence Research Laboratory*.

De Giovanni, L. & Pezzella, F. (2010). An Improved Genetic Algorithm for the Distributed and Flexible Jobshop Scheduling problem, *European Journal of Operational Research*, Vol. 200 (2), pp 395-408.

Deb, K.; Pratap, A.; Agarwal, S. & Meyarivan, T. (2002). A Fast and Elitist Multi-objective Genetic Algorithm: NSGAII, *IEEE Transactions on Evolutionary Computation*, Vol. 6 (2), pp 182-197.

Dowsland, K. A. (1993). Simulated Annealing, Modern Heuristic Techniques for Combinatorial Problems, Ed. C. R. Reeves, *Blackwell Scientific Pub*, Oxford.

Durillo, J. J.; Nebro, A. J.; Luna Dorronsoro B. & Alba E. (2006). JMetal: A Java Framework for Developing Multi-Objective Optimization Metaheuristics. Departamento de Lenguajes y Ciencias de la Computación. University of Málaga. *E.T.S.I. Informática*, Campus de Teatinos.

Fonseca, C. M. & Fleming, P. J. (1995). Multi-objective genetic algorithms made easy: Selection, sharing and mating restriction, *GALESIA*, pp 45-52.

Frutos, M.; Olivera, A. C. & Tohmé, F. (2010). A Memetic Algorithm based on a NSGAII Scheme for the Flexible Job-Shop Scheduling Problem, *Annals of Operations Research*, Vol. 181, pp 745-765.

Frutos, M.; & Tohmé, F. (2009). Desarrollo de un procedimiento genético diseñado para programar la producción en un sistema de manufactura tipo job-shop, *Proceedings of VI Congreso Español sobre Meta-heurísticas, Algoritmos Evolutivos y Bioinspirados*, España.

Giffler, B. & Thomson, G. L. (1960). Algorithms for Solving Production Scheduling Problems, *Operations Reseach*, Vol. 8, pp 487-503.

Goldberg, D. (1989). Genetic Algorithms in Search, Optimization, and Machine Learning, Addison Wesley.

Heinonen, J. & Pettersson, F. (2007). Hybrid ant colony optimization and visibility studies applied to a job-shop scheduling problem, *Applied Mathematics and Computation*, pp 989-998.

Jackson J. R. (1956). An Extension of Johnson's Results on Job Lot Scheduling, *Naval Research Logistics Quarterly*, Vol. 2, pp 201-203.

Johnson, S. M. (1954). Optimal two- and three-stage production schedules with setup times included, *Naval Research Logistics Quarterly*, Vol. 1, pp 61-68.

Kacem, I.; Hammadi, S. & Borne, P. (2002). Approach by Localization and Multi-Objective Evolutionary Optimization for Flexible Job-Shop Scheduling Problems, *IEEE Trans. Syst. Man Cybernetics*, Vol. 32.

Merkle, D. & Middendorf, M. (2001). A new approach to solve permutation scheduling problems with ant colony optimization, *Proceedings of Applications of Evolutionary Computing*, EvoWorkshops 2001, Vol. 2037, pp 484-494.

Muth, J. F. & Thompson, G. L. (1964). Industrial Scheduling, Prentice-Hall Inc.

Olivera, A. C.; Frutos, M. & Casal, R. (2006). Métodos para determinar secuencias de producción en un ambiente productivo complejo, *Proceedings of XIII Congreso Latino-Iberoamericano de Investigación Operativa*, Uruguay.

Panwalker, S. & Iskander, W. (1977). A survey of scheduling rules, *Operations Research*, Vol. 25 (1), pp 45-61.

Roy, B. & Sussman, B. (1964). Les problèmes d'ordonnancement avec contraintes disjonctives, *SEMA*.

Sadeh, N. M. & Fox, M. S. (1995). Variable and value ordering heuristics for the Job Shop scheduling constraint satisfaction problem, Tecnical report CMU-RI-TR-95-39, *Artificial Intelligence Journal*.

Tsai, C. F. & Lin, F. C. (2003). A new hybrid heuristic technique for solving job-shop scheduling problem, *Intelligent Data Acquisition and Advanced Computing Systems, Second IEEE International Workshop*.

Ullman, J. D. (1975). NP-complete scheduling problems. *Journal of Computer System sciences*, Vol. 10, pp 384-393.

Wu, C. G.; Xing, X. L.; Lee, H. P.; Zhou, C. G. & Liang, Y. C. (2004). Genetic Algorithm Application on the Job Shop Scheduling Problem, *Machine Learning and Cybernetics, International Conference*, Vol. 4, pp 2102- 2106.

Zalzala, A. M. S. & Flemming, P. J. (1997). Genetic Algorithms in engineering systems, *London Institution of Electrical Engineers*.

6

A Hybrid Parallel Genetic Algorithm for Reliability Optimization

Ki Tae Kim and Geonwook Jeon
Korea National Defense University,
Republic of Korea

1. Introduction

Reliability engineering is known to have been first applied to communication and transportation systems in the late 1940's and early 1950's. Reliability is the probability that an item will perform a required function without failure under stated conditions for a stated period of time. Therefore a system with high reliability can be likened to a system which has a superior quality. Reliability is one of the most important design factors in the successful and effective operation of complex technological systems. As explained by Tzafestas (1980), one of the essential steps in the design of multiple component systems is the problem of using the available resources in the most effective way so as to maximize the system reliability, or so as to minimize the consumption of resources while achieving specific reliability goals. The improvement of system reliability can be accomplished using the following methods: reduction of the system complexity, the allocation highly reliable components, and the allocation of component redundancy alone or combined with high component reliability, and the practice of a planned maintenance and repair schedule. This study deals with reliability optimization that maximizes the system reliability subject to resource constraints.

This study suggests mathematical programming models and a hybrid parallel genetic algorithm (HPGA). The suggested algorithm includes different heuristics such as swap, 2-opt, and interchange (except for reliability allocation problem with component choices (RAPCC)) for an improvement solution. The component structure, reliability, cost, and weight were computed by using HPGA and the experimental results of HPGA were compared with the results of existing meta-heuristics and CPLEX.

2. Literature review

The goal of reliability optimization is to maximize the reliability of a system considering some constraints such as cost, weight, and so on. In general, reliability optimization divides into two categories: the reliability-redundancy allocation problem (RRAP) and the reliability allocation problem with component choices (RAPCC).

2.1 The reliability-redundancy allocation problem (RRAP)

The RRAP is the determination of both optimal component reliability and the number of component redundancy allowing mixed components to maximize the system reliability under cost and weight constraints. It is known as the NP-hard problem suggested by Chern (1992).

A variety of algorithms, as summarized in Tillman et al. (1977), and more recently by Kuo & Prasad (2000), Kuo & Wan (2007), including exact methods, heuristics and meta-heuristics have already been proposed for the RRAP. An exact optimal solution is obtained by exact methods such as cutting plane method (Tillman, 1969), branch-and-bound algorithm (Chern & Jan, 1986; Ghare & Taylor, 1969), dynamic programming (Bellman & Dreyfus, 1958; Fyffe et al., 1968; Nakagawa & Miyazaki, 1981; Yalaoui et al., 2005), and goal programming (Gen et al., 1989). However, as the size of problem gets larger, such methods are difficult to apply to get a solution and require more computational effort. Therefore, heuristics and meta-heuristics are used to find a near-optimal solution in recent research.

The research using heuristics is as follows. Kuo et al. (1987) present a heuristic method based on a branch-and-bound strategy and lagrangian multipliers. Jianping (1996) has developed a method called a bounded heuristic method. You & Chen (2005) proposed an efficient heuristic method. Meta-heuristics such as genetic algorithm (Coit & Smith, 1996; Ida et al., 1994; Painton & Campbell, 1995), tabu search (Kulturel-Konak et al., 2003), ant colony optimization (Liang & Smith, 2004), and immune algorithm (Chen & You, 2005) have been introduced to solve the RRAP.

2.2 The reliability allocation problem with component choices (RAPCC)

The RAPCC is the determination of optimal component reliability to maximize the system reliability under cost constraint. A problem is formulated as a binary integer programming model with a nonlinear objective function (Ait-Kadi & Nourelfath, 2001), which is equivalent to a knapsack problem with multiple-choice constraint, so that it is the NP-hard problem (Garey & Johnson, 1979). Some algorithms for such knapsack problems with multiple-choice constraint have been suggested in the literature (Nauss, 1978; Sinha & Zoltners, 1979; Sung & Lee, 1994).

A variety of algorithms including exact methods, heuristics, and meta-heuristics have already been proposed for the RAPCC. An exact optimal solution is obtained by branch-and-bound algorithm (Djerdjour & Rekab, 2001; Sung & Cho, 1999). Meta-heuristics such as neural network (Nourelfath & Nahas, 2003), simulated annealing (Kim et al., 2004; Kim et al., 2008), tabu search (Kim et al., 2008), and ant colony optimization (Nahas & Nourelfath, 2005) have been introduced to solve the RAPCC. Also, Kim et al. (2008) solved the large-scale examples by using a reoptimization procedure with tabu search and simulated annealing.

3. Mathematical programming models

Notations and decision variables in the mathematical programming model are as follows.

n : the number of subsystems
m : the number of components
i : index for subsystems ($i = 1,2,\cdots,n$)
j : index for components ($j = 1,2,\cdots,m$)

R_S : system reliability

R_i : reliability of subsystem i

C_S : system-level constraint limits for cost

W_S : system-level constraint limits for weight

r_{ij} : reliability of component j available for subsystem i

c_{ij} : cost of component j available for subsystem i

w_{ij} : weight of component j available for subsystem i

u_i : maximum number of components used in subsystem i

x_{ij} : quantity of component j used in subsystem i (for RRAP)

$$x_{ij} = \begin{cases} 1, & \text{if component } j \text{ used in subsystem } i \\ 0, & \text{otherwise} \end{cases} \quad (\text{for RAPCC})$$

3.1 Reliability-redundancy allocation problem (RRAP)

This study deals with the reliability-redundancy allocation problem in a series-parallel system as shown in Fig. 1.

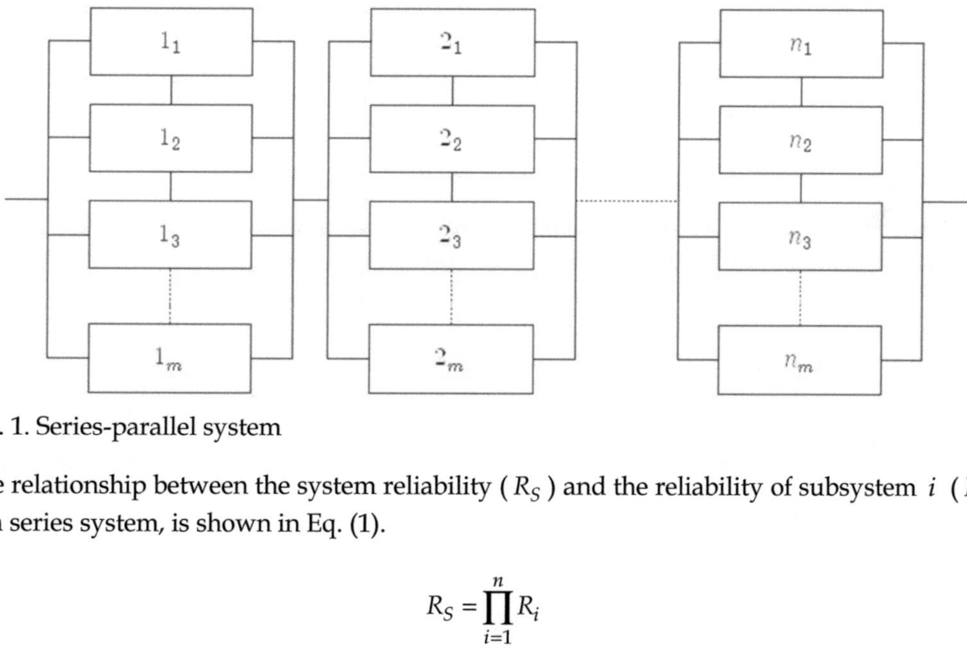

Fig. 1. Series-parallel system

The relationship between the system reliability (R_S) and the reliability of subsystem i (R_i), in a series system, is shown in Eq. (1).

$$R_S = \prod_{i=1}^{n} R_i \quad (1)$$

The relationship between the reliability of subsystem i (R_i) and the reliability of component j available for subsystem i (r_{ij}), in a parallel system, is shown in Eq. (2).

$$R_i = 1 - \prod_{j=1}^{m} \left[1 - r_{ij}\right]^{x_{ij}} \quad (2)$$

Using Eqs. (1) and (2), the mathematical programming model of the RRAP in a series-parallel system is as follows.

$$Maximize \quad R_S = \prod_{i=1}^{n} R_i = \prod_{i=1}^{n} \left\{ 1 - \prod_{j=1}^{m} \left[1 - r_{ij} \right]^{x_{ij}} \right\} \tag{3}$$

$$Subject\ to \quad \sum_{i=1}^{n} \sum_{j=1}^{m} c_{ij} \cdot x_{ij} \le C_S \tag{4}$$

$$\sum_{i=1}^{n} \sum_{j=1}^{m} w_{ij} \cdot x_{ij} \le W_S \tag{5}$$

$$1 \le \sum_{j=1}^{m} x_{ij} \le u_i \ , \ i = 1,2,\cdots,n \tag{6}$$

$$x_{ij} \ge 0 \ , \ i = 1,2,\cdots,n \ , \ j = 1,2,\cdots,m \ , \text{Integer} \tag{7}$$

The objective function is to maximize the system reliability in a series-parallel system. Eqs. (4) and (5) show the resource constraints with cost and weight. Eq. (6) shows the maximum and minimum number of components that can be used for each subsystem. Eq. (7) shows the integer decision variables.

3.2 Reliability allocation problem with component choices (RAPCC)

As shown in Fig. 2, a series system consisting of n subsystems where each subsystem has several component alternatives which can perform same functions with different characteristics is considered in this study. The problem is proposed to select the optimal combination of component alternatives to maximize the system reliability given the cost. Only one component will be adopted for each subsystem.

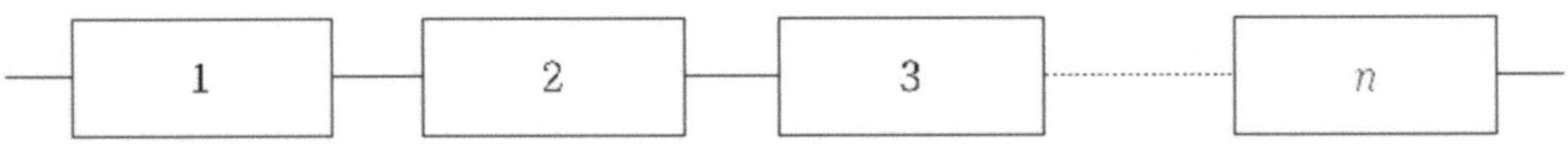

Fig. 2. Series system

Using Eq. (1), the mathematical programming model of the RAPCC in a series system is as follows.

$$Maximize \quad R_S = \prod_{i=1}^{n} \left(\sum_{j=1}^{m} r_{ij} \cdot x_{ij} \right) \tag{8}$$

$$Subject\ to \quad \sum_{i=1}^{n} \sum_{j=1}^{m} c_{ij} \cdot x_{ij} \le C_S \tag{9}$$

$$\sum_{j=1}^{m} x_{ij} = 1,\ i = 1,2,\cdots,n \tag{10}$$

$$x_{ij} = \{0,1\},\ i = 1,2,\cdots,n,\ j = 1,2,\cdots,m \tag{11}$$

The objective function is to maximize the system reliability in a series system. Eq. (9) shows the cost constraint, Eq. (10) represents the multiple-choice constraint which is that the problem prohibits component redundancy, and Eq. (11) defines the decision variables.

4. Hybrid parallel genetic algorithm

The genetic algorithm is a stochastic search method based on the natural selection, reproduction, and evolution theory proposed by Holland (1975). The parallel genetic algorithm paratactically evolves by operating several sub-populations. This study suggests a hybrid parallel genetic algorithm for reliability optimization with resource constraints. The suggested algorithm includes different heuristics such as swap, 2-opt, and interchange (except for RAPCC) for an improvement solution. The suggested process of a hybrid parallel genetic algorithm is shown in Fig. 3.

4.1 Gene representation

The gene representation has to reflect the properties of the system structure. The suggested algorithm for the RRAP represents a gene by one string as shown in Table 1.

Subsystem(Component Alternatives)	1(4)				2(3)			3(4)			
Redundancy & Component	2	1	1	0	1	0	2	0	1	3	0

Table 1. Gene representation (RRAP)

The subsystem in Table 1 indicate the nominal number of subsystem. However, it is not necessary for this number to be one for the composition of a substantial objective function. The "Redundancy & Component" row represents the number of components available for each subsystem. For example, as shown Table 1, subsystem 1 consists of two components of C1, one component of C2, one component of C3. Table 1 can be expressed as shown in Fig. 4.

The suggested algorithm for the RAPCC represents a gene by one string as shown in Table 2.

The subsystem in Table 2 indicates the nominal number of subsystems. However, it is not necessary for the composition of a substantial objective function. The "Component" row represents the available component number for each subsystem. For example, as shown Table 2, a series system uses component No.3 in subsystem 1, component No.2 in subsystem 2, …, and component No.5 in subsystem 6.

4.2 Population

The population of a parallel genetic algorithm consists of an initial population and several sub-populations. The initial population is usually generated by the random and the heuristic generation method. The heuristic generation method tends to interrupt global search.

Therefore, the initial population is generated by the random generation method in this study. The initial population is composed 500 individuals with 100 individuals allocated for each sub-population.

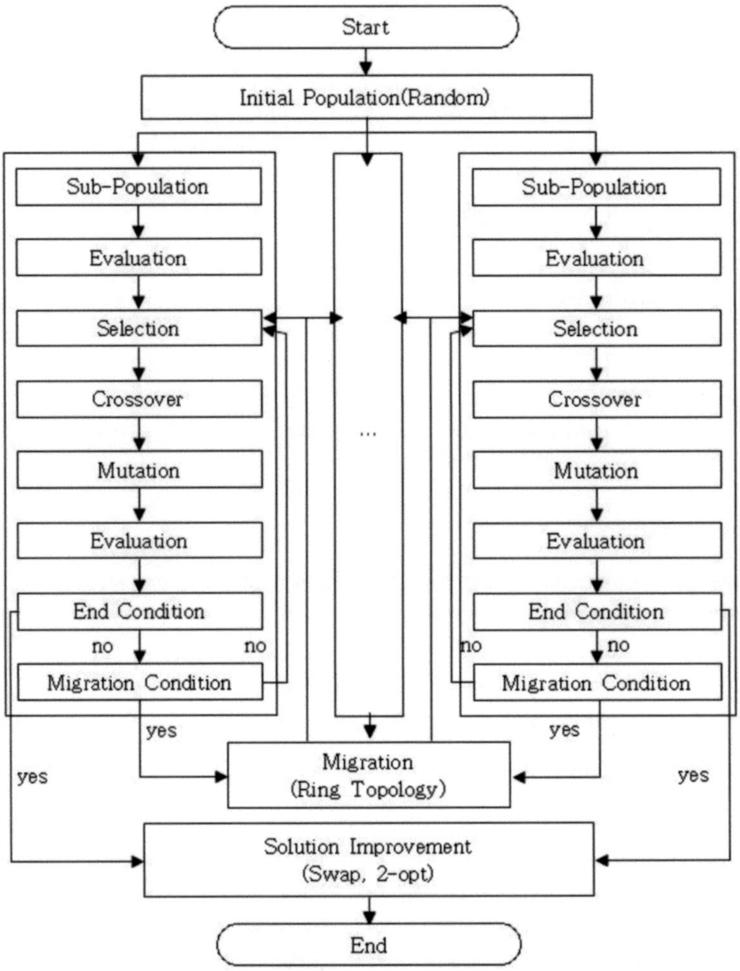

Fig. 3. Hybrid parallel genetic algorithm

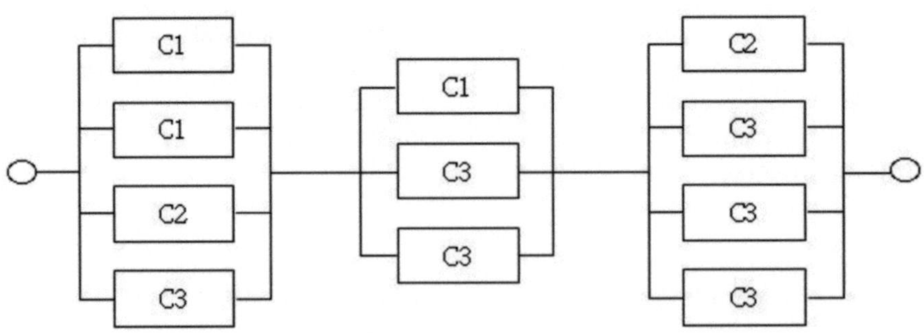

Fig. 4. System structure of Table 1

Subsystem	1	2	3	4	5	6
Component	3	2	4	1	3	5

Table 2. Gene representation (RAPCC)

4.3 Fitness

The fitness function to evaluate the solutions is commonly obtained from the objective function. Penalty functions were used for infeasible solutions by the random generation method in this study. Eqs. (12) and (13) show cost and weight penalty functions, respectively.

$$P_C = \begin{cases} 1, & \text{total cost } \leq C_s \\ \dfrac{1}{total\ cost}, & \text{otherwise} \end{cases} \tag{12}$$

$$P_W = \begin{cases} 1, & \text{total weight} \leq W_s \\ \dfrac{1}{total\ weight}, & \text{otherwise} \end{cases} \tag{13}$$

The multiplication of system reliability and penalty functions related to its cost and weight (except for RAPCC) were used to calculate the fitness of the solutions in the suggested algorithm as shown in Eq. (14).

$$fitness = R_S \cdot P_C \cdot P_W \tag{14}$$

4.4 Selection

The selection method to choose the pairs of parents is applied by the roulette wheel method in the suggested algorithm. The roulette wheel method is one of the most common proportionate selection schemes. In this scheme, the probability to select an individual is proportional to its fitness. It is also stochastically possible for infeasible solutions to survive. The suggested algorithm applies the elitism strategy for the survival of an optimum solution by generation in order to avoid the disappearance of an excellent solution.

4.5 Crossover

The crossover is the main genetic operator. It operates on two individuals at a time and generates offspring by combining both individuals' features. The crossover operator applies a uniform crossover in the suggested algorithm as shown in Fig. 5. The steps of the uniform crossover are as follows.

Step 1. Random numbers were generated for individuals and the individual for crossover was selected by comparing the crossover rate for each individual.
Step 2. The selected individuals were mated between themselves.
Step 3. For each bit of the mated individuals was generated a random number of either 0 or 1.
Step 4. The two offspring bits were generated through a crossover of the two parents' bits when the random number associated with those bits was 1.

P_1	3	5	5	1	1	3
P_2	4	2	2	3	3	5
RN	0	0	1	1	0	1
O_1	3	5	2	3	1	5
O_2	4	2	5	1	3	3

Fig. 5. Uniform crossover

4.6 Mutation

The mutation is a background operator which produces spontaneous random changes in various individuals. The mutation operator applies the uniform mutation in the suggested algorithm as shown in Fig. 6. The steps of the uniform mutation are as follows.

Step 1. The mutation bits were selected by comparing a random number with the mutation rate after Generating a random number between 0~1 for all individual bits.

Step 2. The value of the selected bits were substituted with a new value between 0 and the maximum number of components in each subsystem.

O_1	3	5	2	3	3	5
RN	0.55	0.91	0.43	**0.02**	0.18	0.09
O_1	3	5	2	1	3	5

Fig. 6. Uniform mutation

4.7 Migration

The migration is an exchange operator to change useful information between neighbor sub-populations. Periodically, each sub-population sends its best individuals to its neighbors. When dealing with the migration, the main issues to be considered are migration parameters such as neighborhood structure, the individuals' selection for exchanging, sub-population size, migration period, and migration rate. In the suggested algorithm, the neighborhood structure uses a ring topology as shown in Fig. 7 and the individuals' selection for exchanging is determined by the application of the fitness function. Other migration parameters are shown in Table 3.

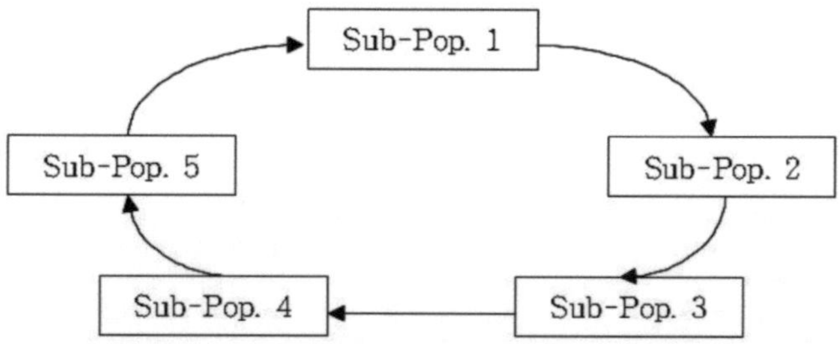

Fig. 7. Neighborhood structure (ring topology)

Migration parameter	Sub-population size	Migration period	Migration rate
Value	100	50	0.2

Table 3. Migration parameters

4.8 Genetic parameters

The genetic parameters include the population size, crossover rate (Pc), mutation rate (Pm), and the number of generations. It is hard to find the best parametric values, so the following parameters were obtained by repeated experiments. The genetic parameters are shown in Table 4.

Genetic parameter	Population size	Crossover rate(P_c)	Mutation rate(P_m)	The number of generations
Value	500	0.8	0.02	1,000~3,000

Table 4. Genetic parameters

4.9 Improvement solution

The suggested algorithm includes different heuristics such as swap, 2-opt, and interchange (except for RAPCC) for improvement of the solution. The swap heuristic was used to exchange each bit which selected two solutions among the five solutions generated by the parallel genetic algorithm. After applying the swap heuristic, a solution of the parallel genetic algorithm was selected by using best fitness. In a selected solution, the 2-opt heuristic performed the exchanging of two bits to enable improvement. The interchange heuristic was applied to each subsystem to exchanging sequences of bits. Finally, a solution of a hybrid parallel genetic algorithm was produced using best fitness after the application of the interchange heuristic.

5. Numerical experiments

5.1 The reliability-redundancy allocation problem (RRAP)

In order to evaluate the performance of the suggested algorithm for the integer nonlinear RRAP, this study performed experiments on 33 variations of Fyffe et. al. (1968), as suggested by Nakagawa & Miyazaki (1981). In this problem, the series-parallel system is connected by

14 parallel subsystems and each has three or four components of choice. The objective is to maximize the reliability of the series–parallel system subject to the cost constraint of 130 and weight constraint ranging from 159 to 190. The maximum number of components is 6 in each subsystem. The component data for testing problems are listed in Table 5.

Subsystem No.	Component choices											
	Choice 1			Choice 2			Choice 3			Choice 4		
	R	C	W	R	C	W	R	C	W	R	C	W
1	0.90	1	3	0.93	1	4	0.91	2	2	0.95	2	5
2	0.95	2	8	0.94	1	10	0.93	1	9	*	*	*
3	0.85	2	7	0.90	3	5	0.87	1	6	0.92	4	4
4	0.83	3	5	0.87	4	6	0.85	5	4	*	*	*
5	0.94	2	4	0.93	2	3	0.95	3	5	*	*	*
6	0.99	3	5	0.98	3	4	0.97	2	5	0.96	2	4
7	0.91	4	7	0.92	4	8	0.94	5	9	*	*	*
8	0.81	3	4	0.90	5	7	0.91	6	6	*	*	*
9	0.97	2	8	0.99	3	9	0.96	4	7	0.91	3	8
10	0.83	4	6	0.85	4	5	0.90	5	6	*	*	*
11	0.94	3	5	0.95	4	6	0.96	5	6	*	*	*
12	0.79	2	4	0.82	3	5	0.85	4	6	0.90	5	7
13	0.98	2	5	0.99	3	5	0.97	2	6	*	*	*
14	0.90	4	6	0.92	4	7	0.95	5	6	0.99	6	9

Table 5. Component data for testing problems

To use CPLEX, this study performed additional steps for transforming the integer nonlinear RRAP into an equivalent binary knapsack problem(Bae et al., 2007; Coit, 2003) as shown in Eqs. (15) to (21).

$$\textit{Maximize} \quad \ln R_S = \sum_{i=1}^{n} \sum_{x_{i1}=0}^{u_i} \cdots \sum_{x_{im}}^{u_i} r_{ix_{i1}\cdots x_{im}} \cdot y_{ix_{i1}\cdots x_{im}} \tag{15}$$

$$\textit{Subject to} \quad \sum_{i=1}^{n} \sum_{x_{i1}=0}^{u_i} \cdots \sum_{x_{im}}^{u_i} \left(\sum_{j=1}^{m} x_{ij} \cdot c_{ij} \right) \cdot y_{ix_{i1}\cdots x_{im}} \le C_S \tag{16}$$

$$\sum_{i=1}^{n} \sum_{x_{i1}=0}^{u_i} \cdots \sum_{x_{im}}^{u_i} \left(\sum_{j=1}^{m} x_{ij} \cdot w_{ij} \right) \cdot y_{ix_{i1}\cdots x_{im}} \le W_S \tag{17}$$

$$\sum_{x_{i1}=0}^{u_i} \cdots \sum_{x_{im}}^{u_i} y_{ix_{i1}\cdots x_{im}} = 1 \,,\; i = 1,2,\cdots,n \tag{18}$$

$$1 \le \sum_{j=1}^{m} x_{ij} \le u_i \,,\; i = 1,2,\cdots,n \tag{19}$$

$$x_{ij} \ge 0 \,,\; i = 1,2,\cdots,n \,,\; j = 1,2,\cdots,m \,,\; \text{Integer} \tag{20}$$

$$y_{ix_{i1}\cdots x_{im}} = \begin{cases} 1, & \text{if } x_{ij} \text{ of the } j\text{th component are used for subsystem } i \\ 0, & \text{otherwise} \end{cases} \tag{21}$$

where, $r_{ix_{i1}\cdots x_{im}} = \ln\left(1 - q_{i1}^{x_{1i}} q_{i2}^{x_{i2}} \cdots q_{im}^{x_{im}}\right)$, $q_{im}^{x_{im}} = (1 - r_{im})^{x_{im}}$, $i = 1,2,\cdots,n$

The experimental results including component structure, reliability, cost, and weight by using a hybrid parallel genetic algorithm are shown in Table 6.

No.	W	Components structure	Reliability	Cost	Weight
1	191	333, 11, 444, 3333, 222, 22, 111, 1111, 12, 233, 33, 1111, 11, 34	0.9868110	130	191
2	190	333, 11, 444, 3333, 222, 22, 111, 1111, 11, 233, 33, 1111, 12, 34	0.9864161	130	190
3	189	333, 11, 444, 3333, 222, 22, 111, 1111, 23, 233, 13, 1111, 11, 34	0.9859217	130	189
4	188	333, 11, 444, 3333, 222, 22, 111, 1111, 23, 223, 13, 1111, 12, 34	0.9853782	130	188
5	187	333, 11, 444, 3333, 222, 22, 111, 1111, 13, 223, 13, 1111, 22, 34	0.9846881	130	187
6	186	333, 11, 444, 333, 222, 22, 111, 1111, 23, 233, 33, 1111, 22, 34	0.9841755	129	186
7	185	333, 11, 444, 3333, 222, 22, 111, 1111, 23, 223, 13, 1111, 22, 33	0.9835049	130	185
8	184	333, 11, 444, 333, 222, 22, 111, 1111, 33, 233, 33, 1111, 22, 34	0.9829940	130	184
9	183	333, 11, 444, 333, 222, 22, 111, 1111, 33, 223, 33, 1111, 22, 34	0.9822557	129	183
10	182	333, 11, 444, 333, 222, 22, 111, 1111, 33, 333, 33, 1111, 22, 33	0.9815183	130	182
11	181	333, 11, 444, 333, 222, 22, 111, 1111, 33, 233, 33, 1111, 22, 33	0.9810271	129	181
12	180	333, 11, 444, 333, 222, 22, 111, 1111, 33, 223, 33, 1111, 22, 33	0.9802902	128	180
13	179	333, 11, 444, 333, 222, 22, 111, 1111, 33, 223, 13, 1111, 22, 33	0.9795047	126	179
14	178	333, 11, 444, 333, 222, 22, 111, 1111, 33, 222, 13, 1111, 22, 33	0.9784003	125	178
15	177	333, 11, 444, 333, 222, 22, 111, 113, 33, 223, 13, 1111, 22, 33	0.9775953	126	177
16	176	333, 11, 444, 333, 222, 22, 33, 1111, 33, 223, 13, 1111, 22, 33	0.9766905	124	176
17	175	333, 11, 444, 333, 222, 22, 13, 1111, 33, 223, 33, 1111, 22, 33	0.9757079	125	175
18	174	333, 11, 444, 333, 222, 22, 13, 1111, 33, 223, 13, 1111, 22, 33	0.9749261	123	174
19	173	333, 11, 444, 333, 222, 22, 13, 1111, 33, 222, 13, 1111, 22, 33	0.9738268	122	173
20	172	333, 11, 444, 333, 222, 22, 13, 113, 33, 223, 13, 1111, 22, 33	0.9730266	123	172
21	171	333, 11, 444, 333, 222, 22, 13, 113, 33, 222, 13, 1111, 22, 33	0.9719295	122	171
22	170	333, 11, 444, 333, 222, 22, 13, 113, 33, 222, 11, 1111, 22, 33	0.9707604	120	170
23	169	333, 11, 444, 333, 222, 22, 11, 113, 33, 222, 13, 1111, 22, 33	0.9692910	121	169
24	168	333, 11, 444, 333, 222, 22, 11, 113, 33, 222, 11, 1111, 22, 33	0.9681251	119	168
25	167	333, 11, 444, 333, 22, 22, 13, 113, 33, 222, 11, 1111, 22, 33	0.9663351	118	167
26	166	333, 11, 44, 333, 222, 22, 13, 113, 33, 222, 11, 1111, 22, 33	0.9650416	116	166

27	165	333, 11, 444, 333, 22, 22, 11, 113, 33, 222, 11, 1111, 22, 33	0.9637118	117	165
28	164	333, 11, 44, 333, 222, 22, 11, 113, 33, 222, 11, 1111, 22, 33	0.9624219	115	164
29	163	333, 11, 44, 333, 22, 22, 13, 113, 33, 222, 11, 1111, 22, 33	0.9606424	114	163
30	162	333, 11, 44, 333, 22, 22, 11, 113, 33, 222, 13, 1111, 22, 33	0.9591884	115	162
31	161	333, 11, 44, 333, 22, 22, 11, 113, 33, 222, 11, 1111, 22, 33	0.9580346	113	161
32	160	333, 11, 44, 333, 22, 22, 11, 111, 33, 222, 13, 1111, 22, 33	0.9557144	112	160
33	159	333, 11, 44, 333, 22, 22, 11, 111, 33, 222, 11, 1111, 22, 33	0.9545648	110	159

Table 6. Experimental results by using HPGA (C=130)

The experimental results compared to the results of CPLEX and existing meta-heuristics, such as GA (Coit & Smith, 1996), TS (Kulturel-Konak et al., 2003), ACO (Liang & Smith, 2004), and IA (Chen & You, 2005) are shown in Table 6. The comparison of CPLEX, meta-heuristics, and the suggested algorithm is shown in Table 7.

The suggested algorithm in all problems showed the optimal solution 6~9 times out 0f 10 runs and obtained same or superior solutions compared to the meta-heuristics. Of the results in Table 7, when compared with the meta-heuristics, 25 solutions are superior to GA, 7 solutions are superior to TS and ACO, and 9 solutions are superior to IA, respectively. The other solutions are the same. The suggested algorithm could paratactically evolve by operating several sub-populations and improve on the solution through swap, 2-opt, and interchange heuristics.

No.	W	Reliability						Number of optimal by HPGA (10 runs)
		CPLEX	GA	TS	ACO	IA	HPGA (This study)	
1	191	0.9868110	0.9867	0.986811	0.9868	0.9868110	0.9868110	8 / 10
2	190	0.9864161	0.9857	0.986416	0.9859	0.9864161	0.9864161	7 / 10
3	189	0.9859217	0.9856	0.985922	0.9858	0.9859217	0.9859217	9 / 10
4	188	0.9853782	0.9850	0.985378	0.9853	0.9853297	0.9853782	8 / 10
5	187	0.9846881	0.9844	0.984688	0.9847	0.9844495	0.9846881	8 / 10
6	186	0.9841755	0.9836	0.984176	0.9838	0.9841755	0.9841755	9 / 10
7	185	0.9835049	0.9831	0.983505	0.9835	0.9834363	0.9835049	8 / 10
8	184	0.9829940	0.9823	0.982994	0.9830	0.9826980	0.9829940	9 / 10
9	183	0.9822557	0.9819	0.982256	0.9822	0.9822062	0.9822557	7 / 10
10	182	0.9815183	0.9811	0.981518	0.9815	0.9815183	0.9815183	9 / 10
11	181	0.9810271	0.9802	0.981027	0.9807	0.9810271	0.9810271	8 / 10
12	180	0.9802902	0.9797	0.980290	0.9803	0.9802902	0.9802902	9 / 10
13	179	0.9795047	0.9791	0.979505	0.9795	0.9795047	0.9795047	9 / 10
14	178	0.9784003	0.9783	0.978400	0.9784	0.9782085	0.9784003	7 / 10
15	177	0.9775953	0.9772	0.977474	0.9776	0.9772429	0.9775953	8 / 10

16	176	0.9766905	0.9764	0.976690	0.9765	0.9766905	0.9766905	7 / 10
17	175	0.9757079	0.9753	0.975708	0.9757	0.9757079	0.9757079	9 / 10
18	174	0.9749261	0.9744	0.974788	0.9749	0.9746901	0.9749261	6 / 10
19	173	0.9738268	0.9738	0.973827	0.9738	0.9737580	0.9738268	8 / 10
20	172	0.9730266	0.9727	0.973027	0.9730	0.9730266	0.9730266	9 / 10
21	171	0.9719295	0.9719	0.971929	0.9719	0.9719295	0.9719295	7 / 10
22	170	0.9707604	0.9708	0.970760	0.9708	0.9707604	0.9707604	9 / 10
23	169	0.9692910	0.9692	0.969291	0.9693	0.9692910	0.9692910	8 / 10
24	168	0.9681251	0.9681	0.968125	0.9681	0.9681251	0.9681251	8 / 10
25	167	0.9663351	0.9663	0.966335	0.9663	0.9663351	0.9663351	8 / 10
26	166	0.9650416	0.9650	0.965042	0.9650	0.9650416	0.9650416	9 / 10
27	165	0.9637118	0.9637	0.963712	0.9637	0.9637118	0.9637118	7 / 10
28	164	0.9624219	0.9624	0.962422	0.9624	0.9624219	0.9624219	7 / 10
29	163	0.9606424	0.9606	0.959980	0.9606	0.9606424	0.9606424	8 / 10
30	162	0.9591884	0.9591	0.958205	0.9592	0.9591884	0.9591884	6 / 10
31	161	0.9580346	0.9580	0.956922	0.9580	0.9580346	0.9580346	7 / 10
32	160	0.9557144	0.9557	0.955604	0.9557	0.9557144	0.9557144	6 / 10
33	159	0.9545648	0.9546	0.954325	0.9546	0.9545648	0.9545648	8 / 10

Table 7. Comparison of CPLEX, meta-heuristics and HPGA (C=130)

In order to calculate the improvement of reliability for existing studies and the suggested algorithm, a maximum possible improvement (MPI) was obtained by Eqs. from (22) to (25) and is shown in Fig. 8.

$$L1(GA) = \frac{R_{HPGA} - R_{GA}}{1 - R_{GA}} \times 100 \tag{22}$$

$$L2(TS) = \frac{R_{HPGA} - R_{TS}}{1 - R_{TS}} \times 100 \tag{23}$$

$$L3(ACO) = \frac{R_{HPGA} - R_{ACO}}{1 - R_{ACO}} \times 100 \tag{24}$$

$$L4(IA) = \frac{R_{HPGA} - R_{IA}}{1 - R_{IA}} \times 100 \tag{25}$$

$L1(GA)$: MPI(%) of GA results

$L2(TS)$: MPI(%) of TS results

$L3(ACO)$: MPI(%) of ACO results

$L4(IA)$: MPI(%) of IA results

R_{HPGA} : system reliability by HPGA

R_{GA} : system reliability by GA

R_{TS} : system reliability by TS

R_{ACO} : system reliability by ACO

R_{IA} : system reliability by IA

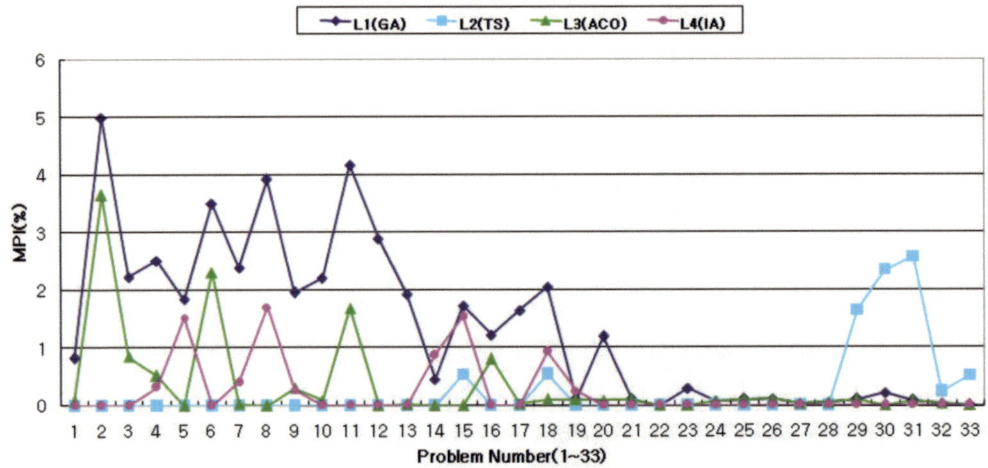

Fig. 8. MPI

The suggested algorithm improved system reliability better than existing studies except for TS in the 1st~20th test problems in which the weight was heavy. In addition, HPGA found superior system reliability compared to TS in the 29th~32th test problems in which the weight was light. The other solutions are almost the same.

Through the experiment, this study found that the performance of HPGA is superior to the existing meta-heuristics. In order to evaluate the performance of HPGA in large-scale problems, 5 more problems are presented through connecting the system data of testing problem 1 (C=190, W=191) in series systems. The large-scale problems consist of 28 subsystems (C=260, W=382), 42 subsystems (C=390, W=573), 56 subsystems (C=520, W=764), 70 subsystems (C=650, W=955) in series systems. After 10 runs using HPGA, the results compared with the optimal solution by CPLEX are shown in Table 8.

No.	Number of subsystems	C	W	CPLEX	HPGA (10 runs)		
					Max	S.D.	Number of optimal
1	14	130	191	0.9868110	0.9868110	0.000021	8 / 10
2	28	260	382	0.9740720	0.9740720	0.000147	6 / 10
3	42	390	573	0.9612374	0.9612374	0.000564	4 / 10
4	56	520	764	0.9488162	0.9488162	0.001095	1 / 10
5	70	650	955	0.9370413	0.9370413	0.001732	1 / 10

Table 8. Experimental results of the large-scale problems

The suggested algorithm presented optimal solutions in all large-scale problems. For the experimental results of large-scale problems 1~4, the suggested algorithm showed the optimal solutions 4~8 times out of 10 runs. The optimal solution to large-scale problem 5 was obtained by HPGA in 1 out of 10 runs.

5.2 The reliability allocation problem with component choices (RAPCC)

In order to evaluate the performance of the suggested algorithm for the reliability allocation problem with multiple-choice, this study performed experiments by using the Nahas & Nourelfath (2005) and the Kim et al. (2008) examples in series. The Nahas & Nourelfath (2005) examples consist of four examples: examples 1, 2, and 3 consist of 15 subsystems with 60, 80, and 100 components, respectively, and example 4 consists of 25 subsystems with 166 components. The budgets are \$1,000, \$900, \$1,000, and \$1,400, respectively. Examples by the Kim et al. (2008) consist of two large-scale examples (examples 5 and 6). Large-scale examples are presented through connecting the system data of example 4. Examples 5 and 6 consist of 100 and 200 subsystems with budgets of \$7,200~\$7,650 and \$14,400~\$15,100, respectively.

To use CPLEX, this study performed an additional step for transforming the nonlinear objective function into the linear function as shown in Eq. (26).

$$Maximize \;\; \ln R_S = \ln\left\{\prod_{i=1}^{n}\left(\sum_{j=1}^{m} r_{ij}\cdot x_{ij}\right)\right\} = \sum_{i=1}^{n}\sum_{j=1}^{m} x_{ij}\cdot \ln r_{ij} \tag{26}$$

The experimental results of examples 1~4 including component structure, reliability, and cost by using CPLEX and a hybrid parallel genetic algorithm are shown in Table 9.

No.	Number of subsystems	Number of components	budget	CPLEX	HPGA		
				Reliability	Component structure	Reliability	Cost
1	15	60	1,000	0.857054	3-4-5-2-3-3-2-3-2-2-2-3-4-3-2	0.857054	990
2	15	80	900	0.915042	3-3-3-4-2-3-3-2-4-1-2-3-4-3-1	0.915042	900
3	15	100	1,000	0.965134	3-3-4-4-3-3-2-2-3-2-2-4-4-4-2	0.965134	995
4	25	166	1,400	0.865439	3-3-3-5-2-3-2-2-3-1-2-3-4-4-1-2-3-3-4-2-3-2-2-3-1	0.865439	1,395
					3-3-3-5-2-3-2-2-3-1-2-3-4-3-1-3-3-3-4-2-3-2-2-3-1	0.865439	1,395
					2-3-3-4-2-3-2-2-3-1-2-3-3-4-1-3-3-3-5-3-3-2-2-3-1	0.865439	1,400

Table 9. Experimental results of examples 1~4 by using CPLEX and HPGA

As found in Table 9, the suggested algorithm presented the optimal solutions in examples 14 and obtained a new optimal solution (3-3-3-5-2-3-2-2-3-1-2-3-4-3-1-3-3-3-4-2-3-2-2-3-1) in example 4.

After 10 runs using HPGA in examples 14, the experimental results including maximum, average and standard deviation values were compared with existing meta-heuristics such as ACO (Nahas & Nourelfath, 2005), SA (Kim et al., 2004), and TS (Kim et al., 2008). The comparison of meta-heuristics and the suggested algorithm is shown in Table 10.

No.	ACO			SA			TS			HPGA (This study)		
	Max	Ave.	S.D.	Max	Ave.	S.D.	Max	Ave.	S.D.	Max	Ave.	S.D.
1	0.85705	0.85705	0	0.85705	0.85705	0	0.857054	0.857054	0	0.857054	0.857054	0
2	0.91504	0.91504	0	0.91504	0.91504	0	0.915042	0.915042	0	0.915042	0.915042	0
3	0.96512	0.96439	0.00050	0.96513	0.96503	0.00033	0.965134	0.965134	0	0.965134	0.965134	0
4	0.86543	0.86491	0.00038	0.86543	0.86536	0.00025	0.865439	0.865439	0	0.865439	0.865439	0

Table 10. Experimental results of examples 1~4 by using CPLEX and HPGA

The suggested algorithm in examples 14 generated the optimal solutions without standard deviation and showed the same or superior solution compared to meta-heuristics.

In order to evaluate the performance of HPGA in large-scale problems, this study performed experiments by using examples in series as suggested by the Kim et al. (2008). After 10 runs using CPLEX and HPGA in examples 5 and 6, experimental results including maximum, standard deviation values, and maximum possible improvement (MPI) compared with existing meta-heuristics such as simulated annealing, tabu search, and reoptimization procedure by the Kim et al. (2008) are shown in Tables 11 and 12. The MPI was obtained by Eq. (27).

$$\%MPI = \frac{(Max - CPLEX)}{(1 - CPLEX)} \times 100 \tag{27}$$

Budget	CPLEX	SA			TS			HPGA (This Study)		
		Max	S.D.	%MPI	Max	S.D.	%MPI	Max	S.D.	%MPI
7,200	0.895758	0.895575	0.001342	-0.1756	0.895758	0.000312	0	0.895758	0.001017	0
7,250	0.900167	0.899438	0.001050	-0.7302	0.899984	0.000305	-0.1833	0.899984	0.000236	-0.1833
7,300	0.904599	0.903866	0.001027	-0.7683	0.904414	0.000390	-0.1939	0.904599	0.000529	0
7,350	0.908866	0.908405	0.001202	-0.5058	0.908866	0.000480	0	0.908866	0.000424	0
7,400	0.913154	0.912601	0.000499	-0.6368	0.913064	0.000337	-0.1036	0.913114	0.000107	-0.0461
7,450	0.917184	0.916815	0.000510	-0.4456	0.917093	0.000494	-0.1099	0.917184	0.000229	0
7,500	0.921141	0.920770	0.000743	-0.4705	0.921141	0.000365	0	0.921141	0.000156	0
7,550	0.925023	0.925023	0.000590	0	0.925023	0.000502	0	0.925023	0.000172	0
7,600	0.929013	0.928269	0.000696	-1.0481	0.929013	0.000445	0	0.929013	0	0
7,650	0.931526	0.931526	0.000388	0	0.931526	0	0	0.931526	0	0

Table 11. Experimental results of example 5 by using CPLEX and HPGA (10 runs)

Budget	CPLEX	TS			TS+SA Reoptimization			HPGA (This Study)		
		Max	S.D.	%MPI	Max	S.D.	%MPI	Max	S.D.	%MPI
14,400	0.802546	0.802218	0.000425	-0.1661	0.802218	0	-0.1661	0.802364	0.000110	-0.0922
14,450	0.806496	0.806167	0.000396	-0.1700	0.806167	0	-0.1700	0.806251	0.000076	-0.1266
14,500	0.810301	0.809890	0.000519	-0.2167	0.809970	0	-0.1745	0.810301	0.000094	0
14,550	0.814290	0.813792	0.000352	-0.2682	0.813792	0	-0.2682	0.813792	0.000182	-0.2682
14,600	0.818299	0.817388	0.000391	-0.5014	0.817798	0.000053	-0.2757	0.817984	0.000003	-0.1734
14,650	0.822160	0.821656	0.000891	-0.2834	0.821656	0	-0.2834	0.822160	0	0
14,700	0.826207	0.824787	0.000709	-0.8171	0.825364	0.000142	-0.4851	0.825774	0.000325	-0.2491
14,750	0.830105	0.829263	0.000815	-0.4956	0.829427	0.000026	-0.3991	0.830105	0.000407	0
14,800	0.833851	0.833428	0.000891	-0.2546	0.833510	0.000026	-0.2052	0.833604	0.000450	-0.1487
14,850	0.837614	0.837448	0.000824	-0.1022	0.837614	0	0	0.837614	0	0
14,900	0.841310	0.840805	0.000786	-0.3182	0.841310	0.000107	0	0.841310	0	0
14,950	0.844856	0.844009	0.000506	-0.5459	0.844856	0.000215	0	0.844856	0	0
15,000	0.848500	0.848332	0.000610	-0.1109	0.848500	0.000027	0	0.848500	0	0
15,050	0.852076	0.851991	0.000722	-0.0575	0.852076	0	0	0.852076	0	0
15,100	0.855751	0.855582	0.000679	-0.1172	0.855751	0	0	0.855751	0	0

Table 12. Experimental results of example 6 by using CPLEX and HPGA (10 runs)

As shown in Table 11, the result of SA and TS gave the optimal solution 2 and 6 times out of the 10 cases, respectively. The suggested algorithm found the optimal solution 8 times for the same cases and it showed the same or superior MPI compared to that of SA and TS. As the results in Table 12 show that, when compared with TS and the reoptimization procedure (TS+SA), the suggested algorithm gave the optimal solution 9 times out of the 15 cases and showed the same or superior MPI than TS and the reoptimization procedure (TS+SA). This is because the suggested algorithm could parallelly evolve by operating several sub-populations and improve the solution through swap and 2-opt heuristics.

Throughout the experiment, this study found that performance of HPGA is superior to existing meta-heuristics. This study has generated one more example, example 7, which is presented through connecting the system data of example 4 in series. Example 7 consists of 1,000 subsystems with \$90,000\$99,000 budgets. After 10 runs using CPLEX and HPGA in example 7, the experimental results including the maximum, standard deviation values, and maximum possible improvement (MPI) are shown in Table 13.

Budget	CPLEX	HPGA		
		Max	S.D.	%MPI
90,000	0.831082	0.830757	0.000681	-0.1924
91,000	0.847706	0.846918	0.000594	-0.5174
92,000	0.860003	0.859647	0.000317	-0.2543
93,000	0.871659	0.871516	0.000183	-0.2228
94,000	0.883369	0.883275	0.000262	-0.0806
95,000	0.895226	0.895185	0.000208	-0.0391
96,000	0.904832	0.904832	0.000079	0
97,000	0.913836	0.913791	0.000055	-0.0522
98,000	0.920716	0.920716	0.000016	0
99,000	0.924869	0.924869	0	0

Table 13. Experimental results of example 7 by using CPLEX and HPGA (10 runs)

As shown in Table 13, the suggested algorithm presented the optimal solution in 3 times out of 10 cases. While the budget increased, the suggested algorithm found the near-optimal solution.

6. Conclusions

This study suggested mathematical programming models and a hybrid parallel genetic algorithm for reliability optimization with resource constraints. The experimental results compared HPGA with existing meta-heuristics and CPLEX, and evaluated the performance of the suggested algorithm.

The suggested algorithm presented superior solutions to all problems (including large-scale problems) and found that the performance is superior to existing meta-heuristics. This is because the suggested algorithm could paratactically evolve by operating several sub-populations and improve the solution through swap, 2-opt, and interchange (except for RAPCC) heuristics.

The suggested algorithm would be able to be applied to system design with a reliability goal with resource constraints for large scale reliability optimization problems.

7. References

Ait-Kadi, D. & Nourelfath, M. (2001). Availability Optimization of Fault-Tolerant Systems, *Proceedings of International Conference on Industrial Engineering Production Management (IEPM 2001)*, Quebec, Canada, August, 2001.

Bae, C. O.; Kim, H. G.; Kim, J. H.; Son, J. Y. & Yun, W. Y. (2007). Solving the Redundancy Allocation Problem with Multiple Component Choice using Metaheuristics, *International Journal of Industrial Engineering*, Special Issue, pp.315-323.

Bellman, R. & Dreyfus, S. (1958). Dynamic Programming and the Reliability of Multicomponent Devices, *Operations Research*, Vol.6, No.2, pp.200-206.

Chern, M. S. (1992). On the Computational Complexity of Reliability Redundancy Allocation in a Series System, *Operations Research Letters*, Vol.11, No.5, pp.309-315.

Chern, M. S. & Jan, R. H. (1986). Reliability Optimization Problems with Multiple Constraints. *IEEE Transactions on Reliability*, Vol.35, No.4, pp.431-436.

Chen, T. C. & You, P. S. (2005). Immune Algorithms based Approach for Redundant Reliability Problems with Multiple Component Choices, *Computers in Industry*, Vol.56, No.2, pp.195-205.

Coit, D. W. (2003). Maximization of System Reliability with a Choice of Redundancy Strategies, *IIE Transactions*, Vol.35, No.6, pp.535-543.

Coit, D. W. & Smith, A. E. (1996). Reliability Optimization of Series-Parallel Systems using a Genetic Algorithm, *IEEE Transactions on Reliability*, Vol.45, No.2, pp.254-260.

CPLEX. http://www-947.ibm.com/support/entry/portal.Overview/Software/ WebSphere /IBM_ILOG_CPLEX

Djerdjour, M. & Rekab, K. (2001). A Branch and Bound Algorithm for Designing Reliable Systems at a Minimum Cost, *Applied Mathematics and Computation*, Vol.118, No.2-3, pp.247-259.

Fyffe, D. E.; Hines, W. W. & Lee, N. K. (1968). System Reliability Allocation and a Computational Algorithm, *Operations Research*, Vol.17, No.2, pp.64-69.

Garey, M. R. & Johnson, D. S. (1979). *Computers and Intractability: A Guide to the Theory of NP-Completeness*, W. H. Freeman and Company, New York, USA.

Gen, M.; Ida, K.; Sasaki, M. & Lee, J. U. (1989). Algorithm for Solving Large Scale 0-1 Goal Programming and its Application to Reliability Optimization Problem, *Computers and Industrial Engineering*, Vol.17, No.1, pp.525-530.

Ghare, P. M. & Taylor, R. E. (1969). Optimal Redundancy for Reliability in Series System, *Operations Research*, Vol.17, No.5, pp.838-847.

Holland, J. H. (1975), *Adaption in Natural and Artificial Systems*. University of Michigan Press.

Ida, K.; Gen, M. & Yokota, T. (1994). System Reliability Optimization with Several Failure Modes by Genetic Algorithm, *Proceedings of the 16th International Conference on Computers and Industrial Engineering*, Ashikaga, Japan, March, 1994.

Jianping, L. (1996). A Bound Heuristic Algorithm for Solving Reliability Redundancy Optimization, *Microelectronics and Reliability*, Vol.3, No.5, pp.335-339.

Kim, H. G.; Bae, C. O.; Kim, J. H. & Son, J. Y. (2008). Solution Methods for Reliability Optimization Problem of a Series System with Component Choices, *Journal of the Korean Institute of Industrial Engineers*, Vol.34, No.1, pp.49-56.

Kim, H. G.; Bae, C. O. & Paik, C. H. (2004). A Simulated Annealing Algorithm for the Optimal Reliability Design Problem of a Series System with Component Choices, *IE Interfaces*, Vol.17, Special Edition, pp.69-78.

Kulturel-Konak, S.; Smith, A. E. & Coit, D. W. (2003). Efficiently Solving the Redundancy Allocation Problem using Tabu Search, *IIE Transactions*, Vol.35, No.6, pp.515-526.

Kuo, W.; Lin, H.; Xu, Z. & Zhang, W. (1987). Reliability Optimization with the Lagrange Multiplier and Branch-and-Bound Technique, *IEEE Transactions on Reliability*, Vol.36, No.5, pp.624-630.

Kuo, W. & Prasad, V. R. (2000). An Annotated Overview of System Reliability Optimization, *IEEE Transactions on Reliability*, Vol.49, No.2, pp.176-187.

Kuo, W. & Wan, R. (2007). Recent Advances in Optimal Reliability Allocation, *IEEE Transactions on systems, man, and cybernetics-Part A: systems and humans*, Vol.37, No.2, pp.143-156.

Liang, Y. C. & Smith, A. E. (2004). An Ant Colony Optimization Algorithm for the Redundancy Allocation Problem, *IEEE Transactions on Reliability*, Vol.53, No.3, pp.417-423.

Nahas, N. & Nourelfath, M. (2005). Ant System for Reliability Optimization of a Series System with Multiple Choice and Budget Constraints, *Reliability Engineering and System Safety*, Vol.87, No.1, pp.1-12.

Nakagawa, Y. & Miyazaki, S. (1981). Surrogate Constraints Algorithm for Reliability Optimization Problems with Two Constraints, *IEEE Transactions on Reliability*, Vol.30, No.2, pp.175-180.

Nauss, R. M. (1978). The 0–1 Knapsack Problem with Multiple Choice Constraints, *European Journal of Operational Research*, Vol.2, No.2, pp.121–131.

Nourelfath, M. & Nahas, N. (2003). Quantized Hopfield Networks for Reliability Optimization, *Reliability Engineering and System Safety*, Vol.81, No.2, pp.191–196.

Painton, L. & Campbell, J. (1995). Genetic Algorithms in Optimization of System Reliability, *IEEE Transactions on Reliability*, Vol.44, No.2, pp.172-178.

Sinha, P. & Zoltners, A. A. (1979). The Multiple Choice Knapsack Problem, *Operations Research*, Vol.27, No.3, pp.503–515.

Sung, C. S. & Cho, Y. K. (1999). Branch-and-Bound Redundancy Optimization for a Series System with Multiple-Choice Constraints, *IEEE Transactions on Reliability*, Vol.48, No.2, pp.108-117.

Sung, C. S. & Lee, H. K. (1994). A Branch-and-Bound Approach for Spare Unit Allocation in a Series System, *European Journal of Operational Research*, Vol.75, No.1, pp.217–232.

Tillman, F. A. (1969). Optimization by Integer Programming of Constrained Reliability Problems with Several Modes of Failure, *IEEE Transactions on Reliability*, Vol.18, No.2, pp.47-53.

Tillman, F. A.; Hwang, C. L. & Kuo, W. (1977). Optimization Techniques for System Reliability with Redundancy-a Review, *IEEE Transactions on Reliability*, Vol.26, No.3, pp.148-155.

Tzafestas, S. G. (1980). Optimization of System Reliability: A Survey of Problems and Techniques, *International Journal of Systems Science*, Vol.11, No.4, pp.455-486.

Yalaoui, A.; Chatelet, E. & Chu, C. (2005). A New Dynamic Programming Method for Reliability and Redundancy Allocation, *IEEE Transactions on Reliability*, Vol.54, No.2, pp.254-261.

You, P. S. & Chen, T. C. (2005). An Efficient Heuristic for Series-Parallel Redundant Reliability Problems, *Computers and Operations Research*, Vol.32, No.8, pp.2117-2127.

7

Hybrid Genetic Algorithm-Support Vector Machine Technique for Power Tracing in Deregulated Power Systems

Mohd Wazir Mustafa, Mohd Herwan Sulaiman*,
Saifulnizam Abd. Khalid and Hussain Shareef
*Universiti Teknologi Malaysia (UTM), Universiti Malaysia Perlis (UniMAP) and Universiti Kebangsaan Malaysia (UKM)
Malaysia*

1. Introduction

The electric power industry is under deregulation in response to changes in the law, technology, market and competition. The aim of deregulation is to optimize the system welfare by introducing competitive environment, mainly among the power producers. Developing fair and transparent power flow and loss allocation method has been an active topic of research, with many transactions taking place at any time.

In the last decades, several power flow tracing algorithms have been proposed in literature mainly from physical flow approach (Bialek & Tam, 1996; Wu et al., 2000; Sulaiman et al., 2008; Pantos et al., 2005) and circuit theory approach (Teng, 2005; Wen-Chen et al., 2004; Mustafa et al., 2008a; Lo & Alturki, 2006). The concept of proportional sharing principle has been proposed by (Bialek & Tam, 1996). This approach has a drawback in handling the transmission losses by introducing fictitious nodes on every lossy branch which will causes the expansion of distribution matrix. The graph method was proposed by (Wu et al., 2000) where the method is basically using the searching technique of the paths and routes from a particular generator to a particular load. The adaptation of the methods from (Bialek & Tam, 1996) and (Wu et al., 2000) has been proposed in (Sulaiman et al., 2008) for tracing the power and loss in deregulated power system. However, the main disadvantage of this approach is it cannot be applied for the circular power flow system. Modification of (Bialek & Tam, 1996) has been done in (Pantos et al., 2005) to trace the real and reactive power by introducing decoupled power flow to overcome the lossy system problem. This method introduces equivalent model of a line for reactive power tracing. The effects of line charging to original generators and loads are integrated. Nevertheless, the actual power contribution from generators to loads has been ignored.

The uses of circuit theory in power tracing have been introduced in (Teng, 2005; Wen-Chen et al., 2004; Mustafa et al., 2008a; Lo & Alturki, 2006). In (Teng, 2005), a method that applies

* Corresponding Author

superposition theorem to trace the power flow and loss in deregulated system has been proposed. The integration of Y-bus matrix with the equivalent impedance of load bus is performed before this integration matrix is inversed into Z-bus matrix. Then, the superposition theorem is applied so that the current injection can be allocated to individual generators. The method that uses basic circuit theory and partitioning the Y-bus matrix to decompose the voltage of load buses as function of the generators' voltage has been proposed in (Wen-Chen et al., 2004). This partitioning technique also has been extended in (Mustafa et al., 2008; Lo & Altuki, 2006). The method from (Wen-Chen et al., 2004) is re-evaluated to represent each load current as function of generators' current and load voltages named as modified nodal equations (MNE) (Mustafa et al., 2008a). However, there are some conditions where the tracing at certain lines or loads could be greater than the power produced by its generation. In (Lo & Alturki, 2006), partitioned Y-bus is applied to design a voltage participation index (VPI) together with the concept of current adjustment factors (CAF) for the reactive power tracing algorithm. CAF is the transformation of complex matrix coefficients for adjustment of non-linearity of the network due to real and imaginary factor interactions. The problem of CAF is it will be very complex if implemented for large system.

In related work based on machine learning, an application of Artificial Neural Network (ANN) into reactive power tracing has been proposed in (Mustafa et al., 2008b). The MNE technique has been utilized as a teacher to train the ANN model. However, ANN is time consuming in the training process. The hybrid of Genetic Algorithm (GA) and Least Squares Support Vector Machine (LS-SVM) to trace the transmission loss has been proposed in (Mustafa e al., 2011). The improvement from (Bialek & Tam, 1996) has been done in tracing the transmission losses. It then is used as a teacher to train the GA-SVM model. However, same with (Bialek & Tam, 1996; Wu et al., 2000; Sulaiman et al., 2008), the technique cannot handle the system with circular or loop flow.

This paper basically proposes the same hybrid technique as proposed in (Mustafa e al., 2011), where the GA-SVM is utilized to trace the real and reactive power from individual generators to loads simultaneously. GA is utilized as an optimizer to find the optimal values of LS-SVM hyper-parameters which are embedded in LS-SVM model. The supervised learning paradigm is used to train the LS-SVM model where the Superposition method (Teng, 2005) is utilized as a teacher. Based on converged load flow and followed by superposition method for power tracing procedure, the description of input and output of the training data are created. The GA-SVM model will learn to identify which generators are supplying to which loads in term of real and reactive power in concurrently. In this paper, IEEE 14 bus system is used to illustrate the effectiveness of proposed method compared to that of the superposition method.

2. Superposition method as a teacher

Superposition method was proposed by (Teng, 2005) where it is based on basic circuit theories including KCL, KVL and superposition law. Same with other tracing methods, this method also requires obtaining the solved load flow prior the tracing can be applied. After converged power flow solution, the power tracing is started by obtaining the contribution of voltages and currents which are using the superposition law concept, equivalent impedance and equivalent current injection. Generators in the system are treated as equivalent current injection which injects the currents into the system by using the following expressions (Teng, 2005):

$$S_{n,G} = \left(P_{n,G} + jQ_{n,G}\right) \tag{1}$$

$$I_{n,G} = \left(\frac{P_{n,G} + jQ_{n,G}}{V_{n,G}}\right)^{*} \tag{2}$$

where n is number of generator, $V_{n,G}$ is the generator bus voltage, $P_{n,G}$ is the real power and $Q_{n,G}$ is the reactive power for the generator bus.

For a load bus i, the corresponding equivalent impedance, $Z_{i,L}$ can be obtained using the following expression:

$$Z_{i,L} = \frac{V_{i,L}}{I_{i,L}} = \frac{\left|V_{i,L}\right|^2}{P_{i,L} - j\left(Q_{i,L} - Q_c\right)} \tag{3}$$

where $V_{i,L}$, $I_{i,L}$ and $S_{i,L} = [P_{i,L}-j(Q_{i,L}-Q_c)]$ are the voltage, current and apparent power of load bus i including the effect of injected MVAR that obtained from the converged load flow solution respectively. The equivalent impedance for each load now is integrated into *Y-bus* matrix where the vector of bus voltages, $\mathbf{V_{BUS}}$ can be obtained as follows:

$$V_{BUS} = Z_{MATRIX} I_G \tag{4}$$

where $\mathbf{I_G}$ and $\mathbf{Z_{MATRIX}}$ are the bus current injection vector and impedance matrix including the effects of the equivalent impedance, respectively.

By using the superposition law, the voltage contribution of each generator to each bus can be obtained as follows:

$$\begin{bmatrix} \Delta v_1^n \\ \vdots \\ \Delta v_n^n \\ \vdots \\ \Delta v_N^n \end{bmatrix} = \begin{bmatrix} z_{11} & \cdots & z_{1n} & \cdots & z_{1N} \\ \vdots & \ddots & \vdots & \cdot^{\cdot^{\cdot}} & \vdots \\ z_{n1} & \cdots & z_{nn} & \cdots & z_{nN} \\ \vdots & \cdot^{\cdot^{\cdot}} & \vdots & \ddots & \vdots \\ z_{N1} & \cdots & z_{Nn} & \cdots & z_{NN} \end{bmatrix} \tag{5}$$

where the effect of each current injection into the system is taken one by one. From (5), voltage at bus i contributed by generator bus n (Δv_i^n) and the voltage of bus i contributed by all generator buses can be written as follow:

$$\Delta v_i^n = z_{in} I_{n,G} \tag{6}$$

$$V_i = \sum_{n=1}^{N_G} \Delta v_i^n \tag{7}$$

The next step is tracing the current in the system. By referring to Fig. 1, the line current from bus i to bus j, Δi_{ij}^{n} and from bus j to bus i, Δi_{ji}^{n} which are corresponding to the voltage contribution of generator bus n, can be obtained using the following equations:

$$\Delta i_{ij}^{n} = \left(\Delta v_i^n - \Delta v_j^n\right) * \left(g_{ij} + jb_{ij}\right) + \left(jc/2\right) * \Delta v_i^n \tag{8}$$

$$\Delta i_{ji}^{n} = \left(\Delta v_j^n - \Delta v_i^n\right) * \left(g_{ij} + jb_{ij}\right) + \left(jc/2\right) * \Delta v_j^n \tag{9}$$

where $(g_{ij} + jb_{ij})$ is the line admittance from bus i to j and $c/2$ is the line charging susceptance.

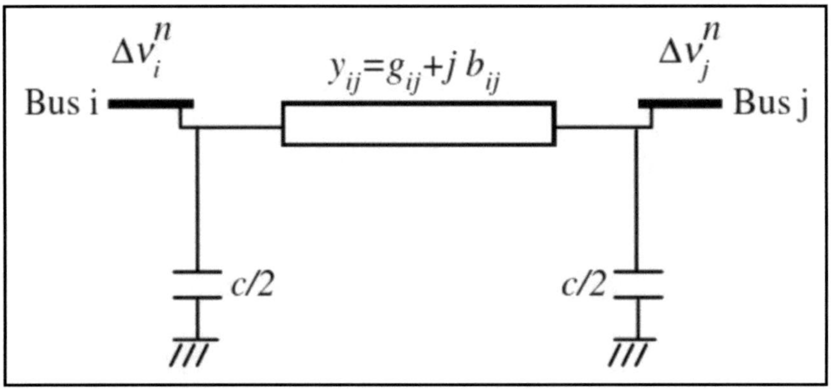

Fig. 1. π-model of transmission line

By referring to (Teng, 2005), the bus voltage can be considered as the force or pressure, which is pushing the current contributed by different generators through the line. Therefore, with a proper manipulation, the power flow contributed by the generator bus n and total power flow can be calculated as follow:

$$\Delta s_{ij}^{n} = \left(\Delta v_1^1 + \ldots + \Delta v_i^n + \ldots + \Delta v_i^{N_G}\right)\left(\Delta i_{ij}^{n}\right)^{*} = V_i\left(\Delta i_{ij}^{n}\right)^{*} \tag{10}$$

$$S_{ij} = \sum_{n=1}^{N_G} \Delta s_{ij}^{n} \tag{11}$$

where Δs_{ij}^{n} is the line power flow produced by generator bus n from bus i to bus j.

To obtain the contribution of individual generator to loads, the same procedure is applied. The current injection from generator n into load bus i, $\Delta i_{i,L}^{n}$ and the total current injection, $I_{i,L}$ can be calculated as follow:

$$\Delta i_{i,L}^{n} = \frac{\Delta v_i^n}{Z_{i,L}} \tag{12}$$

$$I_{i,L} = \sum_{n=1}^{N_G} \Delta i_{i,L}^{n} \tag{13}$$

Since the voltage and current contributions of individual generator have been identified, the power of load bus i contributed by generator bus n, $\Delta s_{i,L}{}^n$ and the total power of load bus, $S_{i,L}$ can be accounted as follow:

$$\Delta s_{i,L}^n = V_i \left(\Delta i_{i,L}^n\right)^* \tag{14}$$

$$S_{i,L} = \sum_{n=1}^{N_G} \Delta s_{i,L}^n \tag{15}$$

Vector $\Delta s_{i,L}{}^n$ is used as a target in the training process of proposed hybrid GA-SVM technique.

3. Function estimation using LS-SVM

Support vector machine (SVM) is known as a powerful methodology for solving problems in nonlinear classification, function estimation and density estimation. SVM has been introduced within the context of statistical learning theory and structural risk minimization. Least squares support vector machine (LS-SVM) is reformulations from standard SVM (Vapnik, 1995) which lead to solving linear Karush-Kuhn-Tucker (KKT) systems. LS-SVM is closely related to regularization networks and Gaussian processes but additionally emphasizes and exploits primal-dual interpretations (Espinoza et al., 2006).

In LS-SVM function estimation, the standard framework is based on a primal-dual formulation. Given N dataset $\{x_i, y_i\}_{i=1}^N$, the goal is to estimate a model of the form:

$$y(x) = w^T \varphi(x) + b + e_i \tag{16}$$

where $x \in R^n, y \in R$ and $\varphi(.) : R^n \rightarrow R^{n_h}$ is a mapping to a high dimensional feature space. The following optimization problem is formulated (Suykens et al., 2002):

$$\min_{w,b,e} J(w,e) = \frac{1}{2} w^T w + \gamma \frac{1}{2} \sum_{i=1}^{N} e_i^2 \tag{17}$$

such that $y_i = w^T \varphi(x_i) + b + e_i$, i=1,…,N.

With the application of Mercer's theorem (Vapnik, 1995) for the kernel matrix Ω as $\Omega_{ij} = K(x_i, x_j) = \varphi(x_i)^T \varphi(x_j)$, i, j=1,..,N, it is not required to compute explicitly the nonlinear mapping $\varphi(.)$ as this is done implicitly through the use of positive definite kernel functions K (Espinoza et al., 2006). From the Lagrange function (Suykens et al., 2002):

$$\zeta(w,b,e;\beta) = \frac{1}{2} w^T w + \gamma \frac{1}{2} \sum_{i=1}^{N} e_i^2 - \sum_{i=1}^{N} \beta_i (w^T \varphi(x_i) + b + e_i - y_i) \tag{18}$$

where β_i are Lagrange multipliers. Differentiating (18) with w, b, e_i *and* β_i, the conditions for optimality can be described as follow (Suykens et al., 2002):

$$\begin{cases} \dfrac{d\zeta}{dw} = 0 \rightarrow w = \sum_{i=1}^{N} \beta_i \varphi(x_i) \\ \dfrac{d\zeta}{db} = 0 \rightarrow \sum_{i=1}^{N} \beta_i = 0 \\ \dfrac{d\zeta}{de_i} = 0 \rightarrow \beta_i = \gamma e_i, i = 1,...,N \\ \dfrac{d\zeta}{\beta_i} = 0 \rightarrow y_i = w^T \phi(x_i) + b + e_i, i = 1,...,N \end{cases} \tag{19}$$

By elimination of w and e_i, the following linear system is obtained (Suykens et al., 2002):

$$\left[\frac{0}{y} \Big| \frac{1^T}{\Omega + \gamma^{-1} I} \right] \left[\frac{b}{\beta} \right] = \left[\frac{0}{y} \right] \tag{20}$$

with $y = [y_1,...,y_N]^T$, $\beta = [\beta_1,..., \beta_N]^T$. The resulting LS-SVM model in dual space becomes:

$$y(x) = \sum_{i=1}^{N} \beta_i K(x, x_i) + b \tag{21}$$

Usually, the training of the LS-SVM model involves an optimal selection of kernel parameters and regularization parameter. For this paper, the RBF Kernel is used which is expressed as:

$$K(x, x_i) = e^{-\frac{\|x - x_i\|^2}{2\sigma^2}} \tag{22}$$

Note that σ^2 is a parameter associated with RBF function which has to be tuned. There is no doubt that the efficient performance of LS-SVM model involves an optimal selection of kernel parameter, σ^2 and regularization parameter, γ. In (Espinoza et al., 2007), these parameters selection are tuned via cross-validation technique. Even though this technique seemed to be simple, the forecasting performance by using this technique is at average accuracy (Lean et al., 2009). Thus by using GA as an optimizer, a more accurate result is expected. In addition, GA is known as a powerful stochastic search and optimization technique. The hybridization of GA and LS-SVM should gives better accuracy and good generalization, especially in real and reactive power tracing problem.

4. Genetic algorithm

Genetic Algorithm (GA) is known as a subset of evolutionary algorithms that model biological processes which is influenced by the environmental factor to solve various numerical optimization problems. GA allows a population composed of many individuals or called chromosomes to evolve under specified rules to a state that maximizes the fitness or minimizes the cost functions. Traditionally, GA is utilizing binary numbers as a representation, but the using of floating and real numbers as representation are becoming popular lately. This paper will focuses on the technique that using floating numbers which has been developed by (R. L & S. A. Haupt, 1998).

If the chromosome has N_{par} parameters (an N-dimensional optimization problem) given by $p_1, p_2, \ldots, p_{Npar}$, then the single chromosome is written as an array with 1 x N_{par} elements as follows:

$$chromosome = [p_1, p_2, p_3, \ldots\ldots, p_{Npar}] \tag{23}$$

GA does not work with a single string but with a population of strings, which evolves iteratively by generating new individuals taking the place of their parents. Normally, the initial population is generated at random. The performance of each string is evaluated according to its fitness. Fitness is used to provide a measure of how individuals have performed in the problem domain. The choice of objective and fitness function is proposed in the next section.

With an initial population of individuals and evaluated through its fitness, the operators of GA begin to generate a new and improved population from the old one. A simple GA consists of three basic operations: selection, crossover and mutation. Selection determines which individuals are chosen for crossover and a process in which individual chromosomes are copied according to their fitness. Parents are selected according to their fitness performance and this can be done through several methods. For this paper, *roulette wheel* selection method is used (Goldberg, 1989).

Crossover is a process after the parents chromosomes are selected from *roulette wheel* method. It is a process that each individual will exchange information to create new structure of chromosome called offspring. It begins by randomly selecting a parameter in the first pair of parents to be crossover at point:

$$\alpha = round\{random * N_{par}\} \tag{24}$$

Let

$$parent_1 = [p_{m1}, \ldots, p_{m\alpha}, \ldots, p_{mNpar}] \tag{25}$$

$$parent_2 = [p_{d1}, \ldots, p_{d\alpha}, \ldots, p_{dNpar}] \tag{26}$$

where m and d subscripts discriminate between the *mom* and *dad* parent. Then the selected parameters are combined to form new parameters that will appear in the offspring, as follow:

$$p_{new1} = p_{m\alpha} - \beta[p_{m\alpha} - p_{d\alpha}] \tag{27}$$

$$p_{new2} = p_{d\alpha} + \beta[p_{m\alpha} - p_{d\alpha}] \tag{28}$$

where β is also a random value between 0 and 1. In this paper, small modification of extrapolation and crossover methods which has been proposed in (R. L & S. A. Haupt, 1998) was done in equations (29) and (30) to obtain the offsprings, as follow (Sulaiman et al., 2010):

$$offspring_1 = [p_{m1}, \ldots, p_{new1}, \ldots, p_{mNpar}] \tag{29}$$

$$offspring_2 = [p_{d1}, \ldots, p_{new2}, \ldots, p_{dNpar}] \quad (30)$$

Although selection and crossover are applied to chromosome in each generation to obtain a new set for better solutions, occasionally they may become overzealous and lose some useful information. To protect these irrecoverable loss or premature convergence occur, mutation is applied. Mutation is random alteration of parameters with small probability called probability of mutation (0-10%). Multiplying the mutation rate by the total number of parameters gives the number of parameters that should be mutated. Next, random numbers are chosen to select of the row and columns of the parameters to be mutated. A mutated parameter is replaced by a new random parameter.

5. GA-SVM for power tracing

In LS-SVM function estimation, the standard framework is based on a primal-dual formulation as explained in section 3. Usually, the training of the LS-SVM model involves an optimal selection of kernel parameters and regularization parameter. In order to find the optimal value of regularization parameter, γ and Kernel RBF parameter, σ^2, the hybrid genetic algorithm (GA) with LS-SVM is proposed. Each chromosome consists of two parameters representing γ and σ^2 in continuous floating numbers that generated randomly. Then each variable are concatenated to construct multivariable string. Fig. 2 shows the example of the chromosome which is can be said as the candidate for solution; for this case is γ and σ^2. The main objective is to find the best combination of these two variables that will produces good generalization of LS-SVM model. The evaluation process is done by using these values in LS-SVM model for training and testing to obtain the mean squares error (MSE) between the output and the target that have been created. The objective function is the value of MSE to be minimized, H as follows:

$$H = \min(MSE) \quad (31)$$

After evaluating each chromosome, the objective function in equation (31) is transformed and normalized to a fitness scheme to be maximized as follows:

$$f = \frac{1}{1+H} \quad (32)$$

The GA properties to find the optimal γ and σ^2 are as follow:

- Selection: roulette wheel
- Crossover probability = 0.9
- Mutation probability = 0.1
- Population = 20
- Maximum iteration = 30

The proposed tracing method is elaborated by designing an appropriate GA-SVM model using LS-SVMlab Toolbox (Pelkmans et al., 2002) for the modified IEEE 14-bus system as shown in Fig. 3. This system consists of 14 buses and 20 transmission lines. The modification has been made for this test system. Initially, the synchronous condenser at bus 3, 4 and 5 are only supporting the reactive power supply for the system. For this case, these synchronous condensers are treated and work as normal generators to alleviate the real power support at generator bus 1. In addition, the modification is made to see the performance of design GA-SVM model for the system with more than two generators. The input samples for training is assembled using daily load curve and performing load flow analysis for every hour of load demand using MATPOWER software package (Zimmerman et al., 2011). Daily load curves for every bus for real and reactive power are shown in Figs. 4 and 5 respectively. Input data and target data for real and reactive power allocation problem for GA-SVM model are tabulated in Table 1. The flow of GA-SVM is depicted in Fig. 6.

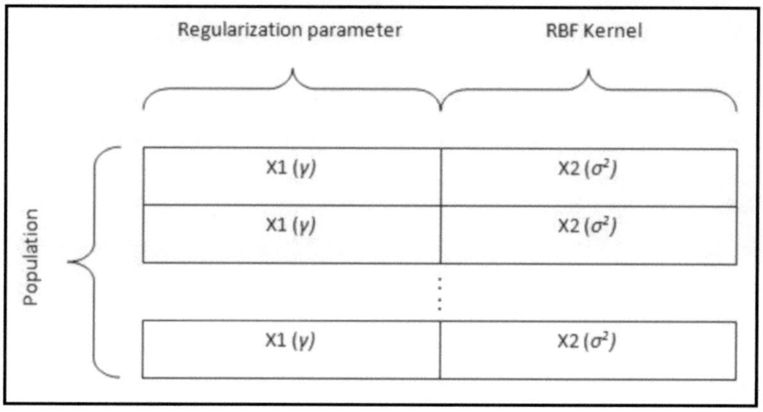

Fig. 2. Chromosome for solution

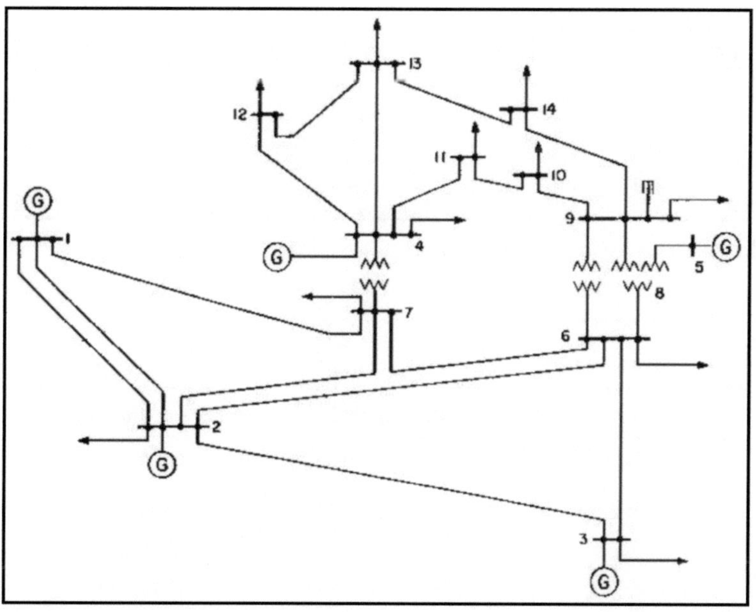

Fig. 3. Modified IEEE-14 bus system

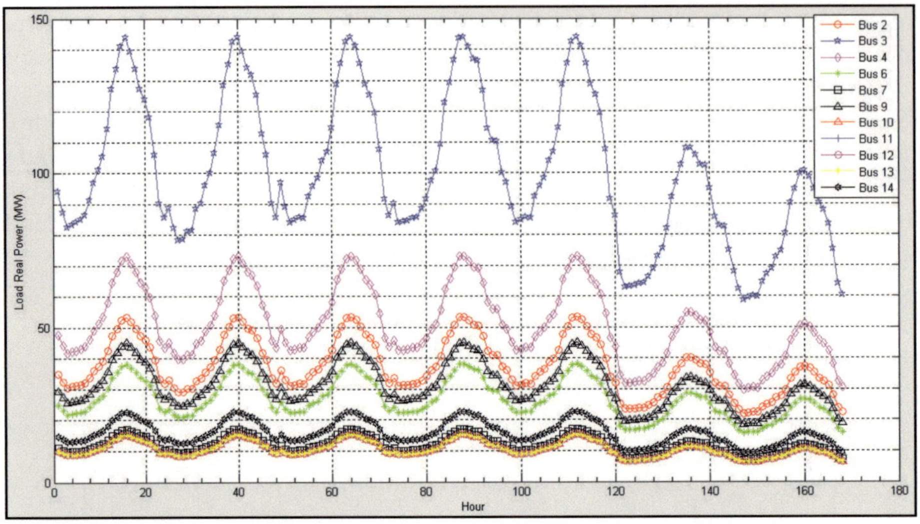

Fig. 4. Daily load curve for real power

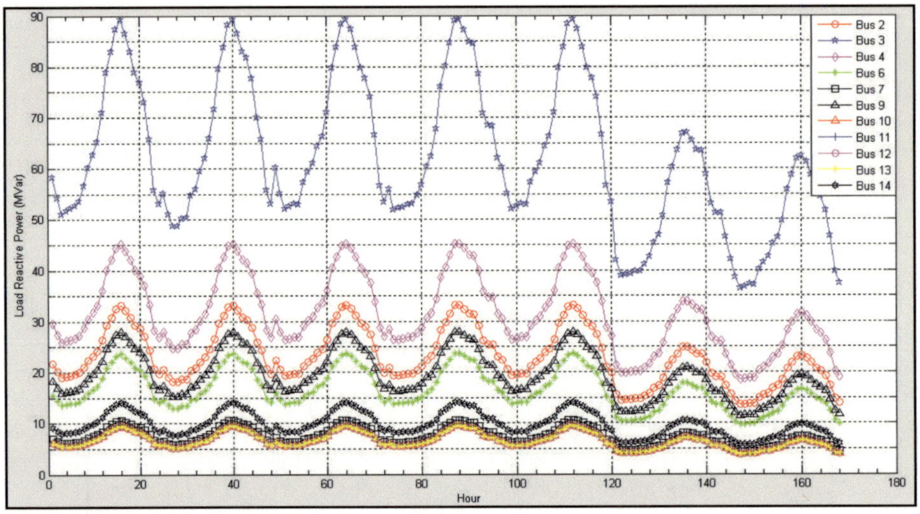

Fig. 5. Daily load curve for reactive power

Input and Output	Description
I_1 to I_{11}	Real load demand (Pd_2, Pd_3, Pd_4, Pd_6, Pd_7,Pd_9, Pd_{10}, Pd_{11}, Pd_{12}, Pd_{13}, Pd_{14})
I_{12} to I_{22}	Reactive load demand (Qd_2, Qd_3, Qd_4, Qd_6, Qd_7,Qd_9, Qd_{10}, Qd_{11}, Qd_{12}, Qd_{13}, Qd_{14})
I_{23} to I_{26}	Scheduled real power generation (P_{G2} to P_{G5})
O_1 to O_{140}	5 generators' contributions to all buses

Table 1. Description of inputs and outputs of the GA-SVM model

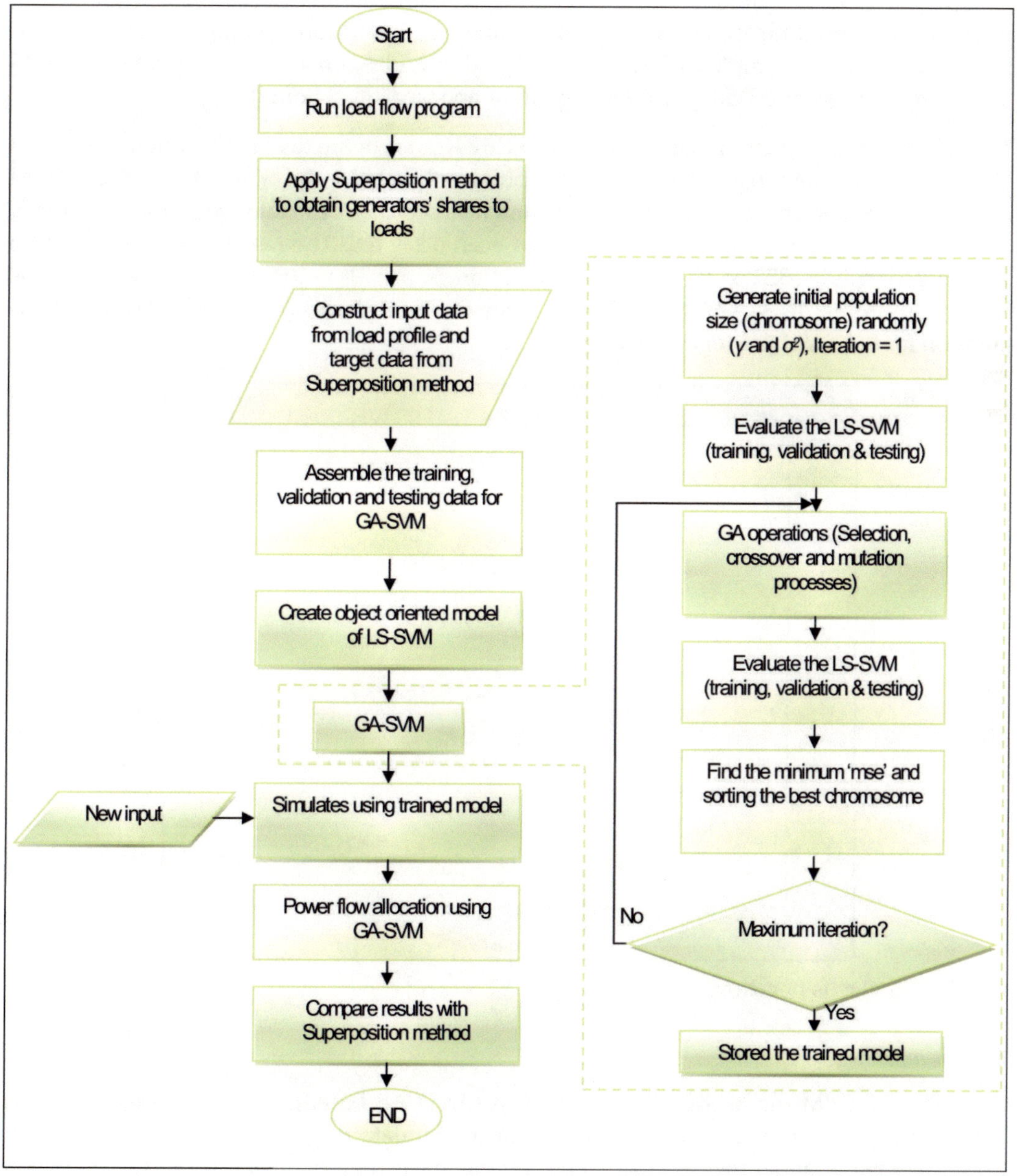

Fig. 6. Flow of proposed GA-SVM

6. Results and discussion

6.1 Training, validation and testing processes

After the input and target of training data have been created, the next step is to divide the data (D and T) up to training, validation and testing subsets. In this case, one week of load profiles data is used for these processes. 48 samples of data (Monday and Sunday) are used for the training, 72 samples (Tuesday, Wednesday and Saturday) for validation and 48 samples (Thursday and Friday) for testing out of one week (168 hours).

The values of regularization parameter, γ and RBF Kernel, σ^2 are decided through the hybrid GA-SVM model that has been discussed previously. From the simulation of GA-SVM model, the final value γ of is set to 913.7632 and σ^2 is set to 9.9813 yields reasonable accuracy of the output of the predictive model that has been designed. The mean square error (MSE) for validation is 3.8322×10^{-5} and for validation is 5.3981×10^{-5} which shows that the estimation process by GA-SVM model is successful. The mean squares error (MSE) versus iteration for GA-SVM model is shown in Fig. 7.

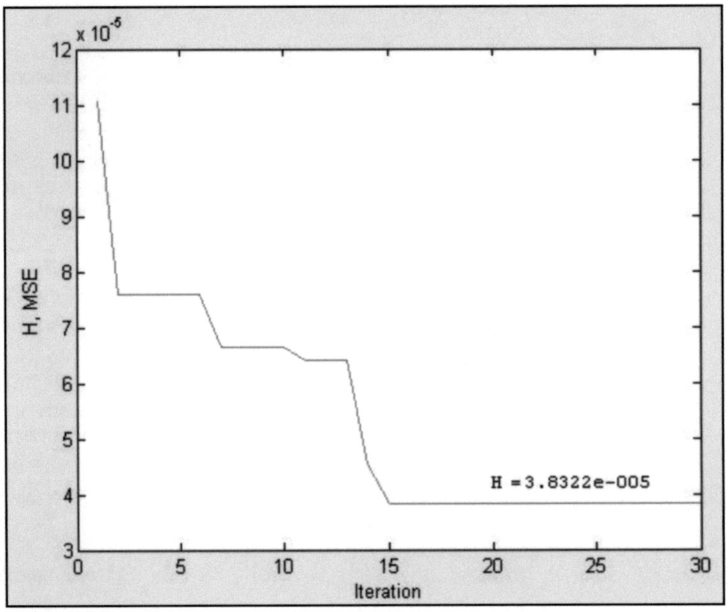

Fig. 7. MSE versus Iteration

6.2 Pre-testing

Once the GA-SVM model has been trained in MATLAB based, the pre-testing process is done where the entire sample of data is used to simulate the model. The obtained result from the trained model then is evaluated with the linear regression analysis. The regression analysis that refers to Generator 2 to real load bus 10 is shown in Fig. 8. The correlation coefficient, (R) for this particular real power allocation is equal to one indicates the perfect correlation between trained GA-SVM with Superposition method results. The MSE value for pre-testing is 4.5401×10^{-5}.

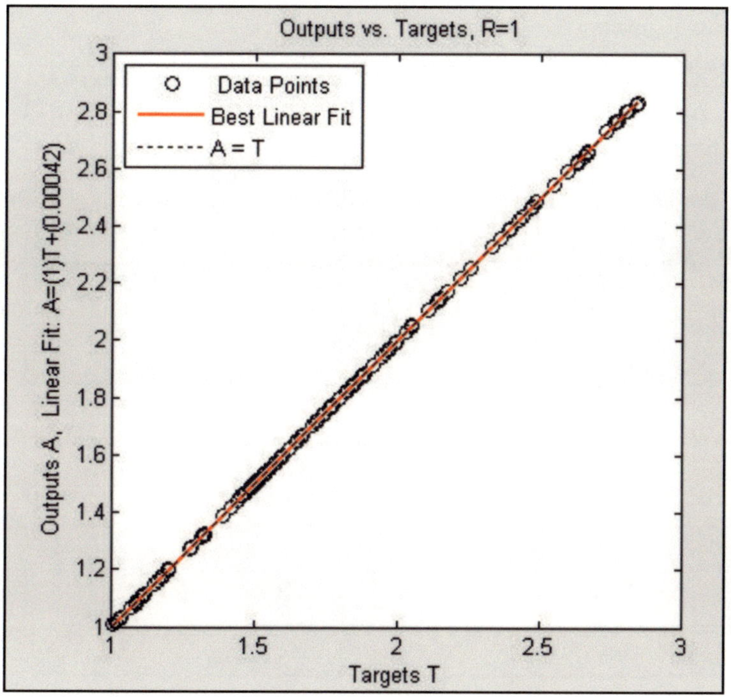

Fig. 8. Regression analysis between hybrid GA-SVM output and corresponding target

6.3 Simulation

The case scenario is that real and reactive power at each load is assumed to increase by 10% from hours 1 to 12 and 20 to 24; and to decrease 15% from hours 13 to 19 from the nominal trained pattern. This also assumed that all generators increase and decrease their production proportionally according to the variation of demands. This simulation aims to observe the effect of increment and decrement of the schedule in load demands. Figs. 9 and 10 show the results of generators' shares at load bus 2 for real and reactive power respectively within 24 hours. The GA-SVM output is indicated by solid lines while the Superposition method is indicated by the points 'o'. From this result, it can be observed that the GA-SVM model can allocates the power flow from individual generators to loads with the same pattern of Superposition method's output.

Contributions of real and reactive power from individual generators to loads on hours 14 out of 24 hours using proposed GA-SVM model and Superposition method are tabulated in Tables 2 and 3 respectively. The results obtained by GA-SVM are compared well with the results from Superposition method. The largest discrepency between generators' share of real and reactive power allocation using GA-SVM and Superposition method are 0.0232 MW at load bus 3 for generator 1 and 0.0187 MVar at load bus 3 for generator 3 respectively. It can be seen that the results obtained utilizing GA-SVM was in conformity with the actual load demand from load flow study although there were small variations in the predicted results. However, the prediction of GA-SVM model was successful since it ables to allocate the ouput of power allocation for new input data with more that 99% accuracy.

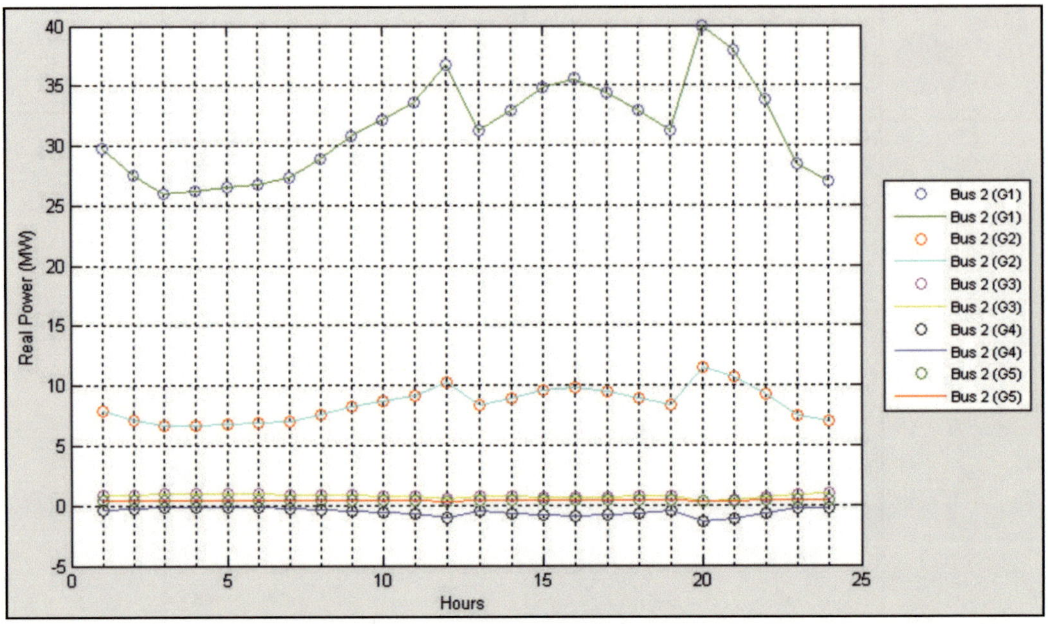

Fig. 9. Real power flow allocation from individual generators to load bus 2 within 24 hours using GA-SVM and Superposition method

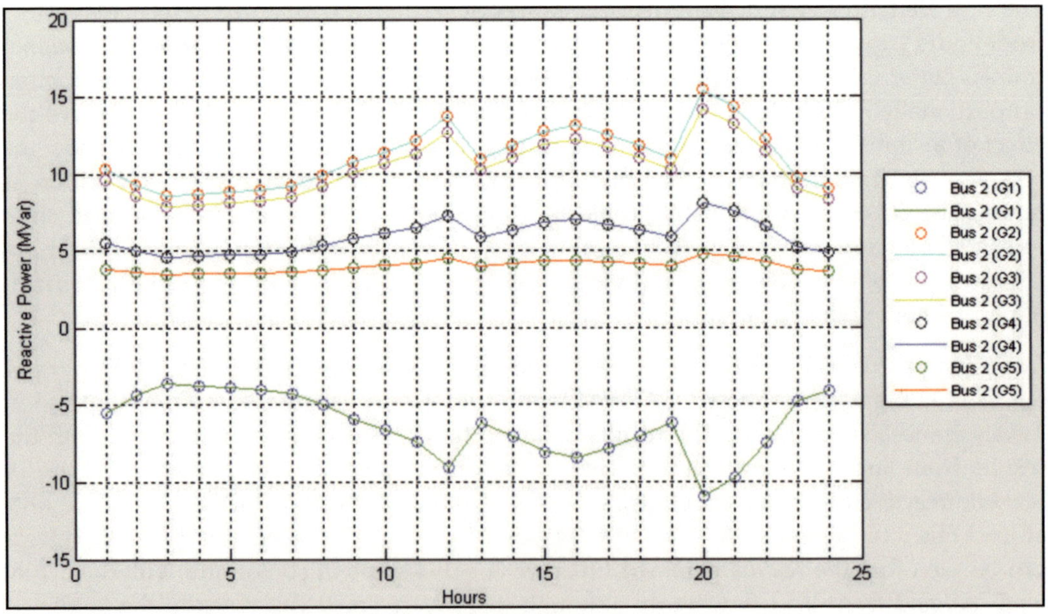

Fig. 10. Reactive power flow allocation from individual generators to load bus 2 within 24 hours using GA-SVM and Superposition method

Bus\Gen	G1		G2		G3		G4		G5		Total		From loadflow	
	P	Q	P	Q	P	Q	P	Q	P	Q	P	Q	P	Q
1	0.0	0.0	0.0	0.0	0.0	0.0	0.0	0.0	0.0	0.0	0.0	0.0	0.0	0.0
2	32.9	-7.1	8.9	11.8	0.7	11.0	-0.7	6.3	0.4	4.1	42.3	26.2	42.3	26.2
3	78.9	-18.5	21.4	27.7	12.0	34.4	-0.4	16.4	2.0	10.6	113.9	70.6	113.9	70.6
4	9.2	-2.0	2.3	3.2	0.4	3.2	1.2	2.7	0.5	1.3	13.5	8.4	13.5	8.4
5	0.0	0.0	0.0	0.0	0.0	0.0	0.0	0.0	0.0	0.0	0.0	0.0	0.0	0.0
6	42.6	-9.9	11.2	14.9	2.3	15.2	0.2	9.4	1.5	6.2	57.8	35.8	57.8	35.8
7	22.8	-5.2	5.8	7.9	0.9	7.8	0.1	5.1	0.6	3.2	30.2	18.7	30.2	18.7
8	0.0	0.0	0.0	0.0	0.0	0.0	0.0	0.0	0.0	0.0	0.0	0.0	0.0	0.0
9	24.9	-5.4	6.3	8.7	1.1	8.8	1.3	5.9	2.1	4.0	35.7	22.1	35.7	22.1
10	8.4	-1.8	2.1	2.9	0.4	3.0	0.6	2.1	0.6	1.3	12.1	7.5	12.1	7.5
11	8.3	-1.8	2.1	2.9	0.3	2.9	0.8	2.2	0.5	1.3	12.1	7.5	12.1	7.5
12	8.2	-1.8	2.1	2.9	0.3	2.9	1.0	2.4	0.4	1.2	12.1	7.5	12.1	7.5
13	8.2	-1.8	2.1	2.9	0.3	2.9	1.0	2.3	0.5	1.2	12.1	7.5	12.1	7.5
14	12.4	-2.7	3.2	4.4	0.5	4.4	1.0	3.2	0.9	1.9	18.0	11.2	18.0	11.2

Table 2. Analysis of generators' contributions to loads on hours 14 using GA-SVM in MW and Mvar

Bus\ Gen	G1		G2		G3		G4		G5		Total		From load flow	
	P	Q	P	Q	P	Q	P	Q	P	Q	P	Q	P	Q
1	0.0	0.0	0.0	0.0	0.0	0.0	0.0	0.0	0.0	0.0	0.0	0.0	0.0	0.0
2	32.9	-7.1	8.9	11.8	0.7	11.0	-0.7	6.3	0.4	4.1	42.3	26.2	42.3	26.2
3	78.9	-18.5	21.4	27.7	12.0	34.4	-0.4	16.4	2.0	10.6	113.9	70.6	113.9	70.6
4	9.2	-2.0	2.3	3.2	0.4	3.2	1.2	2.7	0.5	1.3	13.5	8.4	13.5	8.4
5	0.0	0.0	0.0	0.0	0.0	0.0	0.0	0.0	0.0	0.0	0.0	0.0	0.0	0.0
6	42.6	-9.8	11.1	14.9	2.3	15.2	0.2	9.4	1.5	6.2	57.8	35.8	57.8	35.8
7	22.7	-5.2	5.8	7.9	0.9	7.8	0.1	5.1	0.6	3.1	30.2	18.7	30.2	18.7
8	0.0	0.0	0.0	0.0	0.0	0.0	0.0	0.0	0.0	0.0	0.0	0.0	0.0	0.0
9	24.9	-5.4	6.3	8.7	1.1	8.8	1.3	5.9	2.1	4.0	35.7	22.1	35.7	22.1
10	8.4	-1.8	2.1	2.9	0.4	3.0	0.6	2.1	0.6	1.3	12.1	7.5	12.1	7.5
11	8.3	-1.8	2.1	2.9	0.3	2.9	0.8	2.2	0.5	1.3	12.1	7.5	12.1	7.5
12	8.2	-1.8	2.1	2.9	0.3	2.9	1.0	2.4	0.4	1.2	12.1	7.5	12.1	7.5
13	8.2	-1.8	2.1	2.9	0.3	2.9	1.0	2.3	0.5	1.2	12.1	7.5	12.1	7.5
14	12.4	-2.7	3.2	4.4	0.5	4.4	1.0	3.2	0.9	1.9	18.0	11.2	18.0	11.2

Table 3. Analysis of generators' contributions to loads on hours 14 using Superposition method in MW and MVar

In addition, the GA-SVM model computes the results within 750 ms whereas the Superpostion method took about 15 seconds to calculate the same real and rective power allocation in this simulation process. It would be worth to highlight that better computation time is crucial to improve the online application. For that, the GA-SVM provides the results in a faster manner with good accuracy.

7. Conclusion

The effectiveness of GA in determining the optimal values of hyper-parameters of LS-SVM to solve power tracing problem has been discussed in this paper. The developed hybrid GA-SVM adopts real and reactive power tracing output determined by Superposition method as an estimator to train the model. The results show that GA-SVM gives good accuracy in predicting the generators' output and compared well with Superposition method and load flow study. It is worth to highlight the proposed GA-SVM possesses the following feature:

- The proposed method adopted Superposition method which based on well-known circuit theories as a teacher in training, validating and testing processes.
- Power contributed by each generator may have positive and negative values indicate the direction of the power at load.
- Since the Superposition method is used as a teacher, the tracing method can be utilized in circular or loop flow system.
- The integration of GA and LS-SVM is straight forward and simple by utilizing the toolbox.
- The proposed method provides the results in a faster manner with good accuracy.

The proposed hybrid method can be utilized as generation forecasting management since the power produced by each generator has been traced and identified. Thus the transmission congestion problem can be easily avoided by proper generation scheduling which can be proposed and studied in the future works.

8. Acknowledgment

The authors wish to acknowledge the Ministry of Higher Education (MOHE), Malaysia and Universiti Teknologi Malaysia (UTM) for the funding of this project.

9. References

Bialek, J., & Tam, D. B. (1996). Tracing the generators' output. *Proceeding of International Conference on Opportunities and Advances in International Electric Power Generation*, pp. 133-136, March 19-20, 1996

Espinoza, M.; Suykens, J.; & Moor, B. (2006). Fixed-size Least Squares Support Vector Machines: A Large Scale Application in Electrical Load Forecasting. *Computational Management Science*, Vol. 3, No. 2, pp. 113-129

Espinoza, M.; Suykens, J. A. K.; Belmans, R.; & De Moor, B. (2007). Electric Load Forecasting. *IEEE Control Systems Magazine*, Vol. 27, No. 5, pp. 43-57. ISSN 1066-033X

Goldberg, D. E. (1989). *Genetic algorithms in search, optimization, and machine learning*. Addison-Wesley, ISBN 0-201-15767-5, Reading, Mass

Haupt, R. L., & Haupt, S. E. (1998). *Practical genetic algorithms*. Wiley Pub, ISBN 0-471-45565-2, New York

Lean, Y.; Huanhuan, C.; Shouyang, W.; & Kin Keung, L. (2009). Evolving Least Squares Support Vector Machines for Stock Market Trend Mining. *IEEE Transactions on Evolutionary Computation*, Vol. 13, No. 1, pp. 87-102. ISSN 1089-778X

Lo, K. L., & Alturki, Y. A. (2006). Towards reactive power markets. Part 1: reactive power allocation. *IEE Proceedings-Generation, Transmission and Distribution*, Vol. 153, No. 1, pp. 59-70. ISSN 1350-2360

Mustafa, M. W., Khalid, S. N., Shareef, H., & Khairuddin, A. (2008a). A new method for real power transfer allocation using modified nodal equations. *Proceeding of IEEE 2nd International Power and Energy Conference (PECon 2008)*, Johor Bahru, Malaysia. December 1-3, 2008

Mustafa, M. W., Khalid, S. N., Shareef, H., & Khairuddin, A. (2008b). Reactive power transfer allocation method with the application of artificial neural network. *IET Generation, Transmission & Distribution*, Vol. 2, No. 3, pp. 402-413. ISSN 1751-8687

Mustafa, M. W., Sulaiman, M. H., Shareef, H., & Khalid, S. N. A. (2011). Transmission Loss Allocation in Deregulated Power System Using Hybrid Genetic Algorithm-Support Vector Machine Technique. *Cyber Journals: Multidisciplinary Journal in Science and Technology, Journal of Selected Areas in Renewable and Sustainable Energy (JRSE), January Edition*, pp. 10-19. ISSN 1925-2676

Pantos, M., Verbic, G., & Gubina, F. (2005). Modified topological generation and load distribution factors. *IEEE Transactions on Power Systems*, Vol. 20, No. 4, pp. 1998-2005. ISSN 0885-8950

Pelkmans, K.; Suykens, J. A. K.; Gestel, T. V.; Brabanter, J. D.; Lukas, L. & Hamers, B. (2002). *LS-SVMlab: A Matlab/C Toolbox for Least Squares Support Vector Machines*. Leuven, Belgium: ESAT-SISTA, K. U. Leuven. Available from
http://www.esat.kuleuven.be/sista/lssvmlab/

Sulaiman, M. H.; Aliman. O &, Rahim, S. R. A. (2010). Optimal embedded generation allocation in distribution system employing real coded genetic algorithm. *Proceeding of International Conference on Power Systems Engineering (ICPSE 2010)*, pp. 591-596, ISSN 1307-6892, Penang, Malaysia. February 24-26, 2010

Sulaiman, M. H., Mustafa, M. W., & Aliman, O. (2008). Power flow and loss tracing in deregulated transmission system using proportional tree method. *International Review of Electrical Engineering (IREE)*, Vol. 3, No. 4, pp. 691-698. ISSN 1827-6660

Suykens, J. A. K.; Gestel, T. V.; Brabanter, J. D.; Moor, B. D.; & Vandewelle, J. (2002). *Least Squares Support Vector Machines*. World Scientific, ISBN 981-238-151-1, Singapore

Teng, J.-H. (2005). Power flow and loss allocation for deregulated transmission systems. *International Journal of Electrical Power & Energy Systems*, Vol. 27, No. 4, pp. 327-333. ISSN 0142-0615

Vapnik, V. N. (1995). *The Nature of Statistical Learning Theory 2nd ed.* Springer-Verlag, ISBN 0-387-98780-0, New York

Wen-Chen, C., Bin-Kwie, C., & Chung-Hsien, L. (2004). Allocating the costs of reactive power purchased in an ancillary service market by modified Y-bus matrix method. *IEEE Transactions on Power Systems,* Vol. 19, Np. 1, pp. 174-179. ISSN 0885-8950

Wu, F. F., Yixin, N., & Ping, W. (2000). Power transfer allocation for open access using graph theory-fundamentals and applications in systems without loopflow. *IEEE Transactions on Power Systems,* Vol. 15, No. 3, pp.923-929. ISSN 0885-8950

Zimmerman, R. D.; Murillo Sanchez, C. E. & Thomas, R. J. (2011). MATPOWER: Steady-State Operations, Planning, and Analysis Tools for Power Systems Research and Education. *IEEE Transactions on Power Systems,* Vol 26, No. 1, pp. 12-19. ISSN 0885-8950

8

Hybrid Genetic Algorithm for Fast Electromagnetic Synthesis

Artem V. Boriskin[1,2] and Ronan Sauleau[2]
[1]*Institute of Radiophysics and Electronics of the National Academy of Sciences of Ukraine, Kharkov,*
[2]*Institute of Electronics and Telecommunications of Rennes, UMR CNRS 6164, University of Rennes 1, Rennes,*
[1]*Ukraine*
[2]*France*

1. Introduction

Evolution strategies, implemented in numerical codes, provided researchers with powerful optimization tools capable of finding optimal solutions for a variety of real-world problems. One of the most popular representatives of this family is the Genetic Algorithm (GA) (Barricelli, 1957), which has already been well recognized by the electromagnetic (EM) community (Haupt, 1995; Johnson & Rahmat-Samii, 1997; Weile & Michielssen, 1997; Rahmat-Samii & Michielssen, 1999; Haupt & Werner, 2007; Hoorfar, 2007).

The most attractive features of GA, which are also intrinsic to other evolutionary algorithms (EA), are as follows: they can be applied given limited information about the problem, they do not require initial guesses, and they are able to produce non-intuitive solutions. These capabilities are provided thanks to a two-fold strategy that combines a stochastic global exploration and a local exploitation implemented in the form of an iterative modification and reproduction of already known individuals. The key to success here is the effective division of labour between both.

Different EAs use different ways of balancing between the global and local search, based on the corresponding evolutionary model. A possible bottleneck here is that as soon as a new evolutionary model is introduced, one starts thinking in terms and within the bounds dictated by the analogy used, whereas these bounds are not absolute. They arise from specific tasks addressed by nature and therefore are inherently adapted to "boundary conditions" of specific scenarios. For instance, genetic strategy (Barricelli, 1957) is oriented towards a huge population of diverse individuals and almost unbound time frames. This strategy is rather slow but it aims at the ultimate goal of finding the very best of all possible solutions. This is in contrast to the ant colony (Colorni et al., 1991) and particle swarm (Kennedy & Eberhart, 1995) strategies that naturally serve finding a reasonably good solution during a limited timeframe. Nevertheless, in spite of the formal differences, all population-based EAs have much in common. They share the same goal of finding the global extremum among multiple local ones; they operate with subsets of trial solutions;

they rely on stochastic decision-making mechanisms; and they manipulate with the probability in order to guide the optimization process. The latter is controlled by the selected evolutionary model and evaluation principles, which define the chances of each individual to survive and reproduce in later generations. In addition, all EAs favour improvement of the whole population instead of promoting a single leader. This protects EAs from being trapped in local minima but handicaps the solution convergence rate and may cause stagnation at the later stage of optimization. This also makes sharp distinction between stochastic global techniques and deterministic local ones. Contrary to global ones, local search techniques use cost function gradients to govern the search process. Although criticized for being slow and dependent on the initial guess, local techniques are the only means of learning (Paszkowicz, 2006; Elmihoub et al., 2006). This makes them complementary to EAs and highlights the importance and strong potential of hybridized optimization algorithms, which combine elements of different evolutionary and deterministic models. Such algorithms have been strongly advocated in a number of papers, e.g. (Renders et al., 1996; Haupt & Chung, 2003; Elmihoub et al., 2006); nevertheless they are still rarely used in electromagnetics.

In this chapter, we provide an insight into the general logic behind selection of the GA control parameters (Section 2), discuss the ways of boosting the algorithm efficiency (Section 3), and finally introduce a simple global-local hybrid GA capable of fast and reliable optimization of multi-parameter and multi-extremum functions (Section 4). The effectiveness of the proposed algorithm is demonstrated by numerical examples, namely: synthesis of linear antenna arrays with pencil-beam and flat-top patterns (Section 5).

2. Global and local skills of genetic algorithms

Genetic algorithm (same as any other population-based EA) can be compared with a two-handed machine that uses one hand for random selection of individuals from a given pool of possible solutions and another hand for "cheating" the first one. The cheating is realized in the form of manual weighting the probability of a favourable event to happen. In particular, this is used to promote local search in the neighbourhood of previously found fittest solutions. Different evolutionary strategies incorporate different cheating capabilities whose strength is adjusted by varying algorithms control parameters. A few examples provided below illustrate how the GA skills can be adapted in the favour of either global or local search. Similar mechanisms can be easily identified in other EAs as well.

The terminology used hereafter is borrowed from (Johson & Rahmat-Samii, 1997) whereas a recommended source for detailed information about the properties of GA operators is (Haupt & Haupt, 2004).

In most cases, GA starts with a random seed of a finite number of individuals that constitute the initial population. At this moment any solution within the given design space can be selected and probability of this event to occur equals reverse of the pool volume (the total number of all possible solutions or combinations of parameters). The situation changes for the second and subsequent generations. Here, the number and locations of potential offspring are limited and determined by the previous population. This happens because offspring always preserve properties of parents (at least partially) and therefore they can occur in a limited number of locations dictated by their parents and the crossover/mutation schemes used (Haupt & Haupt, 2004, Chapter 5). Thus, except for the initial step, one never deals with a complete pool of solutions. Instead, as soon as the initial population is randomly generated, one has access only to a subset which includes the current population and its potential offspring. During optimization this trial subset is gradually transformed in a way to include individuals from the most promising regions of the original design space.

To reach this goal, the following sequence of operations is performed at each step of the optimization process. First, the trial subset is expanded by adding new individuals produced via reproduction of already known ones or randomly generated. Then, the quality of new individuals is evaluated and all individuals are ranked according to their cost function values. Finally, the worst individuals are discarded. Hopefully, each iteration moves search towards a region holding the global extremum, thanks to the continuous discarding of individuals which belong to less promising parts of the original design space.

Convergence of this process depends on two factors: (i) the rule that defines interrelation between a population at hand and the corresponding trial subset, and (ii) the criteria used for estimating the individuals' quality, which affects chances of individuals to survive and reproduce. To boost convergence, an additional weighting of individuals in populations can be introduced based on the cost function value or some additional criterion, e.g. taboo (Ji & Klinowski, 2009) or penalty (Paszkowicz, 2009) principles.

The influence of different factors on the GA convergence rate is discussed below.

The role of the population size seems obvious: the larger the size, the more uniform the exploration (or sampling) of the design space is provided. On the other hand, an oversized population slows convergence due to degeneracy of individuals that causes a strong offspring dispersion. This hinders local search because offspring often escape the parent solution's basin. Therefore some optimal size always exists, although it depends on the landscape of the fitness function and properties of the GA operators used. Useful hints on this subject are given in (Linden, 1999).

Two main GA operators are crossover and mutation. They define the size and structure of the trial subset accessible at each step. For instance, if a single-point crossover is implemented in a binary GA, all possible offspring are limited to a few choices that occur along the lines coinciding with the edges of a hyper rectangle with two parents on opposite vertices. The size of this hyper rectangle depends on the distance between parents, whereas sampling density is proportional to the number of crossing points. For instance, the number of potential offspring increases if a double-point crossover is used, whereas a uniform sampling can only be provided if uniform crossover is implemented. For numerical examples the reader could refer to (Haupt & Haupt, 2004, Chapter 5).

Mutation operators also suffer from the problems related to non-uniform sampling (Haupt & Haupt, 2004; Paszkowicz, 2006). Although usually positioned as a source of new genetic material, in practice a binary mutation operator (similarly to the crossover operator) is capable of producing only a finite number of offspring, called mutants, confined to orthogonal lines parallel to the axes. Furthermore, the strength of mutation (spread of mutants' locations) cannot be controlled easily because the change of a single bit in the binary string used for storing optimization parameters (called chromosome) has a different impact on the parameters values depending on the bit position. A partial remedy for the latter is in the Gray coding (Taub & Schilling, 1986) or a continuous representation of variables. But this remedy has a side effect because a non-uniform distribution of potential offspring produced by standard binary crossover and mutation operators has its own hidden sense: it provides denser distribution of potential offspring and mutants in the neighbourhood of their parents that enhances local skills of the algorithms.

Finally, a weighting mechanism is implemented in GA in the form of selection principles that define chances of the fittest individuals to survive and reproduce. Among the popular selection principles (Johnson & Rahmat-Samii, 1997; Haupt & Haupt, 2004), the strongest one (local-search oriented) is the roulette wheel with cost-function weighting. This scheme heavily promotes the best individuals and stimulates local search in their neighbourhood. This increases chances for population degeneracy and thus may negatively affect optimization process by premature convergence to a local extremum. To counterbalance this, a permanent inflow of new genetic material should be provided. This is usually done by choosing a larger population size, higher mutation rate, and/or periodic injection of randomly generated individuals. Sharing the GA searching efforts among several most promising individuals can be realized if a so-called tournament principle is used. This scheme deals with randomly selected sub-groups (instead of the whole population) and in such a manner improves chances of next-to-the-best individuals to survive and reproduce in later generations.

Summarizing the discussion, we would like to highlight the following. Although there are many factors affecting the GA performance, they all serve the same reason: to effectively share the algorithm efforts between the stochastic global exploration and local exploitation. Thus variation of any control parameter can be considered as a contribution towards the enhancement of either global or local skills of the algorithm. This simplification helps a lot when adjusting GA control parameters for a specific problem at hand. Finally, one should remember that GA control parameters constitute a system of counterbalances; therefore variation of any parameters usually requires some adjustment of the others (e.g. a smaller population size should be compensated by a larger inflow of new genetic material, etc.). The additional opportunities for boosting the algorithm efficiency are discussed in the following section.

3. On boosting the algorithm efficiency

There are two complementary approaches for boosting the performance of an optimization algorithm. The first one is based on adaptation of the algorithm control parameters during optimization. The second one is based on the amelioration of the design space landscape. The advantages proposed by each approach are summarized below.

3.1 Adaptation of the algorithm control parameters

As it was discussed in Section 2, selection of the algorithm control parameters (e.g. crossover and mutation schemes and rates) and selection mechanisms affects the global and local skills of GAs. Thus, adaptation of these parameters during simulations enables one to gradually shift the search efforts from the global exploration to local exploitation. The adaptation can be carried out based on different time-varying quantities such as iteration number, population diversity, solution quality, or relative improvement. The numerical examples revealing the capabilities of this approach, as well as an exhaustive review of the literature on this subject, can be found in (Eiben et al., 1999; Boeringer et al., 2005).

3.2 Hybridization of different optimization techniques

An additional degree of freedom for adjusting the algorithm capabilities for global and local search can be gained via hybridization of different optimization techniques. Both global-global and global-local hybrids have been reported so far. The former are typically used to compensate for intrinsic weak points of evolutionary algorithms that come from their natural analogues (Robinson et al., 2002; Salhi & Queen, 2004; Paszkowicz, 2006; Grimaccia et al., 2007); whereas the latter are used for boosting the algorithm efficiency at the later stage of optimization and/or learning purposes (Chelouah & Siarry, 2003; Ishibuchi, 2003; Haupt & Chung, 2003; Elmihoub et al., 2006; Paszkowicz, 2006; Ngo et al., 2007; Quevedo-Teruel et al., 2007; Boriskin & Sauleau, 2011a).

The great potential of global-local hybrids is explained by the distinction and complementarity between the local and global search techniques. Both these features come from the decision-making mechanism implemented in local and global search techniques. The former defines direction where to go (based on the cost function gradient), whereas the latter relies on the elimination principle implemented in the form of a successive dismissal of less promising individuals. In such a way, EAs give preference to the gradual improvement of the entire population instead of promoting a single individual. This is contrary to the local gradient-based algorithms that start from a given initial guess and perform a down-hill movement towards a nearest minimum following the shortest trajectory. Finally, local techniques are the only means of learning. If hybridized with EAs, they can supply the latter with information about cost function gradients, which can be used for introducing additional weights for individuals with better potential for improvement.

The aforementioned tactics are not new. Their pros and cons are well described in (Elmihoub et al., 2006). Nevertheless, the importance of global-local hybridization is still often underestimated, although the marriage of two is a simple and elegant way to achieve the optimal balance between the global and local skills of GA (or another EA).

3.3 Multi-extremum search capabilities

An important feature of EAs is their intrinsic capability for the multi-extremum search. On the way to an optimal solution, EAs sequentially investigate a number of local extrema. Most often, this information is lost as soon as the corresponding individuals are discarded due to lower fitness values or achievement of a stopping criterion. However, some of the next-to-the-best individuals can belong to basins of optimal solutions (or at least the most feasible ones due to some technical constraints not accounted for in the mathematical model). Therefore, search for multiple extrema and proper usage of the optimization history opens the door for development of advanced global optimization algorithms (Moret et al., 1998; Chelouah & Siarry, 2003).

3.4 Modification of the design space landscape

A deciding factor for the solution convergence rate of any optimization problem is a landscape of the corresponding fitness function. Usually it is accepted as something predefined and therefore invariable, although this is not true. Definitely, above all the landscape depends on the problem at hand, but it can also be affected by the style of parameter representation. This includes the chromosome structure (Weile & Michielssen,

1997) and parameter encoding (ODonnell et al., 2003; Boriskin & Sauleau, 2011a). Therefore adjustment of the fitness function landscape can also be considered as a part of the optimization strategy. Indeed, the landscape can be easily modified via mapping (not obviously identical) accounting for the problem-specific information. If properly done, a new design space becomes more optimization-friendly thanks to a reduced dimensionality, smaller size, and/or smoother landscape.

Note that mapping does not require any modifications of the cost-function itself. This constitutes an important distinction compared to (Ioan et al., 1998) and (Farina & Sykulski, 2001), where it was proposed to reduce the computational load by replacing the original cost function by a simplified or approximated cost function. Instead, the mapping only assumes a change in the way of storing optimization parameters that facilitates integration of such an algorithm with external electromagnetic solvers, even those operating in a "black box" mode. Such an approach can be especially effective if many identical parameters are involved, e.g. geometrical parameters describing an antenna topology (Fernandes, 2002; Robinson et al., 2002; Godi et al., 2007; Boriskin et al., 2010; Rolland et al., 2010; Boriskin & Sauleau, 2011b) or phase/amplitude weights in the antenna aperture (Johnson & Rahmat-Samii, 1997; Pérez & Basterrechea, 2007). A few examples of mapping realized on the basis of different encoding schemes are given in Section 5.

3.5 Summary: Recipe for an efficient global optimizer

Summarizing the discussion, a general recipe for an efficient global optimization algorithm can be outlined as follows. Start with an EA, whose control parameters are selected in a way to promote an exhaustive global exploration. Then gradually shift the algorithm efforts in the favour of the pseudo-local search. This can be done via a gradual adaptation of the algorithm control parameters and /or via a switching between different selection mechanisms. In addition, the learning capabilities of local optimizers can be used for determining the improvement potentials of selected individuals, based on the cost function gradients. This knowledge can be used to guide the selection process. If the optimization process shows signs of stagnations, a switching between different EAs can be performed. Finally, top-*N* individuals (if possible, selected from different solution basins) should be extracted and fine-tuned using a local gradient-based optimizer. Such a complementary strategy offers an optimal division of labour between the global and local search, as well as reaching the very bottom of all identified extrema. The latter is very useful for collecting the problem-specific information. To illustrate the discussion, a simple global-local hybrid GA is introduced in Section 4.

4. Hybrid genetic algorithm

In this section we present a global-local hybrid genetic algorithm (HGA) built in line with recommendations outlined in Section 3.5. The algorithm combines a binary GA and a steepest descent gradient (SDG) algorithm. The former is used for the global exploration, whereas the latter is used for tuning the top-*N* individuals produced by GA (hereafter labelled as "GA top-runners") and considered as initial guesses for local optimization.

A distinctive feature of the proposed algorithm is that it aims not only at a single best solution but instead identifies a given number of GA top-runners that are investigated at the later stage with the aid of the gradient-based SDG optimizer. Such a two-step approach enables us to reduce significantly the GA stagnation period at the later stage of optimization and also to guarantee achievement of the very bottom of multiple extrema whose basins are identified by GA. The final solution is then selected among those produced by SDG.

A flowchart of the proposed HGA is shown in Fig. 1. The purpose of each block of the algorithm is discussed below.

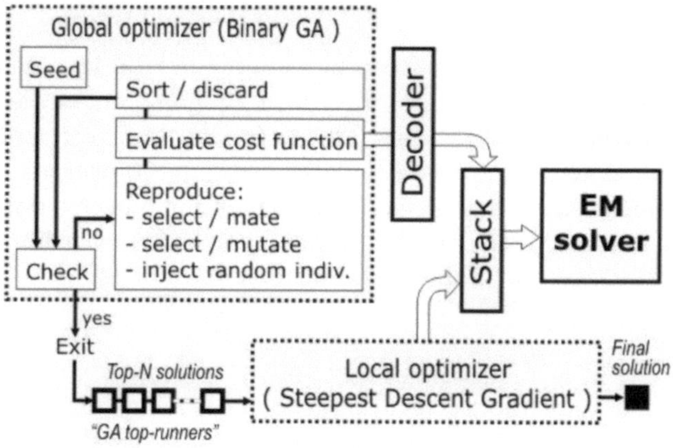

Fig. 1. Flowchart of the HGA

4.1 Global optimizer

The global-local hybridization enables us to let GA concentrate mostly on the global exploration. For this purpose, GA parameters are selected in the following extreme manner that, on the one hand, enhances its global-search capabilities and, on the other hand, strongly promotes pseudo-local search around best individuals: small population size; high mutation rate; periodic injection of randomly generated individuals; no identical individuals (so-called twins) allowed; double-point crossover; uniform mutation. As a counterbalance in the favour of the GA local-searching capabilities, the elitism principle and the roulette wheel cost-function weighted selection mechanism are implemented. The logic behind such a selection of the GA control parameters was discussed in Section 3.

4.2 Local optimizer

For the reported study, the local optimizer is used only for tuning a given number of GA top-runners. To simplify comparison with a standard binary GA, we make SDG algorithm move using the same mesh as for GA, where it is defined by the binary representation of optimization parameters. For simplicity, we disable the "learning function" of the SDG, which means that there are no additional weights introduced in GA selection mechanism and there is no feedback between SDG and GA algorithms after switching between the two.

4.3 Decoder

An important feature of the proposed HGA is a decoder, which is used for communication between GA and EM solver. In contrast to a binary decoder which is an essential part of any binary EA, this additional decoder is used for mapping between the original design space and a new one, which appears due to implementation of specific encoding schemes used for representation of optimization parameters. The decoder is not used for communication between the local optimizer and EM solver because at the final stage of optimization one needs access to the complete pool of parameter combinations corresponding to the original design space.

4.4 Stack

Finally, to avoid the recalculation of the cost function for already known individuals, a stack has been implemented in the form of an array storing parameters of the recently evaluated individuals and their cost function values. This is in line with recommendations given in (Linden, 1999). The optimal size of the stack depends on the complexity of the optimization problem. Our experience shows that a stack with size of three to five populations is usually sufficient. The content of the stack can be updated cyclically: each time a new individual appears it replaces the oldest one in the stack.

4.5 Summary

A combination of the aforementioned features guarantees a high efficiency and reliability of the proposed HGA when solving various optimization problems. It is worth being noted that the performance characteristics of HGA are boosted by letting each algorithm do what it is best suited for, rather than trying to push the optimization process by implementing some deterministic rules, which may cause a conflict with the stochastic nature of the evolutionary strategy. This makes the proposed algorithm very stable and universal. In addition, the performance of the algorithm is strongly facilitated by the amelioration of the design space landscape and elimination of redundant simulations. The effectiveness of the algorithm is demonstrated by solving two multi-parameter optimization problems, typical for EM synthesis (Section 5).

5. Linear antenna array synthesis using HGA

The optimization of antenna arrays has already become classics of the electromagnetic synthesis due to a simple formulation and practical importance, e.g (Haupt, 1995; Johnson & Rahmat-Samii, 1997; Weile & Michielssen, 1997; Rahmat-Samii & Michielssen, 1999; Isernia, et al., 2004; Boeringer et al., 2005; Haupt & Werner, 2007).

To illustrate the performance of the developed HGA, two simple linear array optimization problems are considered, namely phase-only optimization aimed at the minimum side-lobe level (Sections 5.1) and amplitude-phase optimization aimed at a flat-top beam pattern (Section 5.2). In both cases the HGA features are adjusted in a way to let GA perform an exhaustive global search, aiming to identify 10 top-runners to be used as initial guesses for the SDG algorithm. The control parameters are selected as follows: (i) double-point crossover, (ii) uniform mutation with linearly decreasing rate of 20% to 10%, (iii) cost-function-weighted roulette wheel selection mechanism, and (iv) permanent inflow of randomly generated individuals with a rate of 10%. Furthermore, we avoid twins which are replaced by randomly generated individuals each time when identical offspring appear. Finally, to preserve the continuous progress, a few best individuals (~5%) are stored from previous generations (elitism principle). This set of parameters has been approbated on several standard test functions and found to be suitable for various optimization scenarios (these data are skipped for brevity).

In the reported study, we approbate three different encoding schemes, namely: "direct", "relative", and "envelope" ones. The former is a standard encoding scheme when optimization parameters are stored as they are. In the relative scheme, optimization parameters are encoded as differences between neighbours. For most practical cases, this difference does not exceed a half of the parameter variation range. Thus the search domain for new parameters can be reduced by a factor of 2, which means reduction of the entire design space by 2^N parameter combinations, where N is the number of optimization parameters. In case of the envelope encoding scheme, optimization parameters are represented using an envelope line, defined by a polynomial. For the current study the envelope line is constructed as a sum of a few Gaussians. This enables us to replace the original design space with N dimensions by a new one with $3M$ dimensions, where $3M$ parameters are the amplitude, central value, and half-width of each Gaussian, and M is the number of Gaussians used. An empirical rule for selecting the latter parameter is $M = NINT\,(N/10)$, where $NINT$ returns the nearest integer value of the argument. For high-dimensional problems ($N \geq 10$), the reduction of the design space becomes really significant, which strongly facilitates the search for the global extremum.

It is important to note, that in both non-direct encoding schemes the reduction of the design space is obtained via truncation of the original space according to some template defined by the encoding scheme used. Thus it is important to assure that this template "filters" poor solutions and preserve better ones. Definition of such a template is a tricky question. To some extend this is similar to guessing for a class of optimal solutions. It might look like the introduction of a template brings us back to a deterministic optimization scenario, criticised for its strong dependence on the quality of the initial guess, but it does not. As it will be shown below, the selected encoding schemes preserve flexibility sufficient for identification of optimal solution basins for various optimization problems. Once identified, these basins can be effectively studied using a gradient-based local optimizer.

5.1 Test-case 1: Low-sidelobe via phase tapering

The first test problem is the synthesis of a linear array aimed at reduction of the array factor (AF) side-lobe level (SLL) via phase weights optimization. A symmetrical linear array of 31 equally spaced feeds with uniform amplitude weights is considered. The cost function returns a square of difference between the AF SLL for a given phase taper and its desired value. The elements of the array are spaced 0.5λ apart and phase weights are symmetric about the centre of the array with the central element having a phase of zero. Quantization of the phase weights is 4-bit. A trustable reference solution for this test problem can be found in (Haupt, 2007), whereas the one found by the proposed HGA is shown in Fig. 2.

To assess the efficiency of HGA, its performance is superimposed with that of a binary GA whose control parameters are selected in line with general recommendations (Johnson & Rahmat-Samii, 1997). For convenience, parameters of both algorithms are summarized in Table 1.

A typical run of HGA is illustrated in Fig. 3. Here the best and average cost function values are denoted by solid thick lines, whereas cost function values of each individual at each iteration step are denoted by circles. Switching between GA and SDG occurs after 40 generations. The family of ten colour lines shown after 40th generation illustrates the process of tuning the ten GA top-runners by means of the SDG algorithm.

Control parameter	HGA	GA
Population size	50	50
Probability of crossover	Linearly increasing: 65 → 75 %	90 %
Probability of mutation	Linearly decreasing: 20 → 10 %	5 %
Inflow of random individuals	10 %	--
Number of preserved best individuals	5 %	5 %
Selection mechanism	Cost-function weighted roulette wheel	Tournament with sub-population size of 10%
Stopping criterion	40 iterations for GA + as much as needed for SDG	200 iterations

Table 1. Control parameters of HGA and GA algorithms

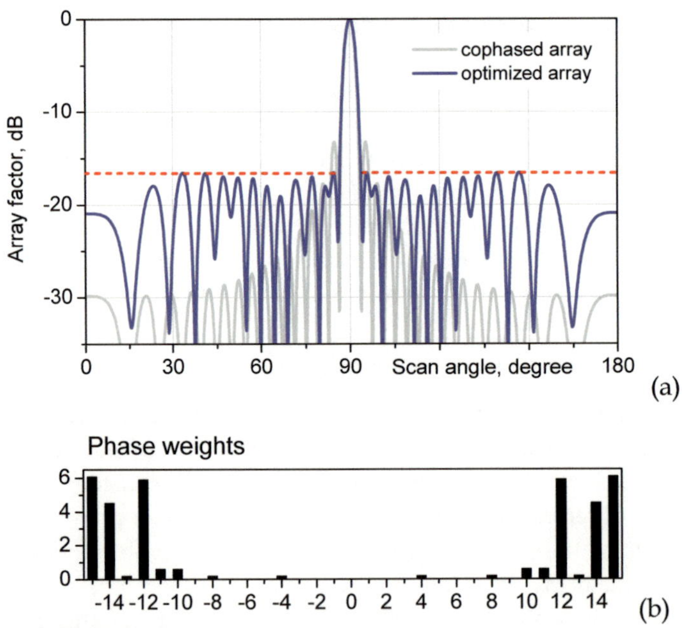

Fig. 2. Optimal solution found by HGA: (a) Array factors of the cophased and optimized arrays, (b) phase weights corresponding to the optimized solution.

The same optimization run represented in terms of AF SLL is shown in Fig. 4. Here it is superimposed with the curve which represents the averaged solution produced by a standard GA. As we can see, the standard GA quickly reaches the AF side-lobe level of approximately -15 dB and spends twice more time to improve solution for another half dB. Such behaviour is typical for GA that continues to explore the entire design space (more or less exhaustively) during all simulation time. This protects GA from "hanging" in local minima but slows down the convergence rate at the later stage of optimization. The proposed HGA is free from this drawback because here GA is used only to identify the optimal solution basins whereas their exploitation is performed in a straight-forward manner using the SDG algorithm, whose performance is based on the cost function gradient. Indeed, we can see that at the initial stage, while HGA is focused on the global exploration, standard GA performs better. Nevertheless, as soon as HGA switches for local optimizer, it catches up and outruns GA in a very few steps.

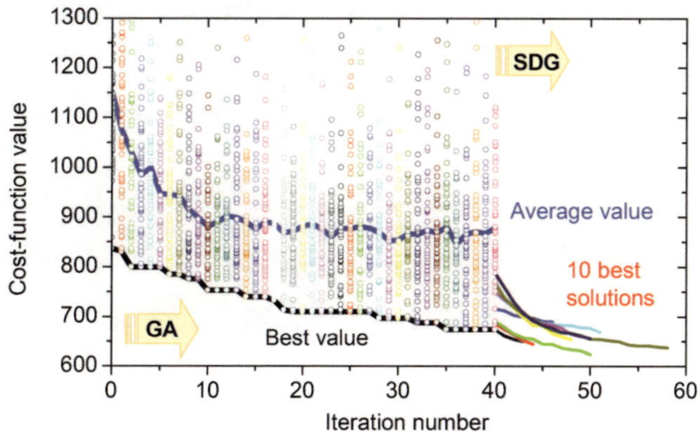

Fig. 3. A typical run of HGA when applied for the linear array synthesis aimed at minimum AF SLL. The AF pattern of the optimized array are shown in Fig. 2.

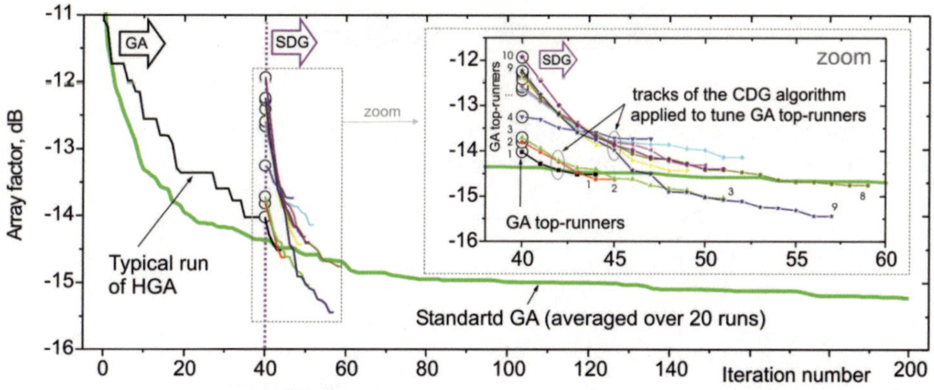

Fig. 4. Comparison between HGA and a standard GA when applied for the linear array synthesis aimed at minimum AF SLL. The HGA run is the same as shown in Fig. 3 but represented in terms of AF SLL. The GA curve is averaged over 20 trials. The inset zooms in on the local optimization stage of HGA.

As already explained, in the proposed hybrid algorithm, GA is used to generate a few best solutions (top-runners) to be then refined using the SDG algorithm. To this end, it is interesting to note that refinement of only the best GA solution (let's label it as a "GA winner") usually does not give much advantage. This is because the winner often belongs to a wide and gently slopping basin, which is optimization-friendly and thus already well examined by GA, whereas most promising solutions are usually located on sides of deep and narrow valleys whose exploration using GA is troublesome. An illustration to such a situation is given in Fig. 4. As we can see, the bottom of the winner's solution basin is reached in four iterations with no significant improvement achieved, whereas the 3-rd, 8-th, and 9-th top-runners demonstrate much better improvement. In particular, refinement of the 9-th top-runner resulted in SLL of -15.4 dB which is approximately 1 dB lower than the final solution found with the GA winner taken as the initial guess.

To get more statistical data, 20 trials have been performed with the same set of parameters (Fig. 5). The obtained data clearly evidence that GA winners rarely appears to be the best initial guess for local search. Therefore evaluation of several top-runners is strongly recommended in order not to waste GA efforts in a hunt for a single winner, which often belongs to a local solution basin. Note that this recommendation remains valid for all tree encoding schemes.

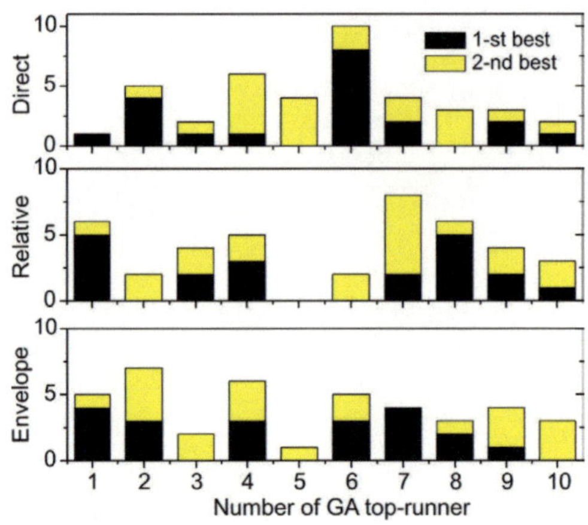

Fig. 5. Number of trials when each of ten GA top-runner, tuned by SDG, finished with the best or second-best result. The total number of trials is 20.

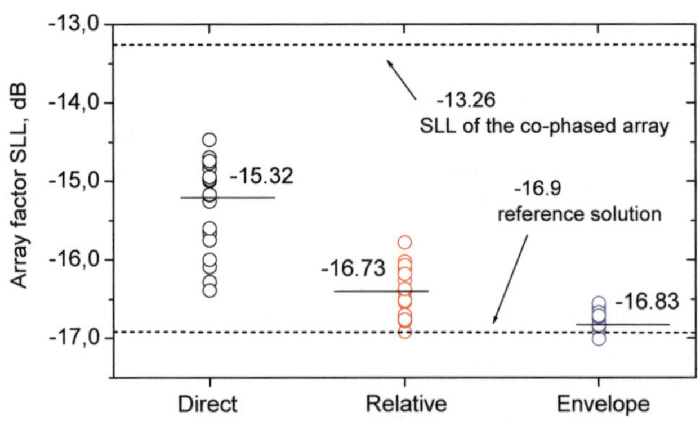

Fig. 6. The final solutions found by HGA in 20 trials applied with three different encoding schemes. The reference solution is borrowed from (Haupt, 1997).

Finally, the impact of different encoding schemes on the algorithm performance is illustrated in Fig. 6. As one can see, the relative and envelope (i.e. Gaussian with M=2) encoding schemes provide much better grouping of final solutions around an improved average value. The better quality of the final solution and the significant reduction of cost function evaluations (see Table 2) are of the primary importance for the EM synthesis because solution of direct EM problems is usually very time consuming.

Algorithm type	No. of optimization parameters	No. of bits per parameter	GA encoding scheme	No. of iterations * (SDG)	Cost function evaluations * (GA + SDG)	Final solution * (SLL, dB)
GA	15	4	Direct	--	10000	-15.18
HGA	15	4	Direct	9.6	3895	-15.32
HGA	15	3	Relative	10.7	4216	-16.73
HGA	6	4	Gauss (M = 2)	11.0	4300	-16.83

* Data averaged over 20 trials

Table 2. Statistical data: HGA vs. standard GA.

5.2 Test-case 2: Flat-top beam via complex weighting

The second test problem is the synthesis of a linear array with a flat-top beam via joint phase and amplitude weights optimization (Fig. 7). This time an even symmetrical linear array of 30 isotropic feeds spaced half lambda apart (d = 0.5λ) is considered. The weights have 4-bit quantization and are symmetric about the centre of the array with the central elements having phase of zero. The pattern template is defined as follows: the flat-top beam parameters are θ_1 = 28° and θ_2 = 30°, the ripples level in the main beam is restricted by F_1=-2 dB, and the highest allowed SLL is -20 dB. The cost function equals the sum of penalties charged for crossing the given corridor (Fig. 7b):

$$F = \sum_{k=1}^{K} \left[\left(F_1 - F(\theta_k)\right) \Big|_{\theta_k \in [0,\theta_1] \cup F < F_1} + \left(F(\theta_k) - F_2\right) \Big|_{\theta_k \in [\theta_2, \pi/2] \cup F > F_2} \right], \quad (1)$$

where K is the number of sampling points, K = 90.

The radiation pattern of the optimized array and its amplitude/phase weights are shown in Fig. 8, and a reference solution is available in (Galan et al., 2011).

To demonstrate the efficiency of the HGA for the considered optimization problem, we compare its performance with that of a standard GA. Parameters of the algorithms are the same as shown in Table 1, except the following: (i) for HGA, the switching between GA and SDG occurs after 50 iterations, (ii) population size for the standard GA has been increased up to 200 individuals in order to compensate for the larger number of optimization parameters (i.e. total of 29, which corresponds to 15 amplitude weights and 14 phase weights). The number of trials has been also increased up to 100.

The statistical data presented in Fig. 9 clearly demonstrate that the proposed HGA significantly outperforms a standard GA in terms of the final solution quality even if the same direct encoding is used, whereas implementation of the advanced encoding schemes leads to further improvement of the stability in the algorithm performance evidenced by the improved quality and superior grouping of final solutions. Once again, the best efficiency is

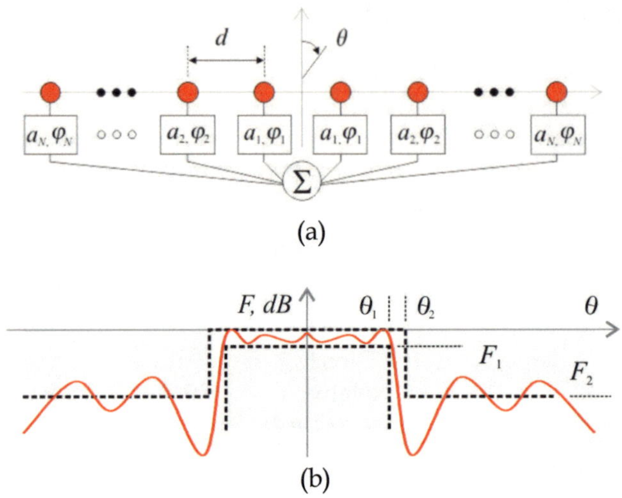

Fig. 7. Linear antenna array under consideration: (a) geometry and notations of the problem, (b) template for the flat-top beam radiation pattern.

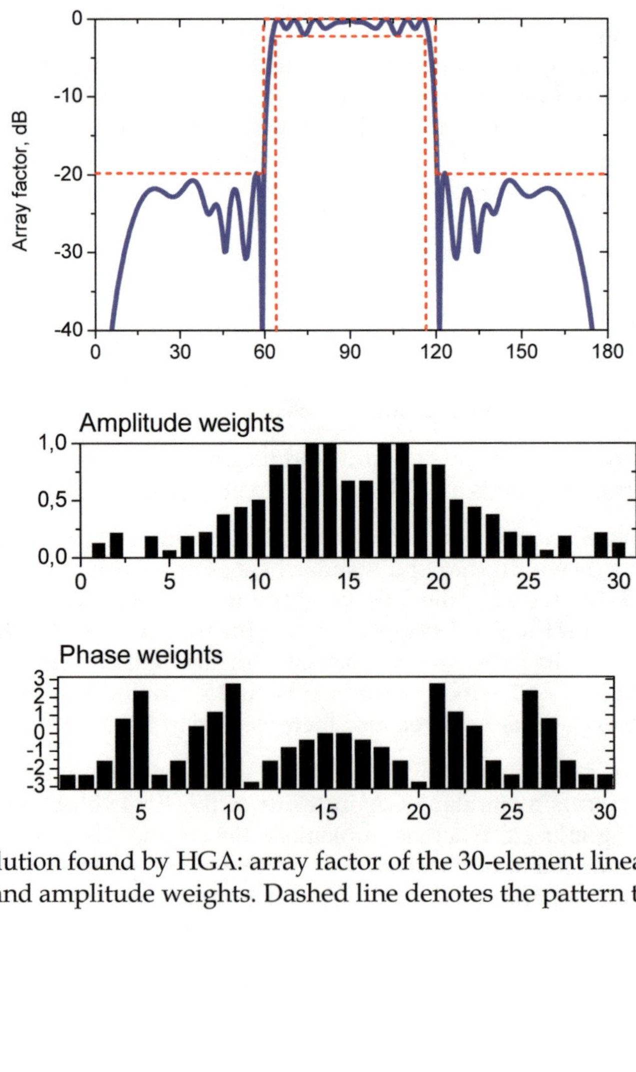

Fig. 8. Optimal solution found by HGA: array factor of the 30-element linear array with optimized phase and amplitude weights. Dashed line denotes the pattern template.

observed for the envelope encoding scheme. Note that this time parameters of two types are involved (i.e. phase and amplitude), therefore the envelope lines for the phase and amplitude weights are reconstructed independently, which explains the increase of the number of optimization parameters up to 12 (two envelope lines build of two Gaussians each). Finally, it is worth being mentioned that the overall computational time (measured in terms of a number of cost function evaluations) is nearly the same for all runs (Table 3), which means that the improved performance is achieved thanks to a more effective optimization strategy.

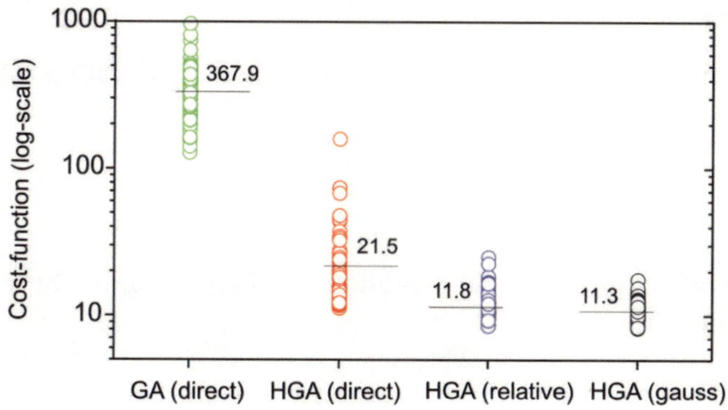

Fig. 9. Final solutions found in 100 trials by a standard GA and HGA with three different encoding schemes. The average values of the final solutions produced are shown nearby.

Algorithm type	No. of optimization parameters	No. of bits per parameter	GA encoding scheme	No. of iterations * (SDG)	Cost function evaluations * (GA + SDG)	Final solution * (cost function)
GA	29	4	Direct	--	20000	367.9
HGA	29	4	Direct	26	17062	21.5
HGA	29	3	Relative	34	21541	11.8
HGA	12	4	Gauss ($M = 2$)	37	23226	11.3

* Data averaged over 100 trials

Table 3. Statistical data: HGA vs. standard GA.

6. Conclusion

In this chapter, the factors affecting the performance of genetic algorithms have been discussed and a few hints on boosting the algorithm efficiency have been provided. In particular, three complementary options have been outlined, namely: adjustment of the algorithm control parameters, hybridisation of different global and local algorithms, and amelioration of the design space implemented in the form of mapping. The discussion has been illustrated by presentation of a global-local hybrid genetic algorithm, whose efficiency in solving multi-parameter problems has been demonstrated through numerical examples.

The main benefits achieved thanks to hybridization of a binary GA and a SDG algorithms are as follows: (i) improved convergence rate, (ii) better quality of the final solution, and (iii) the possibility to investigate multiple local extrema during a single run of the algorithm. These features are of the primary importance for the electromagnetic synthesis. Although the optimal values of the algorithm control parameters may vary for different optimization problems, the general recommendations regarding the logic behind the selection of these parameters are applicable for various optimization scenarios and different evolutionary algorithms.

7. Acknowledgment

This work was supported jointly by Ministry of Science and Education (MSE), Ukraine and Ministère des Affaires Étrangères et Européennes (MAEE), France in the frame of the DNIPRO Program (project N° 24748UH).

8. References

Barricelli, N.A. (1957). Symbiogenetic evolution processes realized by artificial methods, *Methodos*, Vol. 9, pp. 143–182.

Boeringer, D.W.; Werner, D.H. & Machuga, D.W. (2005). A simultaneous parameter adaptation scheme for genetic algorithms with application to phased array synthesis, *IEEE Tran. Antennas Propag.*, Vol. 53, No. 1, pp. 356-371.

Boriskin, A.V.; Balaban, M.V., Galan, A.Yu. & Sauleau, R. (2010). Efficient approach for fast synthesis of phased arrays with the aid of a hybrid genetic algorithm and a smart feed representation, *IEEE Int. Symp. on Phased Array Systems and Technol.*, Boston, MA, pp. 827–832.

Boriskin, A.V. & Sauleau, R. (2011a). Recipe for an efficient hybrid genetic algorithm, *J. Telecommunications and Radio Engineering*, vol. 70, no. 13, pp. 1143–1158.

Boriskin, A.V. & Sauleau, R. (2011b). Numerical investigation into the design of shaped dielectric lens antennas with improved angular characteristics, *Progress in Electromagnetics Research B*, Vol. 30, pp. 279–292.

Chelouah, R. & Siarry, P. (2003). Genetic and Nelder–Mead algorithms hybridized for a more accurate global optimization of continuous multiminima functions, *Eur. J. Operational Research*, Vol. 148, No. 2, pp. 335-348.

Colorni, A. ; Dorigo M. & V. Maniezzo, (1991), Distributed optimization by ant colonies, *Proc. 1st Eur. Conf. On Artificial Life*, Paris, France, pp. 134-142.

Eiben, A.E.; Hinterding, R. & Michalewicz, Z. (1999). Parameter control in evolutionary algorithms, *IEEE Trans. Evol. Comput.*, Vol.3, pp. 124–141.

Elmihoub, T.; Hopgood, A. A.; Nolle, L. & Battersby, A. (2006). Hybrid genetic algorithms - a review. *Engineering Letters*, Vol. 13, pp. 124 - 137.

Farina, M. & Sykulski, J. K. (2001). Comparative study of evolution strategies combined with approximation techniques for practical electromagnetic optimization problems. *IEEE Trans. Magn.*, Vol. 37, No. 9, pp. 3216–3220.

Fernandes, C.A. (2002) *Shaped-beam antennas*, Chapter 15 in *Handbook of Antennas in Wireless Communications*, L.C. Godara, Ed., CRC Press, New York.

Galan, A.Y., Sauleau, R. & Boriskin, A.V. (2011). Parameter selection in particle swarm optimization algorithm for synthesis of linear arrays with flat-top beams, *J. Telecommunications and Radio Engineering*, Vol. 70, No. 16, pp. 1415–1428.

Godi, G.; Sauleau, R.; Le Coq, L. & Thouroude, D. (2007). Design and optimization of three-dimensional integrated lens antennas with genetic algorithm, *IEEE Trans. Antennas Propag.*, Vol. 55, No. 3, pp. 770-775.

Grimaccia, F.; Mussetta, M. & Zich, R.E. (2007). Genetical swarm optimization: self-adaptive hybrid evolutionary algorithm for electromagnetics, *IEEE Trans. Antennas Propag.*, Vol. 55, No. 3, pp. 781-785.

Hoorfar, A. (2007). Evolutionary programming in electromagnetic optimization: a review, *IEEE Trans. Antennas Propag.*, Vol. 55, No. 3, pp. 523-537.

Haupt, R.L. (1995). An introduction to genetic algorithms for electromagnetics, *IEEE Antennas Propag. Mag.*, Vol. 37, No. 2, pp. 7-15.

Haupt, R. & Chung, Y.C. (2003). Optimizing backscattering from arrays of perfectly conducting strips, *IEEE Trans. Antennas Propag.*, Vol. 45, No. 2, pp. 26-33.

Haupt, R.L. & Haupt, S.E. (2004). *Practical genetic algorithms*, 2nd ed., Wiley & Sons, ISBN 0-471-45565-2, Hoboken NJ.

Haupt, R.L. & Werner, D.H. (2007). *Genetic algorithms in electromagnetics*, John Wiley & Sons, New York.

Haupt, R.L., (2007), Antenna design with a mixed integer genetic algorithm, *IEEE Trans. Antennas Propag.*, Vol. 55, No. 3, pp. 577-582.

Ioan, D.; Ciuprina, G. & Dumitrescu, C. (1998) Use of stochastic algorithms for distributed architectures in the optimization of electromagnetic devices. *IEEE Trans. Magn.*, Vol. 34, No. 9, pp. 3000–3003.

Isernia, T.; Pena, F.J.A.; Bucci, O.M.; D'Urso, M.; Gomez, J.F. & Rodriguez, J.A. (2004). A hybrid approach for the optimal synthesis of pencil beams through array antennas, *IEEE Trans. Antennas Propag.*, Vol. 52, No. 11, pp. 2912-2918.

Ishibuchi, H.; Yoshida, T. & Murata, T. (2003). Balance between genetic search and local search in memetic algorithms for multiobjective permutation flowshop scheduling, *IEEE Trans. Evol. Comput.*, Vol. 7, No. 2, pp. 204-223.

Ji, M. & Klinowski, J. (2009). Taboo evolutionary programming: a new method of global optimization, *Proc. Royal Society A*, Vol. 462, pp. 3613-3627.

Johnson, J.M. & Rahmat-Samii, Y. (1997). Genetic algorithms in engineering electromagnetics, *IEEE Antennas Propag. Mag.*, Vol. 39, No. 4, pp. 7-21.

Kennedy, J. & Eberhart, R.C. (1995). Particle swarm optimization, *Proc. IEEE Conf. Neural Networks IV*, vol. 52, pp. 1942-1948.

Linden, D.S. (1999). Rules of thumb for GA parameters, GA monitoring, GA parameter optimization, and enhancement of GA efficiency, Chapter 3 in Rahmat-Samii, Y. & Michielssen, E., Eds. (1999). *Electromagnetic optimization by genetic algorithms*, John Wiley & Sons, New York.

Moret, M.A.; Bisch, P.M. & Vieira, F.M.C. (1998). Algorithm for multiple minima search, *Phys. Rev. E*, Vol. 57, pp. R2535–R2538.

Ngo, N.Q.; Zheng, R.T.; Ng, J.H.; Tjin, S.C. & Binh, L.N. (2007). Optimization of fiber bragg gratings using a hybrid optimization algorithm, *J. Lightwave Technol.*, Vol. 25, No. 3, pp. 799-802.

O'Donnell, T.H.; Altshuler, E.E. & Best, S.R. (2003). The significance of genetic representation in genetic antenna design, *Proc. IEEE Int. Symp. Antennas Propag.*, Colombus, OH, Vol. 1, pp. 149-152.

Quevedo-Teruel, Ó.; Rajo-Iglesias, E. & Oropesa-García, A. (2007). Hybrid algorithms for electromagnetic problems and the no-free-lunch framework, *IEEE Trans. Antennas Propag.*, Vol. 55, No. 3, pp. 742-749.

Paszkowicz, W. (2009). Properties of a genetic algorithm equipped with a dynamic penalty function, *Computational Material Science*, Vol. 45, pp. 77-83.

Paszkowicz, W. (2006). Properties of a genetic algorithm extended by a random self-learning operator and asymmetric mutations: a convergence study for a task of powder-pattern indexing, *Analytica Chimica Acta*, Vol. 566, pp. 81–98.

Pérez, J.R. & Basterrechea, J. (2007). Comparison of different heuristic optimization methods for near-field antenna measurements, *IEEE Trans. Antennas Propag.*, Vol. 55, No. 3, pp. 549-555.

Rahmat-Samii, Y. & Michielssen, E., Eds. (1999). *Electromagnetic optimization by genetic algorithms*, John Wiley & Sons, New York.

Renders, J.M. & Flasse, S.P. (1996). Hybrid method using genetic algorithms for the global optimization, *IEEE Trans. Systems, Man, and Cybernetics*, Vol. 26, No. 2., pp. 243–258.

Robinson, J.; Sinton, S. & Rahmat-Samii, Y. (2002). Particle swarm, genetic algorithm, and their hybrids: optimization of a profiled corrugated horn antenna, *Proc. Inter. Symp. Antennas Propag.* Vol. 1, pp. 314-317.

Rolland, A.; Ettorre, M.; Drissi, M.; Le Coq, L. & Sauleau, R. (2010). Optimization of reduced-size smooth-walled conical horns using BoR-FDTD and genetic algorithm, *IEEE Trans. Antennas Propagat.*, Vol. 58, No. 9, pp. 3094–3100.

Salhi, S. & Queen, N.M. (2004). A hybrid algorithm for identifying global and local minima when optimizing functions with many minima, *Eur. J. Operational Research*, Vol. 155, pp. 51–67.

Taub, H. & Schilling D.L. (1986). *Principles of Communication Systems*, McGraw-Hill, NY.

Weile, D.S. & Michielssen, E. (1997). Genetic algorithm optimization applied to electromagnetics: a review, *IEEE Trans. Antennas Propag.*, Vol. 45, No.3, pp. 343-353.

9

A Hybrid Methodology Approach for Container Loading Problem Using Genetic Algorithm to Maximize the Weight Distribution of Cargo

Luiz Jonatã Pires de Araújo and Plácido Rogério Pinheiro
University of Fortaleza (UNIFOR) - Graduate Program in Applied Informatics
Fortaleza (CE),
Brazil

1. Introduction

It is an agreement that maritime transport of goods occupies an important role in economic development throughout the history. For centuries, port cities were in center of economy, where there were traffic of all kind of products and concentration of industrial factories.

In this background, ship containerization brought great advantages to this process. Its invention in mid-1950s was a key factor in development of modern global commerce by bringing down the cost of transporting and reducing time it takes for loading and unloading cargo (Levinson, 2008).

However, the efficient use of containerization involves new and specialized logistic process, a number of technologies, logistics plans and automated systems to handle a great number of containers. To answer these requirements, computation appears as important tool. For example, software can "determine the order in which the containers are to be discharged, to sped the process without destabilizing the ship" (Levinson, 2008).

The described scenario has been treated in academic literature as the Container Loading Problem (CLP), which was firstly approached by Gilmore and Gomory (Gilmore & Gomory, 1965a). There are some variances of this problem in literature and we approach the Knapsack Loading Problem (3D-KLP), that is, the task of to orthogonally pack a subset of given boxes of various sizes within a single container with fixed dimensions optimizing a criterion such as the total loaded volume.

Still according Dyckhoff (Dyckhoff, 1990) and Wascher (Wäscher et al., 2007), the CLP is a NP-hard problem in the strong sense and belongs to cutting and packing problems problem class. It means there is no known polynomial algorithm that exactly solves the CLP in acceptable execution time.

So, to the described problem, specifically the Knapsack Loading Problem (3D-KLP), this work presents a novel backtracking heuristic that not only maximizes the packed cargo volume but also optimizes its weight distribution. It is the great contribution of present work. Mainly if we consider that the cargo to be packed is composed by items with different densities, which turns the problem more difficult. On the other hand, if we are stowing cargoes of uniform density, weight distribution is not a problem. The figure 1 illustrates a container which mass center of cargo is not necessarily near to its geometric center.

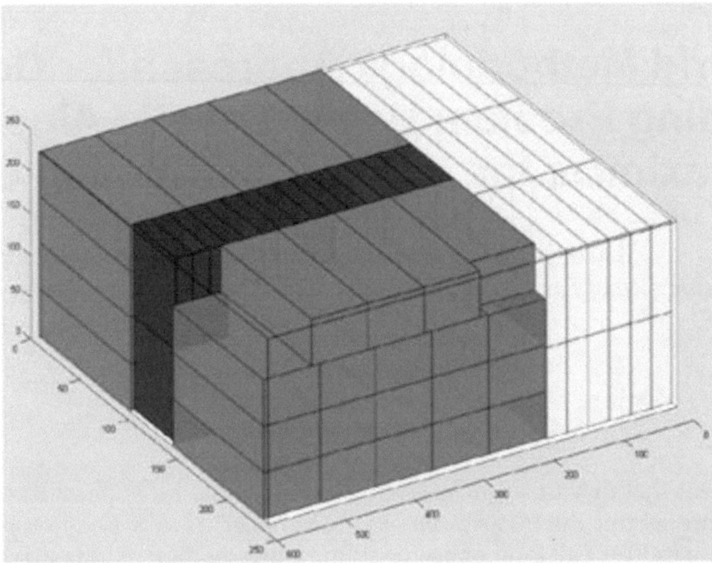

Fig. 1. Different types of packed boxes.

The present methodology is composed by two phases with distinct goals. The first phase is concerned with maximizing the use of container, consequently minimizing the waste of space. It is made by combining a search algorithm, the backtracking, with heuristics that solve integer linear programming models to pack boxes. The second phase executes a Genetic Algorithm to maximize the weight distribution of previously packed cargo. In this work we intend to focus on second phase and consider why genetic algorithm is good alternative to be combined with Heuristics Backtracking.

This work is organized as follows. In section 2 we discuss some related work to solve the CLP, presenting the three main classes of methodologies to approach the problem. In section 3 we present the two phases of our proposed algorithm. We focus in second phase and how we apply a standard genetic algorithm to optimize the weight distribution. Finally, in section 4 we present some computational results. So, in section 5 we make some conclusions regarding the quality of the solutions provided and make some considerations concerning future development.

2. Approaches to solve the container loading problem

In this chapter we present three categories of methodologies existing in theoretical literature on Container Loading Problem: Exact Methods, Heuristics and Hybrid Methods. We discuss these categories and some related work for each category.

2.1 Exact methods

The Container Loading Problem can be modeled as an integer programming problem, as described by Chen (Chen et al., 1993). The proposed model was validated by solving small problems with up to 6 boxes. In other work, Gilmore and Gomory (Gilmore & Gomory, 1963; 1965b) present another {0-1} integer model to solve the CLP using the Simplex method. In this model, the possible coordinates for place boxes belongs to a discrete set and there are {0-1} decision variables to determine if a box is placed is a specific position and other ones to avoid box overlapping. The model in (Gilmore & Gomory, 1963; 1965b) can be unfeasible due to its large number of variables and constraints. Larger the container is higher the number of variables and constraints.

Some characteristics of methodologies that use only exact methods:

- They aim to find the optimal solution;
- They require higher-level computational resources
- Feasible only for small instances.

Due to cited characteristics, few work exist using only exact methods. It is necessary another methodology more feasible that allow us to find good results in acceptable time.

2.2 Heuristics

However exact methods find the best solution, it becomes impractical due to the necessity of high computational resources. Bypassing this problem, much work proposed strategies, heuristics, to avoid applying exact methods. Now we present some known applications in literature.

One of the most known is the *wall building heuristic*. It was firstly described by George and Robinson (George & Robinson, 1980) to create layers across the depth of the container. Each layer is filled in a number of horizontal strips and their dimensions are determined by the first box, taken from a priority queue. A two-dimensional packing algorithm arranges the boxes within the layers. This heuristic can be effortlessly adapted to build horizontal slices.

Many approaches to CLP are based on 'wall-building'. For example, Pisinger(Pisinger, 2002), that presents an algorithm in which the set of layer dimensions are defined through a backtracking algorithm in order to achieve better results. The wall building strategy was also combined with others methods to attend additional requirements. For example Davies and Bischoff (Davies & Bischoff, 1999) build segments, which are composed of one or more walls, which could be rotated and/or interchanged in order to improve the weight distribution.

It is also possible approach the CLP through metaheuristics, that is, computational methods that make few or no assumptions about the problem to be optimized, and try achieve candidate solutions with good measure of quality. These methods, however achieve good solutions in reasonable time, they do not guarantee the optimal solution. In literature we find some works which apply tabu search or simulated annealing in their algorithms with significant improvements.

Genetic Algorithm (GA) has been successfully used to solve the Container Loading Problem. For example, Gehring (Gehring & Bortfeldt, 1997) reduced the 3D-KLP to two-dimension packing problems by arranging items in stacks to the top of container, a strategy based on (Gilmore & Gomory, 1965a). So, a packing sequence of the stacks is represented as a chromosome. The GA process a population of solutions in order to find a good solution, that is, a good packing plan.

Although heuristics methods have better execution time when compared with exact methods, they do not guarantee to find an optimal solution.

2.3 Hybrid methods

We increasingly find papers that seek to combine exact algorithms and metaheuristics to solve combinatorial optimization problems. Conform Dumitrescu and Stuetzle (Dumitrescu & Stuetzle, 2003), these ideas fall under a category of algorithm that has been commonly referred to as *hybrid methods*.

Nepomuceno et al. (Nepomuceno et al., 2007) introduced a successful work in which reduced instances of 3D-KLP are generated by a genetic algorithm, and then solved by linear programming.

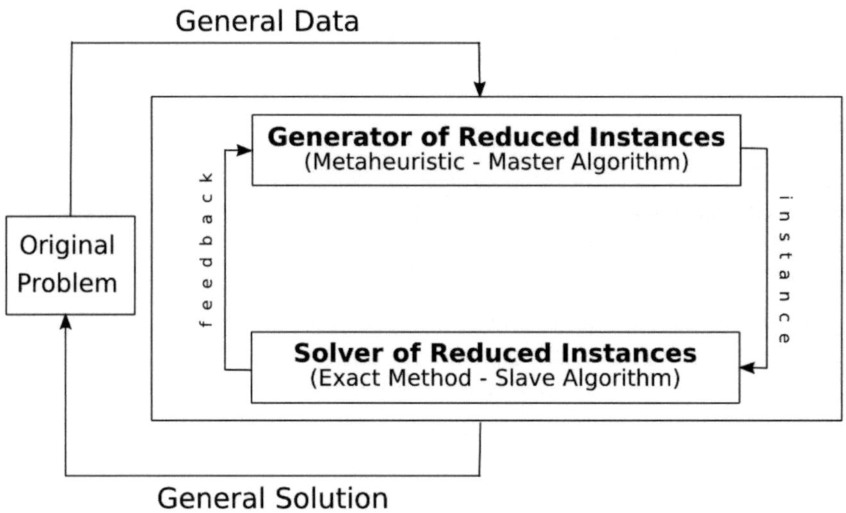

Fig. 2. Flow chart presented in (Nepomuceno et al., 2007).

We also find in literature approaches that combine heuristics methods and local search methods. For example Peng et al. (Peng et al., 2009) combine a basic heuristic algorithm to generate feasible solution from a packing sequence and a search algorithm to find an approximated optimal solution from generated solution.

Thus, once we briefly presented exact, heuristics and hybrids methods and some examples, it is interesting to say that there is no single approach that works better for all problem types or instances. As stated in no free lunch theorem for search and optimization (Wolpert & Macready, 1997), each algorithm is better for a set of specific cases or problem instances while it is worse for other ones.

3. The methodology for 3D knapsack loading problems

As presented in previous works (Araújo, 2011; Araújo & Pinheiro, 2010a;b), the Heuristic Backtracking methodology consists of two independent steps that we call 'phases'. In the first phase, the algorithm is concerned with maximizing the packed volume by combining wall building heuristics with a backtracking search algorithm to choose the best order of proceeding implemented heuristics. In second phase, the algorithm optimizes the weight distribution of cargo by using a classical genetic algorithm to determine a good arrangement of walls, layers and blocks that were built in first phase. This searching for good arrangements does not affect the packed items by previous phase.

In present work we focus the second phase and the justification in we used genetic algorithm in our approach.

3.1 Phase 1 - Heuristics backtracking

In this phase, we are concerned with maximizing the total volume of packed cargo. It is based on Pisinger's approach (Pisinger, 2000) which combines wall building heuristic with backtracking in order to determine the best dimensions of layers. In other hand, we used backtracking to determine the best implemented heuristics to be used although the packing process for each subproblem. The result is a build tree solution.

The Heuristics Backtracking recursively fill the container creating blocks of boxes that are through proposed heuristics. They are in order: XZ Mixed Layer (a), XY Mixed Layer (b), ZY Mixed Layer (c), Partition on X (d), Partition on Z (e), Partition on XZ - Stack (f), Strip Block on X (g) and Strip Block on Z (h). Examples of built blocks are illustrated in figure 3.

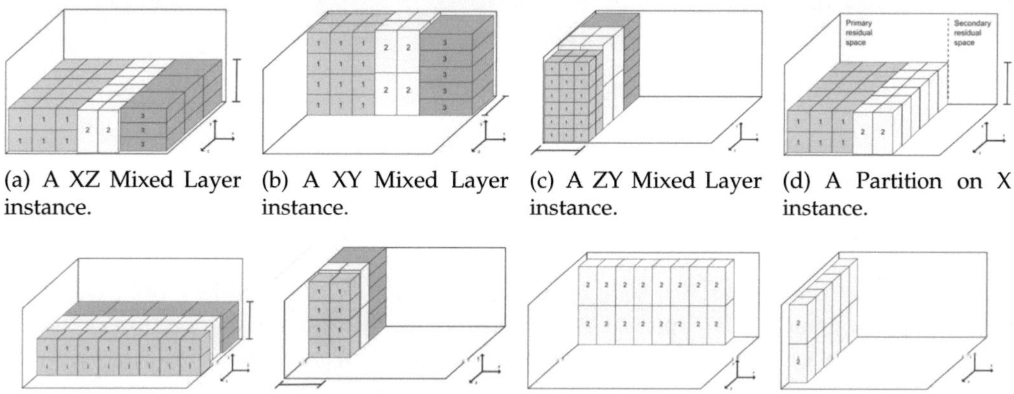

(a) A XZ Mixed Layer instance. (b) A XY Mixed Layer instance. (c) A ZY Mixed Layer instance. (d) A Partition on X instance.

(e) A Partition on Z instance. (f) A Partition on XZ instance. (g) A Strip Block on X instance. (h) A Strip Block on Z instance.

Fig. 3. The used heuristics in the algorithm.

Each heuristic solves a specific integer programming model that aims to maximize the total packed relevance, a non-linear coefficient associated to each box to priories the bigger ones during packing. The adopted relevance value for i^{th} greatest box type in a list of n box types is $r(i,n) = 2^{n-i}$. Therefore, the algorithm lets the smaller boxes to pack in residual space, when it is small. If the model has solution, the algorithm makes the packing and generates the output problem that will be the input problem for the next recursive call to fill the residual space.

As another characteristic, each heuristic accept a small waste of space. This characteristic allows us to find out good solutions that would be discarded if we would accept only optimal solutions.

We use a tree data structure to maintain the solution where each node keeps the received subproblem (input problem), the well-succeeded heuristic to solve it, the list of packed boxes using this heuristic and the residual subproblem, which is the input problem of the next node. Some partitions generate two output problems (Partition on X, Partition on Z and Partition on XZ). In these cases, the node has two child-nodes, firstly solving left-node and its child nodes after right node.

The figure 4 illustrates two solutions for a same problem, the benefit by using backtracking and how it achieves better solutions. A better solution t_2, presented in 4-b, was found switching the used heuristic in second node from first found solution t_1, presented in figure 4-a.

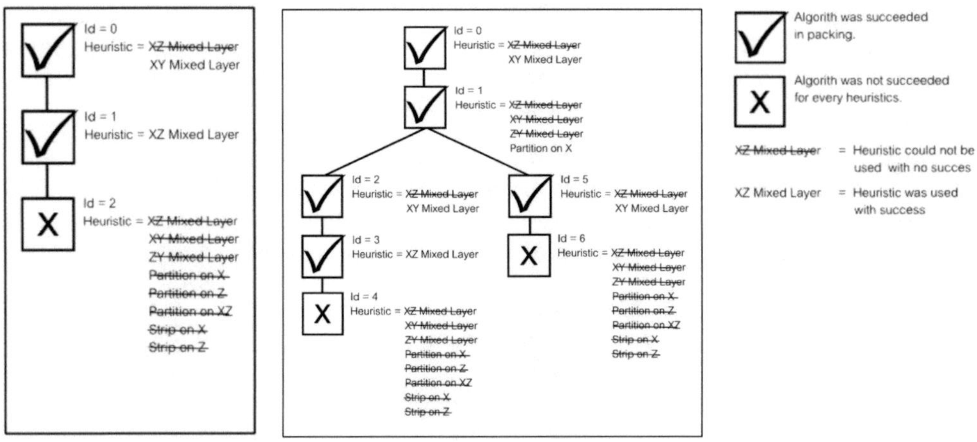

(a) First solution. (b) A better solution. (c) Conventions.

Fig. 4. Solutions for a problem instance.

An important feature of each heuristic regards about the type of built block of boxes, which can be rotated or not. It is explored in the next phase of our implementation, when the algorithm optimizes the weight distribution using a genetic algorithm.

3.2 Phase 2 - genetic algorithm

As previously discussed, the weight distribution of cargo is an important practical requirement to consider during its transport. It is desirable to have the center of gravity of cargo and geometric midpoint of container as close as possible.

Davies and Bischoff (Davies & Bischoff, 1999) presented an algorithm based on Gering's approach (Gehring et al., 1990) to obtain a packing arrangement with a good weight distribution. First, it creates multiple vertical layers across the width of the container. Set of layers called *segments* are rotated or have their positions interchanged in order to improve the weight distribution in a greedy way. The second phase in our methodology is based on idea of rotating blocks of boxes in to optimize the weight distribution without the common trade-off between efficient volume utilization and weight distribution.

The output of the first phase, presented in section 3.1, is a tree solution as exemplified in figure 4-a and 4-b. A node with packed boxes is called *significant node*. In figure 4-b the nodes 0, 1, 2, 3 and 5 are significant nodes. All blocks of boxes that were built using the implemented heuristics can be rotated as illustrated in figure 5. In other words, each built block of boxes can be arranged in either *even rotation* (no rotation) or *odd rotation*.

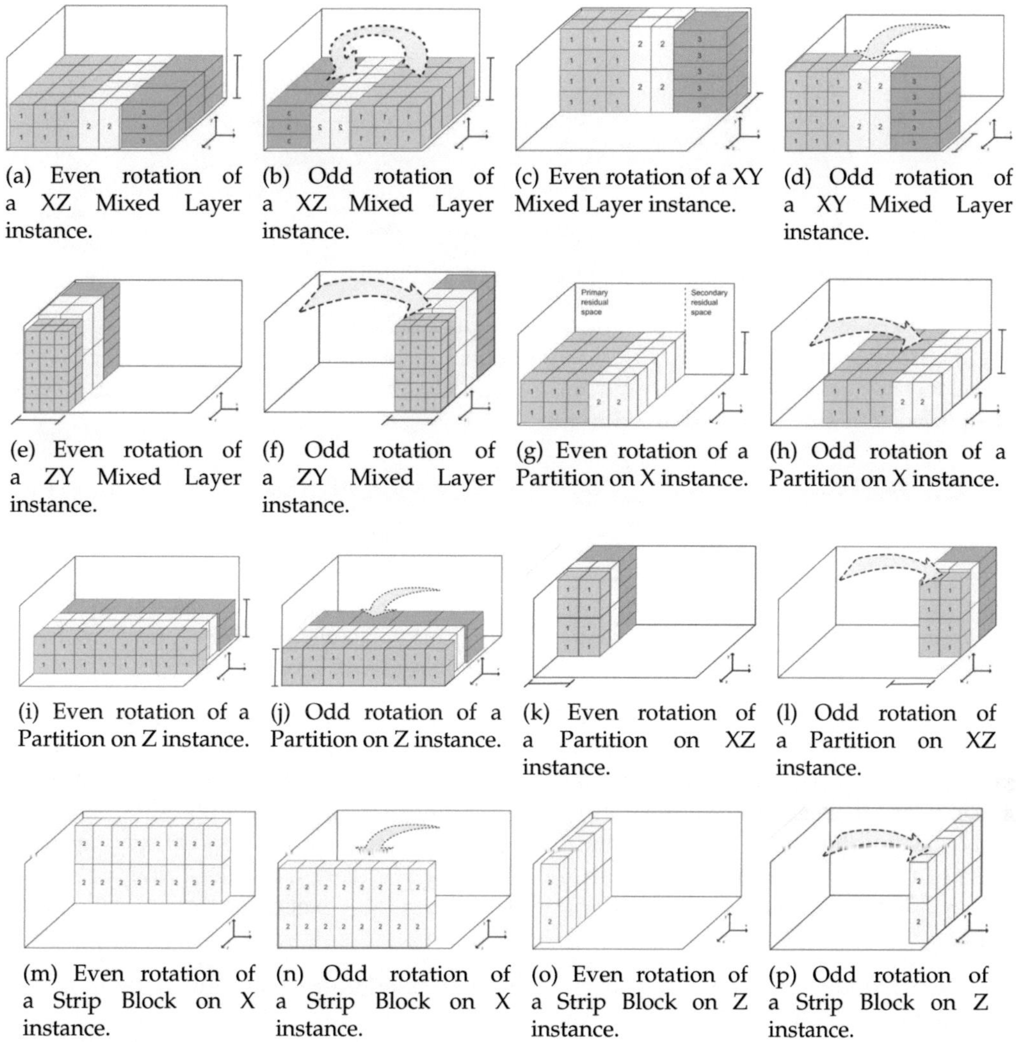

(a) Even rotation of a XZ Mixed Layer instance.

(b) Odd rotation of a XZ Mixed Layer instance.

(c) Even rotation of a XY Mixed Layer instance.

(d) Odd rotation of a XY Mixed Layer instance.

(e) Even rotation of a ZY Mixed Layer instance.

(f) Odd rotation of a ZY Mixed Layer instance.

(g) Even rotation of a Partition on X instance.

(h) Odd rotation of a Partition on X instance.

(i) Even rotation of a Partition on Z instance.

(j) Odd rotation of a Partition on Z instance.

(k) Even rotation of a Partition on XZ instance.

(l) Odd rotation of a Partition on XZ instance.

(m) Even rotation of a Strip Block on X instance.

(n) Odd rotation of a Strip Block on X instance.

(o) Even rotation of a Strip Block on Z instance.

(p) Odd rotation of a Strip Block on Z instance.

Fig. 5. Rotations of heuristics.

From what was defined, it is possible to represent a tree solution with n significant nodes by a binary chromosome with n genes, a gene g_i for each significant node n_i. The statement $g_i = 0$ indicates the block of boxes in n_i should be arranged in *even rotation*. If $g_i = 1$, in the way called *odd rotation*.

To illustrate how the algorithm changes the weight distribution of a tree solution, we chose that one in figure 4-b, with 5 significant nodes. We have in figure 6 two binary chromosomes with 5 genes that differ in value of node 5. It means the algorithm applies rotation to the block of boxes in node 5 of tree solution, which in turn was built through 'XY Mixed Layer', and consequently resulting in a new weight distribution of cargo.

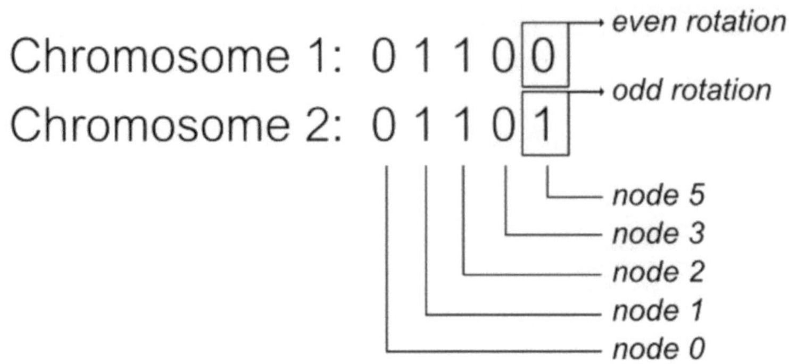

Fig. 6. Different chromosomes obtained from a same solution.

For each individual we can apply an evaluation function that informs us how well the weight distribution is. The proposed evaluation function measures the distance between the geometric center of container and the cargo's center of mass. In both points, y-axis is disregarded. The functions is defined in function 1.

$$f = \sqrt{(x_{gc} - x_{cm})^2 + (z_{gc} - z_{cm})^2} \tag{1}$$

$$x_{cm} = \frac{\sum_{i \in B} x_i w_i}{\sum_{i \in B} w_i}; \quad z_{cm} = \frac{\sum_{i \in B} z_i w_i}{\sum_{i \in B} w_i} \tag{2}$$

where (x_{gc}, z_{gc}) is the geometric center of the container, (x_{cm}, z_{cm}) is the center of mass of the entire cargo, (x_i, z_i) is the center of mass of a box i and w_i its weigh. During implementation we assumed the center of mass as been the geometric center of box.

It is important to note that to calculate the new center of mass from combining the found solution in first phase and a set of rotations described by a chromosome is a very quick operation once it does not change the relative positions of block of boxes. Therefore, it is not necessary to execute again the first phase of implementation. The spent time to evaluate a solution (individual) directly affects the execution time. In a hypothetical scenario, if it necessary 10 seconds to evaluate an individual, a population of 100 individuals that is improved by 60 generations, for example, it leads to a total execution time greater than 16 hours.

In implementation of Genetic Algorithm, which simplified flow cart is illustrated in figure 7, we used its canonical definition:

- Fixed-length binary chromosomes: this size is determined by the quantity of significant nodes of found solution in phase 1;
- Positive fitness domain: once the evaluation is the measuring of the distance between two points, the geometric center of container and the center of mass of cargo, its values is non-negative;
- Fitness proportional selection: the probability p_i of an individual i to be selected to reproduce is $p_i = f_i / \sum_{j=0}^{N} f_j$, where N is the number of individuals in the population and f_i is the evaluation of individual i;
- One-point point crossover.

In next sections we propose a new methodology to compare results from different instances and why we chose genetic algorithm to be used with Heuristics Backtracking.

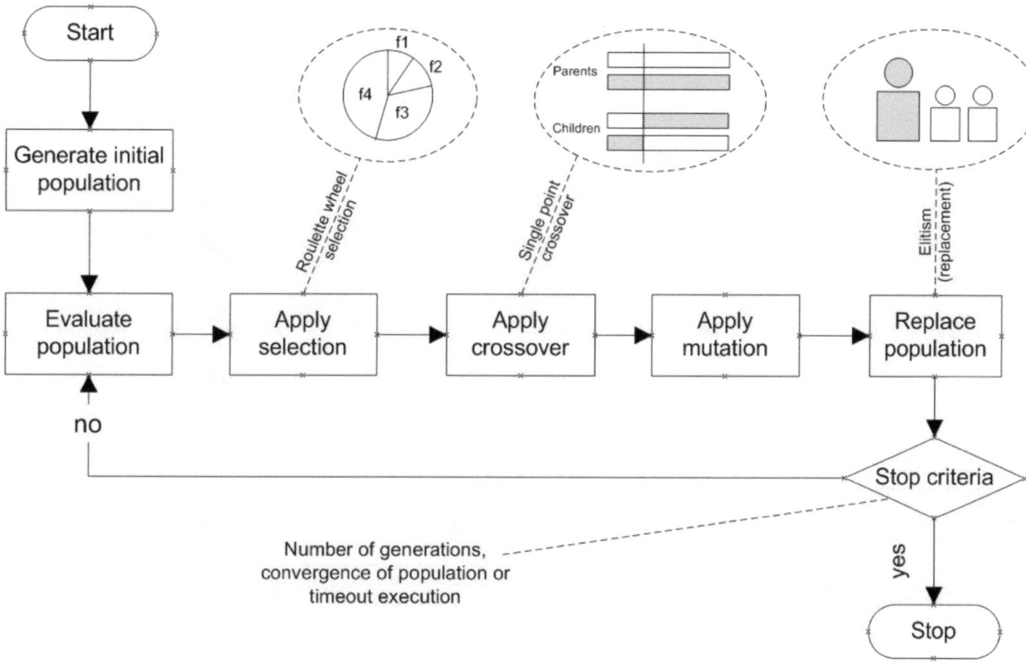

Fig. 7. Simplified flow chart of a Genetic Algorithm.

3.2.1 An approach to compare results regarding weight distribution

There are some known benchmarks in literature to packing problems, including the 3D Knapsack Loading Problem. For example, Bischoff and Ratcliff (Bischoff & Ratcliff, 1995b) proposed a test data for comparing the different approaches for cutting and packing problems. This benchmark and others are cited in section 4.

However, in most of available problems there is no information about weight. In these cases, we can stipulate a formula to define the weight from box dimensions. Moreover, most of these benchmarks differ in many aspects, for example the size of container. In this section we standard the measure to weight distribution requirement in order to facility the comparing between our results and future developments or works, even using different benchmarks.

We stated in previous section about the evaluate function of a solution. It is measured by the distance $d(s)$ between the geometric center of container and the center of mass of the entire cargo in solution s, unconsidered y-axis.

Let it be $Diag$ the length of the diagonal of container floor, where $Diag = \sqrt{W^2 + D^2}$, W and D the width and depth of container, respectively. Thus, we calculate the quality of weight distribution q_{wd} in a solution as follows:

$$q_{wd}(s) = \frac{d(s)}{Diag}$$

To better understand the used variables, they are illustrated in figure 8.

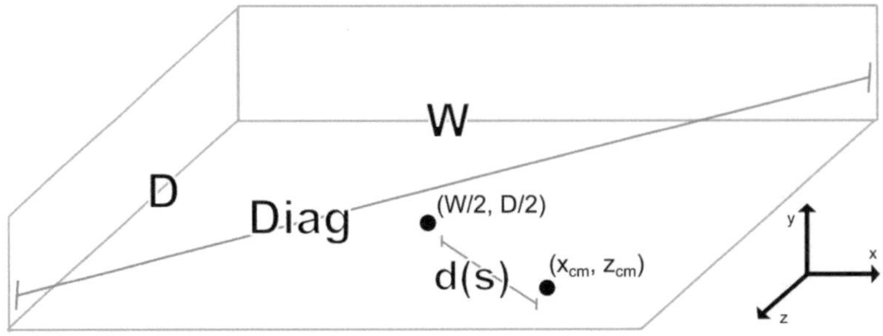

Fig. 8. Variables to measure the quality of the weight distribution of a solution *s*.

Therefore, in section 4, we will present the efficiency of using of container and the quality considering the weight distribution.

In this section, we presented the two phases of proposed methodology including an approach to compare results concerning weight distribution. In next section we present some computational results to prove our approach's efficiency.

4. Computational results

In order to check the quality of generated solutions, we tested some known benchmark test suites that were found in literature. We present computational results for both kinds of problems, two and three-dimensional ones. We also present a case study in which we compared our results with those in use within ESMALTEC, a stove and refrigerator manufacturer in Brazil.

The computational results were obtained using an Intel Core 2 Duo 2.1 GHz with 3 GB of RAM. The operating system is Windows Vista Home Edition. The development platform is Java 6.0 and Eclipse 3.1.1 tool, while the solver utilized was CPLEX 9.0.

Before present results, it is necessary to notice that container loading instances can be classified according its cargo. According to Dyckhoff (Dyckhoff, 1990) and (Wäscher et al., 2007) the cargo can be regarded as *homogeneous* (identical small box types), *weakly heterogeneous* (many items of relatively few different box types) or *strongly heterogeneous* (many items of many different box types). In order to detect in which type of cargo our approach works better, we tested different kinds of problems, as illustrated in figure 9. Instances of CLP are also classified according to the diversity of box types that can be loaded into the container. We evaluate our proposed algorithm on both homogeneous and weakly heterogeneous instances.

In this sense, Bischoff and Ratcliff (Bischoff & Ratcliff, 1995b) proposed a test data for comparing the different approaches for cutting and packing problems. The benchmark library with 700 problems is available on the internet on the website `http://people.brunel.ac.uk/~mastjjb/jeb/info.html`. This collection of test data sets is used to perform a variety of Operational Research approaches. These data sets contain several types of problems, from homogeneous (BR1) to strongly heterogeneous (BR7). In brackets the number of types of boxes. We compare our obtained results average with the following approaches: a genetic algorithm proposed in (Gehring & Bortfeldt, 1997) (GA), the constructive algorithm on (Bischoff & Ratcliff, 1995b)(CA), a constructive algorithm by Bischoff (Bischoff et al., 1995)(HBal), the hybrid genetic algorithm described in (Bortfeldt & Gehring, 2001)(HGA),

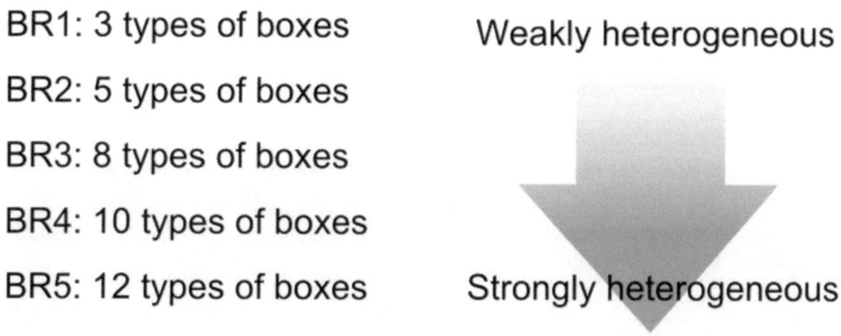

Fig. 9. Types of instances according tue quantity of boxes.

the parallel genetic algorithm in (Gehring & Bortfeldt, 2002)(PGA), a proposed heuristic in (Bischoff, 2006)(PH) and Tabu Search proposed in (Bortfeldt et al., 2003)(TS).

The achieved average results and the standard deviations (σ) by our methodology are represented in columns (HB+GA) and σ, respectively. These results were obtained with timeout execution parameter equals to 10 minutes.

Due to software limitations, for example the maximum number of variables, we tested the first five libraries (BR1 - BR5).

Group	GA	CA	HBal	HGA	PGA	PH	TS	HB+GA	σ
BR1 (3)	86.77	83.37	81.76	87.81	88.10	89.39	93.23	**92.13**	4.07
BR2 (5)	88.12	83.57	81.70	89.40	89.56	90.26	93.27	**91.09**	5.09
BR3 (8)	88.87	83.59	82.98	90.48	90.77	91.08	92.86	90.38	8.45
BR4 (10)	88.68	84.16	82.60	90.63	91.03	90.90	92.40	89.07	7.08
BR5 (12)	88.78	83.89	82.76	90.73	91.23	91.05	91.61	88.17	7.52
Average	88.24	83.72	82.36	89.81	90.14	90.54	92.67	90.17	6.44

Table 1. Comparing some proposals, in %.

An instance of solution of BR1 instance is presented in figure 10.

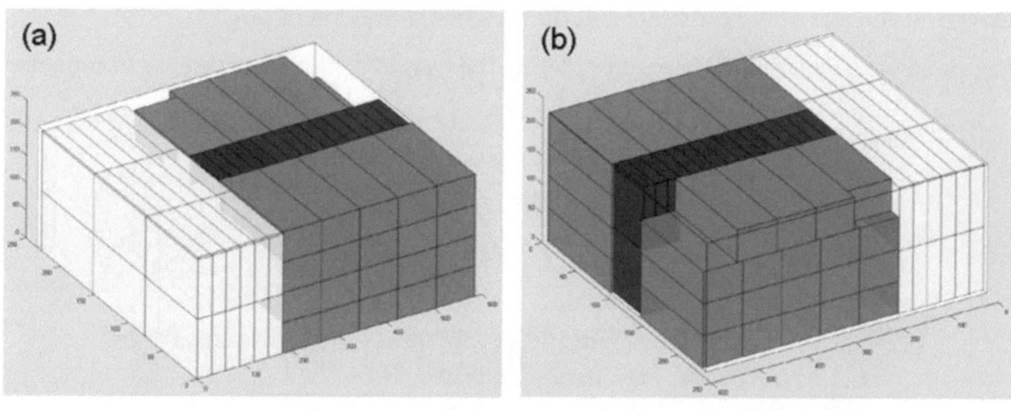

Fig. 10. A packing solution for the first instance form the BR1 set: (a) front view, and (b) back view.

With low timeout execution we achieved good results mainly for BR1 - BR3, the weakly heterogeneous problem instances. It is possible gain efficiency with set up a higher value to timeout execution and by implementing new heuristics to build layers across the container.

In order to prove the efficiency of our algorithm in to find good arrangements such way that a good weight distribution is achieved, we show the obtained results for Bischoff/Ratcliff test cases. We used the following formula to create boxes with different densities: $weight = (width/(2*10^5)) \times (w \times h \times d)$, where $w/(2*10^5)$, where w, h and d represent the width, height and depth of the box, respectively.

We considered the crossing-over parameter equals to 0.75, mutation parameter equal to 0.3, population size equal to 64 and maximum number of generations equals to 100. The table 2 presents the average length of chromosome (length), the less distance between center of mass of cargo and the geometric center of container (dist), the diagonal of container (diag), the average quality of solution (qwd) and its standard deviation (σ) and the execution time in seconds.

Group	length	dist.	diag.	qwd(%)	σ	time(s)
BR1	8.73	100.3	626.87	16	0.19	5.1
BR2	11.01	70.4	626.87	11	0.17	10.7
BR3	15.44	73.5	626.87	12	0.17	31.7
BR4	17.7	75.06	626.87	12	0.19	0.93
BR5	19.97	45.15	626.87	8	0.15	1.04

Table 2. Best-case results of Nepomuceno et al. (Nepomuceno et al., 2007) and the present methodology.

From the table 2 we affirm that chromosome length growing allows to diversify the arrengements of cargo, even and odd rotation discussed in section . However this characteristic needs improving, all weight distribution are relatively near to geometric center of container, using boxes with very different values of density.

The presented methodology achieved good results, mainly to weakly heterogeneous problem instances. However, to Bischoff/Ratcliff test cases, the weight distribution (quality of solution) is better to heterogeneous instances. The algorithm also reduces the common trade-off between an efficient use of container and the weight distribution of cargo.

In figure 11 we compare the results considering the weight distribution and use of container.

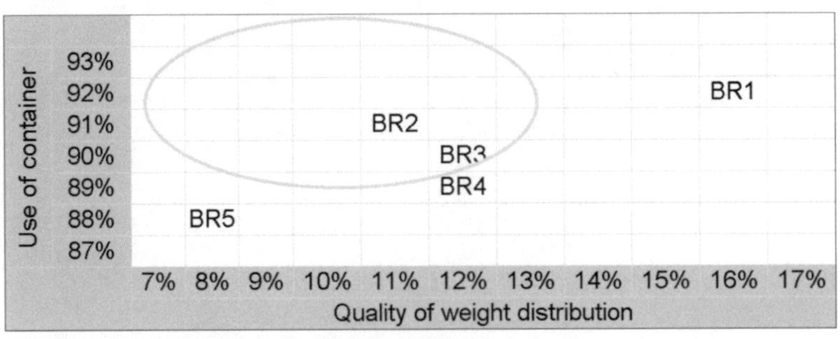

Fig. 11. Comparative of results using different benchmarks.

As we are interested in a maximum use of container and a coefficient of weight distribution (qwd) near to zero, the region we aims is the circle region in figure 11. Thus, the best achieved results were BR2 and BR3. This graphic aims help us to rank the results considering use of container and weight distribution.

5. Conclusion and future work

We introduced a hybrid methodology, the Heuristics Backtracking, an approach that combines a search algorithm, the backtracking, integer linear programming and genetic algorithms to solve the three dimensional knapsack loading problem considering weight distribution.

We discussed about the importance of weight distribution, among others generally unconsidered practical requirements, in practical situations in order to avoid damage of cargo during its transport by ships, trucks or airplanes. We also proposed a needed methodology to compare the quality of solutions 3.2.1, even to different benchmark tests or approaches' results.

Finally, we showed that the Heuristics Backtracking (HB) achieved good results without the commonly great trade-off between the utilization of container and a good weight distribution. Some benchmark tests taken from literature were used to validate the performance and efficiency of the HB methodology as well its applicability to cutting problems.

There are promising lines of investigation. Some of them to improve the already good results mainly regard with use of container and execution time, others to apply the HB to other kind of problems. So, we intend:

- To approach other variants of Container Loading Problem, for example the strip packing, placing boxes on shelves (Hoare & Beasley, 2001), load bearing ability (Ratcliff & Bischoff, 1998) among others;
- To implement heuristics those solve non-linear programming models to avoid many parameterized calls. It will improve the execution time of first phase;
- To improve the weight distribution by increasing the chromosome length. Some built blocks can be rotated in more than one way, so they can be manipulated by more than one gene. This changing will allow us to increase the quantity of discrete values for individuals' fitness;
- To change the backtracking algorithm, equivalent to a brute-force search. It intends to optimize the entire algorithm's time;
- An application of present methodology is in progress to solve cutting problems, similarly to what was made by other hybrid methodologies (Nepomuceno et al., 2008; Pinheiro et al., 2011).

6. Acknowledgements

This work has been financially supported by CNPq/Brazil via Grants #308249 / 2008-9, #473454 / 2008-4, and #312934 / 2009-2.

The authors also acknowledge IBM for making the IBM ILOG CPLEX Optimization Studio available to the academic community.

7. References

Araújo, L.J.P. (2011). A Hybrid Methodology to solve the Container Loading Problem with Weight Distribution and Cutting Problems. *Master's thesis, Graduate Program in Applied Informatics at University of Fortaleza.*

Araújo, L.J.P., Pinheiro, P.R. (2010). Combining Heuristics Backtracking and Genetic Algorithm to Solve the Container Loading Problem with Weight Distribution. *Advances in Intelligent and Soft Computing* 73:95-102.

Araújo, L.J.P., Pinheiro, P.R. (2010). Heuristics Backtracking and a Typical Genetic Algorithm for the Container Loading Problem with Weight Distribution. *Communications in Computer and Information Science* 16:252-259.

Araújo, L.J.P., Pinheiro, P.R. (2011). Applying Backtracking Heuristics for Constrained Two-dimensional Guillotine Cutting Problems. *Lecture Notes in Computer Science* 7030:113-120, to appear.

Bischoff, E.E. (2006) Three dimensional packing of items with limited load bearing strength. *European Journal of Operational Research* 168:952-966.

Bischoff, E.E., Ratcliff, M.S.W. (1995). Issues in the Development of Approaches to Container Loading. *Omega* 23:4:377-390.

Bischoff, E.E., Janetz, F., Ratcliff, M.S.W. (1995). Loading Pallets with non-identical Items. *European Journal of Operational Research* 84:681-692.

Bortfeldt, A., Gehring, H. (1998) Ein Tabu Search-Verfahren für Containerbeladeprobleme mit schwach heterogenem Kistenvorrat. *OR Spektrum* 20:237-250.

Bortfeldt, A., Gehring, H. (2001) A Hybrid Genetic Algorithm for the Container Loading Problem. *European Journal of Operational Research* 131:143-161.

Bortfeldt, A., Gehring, H., Mack, D. (2003). A Parallel Tabu Search Algorithm for Solving the Container Loading Problem. *Parallel Computing* 29:641-662.

Chen, C.S., Lee, S.M., Shen, Q.S. (1993). An analytical model for the container loading problem. *European Journal of Operations Research* 80:6876.

Christensen, S.G., Rousøe, D.M. (2009). Container loading with multi-drop constraints. *International Transactions in Operational Research* 16:6:727-743.

Davies, A.P., Bischoff, E.E. (1999). Weight distribution considerations in container loading. *European Journal of Operations Research* 114:509-527.

Derelia, T., Dasb, G.S. (2010). A hybrid simulated annealing algorithm for solving multi-objective container-loading problems. *Applied Artificial Intelligence* 24:5:463-486.

Dumitrescu, I., Stuetzle, T. (2003). Combinations of local search and exact algorithms. *Applications of Evolutionary Computation LNCS* 2611:211-223.

Dyckhoff, H. (1990). A typology of cutting and packing problems. *European Journal of Operational Research* 44:145-159.

Egeblad, J., Pisinger, D. (2009) Heuristc approaches for the two- and three-dimensional knapsack packing problem. *Computers & Operations Research* 36:1026-1049.

Eley, M. (2002). Solving container loading problems by block arrangement. *European Journal of Operational Research* 141:393-409.

Faroe, O., Pisinger, D., Zachariasen, M. (2003). Guided local search for the three-dimensional bin packing problem. *Informs Journal on Computing* 15:3:267-283.

Gehring, H., Bortfeldt, A. (1997). A Genetic Algorithm for Solving the Container Loading Problem. *International Transactions in Operational Research* 4:401-418.

Gehring, H., Bortfeldt, A. (2002). A Parallel Genetic Algorithm for Solving the Container Loading Problem. *International Transactions in Operational Research* 9:497-511.

Gehring, H., Menschner, K., Meyer, M. (1990) A computer-based heuristic for packing pooled shipment containers. *European Journal of Operational Research* 44:277-288.

George, J.A., Robinson, D.F. (1980). A heuristic for packing boxes into a container. *Computers and Operations Research* 7:147-156.

Gilmore, P.C., Gomory, R.E. (1963). A linear programming approach to the cutting stock problem - Part II. *Operations Research* 11:863-888.

Gilmore, P.C., Gomory, R.E. (1965). Multistage cutting and packing boxes into a container. *Computer abd Operations Research* 13:94-120.

Gilmore, P.C., Gomory, R.E. (1965). Multistage cutting stock problems of two and more dimensions. *Operations Research* 14:1045-1074.

Glover, F., Laguna, M. (1993). Tabu search, In: C.R. Reeves (Ed.), *Modern Heuristic Techniques for Combinatorial Problems*, Blackwell Scientific Publications - Oxford, 70-150. (1993)

Goldberg, D. E. (1989) Genetic algorithms in search, optimization, and machine learning. *Reading, MA: Addison-Wesley.*

Hoare, N.P., Beasley, J.E. (2001) Placing boxes on shelves: a case study. *Journal of the Operational Research Society* 52:6:605-614.

Holland, J.H. (1975) Adaptation in Natural and Artificial Systems. *University of Michigan Press.*

Holland, J.H. (1992) Adaptation in Natural and Artificial Systems, 2nd edition, *The MIT Press.*

Kirkpatrick, S.; Gelatt Jr., C.D.; Vecchi, M.P.: Optimization by Simulated Annealing. Science 220, 4598:671-680 (1983)

Levinson, M.: The box: how the shipping container made the world smaller and the world economy bigger. Princeton University Press. (2008)

Liang, S., Lee C., Huang, S.: A Hybrid Meta-heuristic for the Container Loading Problem. Communications of the IIMA. 73:7:4 (2007)

Loh, T.H., Nee, A.Y.C. (1992) A packing algorithm for hexahedral boxes. Proceedings of the Conference of Industrial Automation, 115-126.

Mack, D., Bortfeldt, A., Gehring, H.: A parallel hybrid local search algorihtm for the container loading problem. International Transactions in Operations Research, 11:511-533. (2004)

Michalewicz, Z. (1992) Genetic Algorithms + Data Structures – Evolution Programs. *New York: Springer-Verlag.*

Morabito, R., Arenales, M.: An and/or-graph approach to the container loading problem. International Transactions in Operational Research. 1:59-73 (1994)

Murata, H., Fujiyoshi, K., Nakatake, S., Kajitani, Y.: VLSI module packing based on rectangle-packing by the sequence pair. IEEE Transaction on Computer Aided Design of Integrated Circuits and Systems. 15:1518-1524. (1996)

Nepomuceno, N., Pinheiro, P.R., Coelho, A.L.V.: Tackling the Container Loading Problem: A Hybrid Approach Based on Integer Linear Programming and Genetic Algorithms. In: VII European Conference on Evolutionary Computation in Combinatorial Optimization (EVOCOP). Berlin: Springer, 2007. v.4446. p.154 - 165. (2007)

Nepomuceno, N.V., Pinheiro, P.R., Coelho, A.L.V. (2008) A Hybrid Optimization Framework for Cutting and Packing Problems: Case Study on Constrained 2D Non-guillotine Cutting. In: *C. Cotta and J. van Hemert (Eds.), Recent Advances in Evolutionary Computation for Combinatorial Optimization*, Chapter 6, pp. 87-99, Book of the Series "Studies in Computational Intelligence"", Vol. 153, Springer-Verlag (ISBN: 978-3-540-70806-3).

Ngoi, B.K.A., Tay, M.L., Chua, E.S. (1994) Applying spatial representation techniques to the container packing problem. *International Journal of Production Research* 32:111-123.

Peng, Y., Zhang, D., Chin, F.Y.L.: A hybrid simulated annealing algorithm for container loading problem. Proceedings of the first ACM/SIGEVO Summit on Genetic and Evolutionary Computation, ISBN:978-1-60558-326-6, pp.919-928 (2009)

Pinheiro, P.R., Coelho, A.L.V., Aguiar, A.B., Bonates, T.O. (2011) On the Concept of Density Control and its Application to a Hybrid Optimization Framework: Investigation into Cutting Problems. *Computers & Industrial Engineering* v.61:3:463-472.

Pisinger, D. Heuristc for the Conteiner Loading Problem. European Journal of Operational Research, 141:382-392. (2000)

Pisinger, D.: Heuristics for the Container Loading Problem. European Journal of Operational Research. 141:143-153. (2002)

Plateau, A., Tachat, D., Tolla, P.: A Hybrid Search Combining Interior Point Methods and Metaheuristics for 0-1 Programming. Int. T. Oper. Res. 9:731-746 (2002)

Ratcliff, M.S.W.: Incorporating weight aspects into container loading approaches. EBMS Working Paper, University College, Swansea. (1994)

Ratcliff, M.S.W., Bischoff, E.E. (1998) Allowing for weight considerations in container loading. *Operations Research Spektrum* 20:65-71.

Wäscher, G., Hauÿner, H., Schumann, H.: An improved typology of cutting and packing problems. European Journal of Operational Research, Vol. 183, No.3. pp.1109-1130. (2007)

Wolpert, D.H., Macready, W. G. (1997) No free lunch theorems for optimization. *Evolutionary Computation, IEEE Transactions* 1:1:67-82

10

Hybrid Genetic Algorithms for the Single Machine Scheduling Problem with Sequence-Dependent Setup Times

Aymen Sioud[1], Marc Gravel[1] and Caroline Gagné[2]
[1]*Département D'informatique et de Mathématique, Université du Québec à Chicoutimi*
[2]*Département Des Sciences Économiques et Gestion, Université du Québec à Chicoutimi*
Canada

1. Introduction

Several researches on scheduling problems have been done under the assumption that setup times are independent of job sequence. However, in certain contexts, such as the pharmaceutical industry, metallurgical production, electronics and automotive manufacturing, there are frequently setup times on equipment between two different activities. In a survey of industrial schedulers, Dudek et al. (1974) reported that 70% of industrial activities include sequence-dependent setup times. More recently, Conner (2009) has pointed out, in 250 industrial projects, that 50% of these projects contain sequence-dependent setup times, and when these setup times are well applied, 92% of the order deadline could be met. Production of good schedules often relies on management of these setup times (Allahverdi et al., 2008). This present chapter considers the single machine scheduling problem with sequence dependent setup times with the objective to minimize total tardiness of the jobs (SMSDST). This problem, noted as $1|s_{ij}|\Sigma T_j$ in accordance with the notation of Graham et al. (1979), is an NP-hard problem (Du & Leung, 1990).

The $1|s_{ij}|\Sigma T_j$ may be defined as a set of n jobs available for processing at time zero on a continuously available machine. Each job j has a processing time p_j, a due date d_j, and a setup time s_{ij} which is incurred when job j immediately follows job i. It is assumed that all the processing times, due dates and setup times are non-negative integers. A sequence of the jobs $S = [q_0, q_1, ..., q_{n-1}, q_n]$ is considered where q_j is the subscript of the jth job in the sequence. The due date and the processing time of the jth job in sequence are denoted as d_{q_j} and p_{q_j}, respectively. Thus, the completion time of the jth job in sequence will be expressed as $C_{q_j} = \sum_{k=1}^{j}(s_{q_{k-1}q_k} + p_{q_k})$ while the tardiness of the jth job in sequence will be expressed as $T_{q_j} = max(0, C_{q_j} - d_{q_j})$. The objective of the scheduling problem studied is to minimize the total tardiness of all the jobs which will be expressed as $\sum_{j=1}^{n} T_{q_j}$.

Different approaches have been proposed by a number of researchers to solve the $1|s_{ij}|\Sigma T_j$ problem. Rubin & Ragatz (1995) proposed a Branch and Bound approach, which quickly showed its limitations. It could optimally solve only small instances of benchmark files of

15, 25, 35 and 45 jobs proposed by these authors. Bigras et al. (2008) have optimally solved all instances proposed by Rubin & Ragatz (1995) using a Branch and Bound approach with linear programming relaxation bounds. They also demonstrated and used the problem's similarity with the time-dependent traveling salesman problem (TSP). This Branch and Bound approach solved some of these instances in more than 7 days. Because this problem is NP-hard, many researchers used a wide variety of metaheuristics to solve this problem, such as a genetic algorithm (Franca et al., 2001; Sioud et al., 2009), a memetic algorithm (Armentano & Mazzini, 2000; Franca et al., 2001; Rubin & Ragatz, 1995), a simulated annealing (Tan & Narasimhan, 1997), a GRASP (Gupta & Smith, 2006), an ant colonies optimization (ACO) (Gagné et al., 2002; Liao & Juan, 2007) and a Tabu/VNS (Gagné et al., 2005). Heuristics such as Random Start Pairwise Interchange (RSPI) (Rubin & Ragatz, 1995) and Apparent Tardiness Cost with Setups (ATCS) (Lee et al., 1997) have also been proposed for solving this problem. For their part, Sioud et al. (2010) introduce a constraint based programming approach proposing an ILOG API C++ model.

Concerning the genetics algorithms (GA), only Sioud et al. (2009) succeeded in proposing an efficient GA, suggesting that this metaheuristic is not well suited to deal with the specificities of this problem. Indeed, the authors have proposed a GA integrating the RMPX crossover operator which takes greater account of the relative and absolute position of a job. Indeed, Armentano & Mazzini (2000); Rubin & Ragatz (1995); Tan & Narasimhan (1997) have shown the importance of relative and absolute order positions for solving the $1|s_{ij}|\Sigma T_j$ problem. The proposed GA outdoes the performance of all the GAs found in the literature but is still less efficient than the Tabu/VNS of Gagné et al. (2005) which represents the best approach found in the literature.

The main purpose of this chapter is to show that GAs can be efficient approaches for solving the $1|s_{ij}|\Sigma T_j$ problem when the different mechanisms of the algorithm are specially design to deal with the specificities of the problem. Indeed, in their respective works, Rubin & Ragatz (1995) and Sioud et al. (2009) have shown the importance of relative and absolute order positions for the $1|s_{ij}|\Sigma T_j$ problem. Thereby, all the used crossover operators into the genetic algorithms from literature maintain the absolute position, or the relative position or both. So, to reach good results, the presented genetic algorithms must ensure the preservation of both the relative and the absolute order positions while maintaining diversification during their evolving. In this context, the presented algorithms will take this into consideration. Indeed, we present, in this chapter, two hybrid GAs for solving the $1|s_{ij}|\Sigma T_j$ where the different mechanisms of the algorithms are specially design to deal with the specificities of the problem. The first hybridization incorporates Constraint Based Scheduling (CBS) in a GA. The hybridization of the CBS approach with the GA is done at two levels. Even, the CBS is used in the reproduction and intensification processes of GA separately. The second hybridization introduces a hybrid crossover in a GA. The proposed crossover uses concepts from the multi-objective evolutionary algorithms and ant colony optimization. Both hybridizations use the specificities of the problem to reach good results.

This chapter is organized as follows: Section 2 presents the used pure GA of Sioud et al. (2009). Section 3 introduce the two hybrid algorithms. The computational testing and discussion are presented in Section 4: we present several versions of hybridizations and compare our results to the Tabu/VNS of Gagné et al. (2005). Finally, we conclude with some remarks and future research directions.

2. Genetic algorithm

Based on the GA proposed by Sioud et al. (2009), we define a simple genetic algorithm. A solution is coded as a permutation of the considered jobs. The population size is set to n to fit with the considered instance size. Sixty percent of the initial population is generated randomly, 20% using a pseudo-random heuristic which minimizes setup times, and the last 20% using a pseudo-random heuristic which minimizes the due dates. A binary tournament selects the chromosomes for the crossover. The proposed GA uses the OX crossover (Michalewicz, 1996) to generate 30% of offspring and the RMPX crossover (Sioud et al., 2009) to generate the rest of the child population. The RMPX crossover can be described in the following steps : (i) two parents *P1* and *P2* are considered and two distinct crossover points *C1* and *C2* are selected randomly, as shown in Figure 1; (ii) an insertion point p_i is then randomly chosen in the offspring *O* as p_i = *random (n - (C2 - C1))*; (iii) the part [*C1, C2*] of *P1*, shaded in Figure 1, is inserted in the offspring O from p_i, from the position 2 shown in Figure 1; and (iv) the rest of the offspring *O* is completed from *P2* in the order of appearance from its first position.

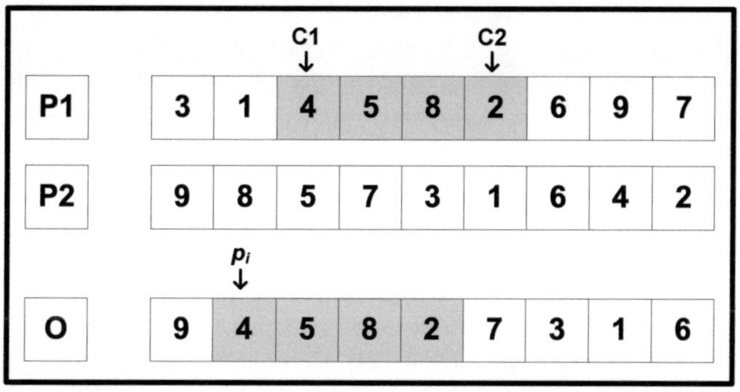

Fig. 1. Illustration of RMPX

The crossover probability p_c is set to 0.8, therefore *n"0.8* offspring are generated at each generation. A mutation is also applied with a probability p_m equal to 0.3. The mutation consists of exchanging the position of two distinct jobs which are randomly chosen. The replacement is elitist and the duplicate individuals in the population are replaced by chromosomes generated by one of the pseudo-random heuristics used in the initialization phase.

3. Hybrid genetic algorithms

Several researchers have attempted to relieve the metaheuristic shortcomings and limitations by modifying the traditional executing for some problems. Indeed, to improve the effectiveness of these methods, some researchers have used metaheuristics variations and hybridizations (Puchinger & Raidl, 2005; Talbi, 2009). In general, hybridization combines two or more methods in a single algorithm to solve combinatorial optimization problems. Hybrid approaches in general and hybrid metaheuristics in particular are gaining popularity because these approaches obtained the best results for several combinatorial optimization problems (Jourdan et al., 2009; Talbi, 2009). Also, according to Blum et al. (2005), the hybridization of metaheuristics is the most promising avenue for improving the quality of solutions in many real applications. Puchinger & Raidl (2005) divide hybrid methods into two categories : collaborative and integrative hybridization. The algorithms that exchange information in a sequential, parallel or interlaced way fall into the category of collaborative hybridization. We talk about an integrative hybridization when a technique is an embedded component of another technique. In this chapter, we introduce first a collaborative hybridization which incorporates CBS approach with the GA at two levels. Indeed, the CBS is used in the reproduction and intensification processes of GA separately. In fact, the CBS approach is integrated in a crossover operator and in the intensification search space process using additional constraints for both of them. Second, we introduce an integrative hybridization at a new hybrid crossover, integrating concepts from two different techniques: archives as in the multi-objective evolutionary algorithms and a transition rule as in ant colony optimization.

3.1 The collaborative hybrid genetic algorithm

Constraint solving methods such as domain reduction and constraint propagation have proved to be well suited for a wide range of industrial applications (Fromherz, 1999). These methods are increasingly combined with classical solving techniques from operations research, such as linear, integer, and mixed integer programming (Talbi, 2002), to yield powerful tools for constraint-based scheduling by adopting them. The most significant advantage of using such CBS is to separate the model from the algorithms which solve the scheduling problem. This makes it possible to change the model without changing the algorithm used and vice versa.

In the recent years, the CBS has become a widely used form for modeling and solving scheduling problems using the constraint programming approach (Allahverdi et al., 2008; Baptiste et al., 2001). A scheduling problem is the process of allocating tasks to resources over time with the goal of optimizing one or more objectives (Pinedo, 2002). A scheduling problem can be efficiently encoded like a constraint satisfaction problem (CSP).

The activities, the resources and the constraints, which can be temporal or resource related, are the basis for modeling a scheduling problem in a CBS problem. Based on representations and techniques of constraint programming, various types of variables and constraints have been developed specifically for scheduling problems. Indeed, the domain variables may include intervals domains where each value represents an interval (processing or early start time for example) and variable resources for many classes of resources. Similarly, various research techniques and constraints propagation have been adapted for this kind of problem.

In Constraint Based Scheduling, the single machine problem with setup dependent times can be efficiently encoded in terms of variables and constraints in the following way. Let M be the single resource. We associate an activity A_j for each job j. For each activity A_j four variables are introduced, *start*(A_j), *end*(A_j), *proc*(A_j) and *dep*(A_j). They represent the start time, the end time, the processing time and the departure time of the activity A_j, respectively. The departure time represents the needed setup time of an activity when the latter starts the schedule.

Figure 2 presents the pseudo-code for the $1|s_{ij}|\Sigma T_j$ problem modeling with the C++ API of ILOG Scheduler 6.0. The main procedure ModelSMSDST calls the two procedures CreateMachine and CreateJob. CreateMachine procedure (lines 3 to 6) uses the class *IloUnaryResource*. This allows handling unary resources, that is to say, a resource whose

```
L1   Modeling SMSDST :
L2
L3     procedure CreateMachine (SetupMatrix)
L4        Create the setup matrix parameter
L5        Create the single machine and associate the setup matrix parameter
L6     end CreateMachine()
L7
L8     procedure CreateJob (ProcessingTimes, StartingTimes, type)
L9        Create a job with a type and processing time
L10       Set a starting time for the created job
L11    end CreateJob()
L12
L13    procedure ModelSMSDST(ProcessingTimes, StartingTimes, DueDates SetupMatrix)
L14       CreateMachine(SetupMatrix)
L15       Define an array for the jobs completion time C
L16       Define a variable for the total tardiness Tard
L17       for each i in NB_JOBS do
L18          job ← CreateJob (ProcessingTimes, StartingTimes, i)
L19          C[i] ← max(0, job.end - DueDates[i])
L20       end for
L21       Tard ← Sum(C)
L22       Minimize (Tard)
L23    end ModelSMSDST
```

Fig. 2. C++ API model for the $1|s_{ij}|\Sigma T_j$ problem

capacity is equal to one. This resource cannot therefore handle more than one job at a time. The use of the setup times in CBS and also with ILOG Scheduler (ILOG, 2003a) indicates that they are resource-related and not activity-related such as is the case in our problem. It is possible to overcome this problem by associating a type for each activity and creating setup times associated with these types. For this purpose, we use the class *IloTransitionParam* which is managing and setting setup times. The setup matrix is then associated to this class which will be related to the unary machine (line 5). Thus, when we calculate the objective function, it is possible to associate the setup times between two distinct types of activities. To model the total tardiness, we must first define a variable *Tard* (line 16). Then we define an array C containing the completion times C_i of the different activities times A_i during the research phase (line 15). When we create the activities in the model, we add a constraint that combines the activities A_i to the corresponding times C_i (line 19). After that, we add a constraint which combines the variable *Tard* with the sum of the C_i in the table C (line 21). Finally, we add a constraint that minimizes the variable *Tard* (line 22). Thus, we obtain the objective function which will be added to the model.

ILOG Solver (ILOG, 2003a) provides several predefined search algorithms named as *goals* and activity selectors. We used the *IloSetTimesForward* algorithm with the *IloSelFirstActMinEndMin* activity selector. The *IloSetTimesForward* algorithm schedules activities on a single machine forward initializing the start time of the unscheduled activities. The activity selector defines the heuristic scheduling variables representing start times, which chooses the next activity to schedule. The *IloSelFirstActMinEndMin* tries first the activity with the smallest start time and in case of equality the activity with the smallest end time. For his part, ILOG Scheduler (ILOG, 2003b) provides four strategies to explore the search tree : the default *Depth-First Search* (DFS), the *Slice-Based Search* (SBS) (Beck & Perron, 2000), Interleaved Depth-First Search (IDFS) (Meseguer, 1997) and the *Depth-Bounded Discrepancy Search* (DDS) (Walsh, 1997) which is used in this work.

The hybridization of an exact method such as the CBS and a metaheuristic such as the GA can be carried out in several ways. Talbi (2002) presents a taxonomy dealing with the hybrid metaheuristics in general. Puchinger & Raidl (2005) and Jourdan et al. (2009) present a taxonomy for the exact methods and metaheuristics hybridizing. In this chapter we present two different approaches of hybridization. The first approach is to integrate the CBS in the GA reproduction phase and more precisely in a crossover operator, while the second approach is to use CBS as an intensification process in the GA.

When we handle a basic single machine model, there is no precedence constraint between activities as is the case in a flow-shop or job-shop where adding constraints improves the CBS approach. The main idea of integrating the CBS in a crossover is to provide to this latter precedence constraints between activities when generating offspring. In this work, we consider only the direct constraints during the crossover. Therefore, the conceived crossover promotes the relative order positions such as the PPX crossover (Bierwirth et al., 1996). The proposed crossover operator is designated *Indirect Precedence Constraint Crossover (IPCX)* and can be described in the two following steps : *(i)* all individuals in the current population are considered and the indirect precedence constraints between jobs concurrently in all the individuals are kept, as shown in Figure 3; and *(ii)* the CBS approach tries to solve the problem while adding the indirect precedence constraints built in the previous step and an upper bound consisting of the objective function value of the best parent. The upper bound is added to discard faster bad solutions when branching during the solver process. As a reminder, the ILOG Solver uses a Branch and Bound approach to solve a problem (ILOG, 2003b).

In the case of Figure 3,we consider a population with 4 individuals. Only the three indirect precedence constraints *(1 before 6)*, *(8 before 2)* and *(9 before 7)* are in the four individuals. So these three indirect constraints are added to the model and will be propagated. Thus, they preserve the relative positions of the pairs of activities *(1,6)*, *(8,2)* and *(9,7)*. After that, in a potential offspring we will find this indirect precedence constraints. Finally, if no solution is found by the *IPCX* crossover, the offspring is generated by one of the pseudo-random heuristics used in the initialization phase. The *IPCX* crossover will be done under probability p_{IPCX}.

Integrating an intensification process in a genetic algorithm has been applied successfully in several fields. The incorporation of heuristics and/or other methods, i.e. an exact method such as the CBS approach, into a genetic algorithm can be done in the initialization process to generate well-adapted initial population and/or in the reproduction process to improve the offspring quality fitness. Following this latter reasoning, the strategy proposed in this section is based on the intensification in specific space search areas. However, we can find in literature only few papers dealing with such hybridization Puchinger & Raidl (2005); Talbi (2009).

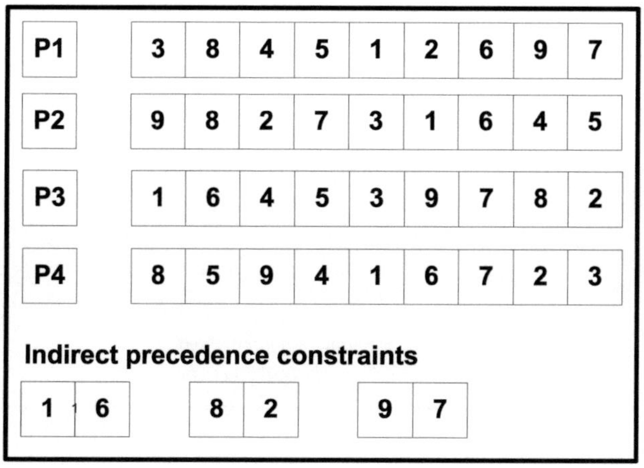

Fig. 3. Illustration of IPCX

In the same vein of the *IPCX* conservation precedence constraints, an intensification process is applied by giving a generated offspring to the CBS approach and fixing a block of α positions. Thus, the absolute order position will be preserved for these fixed positions while the relative order position will be preserved for the other activities. Indeed, the activities on the left of the fixed block will be scheduled before this late block, while the activities on the right will be scheduled after this block. The fixed block size should be neither too large nor too small : if its size is too large, the CBS approach will have no effect and if its size is too small the CBS approach will consume more time to find a better solution. Thereby, at each time this intensification is done, α continuous positions are fixed with $0.2*n \prec \alpha \prec 0.4*n$. We use to this end two different procedures based on the CBS approach. The first one, noted as IP_{TARD}, selects a generated offspring and tries to solve the problem using the CBS approach which minimizes the total tardiness described above while adding an upper bound consisting of the objective function value of this offspring. So as a result, the CBS approach may return a better solution when scheduling separately the activities on the left and the right of the fixed block activities.

Using the similarity of the studied problem with the time-dependent traveling salesman problem (Bigras et al., 2008), the second intensification procedure, noted as IP_{TSP}, works like IP_{TARD} but in this case the CBS approach minimizes the makespan. The makespan optimization aims to minimize the setup times and then, in some specific configurations, will give promising solutions under total tardiness optimization otherwise explore a different areas search space. The makespan criterion is represented by an additional variable Makespan. Its value is determined by $Makespan = \sum_{A_j=1}^{n} max(end(A_j))$. The model minimizing the makespan is similar to that in Figure 2. Indeed, we just delete the declaration of the array C at line 15 and define an activity Makespan with time processing equal to 0 at line 16. Then, a constraint stating that all jobs must be completed before the Makespan start time is added in the loop. Finally, lines 19 and 21 are removed and line 22 minimizes in this case the Makespan end time.

Thereby, an offspring is selected with a tournament under probability p_{IP} and then, one of the two intensification procedures IP_{TARD} and IP_{TSP} is chosen under probability p_{cip} to be applied on this offspring. Figure 4 illustrates the intensification process based on the CBS

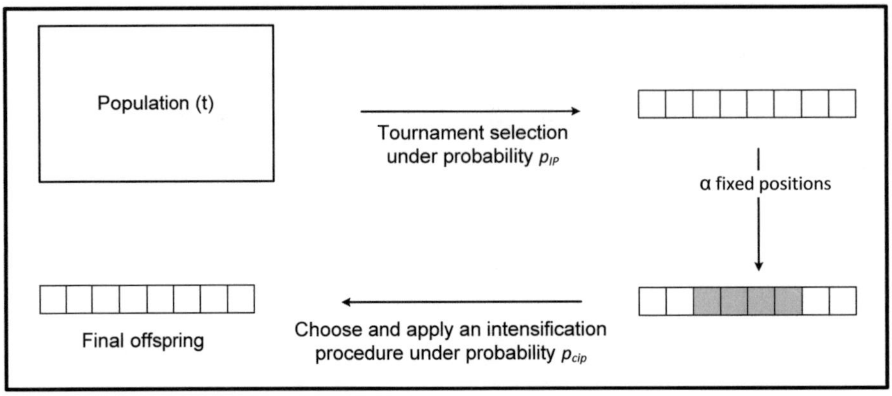

Fig. 4. The intensification process

approach. At each generation, an offspring is selected under probability p_{IP} with tournament selection. After fixing α positions and choosing an intensification procedure, IP_{TARD} or IP_{TSP} under probability p_{cip} , the solver tries to find a solution. If no solution is found the offspring is unchanged.

3.2 The integrative hybrid genetic algorithm

In this section, we introduce the integrative hybrid genetic algorithm which integrates concept from two different techniques : archives as in the multi-objective evolutionary algorithms and a transition rule as in ant colony. This hybridization is done in a crossover noted as *ICX* which evolves in two step : (i) from the first parent, we place the cross section, which represents the section between the two crossover points as the RMPX crossover processing; (ii) use a transition rule to fill the remaining jobs using two lists formed from the second parent.

The transition rule is used in the *ICX* crossover operator as a mechanism taking into account the problem's properties and memory information. After defining the cross section (jobs set from the first parent), the filling section (jobs set from the second parent) is completed using a transition rule adapted to the $1|s_{ij}|\Sigma T_j$ problem, similar to that used by the ant colony optimization (ACO) (Dorigo & Gambardella, 1997) and inspired by the work of Gagné et al. (2002).

From an identified cross section (section from the first parent), it is possible to insert the jobs to the right of this section from the latest job as a classical ant or inversely to the left. First, the number of jobs to be inserted on the right and left of the cross section are determined. Then, two lists from the second parent are built: a job list which will be inserted on the left of the cross section and a jobs list which will be inserted on the right. From the beginning of the second parent, the left list is formed by the jobs not yet placed according to the jobs number to be placed on the left, and the rest of the jobs not yet placed form the right list. In Figure 5 we consider the two parents *P1, P2* and the offspring *O*. Both three positions remain unfilled on the left and on the right of the cross section. Looking through the parent *P2*, the left list is then formed by jobs 9, 5 and 7 while the right one is formed by jobs 3, 1 and 4.

Firstly, we consider the job insertions on the right of the cross section. The second case, very similar to the first, requires only few changes and is subsequently treated further. From the

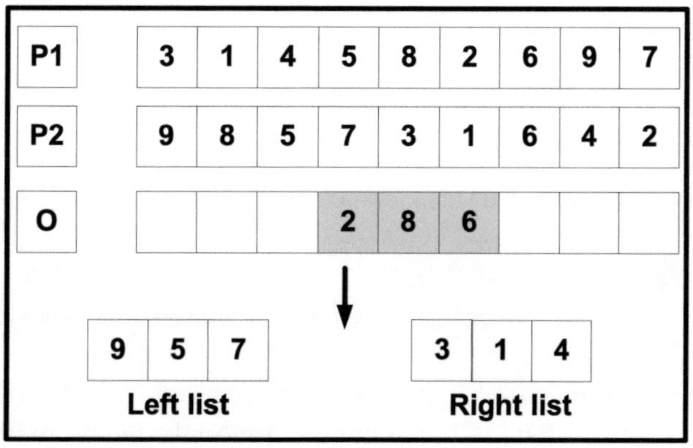

Fig. 5. List construction for the transition rule step

$$j = \begin{cases} arg\ max \left\{ \left[SUCC_{ij}(A_t)\right]^{\alpha} * \left[\dfrac{1}{\overline{s_{ij}}}\right]^{\beta} * \left[\dfrac{1}{\overline{U_{ij}}}\right]^{\phi} \right\} & if\ q \leq q_0 \\ J & if\ q > q_0 \end{cases} \quad (1)$$

where J is chosen according to the probability p_{ij}

$$p_{ij} = \frac{\left[SUCC_{ij}(A_t)\right]^{\alpha} * \left[\dfrac{1}{\overline{s_{ij}}}\right]^{\beta} * \left[\dfrac{1}{\overline{U_{ij}}}\right]^{\phi}}{\sum \left[SUCC_{ij}(A_t)\right]^{\alpha} * \left[\dfrac{1}{\overline{s_{ij}}}\right]^{\beta} * \left[\dfrac{1}{\overline{U_{ij}}}\right]^{\phi}} \quad (2)$$

last inserted job, the choice of the next job is made using the pseudo-random-proportional transition rule expressed in Equations (1) and (2). As in an ACO, in Equation (1), q is a random number and q_0 is a parameter; both are between 0 and 1. The parameter q_0 determines the relative importance of the existing information exploitation and the new solutions search space exploration. Indeed, Equation (2) states that the next job will be chosen by a greedy rule when $q \leq q_0$ or by the probabilistic rule of Equation (2) when $q > q_0$. Equation (2) describes the biased exploration rule p_{ij} adapted to the $1|s_{ij}|\Sigma T_j$ problem when inserting job j after job i.

In Equations (1) and (2), the element $\overline{s}_{ij}$=s_{ij}/MAX s_{ij} are the relative setup times and represents the visibility as in the ACO of Gagné et al. (2002).

We describe in the following, the other two elements of Equations (1) and (2) where two new concepts are introduced : $SUCC_{ij}(A_t)$ which represents the pheromone trail as in an ACO and $\overline{U}_{ij}$ which represents an heuristic for look-ahead information.

In an classical ACO, the pheromone trail contains information based on solution quality. Indeed, in the pheromone matrix, if the intensity of the pheromone value between two jobs i and j increases, then the probability to insert j after i increases. In our case, we construct a matrix $SUCC$ from an archive that stores the best solutions throughout the evolution process as in some cases in multi-objective evolutionary algorithms using the Pareto-optimal concept (Zitzler & Thiele, 1999). This archive is updated at every new offspring creation. The archive size, denoted as N, is equal to the problem size and contains the N best individuals found during the genetic algorithm search.

If n is the number of jobs processed and the archive size, the matrix $SUCC$ is calculated as follows:

$$\textit{For every jobs pair } (i,j) \textit{ where } i \in [1,n] \textit{ and } j \in [1,n]$$

$$SUCC[i][j] = \frac{\textit{number of times that } j \textit{ immediatly succeeds } i}{n} \tag{3}$$

Thereby built from the archive individuals, the $SUCC$ matrix will contain the trail information. Thus, the more job j succeeds job i in the archive individuals, the more important the trail is. This information, then favors the succession of job j after job i in the transition rule. This matrix is calculated as needed from the archive and is updated at each archive update. Consequently, in Equations (1), $SUCC_{ij}(A_t)$ represents the trail quantity that job j immediately succeeds job i in the archive at time t.

In Gagné et al. (2002), the authors have considered a lower bound determined by the tardiness sum of the sequenced jobs and an estimate for the not yet sequenced jobs, as proposed by Ragatz (1993). This lower bound is used as a look ahead function to anticipate the choice of an ant and it is incorporated in the transition rule of their ACO. In this present integrative hybridization, we propose to use an heuristic that also anticipates the choices in the transition rule. However, this heuristic is based on an upper bound of the total tardiness. Indeed, considering a defined cross section in an empty job sequence, we use this heuristic noted as U_{ij} for successively placing the jobs on the right of the cross section first until the end of the sequence. Placing the jobs on the right is very similar and needs only few changes.

Starting from a partial sequence where only the cross section is defined, the heuristic uses the maximum values of processing time $p_{(max)}$ and setup times $s_{ij\ (max)}$ and the minimum due dates $d_{(min)}$ in its calculation to complete the empty positions. Thus, we consider a job sequence Q where a cross section is defined and $Q = [q_0, q_1, ..., q_{n-1}, q_n]$ where q_j is the subscript of the jth job in the sequence. Thereby, the completion time of the jth job in sequence will be expressed as $C_{q_j\ (max)} = \sum_{k=1}^{j}(s_{q_{k-1}q_k\ (max)} + p_{q_k\ (max)})$ while the tardiness of the jth job in sequence will be expressed as $T_{q_j\ (max)} = max(0, C_{q_j\ (max)} - d_{q_j\ (min)})$. In these last two equations, the exact values of processing time, due dates and setup times are used instead the maximum or minimum values for the cross section jobs which are already placed. So, if we want to place a job j immediately after the cross section last job i, then U_{ij} will be defined as $\sum_{j=1}^{n} T_{q_j\ (max)}$.

To better understand how this heuristic works, consider the 9-job example in Figure 6. The first table in this figure shows the respective processing times p_j and due dates d_j.

The second table in Figure 6 presents a partial sequence with only the cross section composed of jobs 2, 5 and 8. The processing time, the related setup times (s_{2-5} *and* s_{5-8}) and due dates of jobs 2, 5 and 8 are used to calculate $\sum_{j=1}^{n} T_{q_j\ (max)}$. We suppose that the right list contains jobs 1, 3, 6 and 7. So, the left list contains the two remaining jobs 9 and 4. Considering the right section filling, we use the maximum values of processing times $p_{\ (max)}$ (the maximum

Job j	1	2	3	4	5	6	7	8	9
p_j	102	100	97	99	96	102	97	107	100
d_j	640	596	602	585	625	635	616	645	608

Q	-	-	2	5	8	-	-	-	-	$\sum_{j=1}^{n} T_{q\,j(max)}$
C_j	120	240	360	456	568	690	812	934	1056	
d_j	585	585	596	625	645	602	602	602	602	
$\overline{T}_{q_j}$	0	0	0	0	0	88	210	332	*454*	**1084**

Q	-	-	2	5	8	1	-	-	-	$\sum_{j=1}^{n} T_{q\,j(max)} = U_{ij}$
C_j	120	240	360	456	568	680	802	924	1033	
d_j	585	585	596	625	645	640	602	602	602	
$\overline{T}_{q_j}$	0	0	0	0	0	40	200	322	431	**993**

Q			2	5	8	6				$\sum_{j=1}^{n} T_{q\,j(max)} = U_{ij}$
C_j	120	240	360	456	568	686	803	920	1037	
d_j	585	585	596	625	645	635	602	602	602	
$\overline{T}_{q_j}$	0	0	0	0	0	51	201	318	435	**1005**

Q			2	5	8	7				$\sum_{j=1}^{n} T_{q\,j(max)} = U_{ij}$
C_j	120	240	360	456	568	666	788	910	1032	
d_j	585	585	596	625	645	616	602	602	602	
$\overline{T}_{q_j}$	0	0	0	0	0	50	186	308	430	**974**

Q			2	5	8	3				$\sum_{j=1}^{n} T_{q\,j(max)} = U_{ij}$
C_j	120	240	360	456	568	670	792	914	1036	
d_j	585	585	596	625	645	602	616	616	616	
$\overline{T}_{q_j}$	0	0	0	0	0	68	176	298	420	**962**

Fig. 6. H_{ij} example

processing time of the right list jobs, here 102) and setup times $s_{ij\ (max)}$ and the minimum due dates $d_{(min)}$ (the minimum due date of the right list jobs, here 602) of the jobs in the right list jobs. We suppose also that the maximum setup times is equal to 20. For the left section filling the maximum values of processing times $p_{\ (max)}$ equal 100 (the maximum processing time of the left list jobs) the maximum setup times $s_{ij\ (max)}$ also equal 20 and the minimum due dates $d_{(min)}$ equal 585 (the minimum due date of the left list jobs). We obtain an upper bound $\sum_{j=1}^{n} T_{q_j\ (max)}$ which equal 1084.

Then for each remaining job in the right list, the heuristic U_{ij} is calculated. So, the respective processing time, due date and setup times following the job 8 (s_{8-*}) are updated and the total tardiness is calculated. For example, if we suppose that job 1 is directly inserted after the cross section and that s_{8-1} is equal to 10, then we obtain the third table in Figure 6. In this partial sequence, we update the setup times s_{8-1} (10 instead of 20) and the due date (640 instead 602). By inserting job 1, the heuristic U_{ij} value equal 993. If we suppose now that job 3 is directly inserted after the cross section and that s_{8-3} is equal to 5, then we obtain the last table in Figure 6. In this partial sequence we update the setup times s_{8-3} (5 instead of 20) and the minimum due date $d_{(min)}$ for the remaining jobs (616 instead 602). For this case, the heuristic value U_{ij} equal 962. The fourth and fifth tables in Figure 6 represent the insertion of the jobs 6 and 7 directly after the cross section, respectively. The heuristic value U_{ij} equal 1005 and 974, respectively.

The normalized values $\overline{U}_{ij}$=U_{ij}/MAX U_{ij} are then used in Equations (1) and (2) to determine which job will be placed. Thus, in the previous example, we obtain $\overline{U}_{8-1} = 0.98$, $\overline{U}_{8-3} = 0.95$, $\overline{U}_{8-6} = 1$ and $\overline{U}_{8-7} = 0.97$. It is obvious that the higher the normalized value, the lower the probability of placing job increases.

Since the cross section is already placed, placing the remaining jobs on the left of this section can be done either from the first offspring position from left to right as a classical ant or inversely from the first cross section position. In both cases, we will have a resulting setup time either at the junction with the cross section if we proceed from left to right, or with the latest job of the previous period (the initial setup time) if we proceed from right to left. During the application of the hybrid crossover *ICX*, we use equiprobable one of the two methods of left insertion.

In the case of placing jobs from right to left, we make some changes in Equations (1) and (2). Indeed, $\bar{s}_{ij}$ and $\overline{U}_{ij}$ are replaced by $\bar{s}_{ji}$ and $\overline{U}_{ji}$, respectively. Also, the matrix $SUCC_{ij}(A_t)$ is replaced by $PRED_{ij}(A_t) = {}^{T}SUCC_{ij}(A_t)$, the transposed matrix of $SUCC_{ij}(A_t)$ from the archive A. In fact, the trace must be built from relevant information related to the predecessors in this case.

So, with these elements, this transition rule uses past, present and future information from the archive, the visibility and the look ahead, respectively. The transition rule is used in this way for all job insertions until the end of the sequence. Finally, the parameters α, β *and* ϕ associated with each transition rule matrix in Equations (1) and (2), can privilege certain elements depending on the characteristics of the problem.

4. Computational results and discussion

The benchmark problem set consists of eight instances, each with a number of jobs of 15, 25, 35 and 45 jobs, and it is taken from the work Ragatz (1993). These instances are available on the Internet at https://www.msu.edu/~rubin/files/c&ordata.zip. The job processing times are normally distributed with a mean of 100 time units and the setup times are also uniformly distributed with a mean of 9.5 time units. Each instance has three factors which have both high and low levels. These factors are due date range, processing time variance and tardiness factor. The tardiness factor determines the expected proportion of jobs that will be tardy in a random sequence. The second instance subset, taken from the work of Gagné et al. (2002), consists of eight instances each with 55, 65, 75 and 85 jobs. These instances which are called "large instances set" are available at http://wwwdim.uqac.ca/∼c3gagne/DocumentRech/ProblemDat
aSet55to85.zip. These instances are also generated similarly as in the smaller instances. All the experiments were run on an Itanium with a 1.4 GHz processor and 4 GB RAM. Each instance was executed 10 times and all the algorithms are coded in C++ language and under the ILOG IBM CP constraint environment using ILOG Solver and Scheduler via the C++ API (ILOG, 2003a;b) for the CBS approach. In order to obtain a reliable comparison, the stop criterion for all the proposed algorithms is 50 000 evaluations. This criterion is used by the Tabu/VNS of Gagné et al. (2005) which represents the best approach found in the literature. First, we

PRB	OPT	GA	CBS	Collaborative hybridization			Ingrative hybridization			TVNS
				CGA^{IPCX}	CGA^{IP}	CGA^{COL}	IGA^{L-R}	IGA^{R-L}	IGA^{OrOpt}	
401	90	0.0	0.0	0.0	0.0	0.0	0.0	0.0	0.0	0.0
402	0	0.0	0.0	0.0	0.0	0.0	0.0	0.0	0.0	0.0
403	3418	0.0	0.0	0.0	0.4	0.0	0.0	0.0	0.0	0.0
404	1067	0.0	0.0	0.0	0.0	0.0	0.0	0.0	0.0	0.0
405	0	0.0	0.0	0.0	0.0	0.0	0.0	0.0	0.0	0.0
406	0	0.0	0.0	0.0	0.0	0.0	0.0	0.0	0.0	0.0
407	1861	0.0	0.0	0.0	0.0	0.0	0.0	0.0	0.0	0.0
408	5660	0.0	0.9	0.0	0.1	0.0	0.0	0.0	0.0	0.0
501	261	0.0	0.4	0.0	0.5	0.0	0.0	0.0	0.0	0.0
502	0	0.0	0.0	0.0	0.0	0.0	0.0	0.0	0.0	0.0
503	3497	0.0	2.5	0.0	0.3	0.0	0.0	0.0	0.0	0.0
504	0	0.0	0.0	0.0	0.0	0.0	0.0	0.0	0.0	0.0
505	0	0.0	0.0	0.0	0.0	0.0	0.0	0.0	0.0	0.0
506	0	0.0	0.0	0.0	0.0	0.0	0.0	0.0	0.0	0.0
507	7225	0.0	1.8	0.0	0.7	0.0	0.0	0.0	0.0	0.0
508	1915	0.0	35.8	0.0	1.8	0.0	0.0	0.2	0.0	0.0
601	12	16.9	41.7	5.7	7.5	2.4	1.0	1.7	0.0	0.0
602	0	0.0	0.0	0.0	0.0	0.0	0.0	0.0	0.0	0.0
603	17587	0.2	6.5	0.8	1.1	0.2	0.0	0.0	0.0	0.0
604	19092	0.2	21.1	0.9	1.3	0.5	0.0	0.0	0.0	0.0
605	228	1.3	122.4	2.6	3.5	0.3	1.0	0.4	0.0	0.0
606	0	0.0	0.0	0.0	0.0	0.0	0.0	0.0	0.0	0.0
607	12969	0.2	17.7	0.6	1.9	0.2	0.0	0.0	0.0	0.0
608	4732	0.2	156.6	0.5	1.2	0.0	0.0	0.0	0.0	0.0
701	97	3.0	20.6	5.3	8.3	2.1	1.2	1.0	0.6	0.3
702	0	0.0	0.0	0.0	0.0	0.0	0.0	0.0	0.0	0.0
703	26506	0.2	2.8	1.2	1.8	0.7	0.0	0.0	0.0	0.0
704	15206	0.3	94.8	1.3	2.1	0.5	0.2	0.2	0.0	0.0
705	200	3.4	72.5	3.2	6.5	1.1	2.3	1.0	0.4	0.2
706	0	0.0	0.0	0.0	0.0	0.0	0.0	0.0	0.0	0.0
707	23789	0.2	20.4	1.0	1.9	0.3	0.0	0.0	0.0	0.0
708	22807	0.3	50.0	1.4	2.1	1.0	0.0	0.0	0.0	0.1

Table 1. Comparison of different approaches for the small problem set

discuss the collaborative and integrative hybridization on the small instances, then only the integrative genetic algorithm on the large instances.

Table 1 compares the results of different approaches and the best results are shaded. In this table, PRB denotes the instance names and OPT the optimal solution found by the B&B of Bigras et al. (2008). These authors have not given information about the execution time of their approach. They only said that some instances have been resolved after more than seven days. The GA column shows the results average deviation to the optimal solution of the genetic algorithm described in the section 3.1 which gives the best results among all genetic algorithms in the literature without an intensification process (Sioud et al., 2009). The GA average CPU time is equal to 13.4 seconds for the 32 instances. The GA generally obtained fairly good results only for the instances 601, 605, 701 and 705. These instances are low due date range and large tardiness factor. Thus, for this kind of instances, "good" solutions may not generate "good" offspring. Furthermore, considering that the tardy jobs are scheduled at the end of the sequence, it may be sufficient to schedule the other jobs by minimizing the setup times. It is the aim of introducing the IP_{TSP} intensification procedures. The CBS column shows the deviations of the CBS approach minimizing the total tardiness defined in Section 3.1. For this approach, the execution time is limited to 60 minutes. It can be noticed that the CBS approach results deteriorate with increasing the instances size and especially for the **4, **5 and **8 instances. The CGA_{IPCX} column shows the average deviation of the genetic algorithm in which the crossover operator *IPCX* is integrated. The probability p_{IPCX} is equal to 0.2 and the CBS approach execution time is limited to 15 seconds. The CGA_{IPCX} average time execution is equal to 12.8 minutes for the 32 instances. The first observation is that the CGA_{IPCX} algorithm is always optimal for 15 and 25 jobs instances. It should be noted that the integration of the IPCX crossover improves all of the GA results and especially for the instances **1 and **5 where the deviation became less than 6%. For example, the deviation was reduced from 16.9% to 6.7% for the 601 instance. Using the direct precedence constraints allows the PCX crossover to enhance both the GA exploration and the CBS search; and consequently reaching better schedules.

The CGA_{IP} column shows the average deviation of the genetic algorithm in which we include the IP_{Tard} and IP_{TSP} intensification procedures under probability p_{IP} equal to 0.1. The CBS approach execution time is limited to 20 seconds for the IP_{Tard} and IP_{TSP}. The CGA_{IP} average time execution is equal to 13.5 minutes for the 32 instances. The CGA_{IP} improves most GA results and specially the **1 and **5 instances but gives worse results than the CGA_{IPCX} and this was expected because in 50% of the cases the intensification procedure minimizes the makespan and not the total tardiness. The CGA_{COL} column shows the average deviation of the GA_{PCX} algorithm where we include the IP_{Tard} and IP_{TSP} intensification procedures. The probabilities p_{IP} and p_{cip} are equal to 0.1 and 0.5 respectively like the CGA_{IP}. The CBS approach execution time is also limited to 20 seconds for the IP_{Tard} and IP_{TSP} in the CGA_{COL}. The CGA_{COL} average time execution is equal to 20.5 minutes for the 32 instances. This hybrid algorithm improves all the results found by the CGA_{IPCX}. These improvements are more pronounced with the integration of local search procedures. The introduction of the two intensification procedures improves essentially the **1 and the **5 instances. Also, the optimal schedule is always reached by CGA_{COL} for the 608 instance. The CGA_{COL} found the optimal solution for all the instances at least one time and this was not the case either for CGA_{IPCX} or CGA_{IP}.

The convergence of both GA and the CGA_{IPCX} algorithms are similar. Indeed, the average convergence generation is equal to 1837 and 1845 generations for GA and CGA_{IPCX}, respectively. Concerning the CGA_{IP} algorithm, the average convergence generation is equal to 1325 generations. So, we can conclude that the two intensification procedures based on the CBS approach are permitting a faster genetic algorithm convergence than the *IPCX* crossover but achieving worse results. The CGA_{COL} average convergence generation is equal to 825 and compared to the CGA_{IPCX}, the introduction of the intensification procedures speeds up the convergence of the solution with reaching better results.

Exact methods are well known to be time expensive. The same applies to their hybridization of them with metaheuristics. Indeed, times execution increases significantly with such hybridization policies due to some technicality during the exchange of information between the two methods (Jourdan et al., 2009; Puchinger & Raidl, 2005; Talbi, 2002; 2009) and this is what has been observed here. However, in this chapter, the solution quality is our main concern. So, we concentrated our efforts on it. Then, because the high consuming time and memory, the collaborative algorithm will not be applied on the large problem set. Finally, we are also aware of the fact that we can't compare the collaborative hybridization with the other approaches because the CBS approach executes more than the 50 000 stop criterion evaluations.

The two row noted as IGA^{L-R} and IGA^{R-L} present the results of the genetic algorithm where the hybrid crossover *ICX* is integrated and the filling section placement is executed by the transition rule, respectively, on the left then on the right (IGA^{L-R}) and on the right then on the left (IGA^{R-L}). The purpose of this comparison is to show the impact of the look ahead element $\overline{U}_{ij}$ in the transition rule.

Indeed, if the results of the two algorithms outperform those of IGA^{1-2}, those of IGA^{R-L} are better than those of IGA^{L-R}, and specially for instances of type **1 and **5. This can be explained by two aspects: (i) in both cases, the look-ahead element $\overline{U}_{ij}$ improves the search for jobs to be placed, by calculating the impact of placing a job in a sequence where some jobs are already placed; and (ii) starting to place jobs on the right allows the transition rule to be more directive concerning the jobs in the beginning of the sequence, specially for instances of **1 and **5 where tardy jobs are usually at the end of the sequence. Similarly, the trace elements, $SUCC_{ij}(A_t)$ and $PRED_{ij}(A_t)$ built from the archive, play an important role to guide the transition rule in order to maintain and preserve the relative order according to an already placed job. Finally, IGA^{R-L} finds optimal solutions at least once except for the instance 704, which is not the case for IGA^{L-R}.

The row noted as IGA^{OrOpt} presents the results of the genetic algorithm IGA^{R-L} where a local search is applied at each offspring creation under probability equal to 0.1. The used local search heuristic in this case is the or-opt (Or, 1976) adapted to the total tardiness. This heuristic is also used by the Tabu/VNS of Gagné et al. (2005) whose results are summarized in the last row in Table 1 and noted as TVNS. In this hybrid algorithm, at each call to the heuristic, we generate a single neighborhood of size 40. The integration of the local search allows the hybrid genetic algorithm to have similar results to those of the Tabu/VNS and improve some average results for instances 604, 607, 701, 703, 704, 705 and 708. The Tabu/VNS achieved better performance only for instances 601 (0.0 against 0.0) and 605 (0.0 against 1.0). Concerning the integrative hybridization execution times, IGA^{L-R}, IGA^{R-L} and IGA^{OrOpt} have an average of 1.6, 1.6 and 2.1 minutes respectively on the small instances group.

Table 2 summarizes the comparison of different algorithms for the large instance set of Gagné et al. (2005). The subrow noted as (B) and (M) present the best and the median deviation of the presented algorithms, respectively. The best results of the B row are shaded in dark gray and the best results of the M row are shaded in gray. Overall, we observe a similar algorithm behavior as in the first group of instances. Indeed, IGA^{R-L}, which gives better results than HGA^{L-R}. Indeed, placing jobs at the end of the sequence before those at the beginning allows the hybrid crossover *ICX* better guiding for job placement using the look ahead element $\overline{U}_{ij}$ and the normalized setup times $\overline{s}_{ij}$ in the transition rule.

It should be noted that IGA^{R-L} lowers the minimum known bound for instances 557 and 858. This can be explained by the nature of these instances and by the fact that the transition rule uses the characteristics of the problems, including due dates and setup times, when calculating the look ahead element $\overline{U}_{ij}$.

PRB	OPT	GA		$IHGA^{L-R}$		$IHGA^{R-L}$		$IHGA^{OrOpt}$		TVNS	
		B	M	B	M	B	M	B	M	B	M
551	183	3.6	5.7	0.3	1.2	0.0	0.7	0.0	0.6	0.1	0.6
552	0	0.0	0.0	0.0	0.0	0.0	0.0	0.0	0.0	0.0	0.0
553	40540	0.1	0.2	0.0	0.1	0.0	0.0	0.0	0.0	0.0	0.1
554	14653	0.3	0.5	0.1	0.3	0.1	0.1	0.0*	0.0	0.0	0.2
555	0	0.0	0.0	0.0	0.0	0.0	0.0	0.0	0.0	0.0	0.0
556	0	0.0	0.0	0.0	0.0	0.0	0.0	0.0	0.0	0.0	0.0
557	35813	0.2	0.3	0.0	0.1	0.0*	0.0	0.0*	0.0	0.0	0.0
558	19871	0.3	0.4	0.0	0.2	0.0	0.0	0.0	0.0	0.0	0.1
651	268	1.6	4.3	0.0	1.0	0.0	0.9	0.0	0.3	0.0	0.2
652	0	0.0	0.0	0.0	0.0	0.0	0.0	0.0	0.0	0.0	0.0
653	57569	0.2	0.3	0.0	0.2	0.0	0.1	0.0	0.1	0.0	0.1
654	34301	0.4	0.6	0.1	0.3	0.1	0.1	0.1	0.1	0.1	0.1
655	2	120.0	185.3	45.0	77.8	17.0	52.0	15.0	25.0	0.0	12.5
656	0	0.0	0.0	0.0	0.0	0.0	0.0	0.0	0.0	0.0	0.0
657	54895	0.2	0.3	0.0	0.1	0.0	0.0	0.0	0.0	0.0	0.1
658	27114	0.4	0.5	0.0	0.3	0.1	0.1	0.0*	0.0	0.1	0.1
751	241	3.2	4.8	0.5	2.0	0.8	1.7	0.2	0.8	0.0	0.3
752	0	0.0	0.0	0.0	0.0	0.0	0.0	0.0	0.0	0.0	0.0
753	77663	0.3	0.4	0.1	0.2	0.1	0.1	0.1	0.1	0.1	0.1
754	35200	0.3	0.7	0.2	0.4	0.1	0.3	0.0*	0.0	0.1	0.3
755	0	0.0	0.0	0.0	0.0	0.0	0.0	0.0	0.0	0.0	0.0
756	0	0.0	0.0	0.0	0.0	0.0	0.0	0.0	0.0	0.0	0.0
757	59735	0.2	0.3	0.1	0.2	0.0	0.1	0.0	0.0	0.0	0.0
758	38339	0.3	0.5	0.1	0.3	0.1	0.2	0.0*	0.0	0.1	0.2
851	384	2.8	5.4	1.3	1.7	0.9	1.6	0.2	0.4	0.0	0.2
852	0	0.0	0.0	0.0	0.0	0.0	0.0	0.0	0.0	0.0	0.0
853	97642	0.3	0.4	0.1	0.2	0.3	0.1	0.0*	0.0	0.0	0.0
854	79278	0.4	0.5	0.2	0.3	0.1	0.2	0.0*	0.1	0.2	0.1
855	283	6.0	7.5	0.5	2.3	1.1	2.0	0.3	1.5	0.0	1.3
856	0	0.0	0.0	0.0	0.0	0.0	0.0	0.0	0.0	0.0	0.0
857	87244	0.3	0.4	0.1	0.2	0.0	0.1	0.0	0.0	0.0	0.1
858	74785	0.3	0.5	0.1	0.2	0.0*	0.1	0.0*	0.0	0.1	0.2

* New lower bound

Table 2. Comparison of different approaches for the large problem set

Nevertheless, for all the introduced algorithms, there are still significant differences for instances **1 and **5, and especially for instance 655 where it exceeds 75%. In these cases, this is due to the low value of the objective function.

The local search integration in IGA^{OrOpt} allows this algorithm to find six other new minimum values for instances 554, 557, 658, 754, 758, 853 and 854. This intensification process improves the genetic algorithm exploitation phase. Also, except for some deviations in instances **1 and **5, IGA^{OrOpt} improves several averages of TABU/ VNS and specially for instances 654, 657, 658, 754, 758, 854 , 857 and 858. Except for the 655 instance, where the deviation is 25% for the average result, TABU/ VNS surpasses IGA^{OrOpt} only in 7 instances (551, 651, 751, 753, 757, 851 and 855) and this with minor deviations. Of these 7 instances, 5 of them are **1 and **5 instances. Finally, in addition to the 8 new minimum values found, IGA^{R-L} and IGA^{OrOpt} also found the best known value for instance 551 while TABU/VNS did not find it. Concerning instances 653, 654 and 753, the best solutions are found by the GRASP of Gupta & Smith (2006).

Concerning the execution times, IGA^{L-R}, IGA^{R-L} and IGA^{OrOpt} have an average of 3.1, 3.1 and 3.9 minutes respectively. Furthermore, these execution times are increased by the transition rule integration in IGA^{L-R} and IGA^{R-L}, and the archive management. Finally, the or-opt local search heuristic increases the execution time by 20% for both the small and the large instance group.

5. Conclusion

In this chapter, we have introduced two hybrid GA to solve the sequence-dependent setup times single machine problem with the objective of minimizing the total tardiness. Indeed, using classical operator, most found GA in literature are not well suited to deal with the specificities of this problem. The proposed approaches in this chapter are essentially based on adapting highly specialized genetic operators to the specificities of the studied problem. The numerical experiments allowed us to demonstrate the efficiency of the proposed approaches for this problem. A natural conclusion of these experimental results is that GA may be robust and efficient alternative to solve this problem.

We describe first a collaborative hybridization where both a crossover operator and intensification process based on Constraint Based Scheduling are integrated into a GA. Indeed, the *IPCX* crossover operator uses the indirect precedence constraints to improve the CBS search and consequently the schedules quality. The precedence constraints are built from all the individual population in the reproduction process. The intensification procedures are based on two different CBS approaches after fixing a jobs block : the first minimizes the total tardiness which represents the considered problem objective function while the second minimizes the makespan which also enhances the exploration process and is well adapted to some instances.

Then, we introduce a hybrid crossover in an integrative hybridization which uses concepts from multi-objective algorithms and ant colony optimization to enhance the relative and absolute job position conservation during the evolving phase. The integrative hybridization introduce the *ICX* crossover which evolves in two steps. Indeed, from the first parent we place firstly the cross section. Then, from two lists formed with the remaining jobs, we use a pseudo-random transition rule to place these jobs. This transition rule uses past, present and future information from the archive, the visibility and the look ahead, respectively. The different proposed adaptations have contributed to the performance of this approach. The use of the archive and the look-ahead information have been shown to improve solution quality also enhancing the relative and the absolute order.

The proposed hybrid GA in this chapter represent very interesting alternatives to find good solutions. In fact, The found results highlight the importance of incorporating specific problem knowledge and specificities into genetic operators, even if classical genetic operators could be used. The two hybridizations have proved effectiveness on sets of benchmark problems taken from literature. Specially, the integrative one which even outdoes the performance of the best approach found in the literature.

For future work, we will work on improving the precedence constraints under the collaborative hybridization. Indeed, it is possible to consider constraints related to a jobs set or to intervals time. Also, it would be possible to employ a chromosome representation based on the start times of activities. Hence, it will be possible to get more accurate combination of start times. Concerning the integrative hybridization, we use it for other scheduling problems in particular and other optimization problems in general, specially real-world problems.

6. References

Allahverdi, A., Ng, C., Cheng, T. & Kovalyov, M. Y. (2008). A survey of scheduling problems with setup times or costs, *European Journal of Operational Research* 187(3): 985 – 1032.

Armentano, V. & Mazzini, R. (2000). A genetic algorithm for scheduling on a single machine with setup times and due dates, *Production Planning and Controly* 11(7): 713 – 720.

Baptiste, P., LePape, C. & Nuijten, W. (2001). *Constraint-Based Scheduling : Applying Constraint Programming to Scheduling Problems*, Kluwer Academic Publishers.

Beck, J. C. & Perron, L. (2000). Discrepancy bounded depth first search, *CP-AI-OR'2000: Fourth International Workshop on Integration of AI and OR Techniques in Constraint Programming for Combinatorial Optimization Problems*, pp. 7–17.

Bierwirth, C., Mattfeld, D. C. & Kopfer, H. (1996). On permutation representations for scheduling problems, *PPSN IV: Proceedings of the 4th International Conference on Parallel Problem Solving from Nature*, Springer-Verlag, London, UK, pp. 310–318.

Bigras, L., Gamache, M. & Savard, G. (2008). The time-dependent traveling salesman problem and single machine scheduling problems with sequence dependent setup times, *Discrete Optimization* 5(4): 663–762.

Blum, C., Roli, A. & Alba, E. (2005). *An Introduction to Metaheuristic Techniques*, Wiley Series on Parallel and Distributed Computing, Wiley.

Conner, G. (2009). 10 questions, *Manufacturing Engineering Magazine* pp. 93–99.

Dorigo, M. & Gambardella, L. M. (1997). Ant colony system: A cooperative learning approach to the traveling salesman problem, *IEEE Transactions on Evolutionary Computation* .

Du, J. & Leung, J. Y. T. (1990). Minimizing total tardiness on one machine is np-hard, *Mathematics and Operations Researchs* 15: 438–495.

Dudek, R., Smith, M. & Panwalkar, S. (1974). Use of a case study in sequencing/scheduling research, *Omega* 2(2): 253–261.

Franca, P. M., Mendes, A. & Moscato, P. (2001). A memetic algorithm for the total tardiness single machine scheduling problem, *European Journal of Operational Research* 132: 224–242.

Fromherz, M. P. (1999). Model-based configuration of machine control software, *Technical report*, In Configuration Papers from the AAAI Workshop.

Gagné, C., Gravel, M. & Price, W. L. (2005). Using metaheuristic compromise programming for the solution of multiple objective scheduling problems, *The Journal of the Operational Research Society* 56: 687–698.

Gagné, C., Price, W. & Gravel, M. (2002). Comparing an aco algorithm with other heuristics for the single machine scheduling problem with sequence-dependent setup times, *Journal of the Operational Research Society* 53: 895–906.

Graham, R. L., Lawler, E. L., Lenstra, J. K. & Kan, A. G. H. R. (1979). Optimization and approximation in deterministic sequencing and scheduling: a survey, *Annals of Discrete Mathematics* 5: 287–326.

Gupta, S. R. & Smith, J. S. (2006). Algorithms for single machine total tardiness scheduling with sequence dependent setups, *European Journal of Operational Research* 175(2): 722–739.

ILOG (2003a). *ILOG Scheduler 6.0. User Manual*, ILOG.

ILOG (2003b). *ILOG Solver 6.0. User Manual*, ILOG.

Jourdan, L., Basseur, M. & Talbi, E.-G. (2009). Hybridizing exact methods and metaheuristics: A taxonomy, *European Journal of Operational Research* 199(3): 620–629.
URL: *http://ideas.repec.org/a/eee/ejores/v199y2009i3p620-629.html*

Lee, Y., Bhaskaram, K. & Pinedo, M. (1997). A heuristic to minimize the total weighted tardiness with sequence-dependent setups, *IIE Transactions* 29: 45–52.

Liao, C. & Juan, H. (2007). An ant colony optimization for single-machine tardiness scheduling with sequence-dependent setups, *Computers and Operations Research* 34: 1899–1909.

Meseguer, P. (1997). Interleaved depth-first search, *IJCAI'97: Proceedings of the Fifteenth international joint conference on Artifical intelligence*, Morgan Kaufmann Publishers Inc., San Francisco, CA, USA, pp. 1382–1387.

Michalewicz, Z. (1996). *Genetic algorithms + data structures = evolution programs (3rd ed.)*, Springer-Verlag, London, UK.

Or, I. (1976). *Traveling salesman-type combinatorial problems and their relation to the logistics of regional blood banking*, PhD thesis, Northwestern University, Illinois.

Pinedo, M. (2002). *Scheduling Theory, Algorithm and Systems*, Prentice-Hall.

Puchinger, J. & Raidl, G. R. (2005). Combining metaheuristics and exact algorithms in combinatorial optimization: A survey and classification, *Proceedings of the First International Work-Conference on the Interplay Between Natural and Artificial Computation, Las Palmas, Spain, LNCS*.

Ragatz, G. L. (1993). A branch-and-bound method for minimumtardiness sequencing on a single processor with sequence dependent setup times, *Proceedings twenty fourth annual meeting of the Decision Sciences Institute*, pp. 1375–1377.

Rubin, P. & Ragatz, G. (1995). Scheduling in a sequence-dependent setup environment with genetic search, *Computers and Operations Research* 22: 85–99.

Sioud, A., Gravel, M. & Gagné, C. (2010). A modeling for the total tardiness smsdst problem using constraint programming., *Proceedings of the 2010 International Conference on Artificial Intelligence, ICAI 2010, July 12-15, 2010, Las Vegas Nevada, USA, 2 Volumes*, CSREA Press, pp. 588–594.

Sioud, A., Gravel, M. & Gagné, C. (2009). New crossover operator for the single machine scheduling problem with sequence-dependent setup times, *GEM'09: The 2009 International Conference on Genetic and Evolutionary Methods*.

Talbi, E. (2002). A taxonomy of hybrid metaheuristics, *Journal of Heuristics* 8: 541–564.

Talbi, E.-G. (2009). *Metaheuristics : from design to implementation*, John Wiley & Sons.

Tan, K. & Narasimhan, R. (1997). Minimizing tardiness on a single processor with setup-dependent setup times: a simulated annealing approach, *Omega* 25: 619 – 634.

Walsh, T. (1997). Depth-bounded discrepancy search, *IJCAI'97: Proceedings of the Fifteenth international joint conference on Artifical intelligence*, Morgan Kaufmann Publishers Inc., San Francisco, CA, USA, pp. 1388–1393.

Zitzler, E. & Thiele, L. (1999). Multiobjective evolutionary algorithms: A comparative case study and the strength Pareto approach, *IEEE Transactions on Evolutionary Computation* 3(4): 257–271.

11

Genetic Algorithms and Group Method of Data Handling-Type Neural Networks Applications in Poultry Science

Majid Mottaghitalb
Dept. of Animal Science, Faculty of Agri. Uni. of Guilan, Rasht, Iran

1. Introduction

The necessity of modeling is well established since the structural identification of a process is essential in analysis, control and prediction. Computer modeling is becoming an important tool in different fields in science including Biology. In Artificial Intelligence research, 'intelligence' is increasingly looked upon not as deliberative reasoning processes alone, but as the ability to exhibit adaptive behavior in a complex world. There have been extensive efforts in recent years to deploy population-based stochastic search algorithms such as evolutionary methods to design artificial neural networks since such evolutionary algorithms are

particularly useful for dealing with complex problems having large search spaces with many local optima(Iba, etal,1996). In recent years, the use of artificial neural networks leads to successful application of different type of algorithm in a broad range of areas in engineering, biology, and economics in which GMDH-type is one.

2. Genetic algorithms

Nature employs the best cybernetic systems that can be conceived. In the neurological domain of living beings, the ecological balance involving environmental feedback, or the regulation of the temperature of the human body, are the examples of cybernetic systems of nature that are fascinating in their accuracy and efficiency (Madala and Ivakhnenko, 1994).

In the 1950s and 1960s several computer scientists independently studied evolutionary systems with the idea that evolution could be used as an optimization tool for engineering problems in different systems (as a collection of interacting, diverse elements that function/ communicate within a specified environment to process information to achieve one or more desired objectives) (Mitchell and Forrest 1994).

Evolution can be considered as the first and highest level of adaptation. It involves the adaptation of a species to global ecological and environmental conditions. This adaptation is a relatively slow process that operates over millennia, although the speed of genetic adaptation may differ widely for individual species.

Genetic algorithms (GAs) are currently the most prominent and widely used models of evolution in artificial-life systems. GAs have been used both as tools for solving practical problems and as scientific models of evolutionary processes. The intersection between GAs and artificial life includes both, although in this article we focus primarily on GAs as models of natural phenomena. Indeed GAs are optimization algorithms that work according to a scheme analogous to that of natural evolution. Literature review reveled that John Holland (Holland 1975) was the first who offered these principles of natural evolution to artificial systems, more precisely to optimization problems, and came up with the notion of GA. A general definition of these algorithms is (Koza 1980):

> *"The genetic algorithm is a highly parallel mathematical algorithm that transforms a set (population) of individual mathematical objects (typically fixed length character strings patterned after chromosome strings), each with an associated fitness value, into a new population (i.e. the next generation) using operations patterned after the Darwinian principle of reproduction and survival of the fittest and after naturally occurring genetic operations (notably sexual recombination)."*

Genetic algorithms as defined by Goldberg (Goldberg, 1989) is:

...search algorithms based on the mechanics of natural selection and natural genetics."

Goldberg offers four differences between genetic algorithms and other search methods.

1. Genetic algorithms work with a *coded* parameter set.
2. They search from a *population* of points in a solution space, rather than from a single point.
3. They only use directly available information provided through a *fitness function*.
4. They rely on *probabilistic transition rules* instead of deterministic rules.

The success of nature in solving many problems nowadays recognized as very difficult for the traditional approaches, have led researchers into studying the biological example. In various abstractions and formalizations, biological systems have been theoretically proven to provide robust solutions to these hard problems. However the models used in the area of biological problems are complex, because of their characteristics and processes. This concept leads to the conclusion that the biological activity generates information with special features, most notable being the following (Fernández and Lozano, 2010):

1. The obtained information from process presents a non-homogeneous structure since of the complexity of the objects alive.
2. The information is emerging from the dynamics of change associated with the functional properties of the studied phenomena.

What structure we need depends, of course, on our aims. We may distinguish roughly between operational and physiological models. An operational model aims to describe behavior realistically, but its structure is not intended to resemble the internal structure of particular biological system. Such models are often referred to as black box models to indicate lack of concern about underlying mechanisms. A physiological model, on the other hand, attempts to take into account more of the physiology that produces behavior, e.g., body and nervous system physiology (Dellaert, 1995).

3. Neural networks

Our brain contains about $\mathbf{10^{11}}$ neurons, each of which is connected to an average of $\mathbf{10^{4}}$ other neurons. This amounts to a total of $\mathbf{10^{15}}$ connections. If these billions of connections were fully random, it can be shown that the brain would be many times larger than it actually is (Happel and Murre, 1994). Massive regressive events of neuronal connectivity in the vertebrate nervous system can be seen as part of the development and maturation of neural functions. The neuron has set of nodes that, connects it to inputs, output, or other neurons, these nodes are also called synapses (See Fig. 1).

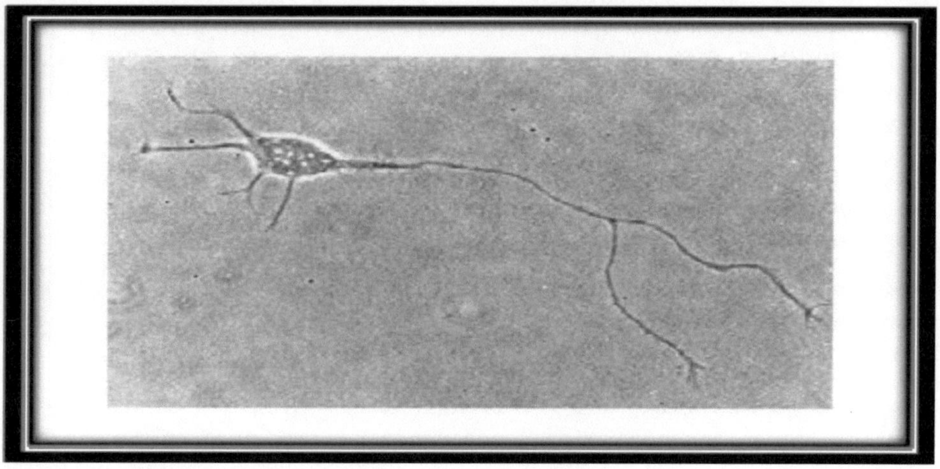

Fig. 1. Schematic structure of a Neuron

A single neuron by itself is not a very useful pattern recognition tool. The real power of neural networks comes when we combine neurons into the multilayer structures, called neural networks (NN) (Fig. 2).

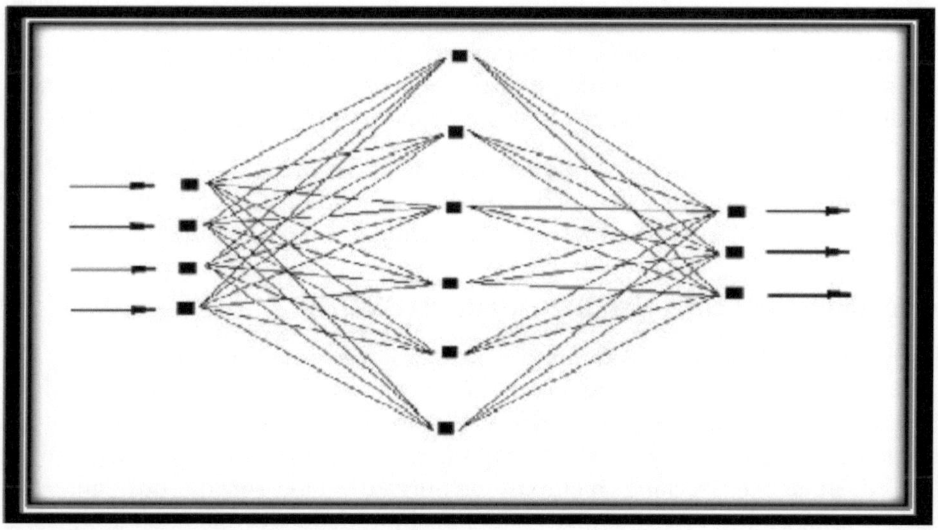

Fig. 2. A Schematic representation of neural net

In a nutshell, a NN can be considered as a black box that is able to predict an output pattern when it recognizes a given input pattern. Once trained, the NN is able to recognize similarities when presented with a new input pattern, resulting in a predicted output pattern. The process of evolution is used as a 'real-world model' that serves as a source of ideas for solving practical and theoretical problems in modeling and optimization.

Researchers from a wide range of fields have discovered the benefits of applying NNs to pattern recognition problems in various systems (including biological system). Artificial NN (ANNs) is a system loosely modeled based on the human brain and are considered as a branch of the field known as "Artificial Intelligence" (AI). The techniques of AI is being applied in this field significantly in recent decades, and among them those known as ANNs, are characterized by their properties of learning and generalization. It's often necessary to take into account their potential for induction, which can be implemented by software (Miroslav Šnorek, 2006).

To understand behavior of model system, we need ways of describing behavior maps and state transition equations. Ideally, behavioral models should fulfill the following requirements (Dellaert, 1995):

1. Versatility
2. Robustness
3. Learning
4. Ontogeny
5. Evolution

NNs are a powerful technique to solve many real world problems. They have the ability to learn from experience in order to improve their performance and to adapt themselves to changes in the environment. In addition to that they are able to deal with incomplete information or noisy data and can be very effective especially in situations where it is not possible to define the rules or steps that lead to the solution of a problem. Once trained, the NN is able to recognize similarities when presented with a new input pattern, resulting in a predicted output pattern. NNs are applied in many fields to model and predict the behavior of unknown systems or systems with complexity (or both) based on given input–output data. Using NNs does not require a priori equation or model. This characteristic is potentially advantageous in modeling biological processes (Dayhof & DeLeo 2001).

There are several methods to obtain inductive models. The Group Method of Data Handling methods, GMDH (Ivakhnenko AG, 1971) is well known and has recently gained popularity as a self-organizing and powerful tool to express complex input–output dependencies.

4. Group Method of Data Handling method (GMDH)

Generally, the connection between input-output variables can be approximated by Volterra functional series, the discrete analogue of which is Kolmogorov-Gabor polynomial. Ivakhnenko (Ivakhnenko, 1966), inspired by the form of Kolmogorov-Gabor polynomial, developed a new algorithm, known as Group Method of Data Handling (GMDH), which are also called inductive learning methods, self-organization, sorting out, and heuristic methods. This approach is substantially different from deductive methods used commonly for modeling. It has inductive nature, i.e., it finds the best solution by sorting-out of possible variants. The framework of these methods differs slightly in some important respects (Madala and Ivakhnenko, 1994).

A major difficulty in modeling complex systems in such unstructured areas as economics, ecology, sociology, and others is the problem of the researchers introducing their own prejudices model. In the mid 1960's the Russian mathematician and cyberneticist, A.G. Ivakhnenko, introduced a method (Ivakhnenko, 1966), based in part on the Rosenblatt perceptron (Rosenblatt, 1958), that allows the researchers to build model of complex systems without making assumptions about internal working. The idea is to have the computer construct a model of optimal complexity based only on data and not on any preconceived ideas of the researchers; that is,by knowing only simple input-output relationship of the system. Ivakhnenko's GMDH algorithm will construct a self-organizing model (an extremely high-order polynomial in the input variable) that can be used to solve prediction, identification, control synthesis, and other system problems (Farrow, 1981).

The algorithm was developed for identifying nonlinear relationships between inputs and outputs. The algorithm provides an optimal structure, obtained in an iterative procedure of partial descriptions of the data by adding new layers. The number of neurons in each layer, the number of layers and the input variables are automatically determined to minimize a criterion of prediction error and thus organizes an optimal NN architecture using a self-heuristics, which is the basis of the GMDH algorithm. (Ivakhnenko,1971). This method is particularly successful in solving problems of modeling multiple entries for a single output (Mutasem, 2004). The main idea of GMDH is to build an analytical function in a feed-forward network based on a quadratic node transfer function whose coefficients obtained by using a regression technique (Farlow, 1984). By means of the GMDH-type NN algorithm, a model can be represented as a set of neurons in which different pairs in each layer are connected through a quadratic polynomial and thus produce new neurons in the next layer, and therefore can be used to map inputs to outputs. Such an NN identification process needs some optimization method to find the best network architecture. This sub-model of ANN is considered as a Self - organizing approach by which gradually more complex models are generated from their performance evaluation (Lemke and Mueller, 2003). The unique feature of GMDH-type NN is that it facilitates, systematically and autonomously, developing optimal complex models by performing both variable and structure identification.

Incorporating Genetic Algorithm to GMDH-type NNs, each neuron is represented as a string, which can be mutated or crossed with each other to form new generations. Thus GA has been used in feed-forward GMDH-type NN for each neuron searching its optimal set of connections with the preceding layer (Vasechkina & Yarin 2001; Nariman-Zadeh et al. 2003).

In the early stage of the development of GMDH theory the similarity between NNs and multilayer GMDH algorithms had been highlighted. (Ivakhnenko 1970) in one of the introductory articles claims that since the differences between perceptron and GMDH are neither significant nor fundamental it is appropriate to call GMDH systems as "systems of perceptron type".

During the modeling procedure, GMDH algorithm involves four heuristics that represent the main features of GMDH theory (Anastasakis and Mort, 2001):

1. Collect a set of observations that seems to be relevant to the object
2. Divide the observations into two groups. The first will be used to estimate the coefficients of model while the second will separate the information embedded in the data into either useful or harmful. Strictly speaking: "no partition of the data, no GMDH".
3. Create a set of elementary functions where complexity will increase through an iterative procedure producing different models.
4. Acording to Gödel's incompleteness theorem, apply an external criterion to choose the optimum model.

A detailed description of a GMDH-type NN terminology, development, application, and examples of using this approach were reported by several researchers (Farrow, 1984; Mueller and Lemke, 2000; Lemke and Mueller, 2003; Nariman-Zadeh et al., 2005). Recently the GEvoM software for GMDH-type NN training (GEvoM 2009) was developed in University of Guilan, Iran.

5. Applications of GMDH-type algorithms in animal and poultry production systems

Contributions to GMDH type of NN, have come from many research areas of different disciplines, and recently, the use of such self-organizing networks has led to a successful application of the GMDH-type algorithm in a broad range of areas in engineering, science, and economics (Amanifard et al., 2008). However, very little research has been conducted on modeling animal and /or poultry growth and production using ANNs.

A series of studies have been conducted to examine the potential use of ANNs in various poultry subjects, such, prediction of ascites in broilers (Roush *et al.,* 1996; Roush and Wideman,2000), the estimation of production variables in the production phase of broiler breeders (Salle *et al.,* 2003), and the comparison of Gompertz and NN models of broiler growth (Roush *et al.,* 2006).

However no attempt was made to use GMDH-type NN in animal agriculture, until 2007, when the results of study was published based on the first work of my group in University of Guilan, Iran (Ahmadi, *etal.,* 2007). The idea behind this work was that, when considering the effects of nutrition on broiler performance, several nutrients may influence the breast meat yield, feed : gain ratio, and number of days required to produce the market body weight; among them, Metabolizable Energy (ME) and Amino Acid(AA) , such as Lysine(Lys) and Methionine (Met) (Hruby and Hamre, 1996 ; Gous, 1998) . In terms of AA, whatever system is used to describe the essential AA requirements for broiler chickens, predicting the performance to be used in deciding the most advantageous dietary AA patterns in practical and useful terms is still difficult, even when the digestibility or availability of AA is specified (NRC, 1994; Sibbald, 1987]. This difficulty is partly due to the nonlinearity of growth responses related to changes in dietary AA concentrations [Hruby and Hamre, 1996, Phillips, 1981]. A more useful method is to model the system, which in turn requires an explicit mathematical input-output relationship. Such explicit mathematical modeling is, however, very difficult and is not readily tractable in poorly understood systems. Alternatively, soft-computing methods, which concern computation in an imprecise environment, have gained significant attention. One of the soft-computing methods is ANNs, which have shown great ability in solving complex nonlinear system identification and control problems.

The optimal structures of the evolved 2- hidden-layer GMDH-type NN that were suggested by GA for performance index (PI) as the system output modeling, were found with 2, 4, and 4 hidden neurons for growth periods 1, 2, and 3, respectively. In the first period, the structure obtained appeared with the GA, which was less complex than in the second and third periods, in which the GA suggested 2 hidden neurons to fit the network. All models constructed from this data set were characterized by a superb response for all input variables from the learning set. The partial descriptions of the GMDH-type NN were found with 2 hidden layers and 2 hidden neurons for growth period, whereas it appeared with 2 hidden layers and 4 hidden neurons for growth periods 2 and 3. In fact, these results revealed the quantitative relation between input (ME, Met, and Lys) and output (PI) variables under investigation, which meant GMDH-type NN may be considered as a promising method for modeling the relationship between dietary concentrations of nutrients and poultry performance, and therefore can be used in choosing and developing special feeding programs to decrease production costs. Also, it can enhance our ability to predict other economic traits, make precise predictions of the nutrition requirements, and achieve optimal performance in poultry production systems. The conclusion remarks of this study were reported as:

4-1- Knowledge of an adequate description of broiler ME and AA requirements can help in establishing specific feeding programs, defining optimal performance, and reducing production costs.

4-2- Calculated statistics indicate that GMDH-type NN provide an effective means of efficiently recognizing the patterns in data and predicting a PI based on investigating inputs.

4-3- The genetic approach could be used to provide optimal networks in terms of hidden layers, the number of neurons and their configuration of connectivity, or both so that a polynomial expression for dependent variables of the process can consequently be achieved.

4-4-The polynomials obtained could be used to optimize broiler performance based on nutritional factors by optimizing methods such as the GA.

In animal and poultry production, feed composition is very important item for diet formulation. Since conventional laboratory techniques for feed analysis is expensive and time consuming, it would be advantageous if a simple means of estimating feed composition could be developed. One year after the first work another study (Ahmadi *etal.,* 2008) was done. The purpose of this study was to examine the validity of GMDH-type NN with a genetic algorithm method to predict the True Metabolizable Energy corrected for nitrogen (TMEn) of feather meal and poultry offal meal (POM) based on their chemical analysis.

All the previously TMEn prediction models reported for poultry by-product meals were based on the regression analysis methods using their CP, ether extract (EE), and ash content. In this study, a soft-computing method of artificial NN (ANN) seemed to be more appropriate for the TMEn prediction of a feedstuff.

The parameters of interest in this multi-input, single-output system that influenced the TMEn were CP, EE, and ash content of the samples. The raw data were divided into 2 parts of training and validation sets. Thirty input-output data lines (12 from FM and 18 from POM

Samples) were randomly selected and used to train the GMDH-type NN model as a training set. The validation set consisted of the 7 remaining data lines (3 from FM and 4 from POM samples), which were used to validate the prediction of the evolved NN during the training processes. The data set was imported into a GEvoM for GMDH-type NN training (GEvoM, 2008). Two hidden layers were considered for prediction of the TMEn model. A population of 15 individual values with a crossover probability of 0.7, mutation probability of

0.07, and 300 generations was used to genetically design the NN (Yao, 1999). It appeared that no further improvement could be achieved for this population size. A quantitative verifying fit for the predictive model was made using error measurement indices commonly used to evaluate forecasting models. The goodness of fit or accuracy of the model was determined by R2 value, adjusted R2, mean square error, residual standard deviation, mean absolute percentage error, and bias (Oberstone,1990).

The results of this study revealed that the novel modeling of GMDH-type NN with an evolutionary method of GA can be used to predict the TMEn of FM and POM samples based on their CP, EE, and ash content(See Fig. 3). The advantage of using the GMDH-type NN to predict an output from the input variables is that there is no need to preselect a model or base the model entirely on the fit of the data. It is concluded that the GMDH-type NN may be used to accurately estimate the nutritive value of poultry meals from their corresponding chemical composition.

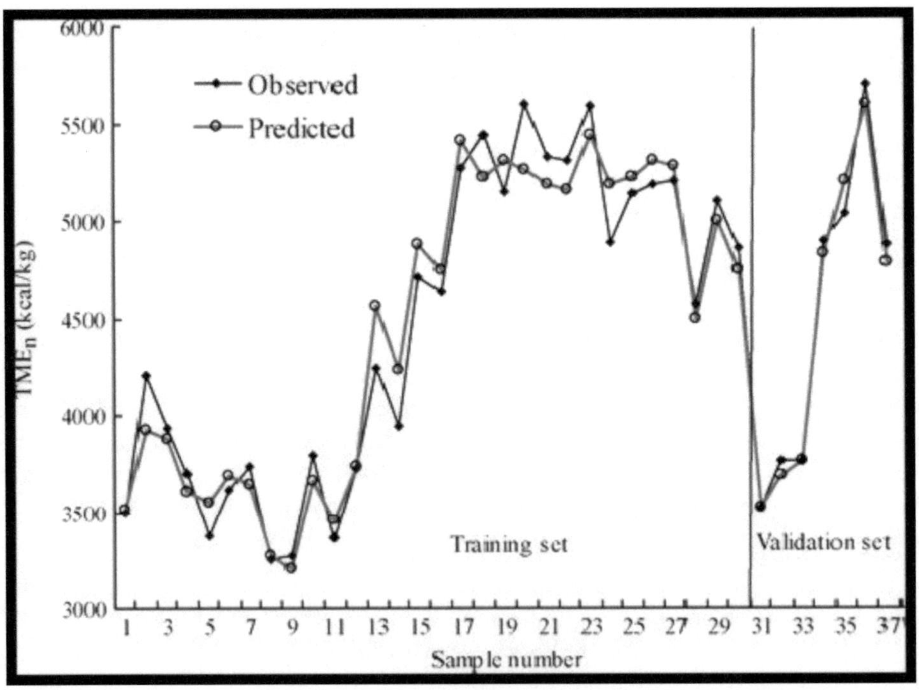

Fig. 3. The comparison of observed and model predicted TMEn values obtained from training (1 to 12 and 13 to 30 are feather and offal samples, respectively) and validation (31 to 33 and 34 to 37 are feather and offal samples, respectively) sets.

The success of poultry meat production has been strongly related to improvements in growth and carcass yield, mainly by increasing breast proportion and reducing carcass fat.

In addition to its measurement in the laboratory using wet chemistry, carcass composition of broiler chickens has been predicted by means of allometric equations, real-time ultrasonography, radioactive isotopes and specific gravity studies (Pesti & Bakalli 1997; Toledo et al.2004; Rosa et al.2007; Makkar 2008). Conventional laboratory techniques for determining carcass composition are expensive, cumbersome and time consuming. Therefore, it would be useful if a simple means of estimating carcass composition could be developed. In this respect, the potential advantages from modeling growth are considerable.

Results obtained from two above mentioned studies urged our group to think about third study in 2010 (Faridi, *etal.*, 2012), aimed at applying the GMDH-type NNs to data from two studies with broilers in order to predict carcass energy (CEn, MJ/g) content and relative growth (g/g of body weight) of carcass components (carcass protein, breast muscle, leg and thigh muscles, carcass fat, abdominal fat, skin fat and visceral fat). The effective input variables involved in the prediction of CEn and carcass fat content using data from the first study were dietary metabolizable energy (ME, kJ/kg), crude protein (CP, g/kg of diet), fat (g/kg of diet) and crude fibre (CF, g/kg of diet). For this purpose, in the current study, GA were deployed to design the whole architecture of the GMDH-type NN, i.e. the number of neurons in each hidden layer and their configuration of connectivity to find the optimal set of appropriate coefficients of quadratic expressions.

Quantified values of bias in this study showed very little under- and over-estimation by the models proposed by the GMDH-type NN, which revealed close agreement between observed and predicted values of CEn and carcass components. The value of R2, a measure of the relation between the actual and predicted values, was high for both studies indicating a strong effect of all selected input variables on output prediction.

In conclusion, the results of the current study showed that a GMDH type NN modeling approach can be a simple but very effective method for predicting carcass composition in broiler chickens based on dietary input variables. This is in agreement with previous studies aimed at investigating the effects of different dietary nutrients on body composition in broilers (Fraps 1943; Donaldson et al. 1956; Kubena et al. 1972; Edwards et al. 1973).

Selection pressure applied by industry geneticists has greatly reduced feed conversion ratio and age to slaughter as well as increased growth rate and yield of edible meat for commercial turkeys. These genetic improvements have occurred along with improvements in nutrition and management (Havenstein et al., 2007).

There has been extensive research conducted to clarify protein, essential amino acids, and energy requirements in poultry. To avoid conventional laboratory and field based techniques problems for determining nutrient requirements alternative methods was offered using GMDH - type NN (Mottaghitalab,*etal.*, 2010). In determining nutrient requirements, the potential benefits from modeling growth in poultry are considerable. This approach has the potential to provide information in several areas for poultry production, including prediction of growth rate and market weights, determination of factors that are truly of economic importance to the operation, general knowledge about the systems involved in production, and determination of more precise nutrient requirements based on sex, strain, protein versus fat accretion, parts yield, and feed intake.

The structures of the 2 hidden layers GMDH-type NN evolved for CE and FE are shown in Figures 4 and 5, respectively. These figures correspond to the genome representation of (abceadaa) and (eeabacdd) for the CE and FE models, respectively, and illustrate the generated relationship between input variables to reach the output. As Figures 4 and 5 show, the optimal structure of the evolved 2 hidden layer GMDH-type NN suggested by GA was found with 5 and 4 hidden neurons for CE and FE, respectively. In most GMDH-type NN, the neurons in each layer are only connected to neurons in the adjacent layer (Farlow, 1984), but for GMDH-type NN developed here, variable a of the input layer for CE is connected to adaa in the second hidden layer by directly passing through the first hidden layer. The same process happens for d and e input variables in the FE model. Such repetition occurs whenever a neuron passes some adjacent hidden layer and connects to another neuron in the next following hidden layer.

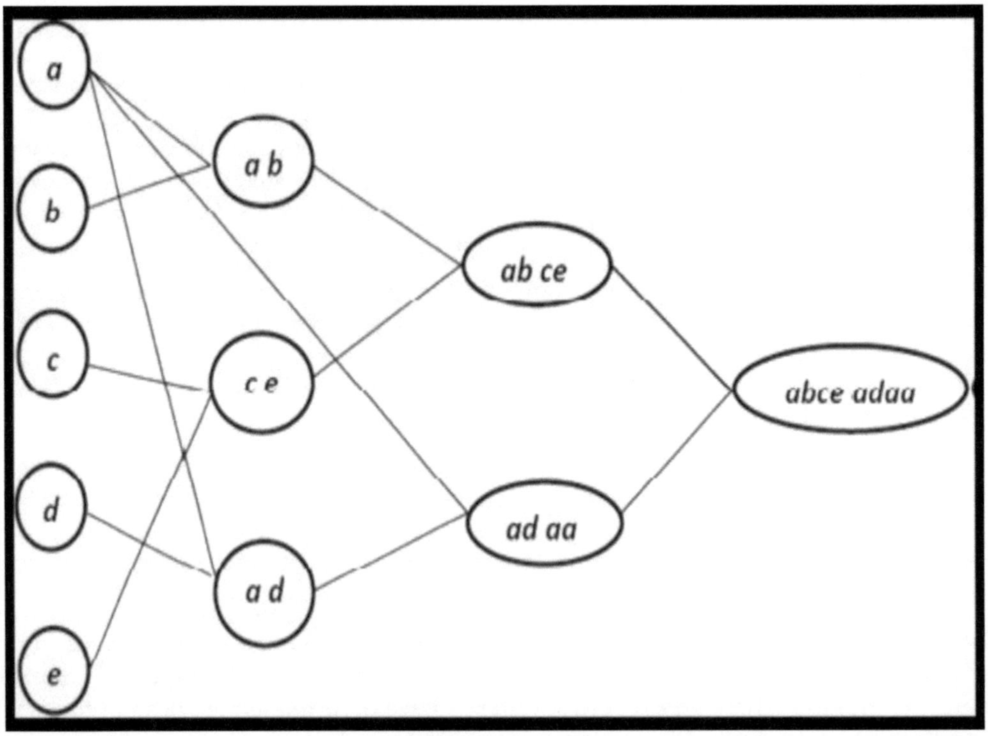

Fig. 4. Evolved structure of the generalized group method of data handling-type NNs for caloric efficiency in tom turkeys. The letters *a, b, c, d,* and *e* stand for input variables of age (wk), ME (kcal/g), CP (% of diet), Met (% of diet), and Lys (% of diet), respectively. This figure illustrates the generated relationship between input variables to reach output.

It appears that all selected input variables in both models had a strong effect on output prediction, which is in agreement with previous studies (Lemme et al., 2006 for amino acid; Noy and Sklan, 2004 for energy and amino acid; Potter et al., 1966 and Waibel et al., 1995 for Met and Lys; and Bowyer and Waldroup, 1986 for protein). Figure 1 shows a very strong effect of age on CE. This result is similar to previous studies aiming to describe the growth pattern of animals with age using growth functions (Darmani-Kuhi et al., 2003; Schulin-

Zeuthen et al., 2008). The calculated values of CE model error measurement showed that the testing set for toms yielded lower values of MS error, mean absolute deviation, mean absolute percentage error, mean relative error, and higher values of R2 compared with the training set.

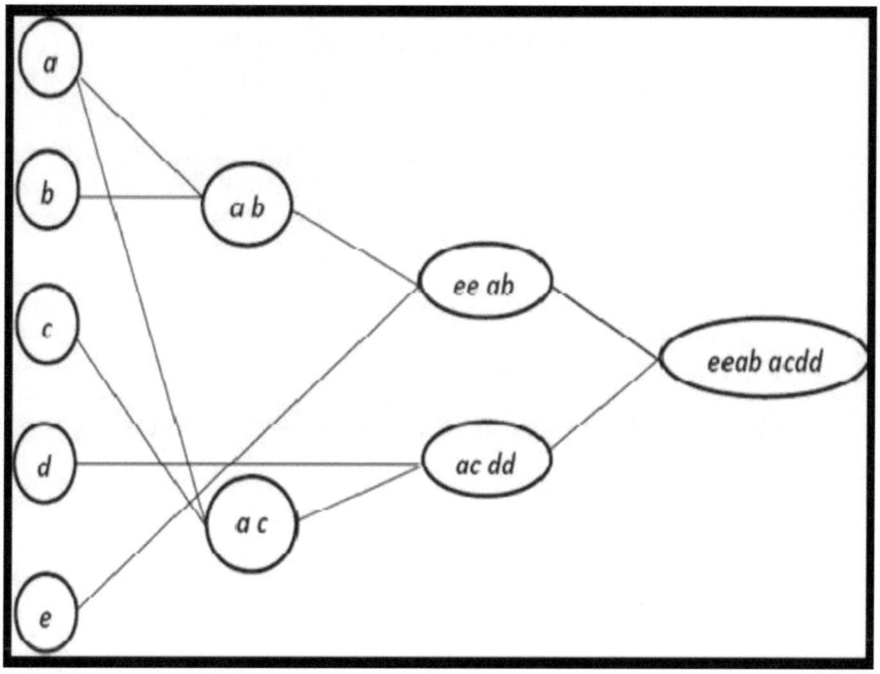

Fig. 5. Evolved structure of the generalized group method of data handling-type NNs for feed efficiency in tom turkeys. The letters *a, b, c, d,* and *e* stand for input variables of age (wk), ME (kcal/g), CP (% of diet), Met (% of diet), and Lys (% of diet), respectively. This figure illustrates the generated relationship between input variables to reach output.

Conducting a sensitivity analysis (SA) on the obtained polynomial equations reveals the sensitivity of model output to input variables. Hence it is necessary to do sensitivity analysis for any proposed model. In other words, SA increases confidence in the model and its predictions by providing an understanding of how the model responds to changes in its inputs. Moreover, the SA identifies critical regions in the space of the inputs, establishes priorities for research and simplifies the model (Castillo et al.,2008; Saltelli et al., 2008).

For such reason and in line with previous work, another study was designed, titled:

"Sensitivity analysis of an early egg production predictive model inbroiler breeders based on dietary nutrient intake" (Faridi et al., 2011).

Although the use of NN and SA techniques has led to successful application in a broad range of areas (Seyedan&Ching 2006;Lee &Hsiung 2009), the use of SA along with NN models is appeared uncommon in poultry science. The aim of the present study was to use the GMDH-type NN to model early egg production (EEP) in broiler breeders (BB) based on the dietary intake levels of ME, CP, and the two first limiting amino acids, methionine (Met) and lysine (Lys). The SA method was utilized to evaluate the relative importance of input variables on model output and to determine the optimum levels of nutrient intake for obtaining the maximum EEP in BB.

In this study, the GMDH-type NN with GA method was used to develop the EEP in BB. By means of the GMDH algorithm, a model can be represented as a set of quadratic polynomials. In this way, GA are deployed to assign the number of neurons (polynomial equations) in the network and to find the optimal set of appropriate coefficients of the quadratic expressions.

The variables of interest in this model were the dietary intake levels of ME (MJ/bird/day), CP (g/bird/day), Met (g/bird/day), Lys (g/bird/day) and weekly egg production (eggs/bird) during early production (from 24 to 29 weeks of age). Datasets were imported into the software GEvoM for GMDH-type NN training (GEvoM 2009).

Results of the developed GMHD-type NN models revealed close agreement between observed and predicted values of EEP. Results showed that the evolved GMDH-type NNs have been successful in obtaining a model for the prediction of EEP in BB. All input variables were accepted by the model, i.e. the GMDH-type NN provides an automated selection of essential input variables and builds polynomial equations to model EEP.

The advantage of using GMDH-type NN is that which polynomial equations obtained can be used to analyze the sensitivity of output with respect to input variables. SA discusses how and how much changes in the input variables modify the optimal objective function value and the point where the optimum is attained. The simple approach to SA is easy to do, easy to understand, easy to communicate, and applicable with any model.

6. Conclusion

The conclusion was that, genetic algorithm in general and GMDH-type NN in particular may be used as a powerful tool to enhance our ability to predict economic traits, make precise prediction of nutrition requirements, and achieve optimal performance in poultry nutrition and production.

7. References

Ahmadi, H.,M.Mottaghitalab,& N.Nariman-Zadeh.(2007).Group Method of data handling-Type NN Prediction of Broiler Performance Based on Dietary Metabolizable Energy, Methionine, and Lysine. J. Appl. Poult. Res. 16:494–501

AHMADI, H., M. Mottaghitalab,N. Nariman-Zadeh & A. Golian. (2008). Predicting performance of broiler chickens from dietary nutrients using group method of data handling-type neural networks. British Poultry Science Volume 49, Number 3, pp. 315—320

Amanifard,N., N. Nariman-Zadeh, M. Borji, A. Khalkhali, & A. Habibdoust. (2008). Modelling and pareto optimization of heat transfer and flow coefficients in microchannels. Energy Conversion & Management, issue 2, Vol.49, pp 311-325.

Anastasakis, L.& N. Mort.(2001).The development of self-organization techniques in modeling: A review of the group method of data handling (GMDH). Research

Report No. 813. October 2001. *Department of Automatic Control & Systems Engineering The University of Sheffield Mappin St, Sheffield, S1 3JD, United Kingdom.*

Bowyer, B. L., and P. W. Waldroup. (1986). Evaluation of minimal protein levels for growing turkeys and development of diets for estimating lysine requirements. Poult. Sci. 65(Suppl. 1):16. Abstr.

Castillo, E., R, Minguez, and C, Castillo.(2008). Sensitivity analysis in optimization and reliability problems. Reliability Eng. and Syst. Safety 93:1788–1800.

Darmani- Kuhi, H. Kebreab, H., E. Lopez, S. and France J. (2003). An evaluation of different growth functions for describing the profile of live weight with time (age) in meat and egg strains of chicken. Poult. Sci. 82:1536 - 1543.

Dayhoff, J. E., & de Leo, J.M.(2001). Artificial NNs: opening the black box. Cancer 91(Suppl.8), 1615–1635.

Dellaert, F.(1995).Toward a biologically defensible model of development.Submitted in partial fulfillment of the requirements for the degree of Master of Science. Department of Computer Engineering and Science,Case Western Reserve University. January, 1995

Donaldson,W.E.,Coombs, G.F. & Romoser, G. L.(1956).Studies on energy levels in poultry rations.1. The effect of calorie-protein ratio of the ration on growth, nutrient utilization and body composition of chicks. Poultry Science 35, 1100–1105.

Edwards, H.M.,Denman,F., Abov-Ashour,A. & Nugara, D.(1973).Carcass composition studies. 1. Influences of age, sex, and type of dietary fat supplementation on total carcass fatty acid composition. Poultry Science 52, 934–948.

Faridi, A. ,. Mottaghitalab, M. , Darmani-kuhi, H. France, J.& Ahmadi. H. (2011). Predicting carcass energy content and composition in broilers using the group method of data handling-type NNs. Journal of Agricultural Science, Vol. 149, No2 , pp. 249-254

Faridi A, M.Mottaghitalab & H. Ahmadi .(2012).Sensitivity analysis of an early egg production predictive model in broiler breeders based on dietary nutrient intake.Journal of Agricultural Science. 150, 87-93

Farlow,S. J. (1981).The GMDH algorithm of Ivakhnenko. The American Statistician.35, 4:210-215

Farrow S.J . (1984). The GMDH algorithm. In self organizing Methods in Modeling: GMDH Type Algorithms (Ed .S. J. Farrow), pp. 1–24. New York: Marcel Dekker.

Fernández,F.H. & F. H. Lozano.(2010). GMDH Algorithms implemented in the intelligent identification of a bioprocess.ABCM Symposium Series in Mechatronics-Vol.4:.278-287

Fraps, G. S. (1943).Relation of the protein,fat, and energy of the ration to the composition of chickens. Poultry Science 22, 421–424.

GEvoM.(2009).GMDH-type NN Design by Evolutionary Method for Modelling. Rasht, Iran: University of Guilan. Available online at:
http://research.guilan.ac.ir/gevom/(verified 20 October 2010).

Goldberg, D. E.(1989).Genetic Algorithms in Search, Optimization and Machine Learning. Addison-Wesley,Reading, Massachusetts.

Gous, R. M. 1998. Making progress in the nutrition of broilers. Poult.Sci. 77:111–117.

Happel, B. L. M. & J. M.J. Murre. 1994. The Design and Evolution of Modular NN Architectures.NNs. 7: 985-1004.

Havenstein, G. B., P. R. Ferket, J. L. Grimes, M. A. Qureshi, and K. E. Nestor. 2007. Comparison of the performance of 1966- versus 2003-type turkeys when fed representative 1966 and 2003 turkey diets: Growth rate, livability, and feed conversion. Poult. Sci. 86:232 - 240.

Holland, J. H.(1975).*Adaptation in Natural and Artificial Systems*. Ann Arbor, MI: University of Michigan Press.

Hruby, M., M. L. Hamre,& C. N. Coon.(1996).Non-linear and linear functions in body protein growth.J. Appl. Poult. Res. 5:109–115.

Iba, H., deGaris, H. and Sato,T. (1996). A numerical Approach to Genetic Programming for System Identification. Evolutionary Computation 3(4):417- 452,.

Ivakhnenko A.G.(1970).Heuristic self-organization in problems of engineering cybernetics.Automatica.l.6:.207-219,.

Ivakhnenko A.G.(1971).Polynomial theory of complex systems. IEEE Transactions on Systems, Man,and Cybernetics.SMC-1, 364–378

Ivakhnenko, A.G. (1966).Group Method of Data Handling-A rival of the method of stochastic approximation.*Soviet Automatic Control*.13:43-71.

Koza,J.R.(1980).*Genetic Programming*. Cambridge, MA: The MIT Press.

Kubena, L .F.,Lott,B.D., Deaton, J.W., Reece, F.N. & May, J.D. (1972). Body composition of chicks as influenced by environmental temperature and selected dietary factors. Poultry Science 5, 517–522.

Lee,C.J. & Hsiung, T. K. (2009).Sensitivity analysis on a multilayer perceptron model for recognizing liquefaction cases. Computers and Geotechnics 36, 1157-1163.

Lemme, A.,U. Frackenpohl, A. Petri, & H. Meyer.(2006).Response of male BUT Big 6 turkeys to varying amino acid feeding programs. Poult.Sci. 85:652–660.

Lemke, F.,and J.A.Mueller. 2003. Medical data analysis using self-organizing data mining technologies. Syst. Anal. Model.Simul.10: 1399–1408.

Madala,H.R.& A.G.Ivakhnenko.(1994).Inductive learning algorithms for complex Systems Modeling. CRC Press:, ISBN:0-8493-4438-7.Boca Raton, Ann Arbor,London Tokyo.

Makkar,H.P.S.(2008).A review of the use of isotopic and nuclear techniques in animal production. Animal Feed Science and Technology 140, 418–443.

Miroslav Šnorek,P.K.(2006).Inductive modeling World Wide the State of the Art.Report of investigation. Dept.of Computer Science and Engineering, Karlovo nam.

Mitchell, M. & S.Forrest (1994).Genetic Algorithms and Artificial Life. Artificial Life, Vol. 1, No. 3, 267-289

Mueller,J.A.,&F.Lemke.(2000).Self-Organizing Data Mining:An Intelligent Approach to Extract Knowledge from Data.Libri Publ. Co., Hamburg, Germany.

Mottaghitalab, M., Faredi, A., Darmani-kuhi, H., France , J. & Ahmadi, H. (2010). Predicting caloric and feed efficiency in turkeys using the group method of data handling-type neural networks. Poultry Science 89, 1325–1331.

Mutasem H. N. M.(2004).An evolutionary method for term selection in the Group Method of Data Handling. Automatic Control & Systems Engineering, University of Sheffield, 11-14.

Nariman-Zadeh,N.,A.Darvizeh,A.Jamali, & A.Moieni.(2005). Evolutionary design of generalized polynomial NNs for modeling and prediction of explosive forming process. J. Mater.Process. Technol. 164–165:1561–1571.

Nariman-Zadeh, N.,Darvizeh ,A.& Ahmad-Zadeh,G.R.(2003).Hybrid genetic design of GMDH-Type NNs using singular value decomposition for modeling and prediction of the explosive cutting process. Proceedings of the Institution of Mechanical Engineers B: Journal of Engineering Manufacture 217, 779–790.

Noy, Y., and D. Sklan.(2004). Effects of metabolizable energy and amino acid levels on turkey performance from hatch to marketing. J. Appl. Poult. Res. 13:241 - 252.

NRC. (1994).Nutrient Requirements of Poultry.9th rev. ed. Natl. Acad. Sci.,Washington,DC.

Oberstone,J.(1990).Management Science-Concepts,Insights,and cations. West Publ. Co.,New York,NY.

Pesti, G.M. & Bakalli, R. I.(1997).Estimation of the composition of broiler carcasses from their specific gravity. Poultry Science 76, 948–951.

Phillips, R. D.(1981). Linear and nonlinear models for measuring protein nutritional quality.J.Nutr.111:1058–1066.

Potter, L. M., A. T. Leighton Jr., and C. E. Howes. (1966). Methionine and lysine supplementation of turkey starting diets containing varying levels of protein. Poult. Sci. 45:1117 - 1118.

Rosa, P.S.,Faria Filho,D. E., Dahlke, F., Vieira, B. S., Macari, M. & FURLAN, R. L.(2007). Performance and carcass characteristics of broiler chickens with different growth potential and submitted to heat stress. Revista Brasileira de Ciência Avícola 9, 181 - 186.

Rosenblatt, F.(1958). The perceptron: A probabilistic model for information storage and organization in the brain.Psychological Review. 68: 386-408

Roush,W.B.& Wideman, R.F.(2000) Evaluation of broiler growth velocity and acceleration in relation to pulmonary hypertension syndrome. Poultry Science, 79: 180–191.

Roush, W.B., Dozier III, W.A. & Branton, S.L. (2006) Comparison of Gompertz and NNs models of broiler growth. Poultry Science, 85: 794–797.

Roush, W.B., Kirby, Y.K., Cravener, T.L. & Wideman JR, R.F.(1996) Artificial NN prediction of ascites in broilers. Poultry Science, 75: 1479–1487.

Salle, C.T., Guahyba, A.S., Wald, V.B., Silva, A.B., Salle, F.O. & Aacimento, V.P. (2003) Use of artificial NNs to estimate production variables of broilers breeders in the production phase. British Poultry Science, 44: 211–217.

Saltelli, A., M. Ratto, T. Andres, F. Campolongo,J. Cariboni, D. Gatelli, M. Saisana and S. Tarantola.2008.Global Sensitivity Analysis.The Primer. John Wiley&Sons,Ltd.

Schulin-Zeuthen, M. Kebreab, E. Dijkstra, J. Lopez, S. Bannink, A. Darmani Kuhi, H. and France, J. (2008). A comparison of the Schumacher with other functions for describing growth in pigs. Anim. Feed Sci. Technol. 143:314 - 327.

Seyedan,b. & Ching, C. Y. (2006). Sensitivity analysis of freestream turbulence parameters on stagnation region heat transfer using a netural network. International journal of Heat and Fluid Flow 27,1061-1068.

Sibbald, I. R.(1987). Estimation of bioavailable amino acids in feeding stuffs for poultry and pigs: A review with emphasis on balance experiments. Can. J. Anim. Sci. 67:221-301.

Toledo, G. S. P., Lopez, J. & Costa,P. T. C.(2004). Yield and carcass composition of broilers fed with diets based on the concept of crude protein or ideal protein.Revista Brasileira de Ciência Avícola 6,219–224.

Vasechkina, E.F. & Yarin, V.D. (2001). Evolving polynomial NN by means of genetic algorithm:some application examples. Complexity International 9, 1–13.

Waibel, P. E., Carlson, C. W. Liu, J. K. Brannon, J. A. and Noll, S. L. (1995). Replacing protein in corn-soybean turkey diets with methionine and lysine. Poult. Sci. 74:1143 - 1158.

Yao, X. (1999).Evolving artificial NNs Proceeding of the, IEEE, Vol. 499, No.9, pp.1423–1447.

12

New Approaches to Designing Genes by Evolution in the Computer

Alexander V. Spirov and David M. Holloway
[1]*The I. M. Sechenov Institute of Evolutionary Physiology and Biochemistry,*
[2]*Stony Brook University,*
[3]*British Columbia Institute of Technology,*
[1]*USA*
[2]*Russia*
[3]*Canada*

1. Introduction

The field of Evolutionary Computation (EC) has been inspired by ideas from the classical theory of biological evolution, with, in particular, the components of a population from which reproductive parents are chosen, a reproductive protocol, a method for altering the genetic information of offspring, and a means for testing the fitness of offspring in order to include them in the population. In turn, impressive progress in EC - understanding the reasons for efficiencies in evolutionary searches - has begun to influence scientific work in the field of molecular evolution and in the modeling of biological evolution (Stemmer, 1994a,b; van Nimwegen et al. 1997; 1999; Crutchfield & van Nimwegen, 2001). In this chapter, we will discuss how developments in EC, particularly in the area of crossover operators for Genetic Algorithms (GA), provide new understanding of evolutionary search efficiencies, and the impacts this can have for biological molecular evolution, including directed evolution in the test tube.

GA approaches have five particular elements: encoding (the 'chromosome'); a population; a method for selecting parents and making a child chromosome from the parents' chromosomes; a method for altering the child's chromosomes (mutation and crossover/recombination); criteria for fitness; and rules, based on fitness, by which offspring are included into the population (and parents retained). We will discuss our work and others' on each of these aspects, but our focus is on the substantial efficiencies that can be found in the alteration of the child chromosome step. For this, we take inspiration from real biological reproduction mechanisms.

1.1 Biological evolution by random point mutations?

Traditional GA, using random point mutations, indicates that such a mechanism would be too slow to account for the observed speed of biological evolution (e.g. Shapiro, 2010). This suggests that other more complicated mutational mechanisms are acting (Shapiro, 1999,

2002; 2010). A number of projects are indicating, indeed, that the design of biological molecular machines, such as gene regulatory circuits, may be unreachable by an evolutionary search from scratch (von Dassow et al., 2000; Kitano, 2004; Shapiro, 2010). A likely solution is that evolution creates complicated molecular machines by operating on previously-evolved simpler domains (motifs, modules) (e.g. Botstein, 1980).

1.2 Building blocks in protein and nucleic acid molecules

In parallel with the computational literature, we use the term 'building blocks' (BBs) for these simpler domains. Biologically, BBs are found in proteins, in which amino acids combine to create functionally and physically distinct regions within the protein (e.g. Voigt et al., 2002); they are found in the semi-autonomous domains of RNA (Ancel-Myers & Fontana, 2005); and they are found in DNA, from nucleosomal and chromatin organization to the organization of gene regulatory regions (Fig. 1). Comparative studies show that BBs are maintained during evolution, and can be shared by quite diverse organisms (Voigt et al., 2002).

The striking conservation of BBs in biological evolution has been noted in GA. It is beginning to be understood how important conservation of BBs is for efficient evolutionary searches in GA (and other fields of EC) (Forrest & Mitchell, 1993a,b; Goldberg, 1989; Holland, 1975; Mitchell et al., 1992). This chapter will discuss recent developments of GA chromosome alteration rules which conserve BBs, and how these relate to developments in directed evolution in the laboratory.

1.3 Nontrivial mutagenesis for molecular evolution in the test tube

As well as increased understanding of the role of BBs in biology and in search mechanisms, there is a growing appreciation for the use of BBs in in vitro, directed evolution experiments. Numerous groups are using evolutionary principles to design and select macromolecules, and it is becoming apparent that random point mutations are not the most efficient means for doing this. The role of crossover in conserving BBs in GA has inspired new techniques in molecular evolution in the test tube (Stemmer, 1994a,b). Methods are now being used to recombine from specific crossover sites to maintain BBs (Fig. 2) and speed the generation of diverse usable progeny molecules.

DNA shuffling (or 'sexual PCR') and in vitro evolution are well advanced fields now, and have been successfully used to design many new biotechnologically valuable enzymes (Sen et al., 2007). Beyond the synthesis of macromolecules, a growing area in systems biology is to investigate the evolution of genes and gene networks, through computation and synthetic biology laboratory work.

1.4 Biological evolution requires complicated mutational mechanisms?

The role of complex methods of mutation vs. simple point mutation is currently an active area of discussion (e.g. Long et al., 2003). In particular, agents such as retroviruses (e.g. HIV) and retroposons are believed to work as highly effective and highly specific mutators (e.g. Brosius, 1999). The crossover mechanism evolved by retroviruses (Fig. 3) shares many similarities with the DNA shuffling/sexual PCR techniques used in in vitro evolution (Fig. 2).

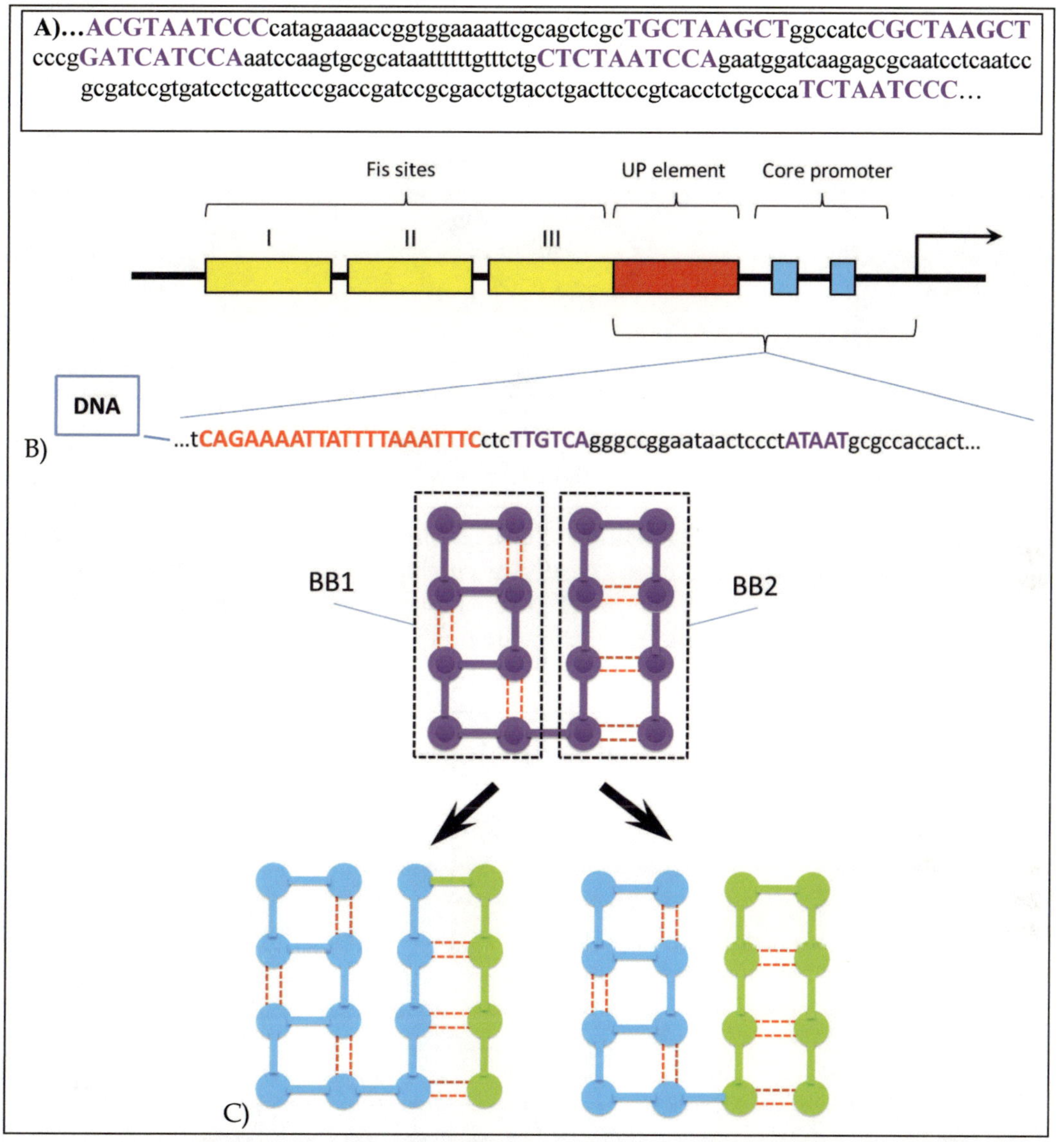

Fig. 1. Some examples of "building blocks" (BBs) in biological macromolecules engaged in keeping and transferring genetic information - polypeptides and nucleic acids. A) The core of the anterior regulatory region of the *Drosophila* (fruit fly) gene *hunchback*, with a cluster of six BBs highly specific for recognition of the Bicoid protein. B) Organization of the bacterial promoter rrnP1 (ribosomal RNA operon promoter) into a series of highly conserved blocks, with between-block spacers of conserved length. C) Illustration of BB disruption in proteins. Black lines represent peptide bonds, red dotted lines represent interactions between amino acid (aa) side chains. Two hybrid proteins are shown. If the first 12 residues (aa's) are from one parent, and the last four residues are from the other parent, three side chain interactions can be disrupted. If the last eight residues come from the same parent, then there is no disruption. Hybridizations that maintained interactions would be most likely to fold properly. (After Voigt et al., 2002)

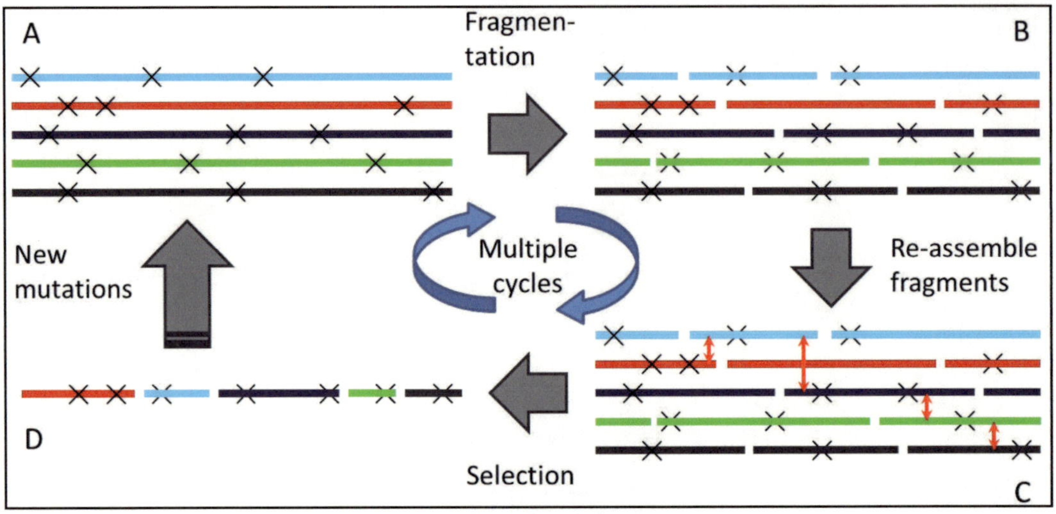

Fig. 2. Schematic of experimental mutation of DNA for in vitro evolution. Input strands can only be cut at specific sites; progeny are created by combining these fragments. BBs are maintained within the fragments, but novel combinations are created in the process. Keeping the BB sequences minimizes structural disruption in the products.

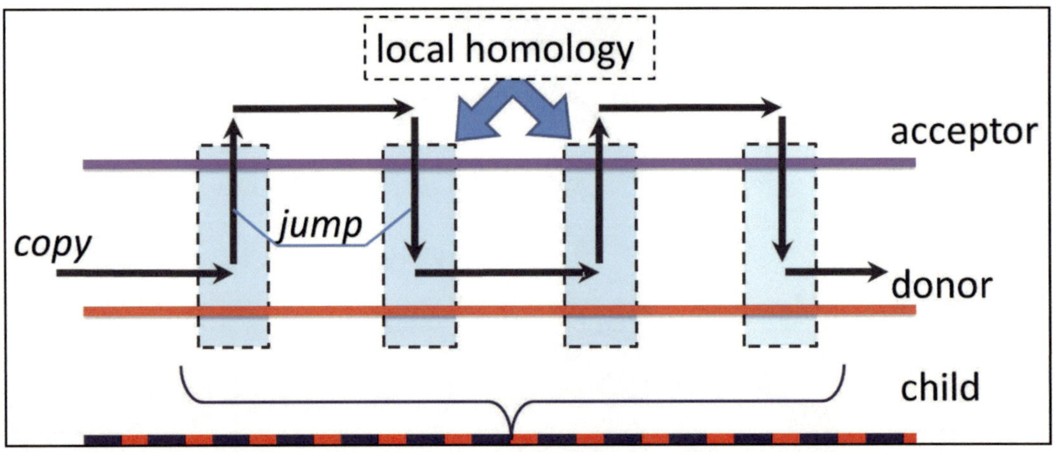

Fig. 3. The overall idea of recombination between two parental RNA strings used by retroviruses. The child sequence is read alternately from the parent strings, jumping between the parent templates at regions of homology (marked by gray rectangles). This is an effective mechanism for genetic diversity in the child, while retaining BBs.

Retroviral recombination usually takes two parent RNA strands to create a child DNA strand (Negroni & Buc, 2001; An & Telesnitsky, 2002; though a three strand mechanism is also a possibility). Development of GA crossover operators that use the retroviral scheme, or extend it to the multiple parent case seen in sexual PCR, can give quantitative understanding of the efficiencies of these techniques, and can provide insight into the biological evolution of retroviruses and retroposons.

1.5 Test tube evolution needs new theoretical considerations

Some in vitro evolution groups are using DNA 'soft computing' on well-defined benchmark computing problems (Chen & Wood, 2000; Henkel et al., 2007). However, theoretical (mathematical) studies of these computations are still at an initial stage (Crutchfield, 2002; Sun, 1999; Maheshri & Schaffer, 2003). A central question is whether theory can offer new approaches to speed up the evolutionary search for macromolecules with desired characteristics or features. This chapter will survey prospective ways to apply new developments in GA crossover operations in order to further the theory and efficiency of in vitro evolution.

We have long been interested in the design of genes with multiple autonomous regulatory elements - these are critical in formation of the early body plan (in particular, we study these genes in the fruit fly, *Drosophila*). We have found that evolutionary searches for such highly structured sequences are very similar to the well-defined Royal Road (RR) and Royal Staircase (RS) computational test functions. By developing GA crossover operators that perform well on RR and RS functions, we are developing computational techniques for solving real design problems for biological and synthetic macromolecules. In particular, we are introducing GA crossover operators that work like retroviral or sexual PCR recombination, and which have the ability to preserve BB architecture. We name our approach Retroviral GA, or retroGA.

This chapter will first (section 2) introduce the RR and RS test functions, and introduce the retroGA technique. Section 3 will show the performance of this approach on the test functions, and on biological gene-structure problems, from bacteria and fruit flies (each with particular challenges as a search problem). retroGA results will be compared with standard GA (point mutation). In section 4 we will discuss the prospects for extending the analytical approach developed by van Nimwegen and co-workers for RR and RS functions to real biological genetic problems, such as the bacteria and fruit fly examples in section 3. We will conclude on the use of the retroGA approach in understanding real biological evolution problems and for aiding the efficiency of directed (forced) molecular evolution in the laboratory.

2. Our approach

We will first discuss the RR and RS benchmark functions, which allow for standardized testing and analysis of BB type evolutionary problems. We will then present our retroGA approach, using retroviral recombination methods (crossover) to preserve BBs during evolutionary searches.

2.1 GA benchmark functions as models of molecular biological evolution

Among the many benchmark tests in EC, the RR and RS fitness functions were specifically invented to study the preservation and destruction of BBs by crossover operators. As such, they can serve as models for many cases of natural and test tube evolution, in which searches proceed with BB preservation. Four RR functions, of increasing complexity, were invented and introduced by Forrest, Mitchell, and Holland to specifically test crossover operations in GA (Forrest & Mitchell, 1993a,b; Mitchell et al., 1992). The related RS functions were devised and introduced by van Nimwegen & Crutchfield (2000; 2001). These well-defined functions allow for analytical (mathematical) study of the evolutionary search behaviour and parameter dependence.

2.1.1 Royal road functions

Royal Road functions were devised to award fitness for the preservation of BBs, and thus to serve as models for natural evolution (van Nimwegen & Crutchfield, 2000). R1, the simplest function, calculates bit string fitness by the number of order-8 schema, or words, in the string. Order does not matter:

s_1 = 1111111***; c_1 = 8
s_2 = *******1111111**; c_2 = 8
....
s_7 = **1111111*******; c_7 = 8
s_8 = ***1111111; c_8 = 8
s_{opt}= 1111111111111111111111111111111111111111111111111111111111; c_{opt}= 64

where the * is a random bit (0 or 1). The fitness value R1 (for string x) is the sum of the coefficients c_s corresponding to each given schema of which x is an instance (c_s is equal to order). The fitness of an intermediate step (such as the combination of s_1 and s_8) is a linear combination of the fitness of the lower level components (e.g. the combination of s_1 and s_8 has fitness 16). The genotype space consists of all bit-strings of length 64 and contains 9 neutral subbasins of fitness 0, 8, 16, 24, 32, 40, 48, 56 and 64. There is only one sequence with fitness 64, 255 strings with fitness 56, 65534 strings with fitness 48, etc. Because fitness proceeds by the build up of words, the fitness landscape for RRs has a subbasin-portal architecture (Fig. 4), in which evolution tends to drift in neutral subbasins, with rare jumps to the next level via portals (creation or destruction of a word).

In searching for fitness functions that are easy for GA and difficult for non-evolutionary methods, a whole family of increasingly complex RR functions was devised (R1, R2, R3, R4; Mitchell, 1996). These showed that standard GA is superior to non-evolutionary techniques on harder problems, but also brought to light that standard GA has substantial weaknesses in the crossover operator. Due to their formal simplicity, theoretical analysis can be carried out on the RR functions to understand the parameters which promote efficiencies.

R2 is very similar to R1, but allows for higher fitness at certain intermediate steps. R3 allows for random-bit spacers of set length between BBs (which are not calculated in the fitness score). The optimal string for R3 is:

s_{opt}=1111111********1111111********1111111*******1111111********1111111********1111111********1111111********1111111.

The most difficult RR function is R4, since one, two, or even four non-neighboring elementary (in our case 8-bit) BBs in the string gives the same exact score (Level 1). The score will only increase if words neighbour, e.g. a pair of juxtaposed 8-bit BBs creates a Level 2 16-bit BB. A Level 3 BB consists of 4 neighboring 8-bit BBs (32 bits in total). Level 4 BBs are 64-bit, composed of eight 8-bit elementary BBs. Level 5 BBs would consist of 16 8-bit BBs. Most current optimization techniques cannot effectively deal with the R4 fitness function.

From the viewpoint of molecular biology, R1 and especially R3 are reminiscent of a key element of the regulatory region of a gene: a cluster of binding sites (BS's), made of short BBs separated by spacer sequences. While the analogy is good, there are several differences to bear in mind. First, usually the positions and order of BS's in such clusters are less restricted (than in the comparable RR), but this depends on the particular gene in question (enhanceosomes vs. "billboards"; see Jeziorska et al., 2009). Second, any BS is not a unique sequence: it is usually a family of related sequences with varying strength (fitness), usually with a conserved core sequence (Stormo, 2000). Finally, proximity of BSs to each other is important for the action of activators and repressors. This is analogous to R4 (e.g. with sub-clustering represented by R4, Level 3), but the biological spacing is somewhat less restricted than in R4. Because of the general parallels between RR and biological structure, we expect RR analysis to shed some light on the evolution of gene regulatory regions, and to be useful as a theory for forced molecular evolution of bacterial and yeast gene promoters. (Where modified or completely artificial promoters can become new molecular tools for bio-sensing, etc.: Haseltine & Arnold, 2007; Lu et al., 2009.)

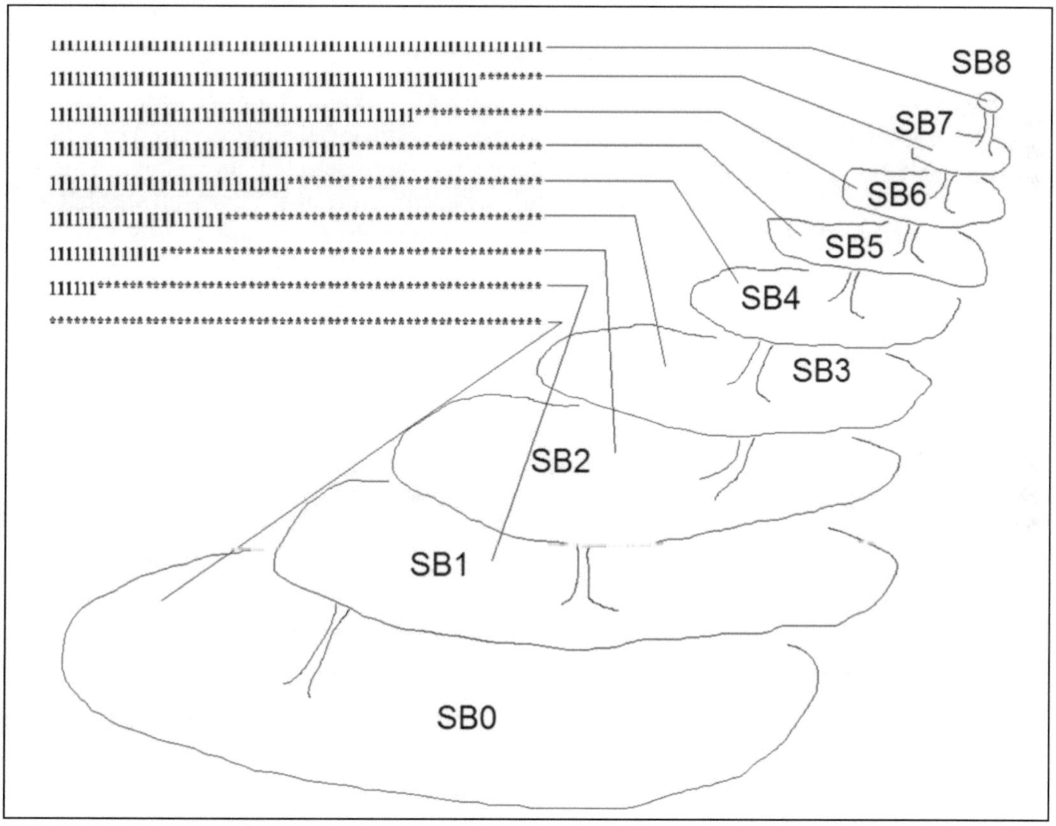

Fig. 4. Subbasin-portal architecture for the R1 function.

2.1.2 Royal staircase functions

These are a generalization of the RR functions in which the subbasin-portal architecture is expressed in a more explicit form (van Nimwegen & Crutchfield, 2000). The RS function we use in this chapter is similar to the 8-bit word, 64-bit string R1 and R2 of the previous section, but order matters (i.e. the string is built up from one end), and fitness for N=8, K=8 RS ranges from 0 to 80:

```
s1 = 11111111********************************************************; c1 = 10
s2 = 1111111111111111************************************************; c2 = 20
..........................................................................................
s6 = 111111111111111111111111111111111111111111111111****************; c6 = 60
s7 = 11111111111111111111111111111111111111111111111111111111********; c7 = 70
sopt= 1111111111111111111111111111111111111111111111111111111111111111; copt = 80
```

This version of RS was used by van Nimwegen and Crutchfield, and we use it in this chapter to be able to compare our results to theirs.

2.1.3 Evolution of gene regulatory regions

Here we develop two prototypical cases in the evolution of gene regulatory regions, highlighting their similarities to the RR and RS test functions. We will present retroGA results on these problems in section 3.

2.1.3.1 Directed (forced) evolution of prokaryotic promoters

Bacterial gene promoters, being simpler than eukaryotic promoters, present good cases for investigating the details of the evolutionary searches producing their structure. For a target sequence (solution) for these sorts of problems, we have selected the sequence of the ribosomal RNA (rRNA) operon promoter rrnP1 in *E. coli*, since it is very well studied and well characterized (Schneider et al., 2003). Core promoters in *E. coli* are approximately 60 base pairs (bp) long and are characterized by several conserved sites with spacers in between. It is believed that while the sequences of these spacers are not significant, their lengths are of extreme importance (Schneider et al., 2003). There are at least four well-conserved features in a bacterial promoter: the starting point (usually 'CAT'); the -10 sequence ('TATAAT' consensus); the -35 sequence ('TTGACA' consensus); and the distance between the -10 and -35 sequences. The rrnP1 promoter sequence contains an AT-rich sequence called the upstream (UP) element (Ross et al., 1998) upstream of the -35 element. UP elements increase transcription 20-to 50-fold (Hirvonen et al., 2001). Its consensus is AAA a/t a/t T a/t TTTT**AAAA, where * indicates a random base, a/t means A or T. In addition, three to five BS's for the Fis protein (FisBS) increase transcription three- to eight-fold (Ross et al., 1990). The weight matrix for the binding sites of this transcription factor has been defined (Hengen et al., 1997). The desired sequence for the rrnP1 promoter therefore includes:

[FisBS]**<~5 bp>**[FisBS]**<~5 bp>**[FisBS]**<~15 bp>**AAA a/t a/t T a/t TTTT**AAAA**<~4 bp>**TTGACA**<16-19 bp>**TATAAT**<5-9 bp>**CAT.

Evolution of the rrnP1 promoter can be viewed as a Royal Staircase fitness function. Starting with the core promoter (s_1), evolution could add the powerful UP element (s_2) and then sequentially add FisBSs (s_3, s_4):

```
s1=*********************************…**********************************************TTGACA***...***TATAAT***...***CAT, c1 = Δ
s2=****************…*****************************AAA a/t a/t T a/t TTTT**AAAA***...***TTGACA***...***TATAAT***...***CAT, c2 = ~35 Δ
s3=*************…*****************[FisBS]*** …***AAA a/t a/t T a/t TTTT**AAAA***...***TTGACA***...***TATAAT***...***CAT, c3 = ~100 Δ
..........................................................................................
sopt=***[FisBS]***…***[FisBS]***…***[FisBS]*** …***AAA a/t a/t T a/t TTTT**AAAA***...***TTGACA***...***TATAAT***...***CAT, copt = ~150Δ
```

where Δ is an arbitrary small fitness value.

Like RS, rrnP1 probably evolved by sequential finding and adding of BBs, with each addition raising the fitness of the promoter sequence (transcriptional efficiency). As with RS, the length and positions of the BBs are conserved during evolution, though not as strictly as the RS function in section 2.1.2.

The simplified rrnP1 test

A major difference between RR and RS functions and functional clusters of BBs in biological macromolecules is the redundant character of the blocks. Functionally very similar blocks can have different sequences, sharing only a common core sequence. I.e. BBs usually are not unique, but are a family of related sequences. Also, compared to RR and RS, biological clusters of BBs include longer spacers (of variable length), and they are usually longer than 64 or 128 elements. Finally, they are not binary, but quaternary (DNA and RNA) (or even consisting of 20 letters, in the case of proteins).

To begin studying the rrnP1 problem (and do so within the RR, RS framework), we can simplify some of these complications: we ignore the redundant character of its 8 BBs and the variability of spacer lengths (see Fig. 1A,B); we assume that all the elements are fixed and/or unique in sequence; and we consider five elements only. The first of these represents the whole core promoter and is modelled by only 6 letters. The second element is the proximal half of the UP element, assumed to have a length of 5 letters. The spacer between the 1st and the 2nd elements is 24 letters. The 3rd to 5th elements are given the same length, with spacers of 15-letter length. We will present results on computing this simplified target in section 3.

2.1.3.2 Genes with multiple regulatory units

In eukaryotic organisms (i.e. non-bacterial), the organization of gene regulatory regions is far more complex. Genes are regulated from cis-regulatory modules (CRMs), which have clusters of BS's for activators and inhibitors, with very important spacer lengths between them to allow for quenching (inhibition) and cooperativity (activation). CRM's can be an arbitrary distance from the gene coding region. Compared to a prokaryotic model, like that for rrnP1, a eukaryotic CRM model must account for evolution of the BS locations and strengths, and be tested, fitness-wise, against a global production capacity. If the BS's are words in the language of gene regulation, CRM's order those words into sentences. Where rrnP1 could be treated as analogous to an RS problem with spacers, a eukaryotic CRM is more analogous to an R4 function, to account for clustering, with the level of the R4 representing the number of BS's in a functional cluster. Since the number of BS's is frequently 2 or 3, this begins to present major computational challenges, since most algorithms are insufficient at R4 Level 2 or 3. If we now begin to consider genes with multiple CRM's, which is common, we must consider at least R4 Level 4, a point at which most algorithms tend to fail. In analogy to language, organization of multiple CRM's is at the level of the paragraph directing a gene's regulation. Such problems may need to be more realistically thought of as higher level RS functions.

Evolution of multiple CRM's in Drosophila

The genes responsible for early body segmentation in the fruit fly, *Drosophila,* form a highly studied network of interacting regulations. These genes code for proteins which transcriptionally regulate the other segmentation genes, and their spatial expression patterns determine where different body parts will form. The regulatory regions for segmentation genes involve multiple CRM's, each of which can control different aspects of the spatial gene expression. It is believed the complex modern regulatory regions evolved by addition of CRM's to a simpler primitive antecedent. We are running computations on the evolution of a number of the segmentation genes.

One example is evolution of the regulatory region of the *hunchback* (*hb*) gene, which forms an anterior-high 'step function' pattern which differentiates the head from the tail end in the embryo. Fig. 5 shows the organization of the 3 *hb* CRM's, and the spatial expression that each is primarily responsible for. *hb* expression is controlled by at least 5 transcriptional regulators (protein products of other segmentation genes): Bicoid, Caudal, Tailless, Huckebein, Hunchback, Giant, Kruppel & Knirps. Available information on the organization of the *hb* regulatory regions is collected in the HOX pro (Spirov et al., 2000; 2002) database (http://www.iephb.nw.ru/hoxpro/hb-CRMs.html).

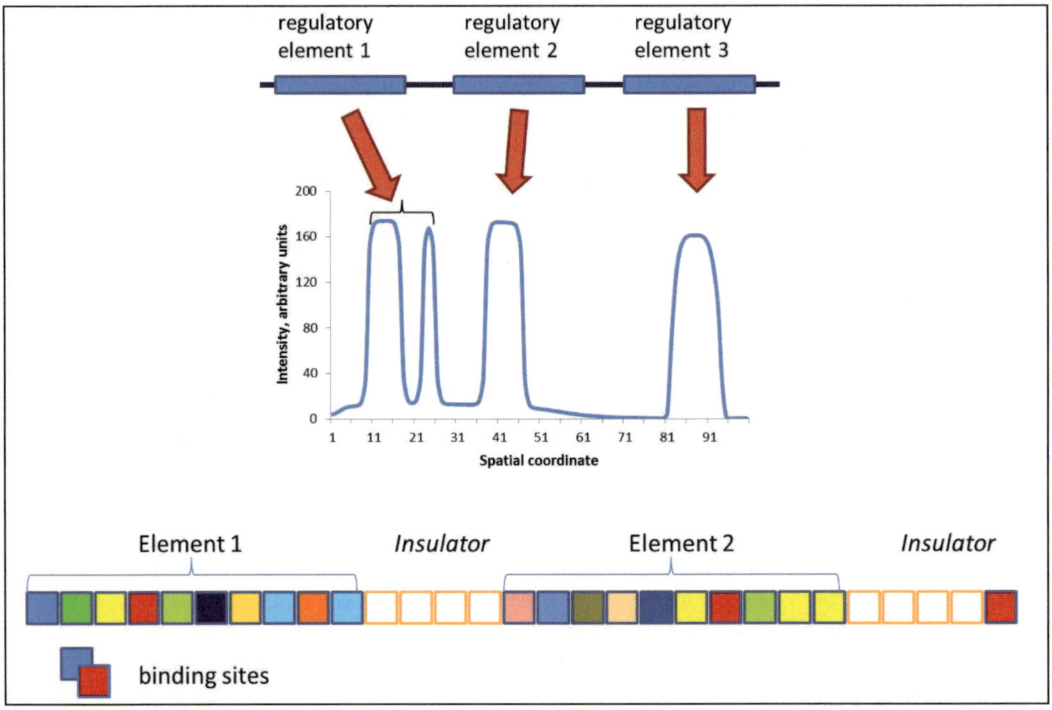

Fig. 5. One of the best studied examples of a gene from the *Drosophila* segmentation gene network - the *hunchback* (*hb*) gene. Bottom: the schematic organization of the *hb* regulatory region, with three separate autonomous regulatory elements (CRMs). Each regulatory element is a cluster of binding sites for, at least, five transcription factors (Bicoid, Caudal, Tailless, Hunchback, Huckebein, Giant, Kruppel & Knirps), shown as colored bars. Spacers (insulators) are also shown. Middle: mature expression pattern for the *hb* gene in an early fruit fly embryo (one-dimensional spatial expression profile, along the main head-to-tail embryo axis). Top: representation of the gene regulatory structure, each responsible for a different aspect of the *hb* expression pattern.

We can study the building up of the modern *hb* regulatory region through computational evolution from a single CRM ancestor. Starting from a single CRM with fitness score = Δ, the evolutionary search finding the 2nd CRM would double the score (2Δ); and so on sequentially to completion (score=3Δ; Fig. 6).

Coding the *hb* problem for computation highlights the levels of abstraction necessary to represent multiple CRMs:

DNA

TTAATCCGTT...***CGAGATTATTAGTCAATTGC***...***GGATTAGC***...***GAAAGTCATAAAAACACATAATA***...
BS for Bicoid&Kruppel Bicoid&Giant Bicoid Hunchback&Giant

Symbolically, CRM level (B for Bicoid, K for Kruppel, H for Hunchback, N for Knirps, G for Giant):

B K B G G B K B H G B K...***N H H/N N H H N H K H H H***
Element 1 Element 2

Symbolically, in octal numbers:

0 1 0 4 4 0 1 0 2 4 0 1...***3 2 2 3 3 2 2 3 2 1 2 2 2***
Element 1 Element 2

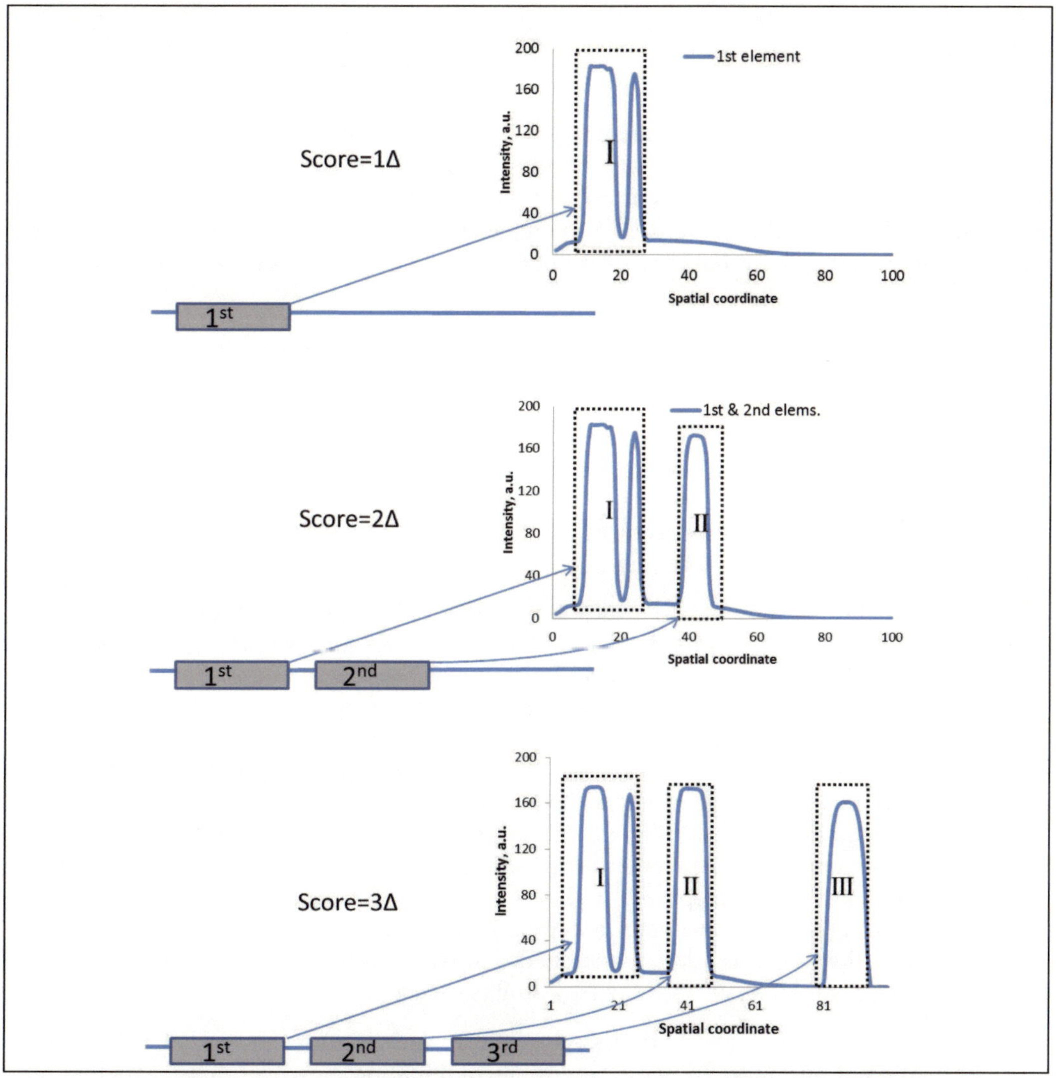

Fig. 6. A simplified scenario for the evolutionary origin of *hunchback* gene organization. A single element would insert into an ancestral gene with no elements, and, due to increased fitness, build up to the gene with three elements. Gene organization and the corresponding patterns of gene expression are shown schematically.

The BS's are finally coded as decimal pairs, where the 1st digit identifies the transcriptional factor and the 2nd digit represents its binding strength. To capture activator cooperativity and inhibitor quenching, neighbouring BS's can be allowed to alter binding strengths. GA and retroGA algorithms can perform crossover operations on these strings to evolve them. In contrast to the rrnP1 problem, where fitness is rated by transcriptional efficiency of the gene, fitness of the *hb* regulatory string depends on how well it produces the required spatial expression pattern. The strings are formal representations of real functional connections between genes in a network. Candidate strings must be solved in a reaction-diffusion model for spatial patterning, and the resulting pattern scored for fitness against experimental data (e.g. profile in Fig. 5).

2.2 The retroGA technique

As discussed in the Introduction, standard GA techniques, specifically through the use of point mutations to generate diversity in the chromosome, can destroy BB's which are important for fitness, slowing evolutionary searches. We have taken inspiration from the mechanisms of retroviral recombination to create crossover operators which preserve BB's. Our innovations are only in the crossover operators, all other actions of the algorithm are as in classical GA.

As discussed above, homology-based PCR techniques (DNA shuffling, sexual PCR) used in test tube evolution may be naturally interpreted as a generalization of retroviral recombination processes (Fig. 3), using n instead of 2 parent strings. Our retroGA operator generates a child string from a given "parent set", combining the function of reproduction and crossover. Crossover points are determined by regions of homology in the parent strings. The parent strings are selected from the population, as in standard GA, by one of several predetermined strategies, such as *truncation, roulette-wheel*, etc. One string is selected as a donor, the others as acceptors (Fig. 7).

In our reproduction and crossover procedure, a first pair of parent candidates is selected. These are the donor and acceptor-1 (Fig. 7). Their sequences are then compared going from left to right for a short distance L_{acc} (where $L_{acc} < L$, L is the length of the whole sequence). If the required zone of local homology is not found, another candidate for acceptor-1 is selected. The number of attempts to find a suitable acceptor is at most N_{acc}. If, and only if, a zone of complete homology of a size no less than L_{hom} symbols ($L_{hom} < L$) is found during an attempt to scan two sequences, do these two sequences become the donor and acceptor-1 pair. Replica generation is then initiated, and takes place in the first n symbols of the donor, from the first element to the last element of the region homologous between the two parents. Replication then jumps to acceptor-1, and acceptor-2 candidates are selected. A search for local homology takes place between acceptor-1 and the putative acceptor-2. If no such region is found, the next candidate is searched. This process is iteratively repeated until the replica (child) is completed, or until the N_{acc} limit is exceeded.

retroGA with point mutations: As discussed in the Introduction, crossover of BB's is more efficient than point mutation. In real retroviral recombination, however, it appears that both processes are present. Template switching between parent RNA strings tends to introduce mutations in the child sequence. For our retroGA, we include this effect by introducing one point mutation in one of a few starting sites in the portion of the child string being copied from the new acceptor. This addition provided speed-up for retroGA on RS, rrnP1-gene and hb-gene searches, but not on RR searches. Further analysis is needed to understand this difference.

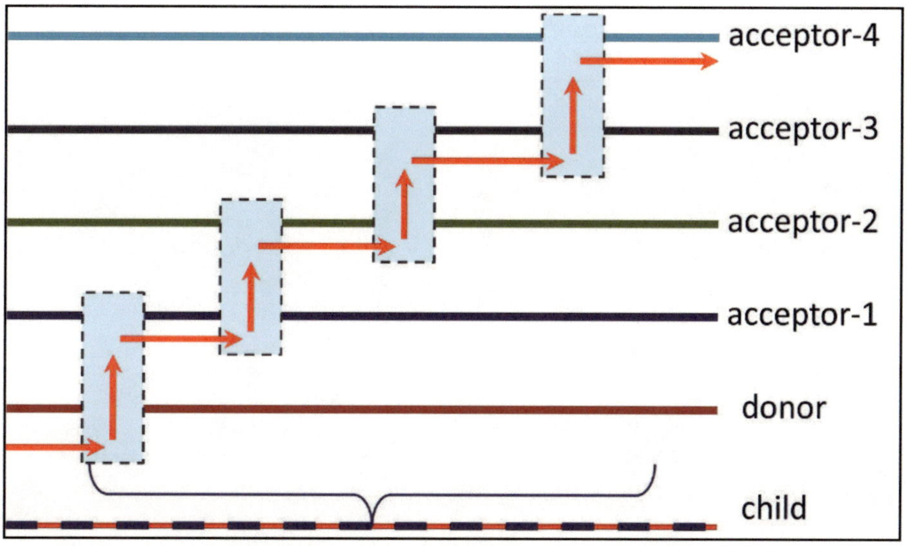

Fig. 7. Principle of the retroGA operator, an analogy to in vitro DNA shuffling techniques. The process of creating the child sequence by the operator starts with the donor-parent. Replication of the child from the donor-parent occurs if there is at least one region of homology (identity) between the donor and acceptor -1 (marked by gray rectangles). The process then jumps onto the acceptor-1 string. An acceptor-2 is found with a region of homology to acceptor-1, and the process repeats, copying from acceptor -1 and jumping to acceptor-2 (which becomes the third parent of the child sequence). The process of jumping from acceptor to acceptor continues until the creation of the child sequence is complete.

3. Results

In this section we present results on the efficiency of retroGA in comparison with standard GA (point mutations only). We do the comparison on RR and RS benchmark tests, as well as on the biological rrnP1 and *hb* gene sequence problems. Because all of these problems share a subbasin-portal type architecture, such computations allow us to begin to characterize the degree to which RR and RS test functions can predict behavior in gene searches. This is especially relevant if we can begin to use the analytical (mathematical) tools that have been developed for the RR and RS test functions to understand the gene search dynamics.

3.1 Crossover operators for RS problems

As a baseline, we have corroborated the RS results of van Nimwegen & Crutchfield (2000; 2001) with point mutation GA. Following their analytical and computational work provides a framework from which to understand the efficacy of our retroGA technique (including for the RS-like rrnP1 problem). In particular, they derived the dependence of the number of evaluations E to achieve the global optimum on the frequency of point mutations q and size of population M (point mutations only and roulette-wheel selection strategy). They found theory and computational experiments to be in good agreement.

We have reproduced their computational experiments and analyzed how average time to achieve a given fitness n empirically depends on n. The case of N = 4, K = 10 is shown in Fig. 8. The averaged time (in the average number of candidate string evaluations) to achieve the n+1 fitness level rises exponentially (Fig. 8A); plotting in semi-log scale confirms this (Fig. 8B).

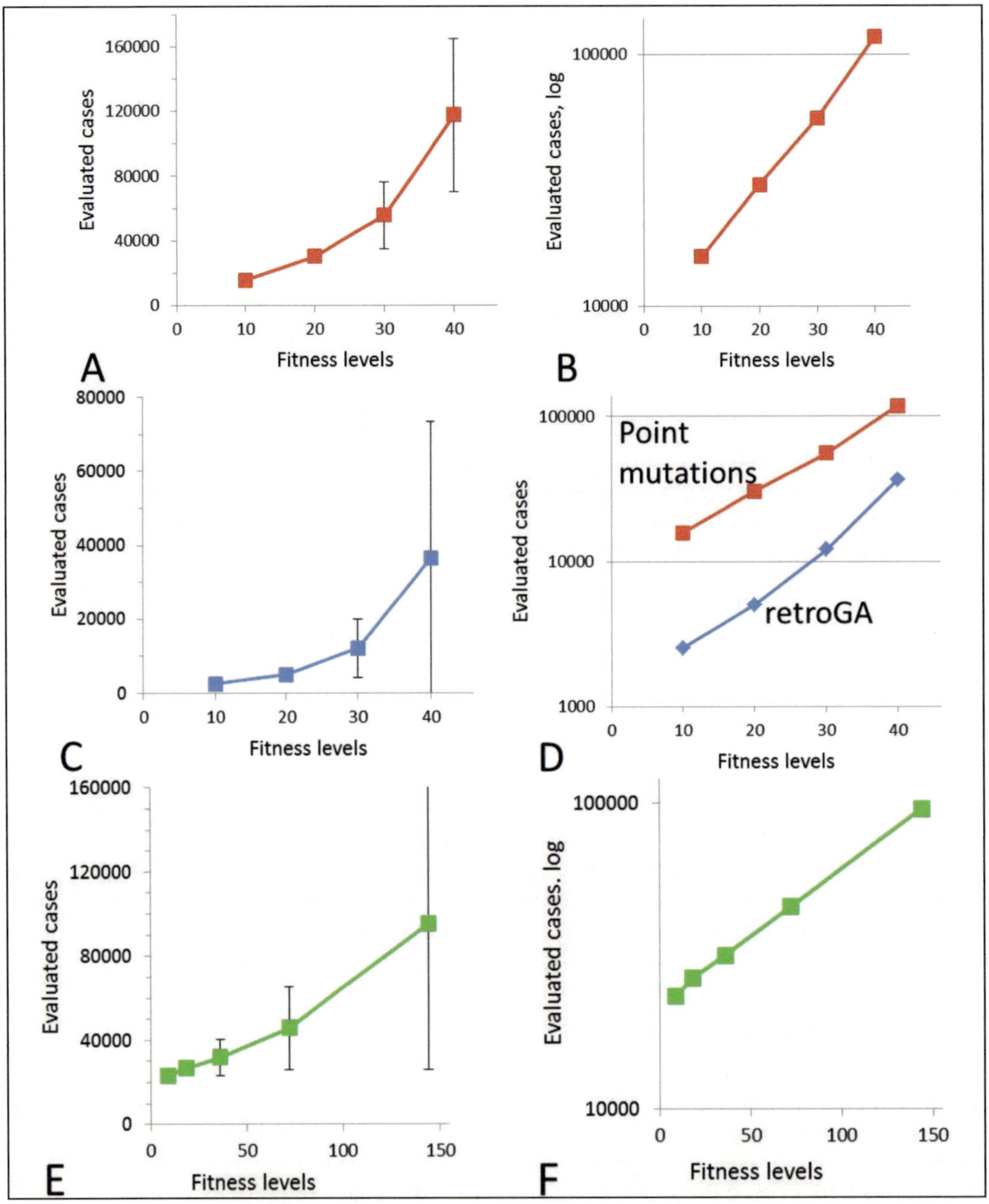

Fig. 8. Average total number of fitness function evaluations to achieve n^{th} fitness level for the Royal Staircase with N=4 blocks of length K=10, in comparison with the rrnP1 gene test.

Evolutionary search with point mutations only (A, B; Cf. van Nimwegen & Crutchfield (2000; 2001)) vs. search by retroGA algorithms (C,D). Each data point was obtained as an average over 200 GA runs. A, B) Corroboration of the van Nimwegen and Crutchfield tests with point mutation only (no crossover). Population size M=30,000; mutation rate q=0.01; roulette-wheel selection strategy. C,D) Our tests with the retroGA operator as the mutation procedure (see text for details). retroGA speeds the search by about 5.5 times compared to point mutations only. M=5,000; truncation selection strategy. E,F) retroGA results on the simplified rrnP1 test function, M=24,000.

3.1.1 retroGA speeds up search on RS fitness functions

Testing both versions of our retroGA operators - crossover without point mutations and crossover with associated point mutations (see section 2.2) clearly shows that the combined crossover/point mutation mechanism is the most effective procedure on RS tests, speeding up searches about five-fold. Fig. 8C,D shows the retroGA crossover/point mutation results for the same RS fitness function as in previous section (N=4, K=10). The RS optimum was achieved in 36,469±36,991 solution evaluations, about 5.5 times faster than by standard GA (point mutations only; ~200,000 evaluations). It can also be seen in Fig. 8C,D, that the retroGA search shows a nearly exponential dependence between search efficacy and the n level, like GA with mutations only (Fig. 8A,B).

3.2 Crossover operators for the rrnP1 problem

We found that the simplified version of the rrnP1 test behaved very closely to the RS tests with N=4, K=10. Though we had initially thought of rrnP1 in terms of RS organization (section 2.1.3.1), we were surprised at the closeness, because the rrnP1 test is specified by quaternary strings (the four DNA letters A, T, G, C) and the string length is about twice the RS test, owing to spacers. The dependence of the search efficacy on the n level is still exponential (Fig. 8E,F) for retroGA on rrnP1, as on RS. retroGA on the simplified rrnP1 (with five blocks) was over five times faster than GA with one-point crossover (crossover rate = 0.01): 95,618±69,575 (Fig. 8E,F) vs. 512,040±48,378 average evaluations. Success on the rrnP1 problem, and the parallels to the well-characterized RS function, suggests that retroGA is an effective technique for prokaryotic gene search problems, and could contribute to real problems of forced (directed) evolution of bacterial promoters in the test tube. We will follow up these connections with modern synthetic biology in the Discussion.

3.3 Crossover operators for R1 - R3 functions

In this section we characterize retroGA performance on R1 to R3. These functions have been well-studied in the literature, and as discussed above, have some of the fundamental motifs necessary for modeling gene organization. Testing retroGA both with and without point mutations after crossover showed little effect (in contrast to RS). The results shown here are for retroGA crossover without accompanying mutation.

We have already reported on the several-fold speed-up of retroGA vs. standard GA for RR problems (Spirov & Holloway, 2010). Here we will focus on the dependence of retroGA performance on key computational parameters. It is known that the R1 – R3 functions behave similarly in computational experiments (Forrest & Mitchell, 1993a,b; Mitchell et al., 1992; Mitchell, 1996). Therefore, we will focus on R1 tests, and present comparisons to R3 performance.

3.3.1 Dependence on population size

Theoretical and computational studies have shown that many performance parameters of R1 depend on population size M (van Nimwegen et al., 1999). With an aim to applying retroGA to real directed molecular evolution problems (in vitro), it is important to characterize the population size dependence (and to connect the theoretical knowledge of R1 to real biological problems). We tested M dependence (Fig. 9) for a set of parameters found to be close to optimal in other tests (see next sub-sections).

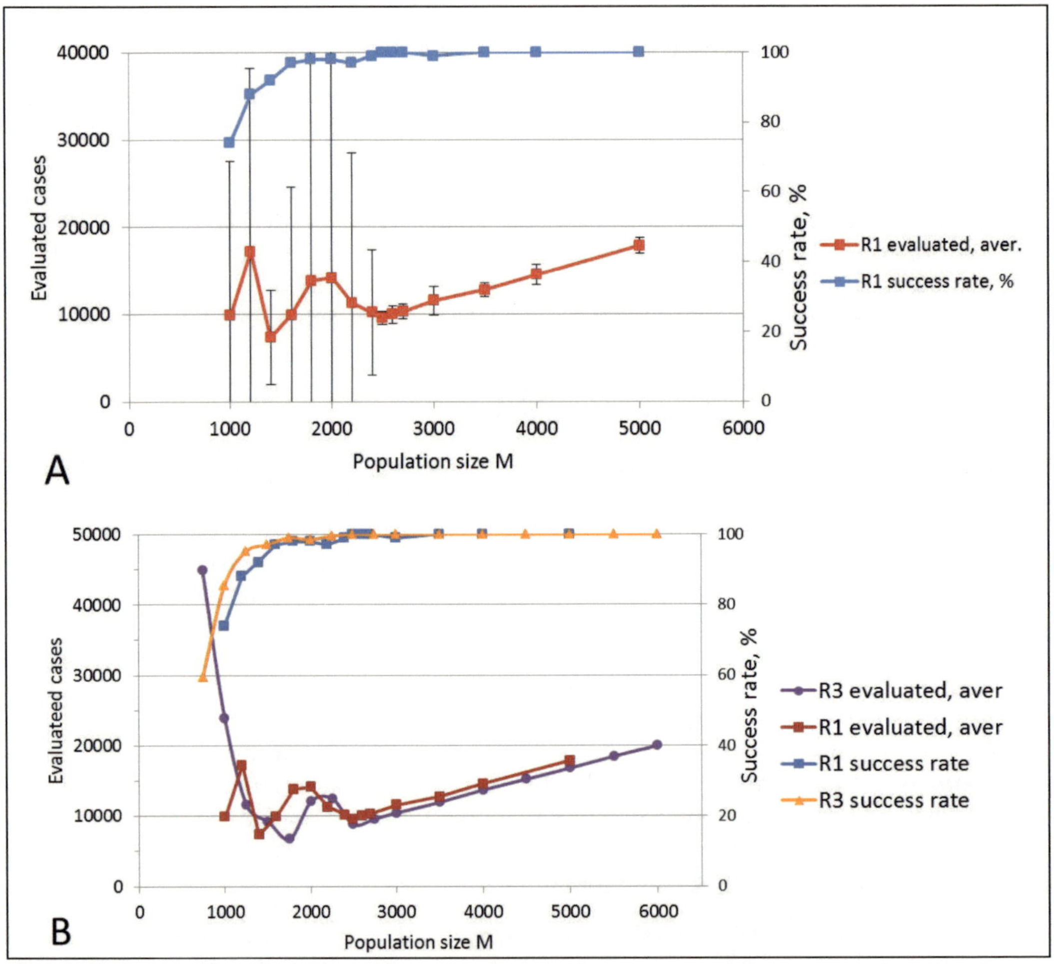

Fig. 9. Royal Road fitness functions 1 & 3: Empirical dependence of average total number of fitness function evaluations on population size M. Each data point was obtained as an average over 100 retroGA runs. Other parameters: limit of acceptor parents N_{acc}=100. A) The R1 tests. B) R1 vs. R3 results.

While retroGA performance, as number of evaluations, is relatively consistent across population size (Fig. 9A, red), there is a relatively narrow window of M from ~2,400 to 2,700 in which number of evaluations and the standard deviation on these are both low. In this range of M, retroGA is about 6 times faster than standard GA (~10,000 vs. ~60,000 evaluations). While M=<2,400 can achieve fast results, the standard deviation is higher and a lower percentage of runs achieve the global optimum (Fig. 9A, blue). For M>2700, the number of evaluations steadily rises with population size. We find that retroGA behaves very similarly on R3 as on R1 (Fig. 9B), as seen earlier with standard GA (Mitchell, 1996). The main conclusion here is that the retroviral crossover is most efficient just as the success rate approaches 100% - small populations are enough for efficient and reliable retroGA searches.

3.3.2 Dependence on retroGA parameters

retroGA algorithms have only three parameters: the maximum number of acceptors N_{acc} to use in synthesizing a child-string (see Fig. 7); the maximum acceptor length to search for local homology L_{acc}; and the maximum length of the local homology region L_{hom} (see section 2.2).

Dependence on number of acceptors, N_{acc}: Even for such a simple problem as R1, a high number of acceptors helps greatly (Fig. 10A). Having only a few acceptors gives a very high number of evaluations; adding acceptors, up to about 40, drops the number of evaluations many-fold. More parents provides a more effective evolutionary search.

Dependence on maximum acceptor length to search for local homology L_{acc}, and on maximum length of local homology region L_{hom}: As explained in section 2.2, in this work we scan each acceptor for local homology for a certain distance from the jump point (see Fig. 7), using length from 2 to L_{acc} to find a homologous sequence of length from 2 to L_{hom}. Fig. 10B shows results for the dependence of efficacy on L_{acc} for the R1 function. The algorithm shows a great increase in efficiency going from L_{acc} ~10% to 20% bit-string length: for the 64 bit test strings, L_{acc} should be over 13 bits. Tests with L_{hom} show a smoother increase in efficiency, and indicate that L_{hom} should be kept over ~40% bit-string length (Fig. 10C).

3.3.3 Time to achieve fitness level *n*

In addition to total number of evaluations, RR and RS functions have been evaluated in terms of epoch duration, the time a population stays at a given level n searching for the solution to the next level n+1. In developing a theory for the R1 problem, van Nimwegen and colleagues (1999), predicted that epoch duration depends exponentially on epoch number (fitness level) n. Computationally, we do see a roughly exponential dependence for standard GA (no crossover; Fig. 11C), though it is not strictly exponential (Fig. 11D, semi-log plot; this in contrast to RS, which shows strict exponentiality, Fig. 8). Interestingly, retroGA with a high level of acceptors shows a linear relationship between number of evaluations and n (Fig. 11A). The dependence becomes exponential again for low acceptor numbers (Fig. 11B). The retroGA operator with many acceptors is far more efficient than standard GA (Fig. 11D) in terms of keeping epoch duration low.

3.3.4 Tests with ternary strings

While the R3 fitness function has strong parallels to the typical clustering of binding sites in gene regulatory regions (Fig. 1A), a major difference is that DNA "strings" are quaternary (four-letter) ones. Here, we check how such dimensionality affects overall efficacy in GA tests. Specifically, we tested R1 with optimized parameter sets (c.f. Fig. 11A) with ternary strings. (Quaternary strings were too computationally intensive for GA for test purposes.)

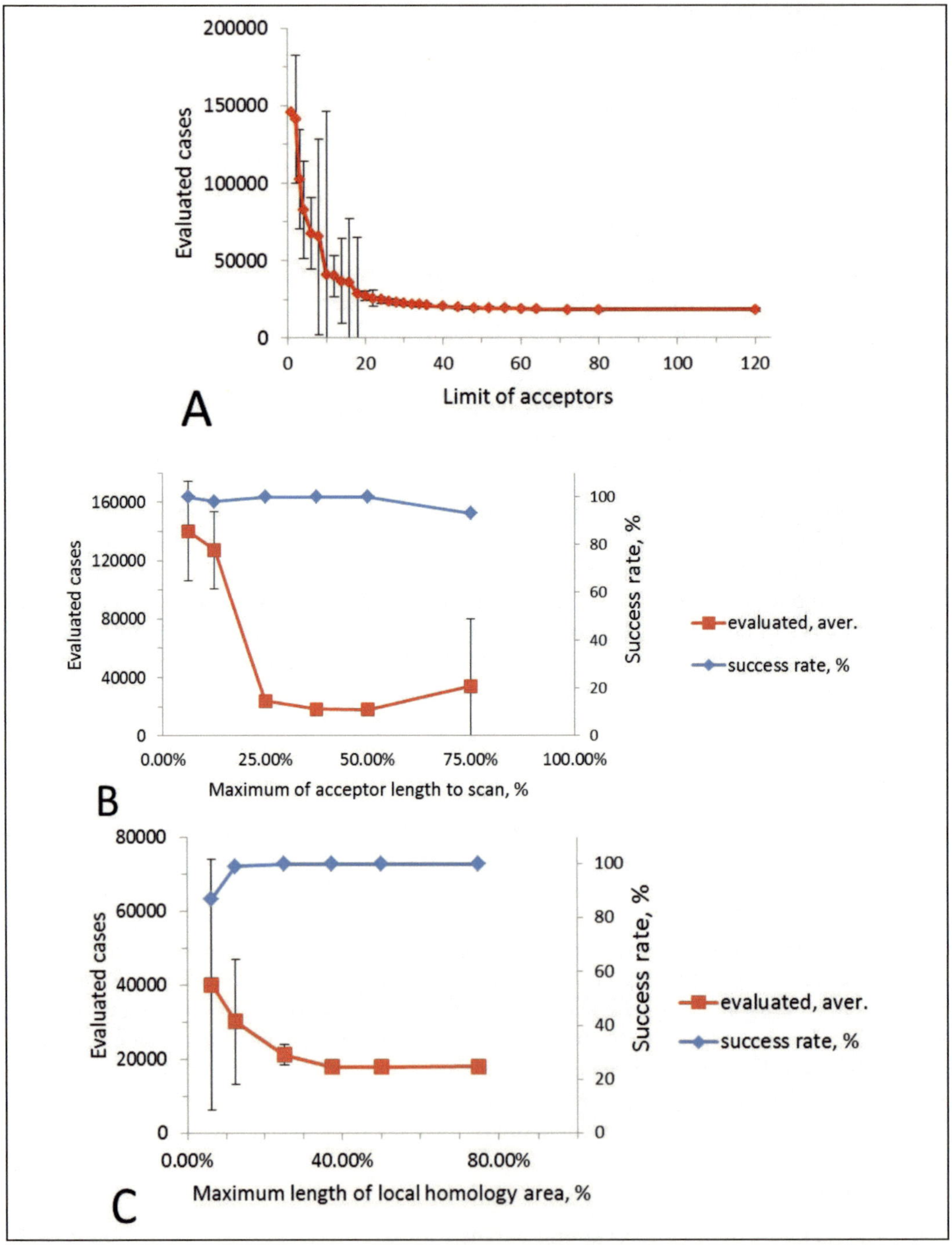

Fig. 10. Tests with the retroGA parameters. Each data point was obtained as an average over 200 retroGA runs. A) Tests on the number of acceptors to use, N_{acc}, for the R1 fitness function. B) Tests on the maximum acceptor length to search for local homology L_{acc}. C) Tests on the maximum length of local homology to find, L_{hom}. M=5,000 in all computations.

Fig. 12 shows the same linear relationship of epoch duration on n found in Fig. 11A for retroGA on binary strings, but the number of evaluations goes up dramatically, with the ternary problem taking ~20 times more evaluations on average than the binary problem (10,893 vs 228,419 - Fig. 11A vs. Fig. 12). There is a large price to pay for increasing the dimension of the problem; we would expect the quaternary problem to be many times slower again.

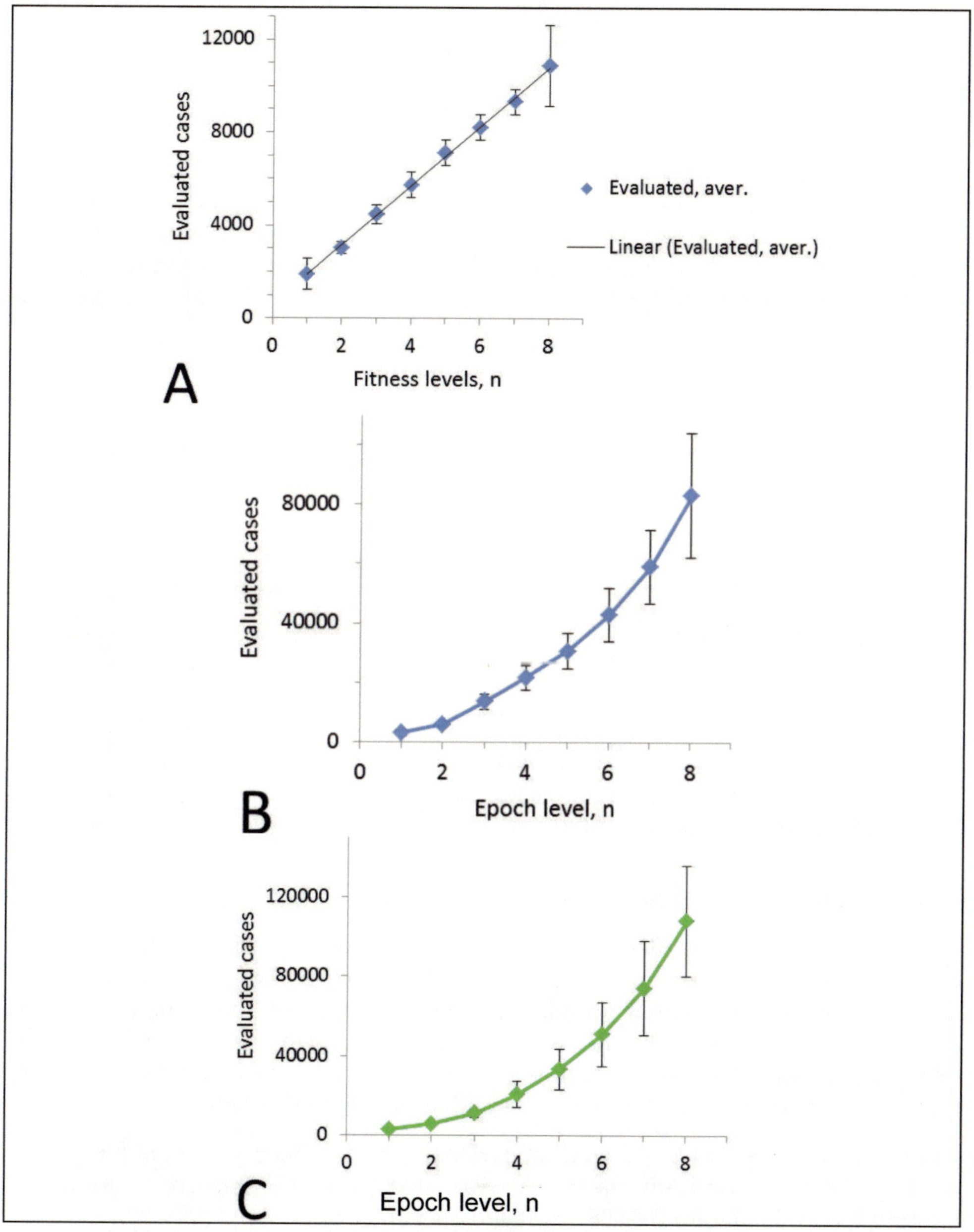

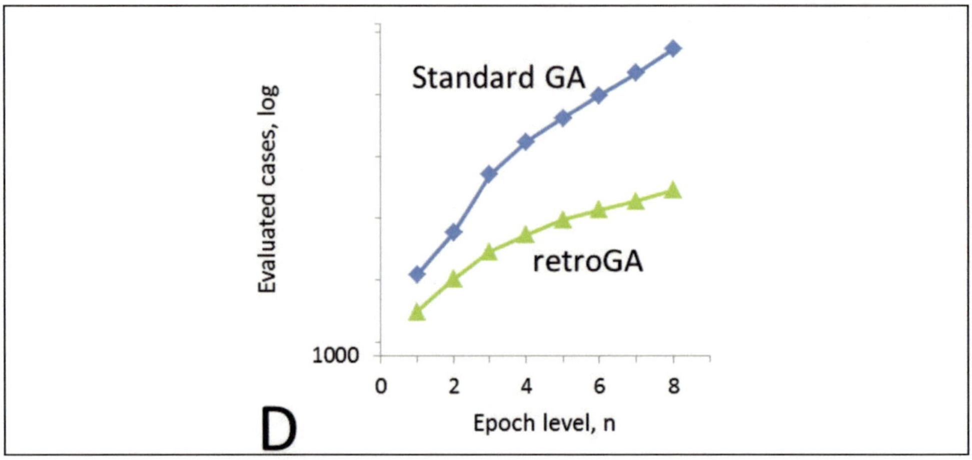

Fig. 11. Epoch durations for the R1 problem: time to achieve fitness level n. Each data point was obtained as an average over 100 retroGA runs. A) retroGA - M=2600; N_{acc}=48; L_{acc}=32; L_{hom}=32. B) retroGA - M=2600; N_{acc}=4; L_{acc}=32; L_{hom}=32. C) Standard GA - M=2600; crossover rate = 0.1; mutation rate = 1/L . D) retroGA vs. standard GA: plots A (green) and C (blue) in semi-log coordinates.

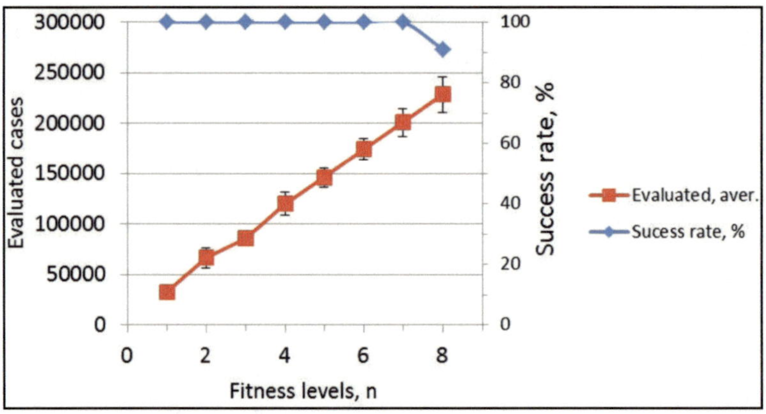

Fig. 12. Epoch duration for retroGA on the R1 problem with ternary strings. Cf. Fig. 11A. Each data point is an average over 100 retroGA runs.

3.4 Crossover to design the *hunchback* gene model

The *hb* gene problem as formulated in section 2.1.3.2 is like R3 in form (N=3; K=16; spacers of length 4), but with octal-digit strings and a substantial level of degeneracy in its three building blocks. The sequential search for CRM's also gives this problem an RS-like character. While the hb search has RR- and RS-like qualities, which should aid in analysis of the problem, the degeneracy of the building blocks is not captured by the test functions, but this does bring the problem closer to real life problems of forced evolution.

We found retroGA (crossover and point mutations) to be an effective method for solving the *hb* gene problem. Specifically, retroGA was over 4-fold faster than standard GA (325,594±59,456 vs. 1,373,246±198,698; averaged over 100 runs).

The *hb* gene problem is the only one in this chapter which has redundant building block sequences. Results show that these blocks are highly redundant. Fig. 13 shows 100 good solutions for the *hb* regulatory sequence. Each row is a solution, with octal-digit represented on an 8-bit grey-scale. There is no discernible pattern outside of the spacer regions (black stripes), illustrating how high the redundancy is in such a problem (for solutions which match the data *well*).

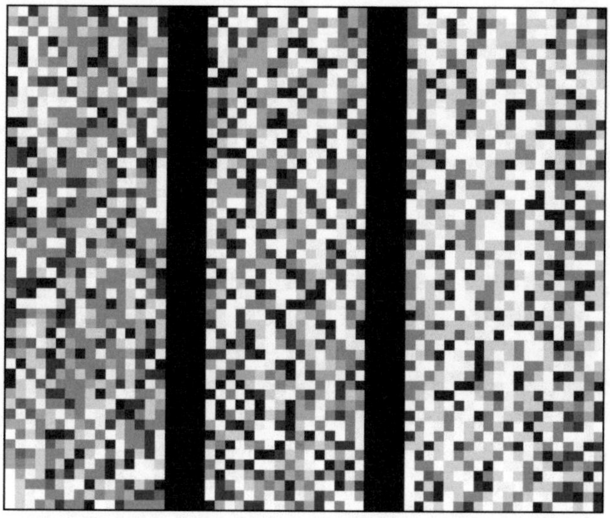

Fig. 13. Grey-scale representation of an aligned stack of 100 good solutions of the *hb* gene problem. Each row corresponds an octal-digit string. The two vertical black columns correspond to two spacer regions of four elements in length each.

4. Discussion

A major aim with this work is to bridge evolutionary computations from benchmark cases, such as Royal Road and Royal Staircase, which are well-understood theoretically (in terms of mathematical analysis), to biological cases, which can serve as a basis for more efficient directed molecular evolution in the test tube and for understanding the mechanisms of biological evolution at the level of gene regulatory sequences.

4.1 Towards a theory of evolution of biological macromolecules

Using analytical tools from statistical mechanics, dynamical systems theory, and mathematical population genetics, van Nimwegen and co-authors (van Nimwegen & Crutchfield, 2000; 2001; van Nimwegen et al., 1999; Crutchfield & Nimwegen, 2001) developed a detailed and quantitative description of the search dynamics for the RS and RR class of problems that exhibit epochal evolution. From this, the authors could analytically predict optimal parameter settings for this class of problems. More generally, the detailed understanding of the behaviour for this class of problems provides valuable insights into the emergent mechanisms that control the dynamics in more general settings of evolutionary searches and in other population-based dynamical systems. By establishing the RR and RS characteristics of gene regulatory problems, we can use this theoretical background to anchor our understanding of more realistic biological search cases.

4.1.1 Royal staircase theory

For RS (point mutation only (no crossover) and roulette-wheel selection strategy), van Nimwegen & Crutchfield (2000) derived an analytical expression for the dependence of the number of evaluations E to achieve the global optimum on the frequency of point mutation q and population size M. Numerical tests (Fig. 14 upper, a) closely follow the analytically predicted dependence (Fig. 14 upper, b). With numerical tests, we found (Fig. 14, (c)) the retroGA operator to have a similar dependence of E on M and Q (Q is the point mutation rate for retroGA; also see Fig. 8). retroGA uses substantially larger populations (M>=2,500) but is several times faster than the standard GA studied by van Nimwegen and Crutchfield. This similar general character of the dependence is promising for extending the van Nimwegen-Crutchfield theory to the case of retroGA crossover.

4.1.2 Royal road theory

van Nimwegen and colleagues (1999) developed an analytical theory for the R1 problem (without crossover and with roulette-wheel selection) and deduced a series of expressions describing the behaviour of this evolutionary search at low mutation rate q. From these, they could predict that high mutation rate would be associated with lower average fitness; they also derived a basis for the exponential dependence of number of evaluations on fitness level. Such predictions are very intriguing for understanding searches and diversity in test tube directed evolution. However, our numerical results with the retroGA operator show a linear relationship of number of evaluations on fitness. This indicates that the analytical results, for the inefficient point mutation operator, may not be seen in biological situations which use more efficient BB-preserving (crossover) operators. Further work is needed to establish the applicability of the point mutation analysis to crossover mechanisms.

4.2 Future prospects for applying the computational results to directed evolution of gene circuits

Our aim is to use the techniques developed in this chapter to aid the directed evolution of bacterial and yeast gene promoters in the laboratory. Several approaches to improve and/or analyze such promoters via directed evolution have been undertaken by experimentalists (Schmidt-Dannert, 2001; Haseltine & Arnold, 2007; Collins et al., 2006). While there is still some gap between the gene models in this chapter and real macromolecular evolution, we hope to have outlined the directions that can be taken for the computational work to provide a stronger theoretical basis for directing and analysing experiments.

We have focused on evolution of sequences, with biological applications in gene promoter structure. The growing field of synthetic biology also includes a great deal of work on designing gene circuits, where large numbers of genes affect each other's expression (e.g. the *Drosophila* segmentation network). Haseltine & Arnold (2007) have identified three primary limitations in using directed evolution to design gene circuits: (a) the evolutionary search space for a genetic circuit composed of many genes is generally too large to explore efficiently; (b) detuning parameters (reducing function) is much easier than improving function; and (c) although selecting for independent properties is possible, it usually requires setting up multiple rounds of screening or selection. In this area, using

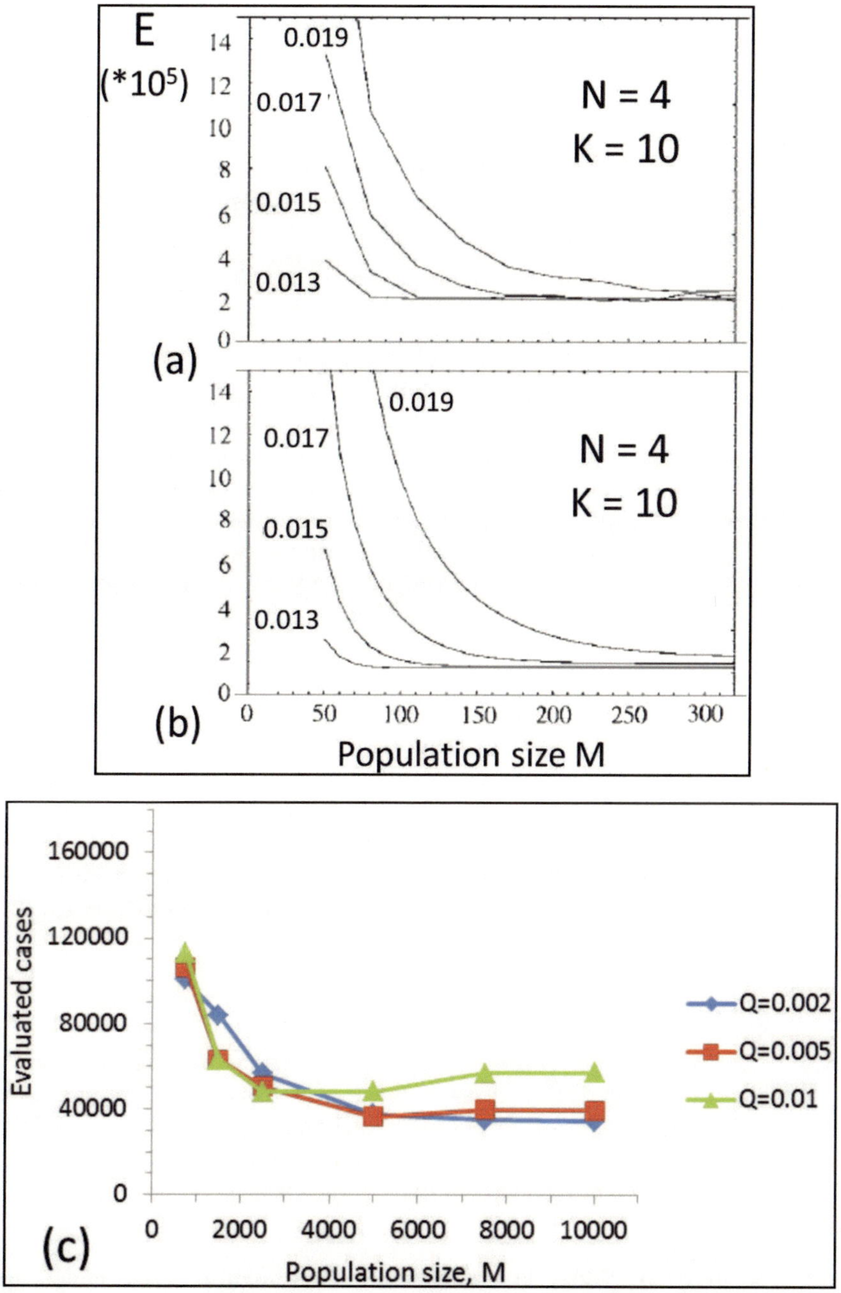

Fig. 14. Dependence of search efficacy E on population size M and mutation rate q. Upper figure: (a) experimentally obtained dependence of E on population size M, each data point is an average over 250 GA runs; (b) shows the theoretical predictions for E as a function of M (van Nimwegen & Crutchfield, 2000). In both, N=4 blocks of length K=10 (c.f. Fig. 8) for four different mutation rates: q ∈ {0.013, 0.015, 0.017, 0.019}. Lower figure (c): Tests with retroGA, showing the empirical dependence of E on M and parameter Q (the point mutation rate for retroGA).

mathematical models to suggest mutational targets can greatly speed up the process and help overcome each of these limitations.

In the wider perspective, an appropriate theory of molecular evolution in the test tube, which includes effective mathematical analysis of new experimental recombination techniques, as described in this chapter, would give a new way to design gene circuits effectively. We hope that the theoretical and computational results discussed in this chapter can facilitate progress in this direction.

5. Conclusion

In this chapter, we have discussed some of the computational issues for evolutionary searches to find gene regulatory sequences. One of the challenges for such searches is to maintain building blocks (meaningful 'words') through genetic change operators. Mutation operators in standard GA frequently destroy such BB's and slow searches. We have introduced the retroGA operator, inspired by retroviral recombination and in vitro DNA shuffling mechanisms, to copy blocks of genetic information. The Royal Road (RR) and Royal Staircase (RS) benchmark functions have been developed for analysing evolutionary searches which preserve BB's. RR and RS theory provide a mathematical framework for understanding the dynamics of searches which have subbasin-portal fitness landscapes. Empirically, we see that retroGA searches share many of the characteristics of RR and RS, but that features, such as multiple parent strings, which can greatly speed up searches, also produce different optimization dynamics than RR and RS. We aim to bridge between RR and RS functions and real biological applications. Through working on specific cases, the rrnP1 and *hb* gene regulatory regions, we are altering simple, binary RR functions to take into account BS clustering and non-binary coding. While real biological problems have a yet higher degree of complexity, our aim is to sketch how EC computations can be used to aid experimental biological work. Computational theory can contribute to both understanding how real gene structures have evolved and to speeding up laboratory work on directed evolution of macromolecules in the test tube.

6. Acknowledgments

AVS wishes to thank Vladimir Fomin for help with hardware and software, Vladimir Levchenko and Marat Sabirov for discussion the results. This work was supported by the Joint NSF/NIGMS BioMath Program, 1-R01-GM072022 and the National Institutes of Health, 2R56GM072022-06. DMH thanks NSERC Canada and BCIT for financial support.

7. References

An W., and Telesnitsky A. (2002). HIV-1 genetic recombination experimental approaches and observations, *AIDS Rev*, Vol.4, pp. 195-212.

Ancel-Myers, L.W. & Fontana W. (2005). Evolutionary Lock-in and the Origin of Modularity in RNA Structure, In *Modularity –Understanding the Development and Evolution of Natural Complex Systems*, pp. 129-141, W.Callebaut and D.Rasskin-Gutman (editors), MIT Press, Cambridge, MA.

Botstein D. (1980). A theory of modular evolution for bacteriophages, *Ann N Y Acad Sci*, Vol.354, pp. 484–491.

Brosius, J. (1999). Genomes were forged by massive bombardments with retroelements and retrosequences, *Genetica,* Vol.107, pp. 209-238.

Chen J. & Wood D. H. (2000). Computation with Biomolecules, *Proc. Nat. Acad. Sci. USA,* Vol.97, pp. 1328-1330.

Collins CH, Leadbetter JR, & Arnold FH. (2006). Dual selection enhances the signaling specificity of a variant of the quorum-sensing transcriptional activator LuxR, *Nature Biotech,* Vol.24, pp. 708–712.

Crutchfield J. P. & van Nimwegen E. (2001). The Evolutionary Unfolding of Complexity, In *Evolution as Computation, DIMACS workshop,* Springer-Verlag, New York.

Crutchfield J. P. (2002). When Evolution is Revolution—Origins of Innovation, In *Evolutionary Dynamics—Exploring the Interplay of Selection, Neutrality, Accident, and Function,* J. P. Crutchfield and P. Schuster (eds.), Santa Fe Institute Series in the Science of Complexity, Oxford University Press, New York, pp. 101-133.

Forrest S., & Mitchell M. (1993a). What Makes a Problem Hard for a Genetic Algorithm? Some Anomalous Results and Their Explanation, *Machine Learning,* Vol.13, (No 2), pp. 285 -319.

Forrest S. & Mitchell M. (1993b). Relative building-block fitness and the buildingblock hypothesis, In D. Whitley (ed.), *Foundations of Genetic Algorithms,* Vol.2, pp. 109-126, San Mateo, CA Morgan Kaufmann.

Goldberg D. E. (1989). *Genetic Algorithms in Search, Optimization, and Machine Learning* (Addison-Wesley, Reading, MA).

Haseltine EL, & Arnold FH. (2007). Synthetic gene circuits Design with directed evolution, *Annu Rev Biophys Biomol Struct,* Vol.36, pp.1–19.

Hengen PN, Bartram SL, Stewart LE, & Schneider TD. (1997). Information analysis of Fis binding sites, *Nucleic Acids Res,* Vol.25, pp. 4994-5002.

Henkel C. V., Back T., Kok J. N., Rozenberg G., & Spaink, H. P. (2007). DNA computing of solutions to knapsack problems, *Biosystems,* Vol.88, (No 1), pp.156 - 162.

Hirvonen CA, Ross W, Wozniak CE, Marasco E, Anthony JR, Aiyar SE, Newburn VH, & Gourse RL. (2001). Contributions of UP elements and the transcription factor FIS to expression from the seven rrn P1 promoters in Escherichia coli, *J Bacteriol,* Vol.183, pp. 6305-6314.

Holland J. H. (1975). *Adaptation in Natural and Artificial Systems* (Ann Arbor, MI Univ. Michigan Press).

Jeziorska DM, Jordan KW, & Vance KW. (2009). A systems biology approach to understanding cis-regulatory module function, *Sem. Cell & Dev. Biol,* Vol.20, pp. 856–862.

Kitano, H. (2004). Biological robustness. *Nat. Rev. Genet.* Vol.5, pp. 826–837.

Long M., Betran E., Thornton K., et al. (2003). The origin of new genes Glimpses from the young and old, *Nat Rev Genet,* Vol.4, pp. 865–875.

Lu T. K., Friedland A. E., Wang X., Shi D., Church G. M., & Collins J. J. (2009). Synthetic Gene Networks that Count, *Science,* Vol.324, (No 5931), pp. 1199-1202

Maheshri, N. & Schaffer D.V. (2003). Computational and experimental analysis of DNA shuffling, *Proc Natl Acad Sci USA,* Vol.100, (No 6), pp. 3071-6.

Mitchell M. (1996). *An Introduction to Genetic Algorithms.* MIT Press.

Mitchell M., Forrest S. & Holland J. H. (1992). The Royal Road for genetic algorithms Fitness landscapes and GA performance, In *Proceedings of the First European Conference on Artificial Life,* Cambridge, MA MIT Press/Bradford Books.

Negroni M., & Buc H. (2001). Mechanisms of retroviral recombination, *Annu Rev Genet,* Vol.35, pp. 275-302.

Ross W, Aiyar SE, Salomon J, & Gourse RL. (1998). Escherichia coli promoters with UP elements of different strengths modular structure of bacterial promoters, *J Bacteriol,* Vol.180, pp. 5375-5383.

Ross W, Thompson JF, Newlands JT, & Gourse RL. (1990). E.coli Fis protein activates ribosomal RNA transcription in vitro and in vivo, *EMBO J,* Vol.9, pp. 3733-3742.

Schmidt-Dannert C., (2001). Directed evolution of single proteins, metabolic pathways, and viruses, *Biochemistry,* Vol.40, pp. 13125–13136.

Schneider DA, Ross W, & Gourse RL. (2003). Control of rRNA expression in Escherichia coli, *Curr Opin Microbiol,* Vol.6, pp. 151-156.

Sen S., Venkata Dasu V., & Mandal B. (2007). Developments in directed evolution for improving enzyme functions, *Applied biochemistry and biotechnology,* Vol.143, pp. 212–223.

Shapiro, J.A. (1999). Transposable elements as the key to a 21st century view of evolution, *Genetica,* Vol.107, pp. 171–179.

Shapiro, J.A. (2002). Repetitive DNA, genome system architecture and genome reorganization, *Res Microbiol,* Vol.153, pp. 447-53.

Shapiro, J.A. (2010). Mobile DNA and evolution in the 21st century. *Mobile DNA,* Vol.1 (No4).

Spirov A.V., Borovsky M., & Spirova O.A. (2002). HOX Pro DB The functional genomics of hox ensembles, *Nucleic Acids Research,* Vol.30, No 1, pp. 351 - 353.

Spirov A. V., & Holloway D. M. (2010). Design of a dynamic model of genes with multiple autonomous regulatory modules by evolutionary computations, *Procedia Comp. Sci,* Vol.1, (No 1), pp. 1005-1014.

Spirov A.V., Bowler T. & Reinitz J. (2000). HOX-Pro A Specialized Database for Clusters and Networks of Homeobox Genes, *Nucleic Acids Research,* Vol.28, (No 1), pp. 337-340.

Stemmer W.P. (1994a). DNA shuffling by random fragmentation and reassembly in vitro recombination for molecular evolution, *Proc Natl Acad Sci USA,* Vol.91, pp. 10747-10751.

Stemmer W.P. (1994b). Rapid evolution of a protein in vitro by DNA shuffling, *Nature,* Vol.370, (No 6488), pp. 389-391.

Stormo GD. (2000). DNA binding sites representation and discovery, *Bioinformatics,* Vol.16, (No 1), 16–23.

Sun F. (1999). Modeling DNA shuffling, *J Comput Biol,* Vol.6, (No 1), pp. 77-90.

van Nimwegen E., & Crutchfield J. P. (2001). Optimizing Epochal Evolutionary Search Population-Size Dependent Theory, *Machine Learning Journal,* Vol.45, pp. 77-114.

van Nimwegen E., & Crutchfield J. P. (2000). Optimizing Epochal Evolutionary Search Population-Size Independent Theory, *Computer Methods in Applied Mechanics and Engineering,* Vol.186, (No 2-4), pp. 171-194.

van Nimwegen E., Crutchfield J. P., & Huynen M. (1999). Neutral Evolution of Mutational Robustness, *Proc Natl Acad Sci USA,* Vol.96, pp. 9716-9720.

van Nimwegen E., Crutchfield J. P., & Mitchell M. (1997). Finite Populations Induce Metastability in Evolutionary Search, *Physics Letters A,* Vol.229, pp. 144-150

Voigt, C. A., Martinez, C., Mayo, S.L., Wang, Z-.G., & Arnold, F.H. (2002). Protein building blocks preserved by recombination, *Nature Structural Biology,* Vol.9, pp. 553-558.

von Dassow, G., Meir., E., Munro, E. M., & Odell, G. M. (2000). The segment polarity network is a robust developmental module, *Nature* Vol. 406, pp.188 - 192.

13

Application of Genetic Algorithms and Ant Colony Optimization for Modelling of *E. coli* Cultivation Process

Olympia Roeva[1] and Stefka Fidanova[2]
[1]*Institute of Biophysics and Biomedical Engineering, Bulgarian Academy of Sciences*
[2]*Institute of Information and Communication Technologies, Bulgarian Academy of Sciences*
Bulgaria

1. Introduction

Classical biotechnology is the science of production of human-useful processes and products under controlled conditions, applying biological agents – microorganisms, plant or animal cells, their exo- and endo- products, e.g. enzymes, etc. (Viesturs et al., 2004). The conventional agriculture or chemistry cannot perform these processes as efficiently or at all. In fact, conventional biotechnology has been the largest industrial activity on earth for a very long time. Modern biotechnology goes much further with respect to control of the biological processes.

Particularly microorganisms have received a lot of attention as a biotechnological instrument and are used in so-called cultivation processes. Numerous useful bacteria, yeasts and fungi are widely found in nature, but the optimum conditions for growth and product formation in their natural environment is seldom discovered. In artificial (in vitro) conditions, the biotechnologist can intervene in the microbial cell environment (in a fermenter or bioreactor), as well as in their genetic material, in order to achieve a better control of cultivation processes. Because of their extremely high synthetic versatility, ease of using renewable raw materials, great speed of microbial reactions, quick growth and relatively easy to modify genetic material, many microorganisms are extremely efficient and in many cases indispensable workhorses in the various sectors of industrial biotechnology.

Cultivation of recombinant micro-organisms e.g. *Escherichia coli*, in many cases is the only economical way to produce pharmaceutical biochemicals such as interleukins, insulin, interferons, enzymes and growth factors. Simple bacteria like *E. coli* are manipulated to produce these chemicals so that they are easily harvested in vast quantities for use in medicine. *E. coli* is still the most important host organism for recombinant protein production. Scientists may know more about *E. coli* than they do about any other species on earth. Research on E. coli accelerated even more after 1997, when scientists published its entire genome. They were able to survey all 4,288 of its genes, discovering how groups of them worked together to break down food, make new copies of DNA and do other tasks. But despite decades of research there is a lot more we need to know about *E. coli*. To find out more, *E. coli* experts have been joining forces. In 2002, they formed the *International E-coli Alliance* to organize projects that many laboratories could do together. As knowledge of *E. coli* grows, scientists are starting to build models of the microbe that capture some of its behavior. It is important to be able to predict how fast the microbe will grow on various sources of food, as well as how its growth changes if individual genes are knocked out. Here is the place of mathematical modelling. Some of recent researches and developed models of *E. coli* are presented in (Covert et al., 2008; Jiang et al., 2010; Karelina et al., 2011; Opalka et al., 2011; Petersen et al., 2011; Skandamis & Nychas, 2000).

Modelling of biotechnological processes is a common tool in process technology. Development of adequate models is an important step for process optimization and high-quality control. In an ideal world, process modelling would be a trivial task. Models would be constructed in a simple manner just to reproduce the true process behaviour. In the real world it is obvious that the model is always a simplification of the reality. This is especially true when trying to model natural systems containing living organisms. For many industrial relevant processes however detailed models are not available due to insufficient understanding of the underlying phenomena. The mathematical models, which naturally could be incomplete and inaccurate to a certain degree, can still be very useful and effective tools in describing those effects which are of great importance for control, optimization, or for understanding of the process. At present the models can be applied in practice since computers allow numerical solution of process models of such complexity that could hardly be imagined a couple of decades ago. Thus numerical solution of the models is the fundament for the development of economic and powerful methods in the fields of bioprocess design, plant design, scale-up, optimization and bioprocess control (Schuegerl & Bellgardt, 2000).

The mathematical modelling of biotechnological processes is an extremely wide field that covers all important kinds of processes with many different microorganisms or cells of plants and animals. The mathematical model is a tool that allows to be investigated the static and dynamic behaviour of the process without doing (or at least reducing) the number of practical experiments. In practice, an experimental approach often has serious limitations that make it necessary to work with mathematical models instead.

Modelling approaches are central in system biology and provide new ways towards the analysis and understanding of cells and organisms. A common approach to model cellular dynamics is the sets of nonlinear differential equations. Real parameter optimization of cellular dynamics models has especially become a research field of great interest. Such problems have widespread application.

The principle of mathematical optimization consists in choice of optimization criteria, choice of control parameters and choice of exhaustive method. Parameter identification of a nonlinear dynamic model is more difficult than the linear one, as no general analytic results exist. The difficulties that may arise are such as convergence to local solutions if standard local methods are used, over-determined models, badly scaled model function, etc. Due to the nonlinearity and constrained nature of the considered systems, these problems are very often multimodal. Thus, traditional gradient-based methods may fail to identify the global solution. In this case only direct optimization strategies can be applied, because they exclusively use information about values of the goal function. These optimization methods provide more guarantees of converging to the global optimal solution. Although a lot of different global optimization methods exist, the efficacy of an optimization method is always problem-specific. A major deficiency in computational approaches to design and optimization of bioprocess systems is the lack of applicable methods.

There are many possible variants such as numerical methods (Lagarias et al., 1998; Press et al., 1986). But while searching for new, more adequate modeling metaphors and concepts, methods which draw their initial inspiration from nature have received the early attention. During the last decade metaheuristic techniques have been applied in a variety of areas. Heuristics can obtain suboptimal solution in ordinary situations and optimal solution in particular. Since the considered problem has been known to be NP-complete, using heuristic techniques can solve this problem more efficiently. Three most well-known heuristics are the iterative improvement algorithms, the probabilistic optimization algorithms, and the constructive heuristics. Evolutionary algorithms like Genetic Algorithms (GA) (Goldberg, 2006; Holland, 1992; Michalewicz, 1994) and Evolution Strategies, Ant Colony Optimization (ACO) (Dorigo & Di Caro, 1999; Dorigo & Stutzle, 2004; Fidanova, 2002; Fidanova et al., 2010), Particle Swarm Optimization (Umarani & Selvi, 2010), Tabu Search (Yusof & Stapa, 2010), Simulated Annealing (Kirkpatrick et al., 1983), estimation of distribution algorithms, scatter search, path relinking, the greedy randomized adaptive search procedure, multi-start and iterated local search, guided local search, and variable neighborhood search are - among others - often listed as examples of classical metaheuristics (Bonabeau et al., 1999; Syam & Al-Harkan, 2010; Tahouni et al., 2010), and they have individual historical backgrounds and follow different paradigms and philosophies (Brownlee, 2011). In this work the GA and ACO are chosen as the most common direct methods used for global optimization.

The GA is a model of machine learning deriving its behaviour from a metaphor of the processes of evolution in nature. This is done by the creation within a machine of a population of individuals represented by chromosomes. A chromosome could be an array of real numbers, a binary string, a list of components in a database, all depending on the specific problem. Each individual represents a possible solution, and a set of individuals form a population. In a population, the fittest are selected for mating. The individuals in the population go through a process of evolution which is, according to Darwin, made up of the principles of mutation and selection; however, the modern biological evolution theory distinguishes also crossover and isolation mechanisms improving the adaptiveness of the living organisms to their environment. The principal advantages of GA are domain independence, non linearity and robustness. The only requirement for GA is the ability to calculate the measure of performance which may be highly complicated and non-linear. The above two characteristics of GA assume that GA is inherently robust. A GA has a number of advantages. It can work with highly non-linear functions and can cope with a great diversity of problems from different fields. It can quickly scan a vast solution set. Bad proposals do not effect the end solution negatively as they are simply discarded. The inductive nature of the GA means that it doesn't have to know any rules of the problem - it works by its own internal rules. This is very useful for complex or loosely defined problems. However, the conventional GA has a very poor local performance because of the random search used. To achieve a good solution, great computational cost is inevitable. The same qualities that make the GA so robust also can make it more computationally intensive and slower than other methods.

On the other hand ACO is a rapidly growing field of a population-based metaheuristic that can be used to find approximate solutions to difficult optimization problems. ACO is applicable for a broad range of optimization problems, can be used in dynamic applications (adapts to changes such as new distances, etc) and in some complex biological problems (Fidanova & Lirkov, 2009; Fidanova, 2010; Shmygelska & Hoos, 2005). ACO can compete with other global optimization techniques like genetic algorithms and simulated annealing. ACO algorithms have been inspired by the real ants behavior. In nature, ants usually wander randomly, and upon finding food return to their nest while laying down pheromone trails. If other ants find such a path, they are likely to not keep traveling at random, but to follow the trail instead, returning and reinforcing it if they eventually find food. However, as time passes, the pheromone starts to evaporate. The more time it takes for an ant to travel down the path and back again, the more time the pheromone has to evaporate and the path becomes less noticeable. A shorter path, in comparison will be visited by more ants and thus the pheromone density remains high for a longer time. ACO is implemented as a team of intelligent agents which simulate the ants behavior, walking around the graph representing the problem to solve using mechanisms of cooperation and adaptation.

In this chapter GA and ACO are applied for parameter identification of a system of nonlinear differential equations modeling the fed-batch cultivation process of the bacteria *Escherichia coli*. A system of ordinary differential equations is proposed to model *E. coli* biomass growth and substrate (glucose) utilization. Parameter optimization is performed using real experimental data set from an *E. coli* MC4110 fed-batch cultivation process. The cultivation is performed in *Institute of Technical Chemistry, University of Hannover, Germany* during the collaboration work with the *Institute of Biophysics and Biomedical Engineering, BAS, Bulgaria,* granted by *DFG*.

The experimental data set includes records for substrate feeding rate, concentration of biomass and substrate (glucose) and cultivation time. In considered here nonlinear mathematical model the parameters that should be estimated are maximum specific growth rate (μ_{max}), saturation constant (k_S) and yield coefficient ($Y_{S/X}$).

The parameter estimation is performed based upon the use of Hausdorff metric (Rote, 1991), in place of the most commonly used metric – Least Squares regression. Hausdorff metrics are used in geometric settings for measuring the distance between sets of points. They have been used extensively in areas such as computer vision, pattern recognition and computational chemistry (Chen & Lovell, 2010; Nutanong et al., 2010; Sugiyama et al., 2010; Yedjour et al., 2011). A modified Hausdorff Distance is proposed to evaluate the mismatch between experimental and model predicted data.

The results from both metaheuristics GA and ACO are compared using the modified Hausdorff Distance. The algorithms accuracy (value of the objective function) and the resulting average, best and worst model parameter estimations are compared for the model identification of the *E. coli* MC4110 fed-batch cultivation process.

The chapter is organized as follows: In Section 2 the problem definition is formulated. As a case study an fed-batch cultivation of bacteria *E. coli* is presented. Further optimization criteria is defined. In Section 3 the theoretical background of the GA is presented. In Section 4 the theoretical background of the ACO is presented. The numerical results and a discussion are presented in Section 5. The GA and ACO adjustments for considered parameter identification problem application are discussed too. Conclusion remarks are done in Section 6.

2. Problem definition

Cultivation process are known to be very complex and modeling may be a rather time consuming. However, it is neither necessary nor desirable to construct comprehensive mechanistic process models that can describe the system in all possible situations with a high accuracy. In order to optimize a real biotechnical production process, the model must be regarded as a step to reach more easily the final aim. The model must describe those aspects of the process that significantly affect the process performance.

The costs of developing mathematical models for bioprocesses improvement are often too high and the benefits too low. The main reason for this is related to the intrinsic complexity and non-linearity of biological systems. In general, mathematical descriptions of growth kinetics assume hard simplifications. These models are often not accurate enough at describing the underlying mechanisms. Another critical issue is related to the nature of bioprocess models. Often the parameters involved are not identifiable. Additionally, from the practical point of view, such identification would require data from specific experiments which are themselves difficult to design and realize. The estimation of model parameters with high parameter accuracy is essential for successful model development.

The important part of model building is the choice of a certain optimization procedure for parameter estimation, so with a given set of experimental data to calibrate the model in order to reproduce the experimental results in the best possible way.

Real parameter optimization of simulation models has especially become a research field of great interests in recent years. Nevertheless, this task still represents a very difficult problem. This mathematical problem, so-called inverse problem, is a big challenge for the traditional optimization methods. In this case only direct optimization strategies can be applied, because they exclusively use information about values of the goal function. Additional information about the goal function like gradients, etc., which may be used to accelerate the optimization process, is not available. Since an evolution of a goal for one string is provided by one simulation run, proceeding of an optimization algorithm may require a lot of computational time. Thus or therefore, various metaheuristics are used as an alternative to surmount the parameter estimation difficulties.

2.1 *E. coli* fed-batch cultivation process

To maximize the volumetric productiveness of bacterial cultures it is important to grow *E. coli* to high cell concentration. The use of fed-batch cultivation in the fermentation industry takes advantage of the fact that residual substrate concentration may by maintained at a very low level in such a system.

The general state space dynamical model described by Bastin and Dochain (Bastin & Dochain, 1991) is accepted as representing the dynamics of an n components and m reactions bioprocess:

$$\frac{dx}{dt} = K\varphi(x,t) - Dx + F - Q \tag{1}$$

where x is a vector representing the state components; K is the yield coefficient matrix; φ is the growth rates vector; the vectors F and Q are the feed rates and the gaseous outflow rates. The scalar D is the dilution rate, which will be the manipulated variable, defined as follows:

$$D = \frac{F_{in}}{V} \tag{2}$$

where F_{in} is the influent flow rate and V is the bioreactor's volume.

Application of the general state space dynamical model (Bastin & Dochain, 1991) to the *E. coli* cultivation fed-batch process leads to the following nonlinear differential equation system

(Roeva, 2008b):

$$\frac{dX}{dt} = \mu_{max}\frac{S}{k_S + S}X - \frac{F_{in}}{V}X \tag{3}$$

$$\frac{dS}{dt} = -\frac{1}{Y_{S/X}}\mu_{max}\frac{S}{k_S + S}X + \frac{F_{in}}{V}(S_{in} - S) \tag{4}$$

$$\frac{dV}{dt} = F_{in} \tag{5}$$

where:

X – biomass concentration, [g/l];
S – substrate concentration, [g/l];
F_{in} – feeding rate, [l/h];
V – bioreactor volume, [l];
S_{in} – substrate concentration in the feeding solution, [g/l];
μ_{max} – maximum value of the specific growth rate, $[h^{-1}]$;
k_S – saturation constant, [g/l];
$Y_{S/X}$ – yield coefficient, [-].

The growth rate of bacteria *E. coli* is described according to the classical Monod equation:

$$\mu = \mu_{max}\frac{S}{k_S + S} \tag{6}$$

The mathematical formulation of the nonlinear dynamic model (Eqs. (3) - (5)) of *E. coli* fed-batch cultivation process is described according to the mass balance and the model is based on the following a priori assumptions:

- the bioreactor is completely mixed;
- the main products are biomass, water and, under some conditions, acetate;
- the substrate glucose mainly is consumed oxidatively and its consumption can be described by Monod kinetics;
- variation in the growth rate and substrate consumption do not significantly change the elemental composition of biomass, thus balanced growth conditions are only assumed;
- parameters, e.g. temperature, pH, pO_2 are controlled at their individual constant set points.

For the parameter estimation problem real experimental data of the *E. coli* MC4110 fed-batch cultivation process are used. Off-line measurements of biomass and on-line measurements of the glucose concentration are used in the identification procedure. The cultivation condition and the experimental data have been presented in (Roeva et al., 2004). Here a brief description is presented.

The fed-batch cultivation of *E. coli* MC4110 is performed in a 2l bioreactor (Bioengineering, Switzerland), using a mineral medium (Arndt & Hitzmann, 2001), in *Institute of Technical Chemistry, University of Hannover*. Before inoculation a glucose concentration of 2.5 g/l is established in the medium. Glucose in feeding solution is 100 g/l. Initial liquid volume is 1350 ml, pH is controlled at 6.8 and temperature is kept constant at 35°C . The aeration rate is kept at 275 l/h air, stirrer speed at start 900 rpm, after 11h the stirrer speed is increased in steps of 100 rpm and at end is 1500 rpm. Oxygen is controlled around 35%.

Off-line analysis
For off-line glucose measurements as well as biomass and acetate concentration determination samples of about 10 ml are taken roughly every hour. Off-line measurements are performed by using the Yellow Springs Analyser (Yellow Springs Instruments, USA).

On-line analysis
For on-line glucose determination a flow injection analysis (FIA) system has been employed using two pumps (ACCU FM40, SciLog, USA) for a continuous sample and carrier flow rate. To reduce the measurement noise the continuous-discrete extended Kalman filter are used (Arndt & Hitzmann, 2001).

Glucose measurement and control system
For on-line glucose determination a FIA system has been employed using two pumps (ACCU FM40, SciLog, USA) for a continuous sample and carrier flow rate at 0.5 ml/min and 1.7 ml/min respectively. 24 ml of cell containing culture broth were injected into the carrier stream and mixed with an enzyme solution of 350 000 U/l of glucose oxidase (Fluka, Germany) of a volume of 36 ml. After passing a reaction coil of 50 cm length the oxygen uptake were measured using an oxygen electrode (ANASYSCON, Germany). To determine only the oxygen consumed by cells no enzyme solution were injected. Calculating the difference of both dissolved oxygen peak heights, the glucose concentration can be determined. The time between sample taking and the measurement of the dissolved oxygen was $\Delta t = 45$ s.

For the automation of the FIA system as well as glucose concentration determination the software CAFCA (ANASYSCON, Germany) were applied. To reduce the measurement noise the continuous-discrete extended Kalman filter were used. This program was running on a separate PC and got the measurement results via a serial connection. A PI controller was applied to adjust the glucose concentration to the desired set point of 0.1 g/l (Arndt & Hitzmann, 2001).

The initial process conditions are (Arndt & Hitzmann, 2001):
$t_0 = 6.68$ h, $X(t_0) = 1.25$ g/l, $S(t_0) = 0.8$ g/l, $S_{in} = 100$ g/l.

The bioreactor, as well as FIA measurement system and the computers used for data measurement from the FIA system and for the process control are presented in Figure 1.

2.2 Optimization criterion

In practical view, modelling studies are performed to identify simple and easy-to-use models that are suitable to support the engineering tasks of process optimization and, especially, of control. The most appropriate model must satisfy the following conditions:

(i) the model structure should be able to represent the measured data in a proper manner;

(ii) the model structure should be as simple as possible compatible with the first requirement.

On account of that the cultivation process dynamic is described using simple Monod-type model, the most common kinetics applied for modelling of cultivation processes (Bastin & Dochain, 1991).

The optimization criterion is a certain factor, whose value defines the quality of an estimated set of parameters. The parameter estimation is performed based on Hausdorff metric. To evaluate the mishmash between experimental and model predicted data a modified Hausdorff Distance is proposed.

Fig. 1. Experimental equipment

When talking about distances, we usually mean the shortest: for instance, if a point X is said to be at distance D of a polygon P, we generally assume that D is the distance from X to the nearest point of P. The same logic applies for polygons: if two polygons A and B are at some distance from each other, we commonly understand that distance as the shortest one between any point of A and any point of B. That definition of distance between polygons can become quite unsatisfactory for some applications. However, we would naturally expect that a small distance between these polygons means that no point of one polygon is far from the other polygon. It's quite obvious that the shortest distance concept carries very low informative content.

In mathematics, the Hausdorff distance, or Hausdorff metric, also called Pompeiu-Hausdorff distance, (Rote, 1991) measures how far two subsets of a metric space are from each other. It turns the set of non-empty compact subsets of a metric space into a metric space in its own right. It is named after Felix Hausdorff. Informally, two sets are close in the Hausdorff distance if every point of either set is close to some point of the other set. The Hausdorff distance is the longest distance you can be forced to travel by an adversary who chooses a point in one of the two sets, from where you then must travel to the other set. In other words, it is the farthest point of a set that you can be to the closest point of a different set. More formally, Hausdorff distance from set A to set B is a maxmin function defined as:

$$h(A,B) = \max_{a \in A} \left\{ \min_{b \in B} \{d(a,b)\} \right\}, \tag{7}$$

where a and b are points of sets A and B respectively, and $d(a,b)$ is any metric between these points. For simplicity, we will take $d(a,b)$ as the Euclidean distance between a and b. If sets A and B are made of lines or polygons instead of single points, then $h(A,B)$ applies to all defining points of these lines or polygons, and not only to their vertices. Hausdorff distance gives an interesting measure of their mutual proximity, by indicating the maximal distance between any point of one set to the other set. Better than the shortest distance, which applied only to one point of each set, irrespective of all other points of the sets.

In this work the Hausdorff metric is used for first time for solving of model parameter optimization problem regarding cultivation process models.

3. Genetic Algorithm

GA originated from the studies of cellular automata, conducted by John Holland and his colleagues at the University of Michigan. Holland's book (Holland, 1992), published in 1975, is generally acknowledged as the beginning of the research of genetic algorithms. The GA is a model of machine learning which derives its behavior from a metaphor of the processes of evolution in nature (Goldberg, 2006). This is done by the creation within a machine of a population of individuals represented by chromosomes. A chromosome could be an array of real numbers, a binary string, a list of components in a database, all depending on the specific problem. The GA are highly relevant for industrial applications, because they are capable of handling problems with non-linear constraints, multiple objectives, and dynamic components – properties that frequently appear in the real-world problems (Goldberg, 2006; Kumar et al., 1992). Since their introduction and subsequent popularization (Holland, 1992), the GA have been frequently used as an alternative optimization tool to the conventional methods (Goldberg, 2006; Parker, 1992) and have been successfully applied in a variety of areas, and still find increasing acceptance (Akpinar & Bayhan, 2011; Al-Duwaish, 2000; Benjamin et al., 1999; da Silva et al., 2010; Paplinski, 2010; Roeva & Slavov, 2011; Roeva, 2008a).

Basics of Genetic Algorithm

GA was developed to model adaptation processes mainly operating on binary strings and using a recombination operator with mutation as a background operator. The GA maintains a population of individuals, $P(t) = x_1^t, ..., x_n^t$ for generation t. Each individual represents a potential solution to the problem and is implemented as some data structure S. Each solution is evaluated to give some measure of its "fitness". Fitness of an individual is assigned proportionally to the value of the objective function of the individuals. Then, a new population (generation $t + 1$) is formed by selecting more fit individuals (selected step). Some members of the new population undergo transformations by means of "genetic" operators to form new solution. There are unary transformations m_i (mutation type), which create new individuals by a small change in a single individual ($m_i : S \to S$), and higher order transformations c_j (crossover type), which create new individuals by combining parts from several individuals ($c_j : S \times \ldots \times S \to S$). After some number of generations the algorithm converges - it is expected that the best individual represents a near-optimum (reasonable) solution. The combined effect of selection, crossover and mutation gives so-called reproductive scheme growth equation (Goldberg, 2006):

$$\xi(S, t+1) \geq \xi(S, t) \cdot eval(S, t) / \bar{F}(t) \left[1 - p_c \cdot \frac{\delta(S)}{m-1} - o(S) \cdot p_m\right].$$

Differences that separate genetic algorithms from the more conventional optimization techniques could be defined as follows (Goldberg, 2006):

1. Direct manipulation of a coding – GA works with a coding of the parameter set, not the parameter themselves;
2. GA searches in a population of points, not a single point;
3. GA uses payoff (objective function) information, not derivatives or other auxiliary knowledge;
4. GA uses probabilistic transition rules (stochastic operators), not deterministic rules.

Compared with traditional optimization methods, GA simultaneously evaluates many points in the parameter space. This makes convergence towards the global solution more probable. A genetic algorithm does not assume that the space is differentiable or continuous and can also iterate many times on each data received. A GA requires only information concerning the quality of the solution produced by each parameter set (objective function value information). This characteristic differs from optimization methods that require derivative information or, worse yet, complete knowledge of the problem structure and parameters. Since GA do not demand such problem-specific information, they are more flexible than most search methods. Also GA do not require linearity in the parameters which is needed in iterative searching optimization techniques. Genetic algorithms can solve hard problems, are noise tolerant, easy to interface to existing simulation models, and easy to hybridize. Therefore, this property makes genetic algorithms suitable and more workable in use for a parameter estimation of considered here cultivation process models. Moreover, the GA effectiveness and robustness have been already demonstrated for identification of fed-batch cultivation processes (Carrillo-Uretaet al., 2001; Ranganath et al., 1999; Roeva, 2006; 2007).

The structure of the GA is shown by the pseudocode below (Figure 2).

```
begin
    i = 0
    Initial population P(0)
    Evaluate P(0)
    while (not done) do (test for termination criterion)
    begin
        i = i + 1
        Select P(i) from P(i − 1)
        Recombine P(i)
        Mutate P(i)
        Evaluate P(i)
    end
end
```

Fig. 2. Pseudocode for GA

The population at time t is represented by the time-dependent variable P, with the initial population of random estimates being $P(0)$. Here, each decision variable in the parameter set is encoded as a binary string (with precision of binary representation). The initial population is generated using a random number generator that uniformly distributes numbers in the desired range. The objective function (see Eq. (16)) is used to provide a measure of how individuals have performed in the problem domain.

4. Ant colony optimization

ACO is a stochastic optimization method that mimics the social behaviour of real ants colonies, which manage to establish the shortest route to feeding sources and back. Real ants foraging for food lay down quantities of pheromone (chemical cues) marking the path that they follow. An isolated ant moves essentially at random but an ant encountering a previously laid pheromone will detect it and decide to follow it with high probability and thereby reinforce it with a further quantity of pheromone. The repetition of the above mechanism represents the auto-catalytic behavior of a real ant colony where the more the ants follow a trail, the more attractive that trail becomes. The original idea comes from observing the exploitation of food resources among ants, in which ants' individually limited cognitive abilities have collectively been able to find the shortest path between a food source and the nest.

Basics of Ant Algorithm

ACO is implemented as a team of intelligent agents which simulate the ants behavior, walking around the graph representing the problem to solve using mechanisms of cooperation and adaptation. The requirements of ACO algorithm are as follows (Bonabeau et al., 1999; Dorigo & Stutzle, 2004):

- The problem needs to be represented appropriately, which would allow the ants to incrementally update the solutions through the use of a probabilistic transition rules, based on the amount of pheromone in the trail and other problem specific knowledge.
- A problem-dependent heuristic function, that measures the quality of components that can be added to the current partial solution.
- A rule set for pheromone updating, which specifies how to modify the pheromone value.
- A probabilistic transition rule based on the value of the heuristic function and the pheromone value, that is used to iteratively construct a solution.

The structure of the ACO algorithm is shown by the pseudocode below (Figure 3).

```
Ant Colony Optimization
Initialize number of ants;
Initialize the ACO parameters;
while not end-condition do
      for k=0 to number of ants
          ant k chooses start node;
          while solution is not constructed do
                 ant k selects higher probability node;
          end while
      end for
      Update-pheromone-trails;
end while
```

Fig. 3. Pseudocode for ACO

The transition probability $p_{i,j}$, to choose the node j when the current node is i, is based on the heuristic information $\eta_{i,j}$ and the pheromone trail level $\tau_{i,j}$ of the move, where $i, j = 1, \ldots, n$.

$$p_{i,j} = \frac{\tau_{i,j}^{a}\eta_{i,j}^{b}}{\sum_{k \in Unused} \tau_{i,k}^{a}\eta_{i,k}^{b}}, \tag{8}$$

where *Unused* is the set of unused nodes of the graph.

The higher the value of the pheromone and the heuristic information, the more profitable it is to select this move and resume the search. In the beginning, the initial pheromone level is set to a small positive constant value τ_0; later, the ants update this value after completing the construction stage. ACO algorithms adopt different criteria to update the pheromone level.

The pheromone trail update rule is given by:

$$\tau_{i,j} \leftarrow \rho\tau_{i,j} + \Delta\tau_{i,j}, \tag{9}$$

where ρ models evaporation in the nature and $\Delta\tau_{i,j}$ is new added pheromone which is proportional to the quality of the solution. Thus better solutions will receive more pheromone than others and will be more desirable in a next iteration.

5. Numerical results and discussion

For parameter identification of model parameters (μ_{max}, k_S, $Y_{S/X}$) of *E. coli* fed-batch cultivation process model, GA and ACO algorithms are applied.

5.1 Application of GA for parameter optimization of *E. coli* cultivation process model

On this subsection we will describe in more details about the application of GA for parameter optimization of *E. coli* cultivation process model.

Solution Representation
The strings of artificial genetic systems are analogous to chromosomes in biological systems. The total genetic package (genotype) in artificial genetic systems is called a structure. In natural systems, the organism formed by interaction of the genotype with its environment is called the phenotype. In artificial genetic systems, the structures decode to form a particular parameter set, solution alternative, or point (in the solution space). Thus a chromosome representation is needed to describe each individual in the population of interest. The representation scheme determines how the problem is structured in the GA and also determines the genetic operators that are used. Each individual or chromosome is made up of a sequence of genes from a certain alphabet. Here applied alphabet consists of binary digits 0 and 1. Binary representation is the most common one, mainly because of its relative simplicity. A binary 20 bit representation is considered here. It has been shown that more natural representations are more efficient and produce better solutions (Chipperfield & Fleming, 1995; Goldberg, 2006; Michalewicz, 1994). The representation of the individual or chromosome for function optimization involves genes with values within the variables upper and lower bounds.

Three model parameters are represent in the chromosome - maximum specific growth rate (μ_{max}), saturation constant (k_S) and yield coefficient ($Y_{S/X}$). The following upper and lower bounds are considered (Cockshott & Bogle, 1999; Levisauskas et al., 2003):

$$0 < \mu_{max} < 0.7,$$
$$0 < k_S < 1,$$
$$0 < Y_{S/X} < 30.$$

Selection Function
The next question is how to select parents for crossover. The selection of individuals to produce successive generations plays an extremely important role in a GA. A probabilistic selection is performed based upon the individual's fitness such that the better individuals have an increased chance of being selected. An individual in the population can be selected more than once with all individuals in the population having a chance of being selected to reproduce into the next generation. There are several schemes for the selection process - roulette wheel selection and its extensions, scaling techniques, tournament, elitist models,

and ranking methods (Chipperfield & Fleming, 1995; Goldberg, 2006; MathWorks, 1999; Michalewicz, 1994). The selection method used here is the roulette wheel selection.

A common selection approach assigns a probability of selection, P_j, to each individual, j based on its fitness value. A series of N random numbers is generated and compared against the cumulative probability, $C_i = \sum_{j=1}^{i} P_j$ of the population. The appropriate individual, i, is selected and copied into the new population if $C_{i-1} < U(0,1) \leq C_i$. Various methods exist to assign probabilities to individuals: roulette wheel, linear ranking and geometric ranking. Roulette wheel, developed by Holland (Holland, 1992) is the first selection method. The probability, P_i, for each individual is defined by:

$$P[\text{ Individual } i \text{ is chosen}] = \frac{F_i}{\sum_{j=1}^{PopSize} F_j}, \tag{10}$$

where F_i equals the fitness of individual i and $PopSize$ is the population size.

The fitness function, is normally used to transform the objective function value into a measure of relative fitness. A commonly used transformation is that of proportional fitness assignment.

Genetic Operators
The genetic operators provide the basic search mechanism of the GA. The operators are used to create new solutions based on existing solutions in the population. There are two basic types of operators: crossover and mutation. The crossover takes two individuals and produces two new individuals. The crossover can be quite complicated and depends (as well as the technique of mutation) mainly on the chromosome representation used. The mutation alters one individual to produce a single new solution. By itself, mutation is a random walk through the string space. When used sparingly with reproduction and crossover, it is an insurance policy against premature loss of important notions.

Let $\overline{X}$ and $\overline{Y}$ be two m-dimensional row vectors denoting individuals (parents) from the population. For $\overline{X}$ and $\overline{Y}$ binary, the following operators are defined: binary mutation and simple crossover.

Binary mutation flips each bit in every individual in the population with probability p_m according to Eq. (11) (Houck et al., 1996):

$$x_i = \begin{cases} 1 - x_i, & \text{if } U(0,1) < p_m \\ x_i, & \text{otherwise} \end{cases}. \tag{11}$$

Simple crossover generates a random number r from a uniform distribution from 1 to m and creates two new individuals $\overline{X'}$ and $\overline{Y'}$ according to Eqs. (12) and (13) (Houck et al., 1996).

$$x'_i = \begin{cases} x_i, & \text{if } i < r \\ y_i, & \text{otherwise} \end{cases}. \tag{12}$$

$$y'_i = \begin{cases} y_i, & \text{if } i < r \\ x_i, & \text{otherwise} \end{cases}. \tag{13}$$

In proposed genetic algorithm fitness-based reinsertion (selection of offspring) is used (Pohlheim, 2003).

Initialization, Termination, and Evaluation Functions
The GA must be provided an initial population as indicated in step 3 of Figure 2. The most common method is to randomly generate solutions for the entire population. However, since GA can iteratively improve existing solutions (i.e., solutions from other heuristics and/or current practices), the beginning population can be seeded with potentially good solutions, with the remainder of the population being randomly generated solutions (Houck et al., 1996).

The GA moves from generation to generation selecting and reproducing parents until a termination criterion is met. The most frequently used stopping criterion is a specified maximum number of generations.

Evaluation functions of many forms can be used in a GA, subject to the minimal requirement that the function can map the population into a partially ordered set. As stated, the evaluation function is independent of the GA (i.e., stochastic decision rules) (Houck et al., 1996).

Genetic Parameters
Some adjustments of the genetic parameters, according to the regarded problem, have to be done to improve the optimization capability and the decision speed. Primary choice of the genetic operators and parameters depends on the problem, as well as on the chosen encoding. The inappropriate choice of operators and parameters in the evolutionary process makes the GA susceptible to premature convergence. Based on performed pre-test procedures and other results in (Roeva, 2008a;b), the GA parameters are set as follows.

There are two basic parameters of genetic algorithms - crossover probability and mutation probability. Crossover probability (xovr) should be high generally, about 65-95%, here – 75%. Mutation probability (mutr) is randomly applied with low probability – 0.01 (Obitko, 2005; Pohlheim, 2003). The rate of individuals to be selected (generation gap – ggap) should be defined as well. In proposed genetic algorithm generation gap is 0.97 (Obitko, 2005; Pohlheim, 2003).

Particularly important parameters of GA are the population size (nind) and number of generations (maxgen). If there are too low number of chromosomes, GA has a few possibilities to perform crossover and only a small part of search space is explored. On the other hand, if there are too many chromosomes, GA slows down. To solve the considered optimization problem the population size is chosen to be 100 after several algorithm performance pre-tests. In the same manner the number of generations is set at 200.

For the considered here parameter optimization, the type of the basic operators in GA is summarized in Table 1. The values of genetic algorithm parameters are listed in Table 2.

5.2 Application of ACO for parameter optimization of *E. coli* cultivation process model

On this subsection we will describe in more details about the application of ACO for parameter optimization of *E. coli* cultivation process model. First we represent the problem by graph. We need to find optimal values of three parameters which are interrelated. Therefore we represent the problem with three-partitive graph. The graph consists of three levels. Every level represents a search area of one of the parameter we optimise. Every area is discretized thus, to consists of 1000 points (nodes), which are uniformly distributed in the search interval of every of the parameters. The first level of the graph represents the parameter μ_{max}. The

Operator	Type
encoding	binary
fitness function	linear ranking
selection function	roulette wheel selection
crossover function	simple crossover
mutation function	binary mutation
reinsertion	fitness-based

Table 1. Operators of GA

Parameter	Value
ggap	0.97
xovr	0.75
mutr	0.01
nind	100
maxgen	200

Table 2. Parameters of GA

second level represents the parameter k_S. The third level represents the parameter $Y_{S/X}$. There are arcs between nodes from consecutive levels of the graph and there are no arcs between nodes from the same level. The pheromone is deposited on the arcs, which shows how good is this parameter combination.

Our ACO approach is very close to real ant behaviour. When starting to create a solution, the ants choose a node from the first level in a random way. Than for nodes from second and third level they apply probabilistic rule. The transition probability consists only of the pheromone. The heuristic information is not used. Thus the transition probability is as follows:

$$p_{i,j} = \frac{\tau_{i,j}}{\sum_{k \in Unused} \tau_{i,k}}, \tag{14}$$

The ants prefer the node with maximal probability, which is the node with maximal quantity of the pheromone on the arc, starting from the current node. If there are more than one candidate for next node, the ant choses randomly between the candidates. The process is iterative. At the end of every iteration we update the pheromone on the arcs. The quality of the solutions is represented by the value of the objective function. In our case the objective function is the mean distance between simulated data and experimental data which are the concentration of the biomass and the concentration of the substrate. We try to minimize it, therefore the new added pheromone by ant i in our case is:

$$\Delta\tau = (1-\rho)/J(i) \tag{15}$$

Where $J(i)$ is the value of the objective function according the solution constructed by ant i. Thus the arcs corresponding to solutions with less value of the objective function will receive more pheromone and will be more desirable in the next iteration.

The values of the parameters of ACO algorithms are very important, because they manage the search process. Therefore we need to find appropriate parameter settings. They are the number of ants, in ACO we can use a small number of ants between 10 and 20 without having to increase the number of iterations to achieve good solutions; initial pheromone, normally it has a small value; evaporation rate, which shows the importance of the last found solutions according to the previous ones. Parameters of the ACO were tuned based on several pre-tests according to the considered here optimization problem. After tuning procedures the main algorithm parameters are set to the optimal settings. The parameter setting for ACO is shown in Table 3.

Parameter	Value
number of ants	20
initial pheromone	0.5
evaporation	0.1

Table 3. Parameters of ACO algorithm

5.3 Objective function

To form the objective function we apply modified Hausdorff distance, which is conformable to our problem. We have two sets of points, simulated and measure data, which formed two lines. We calculated the Euclidean distance $d(t)$ between points from two lines corresponding to the same time moment t. After that we calculate the Euclidean distance from point of one of the lines in time t to the points from other line in the time interval $(t - d(t), t + d(t))$ and we take the minimal of this distances. This is the distance between two lines in time moment t. Thus we decrease the number of calculations comparing with traditional Hausdorff distance because it is obvious that the distance to the points out of the interval $(t - d(t), t + d(t))$ will be large. At the end we sum all this distances between the points and the lines. Thereby we eliminate eventual larger distance in some time moment because of not precise measurement.

When the Least Squares regression is applied as metric, the distance between two lines can be very big and in the same time it is seen that they are geometrically close to each other. This can happen especially in the steep parts of the lines. Applying Hausdorff metrics avoids this, because it measures the geometrical similarity.

Thus, the objective function is presented as a minimization of a modified Hausdorff distance measure J between experimental and model predicted values of state variables, represented by the vector $\mathbf{y}$:

$$J = \sum_{i=1}^{m} h\left(\mathbf{y}_{\exp}(i), \mathbf{y}_{\text{mod}}(i)\right)^2 \rightarrow \min \tag{16}$$

where m is the number of state variables; $\mathbf{y}_{\exp}$ – known experimental data; $\mathbf{y}_{\text{mod}}$ – model predictions with a given set of the parameters.

5.4 Numerical calculation

Computer specification to run all identification procedures are Intel Core 2 2.8 GHz, 3.5 GB Memory, Linux operating system and Matlab 7.5 environment. Matlab is a technical computing environment for high computation. Matlab integrates numerical analysis, matrix computation and graphics in an easy-to-use environment. User-defined Matlab functions are simple text files of interpreted instructions. Therefore, Matlab functions are completely portable from one hardware architecture to another without even a recompilation step.

Because of the stochastic characteristics of the applied algorithms a series of 30 runs for each algorithm is performed. For comparison of the GA and ACO the best, the worst and the

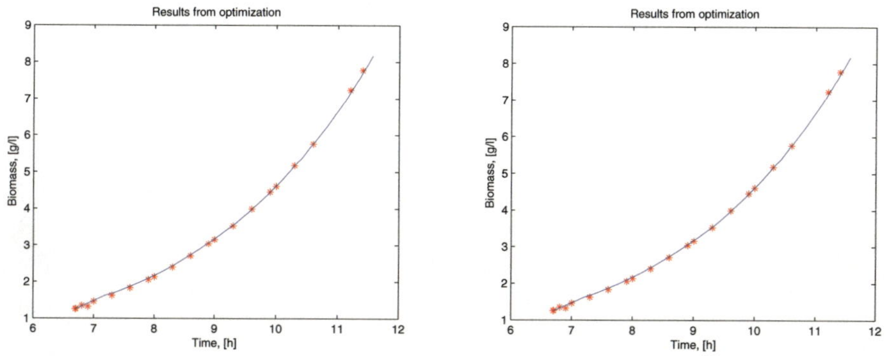

Fig. 4. Time profiles of the biomass, respectively GA and ACO

average results of the 30 runs, for the J value and execution time are watched. For realistic comparison the execution time is fixed to be 1h.

The obtained results are presented in Tables 4 and 5. Regarding the Tables 4 and 5 we observe

Parameters	Average GA	Best GA	Worst GA
μ_{max}	0.5266	0.5537	0.5253
k_S	0.0163	0.0187	0.0164
$Y_{S/X}$	2.0295	2.0318	2.0536
J	2.0699	1.7657	2.3326

Table 4. Results from parameter identification using GA

Parameters	Average ACO	Best ACO	Worst ACO
μ_{max}	0.5444	0.5283	0.5313
k_S	0.0223	0.0174	0.0209
$Y_{S/X}$	2.0256	2.0300	2.0100
J	1.8744	1.6425	2.5322

Table 5. Results from parameter identification using ACO

that the average value of the objective function achieved by ACO algorithm is better than this achieved by GA algorithm. The best value of the objective function achieved by the ACO algorithm is better than this achieved by GA algorithm, but the worst result achieved by ACO algorithm is worst than this achieved by the GA. Thus the interval where the value of the objective function varies is larger when we apply ACO algorithm than GA algorithm. But regarding the average value we can say that the most achieved values of the objective function are close to the best found value. Therefore we can conclude that the ACO algorithm performs better for this problem than GA algorithm.

The objective function is a sum of the modified Hausdorff distance between the modeled and measured data of the biomass and substrate. On Figure 4 with line are represented the values of the modelled biomass and with stars are represented the values of the measured biomass. In most cases, graphical comparisons clearly show the existence or absence of systematic deviations between model predictions and measurements. It is evident that a quantitative measure of the differences between calculated and measured values is an important criterion for the adequacy of a model. We observe that with both algorithms there is coincidence between modelled and measured data. Hence the difference between the values of the objective function achieved by different algorithms comes from the value of the substrate, achieved by them.

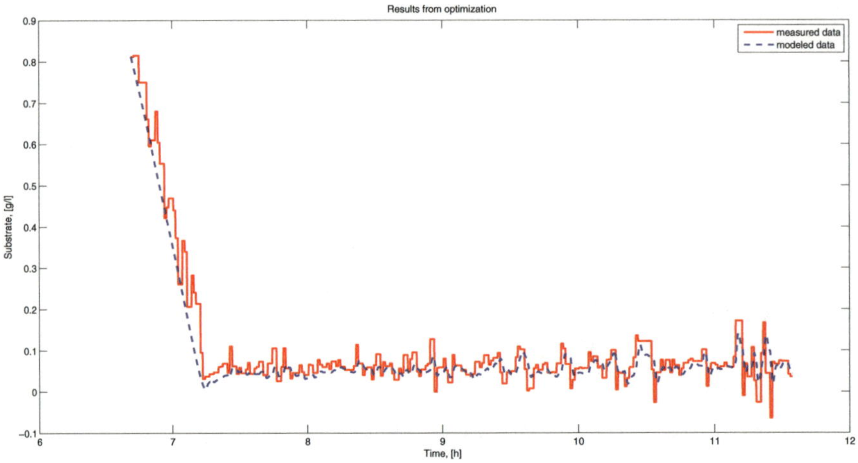

Fig. 5. Time profiles of the substrate: experimental data and models predicted data - best GA result

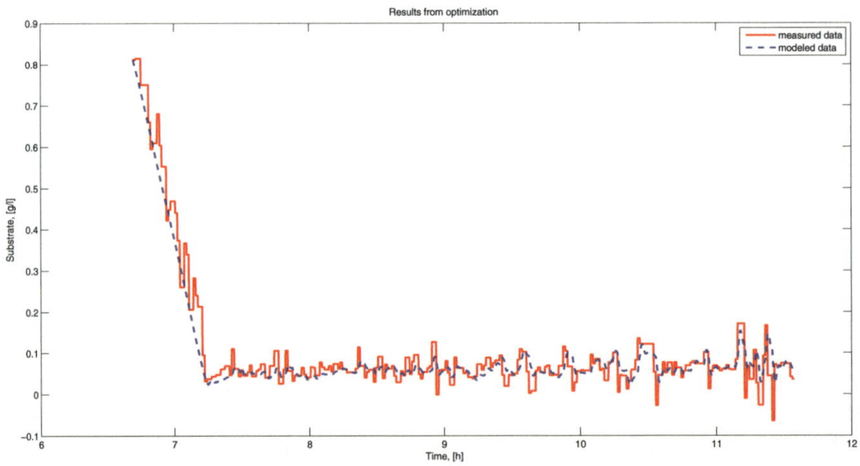

Fig. 6. Time profiles of the substrate: experimental data and models predicted data - best ACO result

On Figures 5 and 6 the modelled substrate is represented by dash line, by solid line is represented the measured substrate. We observe that the modelled data by the ACO algorithm are closer to the measured data than this by the GA algorithm.

On Figure 7 is represented the improvement of the value of the objective function during the execution time. With dash line is represented the improvement of the objective function by GA. With dash-dot line is represented the improvement of the objective function by ACO

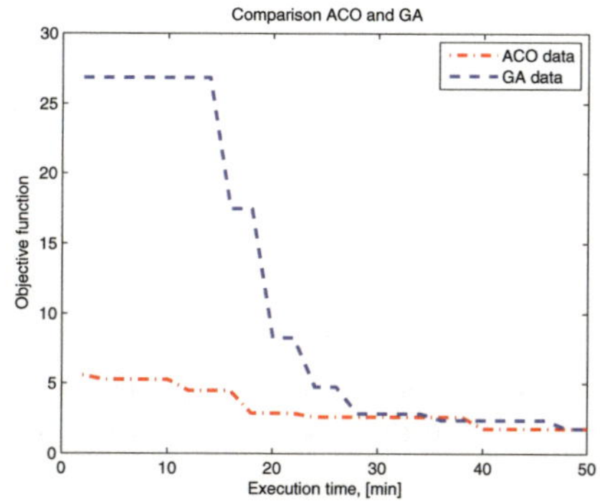

Fig. 7. Improving the objective function during the time

algorithm. The ACO algorithm achieves much better solution at the beginning, because it is constructive method. During the time the achieved values of the objective function by both algorithms become close to each other.

6. Conclusion

In this chapter GA and ACO are applied for parameter identification of a system of nonlinear differential equations modeling the fed-batch cultivation process of the bacteria *E. coli*. A system of ordinary differential equations is proposed to model *E. coli* biomass growth and substrate (glucose) utilization. Parameter optimization is performed using real experimental data set from an *E. coli* MC4110 fed-batch cultivation process. In considered nonlinear mathematical model the parameters that should be estimated are maximum specific growth rate (μ_{max}), saturation constant (k_S) and yield coefficient ($Y_{S/X}$). The parameter estimation is performed based upon the use of a modified Hausdorff metric, in place of most common used metric – Least Squares regression. Parameters of the two algorithms (GA and ACO) were tuned based on several pre-tests according considered here optimization problem. Based on the obtained result it is shown that the best value of the objective function J is achieved by the ACO algorithm. Comparison of the worst obtained results from the two metaheuristics is shown that the GA achieved better estimations than ACO. Analysing of average results it could be concluded that the ACO algorithm performs better for the problem of parameter optimization of an *E. coli* fed-batch cultivation process model.

7. Acknowledgements

This work has been partially supported by the Bulgarian National Scientific Fund under the grants High quality control of biotechnological processes with application of modified conventional and metaheuristics methods DMU 02/4 and TK-Effective Monte Carlo Methods for large-scale scientific problems DTK 02/44.

8. References

Akpinar, S. & Bayhan, G. M. (2011). A Hybrid Genetic Aalgorithm for Mixed Model Assembly Line Balancing Problem with Parallel Workstations and Zoning Constraints. *Engineering Applications of Artificial Intelligence*, Vol. 24, No. 3, pp. 449–457.

Al-Duwaish, H. N. (2000). A Genetic Approach to the Identification of Linear Dynamical Systems with Static Nonlinearities. *International Journal of Systems Science*, Vol. 31, No. 3, pp. 307–313.

Arndt, M. & Hitzmann, B. (2001). Feed Forward/feedback Control of Glucose Concentration during Cultivation of *Escherichia coli. 8th IFAC Int. Conf. on Comp. Appl. in Biotechn*, Canada, pp. 425–429.

Bastin, G. & Dochain, D. (1991). *On-line Estimation and Adaptive Control of Bioreactors*. Els. Sc. Publ.

Benjamin, K. K.; Ammanuel, A. N.; David, A. & Benjamin, Y. K. (2008). Genetic Algorithm using for a Batch Fermentation Process Identification. *J of Applied Sciences*, Vol. 8, No. 12, pp. 2272–2278.

Bonabeau, E.; Dorigo, M. & Theraulaz, G. (1999). *Swarm Intelligence: From Natural to Artificial Systems*, New York,Oxford University Press.

Brownlee, J. (2011). *Clever Algorithms. Nature-Inspired Programming Recipes*. LuLu, p. 436, 978-1-4467-8506-5.

Carrillo-Ureta, G. E.; Roberts, P. D. & Becerra, V. M. (2001). Genetic Algorithms for Optimal Control of Beer Fermentation. In: *Proc. of the 2001 IEEE International Symposium on Intelligent Control*, Mexico City, Mexico, pp. 391–396.

Chen, Sh. & Lovell, B. C. (2010). Feature space Hausdorff distance for face recognition. In: *Proc. of 20th International Conference on Pattern Recognition (ICPR)*, Istanbul, Turkey, pp. 1465–1468.

Chipperfield, A. J. & Fleming, P. J. (1995). The Matlab Genetic Algorithm Toolbox. *IEE Colloquium Applied Control Techniques Using MATLAB*, pp. 10/1–10/4.

Cockshott, A. R. & Bogle, I. D. L. (1999). Modelling the effects of glucose feeding on a recombinant *E. coli* fermentation. *Bioprocess Engineering*, Vol. 20, pp. 83–90.

Covert, M. W.; Xiao, N.; Chen, T. J. & Karr J. R. (2008). Integrating Metabolic, Transcriptional Regulatory, and Signal Transduction Models in *Escherichia coli. Bioinformatics*, Vol. 24, No. 18, pp. 2044–2050.

da Silva, M. F. J.; Perez, J. M. S.; Pulido, J. A. G. & Rodriguez, M. A. V. (2010). AlineaGA - A Genetic Algorithm with Local Search Optimization for Multiple Sequence Alignment. *Appl Intell*, Vol. 32, pp. 164–172.

Dorigo, M. & Di Caro, G. (1999). The Ant Colony Optimization Meta-heuristic. *In: Corne, D, Dorigo, M., Glover, F. (eds).: New Idea in Optimization*, McGrow-Hill, pp. 11–32.

Dorigo, M. & Stutzle, T. (2004). *Ant Colony Optimization*, MIT Press.

Fidanova, S. (2002). Ant Colony Optimization: Additional reinforcement and convergence. *Tech. report IRIDIA-2002-30*, Free university of Bruxelles, Belgium, 12.

Fidanova, S. & Lirkov, I. (2009). 3D Protein Structure Prediction. *J. Analele Universitatii de Vest Timisoara, Seria Matematica-Informatica*, Vol XLVII(2),ISSN 1224-970X, pp. 33–46.

Fidanova, S. (2010). An Improvement of the Grid-based Hydrophobic-hydrophilic Model. *Int. J. Bioautomation*, ISSN 1312-451X, Vol. 14, No. 2, pp. 147–156.

Fidanova, S.; Alba E. & Molina, G. (2010). Hybrid ACO Algorithm for the GPS Surveying Problem, *Large Scale Scientfic Computing*, Springer, Berlin, Vol. 5910, pp. 318–325.

Goldberg, D. E. (2006). *Genetic Algorithms in Search, Optimization and Machine Learning*. Addison Wesley Longman, London.

Holland, J. H. (1992). *Adaptation in Natural and Artificial Systems*. 2nd Edn. Cambridge, MIT Press.

Houck, Ch. R.; Joines, J. A. & Kay, M. G. (1996). A Genetic Algorithm for Function Optimization: A Matlab Implementation, *Genetic Algorithm Toolbox Toutorial*, available at: http://read.pudn.com/downloads152/ebook/662702/gaotv5.pdf

Jiang, L.; Ouyang, Q. & Tu, Y. (2010). Quantitative Modeling of *Escherichia coli* Chemotactic Motion in Environments Varying in Space and Time. *PLoS Comput Biol*, Vol. 6, No. 4, e1000735. doi:10.1371/journal.pcbi.1000735.

Karelina, T. A.; Ma, H.; Goryanin, I. & Demin, O. V. (2011). EI of the Phosphotransferase System of *Escherichia coli*: Mathematical Modeling Approach to Analysis of Its Kinetic Properties. *Journal of Biophysics*, Vol. 2011, Article ID 579402, doi:10.1155/2011/579402.

Kirkpatrick, S.; Gelatt, C. D. & Vecchi, M. P. (1983). Optimization by Simulated Annealing, *Science, New Series*, Vol. 220, No. 4598, pp. 671–680.

Kumar, S. M.; Giriraj, R.; Jain, N.; Anantharaman, V.; Dharmalingam, K. M. M. & Sheriffa, B. (2008). Genetic algorithm based PID controller tuning for a model bioreactor. *Indian Chemical Engineer*, Vol. 50, No. 3, pp. 214–226.

Lagarias, J. C.; Reeds, J. A.; Wright, M. H. & Wright, P. E. (1998). Convergence Properties of the Nelder-Mead Simplex Method in Low Dimensions, *SIAM Journal of Optimization*, Vol. 9, No. 1, pp. 112–147.

Levisauskas, D.; Galvanauskas, V.; Henrich, S.; Wilhelm, K.; Volk, N. & Lubbert, A. (2003). Model-based Optimization of Viral Capsid Protein Production in Fed-batch Culture of recombinant *Escherichia coli*. *Bioprocess and Biosystems Engineering*, Vol. 25, pp. 255–262.

MathWorks Inc. (1999). *Genetic Algorithms Toolbox, User's Guide.*

Michalewicz, Z. (1994). *Genetic Algorithms + Data Structures = Evolution Programs.* Second, Exended Edition, Springer-Verlag, Berlin, Heidelberg.

Nutanong, S.; Jacox, E. H. & Samet, H. (2011) An Incremental Hausdorff Distance Calculation Algorithm. In: *Proc. of the VLDB Endowment*, Vol. 4, No. 8, pp. 506–517.

Obitko, M. (2005). *Genetic Algorithms*, available at http://cs.felk.cvut.cz/~ xobitko/ga

Opalka, N.; Brown, J.; Lane, W. J.; Twist, K.-A. F.; Landick, R.; Asturias, F. J. & Darst, S. A. (2010). Complete Structural Model of *Escherichia coli* RNA Polymerase from a Hybrid Approach. *PLoS Biol*, Vol. 8, No. 9, e1000483. doi:10.1371/journal.pbio.1000483.

Paplinski, J. P. (2010). The Genetic Algorithm with Simplex Crossover for Identification of Time Delays. *Intelligent Information Systems*, pp. 337–346.

Parker, B. S. (1992). *Demonstration of using Genetic Algorithm Learning*. Information Systems Teaching Laboratory.

Petersen, C. M.; Rifai, H. S.; Villarreal, G. C. & Stein, R. (2011). Modeling *Escherichia coli* and Its Sources in an Urban Bayou with Hydrologic Simulation Program – FORTRAN, *Journal of Environmental Engineering*. Vol. 137, No. 6, pp. 487–503.

Pohlheim, H. (2003). Genetic and Evolutionary Algorithms: Principles, Methods and Algorithms. *Genetic and Evolutionary Toolbox*, http://www.geattb.com/docu/algindex.html.

Press, W. H.; Flannery, B. P.; Teukolsky, S. A. & Vetterling, W. T. (1986). *Numerical Recipes - The Art of Scientific Computing*, Cambridge University Press.

Ranganath, M.; Renganathan, S. & Gokulnath, C. (1999). Identification of Bioprocesses using Genetic Algorithm. *Bioprocess Engineering*, Vol. 21, pp. 123–127.

Roeva, O. & Ts. Slavov (2011). Fed-batch Cultivation Control based on Genetic Algorithm PID Controller Tuning, *Lecture Notes on Computer Science*, Springer-Verlag Berlin Heidelberg, Vol. 6046, pp. 289–296.

Roeva, O. (2006). A Modified Genetic Algorithm for a Parameter Identification of Fermentation Processes. *Biotechnology and Biotechnological Equipment*, Vol. 20, No. 1, pp. 202–209.

Roeva, O. (2007). Multipopulation genetic algorithm: A tool for parameter optimization of cultivation processes models. *Lecture Notes on Computer Science*, Springer-Verlag Berlin Heidelberg, Vol. 4310, pp. 255–262.

Roeva, O. (2008a). Improvement of Genetic Algorithm Performance for Identification of Cultivation Process Models. *Advances Topics on Evolutionary Computing, Book Series: Artificial Intelligence Series-WSEAS*, pp. 34–39.

Roeva, O. (2008b). Parameter Estimation of a Monod-type Model based on Genetic Algorithms and Sensitivity Analysis. *Lecture Notes on Computer Science*, Springer-Verlag Berlin Heidelberg, Vol. 4818, pp. 601–608.

Roeva, O.; Pencheva, T.; Hitzmann, B. & Tzonkov, St. (2004). A Genetic Algorithms Based Approach for Identification of *Escherichia coli* Fed-batch Fermentation. *Int. J. Bioautomation*, Vol. 1, pp. 30–41.

Rote, G. (1991). Computing the minimum Hausdorff distance between two point sets on a line under translation. *Information Processing Letters*, Vol. 38, pp. 123–127.

Schuegerl, K. & Bellgardt, K.-H. (2000). *Bioreaction Engineering: Modeling and Control*. Berlin Heidelberg, Springer-Verlag.

Shmygelska, A.& Hoos, H. H. (2005). An ant colony optimization algorithm for the 2D and 3D hydrophobic polar protein folding problem. *BMC Bioinformatics*, Vol. 6, No. 30, doi:10.1186/1471-2105-6-30.

Skandamis, P. N. & Nychas, G. E. (2000). Development and Evaluation of a Model Predicting the Survival of *Escherichia coli* O157:H7 NCTC 12900 in Homemade Eggplant Salad at Various Temperatures, pHs, and Oregano Essential Oil Concentrations. *Applied and Environmental Microbiology*, Vol. 66, No. 4, pp. 1646–1653.

Sugiyama, M.; Hirowatari, E.; Tsuiki, H. & Yamamoto, A. (2010). Learning figures with the hausdorff metric by fractals. In: *Proc. of the 21st international conference on Algorithmic learning theory*, Springer-Verlag Berlin, Heidelberg, pp. 315–329.

Syam, W. P. & Al-Harkan, I. M. (2010). Comparison of Three Meta Heuristics to Optimize Hybrid Flow Shop Scheduling Problem with Parallel Machines. *World Academy of Science, Engineering and Technology*, Vol. 62, pp. 271–278.

Tahouni, N.; Smith, R. & Panjeshahi, M. H. (2010). Comparison of Stochastic Methods with Respect to Performance and Reliability of Low-temperature Gas Separation Processes. *The Canadian Journal of Chemical Engineering*, Vol. 88, No. 2, pp. 256–267.

Umarani, R. & Selvi, V. (2010). Particle Swarm Optimization: Evolution, Overview and Applications. *Int J of Engineering Science and Technology*, Vol. 2, No. 7, pp. 2802–2806.

Viesturs, U.; Karklina, D. & Ciprovica, I. (2004). *Bioprocess and Bioengineering*. Jeglava.

Yedjour, H.; Meftah, B.; Yedjour, D. & Benyettou, A. (2011). Combining Spiking Neural Network with Hausdorff Distance Matching for Object Tracking. *Asian Journal of Applied Sciences*, Vol. 4, pp. 63–71.

Yusof, M.K. & Stapa, M.A. (2010). Achieving of Tabu Search Algorithm for Scheduling Technique in Grid Computing using GridSim Simulation Tool: Multiple Jobs on Limited Resource. *Int J of Grid and Distributed Computing*, Vol. 3, No. 4, pp. 19–31.

14

Multi-Objective Genetic Algorithm to Automatically Estimating the Input Parameters of Formant-Based Speech Synthesizers

Fabíola Araújo, Jonathas Trindade, José Borges,
Aldebaro Klautau and Igor Couto
Federal University of Pará (UFPA)
Signal Processing Laboratory (LaPS)
Belém – PA
Brazil

1. Introduction

The Klatt synthesizer is considered one of the most important formant synthesis. Therefore, this chapter addresses the problem of automatic estimation of Klatt's synthesizer parameters in order to perform the imitation of voice (*utterance copy*), that is finding the parameters that causes the synthesizer to generate a voice that sounds close enough to the natural voice, so that the human ear does not notice the difference. Preliminary experimental results of a framework based on evolutionary computing, more specifically, in a kind of genetic algorithm (GA) called Multi-Objective Genetic Algorithms (MOGA), are presented. The task can be cast as a hard inverse problem, because it is not a simple task to extract the desired parameters automatically (Ding et al., 1997). Because of that, in spite of recent efforts (Breidegard & Balkenius, 2003; Heid & Hawkins, 1998), most studies using parametric synthesizers adopt a relatively time-consuming process (Klatt & Klatt, 1990) for utterance copy and end up using short speech segments (words or short sentences). GA was chosen to peform this task because they are known for their simplicity and elegance as robust search algorithms, as well as for their ability to find high-quality solutions quickly for difficult high-dimensional problems where traditional optimization methods may fail.

This chapter presents the application of GA to speech synthesis to solve the process of *utterance copy* (Borges et al., 2008). With this framework, we use several objective (fitness) functions and three possible ways of operating: *Interframe*, *Intraframe* and/or *knowledge-based* architectures with adaptive control of probabilities distribution and stopping criteria according to the convergence and number of generations. We also intend to fill a gap on the number of research efforts on developing automatic tools for dealing with formant synthesizers and help researchers to compare the performance of their solutions. The possibility of automatic analyzing speech corpora is very important to increase the knowledge about phonetic and phonological aspects of specific dialects, endangered language, spontaneous speech, etc. The next paragraphs provide a brief overview of the Klatt's speech synthesizer, the optimization problem and the approach using MOGA to solve this.

2. Speech synthesis

The voice synthesis consists on producing the human voice artificially, using the automatic generation of voice signal. Aspects as the naturalness or the intelligibility are considered when you evaluate the quality of the synthesized voice. Many researches on voice synthesis have been developed for decades and some headway has been achieved, nevertheless the quality of the terms about the naturalness of the voice produced still presents gaps, principally regarding the adaptations that the speaking can suffer considering the intonation and the emotiveness associated to the expressiveness of the content to be synthesized.

The efforts on producing the voice artificially started around the year of 1779 when the Russian professor Christian Kratzenstein, made an acoustic resonator similar to the vocal tract, where it was possible to produce the vowel sounds. At a later time, in 1791, Wolfgang von Kempelen created a machine where it was possible to produce simple sounds or combiners, and the difference was that the machine had a pressure chamber simulating the lungs, a kind of vibrating shaft that worked like the human vocal cords and a leather tube representing the vocal tract, allowing the emission of vowel and consonant sounds through the emission of its components. In 1800, Charles Wheatstones rebuild a new version of the Kempelen machine which possessed a more sophisticated mechanism and allowed the production of the vowels and great part of the consonants, including the nasal ones.

The researches continued, but with the objective of constructing electric synthesizers. In 1922, Stewart build a synthesizer composed by source that imitated the functionality of the lungs (excitation) and of the resonant circuits that molds the acoustic resonators of the vocal tract. With this machine it was possible the unique static generation of the vowel sounds with two formants. The first device considered a electric synthesizer was the VODER (*Voice Operating Demonstrator*) developed by Homer Dudley in 1939. It was composed by a bar to select the kind of voice (voiced or voiceless) a pedal to control the fundamental frequency and ten keys that controlled the artificial vocal tract. The basic structure of the VODER is very similar to the systems used on the model source-filter. Currently, the technology involving the voice synthesizers evolves and among these the synthesis that stand out are: by concatenation, articulatory, by formants (rules) and most recently based on Hidden Markov Models (HMM).

The speech synthesizer is the back-end of text-to-speech (TTS) systems (Allen et al., 1987). Synthesizers are also useful in speech analysis, such as in experiments about perception and production. Formant-based (Lalwani & Childers, 1991) is a parametric synthesis very eminent in many speech studies, especially linguistics, because most parameters of a formant synthesizer are closely related to physical parameters and have a high degree of interpretability, essential in studies of the acoustic correlates of voice quality, like male/female voice conversion and simulation of breathiness, roughness, and vocal fry.

3. Formant-based and Klatt's speech synthesizer

The techniques for voice synthesis can be divided in three classes: direct synthesis, the synthesis through the simulation of the vocal tract and the synthesis utilizing a model for the voice production (Styger & Keller, 1994). In the direct synthesis, the signal is generated through the direct manipulation of the waveforms. An example of this kind is the concatenative synthesis in which the sound units, like phonemes, are previously recorded and to produce a new sound, these recorded units are concatenated to compose words and sentences. This way, in this category there is no necessity of knowing the mechanisms of voice production. The synthesis through the simulation of the vocal tract has the objective of producing the voice through the simulation of the physical behavior of the organs responsible for the production of the speech. The articulatory synthesis is an example of this category.

The synthesis based on a model for voice production consists on method that utilize the source-filter model (Lemmetty, 1999) which allows the modeling of the vocal tract through a linear filter, with a set of resonators that vary in time. The filter therefore is excited through a source, simulating the vibration of the vocal cords for voiced sounds or the comprehension of the vocal tract in the case of a noise. This way the sound is created in the vocal tract and irradiated through the lips. The synthesis by formants, or based on rules, is one of the most prominent techniques of this category, which is fundamented in a set of rules used to determine the necessary parameters to synthesize the speech through a synthesizer. In this synthesis there are two possible structures for a set of resonators: cascade or parallel, since the combination of the two architectures can be used for a better performance. Among the necessary parameters for the synthesizes based on rules, the fundamental frequency ($F0$), the excitation parameter (OQ), the excitation degree of the voice (VO), the frequency and amplification of the formants ($F1...F3$ e $A1...A3$), the frequency of an additional low frequency resonator (FN), the intensity of the low and high regions (ALF, AHF) stand out, among others.

The Klatt's synthesizer (Klatt & Klatt, 1990) is called a formant synthesizer because some of its most important parameters are the formant frequencies: the resonance frequencies of the vocal tract. Basically, the Klatt works as follows: for each frame (its duration is set by the user, often in the range from 5 to 10 milliseconds), a new set of parameters drives the synthesizer. The initial version of the Klatt was codified in FORTRAN and presented good results on simulations for the production of a variety o sounds generated by the human speech mechanism through the correct furnish of parameters of the source control and resonators. Other versions of this synthesizer were developed, and the KLSYN88 was chosen for this chapter, implemented on C language. The choice was made because its source code was donated to the Signal Processing Laboratory (LaPS - *Laboratório de Processamento de Sinais*) from UFPA by the Sensimetrics Enterprise (*http://http://www.sens.com/*, Visited on March, 2010.). Among the main differences between the KLSYN and the KLSYN88, the number of parameters stands out, because the KLSYN88 has 48 parameters. For a complete description of parameters of Klatt's speech synthesizer, the reader is referred to (Klatt & Klatt, 1990). In the latest versions of Klatt's, six parameters are not used anymore - they all are assumed to be zero, reducing our state space to 42 parameters. The problem to solve is: given an utterance to be synthesized, find for each frame a sensible set of parameters to drive the synthesizer. The number of parameters and their dynamic range make an exhaustive search unfeasible. GA was adopted as the main learning strategy.

4. Genetic algorithm

The GAs are mathematics algorithms from the Computational Intelligence area specifically the Evolutionary Computation (EC), where it searches Nature inspired techniques, the development of intelligent systems that imitates aspects from the human behavior, such as: evolution and adaptation. These possess a search technique and optimization based on the probability, inspired by the Darwinian principle of the evolution of the species, and on genetics where it utilizes the natural selection and the genetic reproduction through the evolutionary operators of selection, crossover and mutation. This way, the most able individuals will have the chance of a longer longevity with higher probability of reproduction, perpetuating the genetic codes for the next generations.

Considering a problem in the GA process, this should be modeled through a mathematical function where the most apt individuals will have a greater or lower result, depending if the object is to maximize or minimize the function. In a population a lot of individuals can exist and each one of them corresponds to a possible solution of the mathematical function. If the function has three variables, for example, each one is represented by a chromosome and their concatenation composes an individual. A chromosome is composed by various characters (genes), each one of them are in a determined position (locus), with its determined value (allele).

The populations are evaluated periodically and it is verified in each one of them which individuals are more able, and these are selected for the crossover. After the crossover, each gene that composes the chromosome can suffer mutation. Following this phase of mutation, a new evaluation of the individuals is made and the ones with greater degree of fitness, that is the ones with the greatest value of the fitness function (performance function), will guarantee the survival for the next population. The genetic operators tend to generate solutions with greater values for the fitness function in which new generations are achieved. This way, the evolutive cycles are repeated until the stop criterion is achieved, it may be: the maximum number of generations, the optimization of the process of convergence or loss of the populational diversity with too similar individuals (do Couto & Borges, 2008).

In addition to the fitness function utilized to measure how much a particular solution will satisfy a condition, the GAs also need another objective function which is the optimization object, it can have a set of restrictions to the values of the variables that compose it. These two functions can be considered identical in optimization numerical problems (Coello et al., 2007).

The GAs present good results, when applied on complex problems that are characterized by:

- Having various parameters that need to be combined in search of the best solution;
- Problems with too many restrictions or conditions that cannot be modeled mathematically;
- Problems with a large search space.

On problems that the optimization with one objective is involved (mono-objective), the GA will try to find an optimal global solution that can be minimum or maximum. In this case, the solution minimize or maximize a function $f(x)$ where x is a vector of decision variables of dimension n, represented by $x = (x_1, ..., x_n)$ belonging to a Ω universe (Coello et al., 2007).

In optimizations with more than one objective function (multi-objective), the task will be the search of one or more optimal solutions, being that none of these can be said to be better than the others considering all of the objectives, because some solutions can bring conflicting scenarios.

5. Multi-objective Optimization Problem

An optimization problem is multi-objective (MOOP - Multi-objective Optimization Problem) when it has various functions that should be maximized and/or minimized simultaneously, obeying a determined numbers of restrictions that any viable solution should obey. An MOOP problem can be characterized by the Equation 1 (Deb, 2001).

$$\left.\begin{array}{lll} \text{Maximize/Minimize} & f_m(x), & m = 1,2,...,M; \\ \text{subject to} & g_j(x) \geq 0 & j = 1,2,...,J; \\ & h_k(x) = 0, & k = 1,2,...,K; \\ & x_i^{(L)} \leq x_i \leq x_i^{(U)}, & i = 1,2,...,n. \end{array}\right\} \quad (1)$$

where x is a vector of n variables of decision $x = (x_1, x_2, ..., x_n)^T$ that consist on a quantity of values to be chosen during the optimization problem. The limit restriction of the variables (x_i) restricts each variable of decision between the limit below $x_i^{(L)}$ and over $x_i^{(U)}$.These limits represent the space values of the variables of decision, or simply the space of decision. The terms $g_j(x)$ e $h_k(x)$ are functions of restriction and a solution x that can not satisfy all of the restrictions and the $2n$ limits will be considered a non factible solution. Otherwise, it is considered a factible solution. The set of all the possible solutions is denominated viable region, search space or simply S. The objective functions $f_1(x)$, $f_2(x)$, ..., $f_M(x)$, together, are the optimization object and can be maximized or minimized. In some cases a conversion of a maximization problem into a minimization problem may be necessary to avoid some conflicting situations.

Differently from a mono-objective problem in which only a function is optimized, and therefore, a single factible solution, on multi-objective problems there is not only one solution, but a set of them, because it is considered that there is not a single solution that satisfies the objective functions simultaneously, and that some solutions are better only on some objectives, and on others not. Even so, the set of solutions needs to be defined and for this the Optimality of Pareto Theory is used.

6. Dominance and optimal Pareto solutions

The terminology of Pareto establish that a vector of variables is considered optimum (x^*), if a non factible vector x exists in which the degradation of a criterion (value of the objective function) do not cause an improvement on at least another criterion, assuming in this case a minimization problem as example. Therefore, there are no solutions better than the others in all criterions but factible solutions (admissible) that sometimes will be better in some criterions, and sometimes they will not.

The multi-objectives optimization algorithms are based on the domination concept and on its searches, in which two solutions are compared to verify if a relationship of dominance is established one over the other. Considering a problem with M objective functions, where $M > 1$, the solution $x^{(1)}$ dominates the other solution $x^{(2)}$ if the two following conditions are met (Deb, 2001):

1. The solution $x^{(1)}$ is not worse than $x^{(2)}$ in all of the objectives, or $f_i(x^{(1)})$ **not** $\prec f_i(x^{(1)})$ for all $j = 1,2,...,M$ objectives;
2. The solution $x^{(1)}$ is narrowly better than $x^{(2)}$ in at least one objective, or $f_j(x^1) \succ f_i(x^{(2)})$ to at least one $j \in 1,2,...,M$.

where it is considered that the operator $\prec$ denotes the worst and the operator $\succ$ denotes the better. If any of these conditions above is violated, the solution $x^{(1)}$ do not dominates the solution $x^{(2)}$. If $x^{(1)}$ dominates $x^{(2)}$ ($x^{(1)} \succ x^{(2)}$) it is possible to affirm that:

- $x^{(2)}$ is dominated by $x^{(1)}$;
- $x^{(1)}$ is not dominated by $x^{(2)}$;
- $x^{(1)}$ is not worse than $x^{(2)}$.

From this analysis considering the concept of optimality mentioned previously, a set denominated optimal solutions of Pareto is made. These solutions are considered as admissible or efficient, being their set represented by $\bar{P}^*$. The correspondent vectors to these solutions are denominated non-dominated. The aggregation of various non-dominated vectors composes the Pareto front (Coello et al., 2007).

The concept of dominance can be applied to define sets of optimal local and global solutions. The optimal local set of Pareto is defined when, for each x element belonging to the $\bar{P}$ set, an y solution does not exist on its neighborhood to dominate another element of the $\bar{P}$ set characterizing the belonging solutions to $\bar{P}$ with a optimal local set of Pareto. If a solution does not exist in the research space that dominates any other member in the set $\bar{P}$ constitutes an optimal global set of Pareto.

In the presence of multiple optimal solutions of Pareto, it is hard to choose a single solution with no additional information about the problem. Because of that, it is important to find as many optimal solutions of Pareto as possible, obeying the following objectives:

1. Guide the search as close as possible to the global optimal region of Pareto and;
2. Keep the populational diversity in Pareto optimal front.

7. Non-Dominated Sorting Genetic Algorithm II

The NSGA-II (*Non-Dominated Sorting Genetic Algorithm II*) is a Multi-Objective Evolutionary Algorithm (MOEA) based on the *a posteriori* technique of search with emphasis in the search for diverse solutions with the goal to generate different elements in the optimal set of Pareto. The process of decision by a solution is made after (*a posteriori*) the realization of complete search by optimal solutions.

This method was proposed in (Deb et al., 2000) as a modification of the original algorithm mentioned in (Srinivas & Deb, 1994). The main characteristics are the elitism, the ranking attribution and the crowding distance. The elitism is used as a mechanism for the preservation and usability of the best solutions found previously on posterior generations. Through the ranking, the algorithm is achieves the ordering of the non-dominated solutions of the population. The crowding distance uses an operator of selection by tournament to preserve the diversity between the non-dominated solutions in the posterior execution stages to obtain a good spread of the solutions.

In the NSGA-II, the population Q_t is created from the parent population P_t, where both have N individuals and are combined to form together the population R_t, size $2N$. After this junction, it is performed an ordering of the best solutions to classify all the population R_t. Even though it requires a greater computational effort, the algorithm allows the checking of a non global domination between the populations P_t and Q_t. With the ending of the ordering of the non-dominated solutions, the new set P_t is created and filled by solutions with different non-dominated fronts $(F_1, F_2, ..., F_n)$. The filling starts with the best non-dominated solution from the first front, following the subsequent ones. As only N solutions can be inserted in the new population, the rest of the solutions is simply cast-off. Each F_i set must be inserted in its totality in the new population, and when $|P_{t+1}| + |F_i| > N$ the algorithm introduces a method called crowding distance, where the most disperse solutions are preferred from the F_i set and the other ones are cast-off. The daughter population Q_{t+1} is created from P_{t+1} using the operators of selection by tournament, crossover and mutation. The Figure 1 shows a sequence of the process of the NSGA-II.

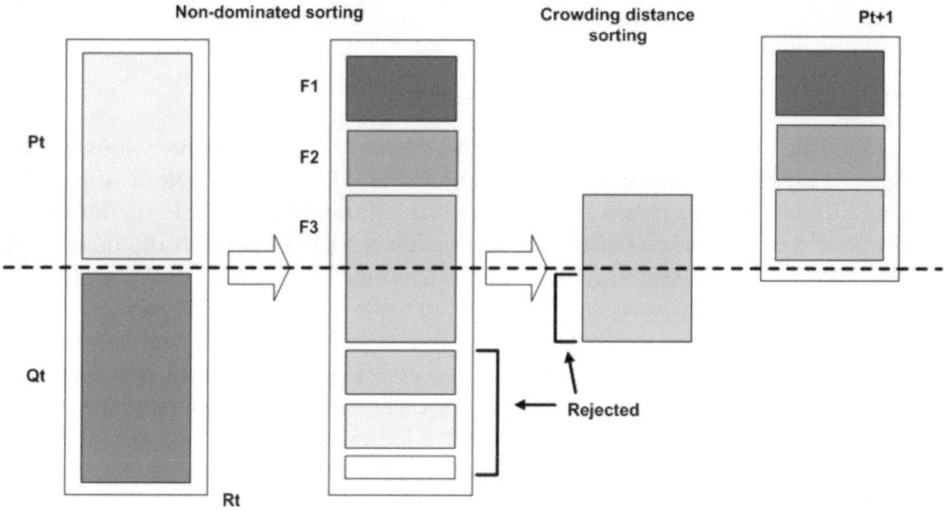

Fig. 1. Diagram that shows the way in which the NSGA-II works - Adapted from (Coello et al., 2007).

To verify the crowding distance, first is calculated the average distance of the two points, both sides of these points, considering all of the objectives. The quantity d_i serves as a estimation of the size of the biggest cuboid that includes the i point without the inclusion of any other point of the population, being called crowding distance. In the Figure 2, the distance from the i-th solution in its Pareto front (filled points) is the average lateral length from the cuboid drew by the dashed lines.

The operator that do the crowding comparison incorporate a modification in the selection method by tournament that considers the crowding of the solution (crowded tournament selection operator). So, the solution i is considered a winner in the tournament by a solution j, if it obeys the following restrictions:

1. The i has the best rank of non-dominance in the population;
2. If both solutions are in the same level, but i has a distance bigger than j $(d_i > d_j)$;

Considering two solutions in different levels of non-dominance, the chosen points are the ones with lower level. If both points belong to the same front, then it is chosen localized points in a region with a less number of points, so, solutions with bigger crowding distances.

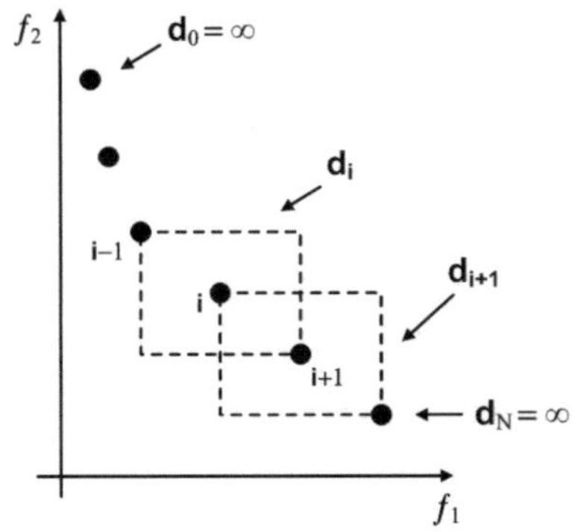

Fig. 2. A graphical illustration of crowding distance.

8. Automatically learning the input parameters

The present chapter has the objective of resolving the issue to estimate the values of the input parameters of a formant synthesizer, as the Klatt for example, aiming to mimicking the human voice. This problem is considered difficult since the parameters specific the temporization of the source and the dynamic values for all the filters. Depending on the quantity of the parameters involved in a possibility of possible combinations can be to big and not viable of being made manually because each parameter has a vast interval of reasonable values. According to Figure 3, it is necessary to estimate initial values for the input parameters of the synthesizer, submitting to the synthesis and then evaluate the synthesized voice through a comparison mechanism with target voice. After the verification, the values of the parameters must be adjusted, that is, new re-estimated values are given as input bringing the synthesis of the voice and a posterior comparison, until the generated voice is as close as possible from the target.

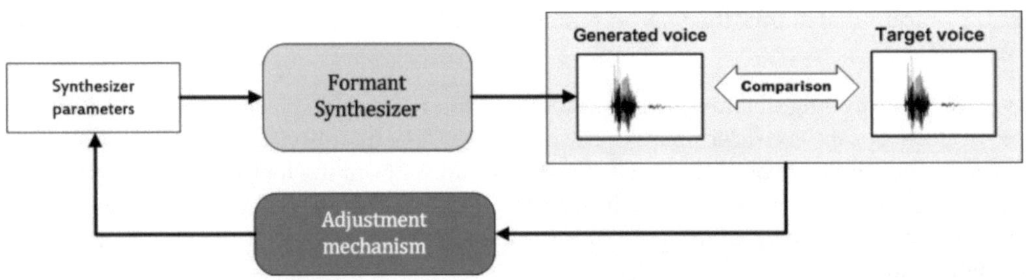

Fig. 3. General problem description.

The Klatt synthesizer is the most utilized among the synthesizers by formants, that is why it was chosen as object of this chapter. Besides that, even not being the focus of this study, the Klatt can be used in TTS systems because it requires low computational cost to produce the voice in high degree of intelligibility, but generally it is hard to reproduce the exact voice signal sound emitted by a human speaker (de Oliveira Imbiriba, 2008).

However, another problem appears in consequence of the option of the formant synthesis that consist in extracting the values of the Klatt's parameters from a voice. These parameters can be generated through the TTS systems, as the Dectalk (Hallahan, 1995), but specifically, to a single speaker. Some tools and techniques that utilize the signal processing appeared to try to extract them of voice and not having them from text files, but the results were not satisfied.

Considering the complexity of the problem, the proposal is to utilize this type of model to estimate automatically the parameters of a formant synthesizer, developing mechanisms of comparison from voices (synthesized and target) e of adjustments of the re-estimated parameters, attaching this methodology to a technique of extraction of the parameters from the voice in which minimizes the degradation of the synthesized voice.

9. GASpeech framework

With the objective of automatizing the imitation of the natural voice (utterance copy), it was developed in LaPS a methodology that uses MOGA. The methodology called *GASpeech* was adapted from NSGA-II algorithm (Deb et al., 2000) and utilizes three architectures, described later.

As illustrated in Figure 4, the *GASpeech* starts with the input text file and as exit there is the synthesized voice. The rectangles represent programs or scripts and the rounded rectangles correspond to files. First, the text files are submitted to *Dectalk* (Bickley & Bruckert, 2002) where it is a TTS system produced by Fonix Corporation. The generated voices by it possess high intelligibility, but are configured to a single male announcer (Paul). A demo version of this TTS was provided to LaPS for academical purposes. The *Dectalk* generate an exit achieve having 18 parameters in which they are mapped to the 13 parameters of the input file from *HLSyn* through the script *DEC2HLSyn*. The *HLSyn* is utilized to generate the input file of the Klatt synthesizer (version KLSYN88), having the 48 necessary parameters to the voice synthesization. But, of the 48 parameters only 42 are utilized because in this chapter the parallel resonators bank is not considered because of its values being always zero.

In possess of the files having the target voice and the corresponding values from Klatt's parameters, the simulation starts in the *GASpeech*. The population is initialized randomically and each individual is a vector composed by 42 parameters according to the motives exposed previously. The initial population is evaluated taking in consideration the objective functions that can be: spectral distortion (SD), mean squared error (MSE) and cross correlation (CC). After the evaluation, a rank is assigned to each individual. Individuals with best ranks are selected to suffer crossover and mutation. As result, a new population is generated and this one will take all the evaluative process and the genetic operators until the total number of generations is achieved or another stop criterion is fulfilled (Figure 5).

The possible architectures are: *Intraframe*, *Interframe*, *Knowledge-based* or a combination of the last two. Considering that a voice file is composed by various frames, in the *Intraframe* methodology, it is believed that each frame is a conventional problem of GA. So, for example, as the target sentence has the duration of one second and each frame of 10 milliseconds (no superposition) , then 100 problems of GA are solved independently. To start the simulation, the population of the first frame is obtained randomically and the user has the option of utilizing a more adaptive model for the crossover and the mutation or operate them with a fix value. In the *Interframe* methodology, the best individuals from the last population from frame t (obtained $rank = 1$) are copied to the frame $t+1$. Considering that it may exist a big quantity of able individuals, only 10% of the population can be copied to a following frame and the other individuals are initialized randomically (Borges et al., 2008).

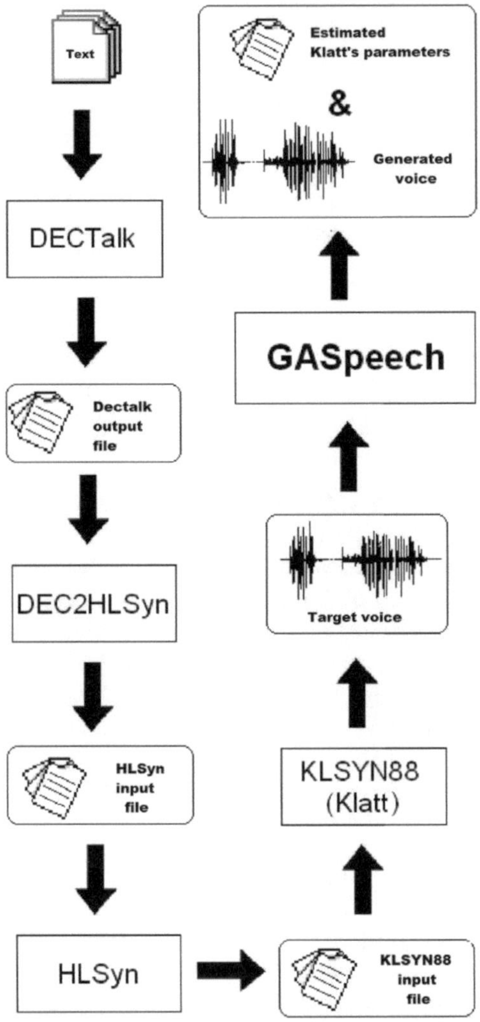

Fig. 4. *GASpeech's* methodology.

In the *Knowledge-based* architecture, for each frame, $N - 1$ individuals from the population are initialized randomically and the last individual is inserted through correct values of the Klatt, applying a random variation. The initial idea consists in that this known individual was extracted from the estimations made in tools such as Praat (Boersma & Weenink, Visited on June, 2011.) and Winsnoori (Laprie, 2010), but these tools do not utilize the same version as the Klatt adopted in this chapter, making it necessary therefore the development of a mapping between the different versions. This architecture also can be utilized in conjunction with a *Interframe*. In this case, besides the insertion of an individual partially known in the population initialized randomically, the best individuals from the previous frame population can be copied to a initial population of the following frame. This way, it is tried to keep a previous knowledge in which is widespread to the following populations, lowering this way the quantity of necessary generations to find the correct value of the Klatt's parameters in each frame.

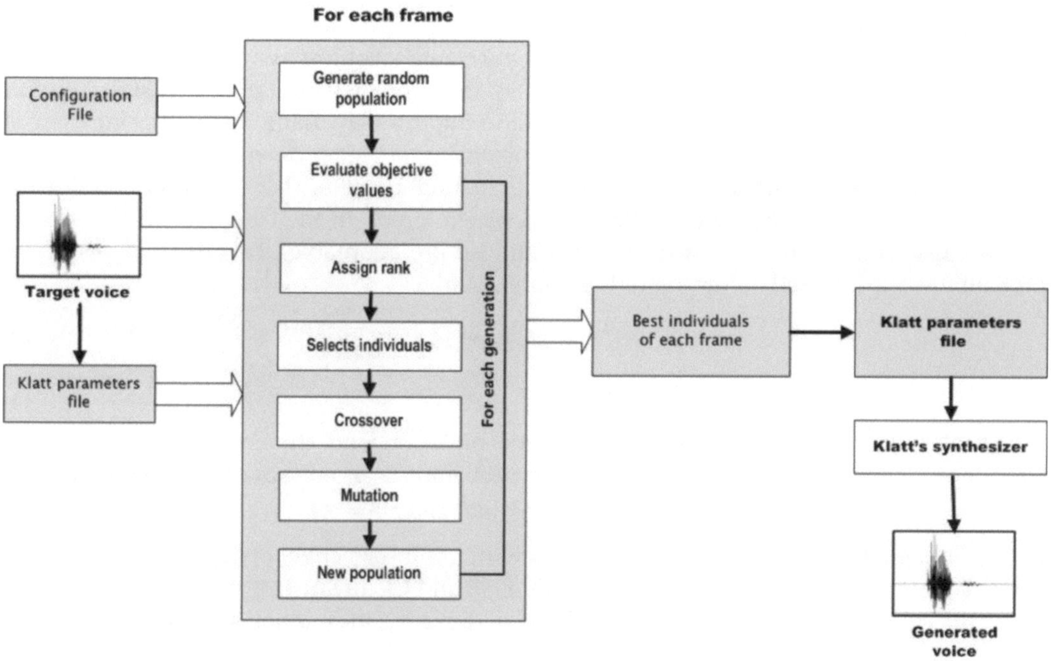

Fig. 5. Functional scheme of *GASpeech*.

The stop criterion defined were three, being them:

- **Convergence:** the simulation is finished when the convergence is obtained, being the convergence parameter (Δ) configured by the user, it can be the SD, the MSE and/or the CC delay.
- **The maximum number of generations:** This criterion is used on traditional GAs and finishes the simulation when the number of generations (*ngen*) is achieved, being this the configured value by the user.
- **The number of generations in evolution:** In this criterion, when the frame achieves the percentage (*ngenwevolve*) of the maximum number of generations with no evolution, the simulation stops. This value is configured by the user and takes in consideration the diversity degree, because when the individuals are the same or too similar, this aspect is not being obeyed.

An individual in the *GASpeech* is composed by a vector of parameters, and in each frame, a single individual must be choose to compose the file with various frames to be synthesized in the end. As the multi-objective optimization can find more than one factible solution, the software is configured to choose the optimal solution of Pareto with lowest value of SD. The fact that the choice befall on the spectral distortion is because this function represents a little better the quality of the generated voice signal, among the other functions. This way, the best individual is the one in which the spectral distortion is lower or equal to 1. If it does not find individuals with this characteristic, the process of decision by the best is used according to the native NSGA-II, based on the elitism, ranking and crowding distance.

On the traditional GAs, the values of the crossover and mutation probabilities are fix, predefined before the initial execution of the algorithm. However, these options can be inefficient since there is a great chance to take the algorithm to minimum places. With it, (Ho et al., 1999) proposed an heuristic, so the parameters could have their values adapted, although controlled. This strategy aims to vary the probabilities mentioned starting with high values and decaying to lower values, considering this way that in the beginning there is little information about the dominion of the problem and a bigger diversity of the population is supposed to exist. In the end of the optimization process, there is some knowledge about the domain and the best solutions must be explored. In the *GASpeech*, if the options of the mutation and crossover probabilities utilized are adaptable, the initial values of the probabilities are lowered according to Equations 2 and 3.

$$p_m^{n+1} = p_m^n - p_m^n x \delta_m \quad (2)$$

$$p_c^{n+1} = p_c^n - p_c^n x \delta_c \quad (3)$$

where δ_m e δ_c are the decreased rates for the mutation and the crossover, respectively, considering a initial value configured for the probabilities of crossover and mutations (p_m^0 e p_c^0) and minimum values that they can assume ($min(p_m)$ and $min(p_c)$).

As mentioned before, the *GASpeech* works with multi-objective optimization and three objective functions are utilized. These are: SD, MSE and CC delay. It was considered that the lower the value of the three objective functions, better is the individual, so, a way of lowering the values of the functions is search.

The SD is calculated through a FFT routine (*Fast Fourier Transform*) that has as objective evaluate the distortion between the synthesized spectrum ($H(f)$) and the target ($S(f)$). The equation is given by:

$$SD = \sqrt{\frac{1}{f2 - f1} \int_{f1}^{f2} \left[20 \log_{10} \frac{|H(f)|}{|S(f)|} \right]^2 df} \quad (4)$$

The MSE is a manner of quantifying the estimated value from the real one (Imbens et al., 2005). The calculation is made through the Mean Squared Error and how it is desired to minimize the error, the Equation 5 must be minimized.

$$MSE = \frac{1}{n} \sum_{j=1}^{n} (\theta_t(j) - \theta_s(j))^2 \quad (5)$$

where n is the number of samples per frame, $\theta_a(j)$ and $\theta_s(j)$ are, respectively, the index samples j of each frame from the waveforms of the target and synthesized voices.

The delay in the CC can be calculated in the following form: consider two sequences $x(i)$ and $y(i)$ where $i = 0, 1, 2...N - 1$. The normalized cross correlation r in the delay d is defined as:

$$r(d) = \frac{\sum_i [(x_i - \overline{x})(y_{i-d} - \overline{y})]}{\sqrt{\sum_i (x_i - \overline{x})^2} \sqrt{\sum_i (y_{i-d} - \overline{y})^2}} \quad (6)$$

where $\overline{x}$ and $\overline{y}$ are mean from the x and y series, respectively.

Considering the delay in the CC the third objective of the *GASpeech*, it is tried to minimize the delay d for which the function r is maximum, where the signals x and y (Equation 6) are frames of the original and synthesized voices. The justification to this fact is that when r is maximum to $d = 0$, it means that the signal has maximum correlation in the moment that there is no delay, then the peaks of these signals tend to be aligned.

10. Experiments

The experiments that are made aim the target-voice generated from the Klatt synthesizer version KLSYN88 where it utilizes 48 parameters. The acquisition of the target voice to the various speech sentences was made from a Dectalk TTS system, to a single speaker, Paul. The sentences were processed one by one, as shown on Figure 6, considering the frequency of 11025 Hz.

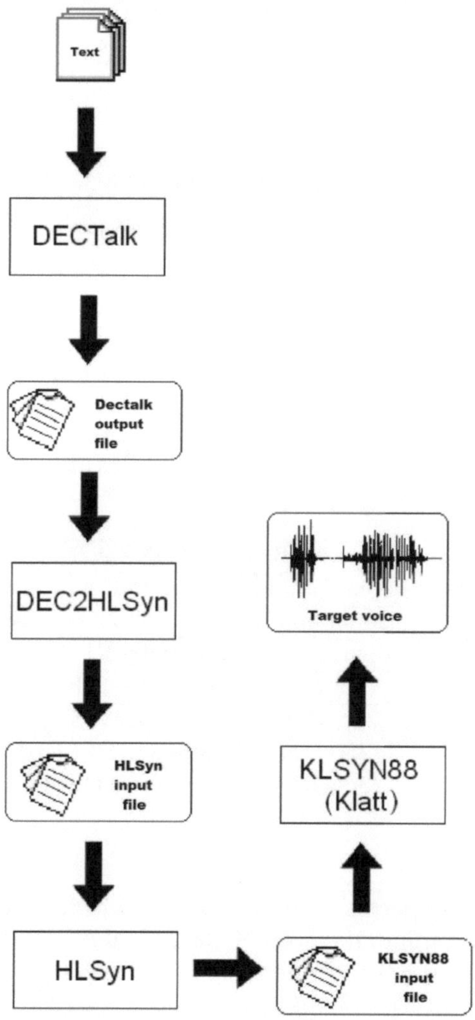

Fig. 6. Preparation of the voice files.

For the experimental effects, nine sentences were chosen considering the variation by phonetic transcription. Each one of them was labeled as shown on Table 1. To evaluate the generated voices it was utilized SD, MSE and CC metrics.

Label	Description
p1007	You don't belong in professional baseball.
p1010	We'll pay you back if you'll let us.
p1013	Draw each graph on a new axis.
p1016	They assume no burglar will ever enter here.
p1032	The wagons were burning fiercely.
p1036	He had four extra eggs for breakfast.
p1069	He recognized his jacket and trousers .
p1074	Our aim must be to learn as much as we teach.
p1159	Blockade is one answer offered by experts.

Table 1. Sentences used.

The experiments made possess as configuration the combinations of the following options:

- **Three objectives**: SD, MSE and CC simultaneously, as objective functions.
- **Two types of architecture**: *Interframe* and the one combined with the Knowledge-based architecture, since the *Intraframe* architecture was less efficient further to the ones mentioned.
- **10 levels of complexity**: the individuals were composed according to the combinations specified on Table 2.

Label	Description
FeB	Formants and bandwidths.
FeBF0	FeB and F0.
20par	FeB and parameters FNP BNP FNZ BNZ A2F A3F A4F A5F A6F AB.
20parF0	FeBF0 and parameters FNP BNP FNZ BNZ A2F A3F A4F A5F A6F AB.
23par	20par and parameters B2F B3F B4F.
23parF0	20parF0 and parameters B2F B3F B4F.
25par	23par and parameters B5F B6F.
25parF0	23parF0 and parameters B5F B6F.
27par	25par and parameters DF1 DB1.
27parF0	25parF0 and parameters DF1 DB1.

Table 2. Levels of complexity.

To initialize a simulation it is necessary a input file in which is generated by the *GASpeech* itself, having the specified configurations on Figure 7. In the example, it is utilized only three Klatt's parameters (F1, F2 and F3) being necessary to inform the value zone that each one of them can receive.

When initializing the simulations it was needed to indicate through the command line the following options:

- **−I <file_name>**: the file of parameters to be passed to the *GASpeech*.

80		**Number of individuals (multiple of 4)**
100		**Number of generations**
1		**Number of goals**
0		**Number of constrains**
3		**Number of real variables (Klatt parameters)**
180	**1300**	**Range of values of the variables (F1)**
550	**3000**	**Range of values of the variables (F2)**
1200	**4800**	**Range of values of the variables (F3)**
0.8		**Crossover probability**
0.024		**Mutation probability**
8		**Distribution index for crossover**
10		**Distribution index for mutation**
0		**Number of binary variables**

Fig. 7. GASpeech's configuration file.

- **−T <file_name>.raw**: audio file (target voice) in the RAW format.
- **−O <file_name>.raw**: name of the output file where its generated in the RAW format too, grouping the best individuals of each frame.
- **−C <value>**: stop criterion based on the informed value.
- **−i <value>**: choose by the *Interframe* methodology with a percentage referring to the best individuals of each frame that will be copied to the next frame.
- **−a**: option to do the adaptation of the values related to the crossover and mutation probabilities.

The utilized values to the parameters during the simulations are described on Table 3.

Parameters	Value
Number of generations ($ngen$)	1000
Population size	200
p_c^0	0.9
p_m^0	0.5
δ_c	0.01
δ_m	0.03
$min(p_c)$	0.1
$min(p_m)$	0.1
Δ	0
$ngenwevolve$	0.3

Table 3. Parameters used in *GASpeech*.

The simulations considered three objectives (SD, MSE e CC), adaptations of crossover and mutations probabilities, *Interframe* architecture isolated and then combined with *Knowledge-based*.

The best results were obtained when it was considered only the formants and the bandwidth (*FeB* – 10 parameters). The *Interframe* methodology combined with the *Knowledge-based* architecture showed slightly better results, being able to find the reasonable solutions in the previous frame, transferring to the next frame. This caused the increase of the investigation power (exploitation) and lowered the quantity of utilized generations to find the correct value of the Klatt parameters to each frame, because of the almost correct values passed through an individual of the population.

The simulations involving 20, 25 and 27 parameters presents an intelligible generated voice, to all the sentences mentioned, considering an subjective evaluation. But, from the simulations with more than 27 parameters, the quality of the voice decays considerably. This degradation still is most evident when the F0 parameter is considered (fundamental frequency). The combination of the *Interframe* architecture with the *Knowledge-based*, brought little improvement regarding the obtained results, reducing only the quantity of utilized generations, until the achievement of the generated voice.

The Table 4 below shows the values of the SD, MSE, and CC obtained to two of the sentences mentioned before (*p*1007 e *p*1010), considering only the FeB, 20, 25 e 27 parameters with the *Interframe* and this architecture combined with the *Knowledge-based*. The values of the metrics indicate that the MSE and the CC presents little variance between the generated files with a good quality of voice and the ones with a degraded voice, except when the voice quality is very bad as in p1007_27par, p1007_27parK, p1010_27par and p1010_27parK. In these cases, the CC values are negative characterizing a delay between target and synthesized voices.

Label	SD	MSE	CC	Subjective
p1007_FeB	0.3176	0	0.0061	Good
p1007_FeBK	0.2271	0	0.0060	Good
p1007_20par	0.7124	0	0.0059	Good
p1007_20parK	0.7415	0	0.0063	Good
p1007_25par	0.6737	0	0.0059	Reasonable
p1007_25parK	0.6146	0	0.0058	Reasonable
p1007_27par	3.2883	0.0084	-0.0223	Bad
p1007_27parK	2.7798	0.0090	-0.0298	Bad
p1010_FeB	0.2991	0	0.0037	Good
p1010_FeBK	0.2671	0	0.0037	Good
p1010_20par	0.6346	0	0.0035	Good
p1010_20parK	0.6534	0	0.0037	Good
p1010_25par	0.6584	0	0.0037	Reasonable
p1010_25parK	0.6363	0	0.0038	Reasonable
p1010_27par	3.3749	0.0098	-0.0168	Bad
p1010_27parK	3.0881	0.0115	-0.0171	Bad

Table 4. SD, MSE and CC values of generated voices.

The SD when evaluated in the file as a whole do not present coherent values according to the values that you can see in *p*1007_20*par* and *p*1007_20*parK* when compared to *p*1007_25*par* and *p*1007_25*parK* because the generated files with *Knowledge-based* architecture are a little better than those generated only by *Interframe* and therefore should have a lower value for SD. However, when the SD frame value per frame is considered (Figures 8 - 11), its behavior can be observed with more detail, with the possibility of identifying which frames were generated with the values of the Klatt parameters too different when compared to the target.

In the following Figures the behavior of the SD value can be observed when the quantity of estimated parameters grows. For each sentence (*p*1007 and *p*1010), simulations were performed using 10, 20, 25 and 27 parameters. In Figures 8 and 9, SD values for each frame is shown using only the *Interframe* architecture and this combined with *Knowledge-based*,

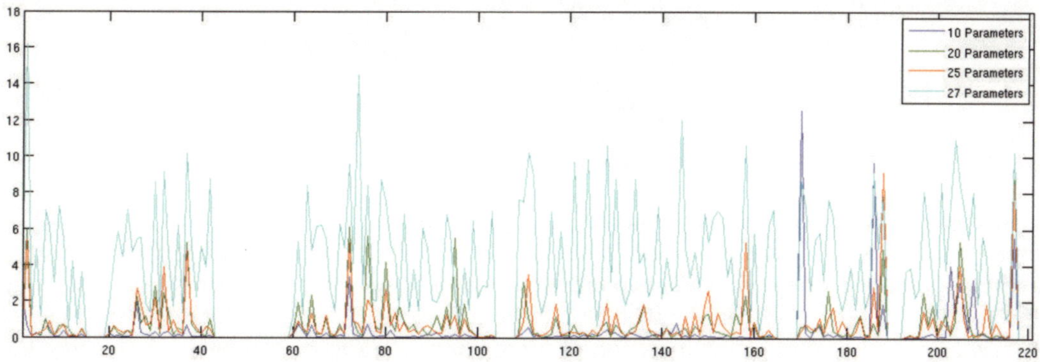

Fig. 8. Spectral Distortion for p1007 sentence with *Interframe* methodology.

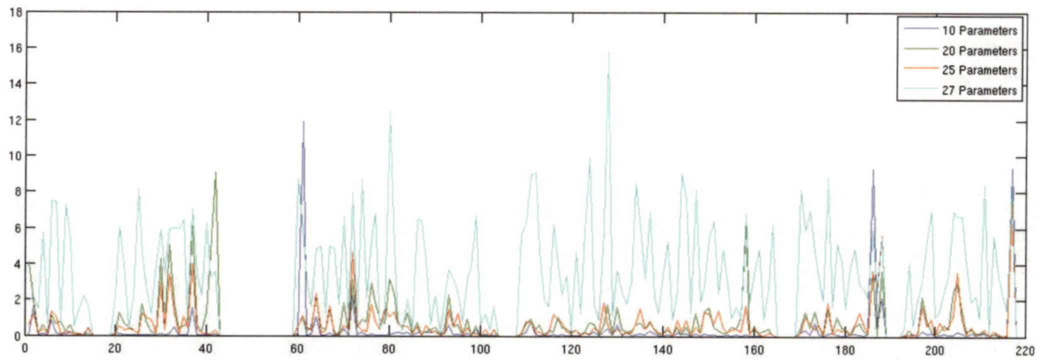

Fig. 9. Spectral Distortion for p1007 sentence with *Knowledge-based* methodology.

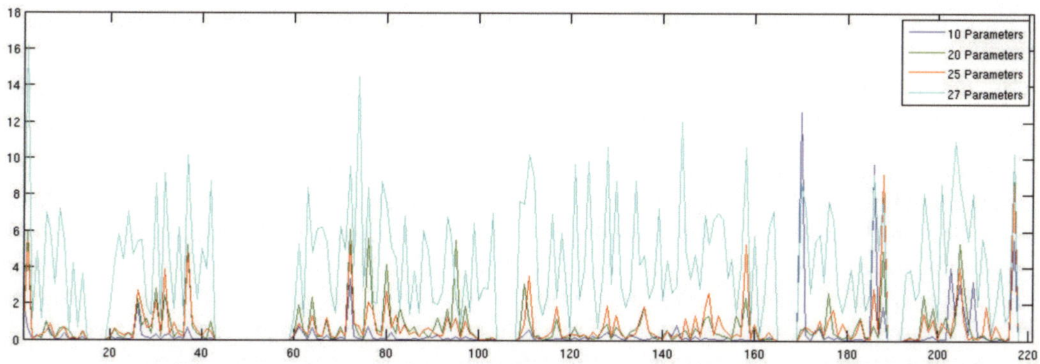

Fig. 10. Spectral Distortion for p1010 sentence with *Interframe* methodology.

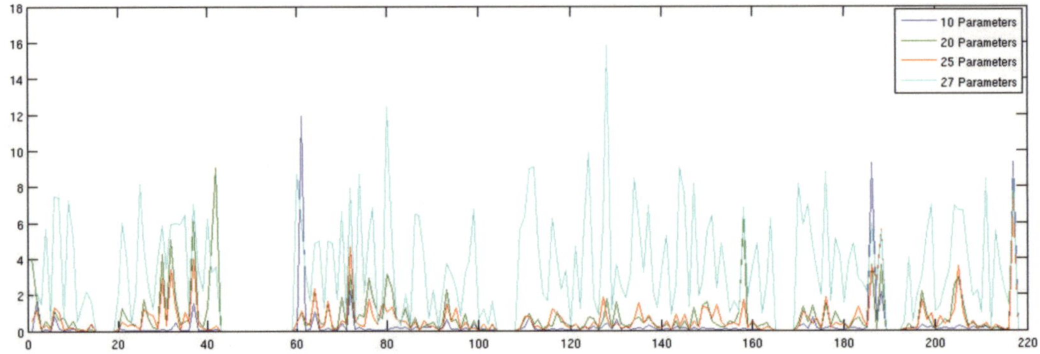

Fig. 11. Spectral Distortion for p1010 sentence with *Knowledge-based* methodology.

repectively. May be noted that the *Knowledge-based* architecture presents lower values of SD by frame compared with *Interframe*, indicating that the partially known individual that is inserted in the population helps to find Klatts parameters value closest to the correct values. The same analysis is true for the sentence *p*1010 as shown in Figures 10 and 11. But it is clear that SD values grows according to the insertion of more parameters to be estimated, indicating the difficulty that the *GASpeech* finds when the increases the amount of the variables involved in the problem.

11. Conclusions

This chapter presented a brief description about the estimation problem of a formant synthesizer, such as the Klatt. The combination of its input parameters to the imitation of the human voice is not a simple task, because a reasonable number of parameters to be combined and each one of them has an interval of acceptable values that must be carefully adjusted to produce a determined voice.

The *GASpeech* used genetic algorithm to estimate the Klatt parameters, however the achieved results were not completely satisfactory, regarding the generated voice when more than 27 parameters are estimated. Good results were achieved only utilizing 10 of the 42 variant parameters. So, careful adjustments is necessary in the framework such as the application of the probabilities of mutation and crossover specific to each Klatt parameter, the utilization of a specific auto-adaptation of these probabilities to a case of real encoding of the variables (Deb et al., 2007) and an specific treatment to better estimate the values of the fundamental frequency due to the fact that an incorrect value of this parameter causes a significant degradation of the quality of the generated voice.

Therefore, it is important to point out that the estimations of the values from the Klatt's parameters, with the objective that they will be as close as possible of the real values, depending on the adequate metric, that really reflect the quality of the produced voice. As seen in the previous session, SD, the MSE, and the CC delay are not adequate when these metrics are calculated considering all frames of the voice files because the metrics values obtained frame by frame is added to obtain an overall average for each synthesized voice file, and in some situations does not reflect the actual quality of voice. Therefore, it is necessary to develop a more efficient mechanism for evaluating the quality of the generated voice as a whole and include it in the *GASpeech* framework.

12. References

Allen, J., Hunnicutt, M. S. & and, D. K. (1987). *From Text-To-Speech: The MITalk System*, Cambridge University Press.

Bickley, C. & Bruckert, E. (2002). Improvements in the voice quality of dectalk reg;, *Proceedings of 2002 IEEE Workshop on Speech Synthesis*, pp. 55 – 58.

Boersma, P. & Weenink, D. (Visited on June, 2011.). Praat: doing phonetics by computer.
URL: *http://www.fon.hum.uva.nl/praat/*

Borges, J., Couto, I., Oliveira, F., Imbiriba, T. & Klautau, A. (2008). Gaspeech: A framework for automatically estimating input parameters of klatt's speech synthesizer, *Neural Networks, Brazilian Symposium on* 0: 81–86.

Breidegard, B. & Balkenius, C. (2003). Speech development by imitation.
URL: *http://cogprints.org/3328/*

Coello, C. A. C., Lamont, G. B. & Veldhuizen, D. A. V. (2007). *Evolutionary Algorithms for Solving Multi-Objective Problems*.

de Oliveira Imbiriba, T. C. (2008). *Aprendizado supervisionado e algoritmos genéticos para obtenção dos parâmetros do sintetizador de klatt*, Master's thesis, Universidade Federal do Pará.

Deb, K. (2001). *Multi-Objective Optimization using Evolutionary Algorithms*, Wiley.

Deb, K., Agrawal, S. & Pratap, A. (2000). A fast elitist non-dominated sorting genetic algorithm for multi-objective optimization: Nsga-ii, *Proceedings of the Parallel Problem Solving from Nature VI*, pp. 849–858.

Deb, K., Sindhya, K. & Okabe, T. (2007). Self-adaptive simulated binary crossover for real-parameter optimization., *GECCO'07*, pp. 1187–1194.

Ding, W., Campbell, N., Higuchi, N. & Kasuya, H. (1997). Fast and robust joint estimation of vocal tract and voice source parameters, *Acoustics, Speech, and Signal Processing, 1997. ICASSP-97., 1997 IEEE International Conference on*, Vol. 2, pp. 1291 –1294 vol.2.

do Couto, I. C. & Borges, J. V. M. (2008). Otimização multi-objetivo aplicada à síntese de voz. Trabalho de Conclusão de Curso apresentado para obtenção do grau de Engenheiro em Engenharia da Computação, do Instituto de Tecnologia, da Faculdade de Engenharia da Computação da Universidade Federal do Pará.

Hallahan, W. I. (1995). Dectalk software: Text-to-speech technology and implementation.

Heid, S. & Hawkins, S. (1998). Procsy: A hybrid approach to high-quality formant synthesis using hlsyn, *Third International Workshop on Speech Synthesis, Jenolan Caves, Australia*, pp. 219–224.

Ho, C., Lee, K. & Leung, K. (1999). A genetic algorithm based on mutation and crossover with adaptive probabilities, *Proceedings of the 1999 Congress on Evolutionary Computation*, Vol. 1, p. 775 Vol. 1.

http://http://www.sens.com/ (Visited on March, 2010.).

Imbens, G. W., Newey, W. K. & Ridder, G. (2005). Mean-square-error calculations for average treatment effects, *IEPR Working Paper No. 05.34* .

Klatt, D. & Klatt, L. (1990). Analysis, synthesis, and perception of voice quality variations among female and male speakers, *Journal of the Acoustical Society of America* 87: 820–57.

Lalwani, A. & Childers, D. (1991). A flexible formant synthesizer, *Acoustics, Speech, and Signal Processing, 1991. ICASSP-91., 1991 International Conference on*, pp. 777 –780 vol.2.

Laprie, Y. (2010). Winsnoori 1.34 - a speech research tool.
URL: *http://www.loria.fr/ laprie/*

Lemmetty, S. (1999). *Review of Speech Synthesis Technology*, PhD thesis, Department Electrical and Communication Engineering - Helsinki University of Technology.

Srinivas, N. & Deb, K. (1994). Multiobjective optimization using nondominated sorting in genetic algorithms, *Evolutionary Computation* 2(3): 221–248.
URL: *citeseer.ist.psu.edu/srinivas94multiobjective.html*

Styger, T. & Keller, E. (1994). *Fundamentals of Speech Synthesis and Speech Recognition: Basic Concepts, State of the Art, and Future Challenges*, John Wiley & Sons Ltd.

15

Solving Timetable Problem by Genetic Algorithm and Heuristic Search Case Study: Universitas Pelita Harapan Timetable

Samuel Lukas, Arnold Aribowo and Milyandreana Muchri
Faculty of Computer Science, Universitas Pelita Harapan, Indonesia

1. Introduction

Almost all education institutes have problem concerning with scheduling, especially university. Many things have to be considered in order to arrange schedule. One of them is availability of lecturers. Not all lecturers are available at any time. Some of them are just available in some time. Therefore, when schedule is arranged, this thing has to be considered. The other things are number of classes and courses offered. Number of classes and courses in university timetable are many. Room availability is other thing, budgeting and many others.

In Indonesian education system, undergraduate students can earn their degree after finishing at least 144 semester credit units. For one unit course, student should attend 50 minutes in class, added by 50 minutes for homework and another 50 minutes for independent activity. In average one course consists of 3 semester credit units. Therefore, to finish their study, students should take about minimum 45 courses. In one semester, students take maximum 24 units and minimum 12 units. Normally, it takes about 4 years of study for a bachelor degree. It means that each semester students have to take minimum 6 courses and maximum about 8 courses unless for the last semester student only take maximum 14 units, one of them is final project which is counted maximum 6 units. Excellence students will finish their study for about 7 semesters. It means that each semester, in average they have to take about 22 units.

It is obvious that within the same semester, all courses have to be scheduled differently one and another so that student can take the course without any overlapping schedule. All of these courses are registered as a group. Since there are four years of study, then the number of different course groups is minimum four for one department.

For a certain department, the number of students in one batch is very big and it is impossible to schedule them for a certain course in one class. Therefore, parallel class most likely will happen. Suppose there are 100 students will take a certain course in the same semester. Since there are only maximum 25 students in one class, then for that course will be opened 4 parallel classes. The schedule of that parallel class does not have to be the same. It depends on the lecturer availability time. In addition, there are also possibilities for a certain course that some classes are merged into one class. Furthermore, there are not one to one mapping between lecturer and courses. One lecturer can teach a number of courses. It will cause making the time table harder.

Universitas Pelita Harapan timetable consists of about 38 departments. The number of students intake each year is about 2000 students. The constraints of the time table are firstly, there are 10 hours lecture time a day and five days a week. Secondly, there are two types of lecture, fulltime and part time lecturer. The part time lecturer maximum is scheduled only 6 units a week, whereas fulltime is maximum 12 units. There is no constraint with the room. However, for some certain courses, there are also laboratory works to be scheduled differently. It is also making the time table harder.

Genetic Algorithm (GA) was powerful to solve assignment problem (Lukas et al, 2005). GA was also used for creating university exam timetable (Burke, et all, 1994). Heuristic search was used for solving scheduling (Joshua and Graham, 2008). This chapter proposes a method for solving this time table problem by using genetic algorithm combined with heuristic search. The role of genetic algorithm is to determine the sequence of all courses to be scheduled in one group, whereas the role of heuristic search is to determine time slots used to schedule the courses (Thanh, 2007).

This chapter will be divided into three main parts. The first part discusses about how genetic algorithm and also heuristic search can solve scheduling problem. Some related works are also included. The second part will be proposed the architecture design of the system. The third part will be shown some experiments and discussion after implementing the system. Chapter will be closed by the conclusion and also some suggestions to improve the system.

2. Principle of genetic algorithm and time tabling

2.1 Principle of genetic algorithm

Genetic Algorithms (GA) are powerful general purpose optimization tools which model the principles of evolution (Davis L. 91). They are often capable of finding globally optimal solutions even in the most complex of search spaces. They operate on a population of coded solutions which are selected according to their quality then used as the basis for a new generation of solutions found by combining (crossover) or altering (mutating) current individuals. Traditionally, the search mechanism has been domain independent, that is to say the crossover and mutation operators have no knowledge of what a good solution would be (Bruns93)(Burke et al.94).

The working principle of a canonical GA is illustrated in Fig. 1. The major steps involved are the generation of a population of solutions, finding the objective function and fitness function and the application of genetic operators. These aspects are described briefly in the subsection below.

An important characteristic of genetic algorithm is the coding of variables that describes the problem. The most common coding method is to transform the variables to a binary string or vector. This initial population formulation process is critical. This step is also recognized as encoding process.

formulate initial population
randomly initialize population
repeat
    evaluate objective function
    apply genetic operators
        reproduction
        crossover
        mutation
until stopping criteria

Fig. 1. The Working Principle of a Simple Genetic Algorithm

GA processes a number of solutions simultaneously. Hence, in the first step a population having P chromosomes called individuals is generated by pseudo random generators whose individuals represent a feasible solution. This is a representation of solution vector in a solution space and is called initial solution. This ensures the search to be robust and unbiased, as it starts from wide range of points in the solution space.

In the next step, individual members, chromosomes of the population represented by a string are evaluated to find the objective function value. This is exclusively problem specification. The objective function is mapped into a fitness function that computes a fitness value for each chromosome. This is followed by the application of GA operators.

Reproduction or selection is usually the first operator applied on a population. It is an operator that makes more copies of better chromosomes in a new population. Thus, in reproduction operation, the process of natural selection causes those chromosomes that encode successful structures to produce copies more frequently. To sustain the generation of a new population, the reproduction of the chromosomes in the current population is necessary. For better chromosomes, these should be generated from the fittest chromosomes of the previous population.

There exist a number of reproduction operators in GA literature, but the essential idea in all of them is that the above average fitness value of strings are picked from the current population and their multiple copies are inserted in the mating pool in a probabilistic manner.

A crossover operator is used to recombine two chromosomes to get a better one. In the crossover operation, recombination process creates different chromosomes in the successive generations by combining material from two chromosomes of the previous generation. In reproduction, good chromosomes in a population are probabilistically assigned a larger number of copies and a mating pool is formed. It is important to note that no new chromosomes are usually formed in the reproduction phase. In the crossover operator, new chromosomes are created by exchanging information among strings of the mating pool.

The two chromosomes participating in the crossover operation are known as parent chromosomes and the resulting ones are known as children chromosomes. It is intuitive from this construction that good sub-strings from parent chromosomes can be combined to form a better child chromosome, if an appropriate site is chosen. With a random site, the children chromosomes produced may or may not have a combination of good sub-strings from parent chromosomes, depending on whether or not the crossing site falls in the appropriate place. But this is not a matter of serious concern, because if good strings are created by crossover, there will be more copies of them in the next mating pool generated by crossover.

It is clear from this discussion that the effect of crossover may be detrimental or beneficial. Thus, in order to preserve some of the good chromosomes that are already present in the mating pool, all chromosomes in the mating pool are not used in crossover. When a crossover probability, defined here as p_c is used, only 100 multiplied by p_c per cent chromosomes in the population are used in the crossover operation and 100 multiplied by $(1-p_c)$ per cent of the population remains as they are in the current population. A crossover operator is mainly responsible for the search of new chromosomes even though mutation operator is also used for this purpose sparingly.

Many crossover operators exist in the GA literature (Zhao, 2007). One site crossover and two site crossover are the most common ones adopted. In most crossover operators, two strings are picked from the mating pool at random and some portion of the strings is exchanged between the strings. Crossover operation is done at string level by randomly selecting two strings for crossover operations.

Mutation adds new information in a random way to the genetic search process and ultimately helps to avoid getting trapped at local optima. It is an operator that introduces diversity in the population whenever the population tends to become homogeneous due to repeated use of reproduction and crossover operators. Mutation may cause the chromosomes to be different from those of their parent. Mutation in a way is the process of randomly disturbing genetic information. They operate at the bit level. When the bits are being copied from the current string to the new chromosomes, there is probability that each bit may become mutated. This probability is usually a quite small value, called as mutation probability p_m. The need for mutation is to create a point in the neighborhood of the current point. The mutation is also used to maintain diversity in the population.

These three operators are simple and straightforward. The reproduction operator selects good chromosomes and the crossover operator recombines good sub-strings from good strings together, hopefully, to create a better sub-string chromosome. The mutation operator alters a string locally expecting a better chromosome. Even though none of these claims are guaranteed and/or tested while creating a chromosome, it is expected that if bad chromosomes are created they will be eliminated by the reproduction operator in the next generation and if good chromosomes are created, they will be increasingly emphasized.

Further insight into these operators, different ways of implementations and some mathematical foundations of genetic algorithms can be obtained from GA literature (Zhao, 2007). Application of these operators on the current population creates a new population. This new population is used to generate subsequent populations and so on, yielding solutions that are closer to the optimum solution. The values of the objective function of the chromosomes of the new population are again determined by decoding the strings. These values express the fitness of the solutions of the new generations. This completes one cycle of genetic algorithm called a generation. In each generation if the solution is improved, it is stored as the best solution. This is repeated till convergence as depicted in Figure 2.

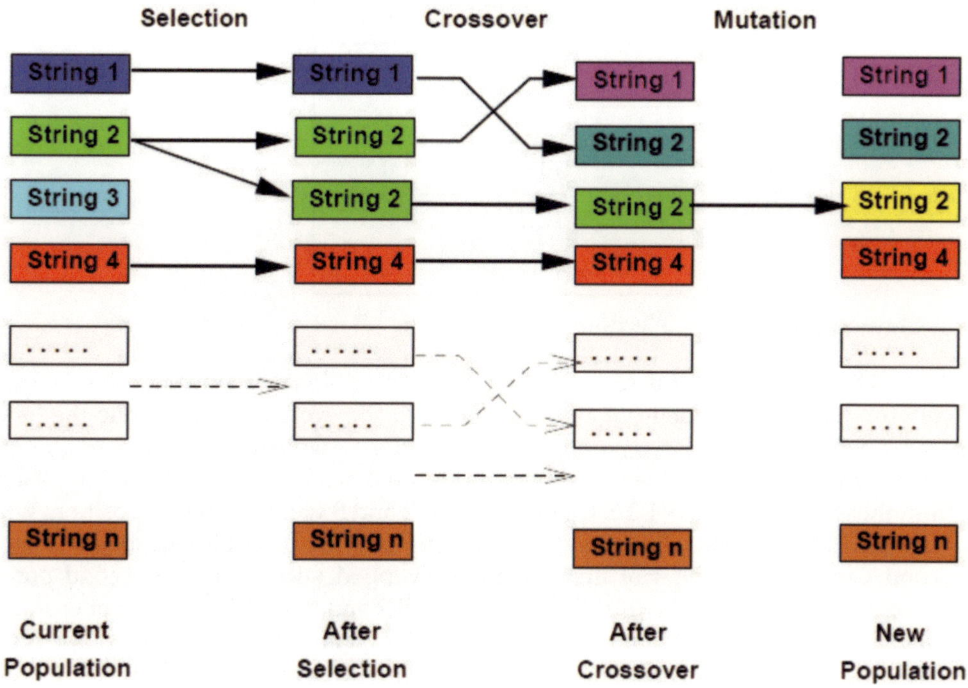

Fig. 2. The basic GA operations

Encoding technique used in this research is permutation encoding. In this technique, chromosomes are coded in the form of integers. Each integer called gene is uniquely assigned to a certain course taught by a lecture. Sequence of integer representing genes in a chromosome, determines sequence of courses to be scheduled (Thanh, 2007). For example a five-gene chromosome represented by 4 2 3 1 5 means that course represented by integer 4 will be scheduled first. Later, it will be followed by course represented by others integer consecutively. Strings length is a total number of courses to be scheduled in a course group. If there are four courses to be scheduled and each of them will be scheduled twice a week, then chromosome length is 8.

Selection is conducted based on truncation selection. Chromosomes are sorted according to their fitness value from the biggest to the smallest. Some chromosomes, started from the smallest fitness strings, will be replaced by new ones (Zhao, 2007). A new chromosome is obtained by reversing the position of all bits in an old chromosome. Unlike other selection methods, the truncation selection does not copy the better chromosome to the population but create a new one. Number of chromosomes to be replaced is obtained by multiplying number of all chromosomes in population with probability of selection. For example, Table 1 contains five-gene sorted chromosomes.

If probability of selection is 0.4, it means that the number of old chromosomes that must be replaced by new ones is 5*0.4 = 2. Then, the position of genes in the last two chromosomes will be reversed. Chromosomes 1 2 5 3 4 will be replaced by 4 3 5 2 1, whereas chromosomes 5 2 3 4 1 will be replaced by 1 4 3 2 5.

Chromosome	Fitness
1 4 5 2 3	1
3 5 2 1 4	0.95
2 4 5 1 3	0.7
1 2 5 3 4	0.5
5 2 3 4 1	0.3

Table 1. Chromosomes before selection

Cycle crossover is applied in this research. The idea behind this method is finding the genes cycle between two parents. Genes that are included in the cycle will stay, while the others will be swapped between the two parents, in order to form two children (Lukas et al, 2005). For example, the two parents used as shown in Figure 3 are 1 5 3 4 2 and 3 4 2 5 1. Genes cycle from those two parents is 1 3 2 1. Then, gene 1, 2 and 3 will stay in that position, while gene 4 and 5 will be swapped. It can be seen that gene 5 of first parent is swapped with gene 4 of second parent, and gene 4 of first parent is swapped with gene 5 of second parent. Therefore chromosomes of the two children are 1 4 3 5 2 and 3 5 2 4 1. Number of crossover is calculated by multiplying number of populations with probability of crossover. It represents how many of chromosomes in population will be crossovered.

In mutation phase, reciprocal exchange mutation is used. Each mutation using this method causes two genes mutated at the same time. First step of this method is determining two gene positions randomly. Then, genes in those positions are swapped (Lukas et al, 2005). For example in chromosome 3 2 5 4 1, the two gene positions chosen are the second and the third. Then, genes in those positions that are gene 2 and 5 are swapped. Chromosome obtained after mutation is 3 5 2 4 1. Number of mutation in population is counted by multiplying chromosome length, number of populations and probability of mutation. Number of crossover and number of mutation must be an even number, because in each crossover, two chromosomes are combined, while in each mutation, two genes are swapped.

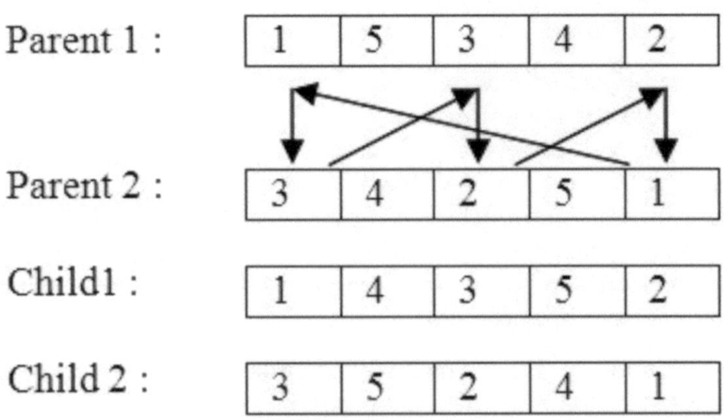

Fig. 3. Cycle Crossover

Fitness value is used to determine how good a chromosome is. It indicates what the objective of the chromosome is. Usually the value is grether than or equal to zero but less or equal to 1. In this research, the objective is to maximize the number of units being able to scheduled divided by total units. So, the more successfully units scheduled courses are, the bigger the fitness value of a chromosome is. Each course has a certain unit. This unit means how many hour students have to spend their time for that course. If a credit of a course is 2, it means that the scheduled course is two hours a week in the timetable consecutively.

2.1 Time tabling

A timetable is essentially a schedule which must suit a number of constraints. Constraints are almost universally employed by people dealing with timetabling problems (Burke and Ross, 1996). Constraints, in turn, are almost universally broken into two categories: soft and hard constraints. Hard constraints are constraints, of which, in any working timetable, there will be no breaches. For example, a lecturer cannot be in two places at once (Erben and Keppler, 1995; Rich 1995). Soft constraints are constraints which may be broken, but of which breaches must be minimized. For example, classes should be booked close to the home department of that class (Erben and Keppler, 1995). In addition to constraints, there are a number of exceptions which must be taken into consideration when constructing an Automated Timetabling system.

In this research, the hard constraints are classrooms must not be double booked, every class must be scheduled exactly once, classes of students must not have two bookings simultaneously, a classroom must be large enough to hold each class booked to it, lecturers must not be double booked, a lecturer must not be booked when he/she is unavailable. Some classes require particular rooms; some classes need to be held consecutively. Whereas the soft constraints are some lecturers have preferred hours to be scheduled, most students do not wish to have empty periods in their timetables, the distance a student walks should be minimized, classes should be distributed evenly over the week, classrooms should be booked close to the home department of that class, classrooms should not be booked which are much larger than the size of the class. In addition, the only exception constraint to be considered is a part time lecturer should be scheduled not more then 6 credit units whereas a full time is 12 credit units.

3. The architecture design of the system

Heuristic search is applied in this research. It uses a 2D matrix called target matrix. This matrix is used to find suitable time slots for scheduling courses (Thanh, 2007). There are six sets applied in this target matrix. They are course code set $M=\{m_1,m_2,\ldots\}$, type course class set $T=\{t_0,t_1,t_2,\ldots\}$, lecturer code set $L=\{l_1,l_2,\ldots\}$, class name set $C=\{c_1,c_2,\ldots\}$, day set $D=\{d_1,d_2,\ldots\}$ and hour set $H=\{h_1,h_2,\ldots\}$. All index set start with one. Only type course class set T has member index zero, t_0. It indicates only for the case that for a certain course of some parallel classes are merged into one class.

There are close relations among course code set, type course class set and also lecture code set. Suppose m_1,t_1,l_1 is one of the relations, it indicates that course code m_1 is taught by lecture code l_1 in type course class code t_1. In addition, c_1,d_1,h_1 is also another relation, it means that at day d_1 on hour h_1 class name c_1 is assigned. If m_1,t_1,l_1 is linked with c_1,d_1,h_1, it means that course code m_1 is taught by lecture code l_1 in type course class code t_1 be scheduled at day d_1 on hour h_1 with class name c_1.

All pairs of course code, type course class and lecture code have to be connected with all pairs of class name, day and hour. This connection is tabulated in a matrix called target matrix. Table 2 is an example of target matrix. Each cell v_{ij} in which i is row and j is column, in target matrix, $V = \{v_{ij}\}$, has three different values, those are :

1. $v_{ij} = 0$ means that certain lecturer time slot represented by this cell is available to be scheduled.
2. $v_{ij} = -1$ means that certain lecturer time slot represented by this cell is not available to be scheduled.
3. $v_{ij} = 1$ means that certain lecturer time slot represented by this cell has already been scheduled.

	m_1,t_0,l_1	m_2,t_1,l_1	m_3,t_2,l_2	...
c_1,d_1,h_1	1	-1	-1	...
c_1,d_1,h_2	1	-1	-1	...
c_1,d_2,h_1	-1	1	-1	...
c_1,d_2,h_2	-1	1	-1	...
c_2,d_1,h_1	1	-1	-1	...
c_2,d_1,h_2	1	-1	-1	...
c_2,d_2,h_1	0	0	0	...
c_2,d_2,h_2	-1	-1	1	...
...	...	...		
# of units scheduled	4	2	1	...

Table 2. Example of target matrix

Number of rows needed is equal to number of class names multiplied by number of lecture days in a week multiplied by number of lecture hours in a day. From Table 2, there are two names of class, c_1 and c_2, are scheduled in the same day and time that is d_1,h_1 and d_1,h_2 for course m_1 taught by l_1. It is possible because the type of class is t_0. It means that it is a merge class of n_1 and n_2. Number of units scheduled of that column is 4. It represents a number of hours has been allocated.

There are six functions that are applied to each cell in target matrix. Those functions are f_m , f_t , f_l , f_c , f_d and f_h, each of which is used to get information about course code, type course class, lecturer code, class name, day and hour respectively. As an example, the value of each function to cell v_{11} are $f_m(v_{11})=m_1$, $f_t(v_{11})=t_0$, $f_l(v_{11})=l_1$, $f_c(v_{11})= c_1$, $f_d(v_{11})= d_1$, and $f_h(v_{11})= h_1$. All of these functions are used to create target matrix.

There are some rules need to be considered in order to fill the target matrix:

1. If $t_x \neq t_0$ and certain course respectively should be scheduled in class name i^{th} then all rows $c_j \neq i$ in that column should not be filled by 1. In addition, if that course can be scheduled at the certain day and hour at that column then that cell at rows c_i is assigned as 1 and others consecutive cells in the same day, as many as unit course of that column, is also assigned 1.
2. If $t_x = t_0$ means that certain course respectively should be scheduled in c_i and c_j class names. Therefore if and only if cell $c_i,d_a,h_b = 1$ then cell $c_j,d_a,h_b = 1$ at that column.
3. For each row, there is only maximum a cell that is equal to 1.The others must be -1 or 0.
4. Course on a column is said to be successfully scheduled only when unit course at that column is a factor of total all 1's cells in that column.
5. If there is a cell in a column of a row c_x, d_i, h_j is equal to 1 then for all row c_y, d_i, h_j have to be set -1 for $c_x \neq c_y$ at that column.

For example, there are 3 courses and 4 lecturers to be scheduled within 2 class names, A and B, 2 days lecture a week and 3 hours lecture a day. There are also two type course classes, namely lecture and lab. It means that $n(M)= 3$, $n(T)=3$, $n(L)=4$, $n(C)=2$, $n(D)=2$, $n(H)=3$. m_1 is course code opened for mixed class name c_1 and c_2 and lectured by l_1, m_2 is course code opened for both class name c_1 and c_2 but their were taught by the some lecturer, l_2 with type course class t_1 as lecture. m_3 is course code also opened for both class, type course class as lab, but with difference lecturer, l_3 and l_4. If course credit of m_1, m_2 and m_3 are 2, 1 and 2 credits and knowing the lecturer's availabilities time, we can produce the initial target matrix, in Table 3. From that target matrix, it can be determined that lecture code l_2 and l_4 are not available for d_1,h_1 and d_2,h_3, while other lecturers are available at any time. These information and other constraints are inputted into the system and saved into databases.

	m_1,t_0,l_1	m_2,t_1,l_2	m_3,t_2,l_3	m_3,t_2,l_4
c_1,d_1,h_1	0	-1	0	0
c_1,d_1,h_2	0	0	0	0
c_1,d_1,h_3	0	0	0	0
c_1,d_2,h_1	0	0	0	0
c_1,d_2,h_2	0	0	0	0
c_1,d_2,h_3	0	0	0	-1
c_2,d_1,h_1	0	-1	0	0
c_2,d_1,h_2	0	0	0	0
c_2,d_1,h_3	0	0	0	0
c_2,d_2,h_1	0	0	0	0
c_2,d_2,h_2	0	0	0	0
c_2,d_2,h_3	0	0	0	-1
# units	0	0	0	0

Table 3. Example of initial target matrix

Suppose that sequence of courses represented by generated chromosome [1 3 2 4] represents m_1,t_0,l_1 ; m_3,t_2,l_3 ; m_2,t_1,l_2 and m_3,t_2,l_4 then, the first course to be scheduled is gene chromosome code m_1,t_0,l_1 and the last is m_3,t_2,l_4. The result of these is shown in Table 4. It can be seen that m_1,t_0,l_1 is successfully scheduled on (c_1, d_1, h_1), (c_1, d_1, h_2) (c_2, d_1, h_1) and (c_2, d_1, h_2). Therefore other columns of those rows are set to -1. M_3,t_2,l_3 and m_2,t_1,l_2 are able to be placed but m_3,t_2,l_4 is failed.

From Table 4, it can be said that the chromosome [1 3 2 4] is able to allocated 8 units out of 10 units for that two classes c_1 and c_2 for 3 courses. The value of 8 over 10 which is 0.8 is called as fitness of that chromosome. If the chromosome is [1 4 3 2] then the fitness is 1. The fitness of a chromosome represents the time table objective. In this case, the objective is to maximize the number of units to be scheduled for each timetable. If number of units scheduled for k^{th} column is $s(k)$, p is a maximum column in a target matrix, $u(j)$ means unit number of jth course to be scheduled for each class name, and t is total courses of each class name, then fitness of a chromosome is defined by (1)

$$fitness = \frac{\sum_{k=1}^{p} s(k)}{n(C) \cdot \sum_{j=1}^{t} u(j)} \tag{1}$$

	m_1,t_0,l_1	m_2,t_1,l_2	m_3,t_2,l_3	m_3,t_2,l_4
c_1,d_1,h_1	1	-1	-1	-1
c_1,d_1,h_2	1	-1	-1	-1
c_1,d_1,h_3	-1	1	-1	-1
c_1,d_2,h_1	-1	-1	1	-1
c_1,d_2,h_2	-1	-1	1	-1
c_1,d_2,h_3	0	0	0	-1
c_2,d_1,h_1	1	-1	-1	-1
c_2,d_1,h_2	1	-1	-1	-1
c_2,d_1,h_3	0	-1	0	0
c_2,d_2,h_1	-1	1	-1	-1
c_2,d_2,h_2	0	0	-1	0
c_2,d_2,h_3	0	0	0	-1
# units	4	2	2	0

Table 4. Example of target matrix after heuristic search

University time table consists of many timetables. Since one degree of each department is designed for four years studies, then each department has at least four time tables for every semester. That is one time table for every batch. No matter is how big a batch in one departement, it has only one time table. It only impacts to the processing time. The bigger the batch is the longer the processing time to produce the time table. It is because not only the number of rows but also the number of columns in the target matrix will be larger.

4. Experiment result

Some experiments are performed to ensure how good the system is. There are 4 course groups from year 1 to year 4. In experiments, we would like making time table for odd semester data 2008 - 2009. Certain number of courses and lecturers to be scheduled in each course group are inputted. For example, in course group year 1 there are 7 courses and 10 lecturers with 2 type course classes (lecture and lab), 2 class names (A and B), 5 days lecture a week and 10 hours lecture a day. Relation among all sets are represented in Table 5.

From Table 5, it can be concluded that $n(M)= 7$, $n(T)=3$, $n(L)=9$, $n(C)=2$, $n(D)=5$, $n(H)=10$. All genes of the chromosome are m_1,t_0,l_1, m_2,t_0,l_2, m_3,t_0,l_2, m_4,t_0,l_3, m_5,t_0,l_6, m_6,t_0,l_5, m_7,t_1,l_6, m_7,t_1,l_7, m_1,t_2,l_8, m_2,t_2,l_9, m_3,t_2,l_9, m_4,t_2,l_{10}, m_6,t_2,l_6. It means there are 13 columns and 100 rows in target matrix. After receiving initial data, such as what is the restricted day and time for a certain lecturer, what room can be used and also the capacity of that room. The system runs with 10 chromosomes in a population and 10 generations are set in the experiment, without considering probability of selection, crossover and mutation, the maximum best fitness value, that is 1, can be achieved. It means that all courses can be scheduled accordingly. Therefore, number of populations and generations does not need to be set high. It means less time is needed to make a schedule. One of the timetables of the course group year 1 is shown in Figure 4.

Course Name	Lecture			Lab		
	A	B	units	A	B	units
ICT (m_1)	Budi Berlinton (l_1)		3	Monika (l_8)	Monika (l_8)	2
Calculus 1 (m_2)	Nababan (l_2)		2	Finela (l_9)	Finela (l_9)	2
Calculus 2 (m_3)	Nababan (l_2)		2			
IPE (m_4)	Sutrisno (l_3)		4	Andree (l_{10})	Andree (l_{10})	2
Discrete Math (m_5)	Samuel (l_4)		4			
Statistics (m_6)	Gunawan (l_5)		3	Gunawan (l_5)		2
Reading Skills (m_7)	Univ (l_6)	Univ (l_7)	2			

Table 5. Relations among the 6 sets

The time table where the class meeting will take place should also be defined. From figure 4, it is clear that every class meeting has their room. Budi berlinton teaches course ICT on

Monday at 7.30 to 10.00 in room B212. The system can define the available room for that class by looking room table in the database. It is easy to search the room by comparing the room capacity, the location etc, from the requirement of that class. After a room is assigned, status of that room is not available any more of that day and hour.

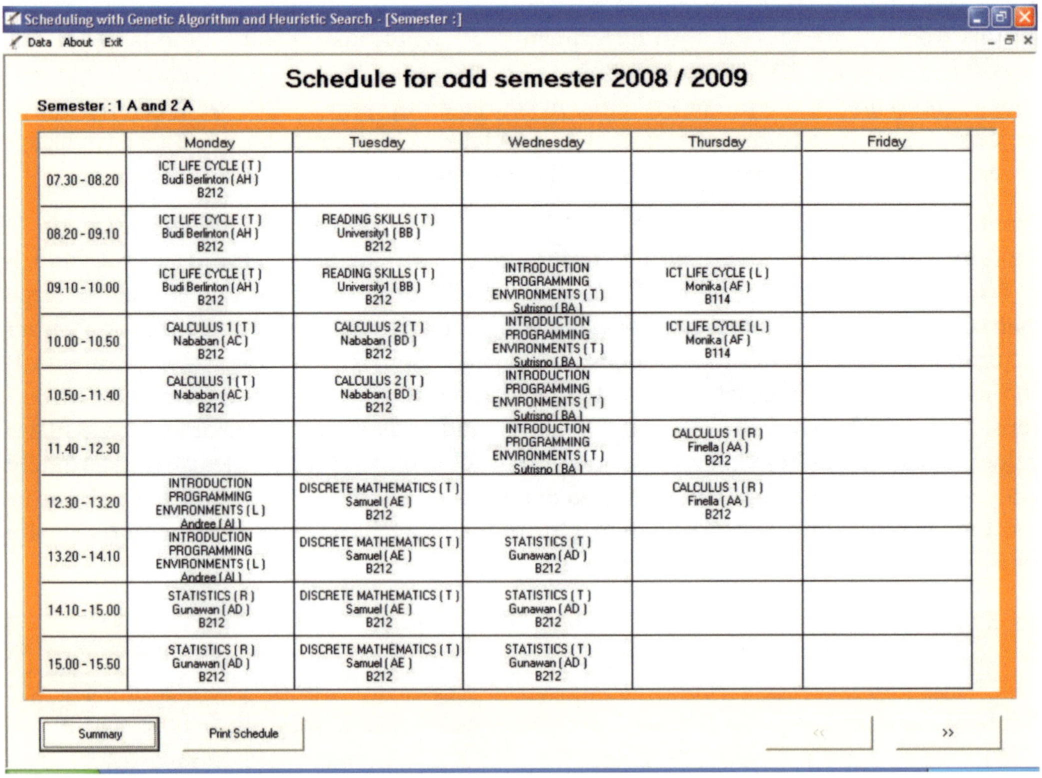

	Monday	Tuesday	Wednesday	Thursday	Friday
07.30 - 08.20	ICT LIFE CYCLE (T) Budi Berlinton (AH) B212				
08.20 - 09.10	ICT LIFE CYCLE (T) Budi Berlinton (AH) B212	READING SKILLS (T) University1 (BB) B212			
09.10 - 10.00	ICT LIFE CYCLE (T) Budi Berlinton (AH) B212	READING SKILLS (T) University1 (BB) B212	INTRODUCTION PROGRAMMING ENVIRONMENTS (T) Sutrisno (BA)	ICT LIFE CYCLE (L) Monika (AF) B114	
10.00 - 10.50	CALCULUS 1 (T) Nababan (AC) B212	CALCULUS 2 (T) Nababan (BD) B212	INTRODUCTION PROGRAMMING ENVIRONMENTS (T) Sutrisno (BA)	ICT LIFE CYCLE (L) Monika (AF) B114	
10.50 - 11.40	CALCULUS 1 (T) Nababan (AC) B212	CALCULUS 2 (T) Nababan (BD) B212	INTRODUCTION PROGRAMMING ENVIRONMENTS (T) Sutrisno (BA)		
11.40 - 12.30			INTRODUCTION PROGRAMMING ENVIRONMENTS (T) Sutrisno (BA)	CALCULUS 1 (R) Finella (AA) B212	
12.30 - 13.20	INTRODUCTION PROGRAMMING ENVIRONMENTS (L) Andree (AI)	DISCRETE MATHEMATICS (T) Samuel (AE) B212		CALCULUS 1 (R) Finella (AA) B212	
13.20 - 14.10	INTRODUCTION PROGRAMMING ENVIRONMENTS (L) Andree (AI)	DISCRETE MATHEMATICS (T) Samuel (AE) B212	STATISTICS (T) Gunawan (AD) B212		
14.10 - 15.00	STATISTICS (R) Gunawan (AD) B212	DISCRETE MATHEMATICS (T) Samuel (AE) B212	STATISTICS (T) Gunawan (AD) B212		
15.00 - 15.50	STATISTICS (R) Gunawan (AD) B212	DISCRETE MATHEMATICS (T) Samuel (AE) B212	STATISTICS (T) Gunawan (AD) B212		

Fig. 4. One example of time table for the first semester.

5. Conclusions and further research

The proposed genetic algorithm and heuristic search are able to solve timetable problem. Although, room has not been included in target matrix, system is able to determine which room is used to a certain cell in time table. However, if the room is one of the critical factor, it should be included in the target matrix. If it happens then it is more likely to create three dimension target matrix instead of adding number of column.

There are some limitations of this research. Firstly, every parallel class of a course group which is represented in one target matrix, has to be scheduled to every course defined in that time table. Secondly, one lecture course can be scheduled only if there is available space consecutively at target matrix at least as much as number of units of the course. If that course has to be split into two segments then the name of that course should be differentiated. It could be assumed as two courses. In the experiment, it is showed that calculus is divided into calculus 1 and calculus 2. Thirdly, the objective of the system is to maximize the number of successful units being able to scheduled, otherwise it should be defined accordingly.

6. References

Burke E.K., Elliman D.G. and Weare R.F. (1993a) "A University Timetabling System Based on Graph Coloring and Constraint Manipulation", *Journal of Research on Computing in Education*. Vol. 26. issue 4

Burke E.K., Elliman D.G. and Weare R.F. (1993b) "Automated Scheduling of University Exams", *Proceedings of I.E.E. Colloquium on "Resource Scheduling for Large Scale Planning Systems"*, Digest No. 1993/144

Burke E.K., Elliman D.G. and Weare R.F. (1994) "A Genetic Algorithm for University Timetabling", AISB Workshop on Evolutionary Computing, Leeds.

Burke E and Ross P (Eds) (1996): *Lecture Notes in Computer Science 1153 Practice and Theory of Automated Timetabling First International Conference, Edinburgh, U.K., August/September 1995, Selected Papers.* New York: Springer-Verlag Berlin Heidelberg.

Davis L. (1991) "Handbook of Genetic Algorithms" Van Nostrand Reinhold

Erben W and Keppler J (1995): A Genetic Algorithm Solving a Weekly Course- Timetabling Problem. In Burke E and Ross P (Eds): *Lecture Notes in Computer Science 1153 Practice and Theory of Automated Timetabling First International Conference, Edinburgh, U.K., August/September 1995, Selected Papers.* New York: Springer-Verlag Berlin Heidelberg. pp 198-211.

Enmund Burke, David Ellimand and Rupert Weare. (1994). "*A Genetic Algorithm Based University Timetabling System*", August 2011, http://citeseer.ist.psu.edu/viewdoc/summary?doi=10.1.1.2.2659

Joshua Poh-Onn Fan, Graham K. Winley. (2008). *A Heuristic Search Algorithm for Flow-Shop Scheduling"*, August 2011, http://www.informatica.si/PDF/32-4/26_Fan - A Heuristic Search Algorithm for Flow-Shop Scheduling.pdf

N.D. Thanh, "Solving Timetabling Problem Using Genetic and Heuristic Algorithms", Eighth ACIS International Conference on Software Engineering, Artificial Intelligence, Networking, and Parallel/Distributed Computing, hal. 472-477, 2007.

Negnevitsky, Michael. (2005). *Artificial Intelligence, A Guide to Intelligence System (2nd)*, Addison Wesley, pp. 222-245, IBN 0-321-20466-2, Harlow, England

Q. Zhao, An Introduction to Genetic Algorithms, 2007.

Rich DC (1995): A Smart Genetic Algorithm for University Timetabling. In Burke E and Ross P (Eds): *Lecture Notes in Computer Science 1153 Practice and Theory of Automated Timetabling First International Conference, Edinburgh, U.K., August/September 1995, Selected Papers.* New York: Springer-Verlag Berlin Heidelberg. pp 181-197.

S. Lukas, P. Yugopuspito and H. Asali, "Solving assignment problem by genetic algorithms using Cycle Crossover", *Universitas Pelita Harapan Computer Science Journal,* Vol. 3, No. 2, Mei 2005, pp. 87-93.

16

Genetic Algorithms for Semi-Static Wavelength-Routed Optical Networks

R.J. Durán, I. de Miguel, N. Merayo, P. Fernández, J.C. Aguado, A. Bahillo, R. de la Rosa and A. Alonso
Optical Communications Group, University of Valladolid, Spain

1. Introduction

Optical communication networks are an excellent option to establish backbone or transport networks due to the high-bandwidth provided by the optical fibres. In this kind of networks the information is transmitted through optical fibres in the infrared domain. Although fibres provide high bandwidth for the transmission of information (around 50 THz), the current electronic technology cannot work at these bit rates. Therefore, a new technology was developed to exploit the bandwidth of the fibre: Wavelength Division Multiplexing (WDM). In this technology, the part of the spectrum used to transmit information is divided into different channels, each one centred in a different wavelength (or frequency). Then, it allows the transmission of several channels through the same fibre by using a different wavelength for each of the channels.

In first optical communication networks, the optical technology was only used for transmission between nodes that were directly connected by means of one or more optical fibres, i.e., adjacent nodes in the physical network. Therefore, when data should be transmitted between two non-adjacent nodes, the information should transverse intermediate nodes in which the information is converted into electrical domain in order to route the traffic through the appropriate output fibre and then transmit the information in the optical domain. In this scenario, the nodes become the bottleneck of the network.

To solve this problem, new optical networks emerged with the capacity of using the wavelength to perform routing functions (Mukherjee, 1997). Thus, a network node can distinguish between traffic destined for other nodes and for itself without any processing, as it is determined by the wavelength and the input port of incoming data. This kind of networks are called Wavelength-Routed Optical Networks (WRONs) and they are based in circuit switching. WRONs allows the establishment of optical circuits between two network nodes (not necessarily adjacent in the physical topology) for the transmission of information. These circuits are called lightpaths. The lightpaths can be permanently (or semi-permanently) established in static (or semi-static) WRON, or established and released on demand in dynamic WRONs.

The objective of this chapter is to show a set of single-objective and multi-objective genetic algorithms, designed by the Optical Communications Group at the University of Valladolid, to optimize the performance of semi-static Wavelength-Routed Optical Networks. The fundamentals of those algorithms, i.e., the chromosome structures, their translation, the optimization goals and the genetic operators employed are described. Moreover, a number of simulation results are also included to show the efficiency of genetic algorithms when designing WRONs.

2. Wavelength-routed optical networks

Wavelength Division Multiplexing (WDM) allows the transmission of several data channels through an optical fibre. Thanks to this technique it is possible not only to use better the huge bandwidth of the optical fibre but also to perform routing in the network nodes in order to avoid the bottleneck that can appear due to the electronic processing. In this context, the concept of Wavelength-Routed Optical Networks (WRONs) was introduced. The basic element in WRON is the lightpath, i.e., an all-optical connection between two network nodes even when they are not adjacent in the physical topology (i.e., when there is not any fibre connecting the two nodes). In this way, the transmission between the two end nodes does not require any electronic processing in the intermediate nodes.

A lightpath should fulfil two conditions:

1. Each lightpath should use the same wavelength in all the fibres that it transverses, unless the network is equipped with wavelength-converters in the nodes, but this is not considered in this work. This restriction is known as the *wavelength continuity constraint*.
2. Two lightpaths cannot use the same wavelength in the same fibre. However, it is possible to reuse wavelengths in different network fibres.

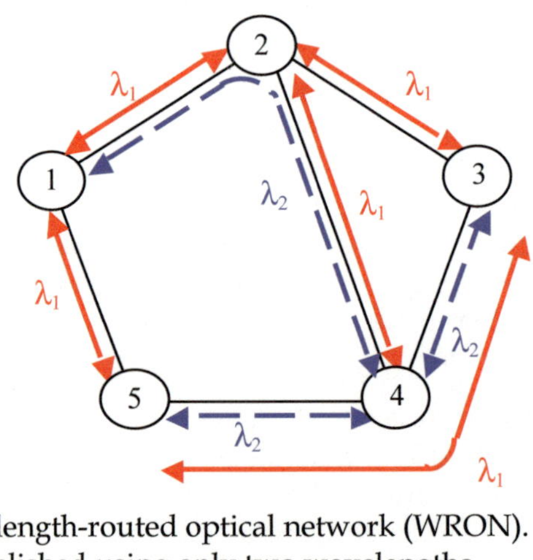

Fig. 1. Example of a wavelength-routed optical network (WRON). Eight bidirectional lightpaths have been established using only two wavelengths

In Fig. 1, a WRON with eight bidirectional lightpaths using only two wavelengths is shown. Moreover, it is shown that a lightpath can be established between adjacent source and destination nodes (for instance, between nodes 5 and 4), or traversing one or more intermediate nodes. For instance, the lightpath between nodes 5 and 3 traverses node 4, which is in charge of properly routing the optical signal with no need to perform conversion to the electronic domain. Note that a lightpath can also be established in a unidirectional way, or even being bidirectional but following different routes and wavelengths for each direction.

In principle, we could think about establishing one lightpath between each source-destination pair (or even more), but this option is not always appropriate. In a network with N nodes, N–1 transmitters (and receivers) are required at each node, and $N(N–1)$ unidirectional lightpaths should be established, so that the number of wavelengths required can be high as well as the cost of the network, due to the number of transmission and reception equipments needed, and to the requirements on wavelength-handling capacity of the optical crossconnects (OXC) and optical add and drop multiplexers (OADM). Moreover, the utilisation of a high number of wavelengths may degrade the quality of the transmission due to physical impairments. This effect can provoke that some of the connections cannot be established due to not reaching enough quality level.

Therefore, instead establishing lightpaths in a permanent o semi-permanent way between each source-destination pair of the network, one solution consists in establishing only a subset of them. In this way, a lower number of transceivers per node and a lower number of wavelengths are required. The drawback is that not all the traffic can be transmitted directly from the source node to the destination node (single-hop communication), but traffic between pairs of nodes which are not directly connected by a lightpath must traverse one or more intermediate nodes where conversion to the electronic domain is performed. Therefore, it is a multihop scenario. Moreover, this solution usually implies a static or semi-static situation as lightpaths are permanently or semipermanently established, although in some cases some of them can be deleted and new ones can be established, for instance to adapt to changes in the traffic offered to the network or to react to network failures.

3. Genetic algorithms

Genetic algorithms (GAs) (Goldberg, 1989; Man et al., 1999) are search algorithms based on the mechanics of natural selection and natural genetics, where stronger individuals are the likely winners in a competing environment. Genetic algorithms represent each solution to any problem as an individual represented by a set of parameters. These parameters are regarded as genes and can be structured on a string or chromosome. The fitness of each individual is the objective parameter that we want to optimize.

An initial population is created, randomly most of the times, and then evolved by means of genetic operators, such as reproduction, crossover and mutation, to form a new population (the next generation) that is hoped to be fitter than the previous one. The reproduction operator creates a literal copy of selected individuals from the parent population in the descendant generation. The crossover operator is applied to pairs of individuals in order to interchange their genetic material. To generate a good offspring, a good mechanism for selecting parents is necessary. Roulette wheel selection is one of the most common techniques. When using this method, the probability of selecting an individual is proportional to its health (or fitness). In this way, good properties should propagate down the generations. On the other hand, the mutation operator makes a random change in the genetic material of a single individual, allowing the GA to explore new corners of the search space and hence avoiding the risk of being trapped in a local optimum. The evolution process is repeated a predefined number of iterations or until another criterion is met. Since individuals from the population become fitter throughout the generations, it is hoped that the final population will contain an optimal or near optimal solution.

Finally, it should be remarked that GAs are generic methods that have to be customized to the particular problems that we attempt to solve. Therefore, the design of the encoding mechanism of the individuals and the different operators of GAs must be adapted to the characteristics of the problem being tackled, since they have a significant impact on the performance of the algorithm.

4. Multi-objective optimization: Pareto optimality with genetic algorithms

Pareto optimality (Man et al., 1999) is based on the concept of the dominant individual. In an n-objective optimisation problem, where $f_i(u)$ is the result of evaluating the individual u according to the objective function i, and assuming that lowest values of $f_i(u)$ are preferred, u is said to be dominated by v if

$$f_i(u) \geq f_i(v) \quad \forall i = 1,2,...,n \tag{1}$$

and if

$$\exists j = 1,2,...,n \text{ such that } f_j(u) > f_j(v) \tag{2}$$

Then, the ranking of an individual is defined as the number of individuals for which it is dominated. The set of optimal individuals is called the Pareto optimal set and it is defined as the set of individuals with ranking zero, i.e., those that are do not dominated by anyone. Hence, each solution that belongs to the Pareto optimal set is characterized because it cannot be simultaneously improved in terms of all the optimization objectives.

Fig. 2 shows an example of a set of solutions provided by a multi-objective method in which each solution is represented in terms of two optimization objectives f_1 and f_2. In both optimization objectives lower values are preferable than higher ones. The number that it is represented near each point (solution) is the ranking of the individual. Moreover, the Pareto optimal set is also represented.

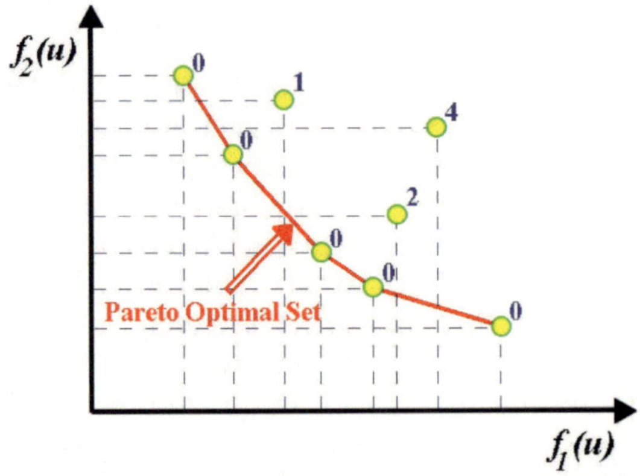

Fig. 2. Examples of the set of solution obtained by a multi-objective method represented in terms of two optimization objectives f_1 and f_2. Lower values are desirable in both objectives.

Pareto optimality can be combined with genetic algorithms in order to solve multi-objective optimization problems. In single-objective problems the roulette wheel method, according to the individual fitness, is utilized as selection process, but when Pareto optimality is combined with genetic algorithms in order to solve multi-objective optimization problem, one possible method to perform the selection is that all the individuals in the Pareto optimal set have the same probability of being selected for a reproduction or crossover stage. Moreover, the selection of the individuals that will take part in the next generation is done by selecting only those solutions from the descendant population which belong to the Pareto optimal set. Then, every individual in the population belong to the Pareto optimal set and all of them have the same probability of being selected for a reproduction or crossover stage.

5. Optimization of semi-static WRON

As it was explained in the previous section, the establishment of a lightpath between each pair of the nodes of the network can be a technical or economical unfeasible option. Therefore, a common solution consists in establishing only a subset of connections. This subset of connections is called the virtual (or logical) topology, and it is the network topology seen by the protocols from the upper layer in the communication protocol tower (Mukherjee, 1997). In Fig. 3 it is possible to see the physical topology (i.e., the physical network where each link of the topology consists of two pair of fibres between a pair of nodes, each one in a direction) from the network shown in Fig. 1. The virtual topology of the network shown in Fig 1 is represented in Fig. 4.

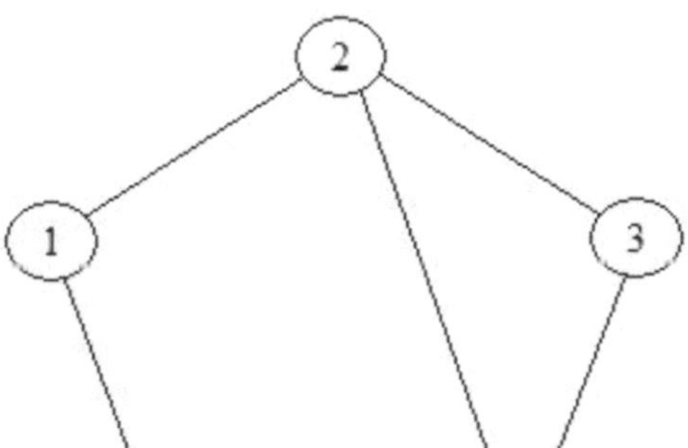

Fig. 3. Physical topology from the network shown in Fig. 1

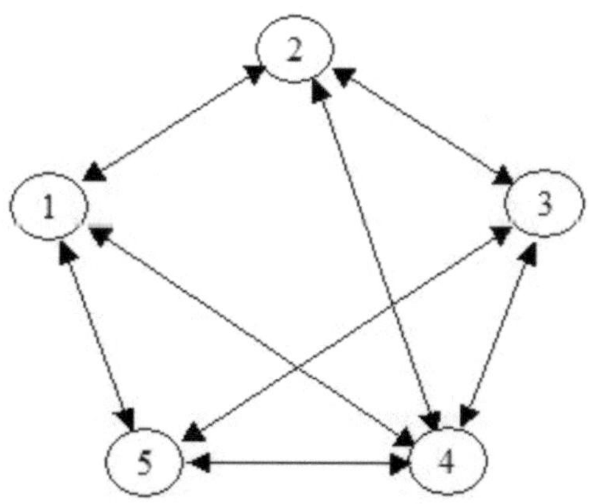

Fig. 4. Virtual topology from the network shown in Fig. 1

5.1 Virtual topology design problem

The optimization problem of designing a virtual topology, given a physical topology and a matrix of traffic to be carried by the network, is shown to be NP-complete. It is usually divided into three subproblems (Mukherjee, 1996):

1. To determine which network nodes should be connected by lightpaths, i.e., to determine the interconnection pattern in the virtual topology.

2. To find a route for each of those lightpaths in the physical network, and to assign an available wavelength to it. This subproblem is known as the static routing and wavelength assignment (RWA) problem.
3. To route traffic on the virtual topology.

Due to the relationship between the three subproblems, some of them are usually solved jointly. The most common method consists in adopting an intermediate solution, and not trying to solve all subproblems jointly nor each subproblem separately. The method consists in solving some of the subproblems jointly. There are a number of possibilities but the most usual one is to solve subproblems (1) and (3) jointly, and then subproblem (2).

Now, we present the mathematical definition of the problem of designing a virtual topology for a WRON, taking into account the three subproblems into which it is divided. The problem can be described as a Mixed Integer Linear Programming formulation (MILP). The notation followed is borrowed from (Dutta & Rouskas, 2000). As an example, the objective of the formulation will be the minimization of the congestion (i.e., the traffic carried by the most loaded lightpath). We describe here all the equations for completeness and then add a constraint for lightpath routing that reduces the computing time required to solve the problem. The following notation is used:

- s and d are used as subscript or superscript and denote the source and the destination of a traffic flow, respectively.
- q is an index to distinguish between the lightpaths between the same pair of nodes.
- i and j denote source and destination nodes, respectively, of a lightpath.
- m and n denote endpoints (nodes) of a physical link.
- f is an index to identify the number of the fibre used among the fibres between two nodes.
- k is the wavelength assigned to a lightpath

Given:

- N is the number of nodes in the network.
- W is the number of wavelengths per fibre.
- Δ is the logical degree of the nodes, i.e., the number of transmitters placed in each node. For simplicity we assume that each node is also equipped with the same number of receivers.
- F is the maximum number of fibres between two nodes.
- Q is the maximum number of lightpaths that can be established between a pair of nodes. In order to do not exceed the logical degree:

$$Q \leq \Delta \tag{3}$$

- $\Lambda^{s,d}$ is the traffic from node s to node d.
- $p_{m,n,f}$ is a binary variable that denotes whether there is a fibre between nodes m and n. $p_{m,n,f}$ takes the value 1 if there are at least f fibres between nodes n and m and takes the value 0 otherwise.

$$p_{m,n,f} \geq p_{m,n,(f+1)} \qquad f \in [1, F-1] \tag{4}$$

- $d_{m,n,f}$ is the propagation delay in the fibre f between the nodes m and n.

- $D_{\min}^{i,j}$ is the propagation delay between the nodes i and j following the shortest path in terms of propagation delay. This value can be estimated using the Dijkstra algorithm modified with the use of weights in the different links (Johnsonbaugh & Schaefer, 2004) and each weight is the propagation delay in that fibre ($d_{m,n,f}$).

Variables:

- $b_{i,j,q}$ is a binary variable that denotes if the lightpath q between node i and node j is established. Note that in this nomenclature i is the source node for this lightpath and j is the destination node. It is important to remark this point since in our definition the lightpaths are unidirectional. $b_{i,j,q} = 0$ means that the lightpath q between nodes i and j is not established. $b_{i,j,q}$ takes the value 1 when this lightpath between these two nodes is established.
- $\lambda_{i,j,q}^{s,d}$ is a variable to represent how much traffic from node s to node d uses the lightpath q between nodes i and j.
- $\lambda_{i,j,q}$ is the traffic that is carried by the lightpath q between nodes i and j.
- $\lambda_{\max}$ is the traffic carried by the most loaded lightpath, i.e., the network congestion.
- $c_{i,j,q}^{k}$ is a binary variable that takes the value 1 if the lightpath between i and j uses the wavelength k, and 0 otherwise.
- $c_{i,j,q}^{k}(m,n,f)$ takes the value 1 if the lightpath between nodes i and j uses the fibre between nodes m and n and uses the wavelength k, and 0 otherwise.

Objective:

$$\text{Minimize } \lambda_{\max} \tag{5}$$

Constraints:

- Degree constraints:

$$\sum_{j=1}^{N}\sum_{q=1}^{Q} b_{i,j,q} \le \Delta \qquad \forall i \tag{6}$$

$$\sum_{i=1}^{N}\sum_{q=1}^{Q} b_{i,j,q} \le \Delta \qquad \forall j \tag{7}$$

Both restrictions limit the number of lightpaths that can be established depending on the maximum number of transmitters, eq. (6) and receivers, eq. (7).

- Routing and wavelength assignment constraints:

$$\sum_{k=1}^{W} c_{i,j,q}^{k} \le b_{i,j,q} \qquad \forall i,j,q \tag{8}$$

$$c_{i,j,q}^{k}(m,n,f) \le c_{i,j,q}^{k} \qquad \forall i,j,q,k,m,n,f \tag{9}$$

$$\sum_{i=1}^{N}\sum_{j=1}^{N}\sum_{q=1}^{Q} c_{i,j,q}^{k}(m,n,f) \le p_{m,n,f} \qquad \forall k,m,n,f \tag{10}$$

$$\sum_{f=1}^{F}\sum_{k=1}^{W}\sum_{l=1}^{N} c_{i,j,q}^{k}(m,l,f) - \sum_{f=1}^{F}\sum_{k=1}^{W}\sum_{l=1}^{N} c_{i,j,q}^{k}(l,m,f) = \begin{cases} b_{i,j,q} & m=i \\ -b_{i,j,q} & m=j \\ 0 & m \ne i, m \ne j \end{cases} \qquad \forall i,j,q,m \tag{11}$$

Eq. (8) ensures that each lightpath uses one, and only one, wavelength. Eq. (9) makes that the same wavelength is used in all the fibres that each lightpath traverses. Eq. (10) avoids collisions, i.e., avoids the possibility that different lightpaths use the same wavelength in the same fibre. Eq. (11) is based on the flow conservation constraints given in (Dutta & Rouskas, 2000) and it is the equation to ensure that the routing of the lightpath over the physical network is continuous along the route.

- Traffic constraints:

$$\lambda_{i,j,q} = \sum_{s=1}^{N}\sum_{d=1}^{N} \lambda_{i,j,q}^{s,d} \qquad \forall i,j,q \tag{12}$$

$$\lambda_{i,j,q} \le \lambda_{\max} \qquad \forall i,j \tag{13}$$

$$\lambda_{i,j,q}^{s,d} \le b_{i,j,q} \cdot \Lambda^{s,d} \qquad \forall i,j,q,s,d \tag{14}$$

$$\sum_{j=1}^{N}\sum_{q=1}^{Q} \lambda_{i,j,q}^{s,d} - \sum_{j=1}^{N}\sum_{q=1}^{Q} \lambda_{j,i,q}^{s,d} = \begin{cases} \Lambda^{s,d} & s=i \\ -\Lambda^{s,d} & d=i \\ 0 & s \ne i, d \ne i \end{cases} \qquad \forall s,d,i \tag{15}$$

Eq. (12) defines the traffic load assigned to the lightpath q between node i and j. The congestion is defined in the Eq. (13). The restriction of eq. (14) avoids that traffic can be routed over a non-existing lightpath. Traffic flow conservation constraints given by Eq. (15) guarantee the conservation of the traffic demand $\Lambda^{s,d}$ along the routes between the source and destination.

In order to speed up the process, one more constraint is added.

$$\sum_{m=1}^{N}\sum_{n=1}^{N}\sum_{k=1}^{W} c_{i,j,q}^{k}(m,n,f) \cdot d_{m,n,f} \le D_{\min}^{i,j} \qquad \forall i,j,q \tag{16}$$

By the Eq. (16) a lightpath can only be established using one of the shortest paths between the source and destination of the lightpath.

5.2 Network provisioning problem

Most network operators have already deployed their fibre networks and they are currently using a set of locations (network nodes) to aggregate and disaggregate the traffic that goes through it. As the cost of the physical installation is the main capital expenditure when a fibre network is built, the optimization methods to be developed in order to upgrade these first generation optical networks to WRONs (while being cost efficient), should use the current physical topologies as an input parameter. Hence, the problem of the design of a WRON starts with the decision about the number of transmitters and receivers that will be used in it and their placement among the network nodes.

On the other hand, WRONs rely on Wavelength Division Multiplexing (WDM) to increase the capacity of the network and also to make the optical routing of the lightpaths. Hence, it is also necessary to determine the number of wavelengths that will be utilized in the network. In this sense, the use of less wavelengths is preferred because it is cheaper as it allows to utilize simpler tunable transmitters and receivers and reduces the complexity of the OXCs.

Therefore, the network provisioning consists of deciding the number of wavelengths, transmitters and receivers and choosing how many transmitters and receivers will be placed in each network node. Note that the optimal solution could require equipping each node with different numbers of these devices. The design of a virtual topology depends on the network provisioning. Hence, in order to design a proper wavelength-routed optical network, the network provisioning and the design of the virtual topology should be considered jointly. However, most of the current methods do not solve both issues together as it is even more complex that only designing the virtual topology. Therefore, it is possible to modify the mathematical definition shown in the previous section to include the problem of network provisioning together with that of virtual topology design. Considering that:

- Tx_{max} is the maximum number of transmitters that can be used in the network.
- Rx_{max} is the maximum number of receivers that can be used in the network. As no lightpath protection is introduced in this formulation and as each lightpath requires a transmitter and a receiver, the number of these to parameters should be equal in order not to waste money.

$$Tx_{\max} = Rx_{\max} \tag{17}$$

- Tx_i is the number of transmitters that should be placed at node *i*.

$$Tx_i = \sum_{j=1}^{N} \sum_{q=1}^{Q} b_{i,j,q} \tag{18}$$

- Rx_j is the number of transmitters that should be placed at node *j*.

$$Rx_j = \sum_{i=1}^{N} \sum_{q=1}^{Q} b_{i,j,q} \tag{19}$$

Then, it is necessary to change Eqs. (6) and (7) by the next two equations:

$$\sum_{i=1}^{N} \sum_{j=1}^{N} \sum_{q=1}^{Q} b_{i,j,q} \leq Tx_{\max} \tag{19}$$

$$\sum_{i=1}^{N}\sum_{j=1}^{N}\sum_{q=1}^{Q} b_{i,j,q} \leq Rx_{\max} \tag{20}$$

5.3 Genetic algorithms to design virtual topologies

In (Durán et al., 2009a) Durán *et al.* propose GALD (Genetic Algorithm for Logical topology Design). GALD is a method designed to solve the full problem of virtual topology design, i.e., to solve the three subproblems shown in section 5.1 jointly. In this section, this work will be presented and complemented with the different versions of the algorithm proposed by the authors. Its chromosome encoding, its translation, the evolution operators used and a summary of performance results will be presented.

5.3.1 Chromosome encoding and translation

The chromosome structure in GALD consists of a sequence of genes where each gene represents a source-destination node pair.

When the chromosome is interpreted in the translation stage, GALD takes each gene in order and tries to establish a unidirectional lightpath between the source and the destination node, subject to the available set of resources. Any of the methods proposed in the literature to solve the RWA problem can be used but a fast method is preferred, hence, we use pre-calculated shortest paths (in terms of propagation delay) in order to solve the routing, and the first-fit heuristic (Zang, 2000) to assign a wavelength to each lightpath. Every time that a gene in the chromosome is read, GALD looks for the lowest available wavelength in any of the shortest paths between the source node and the destination node represented by the gene. If an available wavelength is found, the lightpath is established. Otherwise, the lightpath is not established.

Fig. 5 shows an example of both the chromosome encoding and the translation stage. Each node in the sample network has two transmitters and two receivers, each cable consists of two fibres of the same length (one for each direction), and each fiber is equipped with only one wavelength. When the translation stage takes place, each pair of source-destination nodes (gene) is read from the chromosome. The first three genes are converted into lightpaths because there are enough free resources for their establishment. However, when the algorithm tries to establish the lightpath represented by the fourth gene, it discovers that there is no free wavelength in the shortest path between D and B, therefore this connection cannot be established and is not included in the logical topology. After that, the algorithm tries to establish the lightpaths represented by the final two genes of the chromosome and, as there are enough resources, both of them are established. The resulting logical topology is shown in the figure.

When the chromosome is completely translated, GALD checks whether the logical topology obtained is connected, i.e., there should be at least one possible path in the virtual topology between all the network nodes. If the topology is not connected, the logical topology is rebuilt by first establishing a set of lightpaths forming a Hamiltonian circuit (Johnsonbaugh & Schaefer, 2004, pp. 75-77) and then it continues by trying to establish additional lightpaths according to the information in the chromosome following the method presented above. Then, the traffic is routed in this virtual topology following the shortest paths in terms of hops, similarly as it is done in IP routing protocols.

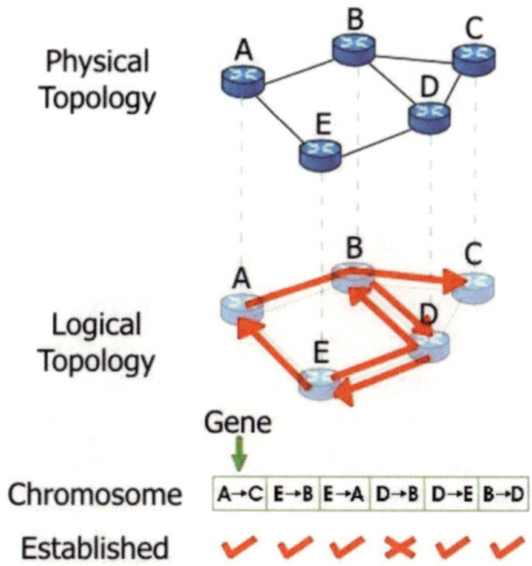

Fig. 5. Example of the proposed chromosome structure and the translation stage.

5.3.2 Initial population

When a new request arrives at the centralized control node to design a virtual topology, it considers the matrix of traffic demands and launches the GALD algorithm. The initial population of GALD is created randomly except one individual that is created following the ideas of a very fast heuristic to design virtual topologies with low congestion: HLDA (Heuristic for Logical topology Design Algorithm) (Ramaswami & Sivarajan, 1996). Hence, the matrix of traffic demand is ordered from the highest to the lowest one. Then, this first individual is created selecting as the first gene the source-destination with the highest traffic demand, the second gene should represents the source-destination pair with the second highest demand and so on. This chromosome will ensure that the health of the fittest individual of the initial population will be better, in most of cases, than the health of the fittest individual of a completely randomly created initial population.

5.3.3 Genetic evolution and operators

During the evolution process (i.e., when the genetic operators are applied), GALD uses the roulette wheel selection mechanism to select the parent individual. Once the first parent (parent 1) has been chosen, it is necessary to decide if a reproduction stage or a crossover stage will take place. The former stage is selected with probability 1- p_{cross} and the later with probability p_{cross}. In the reproduction stage, the individual selected will be copied to the new population without changes. In the crossover stage, it is necessary to select another individual (parent 2) to make the combination and interchange their genetic material. This individual (parent 2) is also selected with the roulette wheel selection mechanism. However, this time the first selected individual (parent 1) cannot be picked out again in order to avoid a veiled reproduction stage. Once both parents have been selected, the crossover operator randomly selects a gene position. Then, the parent chromosomes are divided into two halves by that gene and children are made by interchanging the second halves of their parents. These processes of selection, reproduction and crossover are repeated until the number of individuals in the descendant population (*DP*) is reached.

The mutation operator selects the genes one by one in each chromosome from the descendant population and mutates them according to a probability $p_{mutation}$. If mutation is necessary, the gene is interchanged by another one randomly chosen among the rest of possible values that a gene can take.

After applying the evolution operators, the P fittest individuals from the descendant population are selected to be the parent population for the next generation.

The chromosome structure used for GALD and its translation process makes that each gene position is dominant over the subsequent ones, so it has greater impact on the resulting logical topology. Hence, the crossover and mutation operators are improved by making that there is more probability to choose as crossover point or as gene to be mutated a gene from the first positions in the chromosome than from the latest ones. This is made because when these changes are done in the first genes, the outcomes of applying these operators will be more perceptible.

The stopping criterion is set on the maximum number of generations or on the computation time that the algorithm is allowed to find the solution. One advantage of GALD is that it can be used in a reconfigurable WDM network as the optimization process can be stopped at any time (if required) in order to give the best virtual topology found up to the moment.

5.3.4 Fitness function

As it is explained in section 5.4.1, when the chromosome is translated, the set of lightpaths that will be established are determined, the route and the wavelength used by them is decided, and the traffic is routed over this virtual topology. Then, once the traffic is routed on the virtual topology, the congestion and the delay can be estimated. Different versions of GALD have been presented depending on its fitness function:

- **Traffic Optimization:**
    - **C-GALD** (Congestion optimized - GALD) (Durán et al., 2009a): It is a single-objective version of GALD in which the objective is the minimization of the network congestion (i.e., the traffic carried by the most loaded lightpath).
    - **F-GALD** (Fairness optimized - GALD) (Durán et al., 2009a): a variation to optimize the fairness of the network (whether traffic is uniformly distributed over the established lightpaths). The fairness can be measured by means of the Jain index, which is defined as

$$Jain\ index = \frac{\left(\sum_{i=1}^{L} \lambda_i\right)^2}{L\sum_{i=1}^{L} \lambda_i^2},$$

    where L is the number of lightpaths in the virtual topology and λ_i is the traffic carried by lightpath i. Hence, this index can take values from $1/L$ in the worst case to 1 in the fairest case. So, if the Jain index is close to 1, all lightpaths will carry a similar amount of traffic.
    - **CF-GALD** (Congestion and Fairness optimized - GALD) (Durán et al., 2009a): a version of GALD that optimizes both congestion and fairness. When using this

method, new individuals need to improve both congestion and fairness to be considered as the best topology found until that moment.

- **Delay Optimization:**
  - **MD-GALD** (Mean Delay optimized - GALD) (Durán et al., 2009b): It is a single-objective version of GALD in which the mean end-to-end delay is the parameter employed to evaluate the fitness of an individual. This parameter is estimated using method shown in ((Durán et al., 2009b).
  - **MxD-GALD** (Maximum Delay optimized - GALD) (Durán et al., 2009b): It is a single-objective version of GALD in which the parameter to be optimized is the average end-to-end delay of the most delayed traffic flow.
- **Traffic and Delay Optimization:**
  - **DC-GALD** (Delay and Congestion - GALD) (Durán et al., 2009c): It is a multi-objective version of GALD that employs the classic technique of making a random choice of the fitness criterion (end-to-end delay or congestion, each with 0.5 probability) in order to determine which individuals survive in the next generation.
  - **PDC-GALD** (Pareto optimality of Delay and Congestion - GALD) (Durán et al., 2009c): It is a multi-objective version of GALD, based on Pareto optimality techniques, which jointly optimizes congestion and end-to-end delay.

5.3.5 Results obtained with the methods

Firstly, in Table 1, the performance of C-GALD is compared in terms of network congestion and computing time with that obtained by the MILP formulation shown in section 5.1 with both the basic MILP formulation (Eq. 3 to 15), and with an extension which considers an additional constraint that only allows routing lightpaths through the shortest paths (Eq. 16). The former formulation is denoted by MILP and the latter by SP-MILP (Shortest-Paths MILP). Two networks with different numbers of nodes were used as physical topology and each node was equipped with three transmitters and three receivers. The traffic load between each pair of nodes was set to 0.3 (i.e., the 30% of the capacity of a lightpath). Simulations were made on a computer with a 1.6 GHz Intel Centrino processor and 512 MB of RAM memory, and ILOG CPLEX 10.0 was used to solve the MILP formulations.

	Five-node network		Six-node network	
	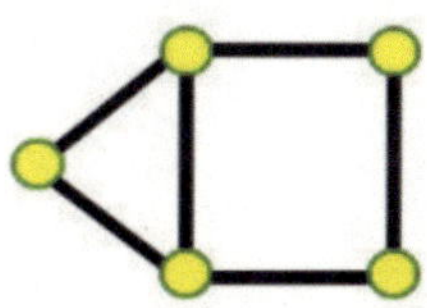		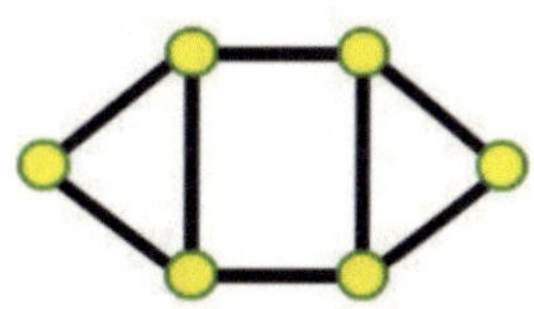	
	Congestion	Execution Time (s)	Congestion	Execution Time (s)
MILP	0.5	15.88	0.7	38060.66
SP-MILP	0.5	1.86	0.7	775.39
C-GALD	0.5	0.01	0.7	1.39

Table 1. Comparison of the congestion of the virtual topologies and the corresponding execution time with the MILP formulations and C-GALD

The results show that all the methods achieve the same results in terms of congestion but C-GALD is the fastest method. It has a computing time which is 180 and 550 times lower than that of SP-MILP in the networks with five and six nodes, respectively. Then, if a network with seven nodes is used, the MILP formulations are unable to find the optimal solution in less than a week using the computer described above. The problem with the MILP formulations is that realistic wide area networks usually have more than seven nodes; hence, the MILP formulations become computationally intractable. On the contrary, C-GALD designs a logical topology in a relatively short period of time and has the advantage of always having a suboptimal solution during the evolution process, thus, this solution can be utilized (if necessary) in a reconfigurable WRON.

In order to evaluate the performance of the different versions of GALD, a simulation study was developed in a simulator based on OMNeT++ using the 14-node NSFNet (Ghose et al., 2005) as network topology and assuming that cables consisted of two unidirectional fibers (one for each direction). The capacity of a wavelength was set to 10 Gbps and the traffic load was normalized by the lightpath capacity. Each node is equipped with five transmitters and five receivers and three wavelength per fibre. Although GALD can be used in networks with or without wavelength converters, we assumed that there were no wavelength converters in the network. The performance achieved by the different versions of GALD is compared with HLDA (Ramaswami & Sivarajan, 1996) as it designs the logical topology with the aim of minimizing network congestion, and it takes into account both the traffic matrix and the availability of physical resources, like GALD does.

In Fig. 6 we compare the congestion obtained when using HLDA (Ramaswami & Sivarajan, 1996) and the tree versions of GALD to optimize the network capacity: C-GALD, F-GALD and CF-GALD. In this last version of GALD, the probability of selecting congestion as fitness function in each generation is set to 0.8, so the probability of choosing fairness is 0.2. We employed uniformly distributed traffic matrixes with different values of the mean traffic load, the creation of 1,000 generations (which takes less than a minute) was selected as the stopping criterion for the three versions of GALD, and the population size was set to two and the descendant size to 12. The corresponding values of fairness are represented in Fig. 7.

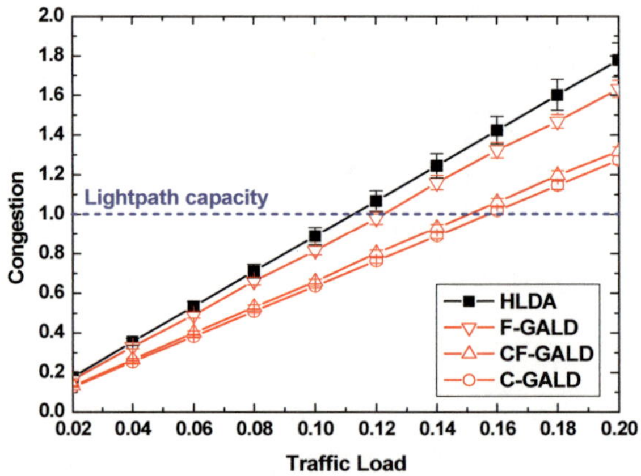

Fig. 6. Congestion value of the logical topologies designed by using HLDA, C-GALD. F-GALD and CF-GALD.

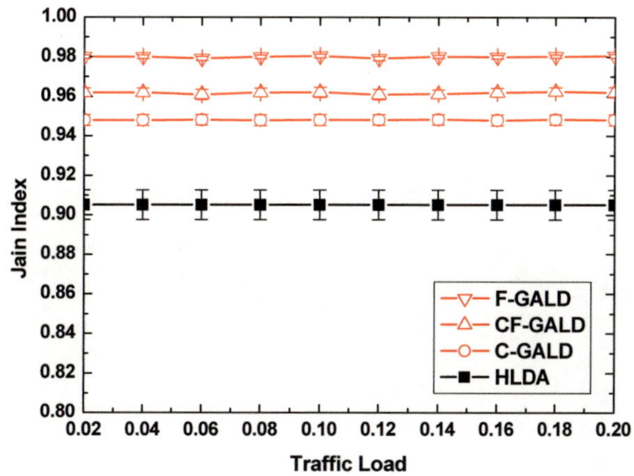

Fig. 7. Fairness of the logical topologies designed by using HLDA, HLDA, C-GALD. F-GALD and CF-GALD .

Fig. 6 show that the congestion of the virtual topologies designed by the four methods grows as the traffic load increases. However, GALD methods always obtain virtual topologies with lower congestion (Fig. 7) and higher fairness (Fig. 8) than those designed with HLDA. In this way, when the mean traffic load is over the 11% of the capacity of a lightpath, the virtual topologies designed by HLDA show a congestion higher than the lightpath capacity and this will cause packet losses. Nevertheless, C-GALD supports traffic loads of up to 0.15 without exceeding the lightpath capacity. Then, the virtual topologies designed by F-GALD, i.e., the version to increase the fairness of the virtual topologies, are the ones that present a higher value of Jain index. Finally, when using the multipurpose version, CF-GALD, there is a trade-off between congestion and fairness, and although the resulting congestion is a little higher than the one achieved with C-GALD, the fairness is better than that obtained with C-GALD.

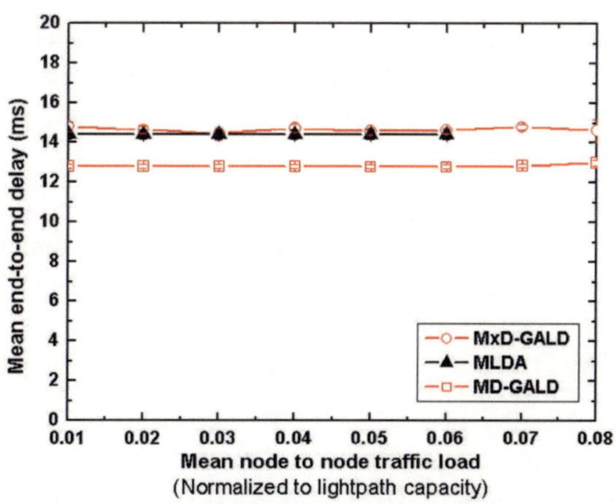

Fig. 8. Mean end-to-end delay of the logical topologies designed by using MLDA, MD-GALD and MxD-GALD. The creation of 500 individuals was the stopping criterion for GALD methods.

Comparing the performance of the versions of GALD to optimize the delay in the same network conditions than the previous study, in Fig. 8, the mean end-to-end delays of the logical topologies obtained with MD-GALD and MxD-GALD are compared with those achieved with MLDA (Ramaswami & Sivarajan, 1996) (an algorithm to design virtual topologies with the objective of minimize the end-to-end delay). The corresponding values of end-to-end delay of the most delayed traffic flow are represented in Fig. 9.

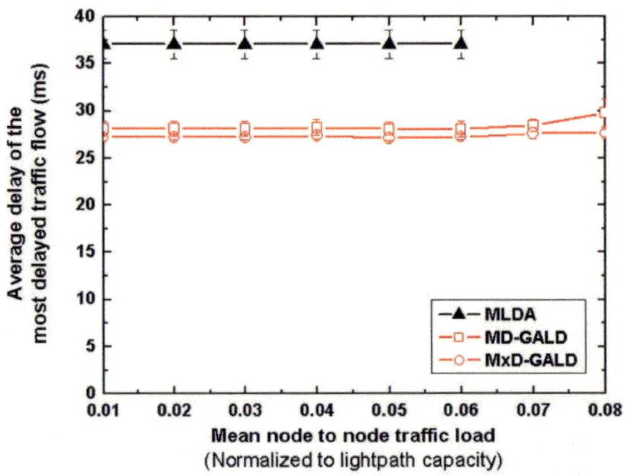

Fig. 9. Average delay of the most delayed traffic flow in the logical topologies designed by MLDA MLDA, MD-GALD and MxD-GALD. The creation of 500 individuals was the stopping criterion for GALD methods.

As shown in Fig. 8, the mean end-to-end delay suffered by the packets in the logical topology designed by all the algorithms has almost the same value for different node-to-node traffic loads because the main component of this delay is due to propagation rather than to processing delays. However, MD-GALD designs virtual topologies that have 10% less average delay than those obtained with MLDA. Moreover, although MxD-GALD is not designed to minimize the average end-to-end delay, it achieves almost the same values than MLDA. Finally, using the network configuration detailed above, the virtual topologies designed by MLDA do not support traffic loads higher than 0.06 (and so the results are not plotted in the figures), while the virtual topologies designed by MD-GALD and MxD-GALD support traffic loads higher than 0.08.

Regarding the average end-to-end delay of the most delayed flow (Fig. 9), both MD-GALD and MxD-GALD design virtual topologies with a significant reduction of this parameter when compared with the one produced by MLDA. In particular, MxD-GALD, which is the most effective algorithm when minimizing this parameter, obtains around 30% reduction when compared to MLDA.

Finally, the advantages of using the multi-objective versions of GALD, mainly PDC-GAPD (i.e., the one with Pareto optimality), will be studied. In Fig. 10 it is shown the results of the virtual topologies obtained by PDC-GALD, DC-GALD, C-GALD, MD-GALD and MLDA assuming a traffic matrix with uniform load of 0.07 between each pair of nodes. Each virtual topology is plotted in terms of its congestion and its mean end-to-end delay. For the genetic algorithms the creation of 1,000,000 individuals was set as the stopping criterion, except for

PDC-GALD. For PDC-GALD we show the results of the initial population (two individuals), the results when 1,000 individuals have been created, and the results when 1,000,000 individuals have been generated

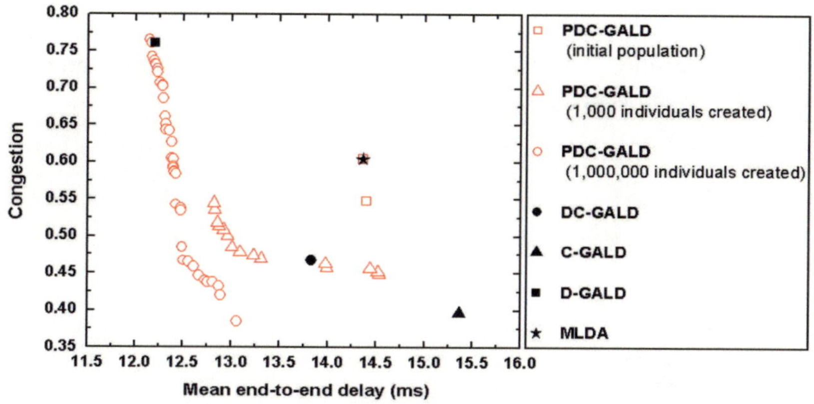

Fig. 10. Mean end-to-end delay and congestion of the logical topologies designed by PDC-GALD, DC-GALD, C-GALD, MD-GALD and MLDA

The first advantage of the method that uses the Pareto optimality in combination with genetic algorithms is that it provides a set of possible virtual topologies (an estimate of the Pareto optimal set) while the other methods only design one (the best topology found until that moment according to the optimization target). This feature of PDC-GALD is very attractive in reconfigurable WRONs, since the network operator can select the virtual topology that better adapts to current network.

Since the first individual of the initial population of PDC-GALD is based on MLDA, obviously PDC-GALD always improves or at least obtains equal results than that algorithm. Moreover, as the number of individuals created increases, the virtual topologies designed by PDC-GALD improve, leading to lower values of congestion and delay. In particular, the virtual topologies found after producing 1,000,000 individuals, do not only get lower values of either congestion or end-to-end delay than the other methods, but they even improve both values, so that PDC-GALD is a very effective method.

Finally, in Fig. 11 and Fig. 12 the congestion and the mean end-to-end delay obtained are compared, respectively, for different traffic loads (randomly generated according to a uniform distribution) for each source-destination pair in the NSFNet with the same configuration than that used in the studies of C-GALD and MD-GALD. The solutions shown for PDC-GALD, are those ones presenting the lowest end-to-end delay (therefore, with the highest congestion) and the ones showing the lowest congestion (hence, with the highest end-to-end delay). The results of the other methods are not shown in order to simplify the figure, but they again got worse results than PDC-GALD.

Fig. 11 and Fig. 12 show that the virtual topologies with lower value of congestion designed by PDC-GALD present a value of this parameter 20% lower than that obtained by the classic multi-objective method, while the end-to-end delay is almost the same for all traffic loads. On the other hand, the solutions with the lowest delay designed by PDC-GALD achieve a reduction of up to 10% in the mean end-to-end delay while the congestion value of this solution is almost the same than the solution found by DC-GALD. Moreover, PDC-GALD designs other logical topologies with congestions and delays between those values.

Summing up, in multi-objective problems, like the one shown in this book chapter, the combination of Pareto optimality with genetic algorithms can give advantages as it does not only provide a set of solution, but the solutions found by it can be better than those obtained with a classic multi-objective genetic algorithm.

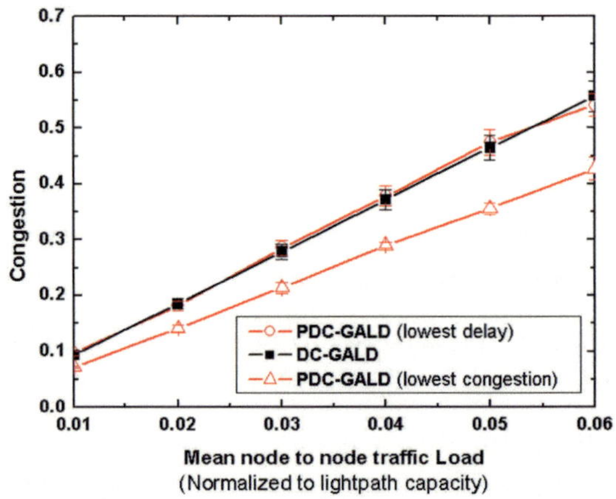

Fig. 11. Congestion of the logical topologies designed by PDC-GALD and DC-GALD

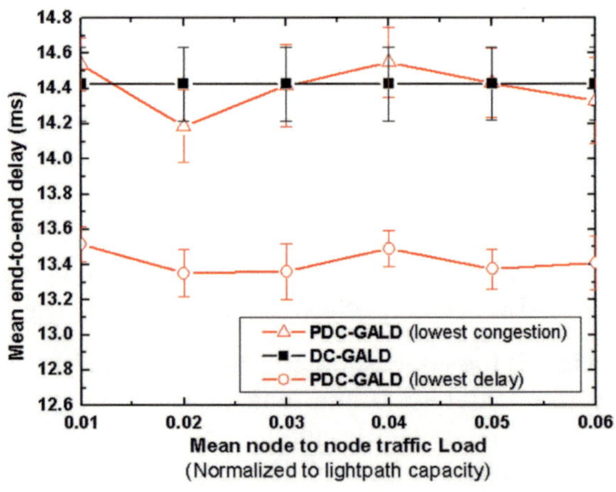

Fig. 12. Mean end-to-end delay of the logical topologies designed by PDC-GALD and DC-GALD

5.4 Genetic algorithms to provision the network and design virtual topologies

In this section, we describe GAPDELT (Genetic Algorithm to Provision the network and to DEsign the Logical Topology) (Durán et al. 2007), a multipurpose method based on the combination of Pareto optimality with genetic algorithms to provision the network and design the virtual topology using the congestion, the number of transmitters/receivers and the number of wavelengths as optimization criteria.

5.4.1 Chromosome encoding and translation

Each chromosome in GAPDELT is composed of a set of $N(N-1)$ genes, where N is the number of nodes in the network. Each gene is a real number between zero and one and is used to determine how many lightpaths will be established between a pair of nodes. For instance, the gene 0 is used to determine the number of lightpaths that will be established from node zero to node one (see Fig. 13) and so on. Furthermore, the genetic information is used to determine in which order the lightpaths will be established.

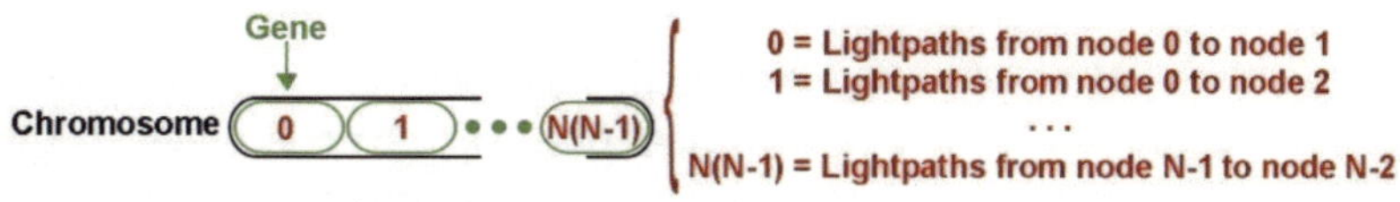

Fig. 13. GAPDELT chromosome structure.

The procedure to translate the genetic information of a chromosome into a network provision scheme and a logical topology follows this pseudo-code:

Step 1. Search for the gene with the highest value in the chromosome.

Step 2. Try to establish the lightpath represented by the gene. Precalculated shortest paths (measured in terms of number of hops in the physical topology) are used for routing the lightpaths and the first-fit heuristic (Zang et al., 1996) is employed to assign a wavelength to each lightpath.

Step 2.a: If the lightpath cannot be established due to lack of free resources, the value of the gene is set to zero.

Step 2.b: If the lightpath is established, a fixed quantity, δ, will be subtracted from the gene. Moreover, a transmitter is assigned to the source node and a receiver to the destination node.

Step 3. Repeat the process from Step 1 as long as there are free transmitters and receivers and as long as there is any gene in the chromosome with value higher than zero. (Thus, note that δ determines the maximum number of lightpaths allowed between a source-destination pair). Otherwise, the translation process finishes, and the resulting resource distribution and the logical topology are the solution represented by the chromosome.

Moreover another version of GAPDELT is presented to solve both the problem of network provisioning and virtual topology design but also ensuring that all the lightpaths of the virtual topology are protected against network failures. Hence, the optimization objectives of P-GAPDELT are also the same ones that GAPDELT but it modifies the step 2 and it does not only offer a lightpath but it also reserves a set of resources to establish a backup lightpath in case the primary one fails. As it is obvious, the primary and the backup lightpath are link disjoint. In order to minimize the resources that will be reserved, P-GAPDELT uses the technique of backup multiplexing in which the reserved resources for a backup lightpath can be also used to provide the redundancy to additional lightpaths if the primary lightpaths are link disjoint.

5.4.2 Initial population

GAPDELT uses as initial population three chromosomes that are designed to ensure that they show either low congestion or low resource utilization and the rest of individuals of the initial population are randomly generated.

The chromosome of the first individual contains the corresponding values of the traffic matrix normalised by the highest value. This individual is inspired in HLDA and has the same objective as the one used in GALD methods. The second individual is a chromosome in which genes that represent lightpaths between nodes that are adjacent in the physical topology are set to δ, and zero otherwise. The third special individual is designed to create a Hamiltonian cycle as the logical topology. These two individuals ensure solutions requiring few network resources.

Then, the rest of individuals are randomly generated setting each value of a gene to a number randomly generated between zero and one. However another modification has been done to find the optimal solutions with different number of resources quickly. The interval between zero and one is divided into σ intervals (parameter defined by the user) and as many chromosomes as desired are generated in the interval $\left[\frac{r}{\sigma},\frac{r+1}{\sigma}\right]$. considering $r = 0,1,\cdots,(\sigma-1)$.

5.4.3 Genetic evolution and operators

In GAPDELT, following the principles of GAs, an initial population of individuals of size P is randomly created. The selection of the two individuals that will act as parents in each crossover process is made randomly among the individuals in the population. In single-objective problems the roulette wheel method according to the individual fitness is utilized as selection process but in GAPDELT, every individual in the population belongs to the Pareto optimal set. The crossover operator is applied to pairs of individuals to interchange a part of their genetic material. It uses the same method than GALD: the chromosomes are divided into two parts by a gene randomly selected (the same in the two chromosome) and the second parts of the chromosomes are interchanged to create two new individuals. The process of crossover is repeated until the descendant population reaches a size of DP that will be proportional to the size of the population ($DP = a \cdot P$). When the process of creating the descendant population is completed, the mutation operator is applied to the individuals in the new population. The mutation operator goes through the genes of the new individuals and it changes the value of the genes randomly according to a probability $p_{mutation}$.

Each time that an individual (or virtual topology) is generated, it is necessary to calculate its goodness according to the fitness functions. Then, the solutions that belong to the Pareto optimal set among the individuals from the descendant and the parent populations will form the parent population for the next generation. When using this technique, solutions which exhibit good performance in many, if not all, objectives are more likely to be produced. Note that the size of the population P, and so DP, will dynamically change depending on the number of individuals that belong to the Pareto optimal set. The evolution process is repeated a number of iterations or until another criterion is met.

A new operator, called vitalization, is designed for GAPDELT. The vitalization tries to increase the health of the individuals similarly as it is done when an individual receives a vitamin. The vitalization is only applied in certain generations, e.g., when the number of individuals generated reaches the user-defined values. When the vitalization is applied, the size of the population is set to three times the current size. In the first third of the new population the current population is copied. Then in the second third, the current population is copied but a certain value between zero and one, called *vitamin*, is subtracted from the genes. If the result is lower than zero, the value of the gene is set to zero. This set of chromosomes can increase the health in terms of resources used (less resources). The third part of the new population is composed by the current population but adding the value *vitamin* to the genes of the current population. If this leads to a gene with a value greater than one, the value of that gene is set to one. The objective of this third part of population is to build solutions with many lightpaths established and so the congestion value of the virtual topologies should decrease. Then, the health of all the population is calculated and the individuals belonging to the Pareto optimal set are considered to be the parents for the new generation.

5.4.4 Fitness function

Each time that an individual is generated and its genetic information is translated into a network provision scheme and a logical topology, its fitness has to be calculated in terms of congestion and number of resources required (transmitters/receivers and wavelengths in operation). To estimate the network congestion, the traffic is routed in the logical topology following the shortest paths measured in number of hops, similar to IP routing protocols. Only those solutions with congestion lower than the lightpath capacity are considered as feasible solutions.

5.4.5 Results obtained with the methods

In order to evaluate and measure the accuracy of both GAPDELT and P-GAPDELT, a simulation study is done using the NSFNet as the physical topology, like in the simulations done to evaluate the GALD method. The maximum number of wavelengths was set to eight and the maximum number of transmitters and receivers to 182. The maximum number of lightpaths between two nodes was fixed to four.

The number of individuals in the initial population was set to 13, three of them were calculated as explained in Section 5.5.2, and the other ones were randomly generated using σ = 9 and a chromosome per interval. The size of the descendant population was two times the size of the parent population. The vitalization was applied each time that 500 individuals were generated and the value of the *vitamin* was set to 0.25. Other configurations for each parameter were analysed, but we finally adopted this one since it led to the best results.

As happens with PCR-GALD, GAPDELT provides as solutions all the dominant individuals in the current population, i.e., an estimate of the Pareto optimal set. However, in this case, the solutions can be represented by the group of three parameters: congestion, number of wavelengths and number of transmitters and receivers used. Hence, in Fig. 14 a three-dimensional colour graph has been used to show the fitness of the set of logical topologies found by the algorithm. Each point in the graph is a solution represented in terms of its number of wavelength, transmitters and receivers in operation and its congestion. In order to show this qualitative result, a random traffic matrix was used in which the traffic demands between a pair of nodes was randomly generated using an uniform distribution with load of 0.1, i.e., 1 Gbps. The creation of one million of individuals was set as stopping criterion.

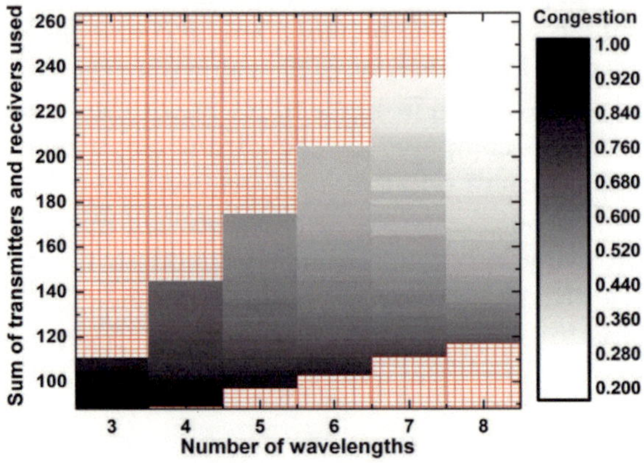

Fig. 14. Fitness of the solutions found by GAPDELT

As it is shown in Fig. 14, GAPDELT obtains in a single execution a high number of feasible solutions. In contrast, if traditional virtual topology design methods were used, it would have been necessary to repeat the execution of these methods a number of times varying the number of transmitters, receivers and wavelengths and also varying the distribution of the transmitters and receivers among the nodes to obtain the same result that GAPDELT can obtain in only one execution.

Moreover, each solution of GAPDELT brings the following information: the number of transmitters in each node of the network (it can be heterogeneously distributed), the number of receivers in each node of the network (it can also be heterogeneously distributed), the number of wavelengths used in the network, the set of lightpaths that should be established in the network, the route and the wavelength that each lightpath has to use and the traffic routing over the virtual topology.

Regarding the results illustrated in Fig. 14, obviously, as the number of resources employed to design the virtual topology increases, the congestion obtained is generally lower. However, as shown by the grated areas in the figure, there are regions where increasing the number of resources does not lead to reductions in congestion, i.e., some resources are wasted in these areas with the corresponding increase in the cost of the network. For instance, in some cases, if the number of wavelengths is increased, but it is not accompanied by an increase on the number of transmitters/receivers, there is no reduction in congestion. GAPDELT detects these situations, leading to solutions with a balanced use of transmitters/receivers and wavelengths, hence optimizing the utilization of resources and improving the cost efficiency of the network.

Fig. 15 shows the number of solutions found, in average, by GAPDELT and P-GAPDELT in a single execution depending on the traffic load. Each value shown has been obtained using 250 traffic matrixes where each value of the matrix has been randomly selected following a uniform distribution with the mean of the traffic load shown in the figures. Results are shown with 95% confidence intervals. The stopping criterion in GAPDELT was set to the creation of 100,000 individual during the evolution process. As can be seen in the figure, as the traffic load increases, the number of solutions found by both version of GAPDELT decreases because there are less solutions with a congestion value under the maximum lightpath capacity. Moreover, GAPDELT achieves to design more virtual topologies than P-GAPDELT as it can use more resources to establish primary lightpaths.

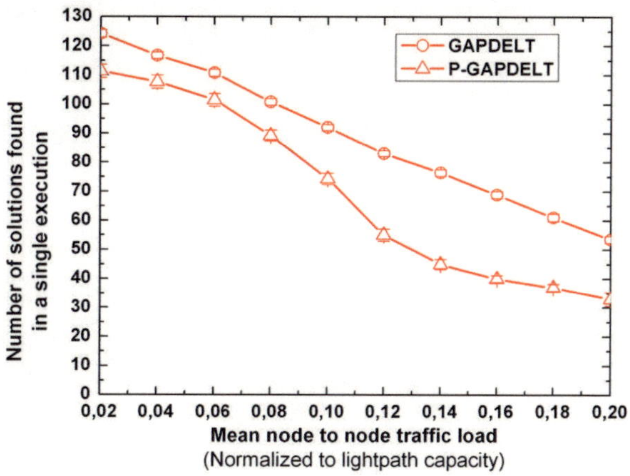

Fig. 15. Number of solutions found, in average, by GAPDELT and P-GALDELT in a single execution

Fig. 16 compares the congestion obtained by GAPDELT, P-GAPDELT, HLDA (when each node is equipped with 13 transmitters and 13 receivers) and HLDA again but using the resource distribution provided by GAPDELT. As GAPDELT methods design solutions with different number of wavelengths used, only the solutions which use eight wavelengths are shown in the figure, and from these solutions, two of them are selected to be plotted: the one with lowest congestion and the one with lowest number of transmitters and receivers. Each value shown has been obtained using 250 traffic matrixes where each value of the matrix has been randomly selected following a uniform distribution with the mean of the traffic load shown in the figures. Results are shown with 95% confidence intervals. The stopping criterion in GAPDELT was set to the creation of 100,000 individual during the evolution process.

The objective of this comparison is to study not only the performance of GAPDELT as a method to design the virtual topology but also to analyse the advantages obtained as a method to solve the network provisioning problem. For higher loads, HLDA cannot find a solution with a value of congestion lower or equal than one (i.e., without exceeding the lightpath capacity) and these are not plotted in the figure.

Firstly, it is possible to see in Fig. 16 that GAPDELT can design virtual topologies for higher traffic loads when HLDA cannot, even when using the resource distribution found by GAPDELT. Moreover, GAPDELT does not only design a set of solutions per execution instead of only one, but it also designs virtual topologies that can reduce in 50% the value of congestion when compared with HLDA. Moreover, the results from Fig. 16 show that the problem of network provisioning and the design of logical topologies are strongly related. In this sense, in Fig. 16 it is shown that when HLDA uses the resource distributions obtained by GAPDELT, it designs virtual topologies with lower congestion than if a uniform distribution of resources among the network nodes is used. Hence, GAPDELT also offers advantages if it is only used to solve the problem of network provisioning.

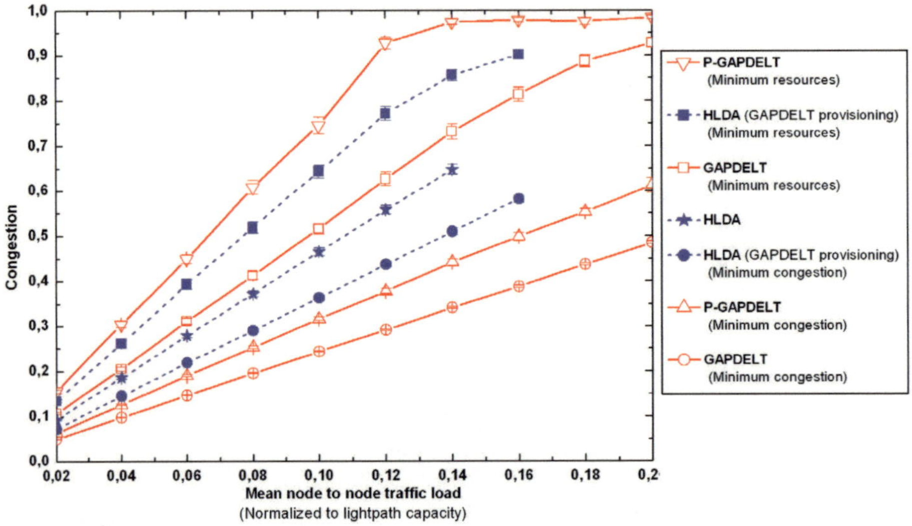

Fig. 16. Comparison of the congestion of the virtual topologies designed by GAPDELT and P-GAPDELT with HLDA for different network loads

As it is obvious, the congestion of the solutions obtained by GAPDELT are lower than those of P-GAPDELT because the former does not need to reserve resources for backup lightpaths and it can establish a higher number of primary lightpaths reducing the congestion but without providing failure protection. However, an interesting result to show the efficiency of the GAPDELT family is that P-GAPDELT can also reduce the congestion obtained by HLDA when the latter is a method to design virtual topologies reducing the congestion and it does offer failure protection.

6. Conclusion

In this chapter, the optimization problems of designing a semi-static wavelength-routed optical network have been described. In this kind of optical networks two problems should be solved: the network provisioning and the virtual topology design. A set of genetic algorithms proposed by the Optical Communications Group at the University of Valladolid to solve these two problem problems have been presented. In this way, GALD methods were proposed to design the virtual topology while GAPDELT methods were created to solve both the network provisioning and the virtual topology design problems. The chromosome structures, their translation, the optimization goals and the genetic operators utilized by each method have been described.

A number of versions of GALD have been developed, each one to optimize a network parameter related with the network capacity (C-GALD, F-GALD) or the delay (MD-GALD,

MxD-GALD). Moreover, a multi-objective method, PCR-GALD, based on the combination of genetic algorithms with Pareto optimality has also been presented. The results from a simulation study show that GALD methods are very good techniques to design virtual topologies as they obtain virtual topologies with better performance than those designed by other methods from the literature.

GAPDELT is a multi-objective algorithm to design both the network provisioning and the virtual topology that minimises the congestion and the number of required resources (in terms of number of transmitters, receivers and wavelengths) and thus the network cost. The method is based on the combination of genetic algorithms and Pareto optimality. Moreover, another version of the method called P-GAPDELT has also been presented to solve the same problems than GAPDELT, but reserving resources to establish backup lightpaths to replace the primary ones when facing network failures. By means of a simulation study, we have shown that both GAPDELT and P-GAPDELT provide a set of solutions, the set of optimal or near-optimal solutions, in only one execution. Moreover, the simulation study done shows that the performance of the solutions found by GAPDELT methods outperform the ones obtained with other methods previously proposed in the literature.

7. Acknowledgment

This research has been partially supported by the FIERRO Thematic Network, funded by the Spanish Ministry of Science and Innovation (TEC2010-12250-E).

8. References

Durán, R.J. et al. (2007). Multiobjective genetic algorithm to design cost-efficient wavelength-routed optical networks. *9th International Conference on Transparent Optical Networks Proceedings*, vol. 4, (Rome, Italy), pp. 96–99.

Durán, R.J. et al. (2009a). Genetic algorithm to design logical topologies in reconfigurable WDM networks. *Photonic Network Communications*, vol. 17, no. 1, pp. 21-33.

Durán, R.J. et al. (2009b). Minimization of end to end delay in reconfigurable WDM networks using genetic algorithms. *European Transactions on Telecommunications*, vol. 20, no. 8, pp. 722-733.

Durán, R.J. et al. (2009c). Joint Optimization of Delay and Congestion in Wavelength-Routed Optical Networks Using Genetic Algorithms. *Photonic Network Communications*, vol 18, no. 3, pp. 233-244.

Dutta, R & Rouskas, G.N (2000). A survey of virtual topology design algorithms for wavelength routed optical networks. *Optical Networks Magazine*, vol. 1, pp. 73-89.

Ghose, S. et al. (2005). Multihop virtual topology design in WDM optical networks for self-similar traffic. *Photonic Network Communications*, vol. 10, no. 2, pp. 199–214.

Goldberg, D.E. (1989). *Genetic algorithm in search, optimization and machine learning*, Addison-Wesley Professional.

Johnsonbaugh, R. & M. Schaefer, Algorithms, Pearson Education, Inc., 2004.

Man, K.F. et. Al. (1999). *Genetic algorithms*, Springer-Verlag.

Mukherjee, B. et al. (1996). Some principles for designing a wide-area WDM optical network. *IEEE/ACM Transactions on Networking*, vol. 4, no. 5, pp. 684–696.

Mukherjee, B. (1997). *Optical Communication Networks*, McGraw-Hill, 1997.

Ramaswami, R. & Sivarajan, K.N.(1996) Design of logical topologies for wavelength-routed optical networks. *IEEE Journal on Selected Areas in Communications*, vol. 14, no. 5, pp. 840-851

Zang, H. et al. (2000). A review of routing and wavelength assignment approaches for wavelength-routed optical WDM networks, *Optical Networks Magazine*, vol. 1, no. 1, pp. 47-60.

17

Surrogate-Based Optimization

Zhong-Hua Han and Ke-Shi Zhang
School of Aeronautics, Northwestern Polytechnical University, Xi'an, P.R. China

1. Introduction

Surrogate-based optimization (Queipo et al. 2005, Simpson et al. 2008) represents a class of optimization methodologies that make use of surrogate modeling techniques to quickly find the local or global optima. It provides us a novel optimization framework in which the conventional optimization algorithms, e.g. gradient-based or evolutionary algorithms are used for sub-optimization(s). Surrogate modeling techniques are of particular interest for engineering design when high-fidelity, thus expensive analysis codes (e.g. Computation Fluid Dynamics (CFD) or Computational Structural Dynamics (CSD)) are used. They can be used to greatly improve the design efficiency and be very helpful in finding global optima, filtering numerical noise, realizing parallel design optimization and integrating simulation codes of different disciplines into a process chain. Here the term "surrogate model" has the same meaning as "response surface model", "metamodel", "approximation model", "emulator" etc. This chapter aims to give an overview of existing surrogate modeling techniques and issues about how to use them for optimization.

2. Overview of surrogate modeling techniques

For optimization problems, surrogate models can be regarded as approximation models for the cost function (s) and state function (s), which are built from sampled data obtained by randomly probing the design space (called sampling via Design of Experiment (DoE)). Once the surrogate models are built, an optimization algorithm such as Genetic Algorithms (GA) can be used to search the new design (based on the surrogate models) that is most likely to be the optimum. Since the prediction with a surrogate model is generally much more efficient than that with a numerical analysis code, the computational cost associated with the search based on the surrogate models is generally negligible.

Surrogate modeling is referred to as a technique that makes use of the sampled data (observed by running the computer code) to build surrogate models, which are sufficient to predict the output of an expensive computer code at untried points in the design space. Thus, how to choose sample points, how to build surrogate models, and how to evaluate the accuracy of surrogate models are key issues for surrogate modeling.

2.1 Design of experiments

To build a surrogate model, DoE methods are usually used to determine the locations of sample points in the design space. DoE is a procedure with the general goal of maximizing the amount of information gained form a limited number of sample points (Giunta et al., 2001). Currently, there are different DoE methods which can be classified into two categories: "classic" DoE methods and "modern" DoE methods. The classic DoE methods, such as full-factorial design, central composite design (CCD), Box-Behnken and D-Optimal Design (DOD), were developed for the arrangement of laboratory experiments, with the consideration of reducing the effect of random error. In contrast, the modern DoE methods such as Latin Hypercube Sampling (LHS), Orthogonal Array Design (OAD) and Uniform Design (UD) (Fang et al., 2000) were developed for deterministic computer experiments without the random error as arises in laboratory experiments. An overview of the classic and modern DoE methods was presented by Giunta et al. (2001). A more detailed description of existing DoE methods is beyond the scope of this chapter.

The schematics of 40 sample points selected by LHS and UD for a two-dimensional problem are sketched in Figure 1.

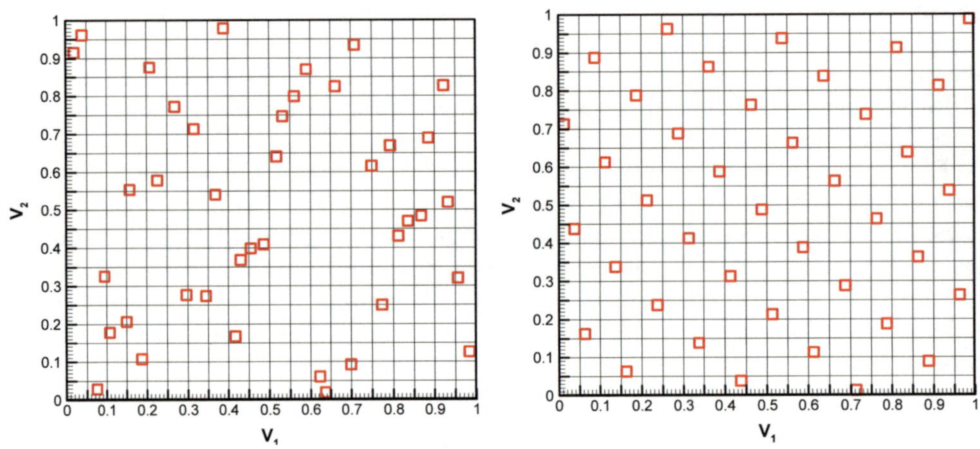

Fig. 1. Schematics of 40 sample points selected by Design of Experiments for a two-dimensional problem (left: Latin Hypercube Sampling; right: Uniform Design).

2.2 Surrogate models

There are a number of surrogate models available in the literatures. Here we limit our discussion to three popular techniques such as RSM (polynomial Response Surface Model), Kriging, RBFs (Radial Basis Functions).

For an m-dimensional problem, suppose we are concerned with the prediction of the output of a high-fidelity, thus expensive computer code, which is correspondent to an unknown function $y:\mathbb{R}^m \rightarrow \mathbb{R}$. By running the computer code, y is observed at n sites (determined by DoE)

$$\mathbf{S} = [\mathbf{x}^{(1)},...,\mathbf{x}^{(n)}]^{\mathrm{T}} \in \mathbb{R}^{n\times m}, \mathbf{x} = \{x_1,..,x_m\} \in \mathbb{R}^m \tag{1}$$

with the corresponding responses

$$\mathbf{y}_S = [y^{(1)},...,y^{(n)}]^{\mathrm{T}} = [y(\mathbf{x}^{(1)}),...,y(\mathbf{x}^{(n)})]^{\mathrm{T}} \in \mathbb{R}^n \tag{2}$$

The pair ($\mathbf{S}$, $\mathbf{y}_S$) denotes the sampled data sets in the vector space.

With the above descriptions and assumptions, our objective here is to build a surrogate model for predicting the output of the computer code for any untried site $\mathbf{x}$ (that is, to estimate $y(\mathbf{x})$) based on the sampled date sets ($\mathbf{S}$, $\mathbf{y}_S$), in an attempt to achieve the desired accuracy with the least possible number of sample points.

2.2.1 Quadratic response surface method

Here we use "RSM" to denote a polynomial approximation model in which the sampled data is fitted by a least-square regression technique. In RSM-based optimization applications, the "quadratic" polynomial model usually provides the best compromise between the modeling accuracy and computational expense, when compared with the linear or higher order polynomial models. An advantage of RSM is that it can smooth out the various scales of numerical noise in the data while captures the global trend of the variation, which makes it very robust and thus well suited for optimization problems in engineering design.

The true quadratic RSM can be written in the following form:

$$y(\mathbf{x}) = \hat{y}(\mathbf{x}) + \varepsilon, \mathbf{x} \in \mathbb{R}^m , \quad (3)$$

where $\hat{y}(\mathbf{x})$ is the quadratic polynomial approximation and ε is the random error which is assumed to be normally distributed with mean zero and variance of σ^2 . The error ε_i at each observation is supposed to be independent and identically distributed. The quadratic RSM predictor $\hat{y}(\mathbf{x})$ can be defined as:

$$\hat{y}(\mathbf{x}) = \beta_0 + \sum_{i=1}^{m} \beta_i x_i + \sum_{i=1}^{m} \beta_{ii} x_i^2 + \sum_{i=1}^{m} \sum_{j \geq i}^{m} \beta_{ij} x_i x_j , \quad (4)$$

where β_0 , β_i , β_{ii} and β_{ij} are unknown coefficients to be determined. Since there are totally $p = (m+1)(m+2)/2$ unknown coefficients in Eq.(4), building a quadratic RSM with m variables requires at least p sample points. Let $\boldsymbol{\beta} \in \mathbb{R}^p$ be the column vector contains these p unknown coefficients. The least square estimator of $\boldsymbol{\beta}$ is

$$\boldsymbol{\beta} = (\mathbf{U}^{\mathrm{T}}\mathbf{U})^{-1}\mathbf{U}^{\mathrm{T}}\mathbf{y}_S , \quad (5)$$

where

$$\mathrm{U} = \begin{bmatrix} 1 & x_1^{(1)} & \cdots & x_m^{(1)} & x_1^{(1)} x_2^{(1)} & \cdots & x_{m-1}^{(1)} x_m^{(1)} & \left(x_1^{(1)}\right)^2 & \cdots & \left(x_m^{(1)}\right)^2 \\ \vdots & \vdots & \ddots & \vdots & \vdots & \ddots & \vdots & \vdots & \ddots & \vdots \\ 1 & x_1^{(n)} & \cdots & x_m^{(n)} & x_1^{(n)} x_2^{(n)} & \cdots & x_{m-1}^{(n)} x_m^{(n)} & \left(x_2^{(n)}\right)^2 & \cdots & \left(x_m^{(n)}\right)^2 \end{bmatrix} \in \mathbb{R}^{n \times p} . \quad (6)$$

After the unknown coefficients in $\boldsymbol{\beta}$ are determined, the approximated response $\hat{y}$ at any untried $\mathbf{x}$ can be efficiently predicted by Eq. (4).

2.2.2 Kriging model

Different from RSM, Kriging (Krige, 1951) is an interpolating method which features the observed data at all sample points. Kriging provides a statistic prediction of an unknown function by minimizing its Mean Squared Error (MSE). It can be equivalent to any order of polynomials and is thus well suited for a highly-nonlinear function with multi extremes. For the derivation of Kriging (Sacks et al., 1989), the output of a deterministic computer experiment is treated as a realization of a random function (or stochastic process), which is defined as the sum of a global trend function $\mathbf{f}^{\mathrm{T}}(\mathbf{x})\boldsymbol{\beta}$ and a Gaussian random function $Z(\mathbf{x})$ as following

$$y(\mathbf{x}) = \mathbf{f}^{\mathrm{T}}(\mathbf{x})\boldsymbol{\beta} + Z(\mathbf{x}), \mathbf{x} \in \mathbb{R}^m, \tag{7}$$

where $\mathbf{f}(\mathbf{x}) = [f_0(\mathbf{x}), ..., f_{p-1}(\mathbf{x})]^{\mathrm{T}} \in \mathbb{R}^p$ is defined with a set of the regression basis functions and $\boldsymbol{\beta} = [\beta_0, .., \beta_{p-1}]^{\mathrm{T}} \in \mathbb{R}^p$ denotes the vector of the corresponding coefficients. In general, $\mathbf{f}^{\mathrm{T}}(\mathbf{x})\boldsymbol{\beta}$ is taken as either a constant or low-order polynomials. Practice suggests that the constant trend function is sufficient for most of the problems. Thus, $\mathbf{f}^{\mathrm{T}}(\mathbf{x})\boldsymbol{\beta}$ is taken as a constant β_0 in the text hereafter. In Eq.(7), $Z(\cdot)$ denotes a stationary random process with zero mean, variance σ^2 and nonzero covariance of

$$Cov[Z(\mathbf{x}), Z(\mathbf{x}')] = \sigma^2 R(\mathbf{x}, \mathbf{x}'). \tag{8}$$

Here $R(\mathbf{x}, \mathbf{x}')$ is the correlation function which is only dependent on the Euclidean distance between any two sites $\mathbf{x}$ and $\mathbf{x}'$ in the design space. In this study, a Gaussian exponential correlation function is adopted, and it is of the form

$$R(\mathbf{x}, \mathbf{x}') = \exp[-\sum_{k=1}^{m} \theta_k \, | x_k - x_k' \, |^{p_k}], 1 < p_k \le 2, \tag{9}$$

where $\boldsymbol{\theta} = [\theta_1, \theta_2, ..., \theta_m]^{\mathrm{T}}$ and $\mathbf{p} = [p_1, p_2, ..., p_m]^{\mathrm{T}}$ denote the vectors of the unknown model parameters (hyper parameters) to be tuned. The schematics of a Gaussian exponential correlation function for one-dimensional problem is sketched in Figure 2.

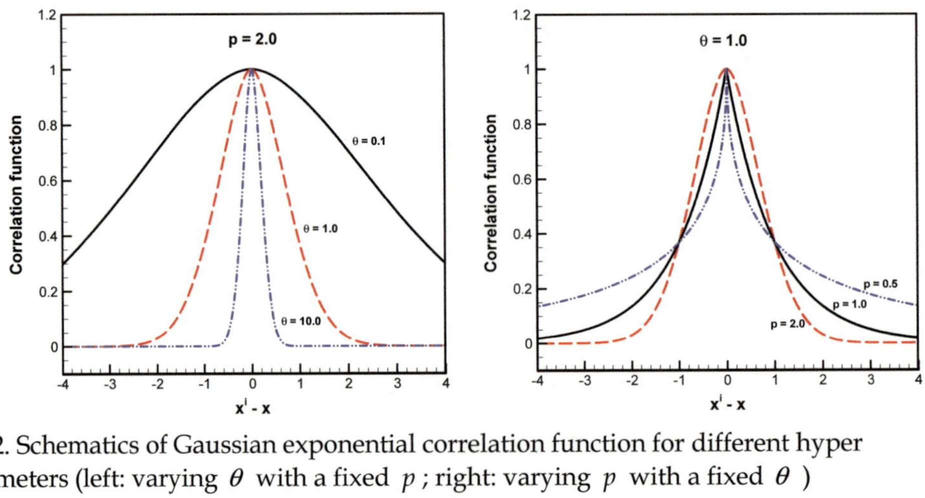

Fig. 2. Schematics of Gaussian exponential correlation function for different hyper parameters (left: varying θ with a fixed p; right: varying p with a fixed θ)

From the derivation by Sacks et al. (1989) the Kriging predictor $\hat{y}(x)$ for any untried $\mathbf{x}$ can be written as

$$\hat{y}(\mathbf{x}) = \beta_0 + \mathbf{r}^{\mathrm{T}}(\mathbf{x})\mathbf{R}^{-1}(\mathbf{y}_S - \beta_0\mathbf{1}), \tag{10}$$

where the generalized least square estimation of β_0 is

$$\beta_0 = (\mathbf{1}^{\mathrm{T}}\mathbf{R}^{-1}\mathbf{1})^{-1}\mathbf{1}^{\mathrm{T}}\mathbf{R}^{-1}\mathbf{y}_S, \tag{11}$$

and $\mathbf{1} \in \mathbb{R}^n$ is a vector filled with ones, and $\mathbf{R}, \mathbf{r}$ are the correlation matrix and the correlation vector, respectively. $\mathbf{R}$ and $\mathbf{r}$ are defined as

$$\mathbf{R} = \begin{bmatrix} R(\mathbf{x}^{(1)},\mathbf{x}^{(1)}) & R(\mathbf{x}^{(1)},\mathbf{x}^{(2)}) & \cdots & R(\mathbf{x}^{(1)},\mathbf{x}^{(n)}) \\ R(\mathbf{x}^{(2)},\mathbf{x}^{(1)}) & R(\mathbf{x}^{(2)},\mathbf{x}^{(2)}) & \cdots & R(\mathbf{x}^{(2)},\mathbf{x}^{(n)}) \\ \vdots & \vdots & \ddots & \vdots \\ R(\mathbf{x}^{(n)},\mathbf{x}^{(1)}) & R(\mathbf{x}^{(n)},\mathbf{x}^{(2)}) & \cdots & R(\mathbf{x}^{(n)},\mathbf{x}^{(n)}) \end{bmatrix} \in \mathbb{R}^{n \times n}, \ \mathbf{r} = \begin{bmatrix} R(\mathbf{x}^{(1)},\mathbf{x}) \\ R(\mathbf{x}^{(2)},\mathbf{x}) \\ \vdots \\ R(\mathbf{x}^{(n)},\mathbf{x}) \end{bmatrix} \in \mathbb{R}^n, \tag{12}$$

where $R(\mathbf{x}^{(i)},\mathbf{x}^{(j)})$ denotes the correlation between any two observed points $\mathbf{x}^{(i)}$ and $\mathbf{x}^{(j)}$; $R(\mathbf{x}^{(i)},\mathbf{x})$ denotes the correlation between the *i*-th observed point $\mathbf{x}^{(i)}$ and the untried point $\mathbf{x}$.

A unique feature of Kriging model is that it provides an uncertainty estimation (or MSE) for the prediction, which is very useful for sample-points refinement. It is of the form

$$\hat{s}^2(\mathbf{x}) = \sigma^2[1.0 - \mathbf{r}^{\mathrm{T}}\mathbf{R}^{-1}\mathbf{r} + (\mathbf{r}^{\mathrm{T}}\mathbf{R}^{-1}\mathbf{1} - 1)^2 / \mathbf{1}^{\mathrm{T}}\mathbf{R}^{-1}\mathbf{1}]. \tag{13}$$

Assuming that the sampled data are distributed according to a Gaussian process, the responses at sampling sites are considered to be correlated random functions with the corresponding likelihood function given by

$$L(\beta_0, \sigma^2, \boldsymbol{\theta}, \mathbf{p}) = \frac{1}{\sqrt{2\pi(\sigma^2)^n |\mathbf{R}|}} \exp\left(-\frac{1}{2} \frac{(\mathbf{y}_S - \beta_0\mathbf{1})^{\mathrm{T}}\mathbf{R}^{-1}(\mathbf{y}_S - \beta_0\mathbf{1})}{\sigma^2} \right). \tag{14}$$

The optimal estimation of β_0 and the process variance

$$\begin{aligned} \beta_0(\boldsymbol{\theta}, \mathbf{p}) &= (\mathbf{1}^{\mathrm{T}}\mathbf{R}^{-1}\mathbf{1})^{-1}\mathbf{1}^{\mathrm{T}}\mathbf{R}^{-1}\mathbf{y}_S \\ \sigma^2(\beta_0, \boldsymbol{\theta}, \mathbf{p}) &= \frac{1}{n}(\mathbf{y}_S - \beta_0\mathbf{1})^{\mathrm{T}}\mathbf{R}^{-1}(\mathbf{y}_S - \beta_0\mathbf{1}) \end{aligned} \tag{15}$$

are obtained analytically, yet depends on the remaining hyper-parameters $\boldsymbol{\theta} = [\theta_1, \theta_2, ..., \theta_m]^{\mathrm{T}}$ and $\mathbf{p} = [p_1, p_2, ..., p_m]^{\mathrm{T}}$. Substituting it into the associated Eq. (14) and taking the logarithm, we are left with maximizing

$$.\ \mathrm{MLE}(\boldsymbol{\theta}, \mathbf{p}) = -n \ln \sigma^2(\boldsymbol{\theta}) - \ln |\mathbf{R}(\boldsymbol{\theta})| \ ., \tag{16}$$

which can be solved by a numerical optimization algorithm such as GA. The hyperparamters tuning strategies are discussed by Toal et al. (2008). Note that the above Kriging formulation can be extended by including gradient information obtained by Adjoint method (Han et al. 2009, Laurenceau et al. 2008) or lower-fidelity data by lower-fidelity analysis code (Han et al. 2010, Forrester et al. 2007).

2.2.3 Radial basis functions

In additional to Kriging, RBFs model (Hardy, 1971) is known as an alternative interpolation method for surrogate modeling. For the RBFs approach by Powell (1987), the approximation of the unknown function $y(\mathbf{x})$ at an untried $\mathbf{x}$ is formally defined as the linear combination of the radial basis functions and a global trend function as

$$\hat{y}(\mathbf{x}) = \sum_{i=1}^{n} \omega_i \varphi(\mathbf{x}) + P(\mathbf{x}), \tag{17}$$

where ω_i are the i-th unknown weight coefficient, $\varphi(\mathbf{x}) = \varphi(\|\mathbf{x}^{(i)} - \mathbf{x}\|)$ are the basis functions that depend on the Euclidean distance between the observed point $\mathbf{x}^{(i)}$ and the untried point $\mathbf{x}$ (similar to the correlation function of kriging model); $P(\mathbf{x})$ is the global trend function which is taken as a constant β_0 here. To ensure the function values at observed points are reproduced by the RBFs predictor, the flowing constraints should be satisfied:

$$\hat{y}(\mathbf{x}^{(i)}) = y^{(i)}, i = 1,..,n \tag{18}$$

Then the additional constraints for $P(\mathbf{x})$ should be imposed as

$$\sum_{i=0}^{n} \omega_i = 0 . \tag{19}$$

Solving the linear equations formed by Eq. (18) and Eq. (19) for ω_i and β_0, and substituting into Eq.(17) yields the RBFs predictor as

$$\hat{y}(\mathbf{x}) = \beta_0 + \boldsymbol{\varphi}^{\mathrm{T}}(\mathbf{x}) \boldsymbol{\Psi}^{-1} (\mathbf{y}_S - \beta_0 \mathbf{1}) . \tag{20}$$

Where $\beta_0(\boldsymbol{\theta}) = (\mathbf{1}^{\mathrm{T}} \boldsymbol{\Psi}^{-1} \mathbf{1})^{-1} \mathbf{1}^{\mathrm{T}} \boldsymbol{\Psi}^{-1} \mathbf{y}_S$ and $\boldsymbol{\Psi}$, $\boldsymbol{\varphi}(\mathbf{x})$ are defined as

$$\boldsymbol{\Psi} := [\varphi(\|\mathbf{x}^{(i)} - \mathbf{x}^{(j)}\|)]_{ij} \in \mathbb{R}^{n \times n}, \; \boldsymbol{\varphi}(\mathbf{x}) := [\varphi(\|\mathbf{x}^{(i)} - \mathbf{x}\|)]_i \in \mathbb{R}^n . \tag{21}$$

When the above RBFs predictor is compared with the Kriging predictor (see Eq. (10)), one can observe that they are essentially similar, only with the basis-function matrix $\boldsymbol{\Psi}$ (also called Gram matrix) and the basis function vector $\boldsymbol{\varphi}(\mathbf{x})$ being different from the correlation matrix $\mathbf{R}$ and the correlation vector $\mathbf{r}(\mathbf{x})$ of the Kriging predictor, respectively. In addition, RBFs differs from Kriging at the following two aspects: 1) RBFs doesn't provide the uncertainty estimation of the prediction; 2) The model parameters can't be tuned by MLE like Kriging. Generally, Kriging can be regarded as a particular form of RBFs.

To build a RBFs model, one needs to prescribe the type of basis functions that only depends on the Euclidean distance $r = \|\mathbf{x} - \mathbf{x}'\|$ between any two sites $\mathbf{x}$ and $\mathbf{x}'$. Compared to the correlation function used for a Kriging model, more choices are available for a RBFs model, which are partially listed in Table 1.

Basis functions	Formulations
Gaussian (GAUSS)	$\phi(r) = e^{-r^2/2\sigma^2}$ (e.g. $\sigma^2 = 1$)
Power function (POW)	$\phi(r) = r^\beta, 1 \le \beta \le 3$ (e.g. $\beta = 1.8$)
Thin Plate Spline (TPS)	$\phi(r) = r^2 \ln(r)$
Hardy's Multiquadric (HMQ)	$\phi(r) = \sqrt{1 + r^2}$
Hardy's Inverse Multiquadric (HIMQ)	$\phi(r) = 1/\sqrt{1 + r^2}$

Table 1. Basis functions for RBFs surrogate model

All the basis functions listed in Table 1 can be classified into two categories: decaying functions (such as GAUSS and HIMQ) and growing functions (POW, TPS and HMQ). The decaying functions can yield positive definite matrix $\mathbf{\Psi}$, which allows for the use of Cholesky decomposition for its inversion; the growing functions generally result in a non-positive definite matrix $\mathbf{\Psi}$ and thus LU decomposition is usually used alternatively. The schematics of the basis functions for one-dimensional problem is sketched in Figure 3.

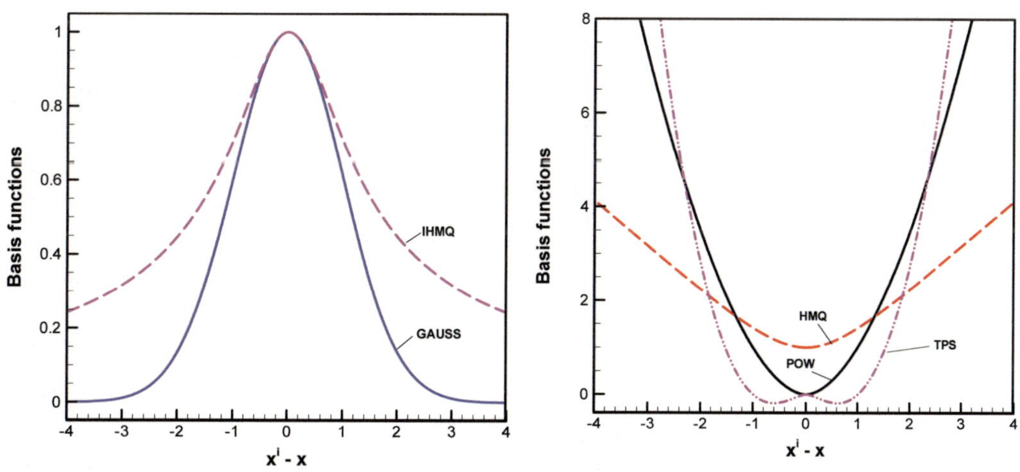

Fig. 3. Schematics of basis functions for Radial Basis Functions (left: decaying functions; right: growing functions).

2.2.4 The big (ger) picture

In addition to what we mentioned above, there are also a few surrogate models available in the literatures, such as Artificial Neutral Network (ANN) (Elanayar et al. 1994, Park et al. 1991), Multiple Adaptive Regression Splines (MARS) and Support Vector Regression (SVR)

(Smola & Schoelkopf 2004). Although these methods are coming from different research communities, the idea is similar when using them for function prediction in surrogate modeling. They are not described in detail here due to the limited space. The readers are referred to read the paper by Wang & Shan (2007) and the books written by Keane et al. (2005) and by Forrester et al. (2008) for more description about surrogate modeling techniques.

2.3 Evaluation of approximation models

An important issue for the surrogate modeling is how to estimate the error of the approximation models. Only when the surrogate model with sufficient accuracy is built can the reliable optimum be obtained. Here we use two variables ($\overline{e}$ and σ_e) to evaluate the error of the approximation models at test points, which are also chosen by DoE method. The average relative error is

$$\overline{e} = \frac{1}{n_t}\sum_{i=1}^{n_t} e^{(i)}, \quad e^{(i)} = \left\| \frac{\hat{y}_t^{(i)} - y_t^{(i)}}{y_t^{(i)}} \right\|, \tag{22}$$

where n_t is number of the test points; $y_t^{(i)}$ and $\hat{y}_t^{(i)}$ are the true value and predicted value corresponding to the *i*-th test point, respectively. The root mean squared error is defined by

$$\sigma_e = \sqrt{\sum_{i=1}^{n_t} (e^{(i)})^2 \Big/ n_t} \ . \tag{23}$$

2.4 Framework of building surrogate models

A Generic framework of building a surrogate model is sketched in Figure 4. Note that the initial surrogate model can be evaluated by Eqs. (22) and (23) and a branch for resampling is denoted by black dashed line in Figure 4.

3. Use of surrogate models for optimization

Suppose we are concerned with solving a general optimization problem as

$$\begin{aligned} \text{Objective} \quad & \text{minimize } \mathrm{y}(\mathbf{x}) \\ \text{s.t.} \quad & \mathrm{g}_i(\mathbf{x}) \le 0,\ i = 1,...n_c \ , \\ & \mathbf{x}_l \le \mathbf{x} \le \mathbf{x}_u \end{aligned} \tag{24}$$

where n_c is the number of state functions which is in line with the number of inequality constraints (assuming that all the equality constraints have been transformed into inequality constraints.); $\mathbf{x}_l$ and $\mathbf{x}_u$ are the lower and upper bound of design variables, respectively; the object function $\mathrm{y}(\mathbf{x})$ and state functions $\mathrm{g}_i(\mathbf{x})$ are evaluated by an expensive analysis code. Traditionally, the optimization problem is solved by either a gradient-based algorithm or a gradient-free algorithm such as GA. It may become prohibitive due to the large computational cost associated running the expensive analysis code. Alternatively, here we are concerned with using surrogate modeling techniques to solve the optimization problem, in an attempt to dramatically improve the efficiency.

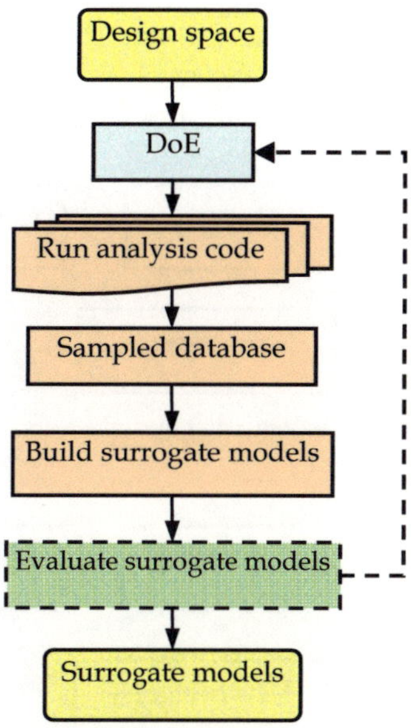

Fig. 4. Frameworks of building surrogate models

3.1 Framework of surrogate-based optimization

3.1.1 A simple framework

The basic idea of using surrogate models in optimization can be quite simple. First, the surrogate models for the object function(s) and state function(s) with sufficient accuracy are built (see Figure 2); second, the optimum is found by an optimizer, with the object function(s) or state function(s) evaluated by surrogate models, rather than by the expensive analysis code. Since prediction with the surrogate models is much more efficient than that by the expensive analysis code, the optimization efficiency can be greatly improved. The comparison of the conventional optimization and surrogate-based optimization is sketched in Figure 5. In addition to improve optimization efficiency, surrogate models also serve as an interface between the analysis code and the optimizer, which makes the establishment of an optimization procedure much easier. One of the examples for such a surrogate-based optimization framework can be found in paper by Han et al. (2010).

3.1.2 A bi-level framework

Although the framework of the surrogate-based optimization sketched in Figure 5. (b) is very intuitive and simple, questions may arise: are the surrogate models accurate enough? has the true optimum been reached? In fact, the optimum gained by the surrogate models is only an approximation to the true optimum (see Figure 5. (a)). One has to refine the surrogate models by adding new sample points, which is to be observed by running the analysis code. The procedure of augmenting new sample point(s) to the current sampled data sets is the so-called "sample-point refinement". The rules of determining the new sample sites towards the true optimum are called "infill criteria", which will be discussed in section 3.2. The flowchart of a surrogate-based optimization with additional process of sample-point refinement is sketched in Figure 6. It can be regarded as a bi-level optimization framework, with the process of building and refining the surrogate models (which needs to run the expensive analysis code) acting as the main optimization and the process of using surrogate models to determine the new sample sites acting as the sub-optimization(s).

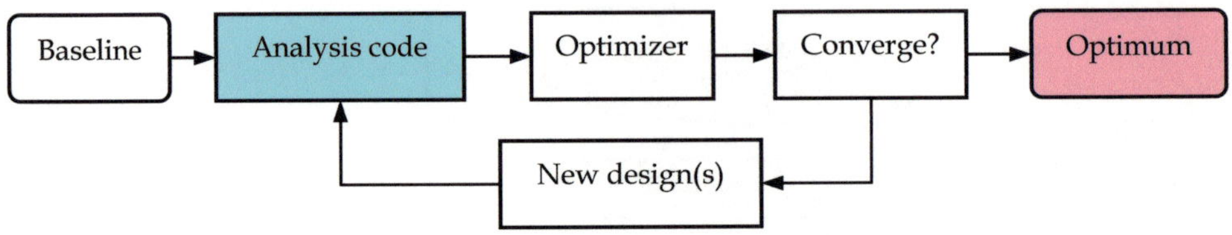

(a) Conventional optimization

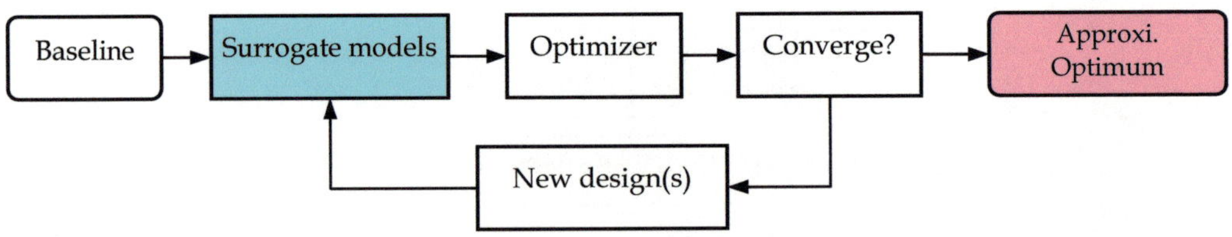

(b) Surrogate-based optimization

Fig. 5. Comparison of frameworks for conventional optimization and surrogate-based optimization with a simple framework

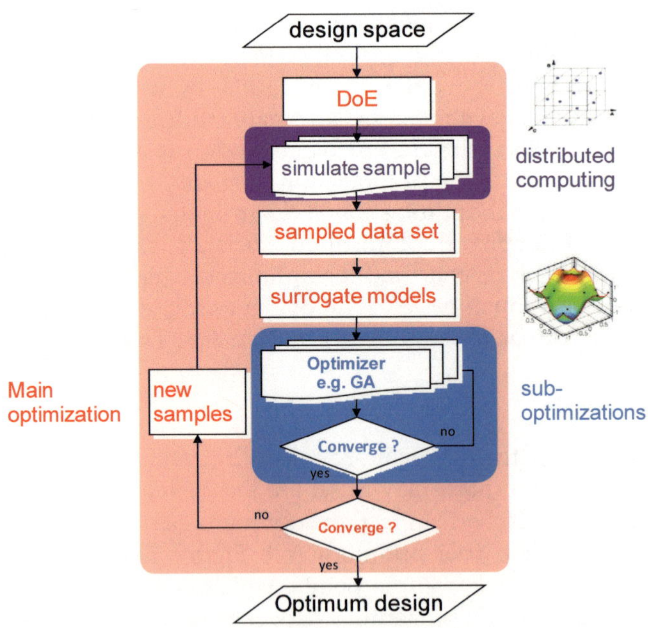

Fig. 6. Flowchart of the surrogate-based optimization with a bi-level framework (main optimization: building and refining the surrogate models which needs to run the expensive analysis code; sub-optimization(s): using surrogate models to determine new sample sites)

3.2 Infill criteria

The infill criterion is related to the determination of the new sample sites by solving sub-optimization problem(s). Three infill criteria are discussed here: Searching Surrogate Model(s) (SSM), Expected Improvement (EI) and Lower-Bounding Confidence (LCB).

3.2.1 Searching surrogate model(s)

Provided that the initial surrogate models have been built, an optimizer such as GA can be used to find the optimum, which in turn can be employed to refine the surrogate models.

The mathematical model of the sub-optimization for determining the new sample site is of the form

$$\begin{aligned} &\text{Objective} \quad \text{minimize } \hat{y}(\mathbf{x}) \\ &\text{s.t.} \quad \hat{g}_i(\mathbf{x}) \le 0,\ i = 1, n_c\ , \\ &\mathbf{x}_l \le \mathbf{x} \le \mathbf{x}_u \end{aligned} \tag{25}$$

where $\hat{y}(\mathbf{x})$ and $\hat{g}_i(\mathbf{x})$ are surrogate models of $y(\mathbf{x})$ and $g_i(\mathbf{x})$, respectively. With the optimal design variables $\hat{\mathbf{x}}_{\text{opt}}$ gained by the surrogate models in hand, one needs to run the expensive analysis code to compute the corresponding true function value and compare it with what predicted by the surrogate models. If the error between them is blow a threshold, the optimization process can be terminated; if not, the new sample point is augmented to the sampled data sets and the surrogate models are rebuilt; the process is repeated until the optimum solution is approached.

This criterion applies for all the surrogate models and is very efficient for local exploitation of the promising region in the design space.

3.2.2 Expected improvement

Surrogate model such as Kriging provides not only an function prediction but also an estimation of the mean squared error (MSE). In fact, the prediction by a Kriging model, $\hat{y}(\mathbf{x})$, at any point can be regarded as a Gaussian random variable with the mean given by the Kriging predictor, and the variance given by the mean squared error, $s^2(\mathbf{x})$ (see section 2.2.2). Viewed in this way, a probability can be computed that the function value at any untried $\mathbf{x}$ would fall below the minimum among the sample points observed so far. Then Expected Improvement (EI) function (Jones et al 1998, Jeong et al. 2005) can be calculated to account for the improvement of the object function we expect to achieve at any untried $\mathbf{x}$. The definition of EI is of the form

$$E[I(\mathbf{x})] = \begin{cases} (y_{\min} - \hat{y}(\mathbf{x}))\Phi\left(\dfrac{y_{\min} - \hat{y}(\mathbf{x})}{\hat{s}(\mathbf{x})}\right) + \hat{s}(\mathbf{x})\phi\left(\dfrac{y_{\min} - \hat{y}(\mathbf{x})}{\hat{s}(\mathbf{x})}\right) & \text{if } \hat{s} > 0 \\ 0 & \text{if } \hat{s} = 0 \end{cases} \tag{26}$$

where $\Phi(\bullet)$ and $\phi(\bullet)$ are the cumulative distribution function and probability density function of a standard normal distribution, respectively. $y_{\min} = Min(y^{(1)}, y^{(2)}, ..., y^{(n)})$

denotes the minimum of the observed data so far. The greater the EI, the more improvement we expect to achieve. The point with maximum EI is located by a global optimizer such as GA then observed by running the analysis code. For this infill criterion, the constraints can be accounted by introducing the probability that the constraints are satisfied. The corresponding sub-optimization problem can be modeled as

$$\begin{aligned} &\text{Objective} \quad \text{maximize } E[I(\mathbf{x})]\cdot\prod_{i=1}^{n_c} P[G_i(\mathbf{x})\le 0] \\ &\text{s.t.} \quad \mathbf{x}_l \le \mathbf{x} \le \mathbf{x}_u \end{aligned} , \tag{27}$$

where $P[G_i(\mathbf{x})\le 0]$ denotes the probability that i-th constraint may be satisfied and $G_i(\mathbf{x})$ is a random function corresponding to i-th state function $g_i(\mathbf{x})$. $P[G_i(\mathbf{x})\le 0]\to 1$ when the constraint is satisfied and $P[G_i(\mathbf{x})\le 0]\to 0$ when the constraint is violated. $P[G_i(\mathbf{x})\le 0]$ can be calculated by

$$P[G_i(\mathbf{x})\le 0] = \frac{1}{\hat{s}_i(\mathbf{x})\sqrt{2\pi}}\int_{-\infty}^{0} e^{-[G_i(\mathbf{x})-\hat{g}_i(\mathbf{x})]^2/2\hat{s}_i^2(\mathbf{x})}dG_i(\mathbf{x}) = \Phi\left(\frac{-\hat{g}_i(\mathbf{x})}{\hat{s}_i(\mathbf{x})}\right) \tag{28}$$

where $\hat{s}_i(\mathrm{x})$ denotes the estimated standard error corresponding to the surrogate model $\hat{g}_i(\mathrm{x})$.

The optimum site $\hat{\mathbf{x}}_{\text{opt}}$ obtained by solving Eq. (27) is observed by running analysis code and the new sample point is added to the sampled date sets; the surrogate models are rebuilt and the whole process is repeated until the global optimum is approached.

3.2.3 Lower-bounding confidence (LCB)

The LCB function is defined as the weighted sum of predicted function value $\hat{y}(\mathbf{x})$ and the standard error of the prediction $\hat{s}(\mathbf{x})$. For an optimization problem of finding the minimum of the unknown function $y(\mathbf{x})$, a simple expression for LCB function is of the form

$$\text{LCB} = \hat{y}(\mathbf{x}) - A\hat{s}(\mathbf{x}), \tag{29}$$

where A is a constant which balances the influence of the predicted function and the corresponding uncertainty. Best practice suggests $A=1$ works well for a number of realistic problems. The corresponding sub-optimization problem can be modeled as

$$\begin{aligned} &\text{Objective} \quad \text{minimize } \hat{y}(\mathbf{x}) - A\hat{s}(\mathbf{x}) \\ &\text{s.t.} \quad \hat{g}_i(\mathbf{x})\le 0,\ i=1,n_c \\ &\qquad \mathbf{x}_l \le \mathbf{x} \le \mathbf{x}_u \end{aligned} , \tag{30}$$

The above optimization problem can be solved via a global optimizer such as GA. Since the point with smallest value of LCB indicates the possible minimum of the unknown function, the optimum site $\hat{\mathbf{x}}_{\text{opt}}$ is then observed and added to sampled data sets to refine the surrogate models. This procedure is performed iteratively until the global optimum is reached.

4. Examples for applications to aircraft design

4.1 Airfoil design

Using an in-house Navier-Stokes flow solver, the objective of the problem is to minimize the drag of an RAE2822 airfoil at the flow condition of $Ma = 0.73$, α=2.7°, $\mathrm{Re} = 6.5\times10^6$, subject to 3 constraints:

$$\begin{aligned} &Objective &:& \quad \text{Minimize} \quad C_d \\ &st. &:& \quad (1)\ Area \geq 0.99\times Area_0 \\ & &:& \quad (2)\ C_l \geq 0.99\times C_{l0} \\ & &:& \quad (3) |C_m| \leq |C_{m0}| \end{aligned} , \qquad (31)$$

where $Area_0$,C_{l0} , C_{m0} are the area, lift coefficient, and moment coefficient of the baseline airfoil, respectively. The first constraint is in consideration of the structural design of the wing to guarantee the volume of the wing; the second one is to enforce a constant lift of the wing in order to balance the weight of the aircraft at cruise condition; the third one is to control the pitching moment of the airfoil to avoid large drag penalty of the horizontal tail paid for balancing the aircraft.

The initial number of samples for Kriging is set to 20, selected by the Latin Hypercube Sampling (LHS). The airfoil is parameterized by 10 Hicks-Henne bump functions (Hicks & Henne, 1978); and the maximum amplitude of each bump is $A^{\max}/c = 0.544\%$. Both of the SSM and EI infill strategies are adopted in the surrogate refinement. Table 2 presents the optimization results of the two optimization method. The optimized and initial airfoils and the corresponding pressure coefficient distributions are compared in Figure 7. Note that the aerodynamic coefficients of the initial airfoil RAE2822 are set to 100. Obviously, the Kriging-based optimization method gives better result, and with higher efficiency, and is more likely to find the global optimum.

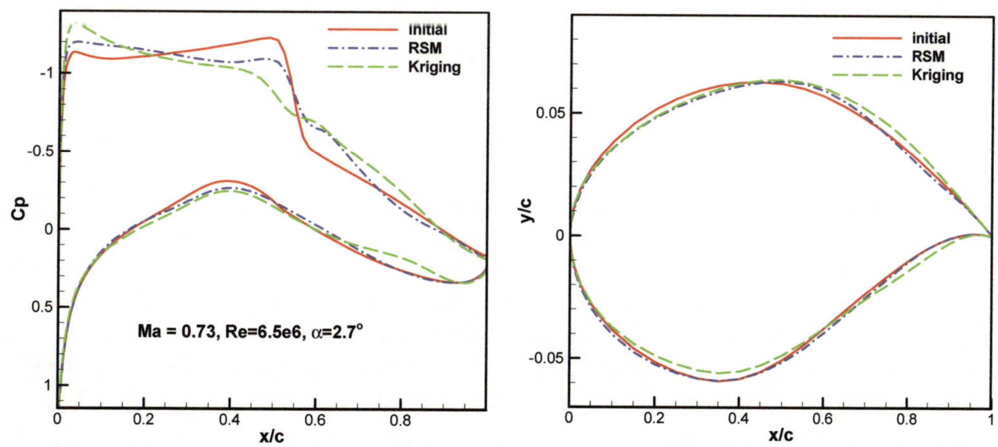

Fig. 7. Aerodynamic shape optimization of a transonic airfoil (RAE 2822) via Kriging and quadratic Response Surface Model (left: pressure distribution; right: airfoil shape); by using Kriging model with Expected Improvement infill criteria, the drag is reduced by 33.6% with only 56 calling of Navier-Stokes flow solver.

	C_d	C_l	$\lvert C_m \rvert$	Area	NS flow solver calls
baseline	100	100	100	100	-
RSM	73.0 (-27.0%)	101.1 (+1.1%)	99.3 (-0.7%)	99.9 (-0.1%)	102
Kriging	70.7 (-29.3%)	101.1 (+1.1%)	96.5 (-3.5%)	100.4 (+0.4%)	57

Table 2. Drag reduction of an RAE 2822 airfoil via Kriging and RSM-based optimizations

4.2 Wing design

Here we are concerned with the preliminary design for a high-subsonic transport-aircraft wing of a wing/body combination, considering aerodynamic, structure and static aeroelastic effect. The calculation of the external flow is carried out by numerical solutions of the full potential equation in conservative form (Kovalev & Karas, 1991). The FEM-based commercial software ANSYS is used for analyzing the structural performance of the wing with double-beams sandwich structure. Weak coupling method is adopted for static aeroelastic analysis.

The optimization objectives are to maximize the aircraft lift-to-drag ratio and minimize the weight of wing for a fixed maximum take-off weight of 54 tons and cruise Mach number of 0.76 at 10,000 meters high. The wing is composed of inner and outer wing. The reference area of wing is 105 square meter. The mathematical model for optimization is of the form

$$\begin{aligned} &\max\ L/D \\ &\min\ W_{\text{wing}} \\ &\text{s.t.}\ \ L \geq 54 && /10^3\text{kg} \\ &\qquad 100 \leq S_{\text{wing}} \leq 110 && /\text{m}^2 \\ &\qquad \sigma_{\max} \leq \sigma_b && /10^9\text{pa} \\ &\qquad \delta_{\max} \leq 1 && /\text{m} \end{aligned} \tag{32}$$

Eight supercritical airfoils are configured along the span. The optimization is subject to 4 constraints. The first constraint is to enforce a constant lift of the wing in order to balance the weight of the aircraft at cruise condition; the second one is to guarantee a near constant wing loading; the third and fourth constraints are to make sure that the strength and rigidity requirements are satisfied. The definition for the limits of design variables is listed in Table 3. The first four design variables define the aerodynamic configuration of the wing. The four remain are for structure design. The detail can be found in paper by Zhang et al. (2008).

The uniform design table, $U100(10^8)$, is used to creates one hundred candidate wings for building surrogate models. The other forty-five candidate wings are created by the uniform design table, $U45(10^8)$, for evaluating the approximation model. For each wing, the static aeroelastic analysis is performed to obtain the responses of lift (L), lift-to-drag ratio (L/D), wing area (S_{wing}), maximum stress (σ_{max}), maximum deformation (δ_{max}) and wing weight

(W_{wing}). Then the average relative errors and the root mean squared errors are calculated to evaluate the approximation models, as listed in Table 4. In this case Kriging and RSM have comparative high accuracy.

Design variable	Unit	Lower limit	Upper limit
Span	m	26	34
Taper ratio		0.2	0.4
Linear twist angle	degree	-3	-1
Sweep angle on leading edge	degree	25	35
Thickness of front-spar web	mm	2	6
Thickness of back-spar web	mm	2	6
Thickness of lower skin	mm	3	7
Thickness of Upper skin	mm	3	7

Table 3. Definition of design variables for preliminary design of a high-subsonic transport-aircraft wing

Parameter	Surrogate model	$\bar{e}$	σ_e	Parameter	Surrogate model	$\bar{e}$	σ_e
L	RSM	0.0360	0.0213	σ_{max}	RSM	0.0563	0.0535
	Kriging	0.0362	0.0213		Kriging	0.0515	0.0522
L/D	RSM	0.0122	0.0099	δ_{max}	RSM	0.0227	0.0241
	Kriging	0.0123	0.0097		Kriging	0.0227	0.0241
S_{wing}	RSM	0.0071	0.0051	W_{wing}	RSM	0.0140	0.0104
	Kriging	0.0071	0.0051		Kriging	0.0142	0.0107

Table 4. Evaluation of modeling accuracy

Then the multi-objective optimization for the supercritical wing is performed based on RSM due to its higher computational efficiency. Weighted sum method is used to transform the multi-objective optimization into a single-objective optimization. Sequential quadratic programming method is employed to solve the optimization. One of the candidate wings with better performance, are selected as the initial point for optimization. The optimal design is observed by running the analysis codes and the results are listed in Table 5. Where $\mathbf{X}^0$ and $\mathbf{Y}^0$ is the initial wing scheme and its response, respectively; $\mathbf{X}^*$ and $\mathbf{Y}^*$ is the optimal wing scheme and its actual response, respectively; $\hat{\mathbf{Y}}$ is the response at $\mathbf{X}^*$ calculated by the approximation models. For the optimal wing scheme, the largest relative error of approximation models is no more than 3 percent. It again proves the high accuracy of the approximation models.

Figure 8 shows the contour of the equivalent stress of the optimal wing. It shows that the stress is larger in the location of intersection of inner wing and outer wing due to the inflexion. Figure 9 shows pressure distribution of the optimal wing. It shows that the wing basically meets the design requirements of a supercritical wing. A little bit non-smoothness of the pressure distribution may be caused by non-uniform deformation of the skin. Figure 10 shows the convergence history of aeroelastic deformation, which shows that fast convergence of the aeroelastic deformation of the optimal wing.

The optimization , together with the aeroelastic analysis of all candidate wings, only takes about two days on a personal computer of Pentium(R) 4 CPU 2.8GHz. If more computers are used to concurrently calculate the performance of different candidate wings, the cost can be further greatly reduced.

	B/m	λ	θ/(°)	Λ/(°)	T_{FS}/mm	T_{BS}/mm	T_{LS}/mm	T_{US}/mm
$\mathbf{X}^0$	34.00	0.244	-1.667	29.444	3.333	3.778	6.556	3.889
$\mathbf{X}^*$	31.69	0.200	-1.563	28.233	2.232	2.000	4.396	4.057
	$L/10^3$kg	L/D	S_{wing}/m^2	$\sigma_{max}/10^9$pa	δ_{max} /m	W_{wing} /10^3kg		
$\mathbf{Y}^0$	51.50	27.81	111.94	0.311	1.191	3.850		
$\mathbf{Y}^*$	53.14	27.40	107.25	0.275	0.991	3.063		
$\hat{\mathbf{Y}}$	54.00	27.45	106.27	0.267	1.000	3.003		
Modeling error	1.61%	0.16%	0.91%	2.97%	0.87%	1.85%		

Table 5. Optimization results when considering the aeroelastic effect

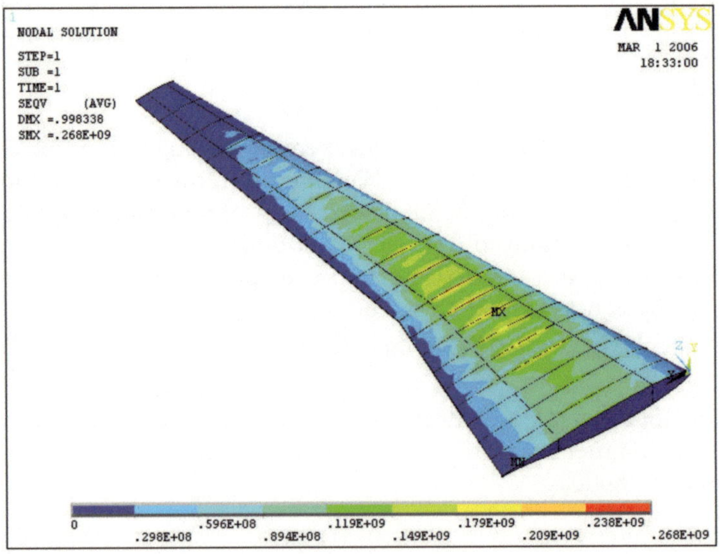

Fig. 8. Contour of equivalent stress of the optimal wing

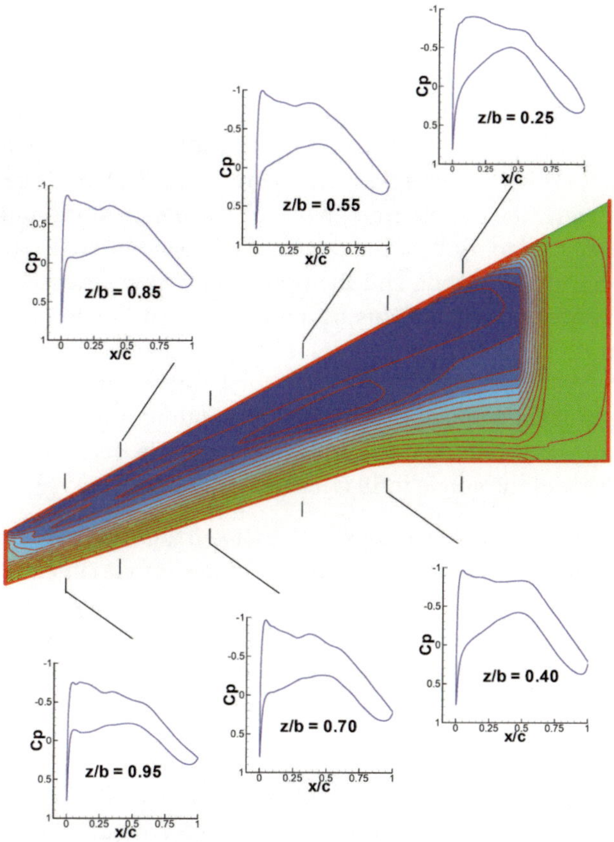

Fig. 9. Pressure distribution of the optimal wing (Ma=0.76, Re=0.257E+08, α=0o)

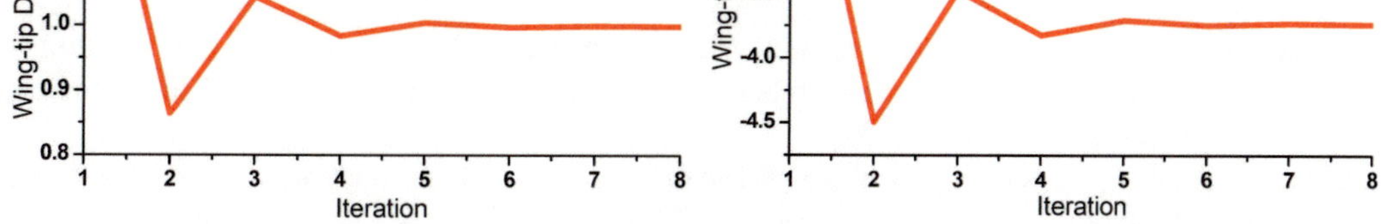

Fig. 10. Convergence history of Y-direction deform and torsion deform on wing tip

5. Conclusion

An overview of the existing surrogate models and the techniques about how to use them for optimization is presented in this chapter. Among the surrogate models, the regression model such as the quadratic response surface model (RSM) is well suited for a local optimization problem with relatively simpler design space; interpolation models such as Kriging or RBFs can be used for highly-nonlinear, multi-modal functions, and thus well suited for a global problem with relatively more complicated design space. From an application point of view, the simple framework of surrogate-based optimization is a good choice for an engineer design, due to the fact that surrogate model can act as an interface between the expensive analysis code and the optimizer and one doesn't need to change the analysis code itself. The drawback of this framework is that the accuracy of optimum only depends on the approximation accuracy of surrogate model and we generally get an approximation to the true optimum. In contrast, the bi-level framework with different infill criteria provides an efficient way to quickly find true optimum without the need of building globally accurate surrogate models. Multiple infill criteria seem to be a better way to overcome the drawback of the single infill criterion.

Examples for airfoil and wing designs show that surrogate-based optimization is very promising for aerodynamic problem with number of design variables being less than about 10. For higher-dimensional problem, the computational cost increases very quickly, which can be prohibitive. Thus, use of surrogate model for high(er)-dimensional optimization problems would become an important issue of future work.

6. Acknowledgements

This research was sponsored by the National Natural Science Foundation of China (NSFC) under grant No. 10902088 and the Aeronautical Science Foundation of China under grant No. 2011ZA53008

7. References

Elanayar, S. V. T., and Shin, Y. C., "Radial basis function neural network for approximation and estimation of nonlinear stochastic dynamic systems," IEE Transactions on Neural Networks, Vol. 5, No. 4, 1994, pp. 594-603.

Fang, K. T., Lin, D., Winker, P., Zhang, Y., "Uniform design: Theory and application," *Technometrics*, Vol. 42, No. 3, 2000, pp. 237-248.

Forrester, A. I. J., Sóbester, A., and Keane, A. J., "Multi-Fidelity Optimization via Surrogate Modeling," Proceedings of the Royal Society A, Vol. 463, No. 2088, 2007, pp. 3251-3269.

Forrester, A. I. J., Sóbester, A., and Keane, A., "Engineering Design via Surrogate Modeling: A Practical Guide," Progress in Astronautics and Aeronautics Series, 226, published by John Wiley & Sons, 2008.

Giunta, A. A., Wojtkiewicz Jr, S. F., and Eldred, M. S. , "Overview of Modern Design of Experiments Methods for Computational Simulations," AIAA paper 2003-649, 2001.

Han, Z. -H., Zhang, K. -S., Song, W. -P., and Qiao, Z. -D., "Optimization of Active Flow Control over an Airfoil Using a Surrogate-Management Framework," *Journal of Aircraft*, 2010, Vol. 47, No. 2, pp. 603-612.

Han, Z.-H., Görtz, S., Zimmermann, R. "On Improving Efficiency and Accuracy of Variable-Fidelity Surrogate Modeling in Aero-data for Loads Context," Proceeding of CEAS 2009 European Air and Space Conference, Manchester, UK, Oct. 26-29, 2009.

Han, Z.-H., Zimmermann, R., and Görtz, S., "A New Cokriging Method for Variable-Fidelity Surrogate Modeling of Aerodynamic Data," AIAA Paper 2010-1225, 48th AIAA Aerospace Sciences Meeting Including the New Horizons Forum and Aerospace Exposition, Orlando, Florida, Jan. 4-7, 2010.

Hardy, R. L., "Multiquadric Equations of Topography and Other Irregular Surface," *Journal of Geophysical Research*, Vol. 76, March, 1971, pp. 1905-1915.

Hicks, R. M., and Henne, P. A., "Wing Design by Numerical Optimization," *Journal of Aircraft*, Vol. 15, No. 7, 1978, pp. 407–412.

Jeong, S., Murayama, M., and Yamamoto, K., "Efficient Optimization Design Method Using Kriging Model," *Journal of Aircraft*, Vol. 42, No. 2, 2005, pp. 413- 420.

Jones, D., Schonlau, M., Welch W., "Efficient Global Optimization of Expensive Black-Box Functions," *Journal of Global Optimization*, 1998, Vol. 13, pp. 455-492.

Keane, A. J., Nair, P. B., "Computational Approaches for Aerospace Design: The Pursuit of Excellence", John Wiley & Sons, Ltd, Chichester, 2005.

Kovalev, V.E., Karas, O. V. "Computation of a Transonic Airfoil Flow Considering Viscous Effects and Thin Separated Regions." La Recherche Aerospatiale (English Edition) (ISSN 0379-380X), No. 1, 1991, pp. 1-15.

Krige, D. G., "A Statistical Approach to Some Basic Mine Valuations Problems on the Witwatersrand," *Journal of the Chemical, Metallurgical and Mining Engineering Society of South Africa*, Vol. 52, No. 6, 1951, pp. 119-139.

Laurenceau, J., and Sagaut, P. "Building Efficient Response Surfaces of Aerodynamic Functions with Kriging and Cokriging," *AIAA Journal*, Vol. 46, No. 2, 2008, pp. 498-507.

Park. J., and Sandberg, I. W., "Universal Approximation Using Radial-Basis-Function Networks," *Neural Computation*, Vol. 3, No. 2, 1991, pp. 246-257.

Powell, M. J. D. "Radial Basis Functions for Multivariable Interpolation: A Review, " *Algorithms for Approximation*, edited by J. C. Mason and M. G. Cox, Oxford Univ. Press, New York, 1987, Chap. 3, pp. 141-167.

Queipo, N. V., Haftka, R. T., Shyy W., Goel, T., Vaidyanathan, R., and Tucher, P. K., "Surrogate-based Analysis and Optimization," *Progress in Aerospace Sciences*, Vol. 41, 2005, pp. 1-28.

Sacks, J., Welch, W. J., Mitchell, T. J., and Wynn, H. P., "Design and Analysis of Computer Experiments," *Statistical Science*, Vol. 4, 1989, pp. 409-423.

Simpson, T. W., Mauery, T. M., Korte, J. J., et al., "Kriging Models for Global Approximation in Simulation-Based Multidisciplinary Design Optimization", *AIAA Journal*, Vol. 39, No. 12, 2001, pp. 2233-2241.

Simpson, T. W., Toropov, V., Balabanov, V., and Viana, F. A. C., "Design and Analysis of Computer Experiments in Multidisciplinary Design Optimization: a Review of How Far We Have Come - or Not," AIAA Paper 2008-5802, 2008.

Smola, A. J. and Schoelkopf, B., "A tutorial on support vector regression," Statistics and Computing, Vol. 14, 2004, pp. 199-222.

Toal, D. J. J., Bressloff, N. W., Kean, J., "Kriging Hyperparameter Tuning Strategies," *AIAA Journal*, Vol. 46, No .5, 2008, pp. 1240-1252.

Wang, G. G., Shan S., "Review of Metamodeling Techniques in Support of Engineering Design Optimization," *Journal of Mechanical Design*, Vol. 129, No. 4. 2007, pp. 370-380.

Zhang, K. -S., Han, Z. -H., Li, W. -J., and Song, W. -P., "Coupled Aerodynamic/Structural Optimization of a Subsonic Transport Wing Using a Surrogate Model," *Journal of Aircraft*, 2008, Vol. 45, No. 6, pp. 2167-2171.